Foodservice Planning

Layout, Design, and Equipment

Foodservice Planning
Layout, Design, and Equipment

Fourth Edition

Barbara A. Almanza
Purdue University

Lendal H. Kotschevar
Professor Emeritus
Florida International University

Margaret E. Terrell

Prentice Hall
Upper Saddle River, New Jersey   Columbus, Ohio

Library of Congress Cataloging-in-Publication Data
Almanza, Barbara A.
    Foodservice planning: layout, design, and equipment / Barbara A.
Almanza, Lendal H. Kotschevar, Margaret E. Terrell. —4th ed.
    p.   cm.
    Prev. eds. by Lendal H. Kotschevar.
    Includes bibliographical references.
    ISBN 0-13-096446-8
    1. Food service management.   2. Food service—Equipment and
supplies. I. Kotschevar, Lendal Henry. II. Terrell,
Margaret E. III. Kotschevar, Lendal Henry, Foodservice
planning. IV. Title.
TX911.3.M27A426 2000
647.95'068—dc21
    99–31236
    CIP

Cover art: © Barbara Maslan
Editor: Neil W. Marquardt
Editorial Assistant: Susan Kegler
Production Editor: Linda Hillis Bayma
Production Coordination and Text Design: Carlisle Publishers Services
Design Coordinator: Diane C. Lorenzo
Cover Designer: Dan Eckel
Production Manager: Laura Messerly
Marketing Manager: Shannon M. Simonsen
Marketing Assistant: Adam Kloza

This book was set in Palatino by Carlisle Communications, Ltd. and was printed and bound by
R.R. Donnelley & Sons Company. The cover was printed by Phoenix Color Corp.

© 2000 by Prentice-Hall, Inc.
Pearson Education
Upper Saddle River, New Jersey 07458

Earlier editions, entitled *Foodservice Planning: Layout and Equipment,* © 1985 by Macmillan
Publishing Company and © 1977, 1961 by John Wiley & Sons, Inc.

Printed in the United States of America

10 9 8 7 6 5 4 3 2 1

ISBN: 0-13-096446-8

Prentice-Hall International (UK) Limited, *London*
Prentice-Hall of Australia Pty. Limited, *Sydney*
Prentice-Hall of Canada, Inc., *Toronto*
Prentice-Hall Hispanoamericana, S. A., *Mexico*
Prentice-Hall of India Private Limited, *New Delhi*
Prentice-Hall of Japan, Inc., *Tokyo*
Prentice-Hall (Singapore) Pte. Ltd., *Singapore*
Editora Prentice-Hall do Brasil, Ltda., *Rio de Janeiro*

Preface

Since this text was first published in 1961, the foodservice industry has undergone considerable change. At that time foods were produced largely from raw materials purchased by the facility and turned into salable products on the premises. Today, much that is sold is purchased in a form that requires limited preparation. The industry has changed from an industry where emphasis was on food production to one in which the emphasis is now on merchandising, from the kitchen to the dining room.

A visit to the National Restaurant Association Show serves to underscore this change. In 1961 there was row upon row of griddles, ovens, deep fryers, and other cooking equipment; pots and pans and other cooking utensils were also prominently displayed. Manufacturers of dishwashers, kitchen sinks, tables, and other units proudly displayed their latest models. There were few foods and most of those were canned or fresh; only a few frozen foods were shown and they required considerable treatment before they were ready for service. Viewers stood and marveled at prepeeled potatoes that stayed white and unblemished. Today one goes to the show and sees row upon row of computers, point-of-sale cash registers, software, and pre-prepared foods that need only minor handling. Tabletop decorations and items that add to the attractiveness of the dining area are found. One cannot help but notice the large number of schools that now advertise their curricula and the many more publishers that now seek to sell magazines, books, and other publications to the industry.

Changes have also occurred that make planning easier. Information is much more available and easier to obtain than in the past. The Internet serves as a vast library at one's fingertips. The use of an AutoCAD computer program now allows relatively unskilled workers to draw plans that meet the highest professional standards. E-mail and facsimile communication facilitate the exchange of information between the planning team members and others. Computers and copying machines can do tasks that formerly could only be done by a publishing house.

In revising *Foodservice Planning: Layout, Design, and Equipment* the authors have sought to reflect these changes as they affect the makeup of food services. Thus, kitchens in foodservice facilities are smaller and dining areas have increased in size in relation to the kitchen. Because foods are now often processed differently, equipment needs and work center design have changed. Newer pieces of equipment may be smaller and mobile for use in different areas. Often they are multipurpose. Newer cooking technologies have created faster, more efficient cooking equipment that specializes in reheating of foods rather than scratch preparation. Storage needs have also changed so that there are fewer raw food materials and more frozen or refrigerated pre-prepared items. Sanitation and safety standards have also risen, requiring the use of different materials or modifications in the facilities or equipment. Finally, increasing operational costs and labor shortages have created unique challenges for the design of restaurants.

Planning and construction of food services has become both easier and more complex because of changes in technology. Keeping up with these changes in the highly competitive hospitality industry has increased the cost of putting up a building and properly equipping it for action. Ways still need to be found to cut costs, while maintaining quality and satisfactory performance. These are the challenges for the future planners.

Barbara A. Almanza
Lendal H. Kotschevar

Margaret E. Terrell, Professor Emerita

(1901–1998)

This book is dedicated to the memory of Dr. Margaret E. Terrell, professor emerita of the University of Washington. She was a pioneer in the field of institution management. Her writing and teaching contributions lent much to the knowledge in her field and to the success of others. A great lady who led the way!

Contents

PART 2   Functional Areas of Food Facilities   113

CHAPTER 5

Space Allocation   115

CHAPTER 6

Checklist for Planning   146

CHAPTER 7

Receiving and Storage   155

CHAPTER 8

Food Processing   166

CHAPTER 20

CHAPTER 21

CHAPTER 22

CHAPTER 23

CHAPTER 24

PART
1

PLANNING

CHAPTER

1

Laying the Groundwork

This chapter provides an overview of the planning process for foodservice facilities and emphasizes why planning is so important to successful food service.

UNIQUE FACTORS IN FOODSERVICE PLANNING

The **plan** for any facility starts with a purpose—the creation of a physical structure designed to suit a particular need. This is accomplished with graphic line drawings and written descriptions of the physical features or equipment needed to produce the contemplated facility. These drawings and descriptions provide much of the information needed to produce the desired facility. There is nothing random about this process. Each line, each number, each graphic presentation, and each written condition or specification details something that must be produced in the facility. The plan for a foodservice facility is no different. It must be a precise, accurate graphic presentation of something that will be recreated as a physical entity to serve food and beverages to people (Figure 1.1).

Specificity of the Plan

Most facility plans have much in common, but foodservice facilities require specialized planning if they are to fulfill the needs of those they are designed to serve. A requirement in any foodservice plan is that it must be for the creation of *that* facility. Experience has shown that the adaptation of plans for one facility seldom suit another facility, resulting in a less than desirable plan.

First of all, foodservice facilities do not fit a general, standardized plan because they differ so widely in type and in what a facility within a type is designed to do. Timing, locations, menu, patrons, and a host of other factors are specific to a facility. For instance, unless you are told about or see the sign of the establishment, you would never know you were in a McDonald's in the Minneapolis airport, because it is so different from the regular McDonald's.

Location and operating conditions require this differentiation. Although colleges and universities serve students as do elementary and secondary schools, the type of patron is so different that very different plans are required for their food services. The setups for the production and service of food and beverages for a nightclub and a nursing home

FIGURE 1.1   Planning must be as carefully done for the outside of a food service as well as for the interior. Adequate parking with easy access to entrances and exits, good lighting, attractive grounds, an inviting entrance, and other outside details must all receive detailed attention. *(Courtesy of National Restaurant Association, Washington, DC.)*

differ widely because of differing patron needs and very probably differing incomes. In the National Restaurant Association's (NRA's) annual reports the NRA lists 31 different kinds of food services totaling more than 799,000 units, very few of which are duplicates in layout and design of any other.[1]

The Three Economic Functions

Economists divide our **economic functions** into three major categories: (1) production, (2) merchandising and retailing, and (3) service. A shoe factory merely produces shoes; a separate shoe store merchandises and sells them. A shoe repair shop services them. Few businesses have to perform all three functions, as a food service is required to do. It must (1) produce the items, (2) merchandise and sell them, and (3) serve them. The requirement to plan adequately so each function meets the facility needs and at the same time coordinate them so the facility is a smoothly functioning unit puts foodservice planning in a separate category when planning facilities. Planning well for two functions, but neglecting the third can create a disaster because they rely one on the other. Like a house of cards, the failure of one causes the entire plan to collapse.

Other food services have additional functions. A hospital food service must support the health function; a casino the gambling function; and an airplane food service the need for food while traveling. In a hotel, the dining and catering facilities support the hotel guests' needs for food and beverages. This need to coordinate not only the three functions together but then to coordinate them into the main purpose of the facility adds to the complexity of the planning.

In some cases the food service may be required to perform only a few of the functions. For instance, a drive-in or take-out service is limited to taking an order, preparing

[1]The actual number is higher because the NRA does not list facilities such as camps kitchens, prison cafeterias, church kitchens, etc.

it, and handing it out. In another kind of food service, production may be limited to merely conditioning already prepared food or beverages for service. Thus, a sandwich shop may dispense only wrapped sandwiches that were prepared and brought in by an outside unit, requiring emphasis only on the merchandising and retailing function. For a hospital, the merchandising requirements to patients may be limited but cannot be neglected for dining facilities attended by employees, medical staff, or visitors. Nevertheless, in *all* types of facilities, whichever number of functions are required to give satisfactory results must receive detailed and careful planning.

Needs to Be Satisfied

The plan for a food service must generally satisfy three factors: (1) the market, (2) the employees, and (3) management. Since food services must merchandise and retail and serve their products, they are intimately associated with their customer market, perhaps more so than any other type of business, and this means that the plan's provision to satisfy the market's needs must receive emphasis. Planners often fail to recognize the need to satisfy employee needs, which results in a plan that may not be completely successful. Employees have needs that must be satisfied when they work in a facility. Of course, anyone will recognize that satisfaction of the needs of management must occur but sometimes planners are so concerned with the satisfaction of this need that they fail to give the other two proper emphasis. In any plan, the three factors should be balanced in emphasis according to the importance of the needs to be satisfied.

The Market.   The main need in any food service is, of course, that it meet its market's need for food. Although it may seem strange, this is often not the reason why a patron selects a particular food service; food may be incidental to the satisfaction of another need or needs. We may choose a particular food service because of social, psychological, convenience, or other needs. Thus, the main purpose may be to attend a banquet or reception to celebrate an occasion. Or, you might be lonesome or just bored and want a change. Today in many families the husband and wife work and it may be much more convenient to load the kids into the car and go to a drive-in to eat. Or, the reason for dining out may be to support a cause, such as to attend a charity dinner.

A large number of individuals, from teens through middle age, "eat and run" at breakfast and lunch. Many are snackers. They are impatient and want quick service, and they readily accept self-service. They are attracted by glamour and change. "Grazing" for their evening meal provides activity, variety, and diversion. Older people with requisite funds and leisure time, persons who are tired or tense, and those who eat out for business or social reasons desire the quieter atmosphere of service dining rooms. Some people eat out because they find the place restful and pleasant (Figures 1.2 and 1.3).

The planner must keep in mind these other needs and provide for them. He or she must know precisely the market the facility is intended to suit and provide adequately to meet their needs. This text gives emphasis to this requirement in discussions that follow.

The Employees.   The second group whose needs should be satisfied is the employees working in the operation. The importance of this factor is often forgotten. Facilities that make work more difficult for employees not only lead to increased costs and poorer quality products and service, but contribute to poorer employee morale with the consequences of high turnover and other problems.

The October 1997 issue of the National Restaurant Association's magazine *Restaurants* (p. 10) summarized a study that was conducted to determine what employees wanted from employers. Ten of the factors most frequently mentioned in the human resources area were, in order of frequency of mention, as follows:

1. A regular paycheck
2. A safe place to work
3. A clean place to work

FIGURE 1.2 A busy dining area can quickly build up considerable body heat, humidity, exhaled air, and undesirable odors. Adequate ventilation is needed to quickly exhaust these and provide a pleasant atmosphere. *(Courtesy of National Restaurant Association, Washington, DC.)*

FIGURE 1.3 Soft colors, good lighting, and well-chosen decorative pieces make for dining satisfaction. Providing good aisle space allows for private conversations but also helps promote guest safety and faster service. Good lighting not only adds to the comfort of guests but to the pleasantness of the surroundings. *(Courtesy of National Restaurant Association, Washington, DC.)*

4. Competitive wage or salary
5. <u>The right equipment for the job</u>
6. Having enough employees to handle the workload
7. Health insurance
8. Working enough hours
9. Paid vacation
10. Workers' compensation insurance.

Three of the first five factors most frequently mentioned (the underlined items, 2, 3, and 5) relate to planning. This is significant and a considerable amount of discussion in this text deals with this problem of producing a well-planned facility to suit the desires of employees in the food service in which they work.

The Management. The third group that must be considered is management. Costs must be controlled if not for profitable operation, then for budgetary reasons. The facility must also function smoothly enough so as to not cause too many management headaches. Good sanitation and safety are growing concerns for management. The consumption of contaminated food or injuries to either employees or patrons can bring about costly lawsuits.

This task of planning in spite of the challenges need not, however, be a frustrating nor tiring one. In fact, it can be one of exhilaration and fascinating preoccupation, almost like playing a game. The challenge is there. How well can it be met? As you proceed, you will experience growing satisfaction as problems are solved and a satisfactory plan emerges.

STEPS IN PLANNING

Normally a plan for a food service evolves along a sort of standard pathway that can be used regardless of whether it is for a total building to be built from the ground up or merely for setting up a plan for an already standing building, or for a modification of an already functioning facility. The steps often follow a standard pattern:

1. A need is found and a decision is made to provide for it. Goals are established. The type of facility and its size are estimated. Everything at this point is conceptual.
2. A location is selected and the feasibility of meeting the need is now investigated. Often this results in a **feasibility study** being drawn up that should indicate whether it can be done, meets the need, is financially supportable, etc. Details that need clarification are investigated and satisfactorily met. Consideration of funds required, money available, and allocation of the funds is made. (An example of what a feasibility plan covers can be found in appendix B.)
3. A decision to move ahead and establish the facility is made. A team is usually set up to provide the expertise needed to prepare a plan. This team consists of personnel representing (1) management, (2) architecture and construction, (3) operations, and (4) building. In recent years the architectural and construction unit has often been enlarged to include specialized expertise in the **engineering** field—electrical, mechanical, etc. This has occurred because of the growing complexity of building codes, technically advanced equipment, etc. Engineering has become so important that it might be looked on as a fifth team member. However in this text we consider engineering to be a part of the architectural team.[2]
4. Research and analysis is now in order. After a statement of the need and goals of the enterprise and a broad definition of its scope and requirements has been

---

[2]An indication of the importance of the engineering aspect for our modern buildings is that frequently the cost for a new food service will be divided into one-third physical building, one-third equipment and furnishings, and one-third engineering.

prepared by management, the other team members now work to provide the necessary information to meet these requirements. The architectural and building members confer with the operation team member(s) to obtain the necessary operational requirements. This provides needed information on the type of equipment required, its placement, space needs, the flow of work, and other areas in which operations should have expertise.

5. Usually the next step is for the architectural and construction members to submit a tentative plan that presents broad details. This plan is critiqued by the team members.

6. The plan is finalized. Often the result is a compromise of the different ideas of the team members. The plan must receive the approval of ownership.

7. The plan with specifications and all other required information is sent out for bidding. Bids are received and reviewed.

8. Often, as a result of bidding, the team members are required to revise and change the plan to coincide with information provided by the bidders. Often these changes are required to meet cost considerations.

9. A final plan is set up and bids once more taken. Management decides on the successful bidders and awards the bids.

10. Construction starts. The team members are involved in seeing that the requirements of the plan are met.

11. When construction is complete, the builder turns the facility over to management. The team members now make their final inspection and certify that the plan's requirements have been met. If not, the factors needing attention are pointed out and must be corrected by the builder before management accepts the work and makes final payment.

BASIC CONCEPTS

It is highly desirable for ownership to identify goals and set standards at the outset of planning. **Goals** are interpreted to mean the general overall criteria needed for proper performance of required functions. For example, the goals for a drive-in specializing in hamburgers might be defined as the service of freshly broiled 4-oz hamburgers in a 2-oz sourdough or regular bun along with good-quality milk shakes and malts, soft drinks, french fries, etc. Maximum time between order and service is established at five minutes. Branded high-quality ingredients would be specified and standards set for preparation methods. Maximum costs of ingredients and labor would be defined.

Standards govern modes, methods, and conditions for reaching specified goals. They are the road map that leads to achievement of goals and should point out acceptable services and quality levels of products required to meet needs in a specific situation. Needs differ and standards vary. There are special expediencies that apply to a particular time, place, and situation that may deserve consideration. Various levels of standards should be formulated to cover all aspects subject to variation, where significant choice of action or selection is to be made. Well-formulated and generally understood standards can do much toward unifying the efforts of a planning group.

Persons in authority are expected to enunciate and approve standards. This may or may not mean that those persons originate standards pertaining to every detail involved. Responsibility for standards rests with each individual who has accepted responsibility for a share in planning as it relates to that person's specific area of activity. This individual is in the position either to propose a standard for approval or to accept an approved standard to govern the action.

Goals and standards should evolve from a clear and comprehensive analysis of needs and circumstances. Often it is necessary to search for basic motives behind stated views and ideas. A member of the hospital medical staff views the role of the foodservice department much differently than does the food production manager. There should be an open-minded appreciation for different viewpoints as they relate to goals. The best plans frequently evolve through compromise. Goals should be realistic and pointed toward the highest standard of quality and performance possible in a given situation. Goals and standards are usually expressed in general terms by those in authority and relate to four aspects of the operation. It is commonly desired that a food facility will do the following:

1. Satisfy the needs of persons to be served with good-quality food that is adequate, appealing, safe, nutritious, and healthful.
2. Function on a basis that is economically sound and within the design that can be created and function on the funds that will be available.
3. Function with a consistently high standard of performance promoting efficient utilization of labor and equipment in clean, safe, attractive surroundings.
4. Cause a minimum of work and time expenditure on the part of persons who should not be directly involved in the operation, such as ownership or the administration, who should not be bothered by worker problems, supply shortages, or service complaints.

It is important to concentrate on the most significant goals and standards and the selection of the best ways to satisfy them. This may mean devising new ways of doing work, utilizing equipment, or using new types of foods. The most important goal or standard in one situation may be service of superior quality regardless of cost. In another, it may be preferable to serve food of acceptable, simple quality at a minimum price. Standards must be specific to the organization according to its requirements.

THE PLANNING TEAM

Owner

Owners or the owners' representative(s) are the pacemakers in food facility planning. They are the decision makers who indicate the character, extent, and cost of the proposed structure. Although they can and frequently should seek advice concerning goals, any ultimate decision is theirs. The goals to be met, procedures to be followed, standards to be maintained, and areas and extent of responsibility granted to planning assistants are important aspects to be determined by owners. A food facility has many aspects calling for special expertise in relation to finance, construction, and adaptation for specific use.

A decision to build is usually stimulated by awareness of kind and extent of need for the food facility as a desirable service and/or as a remunerative investment. Possibilities for financing are explored, both in terms of adequate funds for building and probable income sufficient to support a suitable budget for operation. Consideration is given to the availability of adequate space in a desirable location. To make the most effective use of the experts invited to serve on the team, it is desirable for those in authority to have reasonably accurate and fairly detailed general information on which to base goals, procedures, costs, standards, and operations.

The need for the facility and its size, type, and desirable characteristics are usually presented by the owner or administrator. Thus a superintendent of a hospital or a board of governors decides on a new wing for the hospital and with it the enlargement of the food facilities. A college president may see the need for a new residence hall. A hotel manager may become aware of the need for added banquet space to take care of the convention trade. The extent of the need, the means of financing, and the probability of consumer acceptance will be explored with other interested persons with whom they must act or by whom they are guided. This type of basic information will indicate the feasibility of proceeding with the venture. During this early stage, the size and type of operation may be determined, and the location and general character of the facility outlined with some detail.

Persons engaged to produce plans need to have a reasonably clear concept at the outset of the character, size, and type of services to be provided. Although ideas will grow and change as planning proceeds, much valuable time can be saved by having standards, goals, and limitations reasonably well defined in the beginning. Except for units that are very small, several individuals are likely to be involved in the planning. The greater the number chosen to work on plans, the greater the need for clearly defined goals and standards. Whenever there is more than one individual involved there is room for misunderstanding and misinterpretation, plus differences in standards.

The owner or person in authority is the decision maker and is the number one member of the planning team. The plans will call for accurate and detailed information pertaining to (1) finances, (2) legal aspects, (3) design and construction, (4) essential needs characteristic of the facility, and (5) operational standards and requirements. Persons in authority may be very well informed in important fields of knowledge but lack the information required for designing, building, and operating a food facility. Other team members are chosen to supply essential information. It is the responsibility of each member to supply accurate, complete, and useful information in an understandable form, in time to guide the judgment of the decision maker as it applies to their specific area of expertise.

Architect

The second member of the planning team, the **architect,** is chosen as soon as a decision has been reached to go ahead with the venture. The architect's advice is often sought concerning size, costs, and location even before a final decision has been made to build. The architect interprets the ideas that have been provided by the owner and translates them into a physical plan. The architect provides guidance on architectural design and engineering principles, guides selection of designs and materials, prepares plans and specifications for materials and structures, and supervises construction. Estimates of construction costs are made. After the plans have been completed, the architect will present them and the specifications for bidding and contracting following final approval by ownership. After the contracts are awarded, the architect supervises construction, issues certificates of insurance, and notarizes affidavits and waivers of lien. The architect often contributes valuable information on financial arrangements, legal aspects, decor, and operational points that have been gleaned from experience and knowledgeable observations.

Operation

A person or persons well informed in the **operation** of food facilities of the type proposed should be the third part of the planning team. The choice of equipment, the layout, and the physical factors supporting the essential functions directly influence the success with which the facility will operate. An orderly and logical flow of essential functions and the development of facilities to promote their accomplishment with maximum efficiency and high standards form the basis for layout engineering. The needs, resources, and characteristics of a specific situation govern the functions to be performed. The functions, in turn, will influence the flow of sequence of operations, the equipment needed, and the space requirements. It is often desirable to obtain the services of an interior designer as well as a food management consultant.

Financial aspects confronted by ownership are many and varied. Members of the planning team should be able to supply significant information from their special areas on which many of the decisions can be based. Factors relating to probable patronage, income, operating costs, and upkeep need to be carefully estimated by the food manager. A reasonable budget should be projected for the proposed operation. If building funds are to be recovered through amortization, knowledge is needed about obtainable rates of interest, probable income, and operating costs. Wise judgment is needed to identify the significant services the facility should provide, the important principles to be followed in the organization of work, and the facility's function as a business concern. The feasibility of proceeding with plans for the food facility depends on the ability to establish a budget based on adequate returns for foods and services that are needed and readily acceptable to a sufficient volume of consumers to support the essential costs. Preparation of such a budget calls for accurate determination through careful study of the following:

Extent and duration of needs

Adequacy and suitability of proposed food and services

Probability of patron acceptance, as affected by health, age, mobility, sex, occupation, nationality, food habits, current fashions, and financial and cultural status

Available competition

Financing, the initial costs and amortization, operation, upkeep, and renewal

Amount and source of available funds from grants, available cash, and/or amortization through operation income

Availability and cost of essential materials, services, and labor

Restrictions—legal, administrative, site, space, other.

It is strongly recommended that the person who is to direct the food preparation and service when the facility is completed be a member of the planning team, or be kept closely informed of decisions as planning proceeds. If the manager of the facility is inexperienced, it may be wise to employ a capable and experienced consultant who is well informed in food management. Many foodservice operators know how to operate a food service well, but lack the ability to plan one. Participation of the food manager in planning discussions provides an opportunity to express personal views and to clarify ideas. The success of the operation when the facility is completed will depend to a large degree on this person's understanding and acceptance of the intended organization of work and skill in carrying it out.

Builder

The **builder** selected for the facility may be a fourth member of the planning team. The builder's role in the actual planning may be minor, but very helpful in indicating desirable building materials, construction features, timing of contract awards, and time allowances. Normally, the job of the builder is to take the plan and specifications of the architect and put up the physical structure, which is not a part of planning but is actual accomplishment of the plan. Nevertheless there is a bridge in this instance between the planning group and fulfillment of the plan, and the builder may be able to play some small, but quite important, part in planning.

Sometimes the team may desire to avail itself of the advice of an interior decorator on decorative effects, furnishings and other factors that relate to decor.

In the organization of any planning team, which is usually established by ownership, ample consideration should be given to the use of all four viewpoints. The elimination of any one of them is likely to be hazardous in terms of unnecessary costs and/or an unsatisfactory operation.

The members of the planning team are likely to approach planning with different points of interest and different backgrounds of knowledge. The differences in background and viewpoint can add richly to the fund of information but may at times call for certain refereeing on the part of the owner. A food manager, for example, may suggest an idea that would be impractical from the standpoint of construction, or a design suggested by the architect may interfere seriously with the best flow of work or convenience. Many desirable adjustments can be arrived at through open discussion.

RESEARCH AND ANALYSIS

A food facility that has been cast at great expense from concrete, metal, and labor is not likely to be changed readily even though a satisfactory operation has not been made possible according to the plans. This fact emphasizes the importance of thorough information gathering and evaluation of ideas early in the planning stage. It is the responsibility of each member of the planning team to gather information in their respective areas of specialization that will be helpful to other members of the team. Early investigation or market study should include a careful analysis of needs, tastes, and habits of individuals to be served, their probable number, plus amount and source of income. An experienced foodservice operator should be able to judge the likelihood of patron acceptance of a given type, cost, and amount of food and service.

Gather useful ideas wherever they can be found. Visit establishments that are similar to the proposed facility. Search through current publications. Spend profitable time in forecasting estimates based on actual experience. It is often profitable to talk over estimates with other well-informed individuals. The architect, who must give general estimates of space needs and probable costs, may seek outside advice. Both the architect's and the operator's knowledge can be helpful in a feasibility study. It is important that the collecting of data begin early. A suggested outline for one type of feasibility study appears in appendix B. The outline used needs to be adapted to the specific needs of the particular facility being planned.

The location of the site for the facility is important for success even for nonprofit-oriented units. It is likely to be critical for success in those that are profit oriented. If all of the factors that influence the desirability of site, such as convenience, number of persons near or passing the site at mealtime, attractiveness of location, etc., are fed into a computer, the computer can give helpful assistance in determining the best site. The Oklahoma Restaurant Association in Oklahoma City has found that its computer program on site selection has proven successful in indicating favorable sites. Computer success depends on acute judgment of factors that have a real bearing on attracting and holding the clientele, securing adequate supplies and holding a satisfied workforce, plus bearing on operating expenses.

Sometimes a single detail can prove valuable. Products and their quality and availability on the market should be studied to indicate how materials may be used differently. Trips to equipment dealers and/or manufacturers can also be helpful in indicating costs, items available, specifications, and the names of users of specific models. The opinions of those who have used various pieces of equipment, systems, or designs in layout are valuable. Brief, easy-to-complete questionnaires sent to foodservice operators on significant points of operation or equipment can yield excellent information. Useful time can be spent in the library studying current institution foodservice books and magazines.

Reasonably complete notes should be taken on visits or during study. Keep the notes organized as to subject matter so that specific information can be readily found. Date and state the source of information. Expect the information to fill a large-size notebook. Organize notes so that they can be filed in the notebook or file case according to the classification of the information. One section, for example, might be labeled "Planning Guides" and contain statements of standards and methods that specifically apply. The major part of the notebook might be divided into classifications relating to sections of the facility, such as receiving, storage, and cooking. Under each classification would be filed information relating to standards, space needs, flow of work, ideas for layout, and equipment. Equipment information might include specification sheets for different makes of items to be used.

Studies tend to be most fruitful when information is sought in answer to specific questions. For example, when a facility is being planned for a particular group of people, it is best to know facts about them that relate to the satisfaction of the purpose and success of the venture. What are their tastes, needs, buying power, and probable reaction to the proposed service? Are there social or psychological factors that will influ-

FIGURE 1.4 Guests like to see foods being prepared in an open kitchen such as the one shown here. The planner has not forgotten to make the presentation decoratively attractive. Note the tile and stonework. A large hood placed over food preparation equipment allows odors to be caught that might invade the dining area and negate the merchandising effect of the unit. *(Courtesy of National Restaurant Association, Washington, DC.)*

ence patronage? Current living conditions and changing social customs tend to affect eating habits, and these should be reviewed to ascertain if they are influential in the particular instance. Today Americans are restless, impatient, and mobile. A large percentage of women work outside the home, children eat lunch and sometimes breakfast at school, and many men and women dine in or near their industrial plant. Families often dine out as a group. Fast, informal, inexpensive service is popular. Prices paid for lunch are influenced by budgeted daily allowances. Adequate parking is required for the motor trade. The omission of one consideration or one detail may result in an inadequate plan.

The pleasure value of food makes mealtime ideal for entertaining. Many public restaurants plan entertainment quality into their menus and decor. Dramatic quality in food, surroundings, and service adds enjoyment and reduces the humdrum aspect of everyday living (Figure 1.4). Culinary artists win acclaim by making food not only delectably good but also artistically appealing. Many patrons who relish plain and simple food for daily fare want it to be more imaginative and dramatic for special occasions. Food is used to add drama and special significance to teas, weddings, receptions, professional meetings, and holiday celebrations. The ability to provide special service for a clientele can be facilitated through thoughtful and thorough initial planning.

When the type of establishment has been determined, a careful study should be made of institutions of comparable type. Every aspect, open to observation, that may influence success or failure should be noted. Data should be organized to preserve significant points and avoid confusion as to their relevancy and importance. Notes on visits are likely to be most accurate and complete if made "on the spot," if courtesy permits, or immediately following the visit. The following is a suggested outline for gleaning pertinent information:

Name and address of the operation
Type of operation
General characteristics of patrons
Name and phone number of manager
Manager's education and experience
Type of service and menu pattern and prices
Number served and hours of service
Speed of service (average time from production to consumer)
Storage space and equipment—food, supplies, equipment, laundry
Kind of tableware—removal after meals, cleaning method, handling and storage
Specialty features—menu, service, decor, hospitality
Most popular menu items—volume sold, cost, selling price
Source of supplies and services
Buying—who does it, how often, nature of supplies, volume
Special service provided
Number of employees—production, service, cleanup
Labor sources and rates
Employee training—how much, by whom, for how long
Supervision, amount and type—production, service, cleanup
General plan of layout and approximate space allowances
Analysis of work flow and work timing
Equipment items—production, service, cleanup, office
Condition of equipment and length of service
Amount of items used and how used
Percentage allocation of costs—food, labor, operations, other
General condition and appeal of facility—decor, orderliness, cleanliness
Aspects that appeal most favorably
Aspects that detract most—how they could be avoided or remedied.

When work requirements have been determined, various arrangements of equipment should be studied from the standpoint of flow of work. A minimum of time-consuming motions should be used to accomplish essential functions. Planners need to carefully calculate paths for the logical movement of materials from receiving to storage, through preparation, service, and final cleanup. Utilization of labor-hours and reduction of payroll costs are directly affected not only by the food purchased but also by the equipment selected and a layout that obstructs or promotes efficient work. A job analysis should be made for every position on which effort is regularly expended. Each motion deserves challenge as to whether it is necessary or done the right way, in the right place, at the proper time, and by the right person. Possibly it should be done by machine, combined with another task, or eliminated. We cannot hope to simplify work motions wisely without knowing what the motions are and how much each motion accomplishes. We also need to know the order in which motions are made (see Chapter 4, Analyses of Layout Characteristics).

Preparation of a graphic picture or chart of work flow helps to clarify ideas and uncover blind spots. Accuracy of measurements is important to accuracy of information concerning distances covered and time required. It is necessary therefore at this point of study and research that some preliminary selection of equipment will have been made and measurements secured. Since the study is to explore the advisability of operational schemes, initial plans may be changed or abandoned as a result of the study. Frequently this part of the analysis is still in the conceptual phase, although some of the data and material obtained may begin to work into the actual physical plan or specifications. It is important for planners, especially novices, to remember that these studies are to promote eventual success of the facility, and they should not feel discouraged if ideas and carefully drawn schemes are later discarded. It is extremely desirable to isolate and identify all alternatives, weigh them and the data applying to them carefully, and then make the selection that seems best.

Useful research involves many careful calculations. Before we can evaluate a particular layout, we must determine precisely what work is to be accomplished. Food facilities are being planned today to do full meal preparation starting with basic materials and continuing to completed products, and others are being planned to do no production. The plan selected will determine work to be done and equipment needed. Before selecting one plan over the other, costs, consistency of quality, and dependability of supply need to be evaluated. The vagaries of the markets may present risks to standards and costs that are too great to accept with one type of operation. Good aspects of individuality and special skills developed in production of products in a particular institution may be lost. On the other hand, the quality of food fully produced commercially might be more consistent where labor is less qualified, and it may greatly reduce labor worries in procurement, training, supervision, and maintenance. The planner's calculations should help prevent shedding one set of worries only to assume others that are greater. It is best to evaluate change and look into the future to see what changes are likely to occur and should be considered in planning. Although a plan may satisfy immediate needs, a study of the trend may indicate that the situation and needs are likely to change sufficiently to warrant preparations in the present plan to eventually meet them. It is always highly desirable to obtain as firm a statement as possible from the decision maker or person in authority as to probability of expansion of plans in the future and how soon the changes might occur.

Those in authority need to have convincing proof of value before approving the purchase of costly equipment. Although an item of equipment might be more costly than a very nice house and lot, the amount of labor needed to do the daily task at the current rate for labor might in a surprisingly short time total much more than costly pieces of equipment to do the job. Before the decision maker will be willing to approve the expenditure of large sums, proof must be presented that will justify the cost in terms of improvement of food or services and savings in operational expense.

Every labor minute counts in reducing costs. Calculate the cost of labor employed for the type of work to be done in a unit where a specific piece of equipment is to be used. How much will it cost per minute? A dish washer is likely to receive between 10 and 12 cents per minute. If that person wastes even 15 minutes per day at 12 cents per minute walking a needless distance coping with equipment that is in poor condition or hard to operate or difficult to clean, or in hunting for items that are poorly stored, it will mean the loss of $1.80 per day. This occurring 365 days per year will amount to a loss of $657. In terms of 10 years, the depreciation period for kitchen machines, the loss, compounding interest at 8%, would be about $10,279. The loss for skilled workers, such as cooks and bakers, would be at least double this amount. These figures emphasize not only the need for suitable equipment but also for efficient layout of equipment. Since operation members know food production and how it should be done, they often can point out ways in which costs can be reduced without a loss of essential features (Figure 1.5).

The operation member of the planning team needs to make sure that ideas have been accepted, understood, and approved by those in authority. It can be hazardous to proceed on suppositions. It also is important to be sure that the architect understands recommendations that have been approved and has incorporated them in the plans. The ideas may be as major as a plan of operation or as small as the placement of a power receptacle. There needs to be an established policy concerning the extent of each team member's authority, and it should identify which items require specific approval and by whom. This will give assurance and help to save time for members of the planning team. It is unwise to neglect viewpoints and to fail to do a thorough job of study and research

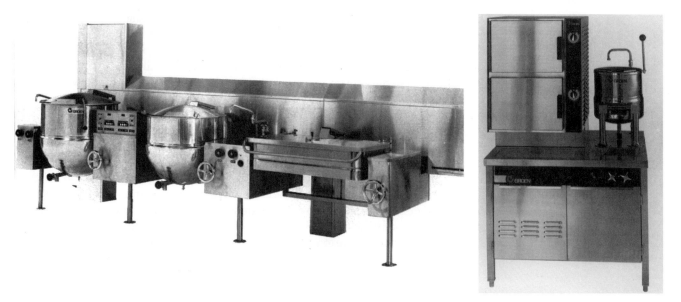

FIGURE 1.5   The operation team member should be conversant with the latest types of equipment and also details available about them that can save space and cost. (a) It is possible to obtain equipment such as that shown already grouped and mounted so in one simple installation all units can be wall mounted. (b) By understanding production needs the operation team member indicates to architects and others on the planning team desirable ways to group equipment to reduce labor requirements and make work easier. *(Courtesy of Groen, Elk Grove Village, Illinois.)*

of all facets affecting a plan. It is said that you can tell how well a foodservice operation has been planned by the time lapse that occurs between the time of its completion and the start of remodeling. Some facilities operate for years without change or modification. Others begin to be remodeled a few days after construction has been completed and operation begun.

COMMUNICATION

Accurate, complete, and understandable communication between team members is very important to successful planning. The differences in background, experience, and points of interest tend to complicate communication between members of the planning team and those who are to share in the realization and operation of the food facility. Words tend to have different meanings for different members of the team and may have still other significance for other persons associated with the project. Forms of communication are needed that will convey ideas precisely. The two forms commonly used for expressing approved requirements are **technical drawings** and **written specifications.** Discussions and pictures are utilized to clarify ideas and to present arguments for or against them, while helping people to visualize the plans. It is important for technical drawings to have a high degree of accuracy in measurements and design. Specifications or word descriptions of materials, conditions, and procedures need to be sufficiently precise to prevent misunderstanding.

Many vague phrases are used that allow for wide interpretation. Familiar in the food industry are "good food," "adequate amount," and "fast service." The speaker is likely to have a definite picture in mind drawn from a specific experience. The listener will immediately picture the meaning in terms of personal experience, which may be drawn from an entirely different background and set of standards. A little thoughtful effort in expressing thoughts precisely can help pinpoint significant aspects. "Adequate amount" may vary widely depending on the type of person to be served. It becomes definite when stated in weight or volume per portion and the number of portions. "Fast service" is a more definite phrase when it is tied to an exact schedule or number served per minute or with limitation of the time lapse from pan to patron.

Good progress in planning springs from a keen awareness of need and a detailed analysis of ways to solve problems. Many standards, particularly those affected by layout designs and specifications, are mathematically measurable. Equipment and layout can be equated to needs and expressed in deck number and size, container capacity, and speed of output. Food goodness, in addition to materials utilized and techniques of preparation, calls for definite handling methods and limitation of time between preparation of the food and its presentation to the customer. Supplying volume requirements depends on batch capacity and speed of output. Protection of palatability involves holding conditions and limits the size of delivery equipment so that the first plates or trays of food are not held and allowed to deteriorate while others are being prepared. Travel distance and mode of travel call for control to shorten time between preparation, dishup, and presentation to the customer. The plan that evolves should meet these and other significant requirements.

In seeking precision of expression planners should analyze the characteristics that can produce the desired results. Such analysis helps to create a plan that can actually be taken to fruition. An analysis of "clean" will indicate the need to identify numerous factors pertaining not only to the product but also to the facilities. For example, all work surfaces will need to be smooth, easily cleaned, nonabsorbent, and free from lodging spots for soil. They will need to be sufficiently durable to permit frequent and vigorous cleaning. Thorough cleanliness will call for food machines that can be taken apart and reassembled easily and quickly. Hand-washing facilities must be convenient to work areas. Suitable cleaning arrangements will be required for the workshop and its equipment.

When writing specifications it is necessary to identify every significant characteristic or condition where choice is afforded. This will include such things as material, design, size, and special operating conditions such as water or power voltage and cycle. The complexity of specifications varies with the amount and type of identification required. Descriptions of manufactured items are simplified when a catalog description is available for reference. On manufactured items, information is needed as to size, model, source of power or heat, material, workmanship, and any other appurtenances or factors desired. Manufacturers usually supply specification sheets for fabricated items for equipment chosen from their company.

Equipment to be fabricated or custom built, where models are not available for examination, requires specifications made in greater detail. Construction details are needed as well as size, material, design, and function. Detail drawings are useful for specifications as well as for shop drawings to guide construction. An architect's or engineer's assistance is likely to be required. The food manager or operator member of the team should work closely with the architect or engineer on the design and approve it when completed. Some equipment manufacturers provide detailed drawings of their equipment or supply graphics of them that can be transferred to a computer for drawing onto plans. (See Figure 1.6.)

Team members should identify items and the size of the equipment plus space relationships for a good flow of work. Satisfactory progress in planning calls for promptness as well as precision of communication.

CREATING A PLAN

Any drawings submitted by team members should be clear and drawn to scale. This can lead to speed in achieving a suitable plan. Members should understand customary modes of expression used on technical drawings and specifications. Many symbols have

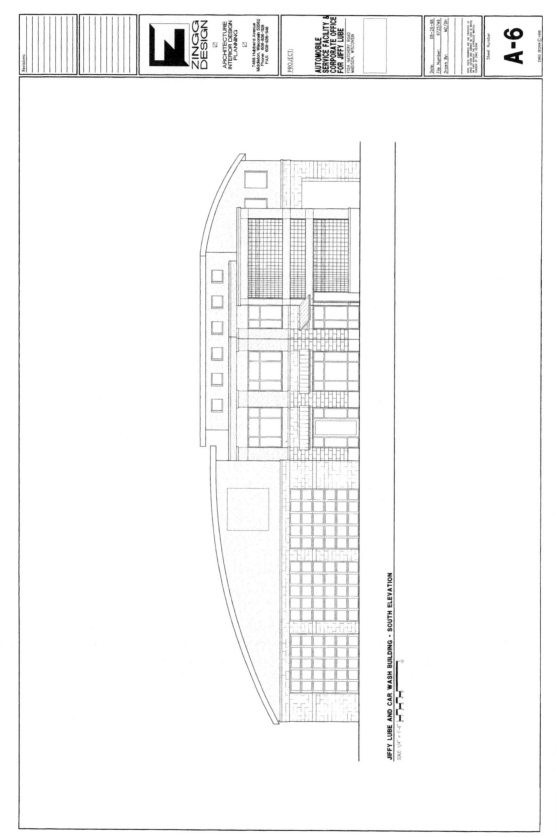

FIGURE 1.6 The use of an AutoCAD computer program allows architects and others to draw plans quickly and professionally with details like those shown in this illustration. *(Courtesy of Zingg Design, Middleton, Wisconsin.)*

specific meanings, and all team members should understand those meanings. If a team member does not know this language and how to interpret scale drawings, perspective, details of construction, and how a series of plans fit together, such as the plumbing, electrical, and other detail plans, reference should be made to such sources of information. **Layout designs,** carefully drawn to scale, are useful in conveying ideas and for study of equipment placement and space relationships. The team members should be able to try out their various schemes before reaching a decision as to the one to recommend. A busy architect should not be expected to respond with a new drawing for each change of mind by a team member.

Sketches should be accurate, neat, legible, and drawn to scale. Lack of accuracy can lead to allowing too much or too little space. Each square yard spells expense to build and maintain as well as increased labor costs. Inadequate space handicaps work progress and the achievement of good standards. Sketch neatness promotes respect for the ideas presented. Architects usually supply a blueprint of the proposed space in a specified scale, such as ¼-in. or 6-mm scale, which means ¼-in. (6 mm) on the drawing represents 1 ft (305 mm) in actual building. The use of graph paper that has ¼-in. (6-mm) squares is sometimes convenient for preliminary sketches.

The use of a computer AutoCAD program or graphics can considerably simplify the task of drawing sketches or plans. Figure 1.6 shows an outside plan of a building drawn by the AutoCAD program. Any lettering required on the drawing can also be done by the computer. If, however, a team member does not have available such a useful tool and must resort to setting up drawings by hand, the following is a useful list of items needed to do such handwork:

1. Drafting table or board that can be positioned for good posture and free, easy motion when drawing. The "working edge" must be true and straight.
2. T-square, preferably with a transparent edge.
3. 45° triangle with an 8-in. (203-mm) side and a 30° × 60° triangle with a 10-in. (254-mm) side. (Test accuracy; these are subject to warping.)
4. Architect's scale rule. [A flat 6-in. (152-mm) rule is popular.]
5. Circle and lettering templates.
6. Drawing pencils: 4H for line drawing, 3H for sketching and lettering, and 2H for tracings to be blueprinted.
7. Sharpener and sandpaper pad for sharpening pencils.
8. Pencil eraser and art gum for cleaning and erasing.
9. Drawing paper that is tough, fine grained, and hard surfaced.
10. Draftsman's tape (preferably) or thumb tacks to fasten the drawing paper to the board.

For team members who do not use graphic drawing programs, the use of templates may help to simplify the work. These are scale drawings of equipment that can be manipulated in various arrangements to afford the best use of space and achievement of work. Figure 1.7 shows some templates made available by an equipment fabricator that can be cut out and used in setting up plans or trying out equipment arrangements. For someone who can use graphics and the computer, this whole task can be done much more easily.

The team member representing operation should list all items of equipment to be used. It is best to separate the list into major equipment, which consists of all items to be shown on drawings, and minor equipment, needed but not shown on drawings, such as pots, pans, and small tools. Specifications that are sufficiently clear and adequate to ensure receipt of the desired item should be given for each listed item. The specifications will be needed not only by the architect but also for full and accurate understanding by bidders.

Knowledge and awareness of measurements are important to effective use of space. The **metric system** of measurement is the one used most widely for world trade. Although it has not been generally followed for everyday use in the United States, it is valuable for food facility planners to be familiar with the terms, abbreviations, and rules

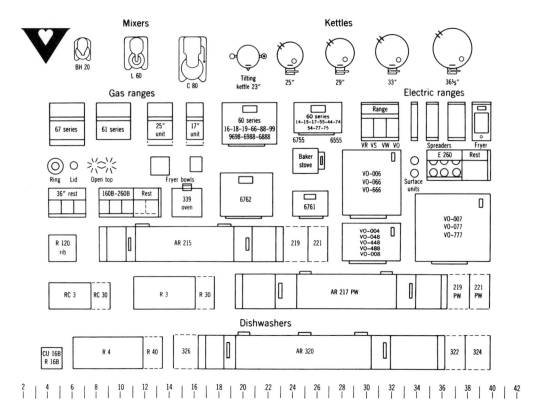

FIGURE 1.7 Equipment fabricators' drawings of their equipment such as these are often made available for use in indicating the details of equipment desired. *(Courtesy of S. Blickman Inc., Weehawken, New Jersey.)*

TABLE 1-1   *Prefixes to Metric Measures*

Multiples and Submultiples	Prefixes	Symbols	Significance
10^6	mega	M	Increase a million times
10^3	kilo	k	Increase a thousand times
10^2	hecto	h	Increase a hundred times
10	deka	da	Ten
10^1	deci	d	one tenth of
10^2	centi	c	One hundredth of
10^3	milli	m	One thousandth of
10^6	micro	μ	One millionth of

Source: Adapted from Thomas Gilbert and Marilyn B. Gilbert, Thinking Metric, *John Wiley, New York, 1973, and L. J. Chisholm,* Units of Weight and Measure, International (Metric) and U.S. Customary, *National Bureau of Standards, U.S. Government Printing Office, Washington, DC 20402.*

of conversion between the metric and the North American system in order to avoid errors. The four metric measurements that will be used most commonly in connection with foodservice planning are those which describe physical quantity, that is, length—expressed in meters instead of inches and feet; weight and mass—expressed in grams instead of ounces and pounds; volume or capacity—expressed in liters in place of pints, quarts, and gallons; and temperature—in degrees Celsius rather than Fahrenheit. The multiples and submultiples of meters, grams, and liters are indicated by prefixes (see Tables 1.1 and 1.2).

TABLE 1-2 *Conversion Factors for Measurements Commonly Used in Food Facility Planning*

Physical Quantity	From	To	Multiply By
Length of area	inch	centimeter (cm)	2.54
	inch	meter (m)	0.025 4
	square inch	square centimeter (cm^2)	6.451 6
	foot	centimeter (cm)	30.48
	foot	meter (m)	0.304 8
	square feet	square meters (m^2)	0.092 903 04
	yards	meters (m)	0.914 4
	square yards	square meters (m^2)	0.836 127 36
	miles	meters (m)	1609.344
	miles	kilometers (km)	1.609 344
Weight and mass	ounce (avoirdupois)	grams (g)	28.349 523
	ounce (avoirdupois)	kilogram (kg)	0.028 349 523
	pounds (avoirdupois)	grams (g)	453.592 37
	pounds (troy)	grams (g)	373.241 721 6
Volume or capacity	cup (liquid)	milliliters (mL)	236.588 236 8
	pint (liquid)	liter (L)	0.473 176 473
	quart (liquid)	liter (L)	0.946 352 946
	pint (dry)	liter (L)	0.550 610 47
	quart (dry)	liter (L)	1.101 221
	quart (dry)	dekaliter (dal)	0.110 122 1
	gallons (liquid)	liter (L)	3.785 411 784

Temperature
Convert Fahrenheit to Celsius (centigrade) by subtracting 32, multiplying by 5, and dividing by 9. To change Celsius to Fahrenheit, multiply by 9, divide by 5, and add 32.

Source: Adapted from Thomas Gilbert and Marilyn B. Gilbert, Thinking Metric, John Wiley, New York, 1973, and L. J. Chisholm, Units of Weight and Measure, International (Metric) and U.S. Customary, *National Bureau of Standards, U.S. Government Printing Office, Washington, DC 20402.*

CHAPTER SUMMARY

The planning of a foodservice facility has some unique requirements; three of the most important are as follows:

1. You must plan for the performance of the three major economic functions. Often these three do not stand alone but must become a supporting part of the main function of the facility such as supporting guest needs for food and beverages at a race track.
2. Every plan must be original; copying the plan of another facility usually results in a poor plan.
3. The plan must satisfy a market, employees, and management.

A plan usually evolves in two stages. The first is entirely conceptual and the second stage is the development of the physical plan. These stages are summarized in the following steps:

1. A need for a food service is seen.

2. A location is selected and a feasibility study is usually conducted to see if the plan is economically sound, practical for satisfying the need, etc.
3. A team to assist in the planning is selected, made up of the owner, architect, operation and builder members. The architect contributes the engineering expertise required, but sometimes engineering is so important that an engineer becomes a fifth team member.
4. Research and analysis is done by the team members.
5. A broad plan is presented and critiqued.
6. The plan is revised and finalized.
7. Bids are taken.
8. Bids are reviewed and the plan may be revised if, for instance, the bids showed that the funds allocated were insufficient. The revised plan is sent out for bids.
9. Bids are reviewed and ownership selects successful bidders.

10. Building proceeds with team members closely following all developments to see that the facility desired is the facility that is actually built.
11. When work is completed, the team members review the facility. If there are deficiencies, the work is not accepted until these are corrected. With acceptance, final payment is made for the work.

The owner team member is responsible for establishing goals and standards and communicating these to the other team members. Establishing the financial limits, arranging for financing, and other matters relating to finance are the province of ownership. The architect is responsible for establishing the plan's requirements and presenting these in a physical plan and specifications and other written material. The architect must meet the financial limitations established by ownership or else advise the owner about why they are inadequate. The operation member is responsible for indicating desirable work flow, kind and placement of equipment, and other matters relating to how the facility is to be used. The builder is responsible for indicating suitable building materials, methods for building, time requirements for completing work, etc. Good communication between team members is needed.

Often team members visit other facilities to gain ideas that might be useful in the new plan. It is also helpful when users of specific equipment are consulted to see if such equipment might be desirable for the planned facility.

A short outline of how to make an actual sketch, drawing, or plan for presentation to the other team members is given. The use of the computer for creating graphics is discussed.

REVIEW QUESTIONS

Instructor: Bring to class a series of plans and show students how the plans are put together. Point out the architectural symbols used in the plans. Demonstrate the use of the drawing equipment and templates. After they have had an opportunity to examine the plans and specifications, simulate a meeting of a planning committee.

It is also advisable that students be introduced to the use of AutoCAD and the use of graphics for setting up plans.

1. Identify symbols used and construction details on architectural plans.

2. Prepare templates for foodservice equipment using a scale of ¼ in. (6 mm) to equal 1 ft (305 mm).
3. Visit a food facility of a specified type and make a report following the outline suggested in the text.
4. Prepare information concerning the food facility visited that would be useful to other members of a planning committee when planning such a facility.
5. Evaluate the ideas that were presented in the simulated planning meeting.
6. Make a copy of a layout as assigned.

KEY WORDS AND CONCEPTS

architect
builder
economic functions
engineering
feasibility study
goals
layout designs
metric system

operation
owner
plan
sketch
standards
technical drawing
written specifications

CHAPTER

2

Foodservice Types: Layout Characteristics

INTRODUCTION

The foodservice industry is composed of a wide number of different units, each designed to meet the needs of a special type of clientele. Proper facilities must be planned for them to function to meet these needs. Today's drive-in must possess unique outside and inside facilities, whereas an industrial cafeteria for factory workers requires an entirely different layout. And a cafeteria in a busy shopping area would be badly planned if it tried to take advantage of the same plan used for a bank's executive dining room. Each foodservice facility must be targeted toward a specific audience, providing the required items and manner of consuming them.

This chapter broadly summarizes some of the more characteristic planning needs of some of our more common food facilities. Such a summary does not imply that a specific food service *must* have such features—wide variations are found because of different situations—but the chapter outlines in general what most facilities of a certain type will usually possess. Planners normally adapt a design from these general features according to the specific needs of the facility they are planning.

Also, in the material that follows mention is made of some planning details that should be considered for a certain type of facility because of their importance to that type of unit. Such details may not be mentioned again in a succeeding section, but this does not mean that they are not important in the planning of another type of unit. Thus, although good ventilation and lighting are mentioned under planning requirements for hotels, and the influence types of service have on space, equipment, and layout needs is mentioned under full-service restaurants, the proper planning done because of these characteristics is important for almost every type of food service. They are not mentioned again because such repetition would defeat the purpose of concentrating on the most essential planning needs for the particular type of facility being discussed.

PLANNING FOR OPERATING AND MAINTENANCE COSTS

A planner of a food facility should strive to create an operation that achieves highest cost savings consistent with adequate food quality and service to patrons. The three largest costs in operating a foodservice facility, in order from most expensive to least, (1) food and beverages, (2) labor, and (3) operating and maintenance costs such as energy for heating, lighting, air conditioning, and cooking, and sanitation and cleaning. The way the food service is planned can directly influence all three, but especially the third, and planners need to keep this constantly in mind. Savings made here can directly influence the operation's ability to operate within desirable cost limits.

Energy

Food services are extremely energy intensive—they are one of the largest consumers of energy in the commercial sector,[1] spending for energy about five times more per square foot of space than offices or retail stores. The Food Service Technology Center (FSTC) of the Pacific Gas and Electric Company in San Francisco estimates that restaurants alone use more than $10 billion of gas and electricity per year. Of this cost in food services, food preparation equipment takes about 35% of the energy dollar. **Heating, ventilating, and air conditioning (HVAC)** are next in cost. Because the amount of heat and moisture developed by food preparation equipment affects the amount of HVAC energy required, any reduction in the first can also create a savings in HVAC costs. Lighting is third in the energy cost hierarchy, so long-life bulbs, efficient ballasts, and reflectors can pay for themselves over their lifetime and also improve lighting conditions in the kitchen, dining, and other areas. Lights that turn on only upon occupancy of the space and turn off when occupancy ends can result in a saving. It is important to remember that poor lighting can significantly reduce worker productivity and thus result in an added cost for labor.

The architects and builders who plan a foodservice facility, should ensure that the building itself is built to conserve energy. Heat transferred into the unit can be a significant factor in hot weather in terms of HVAC energy use, and heat loss through heat transferred out in cold weather can be another. The amount of heat transferred into a building by glass windows when the sun is shining through them can be significant. Glass that keeps this light out or curtains and draperies that shut the sun out can do much to alleviate this cost. Good window glazing can also help. Lights can generate a large amount of heat; in fact, some buildings are now being constructed so as to catch this heat and use it for heating or other energy needs. One hotel reduced the energy costs associated with heating its water, including that used by the pool, by catching such heat. New customized HVAC equipment is now available that can be designed to suit the specific needs of unit spaces rather than the total needs of the facility, in many instances resulting in reduced HVAC costs. The use of humidifiers in extremely dry climates can cool down incoming dry air and add sufficient moisture to make the atmosphere more comfortable. Or, gas-burning desiccant dehumidifiers that dry out humid air, making it easier and cheaper to cool, are now on the market. A polarized additive for refrigeration equipment oil is being marketed that displaces the buildup of oil in condenser and evaporator coils, thus improving heat transfer from the units. If possible, do not recirculate air from spaces where people smoke. Instead, build up a positive air pressure that forces the smoke into air exhaust systems.

The planner should be sure to select energy-saving equipment, providing such equipment gives adequate production and quality performance. Price should not be the sole selection factor. The efficiency rating of insulation on equipment should be investi-

---

[1]Stephen Yborra, president of Energystics, Inc., energy- and-technology consulting firm, as quoted in "Getting a Line on Energy-Saving Measures" *Restaurants USA*, May 1998, pp. 10–11.

gated because the amount of energy used by equipment varies greatly as a result of this factor. High-speed heating units that need only to be turned on to be ready for use are now on the market. These let you avoid turning the heat on early and holding it on so equipment is ready for use, one of the greatest energy-wasting techniques used in the kitchen. **Induction-cooking units** are now available that do not turn on until the cooking unit holding the food is placed onto the induction unit. Immediately a tight magnetic lock occurs between the heating and the cooking units with the immediate development of heat. To remove the cooking unit, the electricity must be turned off, ending energy use. Thus, energy is used *only* during the time needed to cook the food.

Energy firms recommend that operating facilities perform occasional energy audits to ascertain where energy savings might be made or where they might be improved. Anyone planning a facility should do the same and then use this audit to plan energy requirements. Planners can get valuable energy information from the following organizations:

Technical Services Department, National Restaurant Association, 12001 17th Avenue NW, Washington, D.C. 20036; phone: (800) 424-5156

Food Service Technological Center (FSTC), Pacific Gas and Electric, 12949 Alcosta Boulevard, Suite 101 San Ramon, California 94583 phone: (510) 866-5770

U.S. Department of Energy, Forrestal Building, 1000 Independence Ave., S.W. Washington, D.C. 20585

American Society of Heating, Refrigeration, and Air-Conditioning Engineers, 1791 Tullie Circle, N.E. Atlanta Georgia 30329 phone: (404) 636-8400

American Gas Association, 1515 Wilson Blvd., Arlington, VA 22209 phone: (703) 841-8400

Flintridge Consulting (www.primenet.com/flintrd/), 87 E. Green St. #304, Pasadena, California 91105-2072; phone: (626) 795-1171

Cleaning and Sanitation

In this text frequent mention is made of the desirability of equipment that makes cleaning and sanitation easier to accomplish. Rounded corners, smooth, durable cleaning surfaces, and easy access to all areas often are emphasized. Considerable labor and perhaps even materials costs can be saved by selecting the right equipment, right walls and wall surfaces, right floors, and right facilities such that the amount of labor needed to properly maintain them is reduced.

UNIT LAYOUT CHARACTERISTICS

Hotels

The foodservice units in a hotel usually vary more and are more elaborate and extensive than almost any other kind of food operation. Hotel foodservice units run the gamut from fast-food units, ice cream parlors, coffee shops, and snack shops, to cabarets, nightclubs, bars, and lounges to catering services, ethnic restaurants, and upscale dining rooms. They are spread throughout the main floors of the hotel, often making supply difficult. It is not unusual today for a hotel to lease space and have some franchise or independent unit operate a desired food service. The leasing facility will often have a standard plan which they adjust to suit the available space.

Small hotels often have only a coffee shop, while larger ones may require a main kitchen with a number of satellites, a catering section, and other production and dining units. Modest kitchen units can often meet catering needs, if they arise, because the demand is not large. If a central kitchen is to prepare items for other service units of the hotel, the necessary production facilities, storage units to hold production until needed, and shipping units will be required. The equipment and space for the kitchen must be sized to accommodate this increased volume. In the 1990s, you can reduce both space and equipment requirements with the use of value-added items that require limited equipment and time to have ready for service. In some hotels a separate kitchen to provide employee needs is sometimes planned. This employee unit may have some of the characteristics of an industrial feeding unit.

Hotel kitchens usually require more broilers, grills, ovens, and range top units than the ordinary kitchen with specialty equipment such as salamanders (small, upper-shelf broiling units) and rotisseries. Very large steam kettles are needed for the making of stocks and other quantity liquids. Many large kitchens have separate production units, with each unit designed to produce a specific kind of food. Thus, soups and sauces may be prepared in one section and another section is used for preparing vegetables, while a garde manger section is used for preparing cold foods. The bakeshop may have special sections for making ice creams and frozen desserts, another for making candies, etc. Some hotels have retail outlets that sell items to the public, and the production units supporting them should be close by. Even a wine shop with specialty snack and hors d'oeuvre items may be operated.

The amount of an item needed in a given period of time must be known because equipment to be used in its preparation must be properly sized to produce this required amount. Sometimes it is possible to prepare or partially prepare ahead of service needs and then store the item, thus scaling down the amount of equipment needed or its size, but not always. A steak must be fresh from the broiler to have maximum palatability. Green vegetables rapidly lose their color if held any length of time in a hot serving unit. In this text a description of equipment and its use is given and also the approximate amount that it can produce. Manufacturers often give the amounts of items their equipment can produce, but experience has shown these to be grossly overstated. Thus, a 60-gallon stock pot cannot make 60 gallons of soup. To do so, the stock pot would have to be filled to the brim. This is not possible. Some space has to be left for boiling action, mixing, etc. Or, a manufacturer of a griddle may state that the griddle can produce so many hamburgers in an hour, but this time is calculated only on how long it takes to fry the hamburgers, and does not include the time required to put them on the griddle and remove them for another batch or the time needed to scrape the griddle down after several fryings. In this text tested methods are given on how to calculate the actual amounts equipment can produce.

The patron turnover rate influences the amount and size of kitchen equipment required to meet demand. For heavy, peak loads, advanced preparation is often necessary. Good holding equipment helps in the preservation of quality of many items. The required amount of dining room space will be determined by the number to be served, their seating, and their turnover rate. Service stations should be close at hand to expedite removal of used covers and resetting of new ones. Table appointments chosen to harmonize with the restaurant decor should be appropriate for the service and sturdy enough to withstand normal wear. Plans should provide for adequate, close-at-hand storage space for children's high chairs and other equipment. The need for special service areas should be investigated. The provision of a buffet or fast- pickup service can be helpful in satisfying those who want to eat and run. A further definition of such space needs is given in a later discussion in this chapter.

In all types of foodservices good lighting must be present both for worker and guest needs. Some dining areas are often so dark that patrons who lack the best eyesight find it difficult to read menus. Dimly lit areas are also dangerous, contributing to accidents. Glare from lighting can result from lighting that is too strong or improper placement of lights. Good ventilation is also needed and in most cases the kitchen should have a negative airflow so that it pulls air in from dining areas. If the kitchen has more air pressure than the dining areas, a positive flow occurs such that air from the kitchen can flow out to diners, tainting the air with smoke and odors.

It is important to plan for adequate storage space in dining areas where different catering events are held. On some occasions, no tables and chairs are needed, while for others the room is filled with them. A place for storing such items when not in use must be provided and this is often too minimal. Taking advantage of lost space such as that under a stage can be helpful for providing adequate storage space of this kind. Some catering units must be planned so they can be quickly changed to meet special needs. Often they have a fixed stage, but ones that can also be erected to fit a need are also used. A dance floor is often needed, and sound and projection equipment may be required, along with a secure storage area for it. Maximum room capacity must be considered in relation to frequency of demand and probable yearly income from the use of the space. A large area may be partitioned if the partitions are sufficiently soundproof to provide individual unit privacy. If a keynote speaker in one room has to compete with a dance band and gaiety in an adjacent room, someone is sure to leave dissatisfied. The location and equipment for serving pantries and storage areas should be carefully planned in relation to probable use. Cloakrooms or checkrooms, toilet facilities, and traffic lanes should be considered in relation to catering areas and other public areas of the facility. A layout that permits large groups to reach the dining areas without tying up elevators or traffic lanes in general use is desirable.

Room Service.
A number of hotels, motels, and resident clubs provide **room service.** Breakfast usually is in heaviest demand with as many as a fourth of the breakfasts eaten being provided by room service. In this service as in other types of assembled and transported meals, quality depends on protection of the food during assembly and transit. Depending on the preparation required, an order should be delivered within 4 to 15 minutes of the time it was placed. Time stamps that indicate the time the order was received, time it was ready, and time it was picked up for transport to the rooms are helpful in promoting promptness. One of the latest innovations in room service is a specially designed elevator that is equipped to prepare breakfast and other orders for the rooms. Thus, the order can be taken and prepared while the elevator is en route, although supplemental assistance will usually be required for some orders from the main or supplemental kitchen. It is wise to ensure that room service has its own elevator service or ready access to service elevators.

The number of mobile tables required, the amount of equipment, and other room service needs will depend upon the volume and type of service carried. Many hotels and motels now try to restrict room service and have it available for only part of the day. Where the volume warrants, a separate facility may be provided apart from the main production area, but supported by it. Kosher breakfasts are traditionally dairy and for this reason must be prepared in a separate kitchen.

With sufficient volume it is advisable to have a separate room for meal assembly. One of the most common faults in planning room service areas is the failure to provide enough space for tables that must be opened and preset awaiting demand. Such space needs should be calculated and provided. Otherwise there is likely to be a large number of tables in halls or work aisles. This usually is a violation of fire codes and constantly a point of inconvenience and friction.

Bottled goods, beverages, and other required items should be stored in the area. All items required, with the exception of prepared foods, should be readily available. It is desirable to have a counter space for work with storage over or below. Adequate space for orderly storage of supplies and for setting up some parts of orders ahead will help to speed service. If volume is sufficient, a service bar may be provided. A desk with phones will be needed for handling calls. The room service section should be located close to elevators and where the route will permit the shortest, most direct path to the customer with a minimum of delays.

Because of the complexity in planning for such a large facility with such varied requirements, an experienced consultant in hotel foodservice planning should be a part of the hotel planning team.

Motels

Many large motels have catering services for conventions and large parties and offer other foodservice amenities like hotels. In such cases, planning for them may mirror that for hotels, as just discussed. Smaller motels usually find a coffee shop or fast-food unit sufficient to handle their trade. Again, needs will vary according to the type of clientele but most are set up to care for travelers that have limited stays. Many offer room service so planning must provide for this. In some cases a separate dining area is planned where guests can pick up a quick breakfast of juices, coffee, tea, milk, and bakery items. This is often provided as a part of the room charge and usually one person can handle the unit. Operation is often for only a few hours each morning. Some motels find it profitable to offer take-out items that travelers might want so they can eat as they travel. These are often in a display counter near the checkout unit so patrons can see what is available as they leave.

Catering

The two kinds of catering establishments are **on-premise** and **off-premise catering.** The former can be in an operating food service which prepares the food in its regular kitchen and usually serves the event in special rooms constructed for the occasion. If a unit has sufficient catering business, a separation production unit might be planned where the foods and beverages for the event are prepared. In some cases, some of the production may still come from the main kitchen with the separate kitchens doing supplemental and last minute preparation. Off- premise catering units have most of their needs prepared in a special catering unit and then deliver the food elsewhere for serving. Sometimes, only the delivery is done, and someone else does the serving. At other times the items needed are delivered and served. Often there is no kitchen where the off-premise catering event is held. In some cases, an operating food service may prepare food to send out.

The needs of an off-premise unit are so special and complex that its discussion here is not warranted. Not only must a full production kitchen be planned, but with it service equipment that must be stored and delivered. Special transportation equipment is needed including perhaps refrigerated or heated trucks and containers. Often, the caterer rents the dining service equipment such as tables, chairs, linens, dishes, flatwater, and glassware. The caterer might even rent special ovens and other heating equipment. Anyone that must plan such an off-premise unit should obtain a copy of *Off-Premise Catering Management* by Professor Bill Hansen (John Wiley & Sons, Inc., New York City, 1995).

A food production kitchen that is used for catering events must be planned keeping in mind the demands that will be made on it. These can vary from a simple tea with snack to an elaborate eight-course banquet. Answers to the following questions can be of help in planning:

1. What groups will request catering service?
2. What are the sizes and nature of the groups and what foods, beverages, and services, will they need?
3. What space can be made available for special functions and where is it to be located in relation to regular food production or specialized food production and service areas that support it only?
4. At what meal or time of day are these special functions likely to occur? What type of meal or food will be required and what types of service? Will alcoholic beverage service be required that may limit types of service personnel and require special equipment?
5. What facilities will be required for service—tables and chairs, serving equipment, water, refrigeration, electrical outlets, and so forth?
6. What special facilities will be needed by groups—cloakroom, toilets, program equipment such as speaker's podium, sound equipment, screen and projection

equipment, blackboard, dance floor, dressing room, orchestra space, special lighting, other?

7. How frequently will space and equipment be used? What extra costs are involved?
8. Where will catering equipment be stored when it is not in use?

Food goodness, interest, and temperature plus service speed are usual rating values used by patrons when evaluating a caterer. Typical hazards in meeting these values include quality changes due to transportation of foods from production areas to service and the time lost waiting for guest arrival or cocktail enjoyment; plus supply inadequacies due to more patrons than specified, service slowdowns occasioned by overcrowding of space, inefficiencies of temporary help, and insufficiencies in planning and advanced preparation. When catering is well done, there is no part of the food service more liable to flattering acclaim.

It is advisable to utilize but not overload regular staff and equipment in the main kitchen for special catering unless the nature and volume is such that special facilities are required to take care of it. Time and effort load for employees and space and volume capacity for equipment tied into regular production units need to be closely calculated. A certain amount of flexibility is normally built into both staff and equipment to cope with the occasional small increase, but special provisions should be made where catering is expected to be a regular part of the food operation. Such plans should include production, transportation, service, cleanup, space allowances, and equipment storage.

A **catering kitchen** equipped to do some final cooking if located close to the point of service is most likely to serve food of the best quality. Modern, fast-heating equipment makes possible quick final cooking or heating of refrigerated or frozen foods. Such cooking relieves some of the necessity of mealtime transportation and allows for rotation cooking and a more flexible time of service. Many foods can withstand treatment that is usually required of a convenience food with a reasonable degree of excellence. Menus for special meals handled in this fashion should be chosen from such foods. If very large groups are to be served preprepared, frozen, transported, stored, and finished foods, the equipment should be chosen to facilitate such handling. Appropriate size carts should be chosen on which the foods can remain through each of the steps of freezing, transporting, storing, and baking or that will accommodate trays for handling food even to placement on the hot serving table. The cooking equipment might consist of a convection oven only, or may include steam equipment for vegetables and a deep-fat fryer. In other cases, it may be a large complete kitchen.

Remote service pantries should be compactly planned and provide for storage of all necessary dishes, flatware, linen, serving tools, and other equipment. Facilities should be conveniently placed for water, ice, refrigerated milk, coffee, and hot water for tea as well as the containers for the beverage service. Bars for liquor service are frequently necessary in hotels, clubs, and commercial restaurants. If the bar is mobile and the pantry attractive, the pantry may be used as a cocktail bar for direct service and the bar moved aside for mobile dish-up equipment. Provide locked storage on the mobile bar. Hot plates, mixers, and other electrical equipment may be required and provision should be made for sufficient and adequate electrical outlets.

An **assembly-line dish-up** system similar to hospital tray assembly with the use of a traveling belt may be used for rapid banquet service, or the plates may be served at a hot table assembly line and pushed or handed from one server to the next. Advance preparation and portioning of cold menu items should be done and foods refrigerated ahead of time for service. Mobile rack storage will add convenience in transporting the items to the dining area for placement. Trays may be used for plate service or small, attractive, easily maneuverable carts. The carts with plate collars that permit stacking can handle a sizable load repeatedly with less fatigue, especially for women servers. Sufficient landing space for served plates and the filling of carts or trays should be provided at the end of the serving line. Heated mobile dish storage units should be provided in the serving line, as well as sufficient space for backup storage.

Banquet or special service areas may be on other floors or in another building from the food production section. Means of transportation must then be considered. For those located on another floor it is desirable that direct elevator service be provided. Thoughtlessness in relation to catering needs when designing the building can cost many dollars in labor time and sacrifice food quality and prompt service.

The demands connected with catered service are many and varied, and although many of them may have little connection with food service, provision to meet them is a part of satisfactory catering. The group may want special entertainment or dancing during the meal. Orchestra space, stage, dressing rooms, special lighting, sound effects, and other theatrical devices may be needed. A dining area may be used for a morning business meeting and coffee break, a style-show luncheon, and, later in the evening, a dinner dance. Rugs should be removable and a hard floor provided for dancing. Sound equipment may be required for speakers and for transmission of orchestra music. Telephone plug- ins, speaker podiums, projection screens, blackboards, display panels, piano, and other equipment may be required. The kind of establishment doing the catering and the amount of use various equipment will be given will guide planning for its procurement.

It is usually desirable to provide directional signs to the special service rooms in order to guide traffic and save answering repeated questions. A cloakroom and toilet facilities should be provided. Electrical outlets should be suitably located for equipment to be used, either by the servers or the guests. The decor should provide a reasonably neutral background that can easily be varied with decorative features or items provided by groups in carrying out special themes. Provide well-finished tables and chairs of good design that are substantial and snag- proof. Folding equipment or stackables may be used to be readily storable and easily transported. Provide platform trucks or other mechanical equipment for moving them and have adequate storage areas conveniently located.

Restaurant Types

Coffee Shops.   The most common type of restaurant in this country is the **coffee shop.** Many, like Denny's, Country Kitchen, Perkins, etc., are franchised, and standardized kitchen and dining area plans are established by the franchise. Others are single-owner units, often operated by a family, and are sometimes called **mom-and-pop operations.** Coffee shop types are also found in drug stores, shopping centers, and other retail units having a high customer influx. In these settings, they may take on the characteristics of a soda fountain or lunch counter. These often function largely to serve lunch and snack items during the open hours of the facility.

Many coffee shops use what is called the **California menu,** which allows patrons to order a breakfast, lunch, dinner, or snack at any time of the day or night. The decor is usually simple, standardized, and easily maintained. Counter and booth service are provided, and some coffee shops provide table service. Service must be fast and the menu must allow for such quick service. An informal, friendly, cheerful atmosphere is desirable. A significant amount of dinner trade derives from groups of price-conscious people that come for the evening meal. Thus, the dining area and menu must be suitably sized for these groups. Family groups are also prominent for the evening meal, so children's foods must be offered.

Most operations will specialize in a relatively few menu items; items that are overly complicated to prepare are likely to be eliminated. The kitchens of most franchise units must be a sort of combination of a fast-food operation and a full-service operation with some scaling down of both since the meals prepared will not be as extensive as those of a full-service unit and also because many of these operations are now using foods that meet the needs of a meal but come almost ready to serve. Heating in a microwave, broiler, oven, or steamer may be all that is required. The nonfranchise units of this type often require less of the fast-food type equipment and more of a regular restaurant type equipment, but with lowered demand for production.

Good lighting is desirable and display cases should be properly placed and lighted to promote sales. In some operations short-order cooking may occur in the dining area—patrons often like to sit and watch. Such an arrangement calls for special care in planning the hood over the cooking equipment and its pull of air through it to prevent odors from getting into the dining area. Fat odors and a smoky, cluttered appearance can turn away patrons at the door. Step-saving compactness in arrangement is valuable.

Full-Service Restaurants.

Full-service restaurants are often called **white table-cloth restaurants** because many feature such tabletop dressings. Many serve only lunch and dinner; some even serve only dinner. The menu is more elaborate and few fast-food items are offered and these only because some groups that come to dine have children or teenagers that prefer such items. (Although the upscale units of this type will frequently cater to the "expense account crowd" and are not very interested in having children or teenagers as a part of their clientele.) Some have highly specialized menu offerings such as seafood or steaks, or Italian or other ethnic foods. Menus are thus more specialized and extensive, and equipment and layout must be a bit more specialized and extensive to meet these needs. Noise control and an attractive decor are factors that need special attention from planners.

It is important that the planner know what is to be served, how much, and the type of service because service styles will influence planning. An operation featuring a French menu and one featuring a Chinese menu must have entirely different equipment and planning both in the kitchen and dining area. It is thus important to analyze carefully the menu and ascertain equipment and work center needs before starting planning. French style service takes much more (and often much more elaborate) kitchen equipment. Because much of the final preparation in **French service** takes place on a small cart (*gueridon*) at tableside, space must be available in the kitchen for cart movement and storage. A **checker station** is often needed where servers exit the kitchen going into the dining room, so foods can be checked. Food is dished for **Russian service** into tureens, platters, or other equipment and then taken by servers to the table to be served. In **American service,** the food is dished onto serving plates and served to guests at the table. American service usually requires the least kitchen space and equipment.

The space requirements for the dining area are also influenced by the type of service. French service requires more dining space than any other because of the space needed to move around *gueridons,* dessert carts, and other mobile equipment. Oddly, counter service also is a big space user. Normally, 12 to 14 square feet per cover is sufficient for seated service, but counter areas take about 20. Also, in upscale dining units, clubs, and others, where dining is leisurely and the price charged sufficiently high, more space will be allotted. Diners hate to be crowded in and avoid going to places that do so if they wish to have a private conversation or a leisurely meal. An operation that plans a fast turnover and fast service can succeed with much less space. Here the client's motivation in dining is different and rubbing elbows with others is not a problem. It is desirable to plan for wide aisle space for main routes of travel. A desk for the maître d'hôtel should be located at the dining area entrance. Space for a cashier's station is also needed and this is best located where guests leave the dining area.

Full-service restaurants usually have a lounge and bar area. Their planning should fit into the planning of the dining and kitchen areas. It is desirable to have them in proximity to the dining area since guests will tend to stop here before going in to dine. As in all food services the location of restrooms, phone booths, guest apparel storage, etc., should be convenient for guest use.

Drive-Ins and Fast-Food Units.

In the last 50 years **drive-ins** and **fast-food units** have been the fastest growing segment of the industry and today rank among the leaders in dollar volume and first in numbers served. This group includes the typical drive-in, sandwich shops, coffee stands, and other units where patrons can get a quick partial meal and move on. Since the markup is usually modest, the volume produced must be large for the amount of space. As much of the food as possible must be prepared ahead of time or be in a state where it can be rapidly prepared. In a drive-in, only a few minutes should lapse between receiving the order and serving the patron. A unit such as a sandwich shop will have a large part of what it sells prepackaged and in storage ready to take out and hand to the guest. Disposable paper service is standard.

Planners of such units must ensure that there is a smooth flow between receiving and storage units and from these storage units to production and then service. Work centers must be planned so that everything needed is at hand so workers do not move from them. The typical drive-in will have a drive-up window where an order is given from the automobile. The car then moves on to another window where payment is received and perhaps the order handed out, or just payment made with movement ahead in the line to the third window where the order is received. Inside, the planner must provide for a counter where patrons can order, pay, and receive the order. This sequence must proceed in an almost continuous fashion with no delay between steps. The patron then goes to a special section where plastic flatware, napkins, condiments, sugar, etc., can be obtained. From there the patron goes to a dining area with tables that usually seat only four. If more than four people want to dine, patrons push tables together to get the amount of seats needed. After eating the patron takes the tray with the soiled items on it to a trashcan, dumps the soiled items into a slot, and puts the tray above on a shelf. Because McDonald's, Kentucky Fried Chicken, and others have used industrial engineers and top planners, a copy of a plan for one of these units is useful for obtaining *suggestions*. We say suggestions only because the planner must be reminded that every unit has its own peculiar needs and a misplanned unit can result if an existing plan is merely copied.

Parking for those who want to go inside to dine or those who want to stop and eat in their cars must be provided. Attractive parking areas, like pleasant dining rooms, add appeal to the service. They should have a hard surface of fine gravel, cement, or blacktop, and be well lighted and convenient to the unit. Plenty of trashcans should be available and these should be placed such that patrons can deposit their garbage from an open car window. Fast-food units located on highways should have signs that can be sighted ahead so drivers can be apprised of their location. They should not be located on road curves but be clearly viewed from a distance in either direction.

For other types of units, often only an opening onto the street to give service to passersby is needed for the outside contact. Patrons do not enter the unit. They order and receive orders at a counter and then eat them as they move on or move over to a counter where they stand and finish eating. No preparation is necessary. Items like sandwiches and salads are prepackaged. Malts, milkshakes, and coffee are also ready and need merely be withdrawn from holding units. If hot items are offered such as soups, these are prepackaged and held in a heated unit or merely require rapid dish up into a container. These units must have adequate storage areas to hold items at their proper serving temperature. The location must be in a place where there is heavy foot traffic.

Clubs.

Clubs exist to provide special facilities to members. Payment is made through dues and charges made for each service of the club the member uses. Members can sign chits, for which the member is then billed once a month along with dues. Many country clubs where members can play golf, tennis, or other sports have rather elaborate and upscale dining services. Normally, membership is composed of a rather affluent group. Clubs often have facilities for parties, dances, and other social events. City clubs are usually established to provide a place for members to meet, dine, and hold social affairs. Some clubs offer recreation facilities such as swimming pools.

Club dining facilities must be quite extensive to provide for all of the types of food and beverage services needed. For example, a snack and beverage bar may be needed out in the swimming pool area, a dining room would be needed to serve a full menu, and banquet and catering facilities are required for social affairs. Patronage can vary considerably. Some days may see only a few members, while on others the place will be filled. Big catering events demand that the equipment be of sufficient size to prepare large quantities of items.

Club members are often a part of the planning team representing ownership and this can increase the difficulty in planning since they often have little knowledge of the basic planning needs of a club. They direct their planning aims to results, paying little attention to the requirements for meeting them. Members often overplan. In one club a very fine Spanish shawl was used as a display over the entrance to the dining area. The members on the planning team decided that the dishes of the club should have a design taken from this shawl, and the complete needs of the club in dishes were ordered with this design—at great cost. After operating a few months replacement costs because of breakage were so high that a change had to be made to different china at considerable additional cost. This same committee insisted on breaking up the food production facilities into two units, one on one floor and the other immediately above it, increasing labor requirements considerably and causing production problems. Unfortunately, it is usually not possible to avoid having members participate in the planning and dictate their desires. When this occurs, planners should be prepared to meet unfeasible demands with logical facts that are adroitly presented to show members that such planning could be a mistake.

The manager of most clubs manages the dining and beverage services. A chef is often in direct charge and there may also be someone in charge of the dining room, but in large or upscale clubs a food and beverage manager may work under the manager and supervise the dining services. The type of service may be Russian, French, or American. Where members demand it, snack or some types of fast food may also be required. Do not equip areas around the swimming pool with glassware or ceramicware. Use plastic or paper to avoid injuries from broken dishware.

Thus, a planner of dining facilities for a club must first of all understand the kind of club, the cost level the members will support, and the services the members will demand and need. Normally, except perhaps for banquets when a large group is to be served, the space left for each cover is maximum, running sometimes as much as 20 square feet. Members may want to have private discussions at their table and do not want to be crowded. A lawyer taking a client to his or her club to discuss some legal matter does not want people at the next table hearing all of the details. Table sizing must also be adjusted to members' needs. A luncheon club to which business people come may require deuces, trios, or four-seating tables, along with some tables where a large group can gather—some members come to their club to dine, meet friends, and relax and like to meet with their same group each time they come.

Banquet rooms usually have round tables that seat eight. Sometimes square tables that seat fewer are used, but they have drop leafs on each side so that when raised a round table is formed that seats eight. Provision must also be made for long tables to be used for buffets, for speaker's tables, etc. Catering rooms can often be partitioned off for smaller groups. A stage, sound equipment, etc., may also be required. Banquet rooms that also function for social affairs will usually require more seating than regular dining rooms.

Beverage and snack service might be needed just off locker rooms so members can meet and discuss their recreational activities of the day while drinking a beverage or perhaps eating a snack. Again the planner must study the needs—and estimating what really will be needed is often a challenge.

Just as the layout of the dining room depends on the demands that will be made on it, so will the kitchen plan depend on needs. The planner must be sure that all needs are outlined by management and the operation planning members so adequate facilities are provided. If the catering needs are large, a separate catering kitchen might be needed. Separate dining facilities some distance from the main kitchen may also need a small kitchen for the preparation of items that must be prepared at the last minute. The **main kitchen** might supply the longer cooked items such as soups, pot roasts, and casserole dishes. If no separate catering kitchen is planned, the planner must be sure to provide adequate storage space in the kitchen to hold items prepared for the catering activities. Movement of this supply to the catering dining area is best done in mobile equipment if the dining facilities are not next to the kitchen. Thus, the planning of a large club kitchen may follow to a great extent that of the planning for a hotel, whereas a smaller club might find that its dining planning needs resemble those of an upscale restaurant.

Some clubs provide living quarters for members who may eat three meals a day there. Sometimes these members like to eat away from the busy, main dining facilities. If the number is small, special dining facilities and perhaps a small pantry-type kitchen for last-minute preparation needs, with the main kitchen supplying the major food requirements, may be specified. If the number is large, then other more elaborate facilities will be needed.

Bars and Lounges.

Bars and **lounges** are often a part of a foodservice operation and they must receive as much attention in planning as the other foodservice units. Three kinds of bars are used: (1) public, (2) service, and (3) catering. A public bar must be planned for fast, efficient, and pleasant service for patrons who will drop in to have a drink at the bar. The work center for the bartender must be precisely planned so all items are obtained quickly and work proceeds smoothly. Some bars will need to be planned for a group of guests who may want to come in for a quiet drink and leave, while others may want a more informal and lively atmosphere.

A **service bar** is one that prepares drinks for servers who may be working in a cocktail lounge or serving alcoholic beverages in a dining area. These are often out of public view and can be planned solely to give fast, efficient service; decor will not be important. Some facilities, however, have a public bar combined with a service bar in which patrons come to the bar to be served, and the bartenders may also prepare drinks to be served to patrons at tables. The requirements for this dual bar will be much the same as for the public bar, except a place must be planned for the storage of garnishes added by the servers, pigeonholes for checks, etc.

The catering bar is usually of a mobile type carrying a limited supply of alcoholic beverages. They too must be planned for speedy service. An essential in all bars is to provide for good control of supplies, beverages, and cash. With electronic cash registers and the use of preset computer systems and automatic beverage dispensers, the planning of the bar has had to change.

Cafeterias.

Cafeteria-style service facilitates serving large groups quickly with limited personnel. They usually are able to price items lower than service restaurants because they use fewer service personnel. Patrons are able to see the food before making a selection and may limit purchases according to the size of their appetites and money they wish to spend. **Cafeteria service** in public schools permits promotion of nutritionally adequate lunches, and in commercial operations foods may be displayed in a manner that aids merchandising. The service may be adapted to serving a large number within a limited time period, as in mealtime breaks in industrial organizations and between class schedules in colleges and universities.

Food quality protection and traffic control are major considerations when locating the cafeteria counter. It should be as close to the production of hot food, salads, and sandwiches as possible and convenient to patron traffic. The entrance hall should be spacious enough to accommodate persons who will be waiting. Toilet facilities and a cloakroom should be conveniently located near the waiting area. It is a good idea to post the menu with prices and any special information to guide selection in the waiting area. The plan should invite an orderly lineup that will minimize confusion and slowdown in service. Long lines of children in public schools are often less disturbing when the lineup is in a hallway rather than in a part of the dining room. It is desirable for the lineup area and the serving section to be screened from the dining room so as to lessen noise and confusion.

Factors that affect the size and shape of the serving line are (1) the volume of sales, (2) the complexity of the menu, (3) the size and shape of the available space, and (4) the flow of traffic. Simple, **limited-choice menus** are common where there are few patrons to support costs, and where food costs must be kept low and the serving time short. The limited-choice menus may be served from a permanently installed, continuous line in a cafeteria or one made up of mobile units. Where a large number are to be served and will support wide variety to satisfy the many food preferences, there may be multiple counter lines or a shopping center plan of service.

The **shopping center** or **hollow-square plan** speeds service by reducing time spent standing in line (see Figure 2.1). Patrons may pass others to reach the station where their choice of food is obtainable. It is a scatter approach in service that is especially useful in serving large groups that arrive at one time. During the peak periods short lines may form at the most popular points. Space allowance for this and for movement of persons passing each other with trays must be made. Thought should be given to ease of supplying the various stations with foods and tableware during the serving time. When the traffic area is crowded, it is difficult to supply centrally located stations. A shopping center plan may offer grilled items that are cooked to order, hot prepared foods served at a counter, and a variety of cold foods and hot and cold beverages that patrons can serve themselves. Trays are picked up at the entrance, and the tableware, napkins, and condiments are placed near the cashier. Tableware items should be convenient to the dining area where patrons may return for items missed or forgotten.

The quantity of food displayed will influence the length of the counters. Adequate space without crowding is desirable but should be sufficiently filled throughout service to give an impression of plenty. Step-saving compactness is desirable and the display space should not require so much to fill that there are too many leftovers at the end of service. The length of the counter can be reduced by setting food- or dish-dispensing units at right angles to the counter. The worker in an L or U work center counter works from left to right, and can work from surfaces at right angles. It will be convenient for the worker and shorten distance for the patron. The speed of service in a cafeteria line

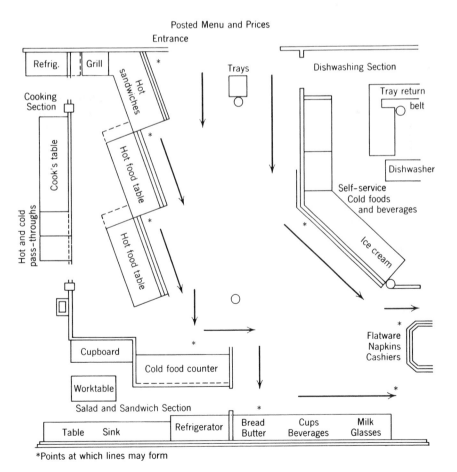

FIGURE 2.1 A shopping center plan in an industrial cafeteria.

is approximately 5 to 8 customers per minute. The variation may be due to amount of selection, promptness of service, and clarity of instructions pertaining to menu offerings, prices, and procedures. Some linear counters serving a set meal and shopping center type cafeterias may achieve a record of 12 customers per minute with items ready for immediate patron pickup.

Some of the major points that merit consideration when planning a cafeteria service layout pertain to (1) features that appeal to patrons, (2) food quality protection, (3) ease and speed in food and dish supply, (4) foods to be promoted, (5) selection habits of patrons, (6) handling of delay points in serving lines, (7) traffic flow, (8) minimizing accident hazards, (9) items for which customers return to serving area, (10) labor economies, (11) menu offerings, and (12) time limitations. Achieving a steady, even flow is a matter of knowing the items required, setting them up in proper sequence to balance serving rate, and providing facilities so that patrons use a minimum of selection time in making choices.

When patrons enter a cafeteria its various aspects should make a pleasant appeal to the senses. The freshly prepared foods should emit aromas that arouse appetite. The colors, design, order lines, and most importantly the cleanliness should be attractive. Patrons touch trays, plates, and flatware and react quickly to smooth, clean surfaces as opposed to those that are gritty, greasy, or wet. Where action is, noise cannot be entirely muffled. Care should be used to eliminate any excesses such as strident voices and clattering pans and dishes. Heavy, commonly used, vitrified tableware is noisy to handle due to its ringing bell-like tone when hit. Careful and minimum handling, plus use of acoustical treatments , will help to reduce noise.

Appearance of delectable quality promotes food sales, and an ensuing experience that is gratifying to the taste encourages patrons to return. Cafeteria counters should provide attractive displays of food and effective means of preserving good quality. The food needs to be seen in the best light, both literally and figuratively. A soft, yet bright light with reds in it can enhance the appearance of meats and entree dishes but not green salads. Clear visibility helps to speed selection and enhances appearance. A counter display should appear suitably bountiful to the last customer. This calls for container-sizes appropriate for the amount of contents. Rotation cooking is far better than use of oversize steam table containers that will be either slack-filled or full of food that will become overcooked and unpalatable by the end of the serving time. Counter openings for pans should permit variation in sizes interchangeably, thus permitting variation according to quantity, sales, and many other factors.

Sanitation is a quality aspect that requires alert vigilance. Careful equipment planning can help in its promotion. Limit possible exposure to contamination, and promote sanitary food- and equipment-handling practices. Provide protective sneeze-guards where foods are openly displayed, and appropriate tools to eliminate hand contact with foods, as well as sanitary means of storing and dispensing dishes, flatware, and napkins. Provide holding temperatures that will discourage the growth of bacteria. Minimize food and equipment handling to the greatest extent possible and in keeping with fast, convenient operation.

In addition to sanitary aspects, methods of food storage will influence qualities of palatability. Temperature, humidity, and length of holding time are significant. Food arriving directly from production usually has the most palatable quality. When quality changes are slight with proper holding, the quality loss is balanced frequently against advantages in utilization of staff time and speed of service. The necessity of having to order and wait for supplies is relieved if foods are at hand when needed. Storage facilities set into the wall between production and service may be an answer. If the hot food requirement is small, a pass-through cabinet may be located opposite the oven and at the end of the cook's worktable. Where supply requirements are large the cabinets may be of a size to accommodate rolling racks of food that have been moved directly from roll-in ovens to heated compartments at the point of service. Short distance and mobility help to lessen transfer time. See Figure 2.2.

FIGURE 2.2 A server removing a tray of portioned desserts from a food rack in a refrigerated cabinet behind the serving counter.

The colorful beauty of fresh fruit and vegetable salads have led many operators to place the salad section at the beginning of the cafeteria line. They are splendid foods to promote nutritionally and a well-arranged display is enticing. This arrangement also has the advantage of hot foods being last so that they lose a minimum of heat. Many patrons, however, prefer to select hot foods first and then choose a salad to go with them. Both arrangements have merit. Arrange foods together that go together or are normally chosen together, such as meat and vegetables. Sales can often be encouraged through locating such foods as soup near salads and sandwiches or ice cream near cake and pie. Balance the workload of employees in terms of motions required for service and item popularity.

Freshly grilled foods and made-to-order sandwiches are among the popular foods that cause traffic delay. This may be solved by placing such items in a separate station that can be bypassed by patrons who are not interested. Some employees alert to usual demands can anticipate orders with enough accuracy to have grilled items ready for almost immediate pickup. Some cafeterias have a signal or communicating system for customers to use for placing orders as soon as they enter the cafeteria line so that they can pick up the orders when they reach that point where they are prepared. In other places, peak loads are supplied by preparing grilled foods ahead and holding them for a short period in a roll warmer. Short delays can often be lessened by preportioning accompaniments such as lettuce, tomatoes, and slices of ice cream rather than cutting or scooping to order.

Planning for accident prevention includes such things as nonslip floors, freedom from obstructions in traffic lanes and blind corners, and protection from burns resulting from food or equipment. Some accident hazards are difficult to avoid due to inattentiveness and resulting spillage by patrons. Alertness in preventing accidents and provision for quick cleanup when they occur are important. It is advisable to have cleanup equipment stored so that it is convenient to the serving area. Accidents cause a disturbing interruption in traffic flow and claim employee attention during a busy period, in addition to discomfort or injury to guests.

When estimating probable traffic flow, consider the time required for patrons to determine and express choices and for servers to comprehend and fill orders. What information is required, and what is readily available? Question extent to which items may be offered for immediate pickup or self-service in terms of customer satisfaction and sanitary protection. Is the layout for traffic flow sufficiently logical or directions clear enough that strangers to the cafeteria will know how to proceed?

Certain items are often forgotten by patrons when picking up meals. These include drinking water, pieces of flatware, and napkins. Many individuals like to return to the line also for beverages, condiments, and other items. Location of such items near the end of the line where they are convenient to the dining area will help to prevent interruption of the traffic flow moving to the cashier. One or more small islands might be placed in the dining area where patrons might select these items. Many of the aspects relating to labor supply, menu offerings, and time restrictions that influence plans will be affected by specific conditions and regulations.

Speed and economy are two major reasons for choosing a cafeteria type of service. The conditions and facilities for the service deserve attention to detail in order to promote these qualities. Consider whether essential supplies and conditions are readily available, such as convenient storage of tools for service; ice bin for ice to use in iced tea, lemonade, or other drinks; items adequately labeled, such as milk, nonfat milk, buttermilk, and chocolate milk; supply storage for uncut pies, cakes, and other foods; a milk dispenser on a turntable so that when one unit is empty another may be turned around for immediate dispensing; adequate display space in proportion to speed of service (to accommodate individual portions or trays of from 6 to 12 portions); wells with drains for ice cream scoops; and a menu board, placed early in line, that is easily read and easily set up. Avoid bottlenecks and provide for easy bypassing of areas where delays may occur, such as those offering numerous choices or which require dishing up, as with soups, hot plates, and some desserts. Estimate about 2 ft (61 cm) linear measurement for each person standing in line.

Speedup facilities, such as extra serving sections, are valuable if there is sufficient demand. Counter shape and length affect speed of service. Right angles slow traffic, whereas straight lines or long curves allow it to move more quickly. Sudden stops or turns are hazards that increase accidents. Limit selection if speed has greater value. Carefully evaluate inclusion of any that hold up movement of the line. Allow sufficient space for a guest to step out of line when waiting for a special order or service.

Providing smooth flow design aids in speeding customers through the line. Tray slides should be sufficiently wide to provide a good base for the trays used. A rail 12 to 14 in. (30 to 36 cm) is desirable for 14-in. (36-cm)-wide trays. Solid construction leads to fewer accidents than rail construction but is less convenient for cleaning. Locating the slide lower than the top of the counter will make it easier to reach over and will lessen the danger of pushing the tray onto the counter. Reduce turns or bends and irregularities to eliminate bumping and spillage hazards. Angles of turn should not be abrupt but curve gradually. A guide on curves helps to prevent accidents.

Dispense tableware in a sanitary fashion. Patrons should be able to pick up items by the handles and not by the end that touches food; silver may be wrapped in napkins. This latter method tends to induce taking more items than required. Coffee urns sometimes boil over and may scald patrons unless equipped with a gooseneck to carry steam and allow hot water to run over the back of the urn close to the drain. Rough edges of metal or glass should be eliminated. Avoid accidents by having traffic lanes clearly lighted, and the path straight, clear, and unencumbered.

Provide an orderly approach to the checker and cashier. Less waiting is required when an unrestricted view of the tray is given for a suitable distance ahead of the checker's stand to permit calculation and quick presentation of the check. Allow for delay space where patrons can search for purse and change without holding up the line. A place for trays during such search and during selection of tableware is necessary.

Self-busing has numerous advantages. When patrons remove soiled dishes to a busing station as soon as they have finished, the table is cleared for use by others. The immediate clearing helps to eliminate a cluttered appearance in the room, especially when patrons during a peak period are leaving the area faster than personnel can handle clearing. It is a labor saver that can benefit price schedules. Some planners locate tray return areas close to where patrons leave the premises.

Industrial Food Services.

Food service for employees may be required by any organization with a large personnel group. It is generally regarded as an effective implement in an industry's personnel relations program. Worker contentment, well-being, and goodwill are the goals. Employees do not rest when they rush several blocks to a lunchroom or perch on top of equipment or squat on the floor during their lunch break. It is important to production on the job for them to be seated comfortably at a table in an orderly, pleasant dining room. A close location; low-cost, good, nourishing food; and an attractive atmosphere are desirable.

There is a considerable range in the amount of subsidy afforded by different organizations for their **industrial food service.** Some furnish space, heat, light, equipment, and janitorial services. There are those that charge for the food cost only. A few serve meals free of charge. The management of the food service may be by the company, which employs and directs a food manager. The company may employ an outside person or agency to whom they turn over the responsibility of the operation on a fee or profit-and-loss basis.

Employees like to see what they are buying and make selections that are within a definitely budgeted amount of money. It is desirable to provide sufficient choice in menu selections to allow for differences in tastes, needs, and buying power. Variety, on the other hand, delays choice and tends to increase production costs. Small- to medium-size cafeterias usually offer a choice of two entrées, two or three vegetables, two or three sandwiches, two or three salads, a salad plate, a variety of breads and beverages, and three or four desserts. Large cafeterias may departmentalize service to hot and cold foods, prepared sandwiches and limited short order, beverages and desserts. This affords greater choice. A scramble-plan in which patrons do not have to keep in line speeds service of a large group and is welcomed by impatient employees. This plan may be used for campus cafeterias also.

Besides meals, fast-food items such as hamburgers, hot dogs, french fries, soft drinks, and milk shakes may be wanted. There will also be a need to service coffee breaks and since these may be limited in time, the service must be planned to be almost instant upon demand. This means that a lot of prepackaged items will be served along with beverages. It has been found that employees often miss breakfast so as they come in to work they rush to the cafeteria to get a prepacked item with take-out coffee and move on to work. In some cases, a special bar or counter can be set up just outside the cafeteria so workers can drop in and out quickly and move on.

Several factors influence probable patronage of an industrial lunchroom. Estimates may be based on a percentage of persons on the payroll, company policies in relation to costs and schedules, convenience of the location, wage scales, time allowance, proposed prices, type of menu, and quality of food and service. A lunchroom rarely serves as many as 85% to 90% of the payroll. The common range is from 50% to 75% of those employed. Cordiality, good food, convenient location, and price have a strong influence on promoting patronage.

Service dining areas may be provided for workers as well as for executives. These may be of the snack bar, counter and booth, or dining room type. The type of facility dictates the type of service offered. Factory workers with a short lunch hour will not favor this more leisurely type of service.

It is good policy to encourage as many employees to have a restful meal period and as adequate nutrition as possible. It is therefore recommended that employees be encouraged to use the dining spaces even if they are consuming items they brought in with them. Often, employees who do this will find it desirable to supplement something they bring from home with something they select at the cafeteria. It is necessary if management wishes to encourage this to plan for such use of the dining area and to provide adequate space for the additional numbers. It is not recommended that a separate space be provided for this since it differentiates among employees. "Brown baggers" should be able to mingle with the others, making the dining occasion a unified period of rest and relaxation.

Planning must consider arrival rate and speed of turnover. It is highly desirable that workers' lunch periods be on a staggered schedule, and the likelihood of this being possible should be ascertained from company management before planning. Assembly-line workers must leave and return to the line all at one time, and staggering is not possible. Where staggering of time is possible, arrival periods of 20 minutes for lunch and 30 minutes for dinner are satisfactory. Some planners use the queuing theory to establish the number of serving lines a facility needs.

Probable growth of the firm and possible changes in policy have an important bearing on lunchroom planning. It is wise to determine whether the kitchen might have to produce food for service elsewhere and whether plant expansion is likely. The length of the breaks and the distance to be traveled to the lunchroom will influence speed of service required. Determine whether more than one type of service will be required, such as an executive dining room, a cafeteria, and mobile service for coffee breaks or meals throughout the plant.

Executive dining room.   Policies differ among companies concerning the desirability of having an **executive dining room.** Some executives feel that it is more democratic to dine with their workers. Surveys indicate, however, that an increasing number of executives favor separate facilities that permit discussions of business matters at the lunch table and promote better acquaintance and fellowship in the group. Features may include a special menu, table service, special decor, carpeting, and air conditioning. Some are served from the main kitchen and serving area. Others have a separate kitchen. Patronage by executives was found to be about 82% where there was a separate dining room and 78% where executives patronized the general cafeteria.

Ethnic Restaurants.   The number of restaurants featuring a specific culture's foods has grown considerably in the last several decades. Chinese, Italian, Mexican, Thai, Indian, Near East, and South American are only a few of the many that exist. Ethnic restaurants require special planning for their equipment and their layout compared to regular full-service restaurants. Storage needs vary. The utensils used both for food preparation and service are typically those used by that culture. The dining area also differs to some extent, although a food service might not go as far as to have patrons sit on pillows on the floor as they do in Near East operations or just sit on the floor as they do in Japan, but in as much as possible, consistent with patron acceptance, an attempt will be made to replicate the culture's ambience. Decor is based on the culture's decor. Even the outside of the building may be considerably influenced by the desire to carry through the ethnic theme.

Unless the planner is completely knowledgeable in the requirements of the facility being planned, it is advisable to use the assistance of an individual who knows thoroughly the production methods, the equipment and work needs, and service customs of the culture. Usually the management members of the team will be able to furnish this information, but, if not, then some outside source must be used.

Health Care Facilities

A wide number of foodservice operations, such as hospitals, health institutes, retirement or convalescent centers, and nursing or rest homes, operate dietary departments which differ from regular food facilities in that they give heavy emphasis to the nutritional and healthful quality of the products they serve. Their patrons are usually people with health problems, infirmities, or other problems that make them in need of medical and/or dietary care. In addition, they may provide food service to employees, doctors, and visitors and even do some catering. A part of their work is consultation and dietary advising of patients. Some may offer instruction in nutrition and diet to nurses, interns, dietary aides, and doctors, which would result in a need for conference rooms, classrooms, teaching equipment, storage for classroom supplies, etc. A few institutions will do dietary research and special laboratory facilities need to be planned to accommodate this research.

Space needed for offices, **therapeutic diet** preparation, and research varies according to the size and type of facility and the organization of the dietary functions. There may be one centrally located office for the manager of the department and assistant dietitians and dietary aides, or there may be separate locations for the therapeutic dietitian, dietary consultant, etc. Those responsible for production should be located near the kitchen. Convenience in consulting with doctors and patients helps determine the location most suitable for the therapeutic staff. Although most modified diets will be prepared in the main food facilities, a special diet kitchen may be required for preparation of special diets. This special kitchen should adjoin the main kitchen, but be separate from other food units as an insurance against error. The number of special diets required is apt to be small, and the equipment often can be of household size.

The **special diet kitchen** needs include shelves for storage and supplies, refrigerator and low-temperature storage, small range with oven, steamer, blenders (1 to 5 liters), dishwashing unit, work counter and tables, cabinets for dishes and equipment, two small carts, utility baskets, pitchers (2 to 5 liters), utensils for cooking and serving, wide-mouth screwtop bottles (100 to 500 mL), graduates (10 to 1000 mL), trays, glasses, dishes, flatware, and pots and pans. The significant value of food to the successful care of patients is cause enough to place emphasis on careful budgeting and planning. Usually the amount of funds available is limited.

Main kitchen needs are approximately the same as those in any kitchen that is preparing a comparable number of meals. The greatest point of difference lies in the highly individualized service of diets and the hazards to product quality imposed by the delivery service to patients. Delay in such transfer damages fragile food quality. Means and methods that help speed service are of special value in this setting.

Employees and doctors are usually provided with a cafeteria-type dining space supplied by the main kitchen, but some may have their own production units or supplemental production pantries; doctors' dining areas may have seated service. Good facilities in this area pay back in employee morale and doctor satisfaction—doctors are important decision makers in where patients go for medical service. A limited dining area, often receiving its prepared foods from the main kitchen, or a snack shop usually serves visitors.

Not all health facilities operate full food facilities. The variety and quality of **value-added foods** on today's market make it possible to considerably reduce kitchen and other needs if such food is purchased and only reconditioned at the facility for service. This may, however, have the disadvantage of locking the food department into this type of service, and if later a decision is made to produce one's own items, the facilities are not suitable for doing so. It is also dangerous to lock the facility into the service of just *one* kind of product such as frozen foods, although this is a bit more flexible in changing to another type of value-added food. Such value-added food comes frozen or chilled, canned, dried, or otherwise preserved. Packaging may be in individual servings or bulk. Costs increase when individual portions are used, but amounts required can be closely controlled. Some meals may come assembled so that the items to be heated can be heated without the temperature of cold foods being disturbed.

The method in which cooked foods are prepared in advance of service needs and stored under refrigeration—has come into wider use. Some may use freezer storage, but this is not usual. This advance food preparation using refrigeration is known as the **cook-chill method.** Items are prepared in large batches—enough for a number of meals—placed very hot into sealed containers, rapidly cooled down, and then stored under refrigeration. This reserve is then withdrawn in amounts sufficient to meet a meal's needs. Various methods are used to bring them to a consumption temperature.

Cold foods such as salads are prepared on the day of consumption. Any of the ways mentioned here for sending foods to patients may be used. When the cook-chill method is used, the planner may choose to plan two kitchen production units, a larger one for preparing the cook-chill foods and a smaller one for reconditioning the cook-chill items and doing preparation required for the present day's needs, such as preparing special items for the doctors' or employees' dining areas. It is now possible to purchase many cook-chill foods already prepared.

Regardless of the source of food and method of preparation or service, certain reasonable, obtainable, quality-production standards need to be established in relation to service. The standards pertain to time allowance in five of the stages of dispatch and presentation of meals and are as follows:

1. Continuous supply of freshly prepared food. For many foods this means a rotation of preparation, timed in terms of the quality depreciation for specific foods.
2. Fast assembly. Search and correct slowdown factors, such as excess motions, too few servers, inadequate space and equipment, slowdowns in the line, and so forth.
3. Short period for meal dispatch. This may mean limiting the size of the carts so meals are not kept waiting after assembly.
4. Shorten distances of travel. Suitable distance both vertical and horizontal should be measured in terms of time.
5. Immediate presentation. Involved at this point is the synchronizing with routine patient care and identification of personnel responsible for presentation of the meals.

The three methods of service commonly used in hospitals are **decentralized service** with serving stations on floors or wards where food is sent for essential treatment and service; **centralized-bulk service,** in which food is sent in trucks for dispensing in corridors near patients' rooms or from a floor pantry; and **centralized service,** in which all of the individual meals are produced, served, and dispatched. The first two are seldom used today, centralized service being considered the most desirable from the standpoint of dietary and quality control. However, we discuss these other means of supply.

Satisfactory means of communication and food transportation in each type of service are needed between the supply source, serving stations, and the patient area. Information concerning supplies, special needs, omissions, and directions is frequently needed. Best satisfaction results when the means of food transport, such as conveyors, elevators, and carts, are used by the food department only. Where general elevators are used, delay of food service may be caused by other traffic.

Decentralized service is favored by those who believe that locating final treatment and service in pantries close to patients' rooms yields best quality. Some of these pantries receive hot food ready for immediate service and other foods are sent for portioning ahead of serving time. Other dietary departments send food to pantries in bulk and expect the preparation of major foods, such as baking of entrees, broiling of chops and steaks, and boiling of vegetables, to be done in the decentralized area. The development of convenience foods and fast methods of conditioning has promoted other plans for preparation and service. In some situations the hot foods are prepared in quantity, quickly chilled or frozen, and held until needed. The meals are set up cold on the serving counter, sent on large carts to the ward where the plates to be heated are pulled from the trays and heated by microwave. The carts that take the meals to the patients hold only four or five trays.

Dishwashing in decentralized service may be done in the pantries or in a central dishroom. If disposable serving units are used, these move to the disposer and only those requiring washing and sanitizing are sent to the dishwashing area. In any case, the dishes and tableware are stored in the pantry. Storage facilities are needed for all items used in setting up trays, such as covers, tray cards, holders, indicators of special diet, flatware and dishes, salt, pepper, sugar, and condiments. Mobile racks are used for preassembly of trays. The amount and type of storage facilities, cooking equipment, tableware dispensers, and serving counters depends on the preparation and service plans used.

Centralized-bulk serving is done from trucks or units stocked in the main kitchen and sent to individual pantries. Service also can be from trucks moved near patients' rooms. Advance setup in the pantries occurs for the trays. Some hospitals have microwave ovens on trucks for rapid cooking of hot foods immediately prior to service. Dishes are usually washed in a central dishroom. The chief advantage of this system is the short time between service and the patient's receiving the food. Disadvantages include extra kitchen trips for omitted items, cumbersome weight and size of trucks, traffic problems in halls and elevators, and simultaneous performance of service in a number of places where supervision may be inadequate.

Centralized tray service has many advantages, which has led to its being almost universally used. In it, the patient trays are assembled in or adjacent to the main kitchen and the foods on them are sent by various transportation methods to the floors and then to the patients (Figures 2.3 and 2.4). Soiled dishes and trays are collected and sent to a central dishwashing room. Floor pantries are used for nourishments and trays held until they can be delivered to patients.

Tray delivery may be (1) placing by hand on a dumbwaiter, moving to the floor, removing and placing by hand on carts where it is moved to the patient's room; (2) placing by hand on a truck that is wheeled to an elevator, moved to the floor, and then to the point of delivery; (3) placing by hand on a small cart and moving via dumbwaiter to the floor, rolling off, and delivering to patients; and (4) moving mechanically from the assembly line on a conveyor to the floor or ward, there removing by hand, placing on a cart, and wheeling to the patient. Service by personnel at one point has been eliminated in the last two methods.

Speed and smoothness of movement of any transport system are desirable. The time lapse between food service and presentation to the patient requires means for retaining sharp temperatures. Large trucks that move slowly and are difficult to maneuver are delay factors. This raises the question of their desirability. Small carts for six or eight trays can be utilized smoothly when plans are synchronized. With food quality depreciation in mind, a standard for the time span between service and patient presentation of the tray

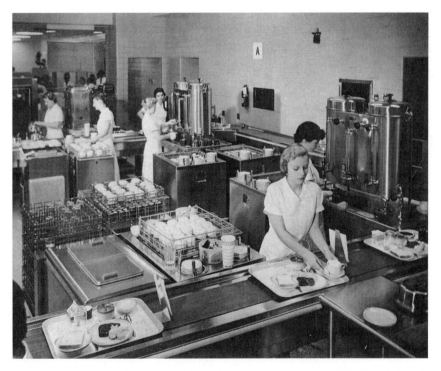

FIGURE 2.3   View of tray assembly and equipment *(Courtesy of St. Francis Hospital, Evanston, Illinois.)*

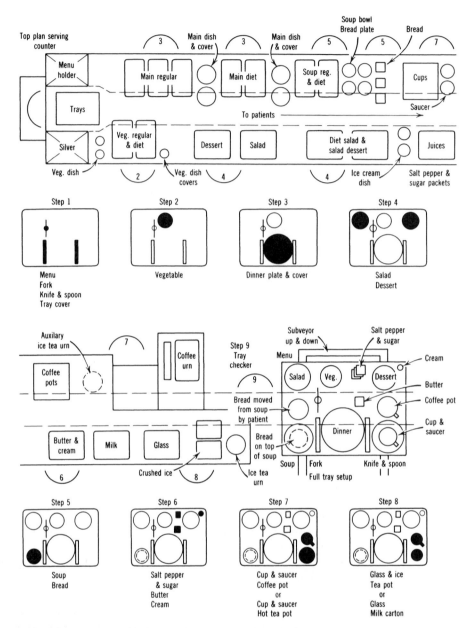

FIGURE 2.4 Steps in assembling a hospital tray. (*Courtesy of Southern Equipment Co., St. Louis, Missouri.*)

should be set. It should include (1) a reasonable rate for trays to come off the assembly line (Figure 2.5), (2) be loaded onto a cart and/or conveyor and discharged, (3) moved to the point of delivery, and (4) be presented to the patient. If food is not protected by some device such as a heated pellet, insulated server, truck that keeps foods hot or cold, or other means, the time limit may be five minutes. Time schedules will involve distance, movement speed, and equipment supply necessary to have carts or other conveyance immediately ready for transporting.

The main virtue of cooked, frozen, and reheated foods is their convenience. If properly selected and handled, the quality may be quite acceptable. The centralized system provides for the service of freshly prepared food, the value of which must be preserved through close control in getting the food to patients promptly and in satisfactory condition. After the time required for a tray to move from the assembly line to the patient is mathematically calculated, it is possible to figure how many units of equipment are required to keep deliveries moving on schedule, how many serving lines and dumbwait-

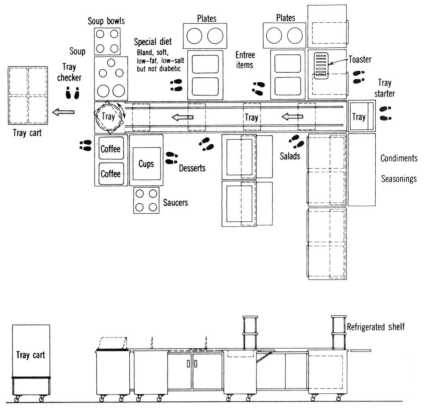

FIGURE 2.5 Floor plan of tray assembly line using conveyor belt and mobile equipment. *(Courtesy of St. Francis Hospital, Milwaukee, Wisconsin.)*

ers (conveyors, elevators, and so forth) are required to serve a given number within the desired length of time, and how many employees are needed at each service point. A sample schedule might call for four trays per minute coming from the tray line, two minutes to check and load eight trays into a cart, one minute for the cart to travel to the floor or ward, one minute to be received and rolled to the farthest point, and one minute to unload and present trays to patients.

Planning must include arrangements for coding trays, giving complete information on a patient's needs in service, and so on. Foods for the trays should also be on hand for immediate placement as soon as the trays reach the servers. Trays may be pushed or moved mechanically on a belt. Trays are pushed by hand only in small operations where the assembly line is later used as a cafeteria for personnel. It is usually augmented by advance assembly of cold items on the trays. Mobile equipment may be moved into position at right angles to the assembly line (Figure 2.6). Reach should be planned for 14 in. (36 cm) to the front and sides. Least used items may be stored farther away or below on shelves. Slanting, overhead shelves, approximately 14 to 18 in. (36 to 46 cm) above the tray, give maximum use of vertical space.

The shortest travel distance for freshly cooked food can be ensured by having the assembly lines located in close proximity to the cooking section. Heated and refrigerated holding cabinets may be needed to hold food close to the serving counter (Figure 2.7). Mechanical means of moving the trays and a layout that permits servers to work simultaneously from both sides expedite tray assembly.

Dishwashing for the various types of service is usually done centrally, as this makes for best use of labor, equipment, and supplies. Some clearing and stacking may be done as dishes are collected or all of this activity may be confined to the dishroom to lessen noise in patient areas and utilize labor to the best advantage. Soiled units may be moved to the dishroom by cart or conveyor. Large hospitals may install two

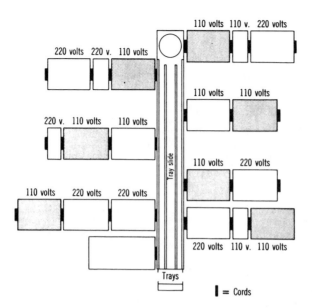

FIGURE 2.6 Electrical requirements for operating the mobile serving equipment *(Courtesy of Institutions Magazine, Chicago, Illinois.)*

dishwashers, one for patients' dishes and the other for personnel dishes. Where a second is installed, it is well for the layout to permit use of either machine to handle the entire load in the event one breaks down. Some sanitary codes require complete separation, with partition between the soiled dish area and the clean dish section of the dishwashing area.

The foodservice facility requirements of **long-term care facilities** such as retirement or rest homes differ little from those of a hospital; modified diets will be needed. In some cases the patrons are mobile, so dining rooms may be needed. Some facilities provide separate apartments or units, so occupants can prepare some of their food there, but most make a requirement that at least one meal a day be eaten in the facilities of the home. Home-type meals are prepared and so the equipping and planning of the kitchen and dining areas can be that of the standard unit. Dining areas should be placed close to the food production units but also convenient to patrons.

When planning for food service for the elderly it is important that psychological aspects be understood. Meals assume a very important role in the life of these whose life patterns have changed from home to institution living and whose emotional satisfactions and securities are limited. Friendliness and conviviality connected with food service can help to offset some of the stresses and frustrations characteristic of aging. Group conversation in family style service has been found to stimulate appetite. The offering of some menu selection encourages decision making, and the residents are helped to retain a sense of personal identity and a feeling that their personal likes and dislikes are being considered.

Attractive table appointments have a beneficial influence. There has been a tendency in some homes to choose extremely durable, unattractive tableware to lessen breakage expense. Durability may be an important economic factor where a fumbling grasp tends to result in more dropping of dishes. Bright, shining, colorful, attractive food containers create values, on the other hand, that should not be ignored.

Convalescent and nursing home food facilities must provide dietary care, so provision for a space for the dietary staff must be included in planning. Frequently the services of a consulting dietitian are used. The units tend to be much smaller than those of hospitals, although commercial food equipment and not household equipment still must be used. An ambulatory dining area for patients may be indicated. A dining service for doctors, nurses, and staff must be provided. A small snack shop for visitors might be a need. The stay of patients in convalescent homes is usually short; in nursing homes the stay may be quite extended. The plan for these units can be much the same as that for a small

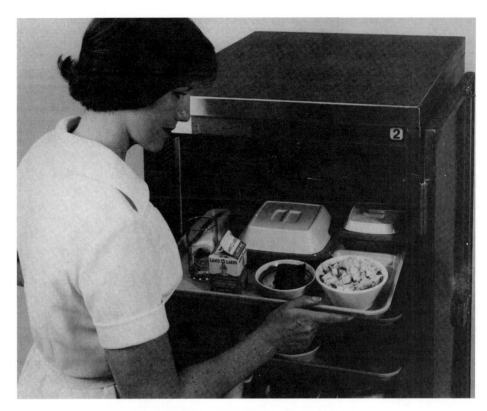

FIGURE 2.7 In the Integral Heating Food Service System only the food in the covered dishes is heated; the remainder of the things on the tray remain cool. Special contacts in the cart provide power to heat the covered dishes. *(Courtesy of 3M, St. Paul, MN.)*

hospital, although some units may be of a size required in the planning of a hospital. Cooking will be done using steam equipment, ranges, and ovens; the use of frying equipment such as grills and deep-fryers may be limited to preparing nonpatient foods.

A health institute requiring a foodservice department is usually a health facility that specializes in one type of illness and tends to be research oriented. The food service may have to be designed more to support the staff rather than patients. However, if dietary research is done, some food units may take on the aspects of a laboratory and the services of someone specializing in such planning may be needed. Separate dining facilities may be needed for staff, doctors, research specialists, and nurses. Some facilities treat outpatients, so a dining room for non-bed patients may be in order. The needs of a dietary staff must be included. For the most part the planning of kitchen and dining facilities may be much like that of a large hospital, with the exception that fewer patient meals will be needed.

Schools

Three types of units are required to meet the needs of most schools, such classification being based on educational status and age. These are primary or elementary, secondary, and units of higher than secondary. In the first, the student will have a set menu and few choices, although the tendency is to have perhaps one or two entrée items and perhaps some beverage selection. These menus will also have to meet specific dietary requirements to meet government subsidy support. The secondary student will be given more choices and often will be allowed to have à la carte items which are beyond the basic dietary requirements. In the third, meals are prepared with free selection being allowed. Little or no dietary restraint is practiced but the students are *encouraged* to select a healthful diet. Plans for each of the three are therefore varied to meet these requirements.

Primary and Secondary Schools.   Primary school kitchens need ovens, steam equipment, perhaps a grill, but no cooking equipment such as deep-fat fryers. A good deal of value-added foods are used. The secondary kitchen resembles a regular coffee shop kitchen but can be blended with the needs of a fast-food unit, since that type of food predominates. A few casserole-type dishes are prepared, but salads and raw vegetables and juices have become popular to the extent that a number of secondary schools have salad bars and juice counters as part of the regular service. The post-secondary school kitchen often resembles that of the ordinary restaurant type and needs to be able to produce three meals a day, while the other two may have to prepare a head-start breakfast and a luncheon. Normally, the service is cafeteria style, but the post-secondary units *may* have table service. These units also may have to do some catering.

Funds available to operate school units are usually very modest in relation to the number to be served. Plans need to ensure the most economical operation in producing suitable meals at the lowest possible price. The unit's success will be considerably tempered by meal costs and by the students' reaction to the food, to the manner in which it is served, and to the personnel with whom the students come in contact.

The plan for dining should help to promote orderly behavior. Students in the primary and secondary units tend to look on the dining period as a recess from classroom discipline. The larger the group, the greater the difficulty in discipline and the less the chance for effective behavior control and perhaps instruction. Separating large dining areas into smaller units helps solve the problem. In one dining plan, long planters with artificial greenery were used to separate a large dining area and in each separate unit different colored chairs and tables were used to further accentuate division. Hand-washing facilities should be provided in convenient relationship to the dining area. It is important to set up a flow plan of entry to the dining area so that service to the tables is continuous and straightforward with little or no criss-crossing.

Primary and secondary programs are often organized into one large centrally controlled unit. A central office is used to administer the program and this may include food and supply storage facilities with a supporting delivery system. Menus are planned for one or two semesters at a time. Many value-added products are used, such as burritos, chilis, pizzas, and hot dogs, so storage for such products must be provided, unless daily delivery is possible. Ovens, steam equipment, and some range space will be needed, but no grills or deep-fat fryers. A dishwashing unit may not be needed if disposable ware is used, but a pot and pan washer may be a good addition. However, a system for collecting and holding a large quantity of soiled disposable ware must be planned.

Plenty of table space should be provided because often a large amount of food is prepared and simply held ready for reheating as service proceeds. Eight-inch ovens are usually specified. Higher ones are seldom needed. If turkeys are roasted, these can be split to lie flat. Quarry tile floors are desirable, but because they are so hard, workers might find it desirable to stand on rubber or other type mats that are more resilient. These can be removed for cleaning outside with hot water and a steam hose.

A number of school systems use a **satellite system** in which the food is prepared elsewhere and delivered to the various schools. Various ways are used to send out the food. Some systems operate central commissaries and send prepared food out in bulk in insulated containers that can be connected to heating or cooling units at the final destination and served from these. Others find that just using insulated containers for the bulk food with no tempering unit at the final destination holds food sufficiently well at proper, safe temperatures. Others may remove the food from the bulk containers to serving counters and serve from there. Or, some may send the food in insulated containers dished into a steam table or other pans so they can just be removed from their containers at proper serving temperatures and placed into heated or cooled counters.

Another type of service is to send the food out in individual portions in paper sacks, foil-wrapped units, or sealed small plastic containers. If the food is to be heated, the latter type of container must be made of special plastic. These individual units are then brought to a proper serving temperature at the final destination. Some schools deliver these foods on carts to the individual classrooms and the students eat there. Others use a cafeteria system and dining area. If these individual unit foods are delivered much ahead of serving time, the satellite kitchen must have the proper holding temperature equipment to provide proper sanitation safeguards. It is not desirable to hold heated foods too long before service since this can harm quality and appearance.

Packaged meals have the advantages of economy, sanitation in food handling, easy assembly, fewer carry overs, and ease of service. Strong disadvantages, though, argue for a cafeteria service: Students are loath to accept foods "sight unseen" and there is less opportunity to teach children to choose foods wisely and to develop good habits in using normal tableware.

Campus Food Services.

Colleges and universities make up the majority of the post-secondary education foodservice units and their foodservice requirements are varied. Types of service units are student unions, coffee shops, cafeterias, fast-food units, snack bars or fountains, residence halls, and club service. In the majority of situations, the institution, faculty, and students are all on tight budgets.

Plans for suitable facilities need to be preceded by a careful analysis of present and future enrollment and conditions. Funds available for building and the policies or conditions that may affect the success of the operation should be considered. The source of funds, the program for repayment of funds, and the possibility for acceptable rates to meet operating costs and loan payments call for thoughtful calculation based on accurate information.

Rates for food service need to reflect all charges to be made against the account. Policies differ as to payment for space, heat, light, repairs, and special services supplied by other campus departments. The extent to which the facility is to be subsidized needs to be determined at the outset. The number of students, their needs and ability to pay given rates, administrative policies, and other sources of college funds will influence decisions.

Labor is a major cost and a worrisome problem on campuses as in food facilities elsewhere. The cost of labor may run from 25% to 40%, depending on the type of service. Characteristics of student help necessitate special planning. Turnover is frequent, and workers are likely to be untrained and inexperienced. The job usually holds little interest for these workers. Their activities must be planned around class schedules that change each term. Simplicity must characterize schedules, work motions, and skills. Assembly-line procedures may be used in processing or serving food during peak periods and for cleanup at the end of the meal periods. Major values lie in helping students earn an education and in having short-period help during peak periods of service.

Campus cafeterias.

Cafeterias have met the common demand by students for speed, convenience, and low cost. Planners should consider effective methods of guiding the choice of balanced meals essential for good health. The use of plate combinations, meal-ticket grouping of foods when pricing, and attractive displays have a beneficial influence on choice. Counter arrangement and special equipment for merchandising may be effective.

Cafeterias providing a choice of food that are open to the general campus may serve both meals and snacks. The serving period may last throughout the day and have both peak and low periods of service. Self-service and self-busing help to lower costs. Simplicity and convenience of procedures are important, such as having a deposit area for soiled dishes on the route out of the dining area. Easy cleanup should be planned. Unsightly litter may be common following service to a horde of students who dash off to class. Hard-surfaced floors and strategically placed soiled dish and paper receptacles make for a cleaner and more orderly appearance when a crowd is served.

Campus food facilities should be in convenient, attractive locations that are reasonably free from noise and distractions. On a large campus where distances are great, consideration should be given to dispersing food units. Near the entrance to the food area, there should be a place for depositing books and coats. The lineup area for the cafeteria should be located in a hall or entry rather than in a lounge where clutter and excessive wear will occur while students wait for meals.

College food services serve as social centers for students, and tables for four, six, and eight may predominate. Students tend to move tables to accommodate larger groups. Provision should be made for ease of movement. Floors and furniture should be chosen for qualities that withstand wear.

Campus coffee shops and snack bars.

Coffee shops and **snack bars** are popular with students if a sociable atmosphere of fun and gaiety and fast service of popular foods are provided. Students respond readily to a friendly, informal atmosphere and enjoy the simplicity that characterizes this type of service. Menus permit freedom of choice, and individual pricing of items makes selection possible for those on the most limited allowance. Check averages tend to be low, but the continuous flow during a day results in an impressive total.

Coffee shop hours vary according to needs and may be scheduled according to the opening and closing hours of other campus food services. The menu offerings may need to supply full meals or snack-type foods not offered in other facilities. It is best to choose a system of operation that provides speed of service and a limited number of items that are the most popular. It should also permit flexible volume and the lowest cost. Menus are usually built around short-order and ready-to-serve foods, such as beverages, grilled foods, and bakery items.

Special catering.

Special catering may supply significant social needs on a campus and varies widely in nature. Economy is best when it is performed through a regular foodservice department. The demands tend to be sporadic. A regular production staff, with some added assistance, usually has the equipment and time to handle the extra load without strain. Space and equipment to meet probable catering requirements need to be incorporated in the initial foodservice plans. This will include work and storage space for special foods, supplies, and equipment, plus dining space.

Time and effort will be saved by having chairs, tables, and cover items stored conveniently on mobile carriers. Speed of service can be promoted by short distances and fast means of transportation. Service may occupy more than one room on one floor or different floors. A direct, straight-line route will help to ensure speed and prevent accidents. Refrigerated storage that will take mobile racks of predished cold foods, such as cocktails, salads, and desserts, can save time and labor. In situations where a great many meals are catered, it has been found desirable to use a traveling belt for plate assembly. The belt carries plates at convenient speed to supply service. Workers place food on plates from both sides without touching the plates, except to place them on and remove them from the belt. Simple repetitive motion helps to develop speed and skill.

Programs are often a part of catered functions. Electrical outlets are required for a public address system, projector, recorder, spotlight, and other program equipment. A portable platform may be requested for a head table, particularly if the room is large. A projection screen, blackboard, display panel, piano, and lectern may be desired.

Cloakroom and toilet facilities for men and for women should be provided. Locate the cloakroom to promote good routing of guests. Rope and stanchions may be desirable for guiding traffic when groups are large. Directional and room signs large enough to be read easily are recommended if there are several dining rooms or a complicated route. Ticket takers or registration clerks may wish table space near the entrance of the dining room.

Campus catering departments are sometimes asked to serve food in buildings other than the one where it was produced. Insulated handling equipment is needed to preserve palatability. If the heated or refrigerated equipment requires electricity it is good to have a long, sturdy extension cord ready for use. Equipment that will ensure easy mobility in handling heavy, bulky food and dishes is highly desirable when catering.

Catering for a campus community may include requests for take-out foods. The foods may be used for teas, receptions, picnics, sack lunches, and home meals. The condition of the food may be ready for immediate service or frozen for later use. Attractive, convenient containers will facilitate handling. The use of disposable containers will avoid the need for keeping track of returnable equipment and making adjustments on costs.

Union buildings.   These are student centers that may incorporate all of the types of food service mentioned, or they may have only a small snack bar. This often depends on whether the union building was built after other food services adequate to serve the campus had been provided. Since the building serves as a center for student recreation, meeting rooms, and offices, it is advisable for it to have some food facilities. Catering needs may vary from refreshments for group meetings, parties, food for banquets in the ballroom, punch for dances, to snacks for those enjoying recreation. The need for food service in this social center is such that planners are well advised to plan the requisite food facility and arrange the remainder of the building around it.

One kitchen may serve many areas in the building if relationships are planned wisely. Transporting food to several floors and to various rooms increases opportunities for accidents and theft. Control of labor and preservation of food quality are constant problems. A close, direct relationship between kitchen and serving stations should be maintained to the greatest extent possible. Mechanized means of delivery of food and return of soiled dishes should be considered. It is important that the layout permit adequate supervision of all production and service areas.

Faculty club.   This service can be an effective implement in creating good personnel relations on a campus. Faculty relationships benefit by having a place where members can meet on a friendly, informal basis, entertain campus visitors, hold social events, and provide occasional family or professional dining. Understanding and respect developed through mutual acquaintance are effective morale builders. Recognition and support by the outside world for outstanding academic achievement are often stimulated through cordial hospitality.

Success of the faculty club requires careful and candid consideration of tastes, spending habits, and common characteristics, as well as specific needs for catering. Food, like the weather, is a common topic of conversation and frequently the proverbial whipping boy for relieving inner tensions. Heavy demands on modest faculty income, combined with a certain sense of insecurity, result in conservative spending habits. Faculty members admire an exclusive atmosphere and would like deluxe service but tend to feel that they should not support it.

Capable help for the short daily period required for noon table service is difficult to obtain, tends to be temporary, and needs constant training and supervision. The number usually served in faculty dining rooms is frequently too small to support labor for service without adding appreciably to meal rates. Higher rates tend to reduce patronage. Therefore plans that present an attractive dining area with self-service in an adjacent room have often been used successfully. The layout should also provide for quiet, inconspicuous removal of soiled dishes.

There are occasions when it is desirable for committees or special groups to be provided with served meals. If rooms are planned in convenient relationship to the kitchen or serving area, such catering can be handled at minimum cost. The possibility of regular or occasional teas, snacks, or coffee service, and the location where they are likely to be needed in the building should be considered and provisions made for storage of certain materials, electric outlets, and water supply. If there are likely to be occasions when persons not connected with food management use the facilities, provision separate from the main kitchen should be made for this. Freedom in the use of the main kitchen frequently leads to misuse of supplies and equipment or, when refused, may arouse irritation. The planner's challenge is to reach the best point of balance between what faculty wants, restrictions it will accept, and costs that members are prepared to pay.

In many faculty clubs the service of liquor is permitted and planning must provide for this. Often a bar in a lounge provides a space for those who wish to have a drink, possibly before a meal, but provision must also be made to serve beverages in banquet or other rooms where dining groups may gather.

Residence halls.   A college or university administration frequently appoints an advisory committee to assist with **residence hall** planning. Members may be chosen to represent the finance office, the student welfare office, and the residence hall management. A fairly intricate task of coordinating the concerns of the three may be required. When planning it is well to know the amount of the schools' subsidy for heat, light, services, and loan payment. Social and welfare programs for student residents need to be considered. It is desirable for the college home for students to be attractive and at the same time sufficiently durable to withstand youthful exuberance and the not uncommon lack of concern for public buildings. Simplicity of design and arrangement tends to be desirable and forced by economic necessity.

The food service is usually designed for the fullest utilization of labor, materials, and equipment in order to minimize costs. Cafeteria service is commonly used for at least a part of the meals in order to promote economy and provide speed of service. The residents may pay for the food and housing on a monthly or a term basis. In large units a checking system is used for admitting those who have made advanced payment for their meals. Providing check points at the door rather than at the end of the line helps to speed movement of the line.

A system is used in some residences in which the residents pay in advance for housing only. Food in the cafeteria is priced à la carte and students may select whatever is offered and pay only for the food selected. Policies may permit students to dine elsewhere than their place of residence whenever they wish to do so, and may permit other campus personnel to dine in the residence hall cafeteria if they desire. This plan has special advantage on a large campus for students who may have classes at a considerable distance from the residence at mealtime, and near other campus food facilities. Students appear to like the system and there is less grumbling about paying for food they don't select or that they are forced to miss.

Table service varies in residence halls from all meals to occasional party meals. In some halls it is used for dinner daily and in others for Sunday and celebration dinners only. Cafeterias have been criticized for encouraging poor social habits. The compromise of using cafeteria service for breakfast and lunch, when time is most limited, and table service for dinner, has been used with success. The size of the dining room is important for congeniality. Very large dining rooms tend to be cold and impersonal. Smaller units create more of a sense of belonging. Units of 100 or less tend to increase sociability.

Mobile Food Services

Many foods and beverages are dispensed by mobile units. Mobile units include trucks operated by the facility, such as special trucks that drive to various parts of a factory to serve workers, thus reducing worker travel time. Other mobile units may be independently operated and drive to strategic locations where they can draw a clientele. Items served include beverages such as tea, coffee, milk, and soft drinks; foods vary from sandwiches, pizzas, ice cream, doughnuts and other pastries, pies, cake, and cupcakes to salads, soups, stews, and full meals. Beer may be sold but no other liquor. Meals-on-wheels is a special service designed to serve those who cannot travel from their homes to get food and are not able to prepare food for themselves. All foods are usually prepared elsewhere and loaded onto the mobile unit just for serving, although some do have units that heat hot dogs, fry hamburgers, and do other limited food preparation. The "Good Humor" ice cream man has been around long enough to become a part of our culture.

Some companies operate large commissaries that send out most of the food items used by satellite units all over the country. Delivery routes may go several hundred or more miles. Items are loaded into large insulated containers and often shipped in refrigerated trucks. The foods needing reheating are reheated at the destination facility. Some shipments are placed into huge shipping containers and loaded by forklift into the truck and then unloaded at the destination by a forklift carried by the truck. At times this delivery is made at night and the container with its contents left on the loading dock. Such containers must be able to be locked for proper security.

The central commissaries preparing the items do so in such large mass quantities that special equipment must be built to prepare it. Thus, steam kettles holding thousands of gallons of a food item may be required. The planning of such facilities is beyond the scope of this text.

Miscellaneous Food Services

Wherever groups live for a period of time or regularly meet at mealtime, there is need for a group-feeding facility. They vary considerably in size, type, and foodservice requirements. Included in this classification are camps and resorts, community kitchens, and kitchens for small clubs and such organizations as fraternities and sororities. Inexperienced hands often work in some of them. Sanitation needs special emphasis because workers may be unfamiliar with sanitation codes in public food service and possess questionable work habits. Equipment appropriate to work requirements and volume needs to be provided. Adequate storage and refrigeration facilities are likely to be important. A study of the specific requirements and conditions will reveal the individual situation peculiarities and needs.

Camps and Resorts. Camps and resorts have certain characteristics in common. Seasonality and remoteness from markets, and perhaps limited utilities and services, may create problems with which plans must cope. Equipment selection will be affected by these factors and by the type of personnel available to operate it. Wide variation in facilities may be demanded. A boy scout camp, a lumbering camp, and a fine resort hotel obviously require different plans. Figures 2.8 and 2.9 show sample plans for kitchens in such facilities.

If the resort is operated as a business to provide food, standards for service will be established on the basis of cost and quality to appeal to a certain class of patrons. Some resorts operate throughout the year and resemble hotels. Those that are seasonal may have different needs that will dictate specific facility and equipment needs. Water supply may be a problem for facilities located remotely from city systems. An adequate quantity of pure water is essential for drinking, cooking, cleaning, and dishwashing. Delivery of supplies may be infrequent to food operations that are remotely located. Suitable and adequate storage may call for careful planning and considerable space. Low-temperature storage may be important for extending storage life when supply is infrequent. Use of power equipment may be curtailed by the amount and type of power available. Dishwashing in camps may be affected by both the power and water supply available. An incinerator is desirable for garbage and trash disposal, especially where bears or other wild animals may invade the area seeking food. Protect foods too from contamination by pests, vermin, or other dangers.

In camps a range area should be provided for preparation of breakfast items, simmering of soup stocks, and cooking of vegetables and sauces. Cabinet ovens are recommended for the preparation of entrées, roasts, and desserts. Worktables are sometimes wood or galvanized iron in the more cost-limited facilities, but in some geographic areas, sanitation regulations do not allow their use. A washable canvas stretched tightly over a wood tabletop is satisfactory for pastry work. Tin-coated steel bowls on mobile racks are desirable for mixing. Mobile racks can save many steps in the preparation and service of meals.

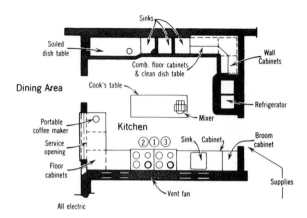

FIGURE 2.8   A small kitchen for community or church, providing for complete cooking and limited baking. Dish-up may be onto plates on a table or from cafeteria plan with hot food dispensed from containers arranged on the serving counters. *(Courtesy of Hotpoint Co., Chicago.)*

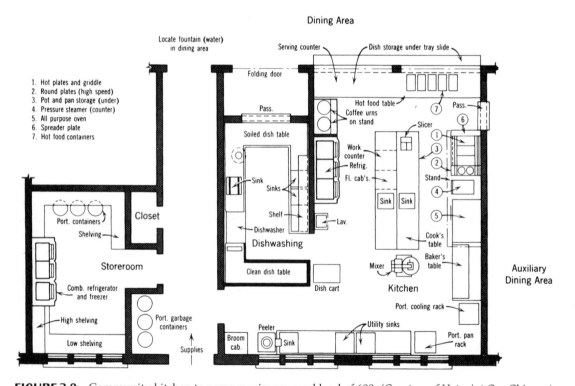

FIGURE 2.9   Community kitchen to serve maximum meal load of 600. *(Courtesy of Hotpoint Co., Chicago.)*

Community Kitchens.

Community organizations, such as churches and clubs, may require a kitchen and dining area. The dining room may be utilized for purposes other than food service. Efficiency may be promoted by planning work space so that either a few can do the work on occasion or many can share in it without confusion or getting in each other's way. Each organization will have specific needs for size, frequency of use, and type of functions for which it will cater.

The equipment requirements and layout will be influenced by the plan for the food preparation and service. Plans in common practice include (1) work done by employed personnel, (2) preparation and service by members appointed by the organization as a committee, (3) contributed food prepared by members and brought in for service, and (4) prepared food brought in by a catering company for service. Plans for (1) and (2) necessitate a completely equipped kitchen; those for (3) and (4) require space for holding, reheating, beverage making, meal setup, and service.

Attitudes toward the food program and the amount of money to be spent will differ greatly. Concern for the food service will be strongly influenced by the funds available and the amount of use anticipated. The common tendency is to seek simple adequacy for minimum cost. Due to irregular use, the rust-free, easy-to-care- for advantages and good appearance of stainless steel equipment should not be overlooked.

In community food units where the food is to be both prepared and served, equipment requirements are similar to those in school lunchroom kitchens of comparable size. Where prepared food is to be brought in, either by members or by a catering firm, adequate space for storing it for final processing is needed. Mobile racks with baking sheets that may be used for shelves or serving trays are convenient. Individual portion salads and desserts may be arranged on the baking sheets and moved to the dining room for service.

The need to provide adequate pot and pan and dishwashing facilities should be stressed. Many pots and pans and large quantities of soiled dishes may accumulate before workers are free to do them. Adequate facilities should be provided for this type of scheduled work.

Small clubs and organizations where members live in require facilities for three meals a day and occasional catering. These types of facilities and boarding houses usually serve a set menu to a given number. Many of the needs are similar to those of a small residence hall. The equipment selection and layout should be based on commercial rather than on domestic requirements.

Vending Services.

Vending services may be mobile or in a fixed location equipped with appropriate equipment for storing and dispensing foods. In mobile service the products are assembled in a central area and may be dispensed some distance away from the production area. Provision is required in this type of vending for suitable temperature holding equipment for foods, appropriate means for transporting it, and seating arrangements for patrons. Successful vending in fixed locations also depends on proper protection of foods to and in the location and some plans for patron comfort while consuming it.

Box lunches are easy to assemble and transport for mobile service and can readily be augmented with hot soup and beverages in vacuum containers. The service can be speedy and requires few employees to serve a large number. Meals for plant employees may be handled also in the manner described under satellite school food service in which hot foods are given final cooking or heating at the point of service. It is now common practice where vending machines are in a fixed location to provide a fast means of heating, such as a microwave, for heating single portions of hot foods.

Vending machines dispensing snack foods or a complete meal are available. Either hot or cold foods may be dispensed. The foods are assembled and packaged in a central commissary kitchen and brought to the machine for loading. A coin, bill, or debit card activates dispensing and, where hot foods are required, may activate heating unless the foods are already hot or to be heated outside the equipment. Some vending machines have automatic cycles of heating for service and cooling down to refrigerated temperatures for holding.

The vending equipment may be owned by the organization requiring the service, the company supplying the food, or a vending equipment firm. If owned by the company served or providing the food, they can prevent many problems through careful selection of the vending equipment. Sanitation standards must be high and it is therefore important to carefully investigate both the record of the equipment and the organization supplying the food. Significant points to consider in relation to the equipment are simplicity of operation, freedom from mechanical failure, servicing record and servicing available by the company, accuracy in dispensing and change making (if this is included), ability to reach parts likely to require servicing, sanitation, and ease of filling. Choose equipment that will provide the specific services required. It is advisable to investigate the record of the equipment and/or the company supplying food before a purchase or contract is made.

Vending may not provide an ideal meal service, but there are situations where making food available in this manner is greatly appreciated. Organizations where the number of personnel to purchase food is inadequate to support a more complete and expensive food operation and those with very irregular patronage over a long span of the day or night, may be served best by a vending operation. Some organizations that provide a well-operated food service find vending of certain items a satisfactory answer for snackers, gripers, and out-of-schedule diners.

Vending equipment for various foods and beverage items shows considerable variety in size and appearance. Plan, for satisfactory appearance, to overcome the heterogeneous aspects. Where the equipment is owned by the company providing the service, it may be possible to set the equipment into a wall and provide a facing that will give a uniform appearance. An attractive decorative scheme may be used to harmonize the whole. Clearly posted menu items with prices will help to guide choices. Machines should be located away from heavily populated traffic areas and in a manner that will help to guide traffic flow in front of them.

Take-Out Foods.
Foods ready to cook or serve immediately are a great convenience for working homemakers and those who entertain without domestic help. Attractive mail-out menus and encouragement of telephone ordering help in building sales. The production equipment and traffic facilities of drive-in restaurants make them especially suitable for handling this business, but downtown locations can profitably utilize this sales potential also because of their nearness to large groups of employed persons. Refrigerated counters displaying these foods near the cashier promote sales. Packaging of items should afford protection in handling and may be used effectively for advertising items, prices, and ordering instructions. Directions for the proper method of reheating are helpful. Foil, plastic, or heavy paper containers are durable and disposable and most can be reheated in an oven. For microwave units sturdy paper or plastic containers may be used.

Transit Food Services.
A significant number of people patronize food services while traveling. Trains, airplanes, ships, and ferries may serve full meals as well as snacks, and some, like cruise ships, serve the most upscale type of cuisine. In fact, eating is a significant part of the attraction for those taking a cruise. Some air travelers may also get a superior type of food service, but in recent years many airlines have scaled down their food service to a bare minimum. Many trains offer full meals, plus snacks and beverages. The shorter the route, the more limited the food service.

Trains.
Trains are usually equipped with a small kitchen that can serve items such as sandwiches and other snack-like foods plus prepare a limited meal menu. Much value-added food is carried and rewarmed to meet the need for entrées. A menu offering a steak, poached salmon, veal stew, and chicken fricassee probably carries the first two as frozen items to be grilled. The last two are frozen or cook-chilled and need only heating to make them ready for service. Soups are canned or frozen. Vegetables are usually canned or frozen. Some deep-fried items may be offered, such as french fries or fried chicken. Fast food items will also be offered.

The kitchen is usually located in the same car as the dining area. With a menu as extensive as that just mentioned, it is evident that in limited space, the kitchen will be crowded and every foot of available linear and horizontal space will be utilized. Normally, the train is provisioned at the start of its journey and resupply is not possible. Thus, an Amtrak leaving Minneapolis, Minnesota, will not be supplied until it reaches Spokane, Washington, where it can take on needed items. The distance is almost 1,500 miles and travel time is about 26.5 hours, during which two dinners, a breakfast, and lunch besides snacks might have to be served. If the average passenger load is around

400 to 500 passengers, this means that a considerable amount of storage for supplies must also be provided.

A planner for such an operation must study the menus offered, calculate the equipment that will be needed, size this equipment to production needs, and provide the necessary space for the foods and beverages required, plus the pots and pans and dishes needed to do the job. In addition, pot and pan washing, dishes and glassware washing, and cleanup needs must be included.

Ships and ferries. Ships' galleys run the gamut from crude, minimal units to those that vie with the most extensive kitchen provided for land operation. A cargo ship with a small crew must provide for the crew's food needs during a long journey. An important factor in maintaining crew morale and satisfaction is the food served, and ships that make long cruises need galleys that can provide a good, substantial level of cuisine. If the cruise period is short, the galley and storage facilities can be more limited.

For long-cruise ships a bakeshop is needed, as well as a fairly well-equipped kitchen. Some ships offer the crew hot meals on the off-hour watches, so prepared food holding equipment must be provided that can keep food in a highly palatable state for these off-hours personnel. Management must provide the planner with the food program schedules to be followed.

Refrigerated, frozen, and other storage space must be carefully calculated to meet the needs of a ship that goes without resupply for long periods. Ferries usually run short distances and so snack-type foods will usually be adequate to meet ferries' foodservice needs. However, some ferries may require extensive service if the travel class demands it and the journey time is long.

Cruise ships that cater to vacationers usually must have food facilities of the most extensive type. It is not unusual to have to provide for bakeshops that have the most elaborate equipment, butcher shops, and cooking spaces that are as extensive as the most luxurious hotel. Normally, the ship is loaded with the supplies needed for the entire cruise and the tons and tons of food taken in at the embarkation point for a cruise is amazing. Complete supply of all needs must be planned for, including water. Besides the main dining area, the ship will probably have specialty food services that serve guests at other times than the main meal. It is recommended that a planner use the advice of chefs, stewards, or others who are acquainted with the foodservice needs of such extensive facilities.

Airlines. A clientele's satisfaction with the food service is generally recognized as having an influence on their contentment with an airline's service. However, competition from "no frills" airlines has made all airlines cut back drastically on such service. Food on planes varies from beverage only, to snack food, to full-course meals, the latter only on extended flights. Most large companies operate their own kitchens, but others may contract for the service. Foods and beverages must be delivered to planes requiring a minimum of preparation for service. Refrigeration and a method of heating are required.

Flight schedules and the number of passengers requiring meals vary. Food must be prepared, specially packed, and ready when needed for transport on schedule to the planes. Intercommunicating radio systems make it possible to transmit sudden changes in count or plane delay quickly. Ease of assembly on the plane, popular foods, and those that will withstand the quality hazards of long storage and customary handling are required. The packages for transporting and holding must be light, sturdy, insulated to protect temperature, easy to handle, and compact. Paper, plastic, or china service may be used.

The central production area of the airline kitchen closely resembles that of any other kitchen. The greatest difference exists in the scheduling of production and the assembly of meals. Time for shipping out orders, instead of meal times, controls production time. The layout for the assembly center should provide for quick, easy assembly of foods, tableware, paper supplies, and meal accessories, such as cream, sugar, salt and pepper, relishes, and containers. A lone worker may work in a semicircle to assemble meals or three or four employees may work assembly-line fashion as with hospital meals.

The storage place for completed meals should be convenient to the loading platform. Each airline uses its own special equipment and requires a special storage space where only its equipment is placed. Special storage is required for liquor. Provision is also needed for ice and other things used in connection with food and beverage service. Handling is facilitated when carts containing meals can be stored, rolled onto trucks, and moved to the planes.

The service of **inflight meals** requires special planning. Planes arrive loaded with soiled equipment. A large mass of soiled equipment must be processed through at one time and in a turnaround time for the equipment of about 1.5 hours, or under special circumstances even less. Thus, the entire lot must be processed, filled with new meals, and ready for loading on another outgoing plane within a very short time. Many items are also not cleaned easily since casserole dishes and other units may have food baked on them that is difficult to remove. Space is needed around the dishwashing and sanitizing area to hold "dead-headed" equipment. Every plane must carry a full load of dishes and other serving equipment even though only a partial load of prepared meals is required. This is done because at the next airport a full meal load is required and the facility will have no equipment unless each plane is fully loaded. Space must be left also for carryover items. While no opened food can be reused, canned pop and other unopened, sealed units may be. The use of disposable ware on planes can solve a lot of ware problems.

Careful planning must occur to see that flow is facilitated. Incoming and outgoing materials must be kept separate, for reasons of sanitation. Loading docks must frequently receive both. Normally a U-shaped plan is best, where incoming materials come in on the left side of the receiving dock, go into washing and sanitizing, then to storage, then to assembly, to production, to loading, and out to the loading dock to be taken away. If separate receiving and loading docks are planned, the flow can be straight line as is the case in the Los Angeles Airport central commissary. Since many tasks are repetitive in preparing trays, dishing-up, and so forth, assembly-line flow with well-planned work centers functions well.

CHAPTER SUMMARY

Various kinds of food services require different planning for the layout, equipment, and dining services and planners need to know what these differences are and provide for them. Energy, HVAC, and sanitation and cleaning costs need to be kept in mind in planning since much can be done to reduce them to a minimum by proper planning without reducing quality and quantity of product produced. Hotel food services can be quite varied. In small units a single coffee shop unit will suffice, while in others the most elaborate of food services will be required. Catering, room service, and other special needs complicate planning. Most smaller motels find that a coffee shop that gives some emphasis to fast foods is sufficient. Other large units require food facilities that equal those of a large hotel. Some do considerable catering and convention business.

There are a wide number of restaurant-type units that use very similar kitchens and dining services, but each type still has special needs. Coffee shops are the most common type and a regular kitchen to produce standard-type meals usually suffices. Full-service restaurants usually need kitchens and dining areas that are rather elaborate and may resemble the kitchen and dining service planned for hotels and motels. Drive-ins and fast-food units usually have streamlined units that offer a limited variety of foods and beverages. They must be able to service people who wish to get food and drive on in their cars. Provision must be made also for on-premise dining. Some clubs limit their food service to one meal a day, such as the luncheon. Others offer a wide range of food and some even serve a resident population as well. The food and level of service is apt to be higher than the ordinary in member-supported clubs. Banquet service and special catering often make up a large part of a club's business. Bars and lounges may serve a limited amount of food as well as beverages, but if they are located close to a main kitchen they may offer a complete menu because supply is so convenient. Most planning will revolve around the service part of these units and not food production.

Cafeterias have kitchens that prepare a wide range of foods and beverages and offer them to patrons in a counter-type service. Their kitchens usually require normal planning. Service is by self-busing although some do have service personnel that stand at the head of the line and take the items patrons select to their table. Some use disposable ware. Industrial food services are used to provide factory workers, office workers, and others with food and beverage. Most use cafeteria service, and the planning of these can usually follow much the same lines that regular cafeterias do although there may be more of a demand for snack and fast foods than in a regular cafeteria.

Health care facilities are hospitals, convalescent and rest homes, retirement and nursing centers, and health institutes. All are distinguished by having dietary departments. Also needing provision are facilities for teaching nutrition, patient counseling, and food services for employees, doctors, and nurses. Some will need a small unit for visitors where a limited menu is served. Nonhospital complements will have foodservice units similar to hospitals but on a smaller scale.

Elementary public schools will serve a limited menu that usually meets the regulations of the federal school lunch program. Many fast foods will be served and these may come ready for service except for bringing to a proper serving temperature. The service is usually cafeteria style. Planners should keep in mind that the learning of good dietary and dining habits is an important part of the program. Secondary schools offer a wider menu that may even include carbonated beverages. Some find salad bars popular. Many elementary and secondary public schools use a satellite system. Normally the school foodservice program is consolidated into one for an entire school district.

Campus food services are varied. Some have coffee shops, cafeterias, or snack shops strategically located around the campus for the convenience of students. These require planning which is standard for these units, but should be designed to serve items favored by young adults. Self-service is frequently used. Residence halls usually have full operating facilities that serve three meals a day. Cafeteria style service is common. The planning of the facilities follows that of standard kitchens and dining rooms. Union buildings often have a variety of foodservice units: coffee shop, snack bars, and full catering units are common. Some may include a faculty club. Often, however, a separate faculty club is operated. These will not only operate to serve the daily needs of the faculty but also meet the needs of a faculty social program where catering and social functions occur. Some operate bars and sell liquor.

A wide number of miscellaneous food services exist and these usually have standard kitchens and dining services varied to meet the special nature of the unit. Some of these units are camps or resorts, community kitchens, vending services, take-out, and mobile food services. The food service on airlines has been considerably simplified in the last decade. Full meal service occurs only on long flights. Snack foods and disposable ware predominate. Central commissaries usually provide the food and beverages. Assembly-line methods are used to assemble foods. Special provisions must be made for the washing of ware. Many must have separate ware washing and storage to keep the ware of different airlines separate and have the ware ready for outgoing flights. The planning for food services on trains, ferries, ships, and other transport units is complex. The matter of supply of needs and their storage until they can be replenished are just two of the many problems a planner must consider if the unit is to function adequately.

REVIEW QUESTIONS

Instructor: Bring to class several plans for a complete building showing the layout and supporting plans (electrical, plumbing, construction details, etc.). Point out the architectural symbols used and what they mean. Demonstrate the use of drawing equipment and templates. Discuss why a building of this type is planned as it is. Indicate some of the essential features a building of this type ordinarily has.

Also demonstrate the use of the computer in drawing plans.

After these two sessions, simulate a meeting of the planning committee to discuss the planning of the building.

It is advisable at this time to inform the students of a term project in which they are to present their own complete plans for a building with the specifications for "X" number of pieces of equipment.

1. How might a planner of a food service reduce HVAC costs? Where can one go to get information on this?

2. What sort of food services might a large hotel in New York City have that caters to conventions as well as travelers and other trade?

3. How does a full-service restaurant differ in plans from a coffee shop?

4. You are an architect and must explain to someone who wants to invest in a hamburger drive-in what sort of a facility must be planned. You make notes for this. Organize these notes for a presentation.

5. Outline some of the needs an off-premise catering facility serving up to several thousand people might have.

6. How does a cafeteria shopping center plan differ from a regular service counter in the ordinary cafeteria?

7. What are the special needs of a plan for a hospital kitchen and dining service over that of an ordinary restaurant?

8. How might the plans for the kitchen and dining space for an elementary and secondary school differ?

9. If you were asked to name the various kinds of food facilities a student union building might have, what would you name?

10. You are a dietitian managing a large school district. You have worked on committees planning food services for new schools. Your church is planning to build a small kitchen to prepare full meals and meet other foodservice needs and you are asked to be on the planning committee. Outline what you would bring to the first meeting of this committee on the needs of the plan. The maximum number to be served a full meal is estimated at about 200. The church plans to rent the facility out to certain civic groups for the purpose of meeting their foodservice needs.

KEY WORDS AND CONCEPTS

American service
assembly-line dish-up
bar
cafeteria service
California menu
catering
catering kitchen
centralized-bulk service
centralized service
checker station
clubs
coffee shop
community kitchen
cook-chill method
decentralized service
drive-in
executive dining room
fast-food unit
French service
full-service restaurant
Gueridon
health care facilities
heating, ventilating, and air conditioning (HVAC)
hollow-square plan
induction-cooking units

industrial food service
inflight meals
limited-choice menu
long-term care facilities
lounge
main kitchen
mom-and-pop operation
off-premise catering
on-premise catering
packaged meals
residence halls
room service
Russian service
satellite system
self-busing
service bar
shopping center plan
snack bar
special diet kitchen
take-out foods
therapeutic diet
value-added food
vending service
white tablecloth restaurant

CHAPTER

3

Operational Factors That Affect Plans

INFLUENCE OF OPERATIONAL POLICIES

Designing a useful plan calls for a knowledge of **operational policies.** The menu pattern, the number to be served, and the style of service provides a general outline for planning, but there are numerous specifics to be filled in that will influence development of a satisfactory layout and selection of equipment. Among these are policies pertaining to desired characteristics of the food and service and the system chosen for operation. Funds available for operation plus local needs and limitations are to be considered.

The food production plans currently in use may be described as follows:

1. Foods are procured unrefined and processed from "scratch" within the facility.
2. The largest percent of the foods are fully processed in the facility with the exception of a few convenience items that offer significant advantage.
3. The majority of foods are purchased fully prepared and only limited preparation is required for a few dishes.
4. All foods are purchased fully prepared and require only final conditioning for service.

The requirement for production equipment, work areas, and storage facilities differ considerably between the plans of operation. Further differences are obvious between the different systems of preparation. The different systems of preparation are aimed at overcoming quality hazards caused by delays in service of prepared foods. Commonly used systems include these:

1. Short-order preparation for immediate service
2. Rotation preparation or batch cooking to supply freshly cooked food at short intervals throughout a serving period
3. Partial preparation with final cooking done by rapid means at the time and place of service
4. The food is fully prepared, chilled or frozen, thawed, portioned, and quickly heated for immediate service.

Short-order cooking calls for grills, broilers, and deep fryers to be located close to the serving area, plus suitable refrigeration for holding highly perishable products before cooking. This differs greatly from the general kitchen process of preparing, chilling, and then reheating for service.

Rotation or batch cooking usually requires normal commercial-size kitchen equipment such as that used in hotels, coffee shops, institutional kitchens, and other similar units. Much of the equipment shown in this text is of that size. Of course, there still will be differences in the size of equipment used between units in this category because of the volume of food required to meet quantity demands. When foods are partially prepared with final cooking later, larger equipment (up to factory size) will usually be needed for preparing huge batches and the high speed units will be microwave, high speed ovens, or other similar fast heating units. The amount of equipment required in the conditioning unit will be limited. The fourth type requires only reconditioning equipment, much as described for the number three type above. If the **cook-chill system** described later in this chapter is used, the type of equipment shown will be used. If the source of food is frozen, the planner must be sure to plan enough frozen space to hold supplies.

Realistic calculation in detail, not suppositions, is needed in determining the most desirable system to adopt for a specific operation. The calculations need to explore and compare costs in preparing all, some, or none of the food served. Acceptability of standards for food and service and the dependability of food and labor supplies are to be considered. Unless the most careful evaluation, supported by reliable evidence, is done before planning and building the facility, the operation is likely to be tied to an impractical system. Detailed study at this point can have long-term benefits. The system of operation will determine the kind and amount of equipment needed and the best layout for efficient work.

There is a wide variation in facilities. Some are designed to prepare everything from basic raw materials and some do no food preparation and are merely service stations. Therefore, space allowance, storage requirements, and specific equipment needs vary. The type of cooking, such as bulk preparation or individual short orders, as well as the extent of cooking need to be known. A different system may be required for each type of variation, and the planner needs to be thoroughly familiar with requirements for the specific system before designing the facility to accommodate it.

One of the first considerations to be made in choosing a system of operation is the menu or foods required to satisfy a particular clientele. Question whether the majority of foods commonly appearing on the specific menus are better in quality prepared by one system or another. Some foods can be prepared in factory quantities, frozen, thawed, and reheated with minimum damage to palatability. Others, with comparable menu classification, would be seriously robbed of appealing qualities. A potted steak, for example, might well survive such treatment, but roast beef could be expected to lose its "pink of perfection."

Preparation of food from "scratch" must be done at some point, and the information in this book is largely based on this premise. How much and what type is done in the individual kitchen depends on the policy and planning of the particular organization or owner. Many factors influence the advisability of one system over another. Although menu demands are a first consideration, **economics of operation** are a close second and involve availability, reliability, and cost of supplies, labor, and management.

Modern markets offer foods at varying stages of preparation. High production costs, especially those for labor, have stimulated attention to foods requiring a minimum of time and skill in conditioning them for service. Such value-added foods as baking mixes, dehydrated potatoes, oven-ready meats, and many other items have labor-saving advantages. Fully prepared menu items have helped to meet problems of labor shortages and lack of training and have given certain uniformity in quality standards. Management needs to be alert in adjusting labor schedules when introducing prepared food in order to offset the higher material cost of the menu items. Practical planners, where there is available food bank capacity, have doubled volume as items were produced of foods that could be frozen, thawed, and reheated without greatly affecting quality, for next use in the menu cycle.

Systems of operation may be distinct, mixed, or combined. Preparation of food from basic raw materials may be done in (1) a food facility kitchen that prepares food for one specific operation only, (2) a commissary kitchen that serves satellite serving units, or (3) a large commercial unit or food factory. All conditions that influence cost of output, such as volume, utilization of labor, variety of items, and amount of elaboration of products, will affect the ultimate cost. It is highly advisable for specific operators to evaluate which system will yield the quality, quantity, and variety of items that will best meet their specific needs.

The separation of work functions and their specialization has been shown to promote efficiency and save labor. A number of both commercial and institutional food services have changed to what is called the cook-chill system in which foods are prepared in bulk, sealed hot in vacuum moisture-vapor-proof wraps, and chilled in ice water (see Figures 3.1 and 3.2). They are then stored under refrigeration just above freezing and only removed from storage when they must be reconditioned for service. Many foods can be held in this form for as much as 60 days without serious loss of palatability or danger from bacterial or other growth.

The cook-chill method has the advantage of completely separating production units from most of service. Foods needed for service are not prepared and served on the same day but withdrawn later from storage and reconditioned for service. This permits the production system to work ahead in preparing foods for the future in large batches. It is readily discernible that such a system could make a significant change in the design

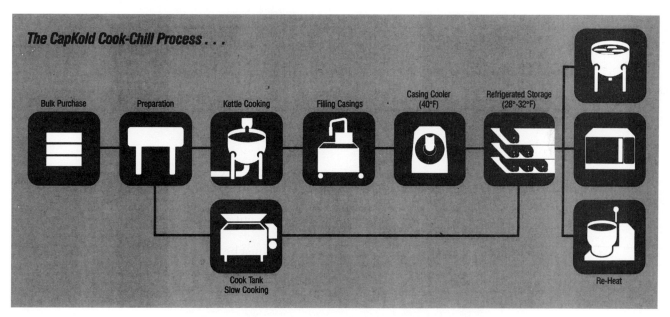

FIGURE 3.1 The steps in the cook-chill (CapKold) process are shown here. Food is purchased in bulk; then prepared for cooking and sent to a cook kettle, which after cooking to proper doneness is then pumped by the kettle to a filler machine. This filler unit can be set to pump a prearranged amount into tough pliable casings that when sealed at 180°F (82°C), is fairly sterile. These pouches are then placed into a high-speed cooler, which tumbles them quickly down to 40°F (2.2°C) so they can be stored under refrigeration and be usable for up to six weeks. The last step shows the food being removed from storage and reheated either in a cooking kettle, an oven, or a tilt kettle. The slow cooking cook tank method shown at the bottom of the figure skips all of the steps mentioned except the storage period and the reheat step. It is a tank that holds a water bath at a very steady cooking temperature—around 200°F (82°C)—or less so plastic-sealed items placed into this bath with their seasonings are slow cooked over a period of hours to come out perfectly cooked, tender, and very flavorful. *(Courtesy of Groen, A Dover Industries Company, Elk Grove Village, Illinois.)*

(a)

(b)

(c)

FIGURE 3.2 Three Groen pieces of equipment used in the CapKold process. (a) The cooking kettle with a tilt-mixing arm. The automatic pump is at the bottom of the kettle. (b) The filling machine. (c) The chiller. *(Courtesy of Groen, a Dover Industries Company, Elk Grove Village, Illinois.)*

of any food facility with production and service units separated by storage and recon-ditioning and no longer linked closely. It is to be expected that the design of kitchens and serving units will change to meet changing methods.

The food factory type of production finds favor especially where a large quantity of similar menu items is required within a specific operation. It is being used by corpo-rations with many units, and within organizations that have similar meal requirements, such as hospitals, nursing homes, and schools. Food may be produced repetitively in batches appropriate to quality requirements for specific dishes and in a manner to best utilize labor time and production costs.

The more meticulous the calculations, the more significant the comparison of costs and desirability between premise-produced food and factory-produced items. The com-parisons should be based on comparable quality, quantity, and choice of items to meet specific menu requirements, and in amounts customarily needed. Cost figures on the part of private production should include costs for (1) raw materials to produce specific quantities of items used daily, (2) daily payroll cost for production, (3) production space needed in excess of that required for final conditioning and service, and (4) production equipment needed in excess of that required for final conditioning and service. The fig-ures for space and equipment should include initial cost plus interest and depreciation, or initial cost and interest for the period of years of life expectancy, such as 20 or 30 years for space and 10 years for equipment. The total cost for each should be divided by the number of years of life expectancy and added to get the cost per year for space and equipment. This figure divided by the number of days per year that the facility will op-erate will give the daily cost. The resulting figure divided by the total number of por-tions produced daily will yield the per portion cost for space and equipment. This added to the portion cost for food, production operating expenses, and labor will give the cost of private-facility produced items. The differences under certain circumstances may ap-pear large, as when serving small numbers. When serving larger numbers, or serving very simply prepared foods, the differences may be negligible or definitely on the side of premise-produced foods.

FACTORS THAT INFLUENCE WORK ACCOMPLISHMENT

Suitable utilization of **man-hours** involves consideration of human factors when plan-ning work areas. It is important that workers be satisfied and able to produce good work in the allotted time with minimum **fatigue.** Conditions to be sought are those that pro-mote a feeling of well-being and a desire to work, and which minimize causes of fatigue. There are two types of fatigue. The first is a tiredness brought on by physical effort and discomfort, and the second by psychological factors, such as monotony, frustration, dis-like of the job, the supervisor, or fellow workers, and low regard for the value of the job. If a worker likes the work, feels that it is important, and has pride in doing it and wants to do it well, a certain buoyancy will be felt that will help to lessen fatigue. The fatigue that is brought on by physical effort and discomfort may be due to one or more of four causes:

1. Physical effort and strain involved in doing the job
2. Length of time engaged in continuous effort, such as length of shift, length of working day, and hours per week
3. Length of time and amount of comfort during rest breaks, plus schedule of breaks during shifts
4. Working conditions in terms of temperature, humidity, light, ventilation, and sounds.

The physical effort and strain in doing tasks that require fast, continuous action, as in mixing ingredients or in chopping vegetables, can be relieved by power equipment.

FIGURE 3.3 When lifting heavy objects, for minimum strain use the force of the legs and not the back. Grasp the object with fingers underneath and keep the weight close to the body.

This   Not this

Awkward positions during work can be tiring. Work levels need to be appropriate for the work to be done and for the stature of persons who do it. A height generally accepted as standard for worktables and ranges used by women is 34 in. (86 cm). This is not always satisfactory. When a worker does hand work, such as rolling pie crust, the work surface should be 2 to 4 in. (5 to 10 cm) below the elbow. A short worker may need a lower surface and a tall worker a higher one. When tools are required for manipulation, such as long beaters or spoons, the height should be such that the worker can stand erect at the work surface with hands flat on the surface with arms straight but not stretched. In this case, a good work level can be 37 to 39 in. (94 to 99 cm). Workers who are tall and have a long reach can usually utilize a higher and deeper work area than those of shorter stature. Height and reach distances will vary, and it is good to know when planning whether men or women are to be employed or persons who are generally short versus those who are tall. Adjustable levels help in overcoming the problem of providing comfortable heights for all workers.

Strain occurs when a worker is required to work at a faster than normal pace and continue for an extended time without a break. Loads greater than one's strength to handle, lifting in a manner that employs weaker muscles, and standing and walking on floors that have little or no resilience tend to induce strain and fatigue (see Figure 3.3). Short-cycle jobs having repetitive motions tend to bore workers who have high mentality. Pace and rhythm are important and must be adapted to the worker's ability. **Pace** and **rhythm in work** can be stimulated mechanically with music or even by a conveyor operating at a suitable speed.

Methods of Counteracting Fatigue

Satisfaction in quality of work and value of the job gives impetus for work. Recognition by management of the individual worker as a valuable person may not be possible to build into the facility, but it is an important factor in promoting satisfactory work in terms of quality and amount of accomplishment. Personal pride and social values are important. The social quality of working with others relieves boredom and imparts enjoyment to work. Social aspects can be promoted by rest breaks and meal periods together in a pleasant atmosphere.

Rest periods improve output through recuperation of physical and nervous energy. Relaxation is most effective when rest periods are management approved and taken in a comfortable place at suitable intervals. Suitable length of periods and frequency will depend on the nature of the work. For the majority of food facility workers, a 10-minute break near the middle of a four-hour shift has been considered satisfactory. Studies indicate that less time is taken for personal needs when suitable rest periods are given (see Figure 3.4).

Plans made for proper body mechanics tend to reduce fatigue. The rate of breathing, heartbeat, blood pressure, and other body functions are increased by unnatural posture. The spine and hips of the body form a structure similar to an inverted T that supports the body weight. The smallest amount of muscle pull results when the weight is in balance or evenly distributed on the T (see Figure 3.5). Workers who must bend over, squat down, stretch up, and lift while working experience a pull on muscles that is fatiguing.

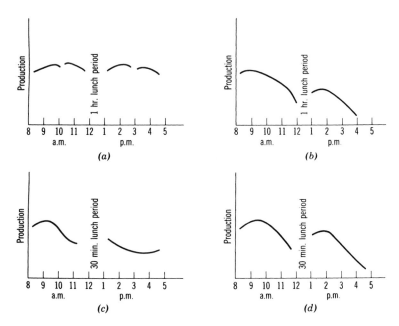

FIGURE 3.4 Production curves under various conditions. (a) Production curve of kitchen worker working at a normal rate with two 10-minute coffee breaks during a shift. (b) Production curve of a worker doing heavy work but not at a fast pace drops toward end of shift when worker is tired. (c) Production curve of a bored worker. Note how when worker sees end of shift approaching, work production increases. (d) Production curve of a worker doing heavy work at a fairly rapid pace.

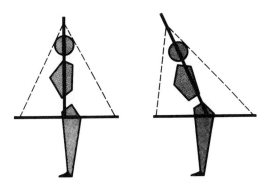

FIGURE 3.5 Body in balanced and unbalanced positions. The head, chest, and trunk of the body rest on an inverted "T" formed by the hips and spine. Correct posture ensures that the weight will be evenly distributed over this "T." Poor posture will impose a heavier workload on some muscles, causing strain and fatigue.

The majority of work in a food facility calls for workers to change position and location repeatedly, and being seated at work would interfere considerably with quantity of work done. There are other situations where repetitive action in one location is necessary and where a worker can be seated while working. A suitable chair will help to reduce fatigue. One that is adjustable in height and sturdily built, with a back support for the spine just below the shoulder blade, allows the worker to hold a good position. The position should be one in which the body is straight from the hips to the neck without bending at the waist.

Sound and Work.   Workers vary in their reaction to **sound.** Noise from outside the work area tends to be more annoying than that in the worker's area. A study made to ascertain the effect of **noise** on workers indicated that, in a factory having an output of 80 units per worker per day, 60 were made when working near a noisy boiler factory and 110 were made when the workers were moved to a quiet work area. In the latter situation errors were also reduced. Noise interferes with attention, annoying workers and affecting their output. Verbal communications are apt to be misunderstood where noise is high.

The Environmental Protection Agency claims scientific evidence supports the recommendation that industrial noise be reduced to 85 **decibels.** The **Occupational Safety and Health Administration (OSHA)** ruling, which went into effect in 1971, stated noise limits to be 90 decibels averaged over an eight-hour day. This is a noise level approximately comparable to that made by a subway train or a 20-ton truck.

In controlling sounds, it is important to understand two physical characteristics of noise, that is, intensity and frequency. Intensity is measured in decibels (dB). One decibel is the lowest sound intensity the average person can hear close to the ear, and 150 decibels is the threshold of pain. The ordinary factory areas may have sound intensities varying from 70 to 110 dB. Noisy restaurants have registered sound intensity of 70 dB. This is comparable to the noise of a vacuum cleaner. Through the use of appropriate controls, noise levels have been reduced by as much as 20 to 30 dB. (See Chapter 16, Sound Control, for further information.)

High sound frequencies are more annoying than low sound frequencies. Low frequencies characterize such sounds as hums, thuds, and rumbles; middle frequencies those of roars and clangs; and high frequencies those of shrill ringing, hissing, or clicks. High-frequency sounds are easier to control than low-frequency sounds. Noises of the impact type of low frequency are annoying if rhythmic. Continuous and meaningful noises are less disturbing.

Noise may be reduced by training workers to work quietly, by choosing or designing equipment to operate quietly, through use of sound-deadening or absorbing materials, and by isolating or closing off noisy areas. Trucks with rubber tires and machines with smooth running parts and freedom from vibration are important in maintaining a quiet workshop. Screens or walls may be placed to deflect sound, and acoustic materials may be used to absorb it. A dropped ceiling helps to capture sound. The suspended ceilings are effective sound absorbers because of the dead air space above them. **Space absorbers,** sometimes called "functional" absorbers, may be used. Proper spacing is necessary to capture sound and absorb it when these are used. Grouping has not been found to be most effective. Absorbers should be hung in such a way that they will not throw shadows or oscillate in drafts.

Music helps in masking sound and in developing rhythms in work. It tends to reduce fatigue. In one instance, it was found to increase productivity 4.7% to 11.4%. It should not be played, however, more than 2.5 hours a day in periods of 12 to 20 minutes. Light, fast music is preferable to slow, somber types.

Light and Work.   Good light helps workers to do a satisfactory job and enjoy their work with a minimum of eye strain. About five of every eight workers lack good vision. Few realize that this may be the cause of fatigue and dislike for the job. The cost of proper lighting will be readily offset by better workmanship, increased productivity, fewer accidents, and less waste due to errors. When planning for light in the work area consider (1) the direction from which it comes, (2) color, (3) diffusion, (4) steadiness, and (5) intensity. (See Chapter 13, Lighting.)

Light should be located to eliminate shadows on the work or glare and excessive brightness in the field of vision. The variation of brightness between the working area and field surrounding the working area should not be greater than 3 to 1, with the working area the brighter. In nonworking areas the contrast can be greater, but the ratio should never be greater than 10 to 1. **Reflectance** levels recommended by a committee studying lighting for kitchens were for ceilings to have a reflection percent of 80, walls 60, equipment 30 to 35, and floors not less than 15.

When selecting **fluorescent lights** choose those that will permit colors to appear natural. Color plays an important role in food enjoyment, and some lights can rob or change the color of food. Some of the highest efficiency fluorescent lights fail to transmit all colors, especially reds, which then give false or off-colors to foods and other items. Fluorescent lights listed in order of satisfactory color quality are cool fluorescent, warm white, and cool white fluorescent. A flickering light or stroboscopic effect may be caused by improper functioning of lighting or by fluorescent lights. It can be eliminated in the latter by the use of 60-cycle current and by the use of two-lamp auxiliaries.

The proper intensity of light is dependent on the kind of work to be done. Measured in **foot-candles,** the following recommendations are made: loading and transporting areas, 10 to 20; rough work, 15 to 35; general work, 35 to 70; and fine assembly, 70 to 150. The committee cited previously that studied kitchen lighting for food facilities recommended general areas, 30, and fine work or inspection, 50 foot-candles. The 1999 FDA Food Code recommends 10 to 20 foot-candles for storage and cleaning and 50 foot-candles for food preparation. We may need to evaluate our standards to meet limitations in energy expenditure. Excess in lighting should be avoided (see Figure 3.6).

The absorption or reflection of light by colors selected for surrounding areas, as well as the psychological effect of colors on workers, should be considered. If color contrast between product and work place is great, eye fatigue may result. Walls of gray or green are restful for workers in bright work areas. Surroundings with proper color selection have been found to reduce absenteeism.

Placement of lights is important in gaining the most benefit. Least benefit occurs when lights are parallel with work areas or immediately over the place where the worker stands, casting working shadows over the work areas. Lights placed perpendicularly or diagonally to work area may help to overcome the shadow effect. Lights should be concentrated on work area and shielded to protect against uncomfortable glare. The fixtures

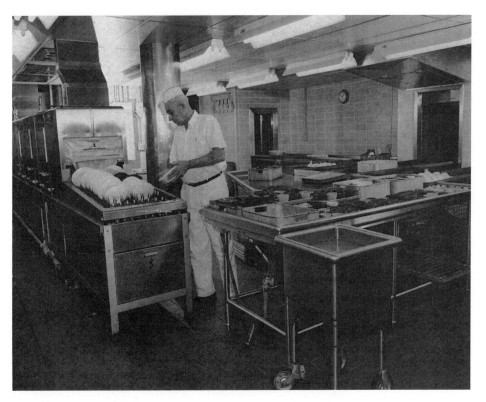

FIGURE 3.6   Well-lighted work areas help to promote good work.

should be designed so as to permit easy, complete cleanability. The lights should be sealed in case of exploding tubes.

Some find that installing lights that have approximately the same lifetime and then operating them until about this time and changing all lights regardless of whether they may have more life is more economical than changing lights as needed. Changing lights individually when they burn out is costly in labor. The number of times lights must be secured, work tools and ladders obtained, and carried to the spot costs more in labor than the loss of the lights in mass changing when most of their hours of operation are already used up.

Temperature and Humidity and Work.   Fresh clean air is invigorating and a suitable temperature in the workshop is necessary for comfort. Such conditions influence the productivity of workers. Individuals fatigue more quickly when temperatures are too high and their limbs tend to stiffen when they are too cold. The feeling of pressure or strain experienced in relation to production rate may be measured in terms of increased rate of heartbeat. Studies made of workers performing in a temperature of 81°F (27.2°C) and relative humidity of 56% showed only a slight increase in heart rate. When temperature was raised to 99°F (37.2°C) and a relative humidity of 75%, the heart rate increased as the day progressed, and fatigue set in. Stiffness of arms and legs develops at temperatures below 50°F (10°C), and fatigue increases with those above 75°F (29.4°C). A temperature that is satisfactory for a moderately active worker is 65°F (18.3°C).

Good **ventilation,** with **air conditioning** where essential, and well-insulated equipment to prevent unnecessary heat loss is helpful in maintaining desirable temperatures. In the average kitchen an **air change** every 2 to 5 minutes is desirable. The undertaking involves not only the bringing in of fresh air but the removal of excess heat and odors, without creating uncomfortable drafts. Hoods over cooking equipment help to remove odors as well as heat.

Draft is a requisite condition for removal of smoke, heat, and steam. Unless it is properly controlled a drafty condition results that is unpleasant for the workers, especially those working near the hood or outlet. **Hoods** are somewhat similar to a vacuum sweeper in that their effectiveness increases in relation to their closeness in proximity to objects to be picked up or removed. Hoods located high above cooking equipment may have their effectiveness nullified by cross currents of air in the room, but they shouldn't be placed low enough to make the draft so strong as to cause considerable discomfort to workers. Workers who are comfortably cool are likely to be more productive than those who are either uncomfortably cool or too warm. A draft or fan should be directed toward the face rather the back of workers for best cooling. Smoke or objectionable odors annoy workers and should be removed as soon as possible.

PROTECTING FOOD VALUES

Food is the "stock-in-trade" of a foodservice facility, so the kitchen designer should be mindful of the important values requiring protection. Included are safety, nutritive content, palatability, appearance, and cost. These are values that may be affected by the adequacy and suitability of the equipment and the convenience of the layout. In some instances the major problem may be coping with high volume, in others protection from **contamination** and preservation of appealing qualities. Food quality is affected not only by the method of processing and cooking, but also by storage methods and time, temperature, humidity, and light.

Palatability standards may be affected at many points between procurement and service of the food to the consumer. It is useful for a planner to trace the route of food from entrance to the kitchen, through preparation, holding for service and service to the consumers, challenging every aspect that affects quality. In some instances time is the enemy to quality, causing loss of freshness of color, flavor, and texture. Time is sometimes in terms of minutes that food is out of refrigeration or between preparation and service. This may influence placement of refrigeration units. Lessening time may call for shortening distances between units of production or between production and service. The best amount of time may relate to speed of heating or rapidity of freezing.

Major concern about light is that there be sufficient candle-power well-placed for seeing work and for the comfort of the workers. On the other hand, light has an effect on the nutritive values of some foods. Light deteriorates the vitamin A and ascorbic acid (vitamin C). Dairy products and most of the fruits and vegetables should be stored, therefore, away from the light.

Temperature and **humidity** are significant elements in the preservation of food quality. The best temperature for holding the various foods differs. Refrigeration slows deterioration in many foods. Bread, however, stales more quickly in a refrigerator than when held frozen or at room temperature. Changes in temperature, caused by the opening and closing of the box during normal use, change the humidity in the refrigerator and can have a drying effect on the food stored. The design of the box may be influenced by this fact. Curtains or baffles can aid in maintaining temperature. A lower temperature is recommended if holding for an extended period of time rather than for temporary storage. Table 3.1 indicates the temperature and relative humidity recommended for fresh fruits and vegetables.

It is possible to destroy the **ethylene gases** that fruits and vegetables give off that cause their ripening. Chemical absorbers that absorb these ethylene gases are placed in refrigerators or other enclosed spaces where fruits and vegetables are held, giving the products stored there a longer shelf life and a better appearance upon use.

The temperature of food when it reaches the consumer may add or detract from the enjoyment of it. Piping hot and refreshingly cold temperatures in food do not last long at room temperature. Time limits between the finish of production and service to consumers may be as important to quality as the time limits in the initial preparation.

TABLE 3-1   *Temperature and Humidity for Storage of Fresh Fruits and Vegetables*

Fresh Fruits			Fresh Vegetables			
Store at 32°F (0°C) and 80% Relative Humidity						
Apples	Figs	Pomegranates	Artichokes	Cauliflower	Horseradish	Radishes
Apricots	Grapes	Prunes	Asparagus	Celeriac	Kohlrabi	Rhubarb
Blackberries	Nectarines	Quinces	Beans, Lima	Celery	Leeks, green	Rutabagas
Cherries	Oranges	Raspberries	Beets	Corn, sweet	Lettuce	Spinach
Coconuts	Peaches	Strawberries	Broccoli	Endive	Mushrooms	Salsify
Cranberries	Pears	Tangerines	Brussel Sprouts	Escarole	Onions, green	Squash (summer)
Dates	Persimmons		Cabbage	Garlic, dry	Parsnips	Turnips
Dewberries	Plums		Carrots	Greens (general)	Peas, green	
Store at 50° (10°C) and 80 to 85% Relative Humidity						
Avocados	Limes	Olives	Beans, green	Okra	Potatoes	Sweet potatoes
Grapefruit	Mangoes	Papayas	Cucumbers	Onions, dry	Pumpkins	Tomatoes (ripe)
Lemons	Melons	Pineapples	Eggplants	Peppers, sweet	Squash (hard shell)	

Commodities Requiring Special Conditions

Bananas for ripening: 58–68°F (14.4–0°C), 90–95% relative humidity.

Bananas, ripe (for holding): 55–60°F (12.8–15.6°C, 75–90% relative humidity.

Pears, for ripening: 60–65°F (15.6–18.3°C), 85–95% relative humidity.

Green tomatoes, for ripening: 55–70°F (12.8–21.2°C), 85–90% relative humidity.

Source: Courtesy of United States Department of Agriculture.

Not only refrigerated temperatures but also prevention of overcooking is involved. Temperature and holding time influence the quality of frozen and/or refrigerated foods. A lower temperature is recommended for holding than for temporary storage because there is less loss or exchange of flavor when the foods are held at a temperature just above freezing.

Ultra violet light, if close enough to items, can destroy microorganisms. UV light is sometimes used in meat curing rooms and other areas where items must be held for fairly long periods of time and could be in danger of spoilage if bacteria got to them.

Adequate managerial supervision can have a strong influence on food quality plus proper utilization of materials and labor time. It is desirable for kitchens and serving areas to be designed with as open a view as possible of the important areas requiring supervision. This means elimination of unnecessary walls and the arrangement of equipment to permit an open view of the major production and serving areas.

ENSURING SAFETY AND SANITATION

Public food operations provide service by people for people. The health and well-being of both groups merit special attention. The safety and sanitation hazards and need for protection are multiplied in relation to the number of food handlers and food consumers involved daily in the operation. Food provides an excellent medium for rapid growth of bacteria and molds, and is very attractive to pests and vermin (see Table 3.2). Requisite handling in food preparation, display, and service makes it easily subject to contamination. Wise planning of layout and selection of equipment can do much to promote **safety** and **sanitation.** The equipment design and the way that it is installed may have an influence on safety and sanitation. All surfaces with which food comes in contact should be smooth, readily cleanable, nonabsorbent, corrosion resistant, and nontoxic. It is recommended that the OSHA regulations and FDA food codes be followed.

Sanitation

All food equipment, walls, floors, and work surfaces should permit easy, thorough, and frequent repeated cleaning. To be cleanable, the equipment and work surfaces, such as cutting boards, should be nonabsorbent and free from cracks or other lodging spots for soil. The surfaces should be smooth and the design such as to permit sanitizing all areas. Machines should be designed for complete dismantling for thorough cleaning. Self-cleaning equipment such as ovens and ventilators is especially desirable.

Equipment should be installed in such a manner as to permit easy access around and under it for cleaning and inspection. Mobility that permits moving items away from the wall or other equipment is desirable. Ranges, fryers, and three-deck ovens are presently designed for sufficient mobility to facilitate cleaning. Wall mounting of permanent fixtures eliminates legs, which interfere with cleaning. Where equipment is fitted to the wall, the fitting should be tight and sealed to exclude vermin or set out sufficiently from the wall at least 6 in. so that vermin cannot lodge behind it. Backsplashes should be on equipment where required. **Stationary equipment,** such as sinks and ranges, when located in the center of the floor, facilitate cleaning and permit workers to work from both sides. When equipment is set on a base or raised platform, the base should be at least 6 in. (10 to 15 cm) high. The base should be recessed to allow for a 4-in. (10-cm) toe space and coved at the floor juncture on a ¾-in. (2-cm) radius. Flat surfaces that must rest directly on the floor or on a base should be sealed to the surface with a mastic or cement to seal against the entrance of vermin.

Traps, drains, pipes, shelves, and bottom surfaces of equipment that are exposed should be at least 6 in. (15 cm) and preferably 8 in. (20 cm) above the floor to permit cleaning under. **Grease traps** need to be placed so as to be readily cleanable. They may

TABLE 3-2 *Foodborne Illness Causes and Prevention*

Contamination	Contributing Factors	Recommendations
Bacteria		
Salmonella	Improper cooking of poultry and egg products; poor hygiene with infected food handler	Thorough cooking of all poultry or egg products; use pasteurized egg products for those that cannot be thoroughly cooked (eggnog, Caesar salad dressing, etc.)
Staphylococcus aureus	Careless handling of food (particularly if employee has open cuts or sores)	Minimize direct contact with food; hand washing; limit time food is between 40–140°F (7–60°C)
Clostridium perfringens	Allowing to stand at room temperature; improper heating and cooling	Thorough cooking and rapid cooling
Clostridium botulinum	Improper processing of canned, vacuum packaged, or sous-vide foods	Thorough cooking; discard questionable foods (can be fatal)
Shigella	Poor personal hygiene; poor fly (insect) control	Minimize direct contact with food; hand washing; rapid cooling; insect control
Listeria monocytogenes	Cross contamination	Thorough cooking (refrigeration will not prevent its growth)
Bacillus cereus	Lack of refrigeration for cooked cereal products (rice, noodles, cooked cereals, etc.)	Keep cereal foods dry in storage; refrigerate cooked cereal foods
Campylobacter jejuni	Cross contamination; poor personal hygiene	Thorough cooking, good hand washing
E. coli 0157:H7	Improper cooking; poor personal hygiene	Thorough cooking (particularly ground meats), hand washing
Parasite		
Trichinella spiralis	Improper cooking of pork or wild game such as bear	Thorough cooking
Viruses		
Hepatitis	Improper cooking of food; poor personal hygiene	Thorough cooking of food; hand washing
Norwalk	Poor personal hygiene	Hand washing
Chemical		
Pesticides, detergents, sanitizers, and other chemicals	Carelessness in use or storage; unlabeled or mislabeled containers	Keep all chemicals well marked and stored separately from food and equipment

be mounted on slightly raised bases coved at the floor. Do not run waste from garbage grinders through grease traps. Spacers should be placed between equipment to seal in areas that may become soil catchers.

Fastenings on equipment should be designed to eliminate projections and ledges. Surfaces should be smooth. Wiring and pipes should be concealed. Hot steam and water pipes are especially difficult to clean and are a hazard to persons working around them. Pipes that must be visible should be of a design and material that will not mar the beauty of the installation. Service lines and utilities can sometimes be hidden by bringing them through the legs of the equipment. The openings for service lines and utilities should be effectively sealed against vermin.

Equipment surfaces should be readily cleanable and sufficiently durable to withstand repeated scrubbing. The structure of the equipment should have a minimum of lodging spots for soil and infestation of pests. The warmth, moisture, and food particles characteristic in kitchens is very attractive to a variety of pests. Some of the pests common in food facilities and suggested methods of control are listed in Table 3.3. The best pest control systems use a combination of sanitation, prevention, and (occasionally) chemicals. Such a system is referred to as **integrated pest management (IPM).**

Provisions for Cleaning.   A firmly established policy pertaining to the responsibility for the care and cleaning of tools and equipment in each work center will greatly help toward promoting good housekeeping practices. It has been generally observed that workers tend to be more careless when an outside person or agency is brought in to do the cleanup. Unless pride and a responsible attitude are developed, only surfaces required for immediate use and equipment that can be sent to the pot washer may be cleaned regularly. Ample hot water, sanitizing materials, and suitable equipment should be provided and accessible to all sections of work. Figure 3.7 lists some critical food temperatures that workers should know about.

Two-temperature hot water is required for dish and pot washing. A **booster heater** may be used to ensure proper temperatures. Although high-temperature water is required for purposes of sanitizing, it is not needed or desirable for general kitchen purposes. Planning should provide water at proper temperatures at points where required.

TABLE 3-3   *Control of Disease Carrying Pests*

Pest	Characteristics	Control Measures
Ants	Attracted to sweet foods, grease, and meats	Clean thoroughly to eliminate food sources
Flies	Feed on human and animal wastes and garbage; while eating they may vomit, deposit fly feces and eggs; serious health hazard	Screen all windows; doors should be self-closing; keep foods covered; garbage should also be kept in covered containers and removed frequently
Cockroaches		
German	Found at any level in a room; can hide in small crevices; can ride into food service in cans and boxes; prefer warm areas; reproduce rapidly; can carry bacteria	Inspect deliveries carefully; keep foods covered; thorough cleaning; control will require an (IPM) program, which may include the services of a licensed pest control operator
American	Found more in the open, or drainage, sewer, and restroom areas; can carry bacteria	Same as for German
Oriental	Found in basements, around water pipes; can carry bacteria	Same as for German
Rodents		
Mice	Can enter through openings the size of a nickel, can ride into food services in cans and boxes; gnawing can cause much damage; reproduce rapidly; carry diseases	Good sanitation; inspect deliveries carefully; traps may be used; may require services of licensed pest control operator
Rats	Can enter through openings the size of a quarter; may also enter around pipes and cracks in foundations of building; gnawing is destructive; reproduce rapidly; carry diseases	Good sanitation; eliminate openings into the building; may require services of licensed pest control operator
Birds	Nest in spaces in gutters, roofs, and roof overhangs; birds themselves and their droppings can be sanitation hazard	Remove nests; keep garbage (food crumbs, etc.) covered; may require services of licensed pest control operator (some birds are protected by state law)

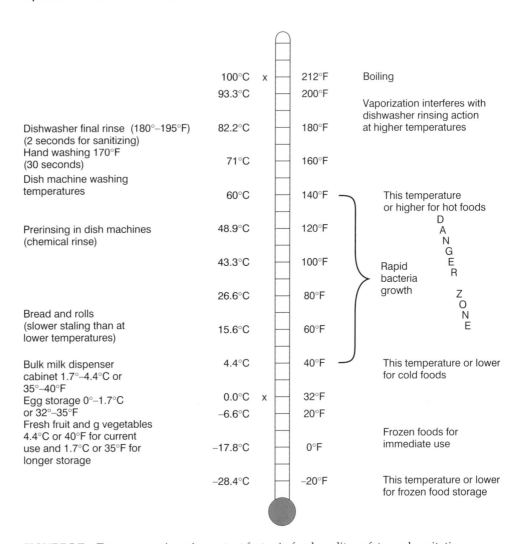

Dishwasher final rinse (180°–195°F)
(2 seconds for sanitizing)
Hand washing 170°F
(30 seconds)
Dish machine washing
temperatures

Prerinsing in dish machines
(chemical rinse)

Bread and rolls
(slower staling than at
lower temperatures)

Bulk milk dispenser
cabinet 1.7°–4.4°C or
35°–40°F
Egg storage 0°–1.7°C
or 32°–35°F
Fresh fruit and g vegetables
4.4°C or 40°F for current
use and 1.7°C or 35°F for
longer storage

100°C   x   212°F   Boiling
93.3°C   200°F
                          Vaporization interferes with
                          dishwasher rinsing action
82.2°C   180°F   at higher temperatures

71°C   160°F

60°C   140°F   This temperature
                           or higher for hot foods
                                              D
48.9°C   120°F   A
                                              N
                                              G
43.3°C   100°F   Rapid   E
                           bacteria   R
                           growth
26.6°C   80°F   Z
                                              O
                                              N
15.6°C   60°F   E

4.4°C   40°F   This temperature or lower
                           for cold foods

0.0°C   x   32°F
−6.6°C   20°F
                          Frozen foods for
−17.8°C   0°F   immediate use

−28.4°C   −20°F   This temperature or lower
                           for frozen food storage

FIGURE 3.7   Temperature is an important factor in food quality, safety, and sanitation.

Hose connections are needed for rinsing floors, flushing a soiled dish table, cleaning mobile equipment, and washing garbage cans. Drains to carry off the scrub water should be provided at locations where needed to remove the water quickly. To prevent odors from coming back into the kitchen, the drains should have traps to collect substances that may coat pipes. All floors should be waterproofed and sloped gradually toward the drains, with about 0.5-in. (1.25-cm) drop at the drain plate to ensure satisfactory drainage (see Fig. 3.8). Floor drains should be provided with flushout valves and should be so located that workers will not have to walk or stand on them.

Utility connections coming from the floor should be minimized and made from the wall where possible. Pipe chases should be put on all vertical lines for gas, steam, electricity, and plumbing leads and designed so as not to harbor vermin. Openings for pipes should be sealed against entry of vermin. Watertight metal ferrules should be installed for all piping and other leads coming through the bottom of equipment, and these ferrules should extend 1 in. above the surface entry area. Drains should be placed in or close to all refrigerated areas and the drainage piped outside. Dripping and leakage from pipes and back-siphonage from drains into the freshwater supply, sinks, and the water bath of steam tables should be prevented. Cooling coils around food should be mounted to protect the food and insulated against condensate. Outlets to sinks should be a minimum of two times the diameter of the water inlet and never less than 1 in. (2.5-cm) above the flood level rim.

FIGURE 3.8 A food facility that has easily cleanable surfaces, movable floor equipment, removable filters in the hood, and well-lighted cooking areas that help to promote sanitation and safety.

Certain metals sometimes used in equipment as well as cleaning agents and pesticides have been the cause of food poisoning. **Toxic metals** that may be found in equipment include zinc, copper, brass, lead, cadmium, bismuth, and antimony. Zinc, which is used for galvanizing iron and steel, is readily attacked by acids in foods. Copper is an excellent conductor of heat and has been popular in some kitchens for cooking pots, especially before the advent of stainless steel. Food pans made of copper require that the surface that comes in contact with food be covered with a noncorrosive, nontoxic metal such as tin. Copper and brass, which contains copper, form a poisonous salt known as verdigris in the presence of air and moisture.

Solder often contains toxic metals such as cadmium, antimony, bismuth, and lead. Where solder is used on surfaces that will come in contact with food it should be made with nontoxic metals, such as tin and silver. Wood surfaces used for cutting boards and table tops made of hard wood such as oak or maple should be in good condition with no open seams, cracks, or gouges, and free from odors or taste that can be imparted to food. Gaskets and packings should be of material that is nontoxic, nonabsorbent, stable, odor free, and fully resistant to foods and cleaning materials.

Safety

"Safe" is the state of being free from hazards. In planning against hazards it is useful to trace the path followed by workers and clients with careful consideration of items or conditions that might cause injury. The degree of awareness and use of care by the individuals strongly influence the occurrence of accidents. The unexpected or "**surprise factors**" account for the largest percentage of accidents. Among the hazardous surprise elements in foodservice facilities are blind corners, cross traffic, irregular surfaces, slick spots on floors, swinging doors, slipping of a knife, equipment out of place, sticking and one-way doors, and unexpectedly hot surfaces. Poor visibility and stairs are conducive to accidents. Fire may result from faulty equipment, poor installation, or maintenance, employees' careless use of equipment, and carelessness in smoking. Some deep-fat fryer fires occur when the operator is not properly attending an operating fryer.

Some of the common human conditions that lead to accidents are lack of training, tiredness, and diverted attention. Workers who have poor work habits and lack interest in and understanding of their work are prone to accidents. Carelessness, excessive hurry, and poor visibility on the part of workers or clients readily lead to accidents. Kitchen work calls for use of power tools, sharp instruments, and high temperatures that cause injury when misused. Both suitable facilities and thorough training and supervision of workers are required for accident prevention. The rate at which accidents occur tends to be highest at a period halfway between their work breaks, as shown in Figure 3.9.

The advent of OSHA has forced many equipment manufacturers to change some of their basic designs and operational characteristics of equipment. For instance, large ovens must have automatic closing and opening contacts allowing the flow of gas or electricity to have automatic safety closure that will shut off the flow of energy into the oven. Such ovens must have free-floating panels on the top so that if an explosion occurs, the greatest part of the force can go up through this less dangerous area. OSHA also requires on many gas ovens motorized damper airflow limit switches, power exhaust blowers, and a purging system for gas, air, and fumes from the oven chambers that will exhaust the oven three times before subsequent ignition can occur. These rules for ovens are an example of the thoroughness with which OSHA has gone through almost every piece of equipment used in food services and has pointed out similar safety requirements.

Fire Protection.   This will include not only the use of fire-resistant materials, but also detection and extinguishing facilities. Dangerous grease fires can be avoided by eliminating all grease accumulation. Elevators, shafts, and ventilating ducts should be able to be sealed off in case of fire. Investigate extinguishing systems and select one that will be most effective and in keeping with local fire ordinances. Steam, carbon dioxide, or water may be piped into ducts for fire prevention. Self-closing louvres may be installed so that ducts close on reaching excessive temperatures. Many new pieces of equipment using steam or gas have instant disconnect systems. In times of emergency they may be crucial to safety. Switches should be placed near exits for equipment that may catch fire, such as fryers. Carbon dioxide portable **extinguishers** should be available as well.

Automatic and manual fire alarms may be installed. Where desirable they may be connected to fire department alarms so that automatic notification occurs. Place alarms next to exits. Include the alarm system as a part of the electrical contract. Have an alarm that is readily distinguished from other sounds. It can be of a general type or coded. In coded type, the area of the fire is indicated. Certain fire ordinances require sprinkler systems and a coded alarm system. Some sprinkling systems give alarm when the water starts to flow. Signals can be sent to predetermined key locations, such as a telephone switchboard, office, or nurses' stations. The system used should prevent undue alarm to

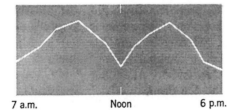

7 a.m.   Noon   6 p.m.

FIGURE 3.9   Accident record in relation to workday. Data compiled by the National Safety Council indicate that there is a sharp rise in accident probability three hours after starting time and three hours after the noonday break. This substantiates the authors' statement that tired workers are accident-prone workers. Monotony and fatigue can be alleviated by work breaks.

building occupants. The National Fire Protection Association and representatives of fire equipment manufacturers can assist in setting up good fire protection facilities. The insurance company and local fire ordinances will have an influence.

Safety Protection.   Plan for sturdy, smooth handrails, 30 in. high (76 cm), firmly installed on stairs. Stair treads, risers, and landings should be standard proportions. Provide adequate protection around floor openings and platforms. Windows and lighting fixtures should be constructed so that their cleaning and maintenance will not be hazardous, particularly from falls. Electrical wiring must not produce fire or shock hazards. Elevators must be equipped with interlocks to prevent operation with the doors open. Floors, ramps, stairs, and all walking surfaces must be rendered adequately nonslip. Provide good lighting.

Moving parts of equipment should be enclosed by guards or castings. Heavy objects should not be stored overhead but placed low enough for convenient use or transfer. Employees should be instructed in body mechanics in relation to proper ways of lifting heavy objects. Employees should not be required to lift loads that will cause excess strain. Some unions limit loads that workers must carry to 50 lb. Provide structure strength for shelves, floors, and other areas sufficient for the greatest load they will bear. Arrange for storage of all toxic materials, such as cleaning compounds, away from areas used for storage of food and equipment and where they will not have to be selected from storage with inadequate light for seeing labels.

Toxic Materials.   Zinc, which is used for galvanizing, is a soft metal that is readily attacked by acids. It should not come in contact with foods. Its use in galvaneal should be restricted to areas where this is not possible. Copper and brass are soft metals that can form **toxic substances,** and these should be well plated with harder metals so that any possibility of reaction with food is eliminated. Antimony, used in gray enamelware, cadmium in plating, and lead, which is a common ingredient in solder, are also toxic.

Safety Codes.   Consult safety codes and suggested standards of the National Bureau of Fire Underwriters, The National Fire Protection Association, American Standards Association, the United States Department of Commerce, the American Society of Mechanical Engineers, National Bureau of Standards, National Sanitation Foundation, United States Bureau of Health, and local ordinances. The requirements of the Occupational Safety and Health Act or, as it sometimes is called, the Williams-Steiger Safety and Health Act of 1970 should be met in all planning. This act establishes many safety requirements in the planning of food services, covering in detail electrical grounding and other electrical requirements, guarding dangerous equipment, the installation and maintenance of fire equipment, the construction of stairways, and rails, and so on. In the first five months of enforcement of this act, the National Restaurant Association reports, "OSHA inspectors conducted 10,668 inspections, found 26,771 violations, issued 2141 citations, and assessed penalties totaling $512,067."[1] Most were because of operational deficiencies but a large number were because of planning failures.

See Safety Check List in appendix C.

---

[1] National Restaurant Association, "OSHA Affects You—Disregard Will Bring Penalties," *NRA News,* reprint, n.d.

CHAPTER SUMMARY

Many operational factors influence the planning of a food facility, and unless planners consider them and make arrangements to accommodate them, the plan will be less than desirable. Such factors involve (1) policies of operation, (2) the environment in which work is done, (3) the need to protect food values, and (4) provisions for safety and sanitation.

The first factor covers such things as how the food is to be received and prepared, held for service, and served. Different types of clientele like to eat at different types of places. A cook-chill method of production requires a very different system than a cook-to-order one. Purchasing value-added foods or purchasing them as raw materials and doing the entire processing on premises also makes a difference.

Under factors that affect work, we find the need for a good environment essential to achieving higher productivity from workers. Energy in workers is not an unending flowing stream; workers have only a limited amount and then they tire and do less work. Assisting workers by providing for well-planned work centers so as to make work easier and quicker to do saves energy. Providing rest after a period of work helps to conserve energy. Workers asked to work at high speeds tire because there is no time for the muscles to rest and relax. Pacing work by proper planning helps save worker energy. Rhythmical work motions save energy. A good heart has rhythm; it gets its rest between beats. Sound, as in music, can help conserve energy, but noise can detract from it. Planning for the deadening of noise, especially at high frequencies, pays off. Good light is essential and a worker doing ordinary work should have at least 50 foot-candles of light on the work surface,

and, if doing finer work, more. Improper temperature and humidity saps worker energy. Having an even, pleasant environment with no drafts that is free of odors helps conserve worker energy.

The third factor, the protection of food values, is most important. Most food should be prepared as close to consumption as possible. The time period for freshness of appearance and best taste in many products is short. Good holding equipment can help prolong this time. Planning a facility so service occurs as soon as possible after preparation is required. The kind of storage products receive is important to final food quality.

Sanitation and safety are factors that planners need to give heavy consideration to. Food must be protected from contamination and deterioration from the moment it is received to the time it is served. A planner should see that the physical facilities and equipment all are easily cleaned and hold up under constant cleaning. Proper storage is needed to prevent food deterioration. Plumbing that reaches high sanitation standards should be sought.

The safety of guests as well as workers must be kept in mind. Main aisles should be planned to be wide enough to permit good flow of the traffic expected to travel through them. Avoid cross traffic and eliminate surprise factors as much as possible. Plan for fire protection and provide proper fire fighting equipment in strategic places for combatting fire. Ensure that the building can be emptied of people quickly if need be. The provisions of OSHA need to be considered. Both employees and guests should be protected from hazards that can harm them.

REVIEW QUESTIONS

1. Choose an employee for observation and note working conditions, manner in which the employee does work, and environmental and any other factors that may be identified as fatigue factors. List these, and recommend ways in which each objectionable factor may be overcome.
2. List ways by which the noise level in the kitchen which has been chosen for observation can be lowered. What provision has been made for control?
3. Evaluate the lighting in the dishwashing area, over the range, where bakery mixing is done, and in the setup and serving areas from the

standpoint of amount of light, placement in relation to the work, freedom from glare, and good color.
4. Use a thermometer to check the temperature in each area of the kitchen. (Permit the thermometer to remain for 10 minutes in each of the areas.) Evaluate the temperature found in each area from the standpoint of worker comfort.
5. Observe the handling of the food from the time it enters a food facility until it is presented to the consumer. List the points at which contamination may occur. Evaluate precautions taken to prevent contamination.

6. List all of the points in a food facility at which a client might be injured. What precautions have been taken to prevent such injury?
7. List the ways in a specific kitchen that an employee might be injured. Inquire whether such injuries have occurred. What precautions are taken to prevent injuries?
8. Observe, if possible, food prepared (a) from raw materials to fully prepared products, (b) in a satellite system in which food is prepared centrally and sent to service units, and (c) commercially and then merely conditioned for service. Evaluate the comparative acceptability of food in each system. Compare the food and labor costs in the different systems.
9. List the points in the food facility at which fire might occur. What precautions have been taken to protect against its occurring?

KEY WORDS AND CONCEPTS

air-conditioning
booster heater
contamination
cook-chill system
decibels
economics of operation
ethylene gases
extinguishers
fatigue
fluorescent lights
foot-candles
grease trap
hood
humidity
Integrated Pest Management (IPM)
man-hours
noise
Occupational Safety and Health Administration (OSHA)

operational policies
pace in work
partial preparation
reflectance
rest periods
rhythm in work
rotation preparation
safety
sanitation
scratch
short-order preparation
sound
space absorbers
stationary equipment
surprise factors
toxic metals
toxic substances
ultraviolet light
ventilation

CHAPTER

4

Analyses of Layout Characteristics[1]

INTRODUCTION

The goal in any layout analysis is to get a detailed concept of work that is to be done. To do this, workers are studied doing work or work is simulated to note the motions required, the distances traveled, and the relationship of equipment to the work. From this the planner can then more closely estimate the type of equipment required, its size, and its placement so work is done in the easiest manner and at the least cost of labor.

The analysis should also indicate the most desirable way to join **work centers** into **sections** and join sections together to make the most desirable layout of the facility. The final layout design will indicate spatial allowances, physical facilities, construction features, and work areas with equipment therein. Some other significant factors resulting from the study that will influence design are quality and quantity of output, cost of operation, time scheduling, shared equipment, character of materials processed and produced, and system of operation.

BASIC UNITS IN PLAN DESIGN

There are three distinct parts in a layout: (1) work center, (2) sections, and (3) the total layout made up of work centers joined into sections. The best plan evolves when work

[1]This chapter, written in 1985 for the third edition, remains little changed for this fourth edition. The reason is that there has been little change in the industrial engineering study methods used and how to do the studies. The big development has been in the use of the computer in recording the data obtained in making these studies along with use of the computer to calculate results and analyze them. In other words, the tried and proven methods of the past, the laws and rules established for industrial engineering studies by Taylor, Mundel, the Gilbreths and other early pioneers in the field, remain much the same. Using the computer to do the recording and then doing the calculations, the analyses, and the drawings are the main developments.

This chapter, however, does not follow into this new area of computer use. The authors recognize it in various places on the chapter, but feel that it is best to stay with the basics, and not go off on a long involved tangent on computer use. The goal of the chapter is to provide information to readers on ways to make industrial engineering studies that will improve equipment placement and result in increased worker productivity when the plan becomes an actual facility. Learning how to use these new computer methods can be a goal of further study.

centers are planned first, then sections, and the sections put together to form the total layout.

Work Centers

A work center is the basic component or unit in a layout. The relationship of work centers to a layout is similar to that of atoms to matter. It is the smallest whole work unit of a layout. Work centers are areas where a group of closely related tasks are done by an individual or individuals, such as one might find in a bakeshop in a mixing center, a panning center, and a baking center. The number of functions to be performed and the volume of material handled determine the number of centers required. In some sections, numerous work centers are needed because the jobs are highly specialized. In a smaller facility fewer work centers may be required, and they may be used repeatedly for the changing tasks done in them.

The space allotted to a work center should be approximately 15 sq ft (1.39 m^2) measuring about 2.5 ft deep (76 cm) by 6 ft long (182 cm) for a worker of medium size (about 5.5 ft or 1.68 m). A worker should be able to do all of the related tasks in the work center without moving from it. This is not always achieved in practice (see Figures 4.1 and 4.2).

Work center size is fairly standard, but it may be adjusted to specific production needs. Workers should not be required to reach or travel farther than the outer area of reach called the **maximum reach.** Most work motions should be within the **normal reach** areas. If heavy objects are lifted or difficult tasks done, these should be within the normal reach areas also. Less frequently made motions may occur in the maximum reach area (see Figure 4.3).

Useful studies of the placement of tools and materials for quick, convenient work in each work center may be made in various ways. It is very helpful to follow the preparation of recipes for representative menu items according to the sequence of activities required noting use of tools, equipment, and materials. Sometimes a simulation may be made in the form of a chalk drawing on the floor that allows the planner to see where the equipment may be placed for best use. Chairs, tables, or other furniture may be used to represent the equipment in the simulation to study the suitability of the location. Observation of work done in a center helps in discovering ways in which time may be saved. Usually observation in an actual work center for several days is sufficient to find the information needed. It is also possible to obtain good information from knowledgeable workers.

Each unit of work done in a center should be challenged with questions of what, where, how, when, who, and why. Work motions should be considered carefully to see if they can be changed, rearranged, or eliminated to improve the work done. The frequency of movements between various pieces of equipment or units in a work center in-

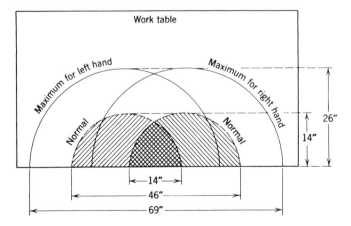

FIGURE 4.1 Chart of maximum and normal work areas for a sitting man of medium size (10% less for a woman of medium size).

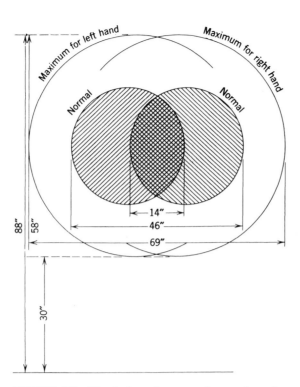

FIGURE 4.2 Chart of maximum and normal work areas for a standing man of medium size (10% less for a woman of medium size).

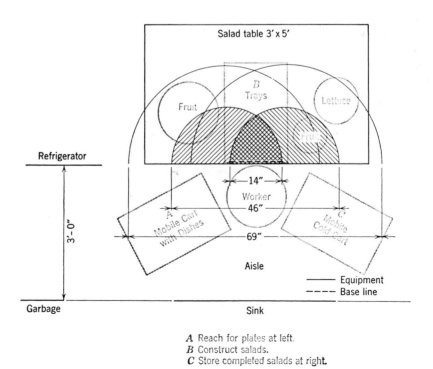

A Reach for plates at left.
B Construct salads.
C Store completed salads at right.

FIGURE 4.3 Chart of maximum and normal reach superimposed over a work area. This procedure is helpful in designing work centers.

dicates the best arrangement of equipment. Distances of reach and keeping work in proper sequence are to be considered. Space allowance should provide for landing areas for food, adequate storage, and temporary holding of foods. Every use of space should be challenged. Flexibility is desirable to accommodate changes in procedures as they occur. The use of mobile equipment may make it possible to change equipment arrangement as work needs change.

Compactness in a work center reduces travel and conserves time and energy. Mobile equipment, when not in use, can be moved aside to allow space for other equipment. Such an arrangement of the work center promotes both compactness and flexibility. Cross-charting is helpful in determining normal relationships of equipment. In a work center where a variety of related tasks are done, special study may be required to ensure smooth progress and prevent confusion in doing work. For example, if a sandwich preparation center needs to be changed to a salad preparation center, the task is more complex than in planning a center for one set of tasks only.

Each work center should be developed by itself. It should be as completely self-sufficient as possible for the work done. Attention needs to be given, however, to other work centers with which it will be closely related or joined. The interrelationships of work centers and the dual use of equipment, especially in smaller facilities, may influence the location of the equipment. If a baker is to use steam equipment in a cook's section, the location of such equipment should be convenient for both workers. Sinks, tables, ovens, and power equipment, such as mixers and slicers, may be used by workers in more then one work center and therefore require special location. Mobility of equipment aids in duality of use when it can be moved from one work center to another. Figure 4.4 shows a well-planned, compact, cook's work center. Mobile equipment that

FIGURE 4.4   A cook's work center with sink, tool drawer, condiment and equipment shelves, ingredient bins, and cooking pots within easy reach. Cold and hot, pass-through cabinets for holding prepared food for the cafeteria are next to the table. (*Courtesy of Robert Whitney and Associates, Los Angeles, CA.*)

can be removed from the center when not needed for use and items brought into the center may be used to provide greater compactness of the center for work. Compactness of work centers helps to reduce time-consuming motion.

Sections

A section is a group of related work centers in which one type of activity occurs. The number of centers in a section varies as influenced by the volume and complexity of work to be done and the time allowance for its accomplishment. In a small establishment, for example, one worker may be able to complete preparation of foods from the raw state to completion for service. In larger places the volume of work may require several workers, working simultaneously to supply the amount of food required within a specific time frame. One center may be required for each of the separate stages of preparation of, say, a cake, such as measuring, mixing, panning, baking, frosting, portioning, and serving centers. The joining of one center with another should be logical and scientific, allowing for a smooth, efficient **flow of work.**

A section is designed after all of the individual work centers have been planned for a section and can be joined together. Location of the centers in the section in terms of proximity will be affected by such factors as dual use of equipment and the number of interrelationships. In a section where a variety of functions are performed, special study may be required to promote smooth progress of work and prevent confusion between centers. Location of supporting areas, such as storage of supplies and equipment needed for specific work, should be close to work centers where there is a high amount of interrelationship.

The location of work centers in a section should follow a careful study of the typical sequence of work to be performed. If foods require preprocessing, such as vegetable paring or meat cutting, the work area and equipment should be close to the center where the food is to be cooked. Eliminating storage and transportation by bringing centers close together so that direct delivery is possible helps to reduce travel and motion and promotes efficiency.

Workers' experience can be valuable in planning placement of equipment or areas of a work center. Similarly, their opinions can be helpful in locating work centers within a section. Workers can rate what they believe are high, medium, low, or practically no relationships between work centers. The data can be compiled in a manner similar to that shown later in Figures 4.8 and 4.9 using work centers instead of items of equipment.

Layout

Centers are combined to form sections and the sections are joined to make up the complete plan or **layout.** Relationships in terms of equipment use, flow of work, and storage of supplies and equipment are important in determining proximity of one section to another. Such factors as preservation of desired qualities and volume of items handled may influence best location of sections. The high temperature of freshly cooked foods promotes placement of the cooking section adjacent to the serving area. The ease of movement of bakery items after preparation allows the bakeshop to be in a more remote area from service, except in kitchens where the cook and baker may need to use the same pieces of large equipment such as mixer, sink, and ovens. The flow of work may indicate the need for a specific section to have a close relationship with several sections. The pot-washing and storage section, for example, may have many pans coming from the serving section that are required for use in cooking, baking, and salad sections.

Striving for compactness of space, locating sections together that have a high amount of interrelationships, and seeking flexibility is as desirable, if not more so, in locating sections as it is in locating equipment in work centers or work centers in sections. Workers' ratings of interrelationships between sections may be as helpful as their rating of interrelationships of work centers. Individual and composite opinions concerning interrelationships of sections in a layout may be charted in the same manner as the charting of equipment in a work center (see Figures 4.8 and 4.9 in a later section).

FLOW OF WORK

The sequence of operations in the processing of materials or the performing of essential functions is called the flow of work. In a food facility it will include work accomplishment and the movement of materials from receiving, through preparation, service, and cleanup. The joining of work centers into sections and sections into a layout should follow certain rules relating to flow of work. Such flow is frequently defined as *a natural and logical sequence of operations in the processing of materials or doing of work.* Normally, the flow of materials is from receiving to storage, to preparation (baking, cooking, and so forth), to holding, to service, to dishwashing and pot washing and other cleanup, to garbage disposal, and so on. This is sometimes changed to increase efficiency.

A basic flow pattern for a facility may be diagrammed on a plan by using arrows to indicate direction of flow. Colored lines may be used to indicate flow of different materials. At the outset the diagram may be a rough sketch on a graph paper plan indicating relationships between sections only. Later these sections may be allocated a specific amount of space with thought given to structural features that may aid or interfere with desirable flow.

Eight basic rules should be remembered when establishing flow in work centers, sections, and the entire layout:

1. Functions should proceed in proper sequence directly, with a minimum of crisscrossing and backtracking.
2. Smooth, rapid production and service should be sought, with minimum expenditure of worker time and energy.
3. Delay and storage of materials in processing and serving should be eliminated as much as possible.
4. Workers and materials should travel minimum distances.
5. Materials and tools should receive minimum handling, and equipment should receive minimum worker attention.
6. Maximum utilization of space and equipment should be achieved.
7. Quality control must be sought at all critical points.
8. Minimum cost of production should be sought.

The flow most suitable for one operation will differ from others according to the manner in which it meets the individual needs of the facility. Change and adjustment are often necessary in adapting a good flow to the specific structural requirements and building shape. A good flow plan is seldom achieved without compromise. The need to make choices may stimulate extra care and thought that will lead to finding a better plan. The flow pattern should follow the functional relationship of work as indicated in Figure 4.5.

Types of Flow

The **straight-line flow** plan is frequently used by industries making a standardized product in large quantities. It may also be called the **unital** or **assembly-line flow.** Materials in manufacture move steadily in a direct line from one process to another. The term *straight line* may be misleading. The layout may actually be in the shape of a circle, parallel, U-shape, L-shape, or other form. Straight line means that the flow of material being processed is continuous or direct in progress. Raw material in such a layout may start at the top floor and progress through various stages of assembly on successive floors until processing is completed at the ground level, with storage and shipping occurring at the lower level. Straight-line flow is used on assembly lines.

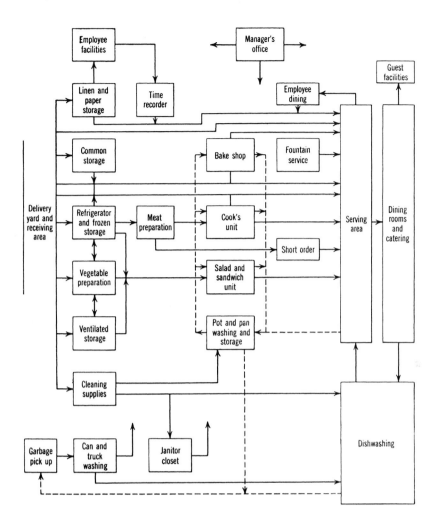

FIGURE 4.5   Flow diagram showing functional relationships.

The **functional flow** plan is often called the **process** or **one-shop plan.** It is adaptable to manufacturing where a number of specialty type products are made. Departmentalization of processing is characteristic. Frequently items are processed to a semifinished point and allowed to accumulate, with storage occurring until a sufficient quantity is obtained for transfer to another processing department. This layout tends to be less expensive to install, but the cost of manufacturing per unit may be higher.

There are advantages and disadvantages to both straight-line and functional flow. Factors that will influence the type best suited are nature of the product, sequence required for processing, and the quantity to be manufactured. The small quantities and the wide variety of products made in food facilities make the functional type of layout advisable. Products made in the various sections, such as pantry, cooking, and baking are quite different in nature and usually cannot be processed on an assembly line. Often food is cooked to order and preparation must await demand. This is best done in functional type layouts. Straight-line layouts are most efficient with continuous production of a large number of products similar in nature.

Plan for the Flow of Work

The flow of work can be traced like the traffic patterns of roads leading into and out of a city. Some activities may vary slightly from others but a most used path will be found that is followed by the greatest number of activities. Begin the plan for the flow of work

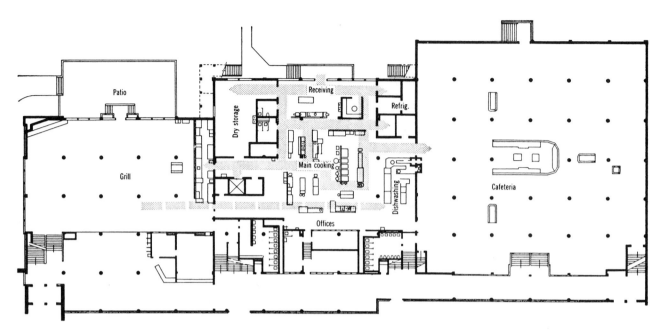

FIGURE 4.6 Example of work flow in an operation designed for varied service and low operating cost. (*The Lodge, Montana State University, Missoula, Montana.*)

with a study of the interrelationships of equipment, supply storage, and sections. The aim is to eliminate excess travel and time- and energy-consuming **crisscrossing** and **backtracking** and to obtain as direct a line of flow as possible.

Having materials and tools within easy reach and essential equipment available and in good condition helps greatly to reduce excess steps and speed flow of work. Flexibility is necessary to allow for changes in flow necessitated by change of activities. Mobile equipment increases flexibility. Mobile equipment, where used, should move in and out easily and permit sufficient space to work around it. In work centers where a variety of related tasks are done, special study is required to promote smooth progress of work and to prevent confusion.

Attention must be directed not only to work flow within a center but also to the flow between it and related centers which make up a section. Flow must also be considered when locating sections in a finished layout. As smooth and direct a flow as possible should be sought between storage of materials to assemble for preparation, to baking, cooking or other treatment, to service. Templates can be used of work centers to arrange their best flow with similar use of section templates to make up the final layout with the best possible flow. Compromises always have to be made. Structural elements often interfere with achieving the most desirable results. One cannot remove a supporting wall to favor a desirable flow. (See Figure 4.6 for an example of work flow through a facility.)

MATERIAL HANDLING

The flow of materials should be considered in establishing the overall flow patterns. Normally, the movement of materials and supplies follows the flow of work, and for this reason the flow patterns for each may coincide. However, at times this may not be true, and in instances where quality and efficiency may be affected suitable modification should be made.

A large amount of time in food facilities may be claimed by the necessary process of **material handling.** Raw materials, tools, and utensils should be placed where they will require as little handling as possible. In transfers and movement the following material handling rules should be followed.

1. **Store at point of first use.** The point of first use will depend on the organization of work in the specific facility. One plan may call for food supplies to be delivered directly to a central storage area that has an adjacent ingredient room. Here the supplies will be opened, checked, and measured into specific recipe quantities to be sent to individual production sections. Control of supplies, care in measurements, and compactness in work areas are counted as advantages of this system. Volume of material handled, variety of menu items produced, and type of food served will influence the desirability of this system. In some establishments it may mean extra handling, extra personnel, and larger space.

Where first use calls for measuring and utilizing materials in specific work centers, it is best to separate supplies into local storage. The utensils and materials will not be in a central area but where they are first needed for work. A pot to be filled with water, for example, will be stored near the sink; yeast, extracts, and other pantry supplies in the bakeshop; and crackers, breads, dairy products, and beverages in the serving section. Central or bulk storage will be used for large market packages that, for economical use of space, are to be divided later for storage in work areas. Frozen foods may be requisitioned in small lots from centralized low-temperature storage and held in a small freezer or ice cream cabinet near the point of preparation. Reach-in refrigerators conveniently located in cooks', bakers', and pantry sections can be time- and step-savers. Where storage is to supply more than one area, the location is usually best where it will be in proximity to the area where the greatest number of trips will be made to it. The meat walk-in refrigerator should be close to the cooks' unit, with material moving from storage to butcher shop to cooks' unit in a straight line.

2. **Allow for economy of motion.** Store according to frequency of use, with the most used items within normal grasp and less used items more remote. Items should be arranged or positioned for easy pickup. A heavy pot or package may have to be where it can be easily lifted in and out. Items should be placed such that others will not have to be moved to reach the desired item. This will influence stacking or placing dissimilar items in front of others on a shelf. The therblig "search" (see page 107) will be reduced if items are placed in plain view and in definite locations. Items for transfer or movement should be, if possible, even with the height of work areas or mobile equipment used for movement.

3. **Use space economically by providing for specific sizes.** Distance between shelves as well as depth of shelves should be considered, with only enough excess space to allow for ease of movement of items into and out of position. Adjustable shelving permits varied spacing where space requirements are likely to change. For easy identification, items stored in front should be similar to those in back of them.

4. **Minimize handling and storage.** Handling is reduced if storage is located and deliveries timed so that items can be placed when and where required by the person who delivers them, such as milk to the serving section or fruit and vegetables to the preparation area. Trucks or pallets provided for weigh-in materials, movement into storage, and from thence on the same unit to the processing area make for savings in handling. Conveyors or mobile storage units reduce handling.

5. **Systemize.** If storage is organized, search and handling will be reduced. If the most frequently used and largest volume products are most convenient to reach, or utensils and equipment are selected for modular size, thus eliminating transfer by making it possible to use in storage, processing, or display and service, the number of handlings will be reduced. Grouping materials for common use and, where desirable, making them mobile increases efficiency. Portable table organizers for servers make it possible to refill table supplies quickly and lay fresh covers. Organized mobile carriers for cleaning materials and equipment will save many steps for workers.

6.   **Use good handling procedures.** Incorporation of safety, sanitation, and security in planning will reduce work. Lift trucks and other mechanized devices should be provided to reduce lifting of heavy items and for handling large volumes of goods.

Some recommend that loads be limited to 35 lb for women and 50 lb for men. Walter et al.[2] recommend a maximum weight of 50 lb (23 kg) for both sexes under optimal conditions. They indicate one can obtain a more accurate limitation by considering not only the object's weight but the horizontal and vertical distance it must be moved, the turning motion required, how frequently the task must be done, and the type of handle or grasping motion involved. Clear aisles and good traffic flow are essential in a layout to reduce material handling.

7.   **Coordinate.** Communication is very significant for ensuring complete and fast relay of information. A satisfactory system will save a great deal of time and effort in a large organization. It is important to select the type that will meet the needs of the specific establishment. Signal lights, buzzers, intercommunicating phones, and electric devices for transmitting writings from a pad in one place to another have been used with success.

THE PARTS OF A JOB

Every job has three parts: "**get ready,**" "**do,**" and "**clean up and put away.**" Employee hours are most productive when spent on the second part. Work planning can do much to see that the most "do" is obtained for the amount of "get ready" and "clean up and put away." Planning the work center to encourage this by sizing equipment properly and planning to have tasks done in quantity when possible is important also. For instance, instead of making cinnamon rolls every morning, it may be better to make them up once a week in a big batch and freeze a six-day supply, thus in one "get ready" and one "clean up and put away" accomplish the entire job. High labor rates emphasize the value of reducing time and motion and increasing efficiency in work centers.

Production done in large batches rather than small ones will make a difference in the size and kind of equipment selected for a work center. Also, equipment placement, interrelationship of work centers into sections, and even the layout may be changed. The operation member of the planning team should inform the committee as to what "get ready," "do," and "clean up and put away" processes are planned.

INDUSTRIAL ENGINEERING WORK STUDY METHODS

Methods used by industrial engineers to study work methods can be useful in planning a foodservice. Some methods relate directly to equipment placement to achieve greatest efficiency, whereas others, like time studies and motion picture studies relate more to improving jobs, but also can yield helpful information because such a study may indicate that a different placement of equipment or a different kind of equipment can improve work methods.

In doing their studies, engineers often use a sort of shorthand or symbols to record what is happening. Thus, in the symbols approved by the American Society of Mechanical Engineers a circle represents an operation and an arrow represents transportation. Other organizations use different symbols, but the most common ones are presented next.

---

[2]Thomas R. Walter, Vern Putz-Anderson, Arun Garg, and Lawrence J. Fine. "Revised NIOSH Equation for the Design and Evaluation of Manual Lifting Tasks," *Ergonomics,* 1983, Vol. 36, No. 7, 749–776.

Motion Symbols

The most commonly encountered symbols are the five approved by the American Society of Mechanical Engineers. These are:

- ○ Operation
- ▷ Transportation
- □ Inspection
- D Delay
- ▽ Storage

Other industrial engineers have simplified the symbols by substituting the small circle for the arrow representing transportation and a triangle for a combination of storage and delay. Some retain the arrow and use it pointed right for forward movement and left for backtracking transportation. A letter may be used inside a symbol for added significance, such as H for hand truck or T for temporary storage. The symbols may be combined when two components of work occur at the same time. A process chart may have a column for recording distance traveled and another for time required for an operation. Table 4.1 illustrates how work symbols might be used in studying a worker making a pie.

Mundel[3] has used similar symbols to indicate flow of products through equipment. These are shown in Table 4.2.

---

[3]Marvin E. Mundel, *Systematic Motion and Time Study*, Prentice-Hall, Englewood Cliffs, NJ, 1955.

TABLE 4-1 Symbols to Indicate Work Flow

Symbol	Action	Definition	Example
○	Operations	Action that creates changes or adds to product.	Baker rolls pie crust.
□	Inspection	Check or inspect quality. No change occurs.	Examines thickness of crust.
○	Transportation	Movement of product by any means.	Places in pan.
▽	Storage	Product awaits work or movement.	Sets aside for finishing.
▽	Delay	Cessation of productive action. Idle but not stored.	Filling boils over and requires attention.
◻	Combined Activity	Work components occuring at one time	Stirs and examines filling for pie.

TABLE 4-2 More Symbols to Indicate Work Flow

Symbol	Action	Definition
○	Operation	A modification of a product that takes place essentially at one location.
○	Movement	A change in location of a product from one place to another, not changing the product's characteristics.
▽	Controlled storage	Storage of a product under control such that a requisition or receipting process is needed to withdraw it.
▽	Temporary storage	Storage of a product under such conditions that it may be moved or withdrawn without a requisition; for example, material banked on skids at a machine.
◇	Quality inspection	The verification of quality of product against a standard.
□	Quantity inspection	The verification of quantity of a product against a standard.

PROCESS CHART

FLOW PROCESS	Type of chart	FOOD SERVICE	Department
ORIGINAL OR PRESENT	Original or proposed	LHK	Charted by
MATERIALS INTO PIE CRUST	Subject charted	May 26, 2000	Date charted

Details	Division of Work	Steps	Feet	Time*	
1. Get mixing bowl	→	6	9	0:35	
2. Weigh flour	○	0	0	1:43	
3. Secure shortening from storeroom	→	28	49	3:03	
4. Weigh shortening	○	0	0	2:22	
5. Weigh salt	○	0	0	1:11	
6. Dump ingredients into bowl	○	0	0	0:18	
7. Set bowl on mixer	→	2	3.5	0:18	
8. Get mixing paddle	→	6	9	0:17	
9. Put paddle on machine	○	0	0	0:08	
10. Start machine; blend ingredients	○	0	0	3:12	
11. Stop machine	○	0	0	0:02	
12. Get cold water at sink	→	4	7	0:29	
13. Add water; start machine	○	0	0	0:07	
14. Blend ingredients	○	0	0	0:40	
15. Stop machine	○	0	0	0:02	
16. Remove paddle	○	0	0	0:07	
17. Take paddle to sink	→	4	7	0:14	
18. Remove bowl and roll to table	○→	7	13	0:18	
19. Store scales and water measure	○	7	13	0:20	
Totals	13○ 7→	64	110.5	13:26	

(a)

FIGURE 4.7   Process chart. (a) Original operations in making pie crust, as shown on a process chart. (b) Revised operations in making pie crust. The summary at the bottom of the process chart shows the savings made in using the proposed method.

The use of engineering work study symbols is shown next in the use of a process chart where the study and improvement of making a pie is demonstrated.

Process Chart

A **process chart** is shown in Figures 4.7a and b, detailing the making of a pie crust until the crust is rolled in the mixing bowl to the table where it is removed, divided, and rolled into pie crusts. Figure 4.7a shows the way the job was originally done and Figure 4.7b shows how the job was changed to improve the task.

PROCESS CHART					
FLOW PROCESS	Type of chart		FOOD SERVICE		Department
PROPOSED	Original or proposed		LHK		Charted by
MATERIALS INTO PIE CRUST	Subject charted		May 26, 2000		Date charted

Details	Division of Work	Steps	Feet	Time*	
1. Get mixing bowl and paddle	→	6	9	0:39	
2. Dump shortening, flour, and salt					
which has been delivered					
preweighed by storeroom clerk	○	0	0	0:19	
3. Put mixing bowl on mixer	→	2	3.5	0:18	
4. Start machine; blend ingredients;	○				
while blending get water at sink	→	4	7	3:16	
5. Stop machine	○	0	0	0:02	
6. Add water	○	0	0	0:07	
7. Start machine; blend ingredients	○	0	0	0:40	
8. Stop machine	○	0	0	0:03	
9. Detach paddle and bowl	○	4	7	0:24	
10. Roll bowl to table	→	7	13	0:14	
11. Paddle to sink	→	4	7	0:05	
12. Scales and water measure stored	○	7	13	0:20	
Totals	8 ○ 5 →	34	59.5	6:08	

Summary					
Item	Present	Proposed	Difference		
Operations	13	8	5		
Transportations	7	5	2		
Steps	64	34	30		
Distance (feet)	110.5	59.5	51		
Time (minutes)	13:26	6:08	7:18		
*Minutes and seconds					

FIGURE 4.7 *Continued* (b)

EQUIPMENT PLACEMENT STUDY

Studies that indicate desirable placement of equipment singly or in groups so as to achieve desirable efficiency are the most useful studies when planning a foodservice facility. The most commonly used studies of **interaction of equipment counts** are presented next.

Worker Opinions on Placement

After a time, a worker working in a work center forms an opinion about how well equipment is arranged to facilitate jobs done. The consideration of these opinions can aid in

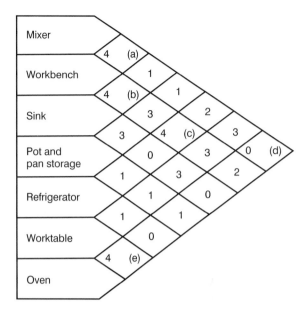

FIGURE 4.8　One worker's rating of the relationship of seven pieces of equipment in a bakeshop work center. Ratings from 0 to 4 are based on comparative-convenience value of close equipment location and shown in the diamond intercepted between specific equipment items.

improving equipment arrangement. If the layout plan is being developed originally with no previous **worker opinions on placement** available, the planner can use his or her own experience.

Figure 4.8 shows a worker's opinion on the convenience of the arrangement of equipment in a work center. The score for the best relationship is 4, while the lowest is 0. Thus, at points (a), (b), (c) and on (e) on Figure 4.8, a high relationship is indicated between the mixer and workbench, workbench and sink, workbench and refrigerator, and worktable and oven, respectively. At point (d), however, a low relationship of 0 is shown between the mixer and oven.

Figure 4.9 shows the total **equipment relation counts** of four workers for the same equipment placement in the same work center as Figure 4.8. The values of the four workers are given on top where the lines between equipment converge, and the average of these appears immediately below.

Table 4.3 shows how **equipment relation counts** are separated into categories A, B, and C. Figure 4.10 shows how work center relationships may be diagrammed and Figure 4.11 indicates how this can be done for sections.

Cross-Charting

Cross-charting can indicate the efficiency of equipment placement. This method of study is especially useful where diverse movements occur and a variety of items are processed in a work center. Movements for more than one product can be charted. Like other types of analysis, an improved method can be compared with an original one, and the relative efficiency of the changes estimated.

A cross-chart may be prepared as follows:

1. Prepare a list of equipment in order of its location. "Issue" or "pickup" is always counted as the first equipment item or location point on this list.
2. Prepare another list of movements made in doing work.
3. Number the movements in the order in which they occur. (Recipes listing order of procedures may be used in preparing this list of movements.)

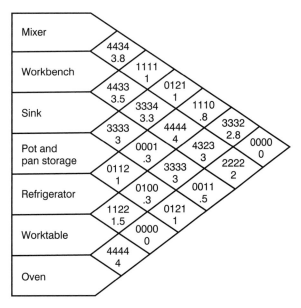

FIGURE 4.9 Rating by a group of workers of the relationship of equipment in the bakeshop work center. (See caption for Figure 4.8).

TABLE 4-3 Breakdown of Interaction Totals into Importance Categories

Work Center Pairs	Total Interactions	Importance Category
Tray service—production (cooking)	3633	A
Production—pot washing	1309	A
Tray service—refrigeration	1255	A
Tray service—tray cart storage	1068	A
Production—meat preparation	936	A
Production—refrigeration	854	A
	Breakpoint	
Tray service—vegetable preparation	509	B
Meat preparation—pot washing	388	B
Dishwashing-tray service	386	B
Tray service—pot washing	381	B
	Breakpoint	
Dishwashing—dumbwaiter and elevator	307	C
Meat preparation—refrigeration	301	C
Bakery—pot washing	292	C
Bakery—production	291	C
Production—dry storage (unrefrigerated)	280	C
Vegetable preparation—pot washing	250	C
Pot washing—dry storage (unrefrigerated)	222	C
Bakery—dry storage (unrefrigerated)	220	C
Vegetable preparation-refrigerated	190	C
Receiving—refrigeration	177	C
	Breakpoint	

Source: A. C. Avery, Increasing Productivity in Foodservice, John Wiley & Sons, New York, 1973.

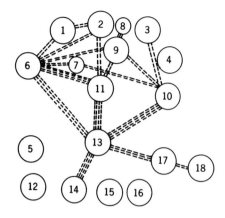

1. Storeroom	7. Meat preparation	13. Tray service
2. Bakery	8. Tray service (branch)	14. Tray cart storage
3. Receiving	9. Vegetable preparation	15. Diet kitchen office
4. Freezer	10. Refrigeration	16. Storeroom (branch)
5. Serving line	11. Production (cooking)	17. Dishwashing
6. Pot washer	12. Dietitian's office	18. Dumbwaiter—elevator

FIGURE 4.10 Work center activity relationship diagram. (*A. C. Avery et al., Increasing Productivity in Foodservice, John Wiley & Sons, N.Y., 1973.*)

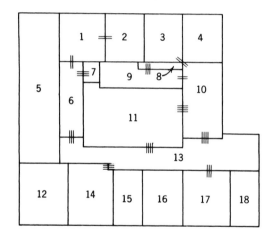

1. Storeroom	7. Meat preparation	13. Tray service
2. Bakery	8. Tray service (branch)	14. Tray cart storage
3. Receiving	9. Vegetable preparation	15. Diet kitchen office
4. Freezer	10. Refrigeration	16. Storeroom (branch)
5. Serving line	11. Production (cooking)	17. Dishwashing
6. Pot washer	12. Dietitian's office	18. Dumbwaiter—elevator

FIGURE 4.11 Work center area activity relationship diagram (assembled). (*A. C. Avery et al., Increasing Productivity in Foodservice, John Wiley & Sons, New York, 1973.*)

4. Draw a square and divide it equally into blocks, with one block more horizontally and one more vertically than the number of items of equipment used. (If there are six items of equipment, there should be seven vertical and seven horizontal square or blocks.)

5. Draw a diagonal line from the upper left-hand corner to the lower right-hand corner.

6. List items of equipment on the left side of the square and from left to right across the top in the same order, using one block for each item of equipment.

7. Leave one empty space on the right side and at the bottom. These empty blocks are to be used for totaling movements.
8. Transfer work movements to the chart by the number of movements on the list. Placement should be guided by three factors: (*a*) equipment *between* which movement occurs, (*b*) number of pieces of equipment bypassed in making the movement, and (*c*) the type of movement. The first factor (*a*) shows travel occurring between two pieces of equipment by placing the movement number in the block where the horizontal and vertical blocks between two pieces of equipment meet. When cross-charting is completed, frequency of movements between equipment can be determined by counting the numbers in the respective blocks. The second factor (*b*) indicates the number of pieces bypassed in making the movement. The number of the movement is placed in that space above or below the diagonal line according to the number of pieces of equipment bypassed. The third factor (*c*) is used to show two types of movements: (1) a movement that does not move a product forward (backtracks), called a **from movement,** and (2) a movement that moves a product forward, called a **to movement.** All *from* movements are placed above the diagonal line and all *to* movements below it.

If equipment is not in line but stands across from each other, the movement number cannot be shown as indicated by factors (*a*) and (*b*). When this conflict occurs, the number should be placed in the proper square as required by (*b*) and circled. An "x" should then be placed in the proper block for step (*a*) above, the first factor guiding placement of numbers. In counting the number of movements between equipment, the circled number is omitted from the count and the "x" is counted instead.

Figure 4.12a and b show cross-charts for an original and improved placement of equipment in a vegetable unit. The work done is peeling and chopping carrots. In the improved placement of equipment in Figure 4.12b, the chopper is mobile and the colander used to hold the carrots is stored under the drainboard on the left side of the sink. The list of equipment set into line for the cross-chart of Figure 4.12a is issue, peeler, drainboard, sink, colander, table, and chopper. In the cross-chart of Figure 4.12b this is changed to issue, peeler, drainboard, colander, sink, chopper, and table. The

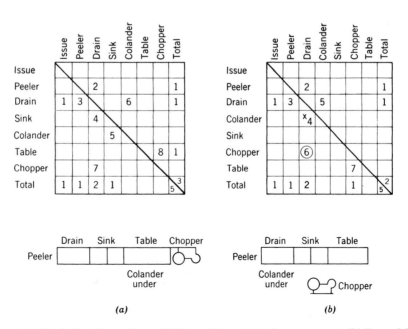

FIGURE 4.12 Cross charts. (a) Record for original arrangement. (b) Record for revised arrangement.

chopper is opposite the sink, and this will necessitate the use of the "x" because the equipment is not in a linear position but across from others. The use of the "x" has been described.

The movements in doing the work are

(a)
1. Issue to drainboard
2. To peeler
3. To drainboard
4. Wash carrots in sink
5. Get colander
6. Colander to drain
7. Carrots in colander to chopper
8. To table for use in salads

(b)
1. Issue to drainboard
2. To peeler
3. To drainboard
4. Wash carrots in sink
5. Get colander from under the top of sink
6. Carrots in colander to chopper
7. To table for use in salads

In Figure 4.12a the motions are recorded as follows:

1. The carrots are brought from issue to the drainboard. This is a *to* motion in that the flow is forward between pieces of equipment. The peeler is bypassed and 1 is placed as shown.
2. The motion is between the drainboard and the peeler, and it is a *from* motion. No equipment is bypassed and the 2 appears in the proper space indicating the movement as shown.
3. The carrots after peeling now move from the peeler to the drainboard, and 3 indicates by its placement it is a *to* motion in which no equipment is bypassed. It is therefore next to the diagonal line in an under position.
4. The carrots move from the drainboard to the sink for washing. Another *to* movement is recorded in which no equipment is bypassed.
5. The worker goes to the table for the colander, which is underneath on a shelf. The movement is between the sink and colander. The number 5 is placed in the *to* area below the diagonal line in the square where the horizontal line from the colander meets the vertical line of the sink. No bypassing occurs.
6. Next, the colander is taken to the drainboard to allow the carrots to drain, bypassing the sink, and this and the fact that it is a backward or *from* motion dictates it be a square away from the diagonal line above it.
7. From the drainboard the colander and carrots move to the chopper. This is a *to* movement and the locations of sink, colander, and table are bypassed. Note that it is three squares from the diagonal line and under the line.
8. The carrots are then moved to the table where they are used for salad. This is a *from* movement with no equipment bypassed.

In Figure 4.12b the first four motions are recorded the same as for Figure 4.12a. Motions 5 and 6 in Figure 4.12a are combined into motion 5. It is a *from* movement from drain to colander where carrots are placed into the colander. Motion 6 is the movement of carrots in the colander to the chopper, which is now opposite the sink. While the chart must show this as a *to* motion bypassing two pieces of equipment—the colander and sink—there is no bypassing actually. Thus, number 6 is shown where it should be showing the bypassing, but a circle is placed around it and the placement of the "x" where number 4 is shows the actual situation. In tabulating, the 6 is disregarded and the "x" is used instead. The carrots in motion 7 are moved to the table for use in salads, a *to* motion with no bypassing.

The *to* movements in each column are then totaled and the sum written on the bottom space intended for this. Similarly, the total *from* movements are written on the space on the right intended for this.

Whenever equipment is placed differently, the cross-chart shows a large number of movement numbers close to and below the diagonal line. Inefficient location is indicated by the numbers distant from the line or above the line. A computation can be made,

1. Rating for Original Arrangement

Blocks from Diagonal Line		Number of Movements		Value
To				
1	×	3	=	3
2	×	1	=	2
3	×	$\frac{1}{5}$	=	$\frac{4}{9}$
From				
1	×	2	=	2
2	×	1	=	2
3	×	0	=	0
4	×	$\frac{0}{3}$	=	$\frac{0}{4}$

Value rating = ⁹⁄₄ or 2¼
(Note: Weighted value rating would be ⁹⁄₄ × ½ or 1⅛).
% Efficiency = ⅝ or 62½%.

2. Rating for Revised Arrangement

Blocks from Diagonal Line		Number of Movements		Value
To				
1	×	4	=	4
2	×	1	=	2
3	×	0	=	0
4	×	$\frac{0}{5}$	=	$\frac{0}{6}$
From				
1	×	2	=	2
2	×	0	=	0
3	×	0	=	0
4	×	$\frac{0}{2}$	=	$\frac{0}{2}$

Value rating = ⁶⁄₂ or 3.
(Note: Weighted value rating would be ⁶⁄₂ × ½ or 1½).
% Efficiency = ⁵⁄₇ or 71%.

FIGURE 4.13   Value and efficiency ratings of cross-charts.

as shown in Figure 4.13, to obtain a value rating for *to* and *from* movements. The various *to* movements are multiplied by the number of blocks away they stand from the diagonal line, and a sum of these results is obtained. This is done similarly for the *from* movements. The sum for the *from* movements is divided into the sum for the *to* movements, giving a value rating. The larger the rating, the more efficient the placement of equipment. A weighted value rating can be obtained. To do this, the sum of *from* movements is doubled in value and divided into the *to* movements. (Multiplying by one-half does this.) Figure 4.13 also shows how an efficiency rating is obtained. The number of *to* motions are added, and this is divided by the sum of the *to* and *from* movements. Perhaps this is the most meaningful figure obtained from these three ratings.

If the cross-chart shows that the number of movements between two pieces of equipment is high, the interpretation should be that these pieces of equipment need to be located adjoining or close together. Direction of flow of work as shown by movements also indicates recommended placement of equipment.

Cross-charting has been shown to be adaptable to computer programming.

Kazarian[4] believes that in cross-charting the weight of products moved between work units should influence equipment placement and has developed a method of cross-charting to show this. Others have pointed out that another factor that must be considered is the frequency with which items must be moved. Consideration of frequency of movement as done in one static example does not indicate the situation completely, because the work done is not static. A varying amount of material will be transferred between work units and this will cause a variation in equipment relationship. Thus weight and frequency of movement both must be recognized in cross-charting. While Kazarian's method can easily be calculated manually, when we add the many permutations that occur with frequency of movement and with the calculation of weight, calculation is best done by computer. However, the computer also makes the Kazarian method easier done than doing it manually.

Often times equipment can help reduce travel and motions required in doing work either by combining or elimination motions or saving space. The combi-oven shown in Figure 4.14 saves space and combines work motions.

---

[4]Edward A. Kazarian, *Work Analysis and Design*, John Wiley & Sons, New York, 1969.

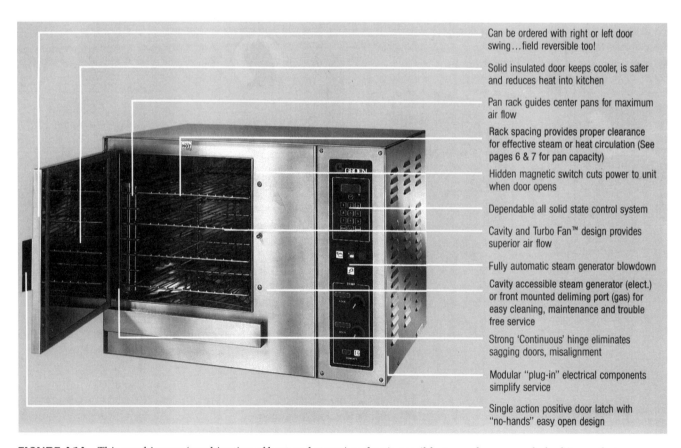

FIGURE 4.14   This combi-oven (combination of heat and steam) makes it possible to produce many baked items that formerly required an oven into which steam was piped. Now the oven produces its own steam, reducing installation costs and resulting in an efficient unit. Manufacturers are constantly striving today to improve equipment to make control easier and better and also make the equipment easier to use. Better products are also made. (*Courtesy of Groen, a Dover Industries Company, Elk Grove Village, Illinois.*)

Man–Machine Chart

A **man–machine chart** is a type of process chart showing the working cycle of a worker and a piece of equipment. The time consumed by each in going through the cycle of work is indicated by a scale in inches. The shorter the time cycle of the operation being charted, the shorter the distance will be per decimal minute of time shown on the process chart. The analyst will chart both the worker and the machine, recording time and operation. Productive time is indicated by a heavy straight line. Idle time is shown by a break in the line. Unloading or loading of a machine is shown by a dotted line. The information obtained may indicate how the work done by man and machine may be better coordinated for maximum achievement (see Figure 4.15).

Sequence Chart

A **sequence chart** is useful in the operational analysis of the complete layout. It is sometimes called a **master process chart** because it is frequently made up of a number of process charts of individual functions. These, when put together, give the complete operation in chronological order. The sequence chart shows when materials are introduced into the process in terms of time, location, and processing sequence, except those involved in material handling. Horizontal lines are used in the chart to show material being introduced into the manufacturing process. Vertical lines are used to indicate processing flow. Where lines intersect and no combination occurs, the symbol used is a small semicircle in the horizontal line at the point where the vertical line crosses it. The symbol is much the same as the one used in electrical drawings to show that no juncture of wires occurs. The motion symbols chosen by Mundel are useful in this type of charting. The chart prepared by Thomas[5] to indicate the flow of products through equipment serves as an excellent example of this type of charting (see Figure 4.16).

Distance Chart

A **distance chart** or (**string** or **travel chart**) portrays the distance a worker or material travels in doing a job or jobs. A scale drawing of the area to be covered by the worker or material travel is required for this. Movements of more than one worker or material, or of worker and material, may be imposed on the same plan by the use of different colors

---

[5]Orpha Mae Huffman Thomas, A Scientific Basis of the Design of Institution Kitchens, doctoral thesis on file at Purdue University Library, 1947.

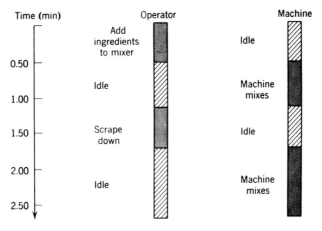

FIGURE 4.15   Man–machine chart showing a partial operation recorded in using a mixer.

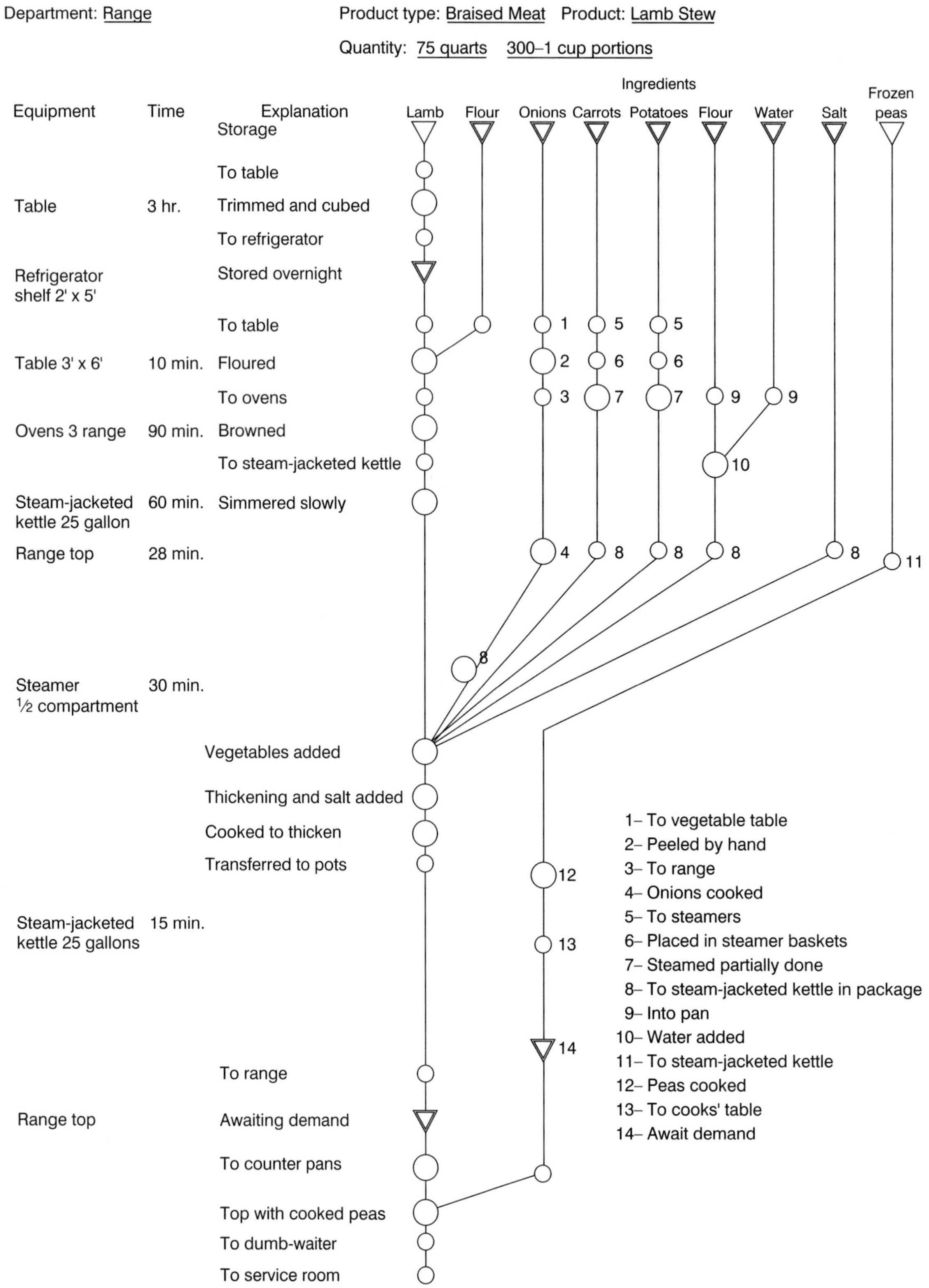

FIGURE 4.16 Master process chart of product through equipment *(Source: O. M. Thomas. A Scientific Basis of the Design of Institution Kitchens, Doctoral thesis on file at Purdue University, 1947.)*

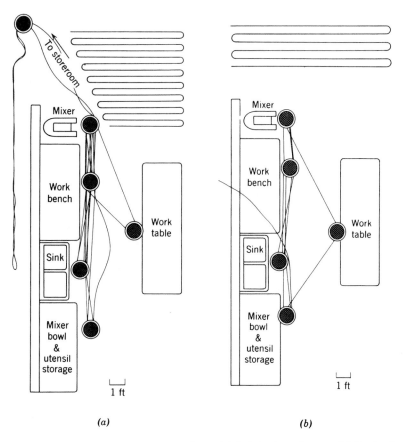

FIGURE 4.17 Distance or string chart. (a) Original work area. (b) Revised work area.

of string. The drawing should be made or mounted on cardboard so as to provide satisfactory firmness. A paper staple should be fastened through the plan at each point to which the worker or material will move. Fasten the string at that point where processing begins. Move the string along the path over which the worker or material moves and over the staple at each point of call. At the end of the process remove the string and measure it. If the drawing is scaled to ¼ in. = 1 ft, then each inch of string will represent 4 ft traveled in the observed process (see Figure 4.17).

JOB IMPROVEMENT TECHNIQUES

A number of engineering study methods are used to improve jobs. In such studies, different placement of equipment may be part of improving the job. This makes such studies helpful in planning a layout.

Time Studies

One of the first techniques used to study work methods was to stand by a worker and record the time taken to make motions or to do a job. It is reliable if done by a keen observer, but it is very time consuming. In certain cases it is the only way to obtain the necessary information. The method is called **time study** charting.

The technique of making time and motion studies is relatively simple. The observer should prepare for timing by first observing the whole operation of the job. In this initial observation an estimate should be made of the worker's skill, effort, technique, and results. Are proper work methods used and are products of good quality? The estimate of these factors, summarized on the timing sheet, will later be required for establishing a present rating factor. The description of the situation should be stated as to product prepared, job done, recipe used, section where work is done, worker observed, and the date and the name of the observer. Standard record sheets usually have space provided for this information (see Figure 4.18). A sketch of the work area with equipment placement is helpful. Starting and stopping period for each element timed should be established before timing is begun. The time for each element usually runs from 0.05 to 0.10 of a minute if therbligs (discussed later) are recorded and longer if an activity or more gross motions are being timed. If time periods are too short, they will be difficult to record accurately; if too long, they will include too much. The elements of the job are written down in units to be timed.

Then the job is timed. The watch for timing should record in decimals of a minute. Timing may be done by one of three methods. One is a **snap-back method** in which the stopwatch hands are started at zero for each element and snapped back to zero at the end. The second is called **continuous method** and is done by recording the time for each element without snapping the watch back. A record is made without stopping the watch. In the third method, two stopwatches are used. They are mounted close together on the observation board and are alternatively activated and stopped at the beginning and at the end of elements. This is an **accumulative method** that permits observation of a longer operation. Readings can be made more easily and accurately when the watch hands are not in motion.

TIME STUDY OBSERVATION AND COMPUTATION

Job _____ Assembling cold plate _____   Section _____ Pantry _____

Date _____ 7/29/2000 _____   Operator _____ J. B. _____

Observer _____ K _____   Recipe used _____ None _____

ELEMENT	OBSERVATIONS (MINUTES) 1	2	3	4	5	6	7	8	Average	% Rating Factor	Allowance Percent	Standard Time
1. Reach for 6 plates and space on pre-positioned tray	— — .12					— — .14		—	.13	90	112	.131
2. Lettuce to plate, left hand; scoop of potato salad to plate, rt hand	.21 — — .09	.08	.10	(12)	.07	.29 .08	.08	.08	.083	90	112	.084
3. Slice ham left hand; cheese with right hand	.27 — — .06	.16 .08	.16 .06	.19 .07	.13 .06	.14 .06	.36 .07	.14 .06	.067	90	112	.068
4. Pickle and olive to plate, alternate hands	.32 — — .05	.21 .05	.21 .05	.23 .04	.18 .05	.19 .05	.41 .05	.19 .05	.050	95	112	.052
5. Store tray in cart at right	.48 — — (16)	.32 .11	.33 .12	.36 .13	.30 .12	.30 .11	.52 .11	.30 .11	.116	90	112	.117

Notes _____

_____   Total standard

_____   per ___ plate ___   .321

_____   ___ tray ___   2.057

Note: Minutes shown above dotted line are cumulative figures, while those below are time for the specific element obtained by subtraction of cumulative figures. Thus, the time .16 for the fifth element "store tray in cart at right" is derived by subtracting .32 from .48. Circled times indicate they were not used in obtaining the average.

FIGURE 4.18   Cumulative time study of a worker setting up cold plates.

Obtaining an accurate picture of a job requires timing it a sufficient number of times to arrive at a good average. When computing, those values that are too high or low are circled and disregarded in making up the average. A *standard time* is the average time multiplied by the percent rating factor multiplied by the allowances made for personal time, delay, or fatigue time loss. A rating factor of 5% is often used for personal needs and 5% to 10% for fatigue slowdown and rest periods. This is called the performance **allowance percentage** and when used, 100% is added to this allowance. Thus if the personal percentage is established at 12%, 112% is recorded. A larger personal allowance percentage is usually required in heavy or difficult jobs. The standard time is shown in the proper space. Standard hourly production can be obtained by dividing 60 minutes by the standard time.

Methods Time Measurement

A technique recently used by Freshwater and others to study work methods has been called **MTM** or **methods time measurement.** This is a method in which pictures are taken at normal speed (16 frames per second). The picture is then played back at normal speed and the work methods studied. It is considered a better method than work sampling because it is more accurate in terms of what is happening, and it covers the actual period rather than a set of random observations. It also is considered better at times than time studies because the work is performed in a less formal situation. Workers tend to tighten up when under observation in time studies. This is why the allowance percentage is given. Furthermore, with MTM it is possible to replay the same task a number of times. In some respects this method resembles simo study (discussed later) except the film is made at normal speed rather than for slow-speed showing.

Picture Analysis

If it is desirable to note travel and wasted motion in a specific work area, pictures may be recorded of fewer motions over a longer period of time with a motion camera set for 1 time frame per second instead of 16 frames per second. When the film is projected, 8 hours of work can be viewed in 30 minutes. This is called **menomotion study.**

One negative may be used to record more than one motion so that movement is shown by one motion being imposed on top of another. This will produce a **stroboscopic picture** showing motion variation (see Figure 4.19).

Still camera pictures may be made to show motions of a small light attached to a body member, such as a hand. With the room in semidarkness, the camera is opened for the period that the motion is made. This picture is called a **cyclegraph** (see Figure 4.20).

Therblig Study

Lillian and Frank Gilbreth were two early engineers who helped formulate the principles of work motion study. They noted in their studies that workers made basic motions that could not be broken down further. They isolated 17 and called them **therbligs** (Gilbreth spelled backwards). They noted that each took about $1/200^{th}$ of a minute, which they called a **wink.** Often they used a **chronometer,** which was divided into 2,000 units and made time recording possible. Placing this chronometer behind a worker made it possible to record the number of winks taken to do a job. Reducing the number of winks in nonrepetitive jobs is difficult, but where a large number of highly repetitive tasks are made time savings can be substantial. The 17 therbligs are listed in Table 4.4.

A job may be studied by an observer making a chart of a worker's motions indicating the therbligs used in sequence or by film taken at high speed and played back at normal speed, making it easy to record the motions. The therbligs taken in either

FIGURE 4.19   A stroboscopic picture. The salad worker is surrounded by portable equipment and prepositioned food supplies. Three basic positions are shown: (1) reaching for salad plates at worker's right, (2) constructing salads (center of picture), and (3) storing salads in portable cart (left).

FIGURE 4.20   An example of a cyclegraph. The paths of light made by a worker's hands as she arranges cheese and sliced meat for a cold plate are studied.

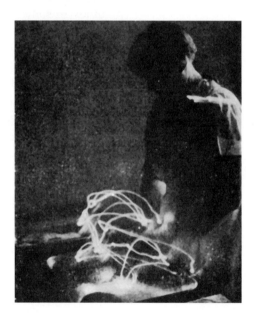

manner are then transferred to a simo (simultaneous) chart. The chart is so named because it charts for a short term the simultaneous motions made by both hands or other parts of the body in doing work. After the motions are recorded, the work is analyzed to see if improvement can be made.

A **simo chart** is valuable in disclosing inefficient motion patterns, idle time, and waste motions. It may lead to improving motion sequence; to improving the placement of foods, tools, or equipment; or to reducing the number of motions made. A reduction of motion, lessening of time, shortening of distance, and the development of a smooth, steady, rhythmic motion tend to increase production and make work easier. The construction of a simo chart from a film is shown in Figures 4.21a–c.

TABLE 4-4   *The Seventeen Therbligs*

Therblig	Symbol	Definition
Search	Sh	The eyes or the hands hunt the object
Select	St	A decision ending with choice of the object
Inspect	I	Examining and evaluating according to standard
Transport	TE	The hand moving toward an object
Grasp	G	Taking hold of an object
Hold	H	A delay in grasp with no movement of the object
Transport load	TL	The object being moved
Release load	RL	Releasing the object
Position	P	The object set into proper position for use
Preposition	PP	Setting into position for future operations
Assemble	A	Joining two or more objects together
Disassemble	DA	Separating two or more objects that are joined
Use	U	Manipulating a tool or device to perform work
Avoidable delay	AD	Stopping the operation
Unavoidable delay	UD	Stopping the work unavoidably
Plan	PL	Mental decision on procedure for action
Rest	R	Cessation of work to overcome fatigue

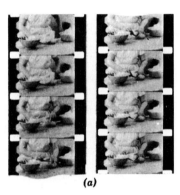

(a)

FIGURE 4.21   Use of film in motion analysis. (a) Film strip of worker trimming lettuce for salad. (b) Record of the film analysis. (c) The next step of recording motions of the simultaneous chart. This vividly portrays idle time for either hand.

The use of films in simo chart work analysis is known as **micromotion study.** The therbligs with an explanation of the work motion and time intervals are frequently transferred first to a **record of film analysis** and from there to a simo chart. Time may be recorded by means of a time device, such as a **microchronometer,** located to appear in the picture, or in terms of camera speed of so many frames per minute. In charting, the motions of one hand are recorded, the film is rerun, and the motions are recorded for the other hand. Idle time is indicated by a heavy black line in the column for the hand that is idle, directing attention to a place for possible improvement.

Work Sampling

Casual, random observations made to see what workers are doing and then charting these observations are called **work sampling.** The observations can be quite detailed or merely indicate on the chart that a worker is or is not busy. The advantage of random sampling is that a large number of different situations can be observed and charted, the theory being that if the observations are random over a period of time almost as good information will be obtained as by standing and observing for a much longer period. One must therefore be sure to take an adequate number of observations to be sure of having an accurate picture of what is occurring. By adding the percentages for times

RECORD OF FILM ANALYSIS

Film Number 52
Date Filmed July 15, 2000
Analysis by LHK
Date July 28, 2000

Operation Trimming lettuce
Operator Hefner
Part Name
Part No.

1 Sheet of 1
Dept. H. Economics

16 frames/sec.

Therblig Symbol	Clock Reading (winks)	Subtracted Time	Left Hand Description	Therblig Symbol	Clock Reading (winks)	Subtracted Time	Right Hand Description	Body Member	Therblig Symbol	Clock Reading	Subtracted Time	Notes
TE	16		To bowl of lettuce	H	16		Holds knife					Frame 1
S	19		Selects lettuce leaf	H	19		Holds knife					not shown
TL	18		Carries lettuce leaf	H	18		Holds knife					Frame 2
P	27		Positions leaf for cutting	H	27		Holds knife					Frame 3
H	29		Holds leaf for cutting	TL	29		Moves knife to cutting position					Frame 4
H	210		Holds leaf for cutting	U	210		Trims off lettuce cups					Frames 5-12
G	17		Picks up waste lettuce	H	17		Holds knife					Frame 13
TL	21		Waste to garbage can	H	21		Holds knife					Frame 14
RL	8		Drops waste lettuce	H	8		Holds knife					Frame 15
TE	16		Returns to pick up lettuce	H	16		Holds knife					Frame 16
			cups to deposit in bowl									
			on left									

(b)

SIMO - CHART

Method
Operation Trimming lettuce
Part Name
Operator Hefner

Film No. 52
Operation No.
Part No.
Charted by LHK
Date charted July 28, 2000

Left hand description	Symbol	Time	Total time in sec	Time	Symbol	Right hand description	Clock
To bowl of lettuce	TE	.50	.50	.50	H	Holds knife	
Selects lettuce leaf	S	.60	1.10	.60	H	Holds knife	
Carries lettuce leaf	TL	.60	1.70	.60	H	Holds knife	
Positions leaf for cutting	P	.90	2.60	.90	H	Holds knife	
Holds leaf for cutting	H	.90	3.50	.90	TL	Moves knife to cutting position	
Holds leaf for cutting	H	2.10	5.60	2.10	U	Trims off lettuce cups	
(continued)						(continued)	

(c)

FIGURE 4.21 *Continued*

Name	Observations										Total	Percent Efficiency
Maria	√	√	0	0	√	0	0	√	√	0	5	50
Tony	0	√	0	√	0	0	√	√	0	√	5	50
Shawna	0	0	√	0	√	0	√	0	√	0	4	40
Terry	√	0	√	√	0	√	0	0	√	√	6	60
Jamal	√	√	√	0	√	0	√	√	0	0	6	60
Carlos	0	√	0	√	0	0	√	0	0	√	4	40

FIGURE 4.22 This chart shows how the work sampling method can be used to estimate worker productivity. At different times observations have been made to determine who is doing productive work. A circle indicates no productive work; a check indicates productive work is being done.

workers are busy and dividing by the number of employees observed, a percentage of efficiency can be estimated. A percentage of 80% or more is usually satisfactory. Figure 4.22 is a sample of random checks made of employees at random periods. To check productivity, write employees' names on a check sheet and go through your operation at different times to determine who is actually doing productive work.

In addition to considering whether classes of change can be made, many of the principles of motion economy and others cited in this chapter should be considered. It is not always possible to arrive at the best method of doing a job, but study will usually indicate a better way. As noted earlier, the Gilbreths were first to state a theory in motion study that has become a byword in the art: "There's always a better way." Even though a job has just been improved, one should always think: "There's always a better way." Usually in analyzing jobs, "before" and "after" situations are shown and a comparison made of any savings incorporated in the "after" way of doing the job. Some of these methods were shown here in the examples used to illustrate the various methods of studying work.

CHAPTER SUMMARY

A foodservice layout is composed of three parts: work centers where workers do specific jobs; sections, which are made up of work centers put together to do a group of related jobs; and then sections put together to create the entire layout. Work centers should be planned so workers can make the most of their work motions within the minimum reach area, with only a limited number of movements being made in the maximum reach area. If possible, workers should not move from their work center to do a job. The flow of work in work centers, sections, and layout should be smooth and flow as directly as possible with little backtracking or crisscrossing. Better flow may sometimes be achieved using mobile equipment so that equipment arrangements can be changed as work methods change. The handling of materials, if possible, should also follow specific rules:

1. Store at point of first use.
2. Use space economically by providing for specific sizes.
3. Minimize storage and handling.
4. Systemize.
5. Use good handling procedures.
6. Allow for economy of motion.
7. Coordinate.

All jobs usually have three parts: (1) get ready, (2) do, and (3) cleanup and put away. The more "do" that can be obtained for the "get ready" and "clean up and put away," the more time and energy will be saved.

In studying jobs to see how to improve them, industrial engineers use symbols to record work motions. The smallest motion that can be studied is a therblig, of which there are 17. Each therblig lasts about $\frac{1}{200}$th of a minute; this time is called a *wink*. Motions that consist of a group of therbligs are called gross motion symbols.

Three kind of studies are made to improve jobs: (1) charting work methods, (2) photographic processes, and (3) process charting. Some of the methods used in charting work methods are (1) time studies—recording time workers take to do work, usually broken down into work motions; (2) equipment relationship—considering worker and planner opinions as to how well equipment is arranged, or counting the number of motions workers make between pieces of equipment in doing work; (3) work sampling—compiling random checks on worker activity to note if productive work is or is not being performed; and (4) cross-charting—evaluating from and to motions made between equipment by assigning a value of 0 to 4 for them, 4 being best, and then listing these on a chart. In many of the charting work methods, the original way of doing work is compiled and studied. From this study, changes are made to the work method so as to reduce the time and energy spent doing a job.

Photographic methods are useful because they make a permanent record of a job which then can be studied for ways to improve it. Menomotion study is the taking of a motion picture at slow speed so as to examine in slow motion how workers are doing jobs. A stroboscopic picture is one where the motions made in doing a job are recorded on one print. MTM (methods time measurement) records work being done on a regular motion picture at regular speed (16 frames per second). High-speed motion pictures are also taken of a worker doing a job. Playing this back at normal speed makes it possible to isolate the therbligs and study how they are done. A simo chart is made from a record of film analysis in which the motions for both hands are recorded. Also shown on the recording is a microchronometer, which shows the time as the work is done.

Process charting studies the work function more than it does the worker's motions, although it is hard at times to separate them. A man–machine chart shows the work cycle of a worker and a piece of equipment. A sequence chart is also called a master process chart and usually covers a group of functions showing the times when materials are introduced in a process. A process chart shows the work motion done along with the time materials are introduced in the function. Distance of travel is also recorded. In a distance or string chart a scale drawing of a work center is marked by small pegs, staples, or other devices so a string can be wrapped around them to indicate where a worker travels in doing work. By unwinding the string and measuring it, transferring the inches of the string into feet according to the scale, one can ascertain how much travel is done for a particular job. In the revised work area, the second string length is compared with the first to find out by how much travel was reduced.

REVIEW QUESTIONS

1. Choose a work section in a production kitchen and identify the work centers in the section. Diagram and evaluate the flow of work in the center.
2. Indicate the relationships in the progress of work in a center with specific items of equipment and with other centers in the section.
3. Diagram the flow of work between sections, using squares to represent sections and arrows to indicate direction of work flow.
4. Observe the flow of work in the entire kitchen and evaluate it in light of the eight basic rules, and state the type of flow that it represents.
5. List the features that meet the basic points, and make recommendations of changes that could be made to improve the flow of work.
6. Prepare a diagram of the kitchen using squares for sections and indicate the route taken by materials using a colored line with arrows to show the path taken. Show place where they originate, are processed, and where use is completed.
7. Make a man–machine chart in which a piece of power equipment is used to facilitate the work.
8. Draw one section to scale (representing the equipment in keeping with the designs commonly used by architects) and use it for preparing a distance chart.
9. Evaluate tool storage and equipment placement in a section in relation to the progress of work. List good points and recommend changes for improvement where needed.
10. Observe a task that is being performed, making note of the materials, motions, and equipment used, the sequence of work, and the character of the finished products. Recommend changes that might be made.

KEY WORDS AND CONCEPTS

accumulative method

allowance percentage

assembly-line flow

backtracking

chronometer

continuous method

crisscrossing

cross-charting

cyclegraph

distance chart

economy of motion

equipment relation counts

flow of work

from movement

functional flow

get ready, do, clean up and put away

layout

man–machine chart

master process chart

material handling

maximum reach

menomotion study

microchronometer

micromotion study

MTM (Methods Time Measurement)

normal reach

process chart

process or one-shop plan

record of film analysis

section

sequence chart

simo chart

snap-back method

straight-line flow

string chart

stroboscopic picture

therblig

time study

to movement

travel chart

unital flow

wink

work center

workers opinions on placement

work sampling

PART

2

FUNCTIONAL AREAS OF FOOD FACILITIES

CHAPTER

5

Space Allocation

INTRODUCTION

Allowing an appropriate amount of space for a food facility calls for consideration of both the building costs and the purpose and economy of operation. It is desirable to allow enough for functional efficiency without excess space to add to building, operating, and maintenance costs. The dining area, for example, needs to be large enough to provide for the number of persons who will require service during a given period of time. If larger than needed, not only will there be excess building expense measured in cost per square foot or meter, but also operating expense measured in labor time for extra steps in service and maintenance. When the area is too small, on the other hand, it is likely to be inadequate for the service load required of it and to provide for the volume of patronage needed to support the operation. Production, storage, and other areas must be similarly allocated.

Adequacy of space is contingent on many factors. Typical of the questions that need answers are the following:

1. How many are to be served, and what are their particular food needs?
2. What is the largest number needing service at one time?
3. What foods are to be offered, and what kind of preparation is necessary?
4. What system of buying, storage, and preparation will be used?
5. What kind of service will be provided and on what schedule?
6. What type and amount of storage will be needed?
7. What are the space needs for maintenance, management office, employee facilities, and patron service?

Answers to these questions call for careful analysis of the current situation plus consideration of probable future changes occasioned by growth, market conditions, competitive influences, and organizational changes. Availability of space and investment funds is likely to temper decisions. Space allowance in relation to investment should be balanced in terms of (1) proposed permanence of the facility; (2) acuteness of need for the specific operation; (3) essentials for operating efficiency; (4) desirable standards in terms of appearance, sanitation, and good quality of production and service; and (5) immediate and future costs, depreciation, upkeep, and maintenance.

Choice of a system of operation has a major influence on space requirements and probable success of the operation. It needs to be determined in relation to needs of the specific operation and the availability of acceptable supplies and services. It is important to be aware of systems being used by similar institutions and the degree of their success. Before adopting any system of operation, evaluate it carefully in relation to the demands of the proposed operation. After a building has been constructed and large equipment installed, it is inflexible in terms of change without a good deal of expense. Requirements for space under the different systems of operation differ considerably. The needs for refrigerated storage, for size of production areas, and the kind and amount of equipment differ for the different systems of operation. Table 5–10 at the end of this chapter lists approximate space allocation for use in preliminary planning. Use of the computer in studying space needs may save time and provide more accuracy than a manual method.

Future needs as well as those that are immediate should be considered. If enlargement is probable, consider where the enlargement is to be made and arrange the initial plan to minimize ultimate cost of enlargement. Market trends and labor supplies are important. Thought should be given to any conditions that may influence patronage volume and/or service demands. Certain neighborhood changes may influence volume.

It is helpful when determining space needs to block out **space allowances** according to functions that the facility is to perform. Calculate area requirements in terms of these factors:

1. Volume and type of service. Counter service, cafeteria, and service dining rooms require a different amount of space per person served.
2. Amount, size, and placement of equipment to be used. Plot out each section with the work space and equipment that will be needed.
3. Number of workers required. Calculate the number needed in each section to perform the volume of work needed to serve the proposed number of consumers. Each worker needs a certain amount of space.
4. Space needed for supplies and other storage. Consider the kind of supplies as well as the amount, and the possible need and cost of frequent deliveries.
5. Suitable traffic areas. Safety and efficiency demands free movement of personnel.

The dining area location and space allowance are usually determined first, the production areas are next in terms of specific relationship to the dining area, and then other sections as required in relation to these. General space recommendations can be suggested but should not be accepted without challenge in terms of the specific facility needs. There are likely to be many variations in meeting the exact requirements.

Ghiselli, Almanza, and Ozaki[1] queried a group of foodservice consultants on kitchen design and reported that the consultants indicated kitchens were smaller than they had been in the past and would continue to shrink in size; that kitchens on the average were about half the size of the dining area; and that type of operation, number of meals per hour, and the choice of menu items—in that order—influenced kitchen size. In view of this latest study the figures reported in Table 5–1 are slightly overstated and should be reduced. They reflect the change that has occurred in space requirements during this period. Planners should not depend on such estimates as these for finalizing space needs. These are general guidelines for preliminary planning only. Space needs should be established on the basis of the special requirements of the facility being planned, the number of workers, the meals to be produced, equipment size, and other requirements specific to the facility. For example, specific building code requirements may change usual standards to something different.

Kazarian[2] in his text *Foodservice Facilities Planning* indicated that estimated square feet requirements varied per seat: 24–32 for table services, 18–24 for counter services,

[1]Ghiselli, R., Almanza, B.A., and Ozaki, S., "Foodservice Design: Trends, Space Allocation, and Factors That Influence Kitchen Size," *Journal of Foodservice Systems*, 1998, Vol. 10, pp. 89–105.
[2]Kazarian, *Foodservices Facilities Planning* (3rd ed.), John Wiley & Sons, New York, 1989.

TABLE 5-1 *Space Allowance per Seat for Various Types of Food Operations*

Type of Operation	Allowance per Seat	
	m^2	sq ft
Cafeteria, commercial	1.49–1.67	16–18
Cafeteria, college and industrial	1.11–1.39	12–15
Cafeteria, school lunchroom	0.84–1.11	9–12
College residence, table service	1.11–1.39	12–15
Counter service	1.67–1.86	18–20
Table service, hotel, club, restaurant	1.39–1.67	15–18
Table service, minimum	1.02–1.30	11–14
Banquet, minimum	0.93–1.02	10–11

20–28 for booth services, and 22–30 for cafeteria services. The kitchen square feet requirements, respectively, were 8–12, 4–6, 6–10, and 8–12 sq ft.

Ghiselli, Almanza, and Osaki in their study mentioned above indicated that the space requirements for various sections of the kitchen varied according to type of operation from 18.7% to 25.3% for storage, 4.7% to 6.2% for receiving, 30.2% to 32.6% for production, 9.0% to 20.2% for kitchen service area, 5.8% to 12% for cleaning, 4.5% to 6.7% for employee needs, and other 4.0% to 9.5%.

They also reported the following order of importance for factors influencing kitchen size: (1) planning more efficient layout designs, (2) using multifunction equipment (see Figure 5.1), (3) simplifying the menu, (4) arranging for more frequent deliveries, (5) using convenience foods, (6) moving equipment to the serving area, and (7) using smaller equipment.

The American Dietetic Association (ADA) and the National Restaurant Association (NRA) have indicated special space needs for individuals with disabilities. Thus, aisle space needs to be about six feet, instead of the standard stated here, to accommodate wheelchairs. Planners should refer to the publications *The ADA in Practice* (1995) and the NRA publication *Americans with Disabilities Act* (1992) to incorporate these requirements into the layout.

DINING AREAS

Space for dining areas is usually based on the number of square feet or meters per person seated multiplied by the number of persons seated at one time.

Space Requirements

Consider patron's size, comfort, and the type and quality of service. Small children may need only 8 sq ft (0.74 m^2) for dining room seating, whereas an adult for comfort would require 12 sq ft (1.11 m^2). **Banquet seating allowance** might be as little as 10 sq ft (0.93 m^2) per seat and a deluxe restaurant as much as 20 sq ft (1.86 m^2) (see Table 5.1). The amount of serving equipment in the dining area and lineup space will influence footage allowance per seat. Space used for other than seating is included in the dining area square footage requirement.

Adequate space for comfort is important. Crowding is distasteful to many people. It is likely to be tolerated more readily by youngsters than by adults. It is more acceptable

(a)

FIGURE 5.1   (a) The use of multifunction equipment saves space by eliminating equipment. This braising pan can not only be used as a kettle in which to boil, simmer, or braise foods, it can also act as a griddle for frying eggs, bacon, hot cakes, etc., or act as an oven for roasting, or as a fry kettle for deep frying breaded veal cutlets, doughnuts, etc. If a small amount of water is added, it can thaw frozen foods or act as a steamer, or a steam table to hold food. (If wheels were put on the legs, it could be rolled into the service line to act as a service table.) In the Cynthia Bishop Kitchen in the State of Texas the only cooking equipment is braising pans, steam kettles, steamers, and ovens. It serves adequately to prepare a full menu. (b) This series of photographs shows cooks using the braising kettle in various ways: (1) Stirring meat, which is being braised; (2) adding vegetables to the braised meat to simmer for a stew; (3) preparing hot cakes; (4) adding shredded cabbage, which will be quickly boiled for only six minutes (the cooking is stopped with the punch of a button, which sends a cooled refrigerant solution into a chamber that surrounds the cooking unit and quickly cools the item down); and (5) stir-frying vegetables. *(Courtesy of Groen, a Dover Industries Company, Elk Grove Village, Illinois.)*

in low-cost quick-service units than in those featuring leisurely dining. Both young and old enjoy having sufficient elbow room and enough space so that dishes of food and beverages are not crowded. Place settings for adults usually allow 24 in. (9.45 cm) and for children 18 to 20 in. (7.09 to 1.87 cm).

All of the areas in a dining room used for purposes other than seating are a part of the square footage (or square meter) allowance for seating. This does not include waiting areas, guest facilities, coatrooms, and similar areas. Excessive loss or use of space for other than seating in the dining area will, however, increase needs. Width and length of the room, table and chair sizes, and seating arrangements and objects used in interior decoration affect capacity.

Service stations may be estimated in the proportion of one small one for every 20 seats or a large central one for every 50 or 60 seats. The advisability of having a central serving station will be influenced by the distance of the dining area from the serving area. It is of special value if production and dining areas are on different floors. Plumbing and wiring, and whether supplies are delivered mechanically, will influence location of the stations. Small substations for silver, dishes, napery, beverages, ice, but-

FIGURE 5.1 *Continued*

ter, and condiments may measure 20 to 24 in. (50 to 61 cm) square and 36 to 38 in. (91 to 97 cm) high. The size of central stations varies from that for a small enclosed room to that of a screened section measuring approximately 8 to 10 ft. (2.44 to 3.05 m) long by 27 to 30 in. (0.69 to 0.76 m) wide by 6 to 7 ft (1.83 to 2.13 m) high.

Table sizes will influence patron comfort and efficient utilization of space. In a cafeteria, for example, where patrons may dine on the trays, it is important that the table be of adequate size to accommodate the number of trays likely to be used. Four trays 14 × 18 in. (36 × 46 cm) fit better on a table 48 in. (122 cm) square than on a table 36 or 42 in. (91 or 107 cm) square. Small tables, such as 24 or 30 in. (61 or 76 cm) square, are economical for seating but are uncomfortable for large people. They are only suitable in crowded areas for fast turnover and light meals. Tables having a common width and height allowing them to be fitted together give flexibility in seating arrangements (see Figure 5.2). These are particularly good for banquet or cocktail bench seating along a wall. Tables in booths are difficult for waitresses to serve if they are longer than 4 ft (122 cm). The width of the booths including seats and table is commonly 5.5 ft (155 cm). A

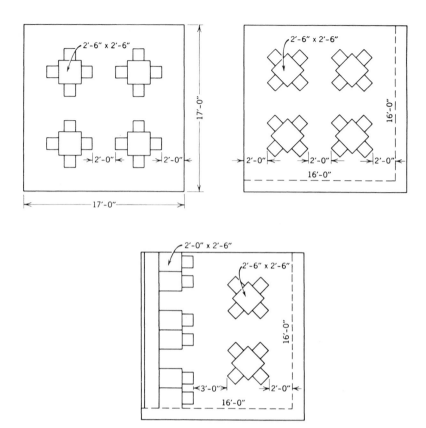

FIGURE 5.2   Variations in the utilization of space, using different table and seating arrangements. Table size 30 in. (0.76 m) square in a room 17 ft (5.18 m) square and in one 16 ft (4.88 m) square.

lunch counter will have a minimum width of 16 in. (41 cm) and a maximum width of 24 to 30 in. (61 to 76 cm). The linear measurement is calculated on the basis of 20 to 24 in. (51 to 61 cm) per seat. The maximum area best served by one waitress is generally 16 ft (4.88 m) of counter. This will allow for 8 to 10 seats. U-shaped counters make maximum use of space and reduce server travel. Space in depth of 8.5 to 11 ft (2.59 to 3.35 m) will be required for every linear foot of counter. This will provide 3 to 4 ft (91 to 122 cm) of public aisle, 2.5 ft (76 cm) for counter width, and 3 to 4.5 ft (91 to 137 cm) for aisle space for employees. A width of 4.5 ft (137 cm) is desirable where employees must pass other workers. Figures 5.2 through 5.5 show various spatial relationships in seating.

Calculate aisle space between tables and chairs to include passage area and that occupied by the person seated at the table. A minimum passage area is 18 in. (46 cm) between chairs and, including chair area, tables should be placed 4 to 5 ft (122 to 152 cm) apart. If wheelchairs are to move between tables the space should be 6 ft. Aisles on which bus carts or other mobile equipment are to be moved should be sized according to the width of such equipment.

The best utilization of space can often be arrived at through a study using templates or scaled models. Moving templates on a computer saves time. Diagonal arrangement of square tables utilizes space better than a square arrangement and yields more trouble-free traffic lanes. Lanes that pass between backs of chairs are likely to be blocked when guests arise or are being seated.

Choose table height in terms of comfort of the diners. This is especially important in schools. In lunchrooms patronized by several grades a compromise height will be needed between 30 in. (76 cm) normally used for adults and 24 in. (61 cm) suitable for children, or two sizes used in different sections of the room. A table to seat four, six, or eight is preferable to longer ones. For guests with disabilities, a table width of 3 ft, 6 in.

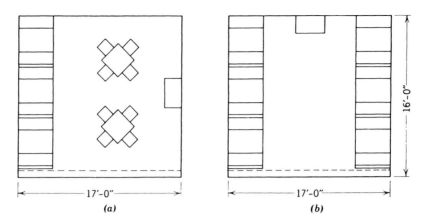

FIGURE 5.3 Seating arrangements affect capacity. (a) Use of booths and tables with serving station has capacity for 20. (b) Booth seating with serving station has capacity for 24.

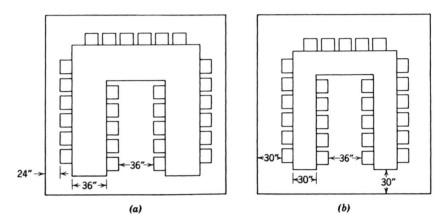

FIGURE 5.4 Table width and aisle space affect capacity. (a) A 36-in. (0.91-m) table in a room 19 ft (5.79 m) square. Capacity: 28. (b) A 30-in. (0.76-m) table in a room 19 ft square. Capacity: 27.

should be provided and the table height should be sufficient to give clearance for arm-rests on wheelchairs.

Number of Persons Allowance

The number of persons to be seated at one time is the second point of information needed for calculation of the dining room size. The total number of seats required at one time multiplied by the space required for each seat will give the total number of square feet or meters needed in the dining area. The number of times a seat is occupied during a given period is commonly referred to as **turnover** or **table turn.** The turnover per hour multiplied by the number of seats available gives the total number of patrons that can be served in an hour. If peak loads, or the largest number to be served at one time, are known, the number of seats required can be estimated.

Turnover rates tend to vary. They are influenced by such factors as the amount of food eaten, the elaborateness of service, and the diner's time allowance. A breakfast meal of few foods may be eaten more quickly than dinner, and a simple fare faster than a many-course meal. Turnover can be quickest where food has been prepared in advance and where patrons serve themselves and bus their soiled dishes. The turnover time is decreased 10% by patrons removing their soiled dishes so tables are available for other guests. Deluxe service for leisure dining, involving removal and placement of several courses, takes the longest time. Although specific turnover may vary from 10 minutes to

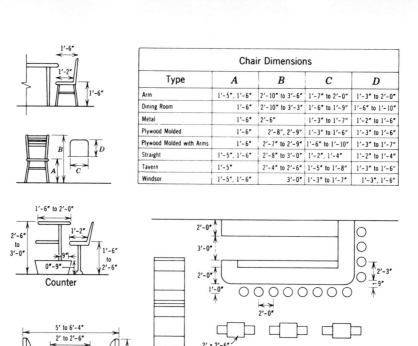

Chair Dimensions				
Type	A	B	C	D
Arm	1'-5", 1'-6"	2'-10" to 3'-6"	1'-7" to 2'-0"	1'-3" to 2'-0"
Dining Room	1'-6"	2'-10" to 3'-3"	1'-6" to 1'-9"	1'-6" to 1'-10"
Metal	1'-6"	2'-6"	1'-3" to 1'-7"	1'-2" to 1'-6"
Plywood Molded	1'-6"	2'-8", 2'-9"	1'-3" to 1'-6"	1'-3" to 1'-6"
Plywood Molded with Arms	1'-6"	2'-7" to 2'-9"	1'-6" to 1'-10"	1'-3" to 1'-7"
Straight	1'-5", 1'-6"	2'-8" to 3'-0"	1'-2", 1'-4"	1'-2" to 1'-4"
Tavern	1'-5"	2'-4" to 2'-6"	1'-5" to 1'-8"	1'-3" to 1'-6"
Windsor	1'-5", 1'-6"	3'-0"	1'-3" to 1'-7"	1'-3", 1'-6"

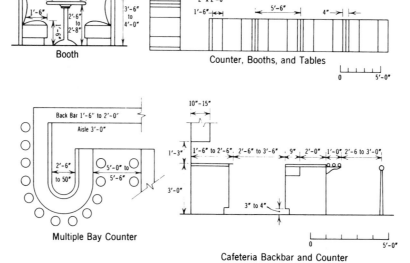

Counter

Booth

Counter, Booths, and Tables

Multiple Bay Counter

Cafeteria Backbar and Counter

Metric Conversion for Feet and Inches Given

ft and in.	meters	ft and in.	meters
9"	0.23	2'4"	0.71
10"	0.25	2'6"	0.76
12"	0.30	2'7"	0.79
1'2"	0.36	2'8"	0.81
1'3"	0.38	2'9"	0.83
1'4"	0.41	2'10"	0.86
1'5"	0.43	3'	0.91
1'6"	0.46	3'6"	1.07
1'7"	0.48	4'	1.22
1'8"	0.51	4'2"	1.27
1'9"	0.53	5'	1.52
1'10"	0.56	5'6"	1.68
1'11"	0.58	6'	1.83
2'	0.61	6'4"	1.93
2'3"	0.69		

FIGURE 5.5 Dining and service area dimensions.

TABLE 5-2 *The Percentage of Tables of Different Sizes Suggested for Food Facilities of Different Types*

Type of Dining Room	Tables for Two, Percent	Tables for Three or More, Percent
Campus commons	30	70
Industrial or business restaurant	60	40
Family restaurant	25	75
Hotel dining room	60	40
Shoppers' tearoom	80	20

2 hours, actual eating time is normally 10 to 15 minutes for breakfast, 15 to 20 minutes for lunch, and 30 to 40 minutes for dinner.

The calculation of occupancy of seats in a dining room must take into consideration a certain percentage of vacancy, except where a given number are seated at one time according to assignment. In table service this has been estimated as 20% of total capacity, in cafeterias from 12% to 18%, and for counter operations 10% to 12%. Many factors influence this percentage, such as patrons arriving at different times, irregular rate of turnover, and reluctance to share a table with strangers.

The table sizes used in the dining room affect occupancy. It is often desirable to provide for groups varying from two to eight, with a predominance in most dining rooms of two persons (see Table 5.2). The "deuces" may be of a size and shape that can be put together to form tables for larger groups. In metropolitan areas where many tend to dine alone, wall bench-type seating and tables for two with a center ridge or line denoting space for one have been used successfully. Chairs with "tablet-arms" that will hold a tray have been used for fast turnover in crowded areas. Table 5–2 indicates the percentage of tables accommodating given numbers that are sometimes suggested for eating establishments of different types.

The utilization of **seating capacity** tends to be greater for cafeterias than for table service. While the patron may spend 25% to 50% of the time seated at the table waiting for service, the cafeteria diner may begin eating as soon as seated. One cafeteria line can serve 4 to 8 patrons per minute depending upon (1) the speed of the servers, (2) promptness of selection, influenced by amount of selection and clarity of information, (3) the convenience of layout, and (4) the type of patrons. At these rates, 240 to 480 patrons will need to be seated within an hour. If the turnover rate is 2 per hour, then from 120 to 240 seats will be used. However, if 15% of the total capacity at the peak period remains unfilled, then between 140 and 280 seats will be required. An additional 14 to 28 seats, or 10%, would be needed if patrons do not bus their soiled dishes. All factors are important.

Patronage estimates for facilities of different types may be guided by the number of persons in residence, enrollments in a school, an industry's payroll, the membership in a club, or the volume of mealtime traffic in an office or shopping area. In each case a certain percentage may normally be expected to dine in the facility. The percentage will be influenced by such factors as its location in relation to other facilities, the patrons' buying power, the prices (as based on subsidy or profit), patrons' time allowance related to speed of service, and the convenience of location.

The patronage estimate for a college cafeteria involves consideration of total enrollment; the number of students who live at home, in organized houses, or residence halls; and competing food facilities on or near the campus. A college residence providing table service may have to allow a seating capacity that is 110% of occupancy if a policy exists of having "special guest" occasions and seating all at one time.

An industrial lunchroom may serve as few as 25% and as many as 90% of the payroll. Clues to probable patronage may be drawn from such factors as nearness to other eating facilities, wage rates, type of work, prices to be charged, length of meal break, policy of permitting or refusing patronage by outsiders, and appeal qualities such as food goodness and an attractive, hospitable atmosphere. The attitude of management toward the lunchroom is likely to influence patronage. Pride in providing good food and appealing service as opposed to a take-it-or-leave-it attitude tends to influence patrons' response.

The size of the hospital dining room should be gauged by the size and the number of the groups who may be served in it, such as employees, patients, or guests. The size and type of hospital will influence the number of personnel likely to be employed and the number of ambulatory patients who may be served in the dining room. The ratio of personnel to patients will vary from 1 to 3, depending on the amount of special care required and the amount of teaching and research done. Food quality, price schedule, and appeal factors will influence the percentage of staff and others eligible to eat in the facility.

School lunch participation has varied from 25% to 90%. It is strongly influenced by the amount of subsidy provided and the prices charged. Where prices are low, the food good, meal selection appealing, and the food service program carefully integrated with the educational program, the percentage can be expected to be high. An acceptable schedule for staggering lunch periods is to be considered when determining seating capacity of the lunchroom.

Capacity for banquet seating needs to be flexible in order to satisfy different types of patrons, kinds of functions, and number of people to be served. Folding tables 30 in. (76 cm) wide are popular. These are obtainable in varying lengths, but 72 and 96 in. (183 and 244 cm) are commonly used. The spacing for the legs should permit comfortable seating when the tables are joined end to end and place settings are laid on 24-in. (61-cm) centers.

Restaurant operators anticipating establishing a business for profit need to determine requisite seating capacity on the basis of the amount of income essential to cover operating costs and provide a suitable profit. Labor, food, and operating costs must be met and a profit realized that covers risk-bearing, effort expended, and **return on investment (ROI)**. Essential income is weighed in the light of probable patronage and probable **average check**. The number of seats provided must be sufficient for the volume of patronage that will yield the income required and that it is reasonable to expect.

Flexibility in seating capacity is desirable. People do not like to be crowded nor do they enjoy the lonely experience of being seated in a huge area occupied by only a few people. Sparse patronage creates the impression of low popularity. Separate rooms, folding doors, screens, or other attractive devices can be used to reduce the size of an area during slack periods. Sections left open should be those easiest to serve. Balconies, backrooms, or other less desirable space can often be used for overflow numbers that occasionally require service.

Dining room operations often need a larger seating capacity at one meal than at others. This may be due either to a variation in numbers or different turnover rates. A residence cafeteria with a main dining room capacity of 600 has an adjoining room to seat 100. The adjoining room is used at dinner time only when a larger number appears for service at one time and because of the fuller meal the turnover is slower. The room is available at breakfast and lunch times for special groups.

Commercial restaurants located in shopping or office areas usually have a heavier demand at noon than at the dinner hour. Rooms used for general patronage at noon may be closed at night or used for private dinner parties. Entrances to these rooms should not require passage through the main dining area. Convenience for serving the special functions is important.

PRODUCTION AREAS

Many factors influence space requirements for production, and consideration of them when planning is essential for ultimate satisfaction. A frequently quoted rule suggests allotting one-fourth to one-half of the area of the dining room as the area size for the production facilities. It can be understood readily that the type and system of production quickly upsets this ratio. It is necessary to make a detailed study of the specific needs. Major points to be considered are as follows:

1. Type of preparation and service. Will preparation be done in quantity or in small individualized amounts on short order?
2. Amount of total production done in the facility. Is the kitchen to fully produce all, some, or none of the food served?
3. Volume in terms of the number of meals served within a given time period. Will the service schedule permit continuing preparation or must the food be ready for the full number to be served at one time?
4. Variety of food offered in the menu. How much choice will be offered in entrées, vegetables, salads, desserts, etc.?
5. Elaborateness of preparation and service. Does the proposed service require individual handwork, different pieces of cooking equipment, and special containers for service?
6. Amount of individual service given. Will special facilities be required for preparing the service, such as a tray line for hospital trays or a setup station for elaborate meals?
7. Seating and service plan, whether on one floor or many. Will food be set up for immediate service in the dining room, or will special means be needed to preserve good condition of food sent to another floor or building for service?
8. Production system used. Will food be prepared and served immediately within the facility, prepared and chilled or frozen for later use, or prepared, temperature-maintained, and shipped elsewhere for service?

Choice of a plan of operation should be preceded by a careful estimate of the potential number of patrons and what they want, need, and are willing to support. There is frequently a wide difference between the quality and quantity of food that people want and the values that they are willing to buy. Elaborate individualized preparation and service is likely to cost a great deal more to set up and operate than one providing limited choice, and quantity production of food that is simply served. The cost of providing space, equipment, and labor required will vary considerably between a foodservice that serves ready-prepared, commercial foods, and one that fully prepares food that is dependably good, adequate, and reliable in supply and suitably individual in character.

New products on the market, new cooking methods, and new equipment available deserve evaluation. The use of preprocessed products has made a pronounced change in the amount of space allotted to the bakeshop, meat-cutting, and vegetable preparation areas. Preprocessed meats now available have eliminated kitchen butcher sections. A large quantity of prepared and refrigerated or frozen fish, poultry, and vegetable products are now being used. This affects both preparation and storage needs. The cost and quality of the market products, their availability, and the frequency of deliveries should be considered (see Figure 5.6).

Refrigeration has become a very important consideration in many kitchens from which food is shipped to other stations or held for delayed service, as well as for preprocessed products. In some kitchens, refrigeration of food at a point when cooking is approximately 90% complete is used to prevent overcooking. The food is chilled and then sharply reheated immediately before service. Hot food held at a palatable temperature for an extended serving period becomes overcooked, losing its fresh appearance, appealing color, texture, and flavor. The cook-chill methods of food handling require space for packaging and carts for moving into storage, as well as space in the refrigerated areas.

Variety in menu selection and elaboration of foods tend to increase space needs in work areas and storage. Small amounts of numerous items do not permit stacking and bulk packaging. Elaboration of food often involves individual portion treatment, with individual casseroles for example, as compared to bulk steam table pans. A hospital food

FIGURE 5.6   Many menu items now come fully prepared, so with just a few minutes of rapid heat input from a microwave oven such as that shown here, they are ready for service. *(Courtesy of Hobart Corporation, Troy, Ohio.)*

service requiring many special diets serves as a common example of menu variety and individual portion treatment imposing special space requirements.

Procedures and equipment used will affect space needs. Garbage, recyclables, and refuse, for example, may require a sizable area for collection and storage awaiting pickup. Disposal or pulper units for food waste, a compactor for garbage, a crusher for cans, and a baler for boxes will greatly reduce space requirements. Frequency of garbage collection and recycle pickups will influence space needs also.

Structural features of the building may influence the utilization of space. Allotting kitchen space for efficient operation is sometimes forgotten when planning the location of ventilation and elevator shafts, support columns, and other floor to ceiling structures. It is important to consider whether the resulting space promotes or defeats forming a layout for efficient work. The location of entrances and exits for a good flow of traffic, window placement for good light and ventilation, and space relationships of sections need to be considered. Elimination of partitions whenever possible reduces space needs and costs and also permits easier supervision.

Kitchens serving a small number of patrons require a larger square footage per meal than those serving large numbers (see Table 5–3). The following data used for industrial cafeteria kitchens show how space needs per meal tend to decrease as the number served increases.

Planners are frequently asked to make estimates of space needs before having an opportunity to ascertain policies or make detailed plans for operation. Figures that are useful in making such estimates are given in Table 5–3. These figures pertain to average full-production kitchen areas found in food facilities of different types. Their use is to be regarded as tentative and to be measured carefully in terms of specific needs. The square footage or meters given is to be multiplied by the maximum number of meals estimated per hour of service in order to find the total space requirement.

TABLE 5-3   *Variation in Kitchen Space in Relation to Numbers Served*

	Area per Meal		Variation in Total Area	
Meal Load	m−	sq ft	m²	sq ft
100–100	0.465	5.00	46–93	500–1,000
200–400	0.372	4.00	74–149	800–1,600
400–800	0.325	3.50	130–260	1,400–2,800
800–1,300	0.279	3.00	223–362	2,400–3,900
1,300–2,000	0.232	2.50	302–465	3,250–5,000
2,000–3,000	0.186	2.00	372–557	4,000–6,000
3,000–5,000	0.170	1.85	511–859	5,500–9,250

TABLE 5-4   *Kitchen Area Allowance per Meal for Food Facilities of Different Type and Size*

		Estimated Maximum Meals per Hour				
Type of Facility		200 or less	200–400	400–800	800–1,300	1,300–7,500
Cafeterias	sq ft	7.5–5.0	5.0–4.0	4.0–3.5	3.5–3.0	3.0–1.8
	m²	0.697–.465	0.465–0.372	0.372–0.325	0.325–0.279	0.279–0.177
Hospitals	sq ft	18.0–4.5	12.0–4.5	11.0–4.5	10.0–4.0	8.0–4.0
	m²	1.67–0.418	1.11–0.418	1.02–0.418	0.929–0.372	0.743–0.372
Hotels	sq ft	18.0–4.0	7.5–3.0	6.0–3.0	4.0–3.0	4.0–3.0
	m²	1.67–0.372	0.697–0.279	0.557–0.279	0.372–0.279	0.372–0.279
Industrial lunchrooms	sq ft	7.5–5.0	4.0–3.2	3.5–2.0	3.0–2.0	2.5–1.7
	m²	0.697–0.465	0.372–0.279	0.325–0.186	0.279–0.186	0.232–0.158
Lunch counters	sq ft	7.5–2.0	2.0–1.5			
	m²	0.697–0.186	0.186–0.139			
Restaurants (service)	sq ft	11.0–4.0	5.0–3.6	5.0–3.6	5.0–3.0	5.0–3.0
	m²	0.092–0.372	0.465–0.334	0.465–0.334	0.465–0.279	0.465–0.279
School lunchrooms	sq ft	4.0–3.3	3.3–2.2	3.0–2.0	2.5–1.6	2.0–1.6
	m²	0.372–0.306	0.306–0.204	0.279–0.186	0.232–0.149	0.186–0.149

Table 5–4 gives space allowances used in planning various kinds of foodservice kitchens. Wide variation in these space requirements can result depending on the kind of production that is done in the kitchen. If the kitchen receives its food from a central commissary or uses largely preprepared foods, the space required will be considerably reduced. Doing many foods from "scratch" may increase it considerably. Again, the information given in Table 5–4 should be considered useful only in preliminary planning. As planning proceeds and needs are more specifically defined, the space requirements can be more accurately determined.

Linear space, depths, and heights for work centers should be controlled in terms of average human measurements. This must include distance to reach and grasp material or equipment used in working. The length and width of the worktable is adjusted in terms of the amount and size of equipment that will rest on it during the progress of work. The linear measurement will vary in terms of the number of workers using it at one time. Table 5–5 shows an example of area allowances.

The width of the table may be 24 to 30 in. (61 to 76 cm) unless dishes or food containers are to rest at the back of the table or on shelves. Tables 36 in. (91 cm) wide are

TABLE 5-5   *General Space Needs in Hospital Dietary Departments*

Section	Area Allowance per Bed			
	m^2		sq ft	
Receiving		0.0642		0.68
Food storage				
Refrigeration		0.1412		1.52
Meat	(0.0557)		(0.60)	
Fruit and vegetables	(0.0557)		(0.60)	
Dairy	(0.0297)		(0.32)	
Low temperature	0.0595		0.64	
Dry bulk storage	0.2230		2.40	
Total storage		0.4237		4.56
Kitchen				
Meat preparation	0.0372		0.40	
Vegetable and salad preparation	0.0743		0.80	
Cooking	0.1858		2.00	
Bakery	0.0743		0.80	
Ice cream (if required)	0.0372		0.40	
Scullery	0.0557		0.60	
Janitors' facilities	0.0111		0.12	
Total kitchen		0.4756		5.12
Staff dining				
Cafeteria	0.1300		1.40	
Auxiliary space (if required)	0.0372		0.40	
Dining room	0.6735		7.25	
Private dining room	0.0650		0.70	
		0.9057		9.75
Dishwashing		0.2044		2.20
Tray setup		0.2044		2.20
Tray truck storage		0.1672		1.80
Offices		0.1858		2.00
Total for Dietary Department		2.6310		28.31

Source: Data adapted from materials compiled by Gladys Knight, Tourist and Resort Section, School of Hotel, Restaurant, and Institution Management, Michigan State University.

preferable when the back of the area is used for such storage. Where two workers work opposite each other, a table 42 in. (107 cm) wide may be used. A work area 4 to 6 ft (1.22 to 1.83 m) long is within convenient reach of the average person. Tables 8 to 10 ft (2.44 to 3.05 m) long are used if two people are working side by side. A height of 34 in. (86 cm) is commonly used as a working height but should be evaluated in terms of specific work done and equipment used. A height 2 in. (5 cm) below the worker's elbow helps to keep the back in a vertical position.

Aisle space should permit free, easy movement of essential traffic. The minimum width for a lane between equipment where one person works alone is 36 to 42 in. (91 and 107 cm). Where more than one is employed and where workers must pass each other in the progress of work, and mobile equipment is used, 48 to 54 in. (122 to 137 cm) are recommended. At least 60 in. (152 cm) are needed for main traffic lanes where workers regularly pass each other with mobile equipment. If workers or equipment must stand in the lane while working, appropriate space should be allowed for this. Thought must be given to space for a door opening into an aisle and for handling large pieces of equipment, such as roasting pans, baking sheets, and stock pots. Main thoroughfares should

TABLE 5-6 Processing Equipment Requirements for a Cafeteria, Based on Menu and Volume Serving Period 11:30 A.M. to 1:00 P.M.

| Menu Item | Portion | | Total | Batch | |
	Size	No.	Amount	Size	Rotation
Soup[2]	1 c (237 mL)	320	20 gal (76 l)	20 gal	—
Roast meat or poultry	4 oz (114 g)	120	30 lb (13.6 kg)	15 lb (6.81 kg)	30 min apart
or boiled meat	4 oz (114 g)	120	30 lb (13.6 kg)	30 lb (13.6 kg)	—
Baked portions of meat, fish, poultry	3 to 6 oz (85 to 170 g)	120	24 to 48 lb (11 to 22 kg)	40 portions	30 min apart
Casserole entrees	4 to 6 oz (114 to 170 g)	240	8 to 12 pans	2 to 3 pans	20 min apart
or stews	1 c (237 mL)	240	15 gal (57 l)	15 gal (57 l)	—
Gravies, sauces	¼ c (59 mL)	480	7½ gal (29 L)	7½ gal (29 L)	—
Baked potatoes	6 to 8 oz (170 to 227 g)	240	240 potatoes	1 or 2 sheet pans	15 min apart
Mashed potatoes	1½ c (118 mL)	240	8 gal (30 L)	2⅔ gal (10 L)	30 min apart
Frozen broccoli	4 to 6 oz (114 to 170 g)	200	8 to 12 pans	2 pans	15–20 min apart
Frozen peas	2½ oz (71 g)	360	60 lb (27 kg)	10 lb (4.55 kg)	15 min apart
Fresh carrots	2½ oz (71 g)	180	30 lb (14 g)	10 lb (4.5 g)	30 min apart
Canned vegetable	2½ oz (71 g)	180	30 lb (14 g)	6 lb (2.7 g)	20 min apart
Sandwich, grilled	4 oz (114 g)	160	40 lb (18 kg)	on order	on order
Sliced foods	2 oz (57 g)	104	13 lb (5.89 g)	all	
Cream pudding	½ c (118 mL)	240	8 gal (30 L)	8 gal (30 L)	—
Cake[2]	2½ oz (71 g)	96	2 sheets	2 sheets	—
Frosting		96			
Cookies	2 oz (57 g)	190	4 sheets	1 to 4 sheets	
Breads[2]	2 oz (57 g)	240	4 sheets	1 to 4 sheets	30 min apart
Beverages[2]	6 oz (170 g)	600	28 gal (106 L)	5 gal (19 L)	15 min apart

[2]Items served daily. Other items adaptable according to equipment needs.

continued

not pass through work centers. The work center should be in proximity to main traffic lanes, with easy access to them. It is important both to avoid distraction from outsiders passing through work centers and to conserve space. Work centers at right angles to traffic lanes are efficient.

Typical menus of the operation should be analyzed to ascertain the production needs. Table 5–6 shows how the analysis for one foodservice menu was made to determine

TABLE 5-6 *Continued*

| Equipment | | Process | Reserve | |
Item	Capacity	Time	for Use	Comments
Steam kettle	114 L (30 gal)	1–4 hr	9:00–1:00	Batch schedule depends on cream or broth soup
Oven 240°F (116° C)	2-pan deck	2–4 hr	7:00–11:30	Pan—305 × 508 mm (12 × 20 in.)
Steam kettle	114 L (30 gal)	2–4 hr	7:00–11:30	May be boiled and held in steam cooker
Slicer			11:00–12:30	Sliced as needed
Oven 325°F (163°C)	2 or 3 2-pan decks	½–2 hr	9:30–12:30	Pan size 305 × 508 mm (12 × 20 in.)
Oven 350°F (177°C)	4 or 6 2-pan decks	½–2 hr	9:30–12:40	Pan size 305 × 508 mm (12 × 20 in.)
Steam kettle	76 l (20 gal)	1–3 hr	8:00–12:30	May be prepared, placed in S.S. pans, held in oven
Steam kettle	38 l (10 gal)	½–1 hr	10:30–12:30	
Oven 400°F (205°C)	4 decks	¾–1 hr	10:30–12:30	Sheet pan size 457 × 660 mm (18 × 26 in.)
Mixer	19 l (20 qt)	¼ hr	11:15–12:45	
5 psi cooker	2-pan deck	15–20 min	11:00–12:40	
Steam kettle	14 kg (10 qt)	10–12 min	11:15–12:45	
5 psi cooker	2-pan deck	15–20 min	11:00–12:40	
Steam kettle	14 kg (10 qt)	10–12 min	11:15–12:45	
5 psi cooker	2-pan deck	15–20 min	11:00–12:30	
5 psi cooker	2-pan deck	5–10 min	11:15–12:40	
Griddle	.61 × .91 mm	10 min	11:15–1:00	
Slicer	(2 × 3 ft)			
Steam kettle	38 l	½–1 hr	9:00–10:00	
Oven	2 decks	½–1 hr	8:00–9:00	Temp. 177°C (350°F)
Mixer	11.4 l (12 qt)	30 min	9:00–9:45	
Oven	1–4 decks	10–20 min	9:00–	Temp 1770°C (350°F)
Mixer			8:00–9:00	
Oven 350°F (177°C)	1–4 decks	20–25 min	10:45–12:15	Retard to bake as needed
Mixer	29 l (30 qt)			
Proof	4 sheets	2 hr	8:45–10:45	
Urns	23–46–23 1 comb. (6–12–6 gal)	10–15 min	11:45–1:00	Brew as needed

equipment requirements. The portion size of menu items times the estimated number of portions required gives the amount to be prepared and this amount can be equated to the equipment size needed. It is important in calculating the size of the equipment needed to know exactly the time required to process batches through equipment. Figuring that six batches can be processed in an hour when the equipment can only handle four can lead to serious misplanning. If the equipment will not process enough portions to last for batch cooking time, more or larger equipment will be needed.

The percentage of floor area covered by equipment varies according to production needs and the type of equipment used. A satisfactory layout may claim less than 30% of total space for equipment, whereas work areas, traffic lanes, and space around equipment for easy operation and cleaning may require 70% or more.

Plans for space-saving compactness require use of actual equipment measurements when planning. Manufacturers' specifications for the food equipment chosen should be secured for this use. Templates made to exact scale for both fixed and mobile equipment are helpful to use in arriving at a suitable arrangement and space allocation.

The allowance of 20 to 30 sq ft (1.86 to 2.88 m^2) per bed is suggested in planning for hospital production and service areas, where full production is done. The need is reduced as the number of beds increases, for example, about 30 sq ft (2.88 m^2) per bed for a 50-bed and 20 sq ft (1.86 m^2) for a 200-bed hospital will be needed.[3] This allowance does not include major storage areas, dining rooms, employee facilities, or floor pantries. Some planners find the data given in Table 5.5 helpful in making rough, preliminary estimates.

Space Needs Based on Equipment Requirements

After the menu plan, probable volume, system of operation, type of service, and time schedule have been determined, an analysis can be made of equipment needs and space requirements for the production area. The condition of the food as procured may require (1) refining, mixing, shaping, and processing, commonly described as "preparation from scratch"; (2) partial processing, as in mixing and whipping dehydrated potatoes or thawing and French frying cut and frozen potatoes; or (3) heating or chilling to palatable temperature fully prepared food, which may be packaged and delivered hot, refrigerated, or frozen in bulk or individual portions.

Space for equipment and work accomplishment will be affected by (1) the activities to be performed, (2) kind and variety of menu items, (3) volume of food required, and (4) type and time schedule of service. Tables 5–6, 5–7, and 5–8 illustrate an example of calculations made for an industrial cafeteria in determining space requirements for equipment.

SERVING AREAS

The highest level of palatability of prepared food is fragile. The location of the serving areas and the equipment used is chosen for its greatest protection. The location may be in the kitchen close to completion of preparation, in the dining room convenient for service to consumers, or as in hospitals, it may be on separate floors where final conditioning is done immediately before service to patients. The shortest time lapse between production and service is in short-order counter service.

Several questions call for answers in determining space needs for serving areas:

1. What type of service is to be used (buffet, table, tray, counter, etc.)?
2. How many are to be served within a given time period?
3. What type of menu is to be served? How much variety is to be offered?
4. Will certain foods in the menu require special treatment or protection?
5. What is the age, status, and state of health of the patrons?
6. Will special equipment be required in the serving area for conditioning food immediately prior to service.
7. Will extra storage be required for special serving dishes or containers?

---

[3]"Ordinance and Code Regulating Eating and Drinking Establishments," *Public Health Bulletin No. 280,* U.S. Public Health Service, Washington, DC.

TABLE 5-7   Equipment Needs Based on Use Time Schedule

Equipment	7:00	7:20	7:40	8:00	8:20	8:40	9:00	9:20	9:40	10:00	10:20	10:40	11:00	11:20	11:40	12:00	12:20	12:40	1:00	1:20
Steam kettles																				
30 gal (114 L) Soup							—	—	—	—	—	—	—	—	—	—	—			
30 gal (114 L) Stew						—	—	—	—	—	—	—	—	—	—	—	—			
1. 10 gal (38 L) Gravy and sauces				—	—	—	—	—	—	—		—	—	—	—	—	—			
2. 2½ gal (9 L) Peas														-	-	-	-			
Steam cooker																				
Deck 1. Vegetables												—	—	—						
or entree ingredients								—	—	—	—									
Deck 2. Vegetables														-	-	-	-			
Range top—Roux, etc.		—	—	—	—	—	—	—	—	—	—	—	—	—	—	—	—			
Griddle													—	—	—	—	—	—	—	
Ovens—Convection																				
Shelf 1 Casseroles Pans 1 and 2[a]												—	—	—						
Pans 7 and 8															—	—	—	—		
Shelf 2 Casseroles Pans 3 and 4													—	—	—	—				
Shelf 3 Casseroles Pans 5 and 6													—	—	—	—				
Shelf 4 Ind. portions Sheet 1									—	—	—	—	—	—						
Shelf 5 Ind. portions Sheet 2										—	—	—	—	—	—					
Shelf 6 Ind. portions Sheet 3											—	—	—	—	—	—				
Shelf 7 Potatoes Sheets 1 and 5[b]												—	—	—	—					
Shelf 8 Potatoes Sheets 2 and 6											—	—	—	—	—					
Shelf 9 Potatoes Sheet 3													—	—	—	—	—			
Shelf 10 Potatoes Sheet 4															—	—	—	—		

[a]Pan size—12 × 20 in. (305 × 508 mm).
[b]Sheet pan size—18 × 26 in. (457 × 660 mm).

Cafeterias

The number of serving lines needed in a **cafeteria** will depend on (1) the number of patrons available for service within a given time period; (2) how much time the patrons have for service, as affected by a set time allowance or their degree of patience; and (3) the serving speed for the specific menu in terms of the number of persons who can be served per minute. Some planners use, as a rough guide, one counter or line for every 250 to 300 patrons served. Arrival time, speed of service, and turnover in the dining room are factors that affect the number of lines required.

The **counter lengths** used varies greatly. It may be one continuous length to serve all of the foods offered, or it may be broken into sections for different parts of the menu. For example, hot food may have two or three lines for service and salads and desserts only one. This may be due partly to popularity of specific parts of the menu and partly to more delay in the service of certain foods. The hot food offering variety may call for selection by the patron and immediate dishing up by the server. The salads and desserts may be ready in advance for quick pickup by the patron. The "shopping type" of cafeteria, in which patrons can go directly to sections that interest them, permits faster movement of patrons through the lines of service.

The variety of foods to be offered and the volume of patrons to be served will influence the counter length that is most suitable. Excess space partially filled is unappealing. Overcrowding on one that is too short usually means that some of the food will not be properly displayed and protected. The average length of counters in college residence halls and hospitals is about 30 to 32 ft (9.14 to 9.75 m), whereas those in school lunchrooms average around 15 to 20 ft (4.57 to 6.10 m). Some commercial counters may

TABLE 5-8 *Equipment Summary With Approximate Dimensions for Floor Plans[a]*

Equipment Items			Dimensions	
No. Type		Size	mm	in.

Processing Equipment

Steam kettles
1 stationary		30 gal (114 l)	914 × 838	36 w × 33 d
1 trunnion		30 gal (151 l)	914 × 838	36 w × 33 d
1 trunnion		10 gal (38 l)	600 × 836	24 w × 33 d
1 or 2 trunnions		2½ gal (9.51)	381 × 432	15 w × 17 d

(2, allow more time for heating and change between batches for rotation)

Steam cooker
1 Cooker		3 compartments 2-pan wide	914× 838	36 w × 33 d

(3 compartments, allow for flexiblity)

Range top
1 section			9014 × 838	36 w × 38 d

(oven a desirable addition for roasting meat or holding food for service)

Ovens
2 convection compartments (stacked)			965 × 1118	38 w × 44 d

(if single-mounted double floor dimensions)
1 conventional		3 deck	1384 × 914	54½ w × 36 d

(1 roasting deck and 2 baking decks)
Griddle			914 × 610	36 w × 24 d

Mixers
1 bench		12/20 qt (11/19 l)	610 × 914	24 w × 36 d
1 floor		30/60 qt (28/57 l)	610 × 914	24 w × 36 d

(can operate with 1, but 2 gives desirable flexibility)
Proof box			1371 × 610	54 w × 24 d

[a]This table summarizes equipment needs indicated in Table 5.6—Processing Requirements and Table 5.7—Schedule of Use.

continued

have an overall length of 70 to 80 ft (21 to 24 m), but counters over 50 ft (15.24 m) are considered inefficient. Twenty feet (6.10 m) is usually considered to be a minimum, but under special conditions and where a limited menu is served, 6 to 8 ft (1.83 to 2.44 m) may be sufficient. To move patrons through service more quickly and smoothly various plans are being used that affect the overall counter length. Some use the continuous counter plan; others separate menu offerings into separate units and patrons shop at the various units to pick up their meals. Counters can be shortened by utilizing mobile equipment for dishes and auxiliary foods.

A useful figure for estimating counter width is 14 ft (4.27 m). This allows 4 ft (1.22 m) for a patron lane, 1 ft (30 cm) for a tray slide, 2 ft (61 cm) for counter width, 4.5 ft (1.37 m) for counter workers, and 2.5 ft (1.07 m) for a back bar. The size of the tray should dictate the width of the tray slide. Counter height needs to be set at comfortable levels for workers and patrons. Schools may have lower counters as well as tray slides, so that the children may see the food and move their trays along a slide as they are served. For little children, 28 to 30 in. (71 to 76 cm) is desirable, with counters that are narrow enough to permit servers to reach across and assist the children. A solid tray slide tends to be freer of accidents than those made of bars or tubing. Compartmented, pastel-colored, plastic trays, measuring 9 × 12 in. (23 × 30 cm) are popular in many schools. Slides for these may be on the server's side of the counter for ease of service and to eliminate spillage or accidents. The child picks up the completed service at the end of the line.

TABLE 5-8　*Continued*

Equipment Items			Dimensions	
No.	Type	Size	mm	in.

Auxiliary Equipment

Refrigerators

	1 box (cook's)		1676 × 914	66 w × 36 d
	1 box (salad and sandwiches)		1676 × 914	66 w × 36 d
	1 box (baker's)		1676 × 914	66 w × 36 d
	1 walk-in with low-temperature compartment		2.4400 × 4.27	96 w × 188 d

Tables

	1 cook's (high shelf, utensil drawer, roll bins)		2438 × 762	961 × 30 w
	2 salad and sandwich (high shelf, utensil drawer, dish bins)		1829 × 762	721 × 30 w
	1 baker's (high shelf, utensil drawer, roll bins) (including sink)		2438 × 762	961 × 30 w
	1 baker's finishing (with dish storage bins)		1829 × 762	721 × 30 w

Sinks

	1 cook's (2 compartments and 2 drainboards)		2032 × 610	80 w × 24 d
	1 salad and sandwich (2 compartments and 2 drainboards		2235 × 610	88 w × 24 d
	1 baker's (single compartment in table)			
	1 (3 compartments, pot and pan, 2 drainboards)		2235 × 610	150 w × 24 d

Pot rack			1829 × 610	72 w × 24 d
Food racks				
	2 bakery		508 × 762	20 w × 30 d
Kitchen carts				
	2 2-shelf, table height		610 × 914	24 w × 30 1
	1 2-shelf, utility		508 × 762	20 w × 20 1
Slicer stand			610 × 914	24 w × 36 1

[a]This table summarizes equipment needs indicated in Table 5.6—Processing Requirements and Table 5.7—Schedule of Use.

When determining the number of serving lines needed, consideration is to be given to the time allowance of the patrons, the serving speed in terms of persons served per minute, and the total number to be served within a given time period. Various factors affect these points. Are the patrons on a set time allowance, or are they free to take as much time as their patience for food allows? How many of the foods to be selected are prepared ready for pickup and how many must be prepared or served to order? Some operations give customers who must wait in line a number so the customer can be seated while waiting. When the order is ready, the customer picks it up. This avoids congestion at the serving line and avoids having to provide space for those waiting in line. Is the choice of food limited or are there several choices calling for decisions on the part of the patrons? Will information about choices, ingredients and prices, be readily available or given only upon request? The rate of patrons passing the cashier's stand or completing their food selection may range from 5 to 15 per minute depending on the number of slowdown factors such as preparing or dishing up to order, asking questions, insufficient servers, awkward arrangement, and accidents. Arrival rate, speed of service and menu selection are factors that strongly influence the number of lines required.

Service space in hospitals depends on whether central, floor, or ward service is used. Food sent to the floors or wards may be in bulk quantity to be served in the pantry or may be set up on a central serving line and the pantries used for a few items such as beverages. A dietary department using the cook-chill system may set up cold trays in the central unit and pull plates for heating in the ward pantry. Modified diets may be handled in a special diet kitchen or may be handled on the central serving line. Whatever system is used, space must be allowed for bulk-food trucks, tray trucks, small-tray carts, or special dispensing units that are to be used.

Short-order units where food moves directly from production to the consumer require the least service space. Next to this are those restaurants or coffee shops in which servers go to points of production, such as grill section, salad section, and dessert section to pick up orders. Larger dining rooms may have a kitchen serving section and serving stations in the dining areas. The units requiring the most space are those furnishing elaborate or highly individualized production and service.

RECEIVING AND STORAGE AREAS

Receiving personnel will need at least space for a desk and perhaps a file at the receiving area. Other equipment may be needed. An office may be planned at the receiving point for use by receiving personnel. This should be equipped with proper file cabinets, computer, Internet services, fax, etc. The computer should be connected to the main computing system of the facility so information from receiving can be transferred over to other units needing it.

Space allocation for receiving and storage should be based on specific needs. Calculation of needs is to be based on the menu to be served; the temperature and humidity requirements of the items to be stored; availability, reliability, frequency, and cost of deliveries and/or the obtaining of supplies; and the largest volume for which provision must be made. Systems that have been recently introduced in the purchasing, processing, and handling of foods have changed storage needs. Short-period holding of processed foods has increased space requirements for refrigerated storage and reduced the space needs for common storage. Mobile storage units have been found to increase flexibility and increase utilization of storage space.

Suitable and adequate space is needed for the receiving and checking in of supplies as they are delivered. Truck-bed height for delivery platforms and roll-in level for refrigerator floors help greatly in the movement of supplies. Cases of 6/10 cans stacked 6 cases high on flat trucks will have a bearing weight of approximately 250 lb (113 kg) to 300 lb (136 kg) per sq ft (0.93 m^2). Where heavy items, such as 10-gal (38-liter) cans of milk, are stored, bearing weights may be increased. One case of 6/No. 10's, 24/No. 2½'s, or 24/No. 2's weighs approximately 51 lb (23 kg) and occupies 1 cu ft (0.028 m^3).

The storage area should be organized to promote quick location of items and convenience in handling. Where possible, items should be stored at points of first use and in a manner that facilitates inventory taking and prevents theft. Material handling is minimized when delivery personnel can put deliveries where they are to be checked in and stored. Convenience is the key for promoting this. Deliveries often arrive during busy hours of production. It is important that areas be so planned that delivery people and their loads will not get in the way of kitchen workers.

Common Storage

Items to be held in common storage are characterized by variety in size, use, and character. Major supplies usually include canned and bottled goods, cereals, pastes, sugars, flours, condiments and fats, soups, paper supplies, and laundry supplies (see Table 5–9). It is desirable for safety that soaps and other cleaning materials that may be injurious to health be stored in a separate area from food and equipment. Heavy items should be

TABLE 5–9 *Measurements of Representative Storage Items (for use in determining interspace, width, and linear space of shelving)*

Product	Package	Approximate Capacity wt./vol.	kg	Height in.	cm	Width of Diameter in.	cm	Length in.	cm
Refrigerated									
butter	box	64 lb	29	12	30	12	30	14	36
cheese	wheel	20–23 lb	9–10	7½	23	13½	34		
eggs	case	45 lb	20	13	33	12	30	26	66
milk, 10 gal	can	80 lb	36	25	64	13½	34		
½ pt	case	24/8 oz	227 g	10½	27	13	33	13	33
½ pt	case	24/8 oz	227 g	7	15	13	33	19	45
margarine	box	60 lb	27	10	25	14	36	17½	44
meat, portions	tray	40 lb	18	3	7.6	18	46	26	66
cuts	box	140 lb	63.5	6	15	18	46	28	71
cuts	box	50 lb	23	10	25.4	10	25.4	28	71
apples	box	35–40 lb	16–18	10½	27	11½	29	18	46
	carton	40–45 lb	18–20	12	30	12½	32	20	51
berries	crate	36 lb	16.3	11	28	11	28	22	56
cherries, grapes	lug	25–30 lb	11–14	6	15	13½	34	16	41
citrus	crate	65–80 lb	29–36	12	30	12	30	26	66
	carton	45–65 lb	18–29	11	28	11½	29	17	43
cabbage	crate	50–80 lb	23–36	13	35	18	46	22	56
cauliflower	crate	40 lb	18	9	23	18	46	22	56
celery	crate	55 lb	25	11	28	21	53	24	61
lettuce	crate	40–50 lb	18–23	14	36	19	48	20	51
	carton	40 lb	18	10	25.4	14	36	22	56
tomatoes	box	30 lb	13–14	7	18	13½	34	16	41
Frozen Food									
eggs or fruit	can	30 lb	13	12½	32	10	25.4		
fruit	carton	5 lb	2.3	3	7.6	8¼	22	12	30
fruit juice	case	12/30 oz	850 g	6	15	12	30	16½	42
ice cream, 2½ gal	carton	20 lb	9	10	25.4	9	23		
meat	carton	10 lb	4½	2½	6.4	9½	24	13½	49
vegetables	carton	2½ lb	1.13	2½	6.4	5	12.7	10	25
	case	12/2½ lb	1.14	10	25.4	10	25.4	16½	41
Dry Stores									
fruit and vegetable	No. 10 can	104 oz	3	7	15	6¼	15.9		
juice cans	No. 3 cyl	46–52 oz	1.3–1.5		15	4¼	10.8		
fruit can	No. 2½	28 oz	0.79	4¹¹⁄₁₆	11.9	4¹⁄₁₆	10.3		
fruit and vegetable	No. 2 can	20 oz	0.57	4⁹⁄₁₆	11.5	3⁷⁄₁₆	8.7		

positioned to reduce lifting and facilitate dispensing. Drums of liquids such as oil or vinegar should have spigots and be located on cradles or be equipped with pumps. Table surfaces and scales should be located for convenient issuing of dry stores. Plan to have all products 6–8 in. (15–20 cm) above the floor or movable to facilitate cleaning. Limit the height of top shelves for easy reach without the aid of stool or stepladder. The average vertical reach for men is 84.5 in. (2.15 m) and of women 81 in. (2.06 m). Use of the top shelf for light, bulky packages, such as cereal, is recommended.

The maximum stack height for cases that are handled without the aid of a motorized lift is 72 in. (1.83 m). Accessibility of items that differ in shape as well as volume will govern the number of stacks needed. A total of 3 cu ft (0.85 m³) per stack is estimated to

TABLE 5-9 *Continued*

Product	Package	Approximate Capacity		Height		Width of Diameter		Length	
		wt./vol.	kg	in.	cm	in.	cm	in.	cm
Dry Stores									
fruit, vegetable soup	No. 303 can	16 oz	0.45	6 6/16	11.1	3 3/16	8.1		
juice, pork and bacon	No. 1 tall	12 oz	0.34	4 11/16	11.9	3 1/16	7.8		
fruit, soup, vegetable	No. 1 picnic	10 oz	0.28	4	10.2	2 11/16	6.8		
fruit, vegetable, and specials	No. 8Z tall	8 oz	0.23	3¼	8.3	2 11/16	6.8		
canned foods	case 12/No. 3 cyl	46 oz	1.3	7½	19	12½	32	19	48
canned foods	case 6/10	104 oz	2.9	7½	19	12½	32	19	48
canned foods	case 24/No. 2	20 oz	0.57	9½	24	12	30	16½	42
canned foods	case 24/No. 2½	28½ oz	0.80	9½	24	12	30	16½	42
macaroni	box	20 lb	9.07	6	15	9	23	21½	55
lard	can	50 lb	22.7	15	38	12½	32		
oil, vinegar	glass jar	8 lb	3.63	8½–12	22–30	8½	16.5		
oil	5 gal can	40 lb	18	14	36	9½	24	9½	24
shortening	carton	50 lb	22.7	13	33	12½	32	12½	32
storage	garbage can	33 gal	125 L	26	66	20⅜	52		
	garbage can	20 gal	75.7 L	26	66	16	41		
sugar, flour, potatoes	sack	100 lb	45.4	8–11	20–28	18	46	33	84
soap, or other	barrell or drum	50 gal	189 L	34¾	88	22¾	56		
straws	carton	500 count		6	15	7	18	9½	23
paper towels	case	25 pkgs/110 count		15	38	18	46	21¾	55
fixture napkins	case	20 pkgs/500 count		15	38	19½	51	28	71
paper cups	carton	50 cups/16 oz		3¾	9.5	3¾	9.5	22	56
	carton	50 cups/5½ oz		3½	8.9	3½	8.9	21	53
	carton	50 cups/4 oz		3	7.6	3	7.6	19	48
portion cups	carton	250 cups/1 oz		1¾	4.4	3⅜	8.2	14¾	37
tumblers, glass	case 6 dz	9 oz	255 g	9¼	24.7	12½	32	13½	34
Linen									
aprons	laundry fold 4 only			1	2.5	9	23	14	36
tablecloths	laundry fold 4 yds			1	2.5	12½	32	18	46
table pads	laundry fold 4 yds			4	10	14	36	18	46
uniforms	laundry fold 1 only			1	2.5	11	28	18	46
waiter coat	laundry fold 1 only			1	2.5	10	25.4	15	38

include floor space covered by the case of canned food, plus a share of aisle space. One thousand cases piled eight high in 125 stacks will require 375 sq ft (34.9 m^2) or a storage area approximately 20 × 20 ft (6.1 by 6.1 m). Storage room aisles may be as narrow as 36 in. (91 m), but 42 to 48 in. (1 or 1.2 m) are preferred. Wider aisles may be required if motorized equipment is used. A 36-in. (0.91-m) skid on a hydraulic jack needs maneuvering room. If rolling bins or garbage cans on dollies are used for storage, plan the location for these. If cans or bins are under shelves, adjust the height of the bottom shelf to clear and allow for space for easy removal of food from the containers. Fixed shelving needs to be planned to accommodate sizes of items to be stored. Consider both interspace and depth suitable. Condiment bottles, cereal packages, and canned goods differ in package size and stacking quality. The depth of a shelf should accommodate either the width or length of the case, and the interspace should be adequate for the number to be stacked one on top of another. Allow 1.5 to 2 in. (3.8 to 5 cm) as free space for ease of positioning. Add thickness of shelving to interspace when stating measurements between centers.

Root Vegetable Storage

Root vegetables need cool, dark storage at 50 to 60°F (10 to 15°C) and a relative humidity of 85% to 90%. Allow for good ventilation by cross-stacking sacks on a floor pallet. A 100-lb (45-kg) bag of potatoes takes approximately 3 cu ft (0.085 m^3) of space, including aisle space. The bags should not be stacked higher than 6 ft (1.83 m). The method for ensuring good air circulation and the means of maintaining desired temperature in areas where there is likely to be injurious extremes in temperature are to be considered. Length of holding time for products held in ventilated storage should be considered also.

Refrigerated and Low-Temperature Storage

Many factors affect space needs for refrigerated and low-temperature foods. Specific menu offerings, volume, and required holding time are significant factors. The economics of deliveries in terms of frequency and cost may influence total amount to be stored. Small-volume operations are often required to receive supplies for a longer period for volume to offset the delivery costs. This tends to be true also when the operation is remote from the supply center. Financial aspects in preserving food quality and in avoiding unnecessary cost in construction and maintenance point to the wisdom of making careful calculation of needs for the specific operation. Across-the-board figures should be used for early estimates only.

Allocations used for convenience in preliminary planning may be as follows: 20% to 35% for meat (portion-ready meats require one-half to one-third less space than carcass or wholesale cuts); 30% to 35% for fruits and vegetables; 20% to 25% for dairy products, including those in serving areas; 10% to 25% for frozen foods; and 5% to 10% for carryover foods, salads, sandwich materials, and bakery products. A requirement of 15 to 20 cu ft (0.42 to 0.57 m^3) of refrigeration per 100 complete meals has been used also by some planners. Others state that 1 to 1.5 cu ft (0.03 to 0.04 m^3) of usable refrigerator space should be provided for every three meals served. Analysis of several successful installations showed approximately 0.25 to 0.50 cu ft (0.007 to 0.009 m^3) per meal served; additional low-temperature or refrigerated space in reach-ins was not calculated. In some climates, refrigerated space must be provided for dried fruits, nuts, cereals, and other foods to prevent weevil and insect infestation. It can be readily understood that the major use of frozen prepared meals will strongly affect requirements.

A walk-in refrigerator is feasible for an operation serving 300 to 400 meals per day, and refrigerated pass-throughs can be added when 400 to 500 meals are served per day. A walk-in 5 to 6 ft (1.5 to 1.8 m) wide does not permit storage on both sides with adequate aisle space. Storage space of 1.5 to 2 ft. (0.46 to 0.61 m) should be allowed on either side of the aisle. If crates or cases are stored, this may have to be wider. Walk-ins that are 8 to 9 ft (2.44 to 2.74 m) wide and 10 ft (3.05 m) long are minimum size. This allows for a storage area on each side 30 in. (0.76 m) wide and an aisle 3 to 4 ft (0.91 to 1.22 m) wide. If added width is desired for storage space in the center, allowance for storage area of 3 ft (0.91 m) and 42 in. (1.60 m) minimum aisle width may be provided. Walk-ins without aisles between shelves save space if shelves are on wheels and slide out easily. Large walk-ins may be designed for lift-truck operation, with doors opening from the receiving dock on one side and into the kitchen opposite. If this is done and lift trucks are used, space must be allowed in storage aisles for their working and turning. Doors should be a minimum of 42 in. (1.06 m) wide to permit large crates and containers or be sized to accommodate measurements of mobile equipment. Doors to low-temperature areas usually are planned to open into refrigerated areas to lessen temperature change. If this is not done a heating device may be needed on the door gaskets to prevent their freezing tight from condensation. About 12 to 15 sq ft (1.1 to 1.4 m^2) must be kept free for every door opening. About 45 lbs (20 kg) of frozen food, if stacked in cases, can be stored per cubic foot. About 30 to 35 lb (14 to 16 kg) of refrigerated food can be stored per cubic foot (or meter).

SANITATION AREAS

Dishwashing Area

Answers to the following questions will help guide space allocation. Will dishes be washed by hand or by machine? Will prerinsing be done by hand or by machine? If manually, will an overhead spray be used to rinse dishes in loaded baskets, or will a flush of water be used for scraping individual pieces? Will refuse be removed through a disposal unit? Will a soak-sink be used for dishes and silver? Are glass and silver washers to be used? What type of equipment will be used for moving washers to be used? What type of equipment will be used for moving and storing clean tableware? What storage will be provided for detergents, special cleaning equipment, and extra tableware? Figure 5.7 shows two popular sizes of dishwashers.

The cleaning of tableware calls for a soiled-dish table large enough to receive the volume of dishes likely to arrive at one time, without hazardous pileup. Space needs will also be affected by the manner in which the dishes arrive, whether in bus boxes, on carts, on trays, or by means of a traveling belt. The table must be spacious enough for scraping, stacking, and placing in baskets or on a machine conveyor or into a prerinsing operation. When everyone eats and leaves at one time, soiled dish space must be increased or mobile equipment can be used to carry the additional load. The number of workers who will be assigned to handle the dishes will affect space needs. The machine capacity and dimensions will be chosen in relation to the volume to be handled within a given time period. The dimensions may be only 30 to 36 in. (0.76 to 0.91 m) for a single tank

(a)

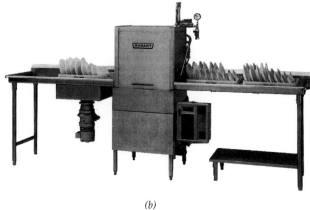

(b)

FIGURE 5.7   Two good single-tank dishwashing space savers are shown here. (a) A small dishwasher measuring overall 33¾″ × 23¹⁵⁄₁₆″ × 26¾″ overall, with a capacity of doing over 400 dishes per hour, 25 dishes per rack. (b) A larger dish machine capable of doing more than 1,000 dishes per hour. *(Courtesy of Hobart Corporation, Troy, Ohio.)*

machine, 60 to 72 in. (1.52 to 1.83 m) for sinks, or 7 to 30 ft (2.13 to 9.14 m) or more for a conveyor-type machine.

The clean-dish space, whether a part of the machine or the dishtable, should be large enough for dishes to stand and air-dry before stacking. The space for rack-type machines must be sufficient for at least four racks, a stack of trays, and three or four racks of dishes. For low-temperature dishwashing there should be space for six racks. In calculating total space, it is usually recommended that the clean-dish area occupy 60% and the soiled-dish table area 40% of the total dishtable space. More clean dry space is needed when low-temperature dish machines are used because it take the clean ware longer to dry.

Cups, glasses, and silverware need special treatment. It is convenient to have a shelf over the scraping table to hold baskets for cups and glasses that are to be put through the washer. The soak sink for silver may be a bus box filled with water or a mobile container that can be beside the scraper or rolled under the dishtable. A table surface is desirable for sorting, treating, or inspecting silver and other tableware. Where mobile storage equipment is used for dishes more space is needed in the dish room than where one cart is used for transporting to storage areas and is repeatedly loaded and unloaded. If a washer and drier is to be used for kitchen towels, space should be allowed in the dishroom for this equipment.

Pot and Pan Section

Provide a soiled utensil collection area adequate for the largest number that normally arrives in the section at one time. The busiest periods are likely to occur when preparation containers are emptied for service and immediately following service when service equipment is brought from the serving area. Equipment for scraping refuse from equipment will be needed. A disposal unit or a removable strainer over a drain and an overhead spray for rinsing may be used.

When allowing space for the pot and pan section, 40 sq ft (3.74 m^2) is generally regarded as a minimum for the smallest unit. The free work aisle between sinks and other equipment should be 4 ft (1.22 m) wide. The space allowance above the minimum will vary widely according to equipment used and the volume of pots and pans handled. Less space will be needed in relation to the maximum load where a mechanical washer is used, and fewer labor hours will be spent in handling a large volume per unit handled. There should be three sinks. The bottom of the potwashing sink and rinse sink should be at thumb tip level of an average-height worker, and the soak sink 6 in. lower.

Miscellaneous Sanitation Areas

Proper sanitation calls for the thorough washing of mobile equipment used in the preparation and service of food. The area should be one where splashing can be confined and where satisfactory drainage is provided. A hose supplying a flood of water with suitable force, a steam hose, and adequate ventilation are needed. The size and type of equipment to be handled govern space needs. Garbage cans washed in this area should have a rack for draining and storage.

A storage area for emergency cleanup equipment is needed in convenient relationship to dining area work sections. Spillage and breakage create unsightliness and are accident hazards. Immediate care usually does not require heavy or large equipment but may be handled by a small broom, dust pan, mop, and bucket not used for major cleaning. Thoughtful planning will help in locating small, inconspicuous cleanup closets near various areas for quick emergency cleanup.

Major cleaning equipment will depend on the floors, finishes, and furniture to be cleaned. Determine whether a power sweeper, scrubber, and waxer are to be used. Space may be required for storage of janitor supply carts and for miscellaneous replacement items, such as light bulbs. Provision will be needed for storing, emptying, cleaning, and filling mop trucks and for cleaning and air-drying wet mops.

EMPLOYEE FACILITIES

Facilities for employees may include locker and lounge area, toilets, showers, time-recording equipment, hand basins near work areas, and dining room. An employee entrance should be so located that the employees may go directly to the dressing rooms without passing through dining or production areas.

Locker and Lounge Area

Employee possessions should be protected in a suitably safe and sanitary condition while employees are at work. Whether individual lockers or common cupboard, sufficient space should be provided for personal clothing to hang without crowding and wrinkling. Individual parcel lockers should be provided for storage of purses and other valuables. The height of the space for clothing should permit the longest garments to hang straight without wrinkling. The depth from front to back should be a minimum of 20 in. (0.51 m).

Suitable size for an employee lounge depends largely on scheduling of workers, location, and rest period policies of individual establishments. Many operators discourage lounging in dressing rooms and recommend that the employees' dining area be used for rest breaks. Others having broken shifts in employee schedules favor an extra room for lounging. In all cases benches or chairs are to be provided on which workers may sit when changing clothes or shoes.

Toilets and Showers

The location of toilet facilities near work areas is preferable to a remote location in order to promote good health habits, lessen loss of labor time, and permit closer employee supervision. Separate facilities should be provided for men and women. They should be separated from food areas by a hallway or a double entrance. Supply one washbowl for every 8 or 10 workers, one toilet for every 12 to 15 workmen, and one urinal and one toilet stool for every 15 men. Toilet compartments measure approximately $3 \times 4.5 \times 5$ ft ($0.91 \times 1.37 \times 1.52$ m).

The type of employees, the climate, kind of work, and conditions of work will influence the need for shower facilities. Showers are appreciated and used by employees working in hot, humid kitchens. Food managers have regarded showers as essential in areas where there are likely to be inadequate bath facilities in the homes. Experience has demonstrated that they are little used in localities where the weather is cool most of the year, the work areas well ventilated, and workers drawn from an income group that has good facilities in their homes.

Time-Recording Equipment

Provide space for a recorder or time clock near and within view of management. Wall-hung card racks of sufficient capacity to accommodate the total number of workers, both full and part time, who are likely to be employed during an accounting period will be

needed. Space estimates may be based on a clock recorder approximately 18 in. wide ×
12.5 in. deep × 18 in. high (45.7 × 32 × 45.7 cm) and a rack for 50 cards approximately
1.5 × 2.5 × 34.5 in. (3.8 × 6.4 × 88 cm).

Employee Dining Area

Ascertain the largest number to be accommodated at one time and allow 12 sq ft (1.12
m^2) per person. The comfort and appearance of the employees' dining area may be an
important rest and employee-satisfaction factor.

General Considerations

The size of employee facilities has been found to vary widely. Small operations may
not supply lockers and may have only a toilet and lavatory for workers. Some do not
provide a separate dining room. Expediency in allowing ample space may be tempered by cost of space, available room, and acuteness of need. Total space may be increased where main toilet and locker rooms are remotely located and additional facilities are provided near work areas. It may be decreased where the food facility is a
part of a larger organization providing facilities for other workers, as in a hospital or
a hotel.

OFFICE SPACE

Space needs for an office depend largely on the number and type of activities that
are to be performed there, the number and type of equipment items to be used, and
the number of people who are likely to be there at one time. Will it be used for employee or purchasing conferences while another person is doing accounting? Will
table space be needed for assembling material or holding typewriters, calculators,
computers, or phones? Adequate space will be needed for files. The smallest office
inside an enclosure, to be occupied by one person only, should measure 6 × 8 ft (1.83
× 2.44 m). Ventilation will be of special concern in an area this small. If enclosed by
glass on at least two sides, it will give an impression of greater spaciousness. A space
96 sq ft (8.99 m^2) or, preferably, 108 sq ft (10 m^2) may be sufficient to accommodate
two people.

GUEST FACILITIES

Comfort and cordiality should characterize the entrance and waiting area for guests. The
size of the area should be based on probable need for waiting, type of service, and number of persons likely to congregate at one time. If there is a lounge or hallway adjacent
to the dining room, this may provide some waiting space.

Locate the public telephone, coat rack, and toilet facilities in convenient relationship to the waiting area. In college dining rooms provide ample space for books as well
as coats. In residences, a hallway approaching the dining room will lessen wear on the
lounge. Attractive benches or seats are recommended.

The approximate space needs given in Tables 5–10 are useful in making early estimates before more accurate figures have been obtained. They should be regarded as tentative, to be replaced by those gained through careful study and planning.

TABLE 5-10 Approximate Space Allocation Suggested for Preliminary Planning[a]

	Cafeteria			Lunch Counter			Restaurant			Hospital		
	Percent	sq ft	m²	Percent	sq ft	m²	Percent	sq ft	m²	Percent	sq ft	m²
Total space	*100*	*5700*	*529*	*100*	*2400*	*223*	*100*	*4800*	*446*	*100*	*5250*	*488*
Dining area	*40*	*2280*	*212*	*50*	*1200*	*111*	*50*	*2400*	*223*	*18*	*945*	*88*
Service and guest facilities	*21*	*1197*	*111*	*18*	*432*	*40*	*7.5*	*360*	*33*	*9*	*472*	*44[b]*
										20	*1050*	*96[c]*
Production	*18*	*1026*	*95*	*12*	*288*	*27*	*21*	*1008*	*94*	*22*	*1156*	*107*
Meat preparation and cooking		200	19					200	19		220	20
Bakeshop		200	19					200	19		200	19
Cold foods		106	10					120	11		132	12
Vegetable preparation		120	11					108	10		132	12
Traffic lanes and other		400	37					380	35		472	44
Storage areas	8	456	42	5	120	11	8	384	36	11.5	604	56
Receiving		56	5					48	5		56	5
Common-dry		240	22					192	18		316	29
Refrigerated		160	15					144	13		232	22
Cleaning areas	7	399	37	8	192	18	7.5	360	33	10	525	49
Dish and truck wash		230	21					216	20		315	29
Pot washing		60	6					60	5		80	7
Trash, can wash, and other		109	10								130	12
Employee areas	4	228	21	5	120	11	4	192	18	4.5	236	22
Toilets, lockers		108	10					84	8		116	11
Dining room		120	11					108	10		120	11
Office	2	114	11	2	48[d]	5	2	96	9	5	262	24

[a]Maximum meals per hour: cafeteria, 450; lunch counter, 250; restaurant, 320; hospital (175 beds central service). Seats in dining room: cafeteria, 200; lunch counter, 100; restaurant, 200; hospital—for staff. Note that totals are italicized.

[b]Personnel.

[c]Patients; the combined personnel and patient needs will give total space needs.

[d] A portion of another area may be used and not enclosed.

CHAPTER SUMMARY

A number of factors should be considered when allocating space in a foodservice plan. Information helpful in such allocations are

1. Volume and type of service
2. Equipment size, amount, and placement
3. Number of workers used
4. Supply and other storage space
5. Suitable traffic areas.

The need for future additional space should be investigated. Dining space can be as low as 10 sq ft per person for small children or crowded banquets and as high as 20 sq ft or more for deluxe restaurants, clubs, etc. For the ordinary dining room, 12 sq ft is a minimum. Counter space takes about 20 sq ft per seat.

Table sizes vary but for a table seating four about 42 to 28 sq ft is considered adequate. Cafeterias should fit their table size to the size needed to accommodate trays. The number of seats in a dining space times the square feet allocated per seat will give the *approximate* number that a dining room will hold. Vacancies at tables will reduce this number usually. The number that can be served in a given time depends on the number of seats, the vacancy rate, and the turnover rate per seat.

Production areas often take about one-third to one-half the space of the dining room they serve, but this should be looked on as a very rough guide in determining any space allocation. Rough guides also exist indicating production space needs per number of seats in the dining area. Worktable sizes, sink drain board space, and other such equipment sizes depend on the need for such space. Aisle space should be about 36 to 42 in. when a worker works alone, but 48 to 54 in. when more than one worker works in an area and there is passing. Main traffic lines should be at least 60 in. and more if large equipment will be moved through them. Traffic lanes may take up as much as 70% of the production space.

The most efficient food dispensing counter in a cafeteria will measure between 20 and 50 linear feet. A back bar, worker aisle space, counter width, tray slide, and patron space need a minimum of 14 ft. Storage space should be planned to hold the estimated amount of supplies or equipment to be stored there. Sufficient aisle space should be planned. If heavy equipment is to be moved in the area, such as might occur in a warehouse, the planner should provide sufficient space for movement and maneuvering of such equipment. A moderately large operation will require a common storage space at ordinary room temperature but with good ventilation; a root vegetable space providing dark storage and good ventilation at 50° to 60°F; a refrigeration space with adequate temperature and humidity controls; and a low-temperature space at 0° to −10°F or lower. Guides are available for allocating storage space for meats, fruits and vegetables, etc.

The space around dishwashers and accompanying equipment should be ample enough to permit worker passage while carrying loads and moving equipment in and out. Landing tables for soiled ware need to be planned to suit the loads carried. Similarly, the clean dish area should be roomy enough to allow trays of dishes coming from the machine to stand for a short time until they finish drying. The result is more sanitary dishes when such space is provided. The smallest size recommended for a pot and pan cleaning unit is 40 sq ft but for large units a much larger space is required. Calculate space needed based on end of the meal loads when the largest number of pots and pans arrive. Some large units will find it feasible to use a mechanical pot and pan washer.

Provide for an area to handle cleaning supplies and equipment for care of the dining area. Employee facilities such as lounges, toilets and showers, dressing rooms, and lockers should be provided. Time-recording equipment usually takes little space because it should be wall mounted and in hallways where employees pass on their way to work. Some units allow employees to eat in the dining area during off-hours. A small facility may provide an employee dining space in a corner of the kitchen, while one with more employees might have an employee dining area equipped with a service pantry. The space need will be decided by management and the number of employees.

Guest facilities should provide telephoning space, cloakrooms, toilets and other space where those who are to dine can wait, if necessary.

REVIEW QUESTIONS

1. Select three food facilities of different types (college, industrial, fast-food chain, school lunch, hospital, other) and find out for each:
   a. The number served at each meal (including personnel)
   b. The kind of meals served and the hours of service
   c. Amount of food fully prepared, amount used that has been preprocessed, and amount used that has been fully prepared commercially
   d. Seating capacity of the dining area.

2. For one of the facilities you chose in Question 1, find out the dimensions in square feet or meters in:
   a. Dining areas
   b. Kitchen areas
   c. Storage, both common and refrigerated
   d. Employee areas
   e. Guest facilities
   f. Office.

3. For one of the facilities you chose in Question 1, during a peak hour of service, find out how many were checked past the cashier and calculate the number served per hour.

4. Observe in a dishwashing area and evaluate whether there is a holdup of activity at any point during the peak period for dishes arriving from the dining area. Is it due to inadequate space or lack of employees?

5. Prepare an analysis of equipment needs based on a given system of operation, a timetable for equipment use, and a summary with equipment dimensions for floor plans.

6. A fast turnover coffee shop with a dining area of 40 ft × 50 ft is being planned with a 10-ft long counter holding 10 seats. It will have no food preparation because all prepared food will come from the kitchen. Approximately how many seated service seats can be planned from the remaining space? Here is the calculation:

   10 counter seats × 20 sq ft per seat = 200 sq ft needed for the counter
   40 ft × 50 ft = 2,000 sq ft
   2,000 sq ft − 200 sq ft = 1,800 sq ft available for seated service
   1,800 sq ft/12 sq ft per seat = 150 seats or
   1,800 sq ft/18 sq ft per seat = 120 seats

   Answer: Approximately 120 to 150 seats.

KEY WORDS AND CONCEPTS

average check
banquet seating allowance
cafeteria
counter length
lunch counter
Return on Investment (ROI)

school lunch
seating capacity
space allowances
table sizes
turnover (table turn)

CHAPTER

6

Checklist for Planning

Because of the numerous details involved in the planning of a food facility, it is easy to overlook significant items. Therefore, a checklist is helpful to guide thinking so as to cover all of the important items requiring attention. Some similarity exists as to functions in establishments producing and serving food, although the manner in which they are performed may differ. Of course, the requirements of a specific food facility must be taken into consideration when planning, but characteristics common to most food facilities give value to the following comprehensive list, which can then be tailored to a specific facility.

A PLANNING CHECKLIST

When planning a food facility it is a good idea to have a checklist which the planner can use to safeguard against omissions that might subtract from the overall operational value of the facility. The following list provides reminders to planners of things to include.

1. Preliminary Analysis
   a. Facility needed—type, patronage potential, probable income and source of funds, extent and characteristics of need.
   b. Probability of permanence—possibility for growth, likelihood of competition.
   c. Selection of planning committee—ownership, architect, food consultant.
   d. Financing—money available, probable expense, limitations, estimated income and expenses. Do feasibility study.
   e. Site selection—location, conditions of procurement, local codes or other legal restrictions.
   f. Availability of labor, materials, and utilities for operation.
   g. Trends that may affect success of operation—population changes, competition, traffic flow, authoritative regulations, food customs, or requirements.
2. General Considerations
   a. Character of the facility, number to be served, type of service, menu, serving hours, seating capacity, prices, theme and decor.

    b. Policies relating to standards—quality of materials and construction, safety, sanitation, lighting, appearance of the facility.

    c. Policies relating to standards for food and service—quality of food and service, selection, portion sizes, prices, hours of service, special purposes to be served (physical, social, educational, economic).

    d. Schedule of construction and completion—labor supply or bidding advantages, seasonal influence, specific needs.

    e. Budget allowances for building, plumbing, lighting, equipment, designing.

    f. Bidding and contracting procedures.

    g. Code requirements—zoning, fire, sanitation, plumbing, electrical, structural, and other.

    h. Building design and materials:

        Permanence and ease of alteration for future expansion.

        Type and harmony with structures nearby.

        Original cost and upkeep.

        Relations to functions—weight stresses, space allotment, work flow.

        Advantages—patron appeal, ease of maintenance, durability.

    i. Traffic needs—entrance and exit, parking, delivery, and trash removal.

    j. Landscaping.

3. Physical Plant and Utilities

    a. Gas—safety pilot, drainage, ventilation, venting, proper pipe size.

    b. Electricity—proper voltage, proper grounding, adequate and convenient outlets, well-located and adequate panel.

    c. Water—safe, right temperature and pressure, convenient supply in sections, adequate amount, degree of hardness.

    d. Steam—right pressure, right places in dishwashing, cooking, and cleaning sections, in hoods for fire prevention. Steam boiler compounds may require a separate boiler for steamer use.

    e. Plumbing—adequate waste lines, prevention of back siphonage, sufficient drop in lines from disposals that bypass grease traps, provisions for cleanout of grease traps, proper venting, well-placed drains.

    f. Ventilation—exhaust hoods over dishwashers, pot washers, coffee urns, cooking equipment, and steam tables; filters removable and of a size to pass through dishwasher; air change every two to five minutes in kitchen; air conditioning protected from excessive loss from ventilation; cleanout ducts and access panels provided.

    g. Lighting—right kind and amount for specific area needs, freedom from glare and sharp contrast, easy-to-change, clean lights and fixtures.

    h. Refrigeration—compressors, evaporative condensers, cooling tower. Can condensers be located to reduce load on working area ventilation?

4. Receiving and Storage

    a. Ventilated storage for temporary holding of perishable foods.

    b. Ventilated root storage.

    c. Proper sizing and facilities at receiving dock.

    d. Storage with proper temperature and humidity for refrigerated (meat, dairy, fruits, and vegetables) and frozen foods.

    e. Common or dry storage for staple supplies.

    f. Areas for cleaning supplies and equipment conveniently located.

    g. Space for equipment replacement and paper supplies appropriate in size and location.

    h. Linen supply storage.

    i. Valued storage separately locked off.

Items, facilities, and equipment to be checked:

Covered dock and receiving area properly sized to handle deliveries.

Garbage storage area.

Scales—mobile, floor level, table.

Conveyors—(convenient access) elevator, dumbwaiter, belt or gravity, chute.

Mobile equipment—hand truck, dollies, platform truck, hydraulic lift.

Storage equipment—pallets, barrel cradles, platforms or tables for sacks, bins or mobile containers, cans on dollies, shelving that is adjustable, fixed, or mobile.

Temperature and humidity indicators and controls in refrigerated areas.

Refrigerators with hard-surfaced floors and walls, self-defrosting, adequate drains, flush floors for walk-ins, escape provision for anyone locked in, easy opening of door for low-temperature compartment, well-lighted interiors, adequate insulation, rail tracks, wire baskets.

Adequate storage provided in sections for supplies and equipment (service, banquet, or processing sections).

Adequate insulation of walls and ceiling and plastic door straps.

5. Food Preparation
   a. Vegetable cleaning and preparation.
   b. Meat preparation.
   c. Cooking section.
   d. Bakeshop and dessert section.
   e. Salad and sandwich making or pantry section.
   f. Short-order and breakfast section.
   g. Catering unit supplying take-out foods, special diets, and party service.
   h. Fountain item preparation.
   i. Catering needs.

Items, facilities, and equipment to be checked:

Flow of processing in logical sequence.

Adequate aisle space.

Minimum of—distance traveled, outside traffic in work areas, material handling, fixed space for little-used equipment, backtracking and cross traffic, accident hazards.

Maximum utilization of equipment, space, labor time, and motion.

Use of transportation devices—vertical and other as required.

Adequate equipment in section to meet work requirements.

Adequate handwashing sinks to meet sanitation codes.

Vegetable Preparation

Rack for root vegetables	Vegetable cutter and attachment rack
Platform truck	Mobile storage containers, racks
Peeler	Mobile mixing bowls
Cleaning sink and drainboards	Work table with storage for small
Waste disposal	utensils
Knife rack	Wire baskets

Meat Preparation

Meat block	Slicer
Butcher's bench	Tenderizer
Chopper and grinder with tamper	Saw
Overhead conveyor	Sink and drainboard
Twine holder	Work table with drawer

Knife rack, tool rack
Molder or patty machine

Utility cart
Breading equipment
Mobile tables

Cooking Section

Ranges, griddle, broiler,
  salamander
Deep-fat fryer
Roast ovens
Steam kettles—water faucet and
  drains
Steam cookers and drains
Hood—lights and removable
  filters
Utility carts
Mixer
Pot rack and attachment storage
Slicer
Can opener
Scale
Fat filter

Knife rack
Cook's table with spice bins and small
  equipment drawer
Mobile or fixed bins
Sink and drainboard
Worktables
Electrical outlets for equipment
Fire extinguisher
Garbage cans on dollies
Utensil shelves
Hot food table, bain marie, or mobile
  hot food cabinet
Mobile dish storage, heated
Refrigeration and low-temperature
  storage

Short-Order, Fountain, and Breakfast Preparation

Griddle
Broiler
Egg cooker
Dish storage, regular, refrigerated,
  and heated
Refrigerator
Sink and drainboard
Worktable with cutting board
Frozen dessert cabinet
Ice cream storage
Oyster stewer
Waste disposal
Table mixer
Roll warmer
Slicer
Pastry cabinet
Hot plate
Hood—shelf type with removable
  filters
Soup warmer

Serving or pickup counter
Waffle irons
Coffee maker
Cream dispenser
Iced tea dispenser
Toaster
Butter dispenser
Beverage mixer
Carbonator and CO_2 tanks
Soft ice cream mixer
Ice bin
Equipment and tool storage and racks
Storage for glass and paper service
Dipper well with running water
Juice extractor
Malt dispenser
Fudge warmer
Glass washer
Cold pan
Mobile tables and carts

Garde Manager and Seafood

Serving counter
Cold pan
Ice bin
Slicer
Cold plate refrigerator
Dish storage

Sinks and drainboard
Waste disposal
Reach-in refrigerator
Utensil and tool storage
Seafood bar
Table and mobile carts

Banquet Kitchen

(Add facilities and equipment from Cooking Section, Salad and Sandwich Making, and Housekeeping and Sanitation Section as required. *See* Waitstaff and Bussing Facilities also.)

Service bar
Refrigerator salad storage
Tray storage, mobile or fixed
Hot food trucks
Hot food storage
Setup counters
Dish and glass storage
Roll warmer

Waste disposal or garbage facilities
Dumbwaiter or elevators
Linen storage
Mobile equipment
Ice cream storage and fountain supplies
Dessert storage
Banquet equipment storage
Can opener

Salad and Sandwich Making

Refrigerated storage with tray
    slides
Mobile storage containers
Mobile dish storage
Spice and dressing containers
Mixing bowls
Cutting boards
Food cutter

Mobile racks
Worktable with utensil drawer and tray
    shelves
Toaster
Electrical outlets for slicer, toaster,
    juicer, etc.
Can opener
Bread cabinet

Bakery

Baker's bench with spice bins and
    utensil drawer
Mobile bins
Worktables as required
Wooden tables for cutting and
    makeup
Scale
Mixers and storage for bowls and
    attachments
Bowl dolly
Mobile mixing bowls
Tilting steam kettle, water faucet,
    drain
Lighted oven
Hood with lights and easily
    removable filters
Electrical outlets for mixer, roller,
    proof box, scale, warmers, etc.
Marble-top table

Batch warmer
Can opener
Dough divider and rounder
Molder
Dough roller
Dough trough
Proof box with humidifier
Sinks and drainboard
Refrigerator and low-temperature
    storage
Dough retarder
Mobile racks and storage shelves
Power sifter
Doughnut machine and fryer
Mobile dish storage
Utility carts
Landing racks, mobile
Pastry stove
Bread slicer

If ice cream is made:

Ice cream freezer
Hardening cabinet
Storage cabinet
Work table
Sinks and drainboard
Mixer

Scale
Refrigerator
Supply cabinet
Stove
Steam kettle
Special equipment and its storage

6. Housekeeping and Sanitation
    a. Soiled dish collection, transportation, and washing.
    b. Dish, glass, and silver handling, storage and dispensing.
    c. Pot and pan washing and storage.
    d. Garbage disposal, can washing, and storage.
    e. Mop truck filling, emptying, cleaning, and storage.
    f. Mop cleaning and drying.
    g. Storage space for catering equipment, such as folding chairs, flower containers,
        and special tables.

Items, facilities, and equipment to be checked:

Quiet, inconspicuous soiled dish disposal.

Clean, neat, attractive uniforms and linens.

Provision made for sanitary cleansing and handling of facilities and equipment.

Design and materials—easily cleanable, durable, and proofed against insects and vermin.

Food and equipment protected from contamination.

Adequate, well-kept equipment and facilities.

Adequate handwashing sinks to meet sanitation code.

Dishwashing

Collection area, busing port, or conveyor for soiled dishes

Soiled-dish table with scrap block, waste disposal or pulper, sorting space, and storage space for cups, glasses, silver

Dishwasher with detergent dispenser and rinse injector, water softener, booster heater, hood, hose for cleaning, and rack return

Silver washer and dryer, dip sink, burnisher

Locked storage for valuable silver

Clean dish table or machine extension

Sink for glass washing or glass washer and table

Adequate light

Mobile storage, glasses, cups, etc.

Cart space

Storage for detergents and other cleaning materials

Splash guards on rack-type machines

Detarnishing sink

Pot and Pan Washing

Pot washer or pot sink (three compartments) tables, overhead spray

Waste disposal

Pot storage, fixed or mobile

Pot scrubber

Mobile soiled and clean pot table

Garbage Disposal and General Cleaning

Garbage cans or waste disposal

Garbage disposal area, refrigerated

Janitor's closet

Hot water and steam hose

Detergent and supply storage

Kitchen lavatories, waste container, soap and towel dispenser

Adequate storage area

Can washer

Garbage can storage

Well-placed floor drains

Mop truck and facility for filling, emptying, cleaning, and storage

Mop sink

Drying rack for mops

Recycling containers

Can crusher

Baler

Linens

Towel washer and drier

Soiled linen hampers and bags

Sorting table

Linen storage: uniforms, aprons, towels, table linens

Banquet and Catering Equipment

(Storage facilities for banquet equipment, tables, chairs, serving equipment, etc.)

7. Display and Service of Food
   a. Dining area with adequate, comfortable seating.
   b. Storage facilities with appropriate temperature control and sanitation protection with provision for display as needed.

c. Provision for necessary beverage and water supply.
d. Storage for dishes and serving equipment and supplies.
e. Properly placed checker's and cashier's stations.
f. Menus or menu boards.
g. Adequate handwashing sinks to meet sanitation codes.

Items, facilities, and equipment to be checked:

Inviting, attractive, and comfortable dining and service areas.

Facilities to preserve quality and sanitation of food.

Provisions for quick, quiet, appealing service.

Adequate lobby or waiting area.

Good intercommunicating system.

Dining Areas

Tables, chairs, booths, settees,
   benches
Waitstaff service stands,
   counters, wagons
Bus stands or tray stands
Dish conveyors to soiled-dish
   area, carts, dollies, belt
   conveyors, subveyors
Counters, service, cafeteria,
   cashier, retail sales, cigar,
   candy, gift

Cash register
Rugs
Adequate lighting
Clean, comfortable air
Water and ice supplies
Condiment and linen supplies
Silver, glasses, dishes available

Coffee Shop or Fountain Luncheonette

Counter, stools, benches,
   booths
Cream dispenser
Soft drink dispenser
Carbonator and CO_2 tanks
Refrigeration
Back counters
Milk dispenser
Juice dispenser and extractor
Iced tea dispenser
Butter dispenser
Soup warmer
Syrup heater
Malt dispenser
Ice bin
Drink mixer
Sinks and work areas
Waste disposal
Counter dish and glass washer
Fudge warmer
Toaster

Toast and bread unit
Hot food table
Sandwich unit
Coffee maker and warmer
Water station
Broiler
Griddle
Grill
Deep fryer
Hot plate
Hood
Egg boiler
Waffle baker
Roll warmer
Pastry and salad display cases
Ice cream cabinet
Disher well
Dish conveyor, cart, belt, etc.
Soft ice cream machine
Hot chocolate dispenser

Cafeteria, Canteen, or Buffet

Serving counter
Coffee-making equipment
Cream, milk, iced tea dispensers
Ice bin

Guard rail
Back counters
Short order counter
Grill and griddle

Mobile dish storage equipment	Broiler
Ice cream cabinet	Hot plate
Disher well	Menus and menu board
Water cooler and fountains	Vending machines
Canteen carts	Juice extractor and dispenser
Napkin, silver dispensers	Hot chocolate dispenser
Roll warmer	Tray slide and guard rail or call window

Bar, Service or Public

Workboards	Linen storage
Sinks	Supply storage
Ice bins	Drink mixer
Bottle cooler	Blender
Beer dispenser	Refrigerator
Glass and dish storage	Back or center bar
Stools, booths, tables, and chairs	Portable bars

Room Service

Portable tables	Toasters
Portable heaters	Supply cabinet
Refrigerator	Water and ice
Setup area	Phone
Linen and other storage area	Desk
Dish, covers, and other storage	File

Waitstaff and Bussing Facilities

Tray stands	Setup tables
Water stations	Serving wagons
Ice bins	Pastry cart
Water bottle storage	Garnish sink
Wait staff stations	Linen, silver, and other storage

8. Guest Facilities
   a. Entrance inviting and convenient.
   b. Comfortable waiting area, attractive chairs or benches, ashtrays, cigarette vending, phone.
   c. Coat and hat racks or checkrooms, parcel and umbrella storage.
   d. Toilet facilities, conveniently located, clean, attractive, adequate.
   e. Dining room, good traffic flow, cheerful, attractive, well-lighted, comfortable.
   f. Telephone affording reasonable privacy.
9. Employee Facilities
   a. Convenient entrance.
   b. Toilet, locker, and dressing room space equipped with:

coat cabinets	handwashing sinks	mirror
lockers	soap dispenser	chair or bench
toilets	towel dispenser	
urinals	waste container	

   c. Kitchen lavatories, soap dispensers, towel dispensers, paper cup dispensers, fountains, waste containers.
   d. Time clock and card rack.
   e. Bulletin board.
   f. Dining room.
   g. Clock.
   h. First-aid supplies.

10. Management and Supervisory Facilities
    a. Privacy for conferences and business.
    b. Freedom from unnecessary distraction.
    c. Safety of money, files, and records.
    d. View for supervision of operations, control of supplies, food processing, and service.
    e. Suitably equipped for work.
    f. Control panel for lights and utilities.
    g. Sound equipment control.

Items, facilities, and equipment to be checked:

Desk, table, and chairs.

Computer and printer.

Copy machine.

Fax machine.

Files—recipe, inventory, letter.

Machines—typewriter, calculator, adding machine, telephone.

Books—accounting, recipe, policies and procedures.

Cabinets for coats and supplies.

Safe.

Private toilet and dressing room.

Wastebaskets.

First-aid Supplies.

REVIEW QUESTIONS

1. Identify materials used for:
   a. Hood over cooking equipment.
   b. Floor and walls.
   c. Workables and bins.
   d. Refrigerator shelving, storeroom shelving, dish bins, or shelving.
   e. Pots, pans, and tableware.
2. List locations of the following:
   a. Electrical outlets for equipment.
   b. Water sources for work sections.
   c. Scales; state model and use.
   d. Bins for food; state whether mobile or stationary.
3. List all items of equipment in:
   a. Serving area.
   b. Dishwashing area.
   c. Office.
   d. Personnel facilities.
4. Trace path of food from receiving to service in terms of sanitary handling methods. List points where there is:
   a. Satisfactory protection.
   b. Possibility of contamination.
5. What methods used or conditions exist that:
   a. Promote good standards.
   b. Cause poor results.

CHAPTER

7

Receiving and Storage

A well-planned and executed receiving and storage system must exist to see that goods received are properly accounted and cared for. Loss and/or misunderstanding can arise at a number of points. A number of people are normally involved in the placing, taking, and filling of orders and receiving of goods. Many of the items are subject to deterioration and misappropriation. Lack of organization can lead to loss of labor time in hunting for items.

An adequate system for protection of goods extends from the time material is ordered until it has been used. The record of an order should give date, company from which ordered, amount ordered, description or specification of goods, price, and time when delivery is promised. The deliveries should be received and examined by an authorized person, who should direct where the supplies are to be placed. Materials hastily delivered and signed for by any person who happens to be handy can lead to loss of both material and worker time. Materials should be placed for best convenience for use and most satisfactory protection while stored. An inventory should be maintained that reflects all issues for use, and amount in stock.

RECEIVING

The **receiving** of goods involves examination to ascertain that the amount and kind ordered and charged for are delivered. Rectifying errors can be done most easily while the deliveryperson is present to acknowledge the error and return unacceptable material to the company. The space allowed for receiving should be sufficient for the volume and type of merchandise normally delivered and required to occupy the area until examination has been completed. The kind of examination of many of the bulky shipments of packaged goods allows them to be placed directly in storage under the supervision of the receiving clerk. Many items require minimal inspection and merely call for package, label, and count. Others, such as meat cuts, may call for opening packages to inspect quality, sizing of cuts, count, temperature, and weight. Time and money can be saved by providing facilities that will require a minimum of rehandling and permit direct transfer to points of use or storage. The use of mobile equipment or the use of conveyors facilitates such a goal. Many deliveries are heavy and bulky and should require a minimum of movement. The material flow from receiving to storage and then

FIGURE 7.1   An unloading dock at proper height for truck deliveries. Note antipest fans over receiving doors, portable platform scales conveniently placed, and reflector-type lights providing good illumination. *(Courtesy of Sky Chef, Los Angeles.)*

to processing should be as short as possible and cause a minimum of interruption of work in sections.

Locate the receiving area where it will be convenient for the delivery of supplies, and where the arriving material is close to storage or points of use. The delivery point is usually a "back door" area with space for trucks and other delivery equipment. Small units may have only a desk located here, but a larger unit may have an office for handling receiving matters. These places should be located so as to have a clear, unobstructed view of the entire receiving dock. Scales and other equipment will also be available. Figure 7.1 shows a well-planned delivery or **receiving dock.**

The size of the receiving area for a specific food facility is influenced by the nature and volume of materials received and going out at any one time. Some may be measured in terms of a hand truck and others in terms of a carload of merchandise. Satellite units receiving hot food in heated trucks or serving carts need space for the carts and perhaps electrical outlets for maintaining desired temperatures. **Pallet delivery** of quantities requiring the use of a fork truck need space for essential maneuvering of the truck. A stairway from the ground to the receiving dock level should be provided. Immediate removal of supplies from the delivery carton calls for space for refuse.

Floor bearing weight should be studied and given adequate support to hold heavy loads. In addition to the weight of the merchandise, it is necessary to include the stress of carts, fork trucks, and other transportation equipment. Provide a floor that can be easily scrubbed and rinsed, and has adequate drains. A hose connection will be needed, and it is best to provide storage for cleaning supplies near this area.

Movement of shipments from truck to **receiving dock** requires that the dock be close to the same height as the truck body. A problem is presented by heavy van trucks having a higher body than the smaller light delivery trucks. In order that both may use the same dock, the dock can be built for the heavier units and a movable platform provided that can be put in place before the lighter unit backs up, thus raising it to the proper height. Where deliveries are substantial, adding an adjustable platform that raises or lowers to meet the proper level of the truck is possible. Ordinarily, facilities will find that a **delivery dock** 2.5 to 3 ft (0.76 to 0.91 m) and 9 ft (2.44 m) deep is adequate, with the length varying as needed. Door openings should be large enough to allow free passage of supplies and equipment; 3.5 and 5 ft (1.07 and 1.2 m), respectively, are usually considered standard for single and double doors, but this may vary according to needs. Doors should be self-closing. Supplies may be moved into the facility by means

FIGURE 7.2 A scale that quickly and accurately weighs items and can do required calculations automatically is a big help in good storage management. *(Courtesy of Hobart Corporation, Troy, Ohio.)*

of gravity slides, conveyors, elevators, motor-moved skids or platforms, platform trucks, dollies, hand trucks, and various carts.

Equipment in the receiving area should include an inspection table, scales, and container-opening tools, such as a crow bar, claw hammer, short-bladed sharp knife, and can opener. There must be space, place, and equipment also for record keeping. Accurate scales of appropriate size are essential. Freight scales level with the floor are recommended for large operations and smaller portable scales for small quantities and for weighing individual packages. Scales are available that can stamp the weight, date, and time and thus provide a useful record (see Figure 7.2). With proper programming, this information can be automatically transferred into a computer. Locate scales in proper lines of flow from receiving to storage or direct delivery.

STORAGE

The organization of **storage** should promote securing products for use with a minimum of motion and search and should provide protection and preservation in keeping with the specific needs of the various items. Motion and search are minimized when products are stored at the point of first use. The location in storage calls for consideration of various factors, such as volume and nature of the products, frequency of use, as well as their degree of fragility or perishability. The volume used, the frequency of deliveries, and the size and economics of the establishment have to be considered.

Maintaining compactness for work efficiency in work sections tends to limit available space for supply storage, especially if items are bulky. The convenience in handling, however, merits evaluating the amount of storage possible with minimum work interference, with consideration of splitting the shipments received. In some units, the money for space and equipment may prohibit proliferation of refrigerators or other storage compartments. Institutions that use a large volume may be able through frequent deliveries to lessen amounts carried in stock. Operations that require only a small volume and those located a considerable distance from supply centers may find it necessary to buy in sufficient quantity to support delivery costs. The cost for man-hours and the time that can be saved by having supplies at hand for work have sufficient economic value to merit storing at point of first use whenever possible.

When planning storage, differentiate between **local** (unit) and **central** (distant) **storage** needs. If space is provided at the local work unit, many supplies can be delivered and held directly there, saving time and labor. Central storage should be provided for items to be held for longer periods or that are sizable in bulk. Policies of management should be ascertained before allowing larger holding areas in local units than those required for use in a short time, such as a day's use. It may not be desirable to have a lot of items stored in units in terms of safety against misappropriation and compactness of the work center. Management may prefer to have items stored in a central unit where there is better accountability and control.

The nature of the different products and their specific holding requirements will cause storage needs to vary. The storage needs for the different forms of potatoes serve as an example. They may be purchased as field potatoes in 100-lb sacks, as processed potatoes ready for cooking, as dehydrated potatoes ready for whipping, and as frozen precooked supplies that are to be thawed, reheated, and served. Storage requirements will vary from cool, dark space, to common and frozen storage.

The type of establishment will have an influence on storage needs. Short-order houses offering a limited menu will have different needs than an institution providing complete menus and several choices. The service of vegetables has been eliminated from many menus in specialty restaurants, except for the simplest salads, such as sliced tomatoes, cole slaw, and tossed lettuce. School, college, military, and industrial food units responsible for full nutrition of the diners use large quantities of fresh, frozen, and canned fruit and vegetables. Where ample space is available without a great deal of extra expense, managers of large establishments have sometimes found it advantageous to purchase in large quantities at "harvest prices" and store the merchandise until needed.

The storage space in work areas should be provided in a quantity and manner that will not interfere with efficient compactness of the area. It is sometimes necessary to work out a compromise between unit and central storage, with provision for daily storage only in the work section. When this is done, handling is facilitated if space is allowed for moving the supplies from one location to the other in a cart. Easy movement of the carts requires level floors and door size and compartment space large enough to admit the carts. Similar requirements exist where large quantities of convenience foods or precooked meals are moved to storage and then to units for final processing. Moving and storage in cart quantities will reduce handling time and costs. Adequate protection includes protection against theft as well as providing proper temperature and humidity. Lockable carts are available for small-quantity unit stores, as well as built-in cabinets.

Central storage areas should be equipped with a scale of appropriate capacity for issuing supplies. There should be a table or ledge on which to write a record of supplies coming in or being issued. Equip all storage areas with an inside release and/or signal system to prevent any person being locked in. Install thermometers at points where they will be easy to check. Design areas for easy, thorough cleaning and sufficient air circulation to prevent stagnant off-odors and to allow ventilation and even refrigeration in the refrigerated areas.

Allowance of appropriate space and the location of supplies for storage will be affected by the plan or system of operation. This point can be readily appreciated through consideration of the needs in an operation that fully prepares bakery products versus one that purchases them ready-made, or one that supplies short-order meals versus full menu offerings, and those that have a full production kitchen versus commercially produced, precooked, frozen meals. The organization of work will influence storage space requirements also. Where stores are all issued from a central area, weighed correctly for use in specific recipes, and supplies allotted for daily needs, space and facilities will need to be provided in the storage area for this aspect of production. Where this is done the storage space may be reduced in the work areas.

TYPES OF STORAGE

The location of storage areas should be determined in relation to those sections that depend on them for space or supplies. Different types of storage may be classified in terms of location as central or unit; in terms of temperature such as common, ventilated, or refrigerated; or in terms of use such as baker's pantry, or cleaning supplies.

1. General Dry Storage
   a. **Staple food supplies.**
   b. **Nonfood supplies** used in connection with food service such as paper supplies.
   c. **Cleaning supplies and equipment.**
   d. **Linen.**
   e. **Baker's supplies.**
   f. Trash and recyclable storage.
   g. **Equipment storage,** such as dining room chairs, tables, program equipment, flower vases, tableware, equipment supplies, and light bulbs.
2. Ventilated Common Storage
   Used for short-period holding of fruits, vegetables, and some cooking fats.
3. Refrigerated and Low-Temperature Storage
   a. Dairy.
   b. Meat, fish, and poultry.
   c. Fruits and vegetables.
   d. Frozen foods.
   e. Garbage in certain institutions and in hot areas.

General Dry Storage

Factors to remember when locating the **general dry storage** area include cost of labor time of employees coming from different units to procure supplies; easy movement of heavy products by cart to areas of the kitchen; good ventilation; security; and reasonably easy maintenance of 60 to 70°F (15.5 to 21.1°C) temperature. Although a temperature of 70°F (21°C) is generally considered acceptable the lower temperature of 60°F (15.5°C) can often be maintained by locating the area where it will not get heat from the sun, heating equipment, or from transmission by heated areas. Insulation of hot pipes that must pass through the area will help in holding the proper temperature. Dry storage areas should not go over 100°F (37.4°C).

Protect the products in storage. Many of the products normally kept in the general storage area can be damaged quickly by excess moisture, which may come from sweating walls, dripping pipes, or subsoil dampness. Keep all products off the floor and away from walls that are not impervious to moisture. Screen against insects and vermin. If any vermin are discovered, use effective extermination means immediately before either insects or vermin have a chance to multiply. See Table 3–3, Control of Disease-Carrying Pests. Even areas in which the best housekeeping practices are followed can become infested by pests riding into the establishment on food and clean laundry packages.

Satisfactory housekeeping calls for all materials to be stored off the floor at least 6 in. (15 cm) in or on mobile containers or on floor racks. Hydraulic packs may be provided to move bulky supplies on **skids** or **slatted racks** 8 to 12 in. (20 to 30 cm) high. Clearly labeled metal or plastic containers on wheels or **dollies** provide useful storage for loose bulk items, such as rice, beans, milk solids, and sugars. Rolling bins, interchangeable with those used in work sections, such as those for the cook and baker, save extra handling.

Provide suitable clearance for movement of materials and utilization of space. Shelving over mobile bins must provide for overall bin height and sufficient space for lifting the lid and removal of products. The space allowance may be least when the bin can be moved forward and the lid slid back. Having a place for the lid (as with a garbage can type of lid) presents a problem when it is removed for getting material from the container.

Adjustable shelving is desirable to allow for spacing and because it is vermin proof. It should be sturdy enough to support loads without sagging or collapsing. Locate shelving at least 2 in. (5 cm) from walls. If the size and shape of the room will permit, arrange so that shelving is accessible from both sides. Consider both interspace and depth suitable for a given number and types and sizes of packages likely to be stored on either the fixed or movable shelves (see Figures 7.3 and 7.4). Condiment bottles, cereal packages, and canned goods due to difference in size and shape require different al-

FIGURE 7.3   A sturdy dunnage rack that may be stationary or on casters, and wire shelving that may be erected as needed. *(Courtesy of InterMetro Industries Corp., Wilkes-Barre, PA)*

lowances. Store in standard lots, such as number in a case, to facilitate inventory. The shelf width should fit either the width or length of the case and the interspace should be adequate for the number of cans or cases to be stacked on top of one another. Allow 1.5 to 2 in. (3 to 5 cm) excess in an interspace for ease in positioning and removing packages.

Safety and sanitation call for cleanable surfaces, prevention of tumbling of heavy stacks and collapsing of shelves, plus elimination of hazardous climbing on ladders, stools, or boxes, and excess lifting. Position heavy items so as to reduce lifting and facilitate dispensing. Drums of oil and vinegar or cleaning supplies should be equipped with pumps or located on cradles and have spigots. Limit the height of top shelves to 6 ft (1.8 m) for easy reach without the aid of a stool or stepladder. The average vertical reach of men is 84.5 in. (21.5 cm) and of women 81 in. (20.6 cm). Use the top shelf for light, bulky packages, such as cereals, or items used infrequently. Issuing of many bulk items, such as beans and rice, requires weighing. A table and scales should be positioned conveniently for this purpose.

Equipment and Tools.

A box opener is needed to lift tops and pull out nails, and a box cutter for corrugated board cartons. Suitable carts and hand trucks facilitate moving supplies. Vermin-proof storage containers on casters or dollies are desirable for moving when issuing supplies or cleaning floors. Tools commonly needed include a crowbar for opening large heavy crates, pliers, hammer, screwdriver, and spindle or clip board for orders and delivery slips. Scale capacity for receiving and issuing products from the largest to the smallest items normally handled will be needed, plus grocery type, aluminum or plastic scoops for such dry products as beans and rice. Supply a sturdy step

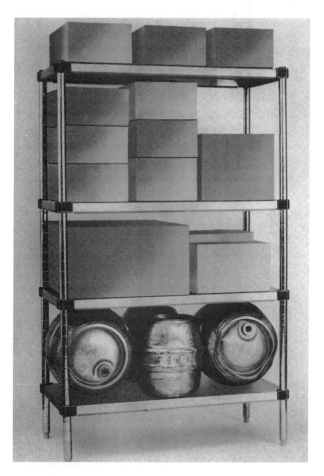

FIGURE 7.4 Storage shelving spaced in 2-in. (3-cm) intervals to accommodate different size packages. *(Courtesy of InterMetro Industries Corp., Wilkes-Barre, PA)*

stool or ladder as needed. A sturdy worktable should be provided with or near scales and packaging materials to handle bulk supplies.

Nonfood Supplies.

Paper supplies, cleaning equipment, equipment parts, and replacement supplies may be located together or separately, according to use, volume handled, and flow of traffic. Some storage may be provided in work sections. The bulkiness of paper supplies requires auxiliary storage to protect compactness in the serving area. It is desirable to have sufficient space in the work section to provide supplies through the peak periods or until a break in service permits replenishing.

Cleaning Supplies and Equipment.

Certain of the cleaning materials are toxic and corrosive. It is important for safety that these be stored away from food and equipment storage and clearly marked to eliminate possible error of their being used in food. It is desirable that they be stored close to cleaning areas, such as a dishwashing room or janitor's area. Janitor areas should have racks or wall pegs for hanging brooms and mops. Mops used where there is greasy soil should not be used in other areas. Shelves are needed for sundry supplies and inverted buckets. Good light and ventilation are important. Janitor's closets should have hard-surfaced walls and nonslip floors.

Linen and/or Laundry Room.

The space allowed will be influenced by the policies of the operation related to owning, laundering, or using services of a supply laundry. If the institution owns and launders the linens, it will require laundry, mending and pressing equipment, and space for the entire stock. Rotation of supplies with a supply laundry tends to reduce the total stock stored at one time. Some institutions find it desirable to have a domestic washer and drier for kitchen towels. The unit should be installed near the linen storage.

Linen storage should include shelving for linens, rods for hanging uniforms, and a counter for sorting and counting material to be sent out or received. Allow sufficient shelf space for storing uniforms according to size and other material according to size, type, and use. The type of fold given linens will govern size needed. If napkins are stored flat and not folded, the space would be wide and deep enough to hold them. The size of tablecloths and their fold will affect space requirements. Provide metal tab holders for listing item and size. A shelf, table height, and projection 12 to 18 in. (30.5 to 45.7 cm) beyond the other shelves, may be used for packages while shelves are being filled. A cart or mobile table may be used instead, if space permits. Aisle space between shelving should be 42 to 48 in. (109 to 122 cm) wide. Have a table area where packages of clean linens may be opened and checked and where soiled linens may be sorted and counted.

Provide for collection of soiled linens. Mobile carts on which open bags or hampers can be hung are useful for soiled linen collection. Server stations may have nonabsorbent containers for soiled table linen or washable laundry bags placed near the deposit area for soiled dishes or in passageways through which servers pass. Good ventilation is required, and frequent removal of these linens is desirable. Wet linen may sour or mildew quickly, and it is a good idea to provide a drying rack for it.

Garbage and Recyclable Storage.

The garbage and recyclable collection area should be located for easy pickup. Refrigeration is sometimes required. Good ventilation is important. Allow adequate space for trash as well as empty crates, plus boxes or other containers that are to be returned. The garbage and recyclable can cleaning area should be close to the collection and holding area. Provide a steam hose and/or can washer and a rack for can drainage and storage. A pipe platform over which cans can be inverted has been found to be satisfactory for this purpose. Provide sufficient space for the full complement of cans and for carts that are to be washed in the area. Provide hard-surfaced, moisture-proof strong walls and floors. Truck movement of heavy containers requires steel jambs on doors and shields or bumpers on doors and walls.

Equipment Storage. Multipurpose use of rooms, such as school lunchrooms or hotel banquet areas, requires the repeated moving of tables and chairs. Labor savings and the protection of these furnishings will depend on suitable methods of handling and storage. Stackable units and appropriate trucks or dollies for moving can save both labor and equipment. Adjacent cabinets or storerooms lessen moving time and should be included in the original planning. Under-stage storage may be used for folding chairs on low dollies (see Figure 7.5).

Equipment storage is needed for new, surplus, or replacement equipment, and that which is infrequently used but required for special purposes. This storage may be centrally located or separated into use areas. Where it is kept together, it is smart to locate it near the point of most frequent use, such as catering. Folding tables and chairs represent the largest volume generally found in such storage. Platform trucks or special dollies greatly facilitate movement and handling of these. It is customary for establishments to have a reserve supply of china, glassware, flatware, and other table appointments regularly used in quantities equal to approximately 10% to 20% of that required for current use. It is suggested that establishments with a limited need for flower arranging provide for this is in the vegetable preparation section where sinks, knives and carts are available for such work. Storage of vases, frogs, tools, and decorations may be located where they will be convenient to the area where used. In large facilities using many flowers, a separate area may be provided with storage, sink, and work area.

Special, lockable storage is required in facilities that handle costly items and those highly susceptible to theft, such as candy, cigarettes, and alcoholic beverages. Wine storage needs special shelving to keep corks moist.

Ventilated Common Storage

Satisfactory use of a **ventilated common storage** area, which does not have mechanical means of heating or refrigeration, depends on current weather conditions. Extremes in temperature for several months of the year will limit this type of storage to the short period between delivery and preparation for other storage. Foods that may be held for two or three days at temperatures ranging from 50 to 60°F (10 to 15.6°C) include under-ripe avocados, bananas, grapefruit, lemons, limes, melons, cucumbers, eggplant, potatoes, squash, and firm tomatoes. A temperature of 65 to 75°F (18.3 to 24°C) is suitable for ripening rooms for bananas, avocados, tomatoes, pears, apples, and similar items. Potatoes should be stored at 50°F (10°C) if they are to be used soon, otherwise at 40°F (4.4°C) or below, and removed three weeks before use into 50°F (10°C) storage to allow sugars to develop into starch. See Table 3–1.

FIGURE 7.5 Under-stage storage for chairs in a multipurpose room. *(Courtesy of Haywood Union High School District, Hayward, California.)*

Refrigerated and Low-Temperature Storage

Modern food facilities show marked changes from a decade ago in their use of **refrigerated** and **low-temperature storage.** Many of the changes have been occasioned by the processing and/or use of precooked meal items (convenience or value-added foods). Commissary or central kitchen units are more common where foods are processed and sent to satellite units for service. These foods may be refrigerated for a short interim holding or frozen for longer holding or farther shipment. Blast freezers which provide fast freezing are needed by processing kitchens where initial freezing is done.

Good quality in frozen foods requires (1) understanding the characteristics of the specific food item, (2) fast-freezing and storage at low temperature, (3) packaging to shut out air and protect the product, and (4) maintenance of uniform temperature. Quality loss speeds up approximately five times for every 5 to 10° rise in temperature from 0 to 30°F (-18 to -1°C). Very few products are improved by freezing. Quantity needs should be carefully calculated so that frozen foods have a rapid turnover while their quality is at its best. This will help also in preventing excessive installation expense for larger space and heavier refrigeration equipment.

Refrigerators, in the average kitchen, must respond to repeated variations in temperature due to the continual opening and closing of doors. Such holding is unsatisfactory for long period holding of refrigerated items. Commercial warehouses are likely to be better equipped for the longer period holding of fruits and vegetables. The commodities held at temperatures just above freezing and with 80% relative humidity show less loss of flavor and dehydration than those at higher temperatures and lower humidity. Certain fruits and vegetables, such as papayas, pineapples, bananas, avocados, some of the citrus fruits, green beans, cucumbers, peppers, potatoes, sweet potatoes, and tomatoes, are preserved better when held at 50°F (10°C) with 85% relative humidity. Low-temperature storage should be 0°F or preferably lower.

Compartments in **refrigerated storage** and **low-temperature storage** areas should be sized for the volume and method normally used for handling loads, whether by mobile cart or portable tray. Variations between requirements in the processing unit and the serving area are to be kept in mind by the planner. Where both activities are performed in the same establishment, pass-through refrigerators may serve as a highly desirable convenience even though the double entrance lessens insulation values and increases possibilities for temperature changes, plus there is a dehydrating effect on foods brought about by the temperature changes.

Cleanability that promotes sanitation is a significant need in these areas. Hard-surfaced, easily cleaned floors, walls, and fixtures are needed. The use of smooth, nonabsorbent materials is desirable. Drains should be provided for removal of scrubbing water and condensate. These may be located in or immediately outside the door opening to the compartment if they may freeze up inside. Care should be used to avoid a floor irregularity that might be hazardous to footing or cause the jarring of rolling carts carrying fluid foods. Satisfactory refrigeration requires uniform ventilation in all areas of the compartments. Provide lighting that will illuminate all areas adequately. In walk-in refrigerators equipped with locks provide an inside lock release and alarm system.

CHAPTER SUMMARY

The planning of receiving and storage facilities must result in facilities that promote high efficiency, the preservation of quality, and security. The planner should also provide for adequate recordkeeping facilities.

The receiving area should be planned to adequately receive loaded trucks, weigh in and inspect deliveries, and provide good sanitation and security. The floor should withstand the rugged wear it gets and be able to carry the heavy loads placed on it. Receiving and storage should be planned as close together as possible.

Storage units should suit the product needs stored there. Many units will require a well-ventilated room-temperature area often called a general dry storage area; potatoes, onions, and some other products are best held in a dark, cool, dry area at about 50° to 60°F; a refrigerated area to hold dairy products, meats, fish and poultry, fruits and vegetables; and in some areas garbage may have to be held under refrigeration. A low-temperature area is needed to hold frozen items. A separate dry storage area may be needed for the storage of paper goods and other nonfood supplies. Cleaning materials and substances that might be toxic should be stored separately by themselves. There will be a need to store pots and pans, mobile equipment, dining room equipment and supplies, etc. The storage needs are wide and varied. Those who operate the facilities often complain there is never enough.

Provide for good security, cleaning, and protection from insects and animals. Water should be available for the hosing down of refrigerators and other spaces when they need cleaning. Good drainage should be provided. The collection of trash and recyclables is a factor to consider and the space provided should be such as to be out of the way from where other items are stored. If weighing equipment and other equipment for handling items are required, provide for these. Spaces should be planned so mobile equipment used to carry goods can be moved in and out. Shelving should be strong enough to bear loads, provide for adequate identification of items, and be easily cleanable. Goods should not rest on the floor. Often they can be stored on pallets. The dining area will need a place for storing linens and laundry. Trash and garbage storage must be considered. Refrigerated storage should be under 40°F. Low-temperature storage should be 0°F or less. Workers and guests will have storage needs.

REVIEW QUESTIONS

1. Select three food operations of different types; state amount of preparation done in the establishment and system of operation (short-order, satellite, or other).
2. List for each the amount of space devoted to each kind of storage and where located.
3. Indicate for each how frequently food orders are placed, and how often deliveries are received for staple supplies, meats, dairy products, paper supplies, and laundry.
4. Describe methods and equipment used for receiving supplies.
5. Trace the movement of supplies from central storage and from refrigerated storage, and evaluate in terms of convenience.
6. List and evaluate the storage equipment (shelving, carts, bins, other) in terms of
   a. Convenience and adequacy for use.
   b. Safety for supporting load limits.
   c. Cleanability and sanitation.
   d. Suitability in terms of cost and convenience.
7. Evaluate methods of receiving and storage in terms of protection of safety, sanitation, convenience, and cost.

KEY WORDS AND CONCEPTS

adjustable shelving
Baker's supplies
central storage
cleaning supplies and equipment
delivery dock
dollies
equipment storage
floor bearing weight
garbage and recyclable collection area
general dry storage
linen storage
local storage

low-temperature storage
nonfood supplies
pallet delivery
receiving
receiving dock
refrigerated storage
skids
slatted racks
staple food supplies
storage
trash and garbage storage
ventilated common storage

CHAPTER

Food Processing

Many factors influence quality and economy in foodservice operations. In recent years a proliferation of fully prepared products has become available on the market. Increased use of **value-added** or **ready-prepared foods** in the home has created a greater acceptance of commercially prepared foods. High labor cost for preparation in small quantity has put food items commercially produced in large volume in a more favorable, competitive position. Operators who prize quality, individuality, and flexibility in the foods produced for service insist on fully producing the foods served. Maintaining a desirable degree of excellence calls for skill in selection, training, and supervision of employees who are to produce and serve the food. Shortage of well-qualified help and acute financial conditions have a strong influence on choice of the system of operation to be followed. Enduring success ultimately requires giving consumers what they want, need, and are willing to support.

The varying extents of food processing performed in public food facilities may be listed as follows:

1. Complete production of foods:
   a. for immediate service in adjacent dining rooms.
   b. to be chilled, then reheated for delayed service.
   c. to be shipped hot or cold to satellite units for service.
2. Full preparation of part of the food served and utilization of many items commercially prepared ready for cooking, such as fish sticks, french fries, and preprocessed vegetables.
3. Final conditioning for service of food that has been fully prepared commercially.

Advanced calculation of values and formulation of policies are needed to prevent a facility being tied to a system that will not be the most advantageous. It is easy to be overly enthusiastic about certain values and miss having greater benefits in a specific situation. Those who try to eliminate labor problems by using ready-prepared food may be equally harassed by food selection and supply problems and standards control. Those who believe the ready-prepared foods to be a sure route to fairly uniform quality may eliminate opportunities for variety and quality freshness desired by a specific clientele or fail to gain a versatility needed to meet changing conditions. The most practical and thorough calculations and research are required in arriving at the basic decision as to which system to use. In addition, whatever system is chosen should be examined for possible flexibility if a desirable change may need to be made later.

In this text, information is given relating to **complete food processing,** but from time to time notations will be made as they relate to different systems. The **basic functions of food production** must occur even though they may not be done in the facility where the food is served. Specific systems are simplified by eliminating one or more of the basic functions performed in the unit. It is essential, because all of them must be performed somewhere, that all steps be covered in a basic text of this kind and then decisions may be made as to which ones to include in the specific plan.

Three general steps make up the full processing procedure: (1) preliminary preparation, (2) cooking of foods or manipulating of materials for salads, sandwiches, and desserts, and (3) **finishing** and **portioning** for service. In a small kitchen, one cook or department may perform all functions. In large establishments, each step may have subdivisions. The work in well-organized sections will be performed by definite persons on a specified time schedule according to established standards and procedures.

Planners of production units with the goal of efficient work will be mindful of time, place, persons, and method in relation to essential functions. Usually most of the full-time and highest salaried workers are employed in the processing sections. The questions of who, where, when and how need answers that will maximize their production abilities. It is important that standards of quality be defined and quantity needs be determined so that proper equipment, convenient arrangement, and adequate space will be provided. A flow of work that produces the quality standards and the quantity requirements on schedule, with the fewest workers and the least amount of effort, should be developed regardless of the **production plan.**

PRELIMINARY PREPARATION SECTIONS

Fruit and vegetable preparation plus meat cutting make up the major part of preliminary preparation. The fairly simple, routine nature of fruit and vegetable preparation makes it possible for workers having limited knowledge and experience to perform the work satisfactorily. They are paid less than those doing meat cutting, which calls for special skill and knowledge. Some of the duties in these sections may be filled by workers from other areas. It is important for planners to know local conditions, wages, and the management's buying policies before allotting space or designing a layout for these areas. This is especially significant if certain units are to be eliminated and processed items obtained. Local market conditions are likely to influence this. The advisability of allowing for a given amount of flexibility in the preliminary preparation sections will be influenced also by future trends, changes in methods of processing and marketing, grading variations, different products on the market, and different needs in the facility.

A computer can be useful in studying the advisability of including space and equipment for preliminary preparation sections. Most of the value aspects, such as levels of quality and market dependability, can be coded. Costs of labor, space, equipment, and supplies can be weighed most easily if changed to a common denominator, such as time period, cost per minute, hour, or day. Availability and skill of labor (few cooks are proficient in meat cutting) require consideration. Some factors may be coded as absolute restrictions, such as space limitations and time restrictions and others with varying levels of acceptability.

The volume used will have considerable influence on the economic advantage of one system of purchasing over another. Cost of labor, space, and equipment in vegetable preparation, for example, is likely to be less per given volume per week when the volume used is large than when it is small, since there are more units to share costs and compete with purchase prices.

Vegetable and Fruit Preparation Sections

Characteristics of fruits and vegetables emphasize the relationship of this section with others. The bulk, weight, and soil typical of much of the merchandise make a minimum of movement desirable in getting it into the initial processing area. Its liability to spoilage calls for limiting time in getting it into suitable storage or use. Empty crates and bulky refuse require disposal quickly to clear space. After preliminary processing is done and materials stored, items move to the cooking and pantry sections. Economy in handling, insurance of sanitation, and protection of quality stress the importance of good flow of this material. Convenient relationships should be maintained between (1) receiving of supplies, (2) work area or storage adjacent to the work area, (3) trash or garbage space, and (4) refrigeration adjacent to section where processing will be continued (that is, cooking, salad or sandwich making, and serving area).

Where heavy or bulky loads are handled, time and labor will be saved by moving on wheels or other labor-reducing means. Many types of platform and hand trucks, kitchen carts, and storage bins are available to fit various uses from receiving through the several stages of processing. When selecting transportation equipment and planning storage, thought should be given to minimizing rehandling. Placing vegetables for cooking in steamer baskets and/or steam table pans as prepared can save rehandling time. Receiving and initial preparation may be performed on one floor level and the refrigerator and production section may be on another. Any flow that increases distance adds to the importance of study to reduce transportation of materials. See Table 8–1.

The work in the **fruit and vegetable preparation section** usually forms into three work centers: (1) cleaning, (2) paring, and (3) trimming, shaping, and chopping. Where the volume handled is small, all of the activities may be performed in one work center. When the quantity is very large, an assembly line production may be used, and one center completely separated from the others. Simplified and repeated motion in such activities make it possible to develop rhythm of work and increases speed of accomplishment. Worker qualifications and essential instruction may also be simplified for work that does not require constantly changing motion and decision making.

Potato paring has been largely eliminated because there is a dependable, reasonably priced supply of potatoes available in popular forms ready for cooking. Large-volume operations and those where supplies are less readily available may find it expedient to perform this function within their own establishment. In addition to the sacked field potatoes needed for baking or boiling, the market has a wide range of dried, dehydrated, frozen, or chilled products available. About 62% of the potatoes used currently in institutions are **preprocessed** potatoes.

Pared potatoes and root vegetables should be stored close to the peeling area. In multiple-function centers, it is often desirable to have mobile peelers that can be rolled out of the way when not required for use. In very large kitchens using a huge volume of pared potatoes and vegetables, it is useful to have a mechanical lift for gravity feeding to the peeler, and a moving belt under the peeler outlet for carrying the potatoes under a rinse spray to the worktable where eyes and spots are removed. They are next dropped into a water bath or an antioxidant solution. The sink for this final bath may be shallow and located at the end of the belt or eyeing table. In some operations the peeler is adjacent to a sink or empties over an inspection table leading to a sink that is a part of another work counter. Plan small tool storage in a drawer or rack in a table and space for pans and mobile equipment under the table or adjacent to this work area.

The work done in the cleaning center requires a two-compartment sink. Size will depend on the quantity of bulky vegetables and fruits to be cleaned. The work in this center bears a close relationship to the third center where trimming, shaping, and chopping are done. It may be combined with it for short, convenient movement of supplies. If possible, the entire length should be limited to 8 ft (2.5 m) for step-saving compactness. Limiting sink depths to 12 to 14 in. (30.5 to 35.5 cm) makes for convenient reach. A drain basket, made to fit between and be suspended from the sides of a sink compart-

TABLE 8-1 *Fruit and Vegetable Storage with Section of First Use (See Table 5.9 for container measurement)*

Commodity	Wholesale Package	Approximate Weight	Recommended Storage	Section of First Use
Fruits				
Apples, fresh	box or carton	30–40 lbs (16.3–19 kg)	Refrigerated	Pantry or bakeshop
Pie, frozen	can	30 lbs (13.6 kg)	Low temperature	Bakeshop
Pie, canned	case, 6/10	48 lbs (21.8 kg)	General dry	Bakeshop
Apricots, fresh	lug	24–26 lbs (10.9–11.8 kg)	Refrigerated	Pantry or bakeshop
Frozen	can	30 lbs (13.6 kg)	Low temperature	Bakeshop or pantry
Canned	case, 6/10 or 24/2½	48 lbs (21.8 kg)	General dry	Bakeshop or pantry
Bananas	carton	20–40 lbs (9–18 kg)	Cool, 65°F (18°C)	Pantry or bakeshop
Berries, fresh	12/pint flat	7–9 lbs (3.2–4.1 kg)	Refrigerate	Pantry or bakeshop
Frozen	can	30 lbs (13.6 kg)	Low temperature	Bakeshop or pantry
Canned	case, 6/10 or 24/2	48 lbs (21.8 kg)	General dry	Bakeshop or pantry
Cantaloupes	jumbo crate	18–45 lbs (8.2–20.4 kg)	Refrigerate	Pantry
Cherries, frozen	can	30 lbs (13.6 kg)	Low temperature	Bakeshop
Cranberries, fresh	carton, 1/lb bags	24 lbs (10.9 kg)	Refrigerate	Pantry
Grapefruit and oranges	4/5 bu. carton or box	42–45 lbs (19–20.4 kg)	Refrigerate	Pantry
Grapes, table	lug or carton	24–28 lbs (10–12.7 kg)	Refrigerate	Pantry
Honeydew melons	jumbo flat carton	45–50 lbs (20.4–22.7 kg)	Refrigerate	Pantry
Lemons	carton	38 lbs (17.2 kg)	Refrigerate	Pantry, cook, bakeshop
Peaches, fresh	Sanger lug	19–22 lbs (9.6–10 kg)	Refrigerate	Pantry or bakeshop
	Los Angeles lug	22–29 lbs (10–13 kg)	Refrigerate	Pantry or bakeshop
Frozen	can	30 lbs (13.6 kg)	Low temperature	Bakeshop or pantry
Pineapples, fresh	crate or carton	35 lbs (15.9 kg)	Cool storage	Pantry
Canned	case, 6/10 or 24/2	48 lbs (21.8 kg)	General dry	Pantry or bakeshop
Plums, fresh	lug or carton	26–30 lbs (11.8–13.6 kg)	Refrigerate	Pantry
Canned	case, 6/10	48 lbs (21.8 kg)	General dry	Pantry or bakeshop
Watermelons	cartons, 3, 4, 5	55–80 lbs (20.4–36.3 kg)	Refrigerate	Pantry
Vegetables				
Asparagus, fresh	Pyramid crate	32 lbs (14.5 kg)	Refrigerate	Preprocess or cook
Frozen	case, 12/2½ lbs	30 lbs (13.6 kg)	Low temperature	Cook
Beans, fresh	carton or hamper	28–30 lbs (12.7–13.6 kg)	Refrigerate	Preprocess or cook
Frozen	case, 12/2½ lbs	30 lbs (13.6 kg)	Low Temperature	Cook
Canned	case, 6/10	48 lbs (21.8 kg)	General dry	Cook or pantry
Dry	sack	10–1000 (4.5–48.3 kg)	General dry	Cook

TABLE 8-1 *Continued*

Commodity	Wholesale Package	Approximate Weight	Recommended Storage	Section of First Use
Vegetables (cont.)				
Beets, fresh	crate, 24 bunches	36–40 lbs (16.3–18.1 kg)	Cool storage	Cook
Broccoli	pony crate	40–42 lbs (18.1–19 kg)	Refrigerate	Cook
	carton, 14 bunches	20–23 lbs (9–10.4 kg)	Refrigerate	Cook
Broccoli, frozen	12–2½ lb	30 lb (13.6 kg)	Frozen	Cook
Brussels sprouts	drum or carton	25 lbs (11.3 kg)	Refrigerate	Cook
Brussels sprouts, frozen	12–2½ lb cartons	30 lbs (22.7 kg)	Frozen	Cook
Cabbage	crate or bag	50–60 lbs (22.7–27.2 kg)	Cool storage	Preprocess or cook
Carrots, bunches	carton	23–27 lbs (10.4–12.2 kg)	Cool storage	Preprocess or cook
topped	crate or bag	50 lbs (22.7 kg)	Cool storage	Preprocess or cook
Frozen	12–2½ lb cartons	30 lbs (22.7 kg)	Frozen	Cook
Cauliflower, wrapped	carton of 12–16	18–24 lbs (8.2–10.9 kg)	Refrigerate	Preprocess or cook
	crate	45–50 lbs (20.4–22.7 kg)	Refrigerate	Preprocess or cook
Cauliflower, frozen	12–2½ lb cartons	30 lb (22.7 kg)	Frozen	Cook
Celery	crate	55–60 lbs (24.9–27.2 kg)	Refrigerate	Preprocess or pantry
Corn, fresh	crate or bag	40–50 lbs (18.1–22.7 kg)	Refrigerate	Preprocess
Frozen	case, 6/5 lbs	30 lbs (13.6 kg)	Low temperature	Cook
Canned	case, 24/2	48 lbs (21.8 kg)	General dry	Cook
Cucumbers	lug or carton	28–32 lbs (12.7–14.5 kg)	Refrigerate	Pantry
Eggplant	bushel basket or crate	30–34 lbs (13.6–15.4 kg)	Refrigerate	Preprocess or cook
	lug	20–22 lbs (9–9.9 kg)	Refrigerate	Preprocess or cook
Lettuce, iceberg	carton	40–45 lbs (18.1–20.4 kg)	Refrigerate	Preprocess or pantry
Romaine	crate, carton, basket	25–35 lbs (11.3–15.8 kg)	Refrigerate	Preprocess or pantry
Onions, dry	sack or carton	48–50 lbs (21.8–22.7 kg)	Cool dry	Preprocess
green	carton	15–18 lbs (6.8–8.3 kg)	Refrigerate	Pantry
Parsnips	sack or bushel basket	50 lbs (22.7 kg)	Cool dry	Preprocess
	lug	30 lbs (13.6 kg)	Cool dry	Preprocess
Peas, fresh	hamper or crate	28–30 lbs (12.7–13.6 kg)	Refrigerate	Preprocess
Frozen	case, 6/5 lbs	30 lbs (13.6 kg)	Low temperature	Cook
Potatoes	sack	100 lbs (45.3 kg)	Cool dry	Preprocess
	carton	50 lbs (22.7 kg)	Cool dry	Preprocess
Squash, summer	bushel basket or crate	40–45 lbs (18.1–20.4 kg)	Refrigerate	Preprocess
	lug	24 lbs (10.9 kg)	Refrigerate	Preprocess
Winter	individual	any quantity	Cool dry	Preprocess
Rutabagas	sack	50 lbs (22.7 kg)	Cool dry	Preprocess
Tomatoes	lugs, flats, cartons	20–40 lbs (9–18.1 kg)	Refrigerate	Pantry
	baskets	9–20 lbs (4–9 kg)	Refrigerate	Pantry

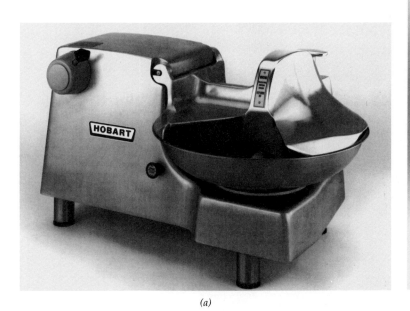

(a)   (b)

FIGURE 8.1 Equipment such as this (a) food chopper, which quickly chops vegetables, nuts, breads into crumbs, and other products needing fine division, and (b) food processor, which slices, dices, shreds, grates or makes products into julienne sizes, makes for easier, faster, and better work in the food preparation room. (*Courtesy of Hobart Corporation, Troy, Ohio.*)

ment, is useful when washing fruits and vegetables by using an overhead spray. The basket may be perforated steel, strong, firm plastic, or heavy wire mesh. The weight and size should be suitable to lift when filled. A basket 18 in. (46 cm) wide may be fitted into a mobile cart designed for 18-in. (46-cm) modular pans and moved into storage. The pans may be placed on the table during work and require less stooping or reaching than cans on dollies. Choose storage containers to minimize handling as fruits and vegetables move to the next processing sections, such as pantry or cooking. Cooking is frequently done in steam table pans or containers. These may be placed on trucks and moved into storage until needed.

Motor-driven equipment, such as choppers, grinders, and shredders, is used in the third center (Figures 8.1 and 8.2). The hazards common to the use of this equipment make an arrangement desirable in which the operator will not be liable to bumping or distraction of attention. The equipment is likely to have several loose parts and attachments requiring storage. A wall rack close to the machine may provide both convenience and protection of cutting edges. Certain machines may be needed in more than one center for only a limited time, and, if mounted on wheels, these could be used without duplication and pushed out of the way when not needed. Mobile carriers for such equipment should be equipped for storage of blades and attachments to provide for rapid change of work center arrangement.

Equipment shared by workers in two or more areas should be central to the respective areas for convenience. Equipment storage is an example. Cooking and storage pans, mixing bowls, and cutting tools are needed in more than one center. Various items on mobile equipment, such as bowls on mobile racks and storage carts, require space that should be provided nearby. A **disposal unit** or garbage container will be needed for

FIGURE 8.2   This mixer, blender, and chopper is a useful tool for the pantry, cooking section, or bakery and often requires placement where it can serve multiple sections. Or, it can be equipped with lockable wheels and wheeled in and out of work centers, as needed. (*Courtesy of Hobart Corporation, Troy, Ohio.*)

refuse from trimming, cleaning, and sorting. The kitchen areas having a major need for garbage disposal include (1) the fruit and vegetable preparation section, (2) the scraping area in the dishwashing section, and (3) the potwashing section. Small operations that can afford only one power disposal may find it desirable to organize work and arrangement so that refuse from more than one section can utilize a disposal unit located in the center where it is most needed, such as dishwashing.

Meat Handling

The cost and popularity of meat on menus, in addition to its nutritive values, give meat handling outstanding importance. Usually the most skilled and highest salaried employees are given responsibility for its handling or preparation. Meat quality is highly perishable, being subject to absorption of off-flavors, dehydration, and spoilage. The cost of labor and perishability of the product highlight the importance of proper equipment, strict sanitation, and a layout for efficient work.

Very few facilities currently have fully equipped **meat sections.** Large commissary installations and those established for many years may have them. Satisfactory economics will also call for them to have skillful meat cutters and suitable outlets for all the meat processed from carcass and other wholesale cuts. A modified amount of meat cutting occurs in many restaurants featuring steaks, chops, and roasts. This tends to be sufficiently repetitious to require somewhat less skill and less costly and extensive equipment. Instead of buying full carcasses, wholesale cuts or lesser units are bought. The meat may be aged in restaurant storage, and for this reason special space and facilities may be required. When needed for use it is processed ready for cooking. If freshly cut, it will have best quality.

Cuts of meat made to exacting specifications are available from packing houses and butcher shops in metropolitan areas. The majority of food operators rely on this service. Although the price of the fabricated meat appears high in comparison with the price per pound of carcass meat, it is usually found to compare well on a cost per portion basis. Part of the advantage lies in having uniform portion size, in freedom from having to utilize all of the various cuts in a carcass for specific types of menus, and in having exact, immediate knowledge of portion costs. Full realization of values is likely to depend in considerable degree upon the knowledge and skill of the buyer in making specifications and of the receiving clerk in recognizing and checking the extent to which the merchandise meets specifications when it is delivered.

The majority of cooks currently have little knowledge and skill in or time for meat cutting. There is a limited amount required in general preparation of meals for which appropriate equipment is needed, even with the purchase of fabricated meats. The cook's sink should be of adequate size of poultry cleaning or work with other bulky items. A heavy cutting board on the table may substitute for a butcher's block. A utility table, perhaps mobile, in the cook's section may be used for the meat grinder and possibly a cuber, scales for roasts and portions, and a slicer. If the slicer is mounted on a separate mobile table, it may be used by pantry workers as well (Figure 8.3).

Keep meat refrigerated. Use extra care in locating storage for meat as it is received, processed for cooking, and for supplies during a cooking process such as grilling or broiling. The nearer to freezing temperature that fresh meat is held the less the exchange of flavors and danger of microbiological growth. Temperatures from 34 to 38°F (1.1 to 3.3°C) are recommended as suitable for holding fresh meat. Repeated opening of a

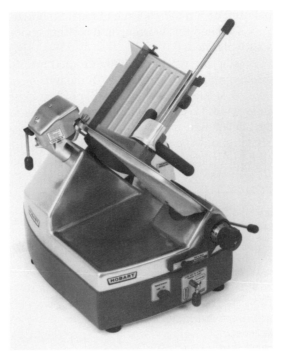

FIGURE 8.3 A meat slicer such as that shown here can quickly and neatly cut portions of meat, cheese, bread, etc., much easier than it can be done with a knife. (*Courtesy of Hobart Corporation, Troy, Ohio.*)

refrigerated compartment changes the temperature and has a drying effect on the meat. This point is good to remember when sizing the compartment and considering the door size. Location and convenient level of reach are significant to work efficiency where frequent reference is made for supplies. Space shelves appropriate to package size and/or trays of meat prepared for cooking. If carcass meat is handled, have an overhead track extending from the receiving area into the refrigerated holding area adjacent to the cutting or work center. Prevention of objectionable exchange of flavors calls for fish to be held in a separate compartment from fresh meat. A covering of cracked ice helps to prevent drying of fish and the escape of odors.

In 1997, after a series of outbreaks of illness and some deaths caused by **E. coli 0157:H7** in meat and other foods, President Clinton issued a new order requiring that meats be inspected by a new method, strengthening what was derisively called the **"smell and poke" method** of meat inspection used by the USDA. The new method is called **Hazard Analysis Critical Control Points (HACCP)**. HACCP is a preventive system that requires the operation to set up a seven-step system to ensure food safety:

1. Assess the hazards.
2. Identify the critical control points (CCP).
3. Set up control procedures and standards for the CCP.
4. Monitor the CCP.
5. Take corrective actions.
6. Set up a recordkeeping system.
7. Verify that the system is working.

HACCP is thought to hold great promise for minimizing the risks of foodborne illness. It was originally developed by the Pillsbury Company to protect the food for astronauts in space where foodborne illness could not be allowed. It has already been implemented in food processing establishments. Implementation in foodservices is also occurring. Proper follow-through is provided by inspectors who review records to make certain that operations are implementing HACCP properly.

In addition, meat must now carry with it a warning label on its handling and cooking. Such a label used on a retail package of meat is shown in Figure 8.4. It is important that foodservices also heed this warning and see that good sanitation practices are possible for the facility planned.

In a butcher shop the work is usually divided into three work centers: (1) whole carcasses are broken into **wholesale cuts;** (2) meats are shaped into cooking portions, such as roasts, chops, steaks, or patties; and (3) poultry is dressed and fish is cleaned and descaled (requires a sink). Where carcass meats are broken down, a meat hook will be needed near the block where a carcass can hang and from which cuts may be placed on the block. The block should be far enough from other equipment to allow the butcher to work around it and for large cuts to project beyond the edge. A conveniently located

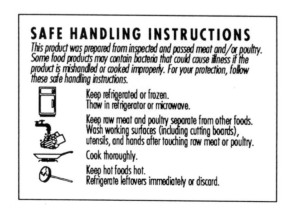

FIGURE 8.4   All meat products sold today must carry these safe handling instructions.

hand or power saw will be needed. A rack should be on or near the block for the cutting and boning knives. A twine holder for tying roasts should be within easy reach above the block.

A power saw is used for breaking up carcasses and for making portion cuts. It should be located so that a cart with meat may stand on one side and a table or cart for pans of portions on the other. Avoid placing a power saw where the butcher is likely to be interrupted or have his or her attention diverted, as in areas where others may need to pass through.

The activity of the second center may be done at the **meat block** or **meat saw.** Depending on menu requirements, this center may need a food chopper and patty shaper, cuber, cutting block, and knives and scales for shaping portions. Pans should be stored within reach and mobile equipment supplied for moving the portioned material to the cooking section and refrigeration. A table drawer is needed for miscellaneous equipment and such supplies as larding needle, knife sharpener, parchment, and wax paper. Linear space requirements may be reduced through the use of mobile tables or carts that can be moved through processing from table to machine and back to table. A thick wooden cutting block on the table will lessen need to travel to the main block for small trimming and cutting.

The flow of work in fish and poultry preparation is likely to proceed from cart to sink to table. Position the knife racks for convenient reach and handling. The **cutting board** for work with fish and poultry should be absorption proof and thoroughly cleanable, such as plastic or hard wood. Thorough cleaning requires use of detergents and sanitizing chemicals. Plastic cutting boards can be sent through the dish machine for cleaning and sanitizing. The table on which portioning and panning are done may be a separate one or the same one used for the final preparation of food.

Arrangement of meat cutting sections varies according to need and organization of work. In many facilities the block is placed opposite the sink and against a table. This allows freedom for working on three sides and movement of items to the table within the maximum reach area. Ample space needs to be allowed for a cart to stand beside the saw and block or to move along the table while work is proceeding.

Provide good light in this section, at least 50 to 60 foot-candles. Place light sources so as to avoid glare or shadows on the work. Floors should be hard-surfaced and non-skid type. Place drains and slope floor toward them for proper cleaning and where drain depression will not be in a frequently used passage or be a footing hazard. Walls should be hard-surfaced and washable. Cantilevered tables and equipment permit easy cleaning and mobile cart storage.

COOKING SECTIONS

The **cooking sections** include not only where entrees, vegetables, and sauces are prepared but also the pantry and bakeshop. The hot food area in which the chef or cook presides is generally considered the heart of the kitchen. The chef or cook is usually held responsible for the amount and quality of the work done in the cooking section. In operations where there is a cook-manager, this person supervises the activities of the entire kitchen. Supervision is facilitated when equipment is arranged in such a manner as to permit a view of the important production areas.

There are reasons for giving preference in arrangement and location of the hot food section. The materials used and labor time are the most expensive. The items produced tend to have the highest popularity rating and lose important pleasure qualities most rapidly after preparation has been completed. A planner's challenge is to find the shortest route in the work flow from garden patch to cooking pot to paying patron. The hot food section should usually be given preference of location in relation to flow of work, service, and supervision. When choice must be made in terms of proximity to auxiliary units and other sections, precedence should be given where labor time can be minimized and fast service and protection of fragile food qualities ensured.

Material Flow

The flow of raw materials will come from three main sources: (1) the meat and vegetable preparation sections, (2) dry or common, refrigerated, and low-temperature storage areas, and (3) direct delivery. Unless processed foods are refrigerated or frozen for delayed cooking, they will flow from the cooking section to points of service. Intermediate holding between preparation and service may occur in hot serving table, **bain marie,** hot cart, **pass-through refrigerated cart,** or other type of unit. Various means are used to shorten the distance between final preparation and service. One consists of locating a part of the cooking equipment, such as a grill for filling short orders, in a cafeteria lunch counter, as shown in Figure 8.5, or by using a pass-through to service in cafeterias and less formal table-service dining rooms. Food partially processed in a main kitchen may be sent to a service kitchen for final cooking, as in a decentralized service hospital. Some hotels send prepared foods to a grill or coffee shop to supplement the grill items prepared locally and to provide a more adequate menu selection. To ensure palatable food temperature for patients' meals, some hospitals utilize mobile microwave units and food on carts and do the final preparation close to the patient's room.

Cooking Functions

The functions in the cooking sections may be grouped according to treatment required and type of cooking done. Treatment will involve seasoning, mixing, shaping, breading, and panning. Cooking can be done by steam in cookers and kettles; by dry heat in

FIGURE 8.5   A grill is located at the end of a serving line for preparation of hot sandwiches. Perishable supplies are held in a pass-through refrigerator. (*Courtesy of Robert Whitney and Associates, Seattle, Washington.*)

ovens, ranges, grills, and broilers; by deep-fat frying by induction heating; by infrared heat; and in limited degree by microwave. Layouts for step-saving should provide not only for flow of materials in processing but also minimize backtracking in inspection, processing, and procurement of supplies. The variety and volume of items to be prepared will influence equipment needs and the forming of work centers. Work centers are often formed around a particular type of preparation, such as vegetable cooking, soup and sauce making, and meat cooking. In small establishments the various functions will be consolidated into one or two work centers. Simplification of menus to eliminate functions often helps to simplify equipment needs and increase production efficiency.

Detailed consideration should be given to individual work centers, the close coordination of the centers with others in the section, and the section with other sections of the facility (see Figure 8.6). This includes planning for:

1. Good supervision. Make sections easy to supervise by avoiding unnecessary obstructions, such as posts, walls, and tall equipment, to a view of important production areas.
2. Freedom from interruption of work. Avoid through-traffic in sections. Workers from other sections should not have to pass through to get supplies or to use equipment. Servers should not be permitted to enter work sections. Their area and traffic flow should be located so that they will move smoothly in a definite direction.
3. Good equipment-use relationship with others who require periodic use of certain items of equipment. The baker and the cook may need to share ovens, **tilt kettles,** and steam cookers. In small kitchens, one mixer may serve both sections. The pantry worker may need to steam potatoes, cook eggs, or prepare dressing using equipment in the cooking section. Where equipment is used by workers from

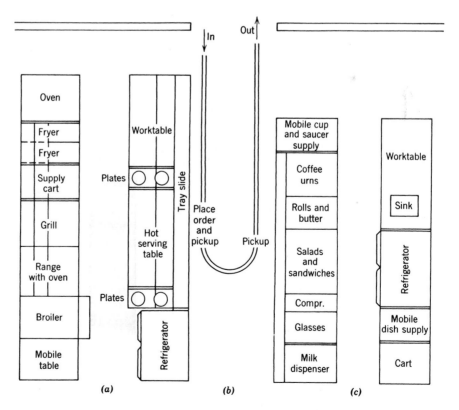

FIGURE 8.6 Plan for a service restaurant showing A—cooking section, B—servers' route, and C—pantry section.

more than one center, it should be mobile or so placed that it can be used with the least interference in a given center. If mobile, it may be moved to other work centers. The way it is used and the condition in which it is left may give rise to arguments that good planning can help to prevent. The prerogative of ownership are less definite when equipment has no fixed location.

4. Step-saving calls for close proximity to pot and pan storage and washing and to storage of frequently procured supplies.

The **minimum work center width** should be 9 ft (2.74 m) and the **maximum work center length** recommended is 6 ft (1.83 m) to confine work within a maximum work area for a normal person. The simplest section consists of one work center having a range top with oven below and a table parallel. Roasting, baking, and oven broiling may be done in the oven, and stewing, soup making, and other cooking on the range top. From this simplest center, gradual extension may be made until a section is formed of many highly specialized centers. Traffic flow and suitable supervision become more difficult as the section size is increased. The specialized work centers tend to be less complex, however, than the work center that incorporates all of the cooking functions. Ranges with ovens require extra stooping and lifting, but they are used where space limitations or other factors make them the most desirable.

The size of the cooking sections and the number of work centers required are affected by a number of factors. The most important are the volume of food to be processed, amount, and type of processing required. As quantity increases, the labor required is likely to increase also. There is a point when it is economical to break down functions between two or more workers rather than allow each to begin and complete entire functions. In this instance a product may be partially processed in one center and delivered for completion to another adjoining it. Such a plan may result in shorter and more repetitive motion that lessens production time. Coordination of work must be carefully planned where workers share in processing. Where centers process entirely different products, less coordination is required.

The type of service and the type of menu will influence the makeup of the section. A drive-in or fast-food operation may require only a grill and a french-fryer (Figure 8.7). In certain facilities, cooking functions may be divided into separate sections. A hospital diet kitchen may process certain foods. A special kitchen may prepare food for hotel banquets. A breakfast unit may prepare eggs, waffles, hot cakes, and French toast in a pantry or serving area separate from the cooking section. A cooking section where waiters and waitresses come in and pick up their orders differs from that of a cafeteria. Short-order and complete meal preparation functions differ, and meeting their needs may cause basic differences in plans for the cooking section. A facility specializing in prime beef ribs and baked or french-fried potatoes will not need the extensive equipment required by a large facility offering a wide menu choice. The work and equipment needs are also simple in cooking sections assigned to thawing and completing the preparation of preprocessed foods. The trend is toward simplified menus and a reduction of functions performed by cooks. More quality control is possible and less supervision, labor, equipment, and space are required.

Specific methods of preparation, schedule of service, and organization of staff will influence the makeup of the cooking section. An operation open 24 hours a day and serving drop-in trade has different needs from one preparing three meals daily at scheduled times. A kitchen organized under an executive chef, a pastry chef, and a steward will differ in many details from one where a dietitian directs preparation. Procedures will vary. Where it may be necessary to oven-prepare hamburgers for a school lunch, a lunch counter may grill them to order and another restaurant may broil them. More steam-jacketed kettles and cookers are used in certain operations than in others where range-type cooking is greater. The amount and specific type of preprocessed foods used will affect equipment needs and organization of work. A thorough analysis of the requirements is necessary before planning this important section.

FIGURE 8.7 In spite of the admonition for reasons of health to avoid fatty foods Americans are eating increased quantities of fries each year. Using a modern deep fryer, which has the ability to maintain proper frying temperatures, reduces fat intake into the product and lessens the amount of fat consumed. (*Courtesy of Hobart Corporation, Troy, Ohio.*)

Layout Design

Take time to detail all functions that are to be regularly performed in the cooking section. List in order of performance each activity and the equipment required for doing it. Separate activities according to the number of employees required to do them and the number of work centers needed. A satisfactory section for one food facility may be unsuitable for another. For best performance the section must be custom fitted to specific needs, even though certain basic patterns may be helpful in planning new sections.

The arrangement of equipment and work centers may be linear, parallel, square, L- or U-shaped. The minimum width of 9 to 19 ft (2.74 m to 3.05 m) includes a work table 2.5 to 3 ft (0.76 to 0.91 m) wide, an aisle 3.5 ft (1.07 m), and a range top 3 ft (0.91 m) deep. Have work aisles 3.5 to 4 ft (1.07 to 1.22 m) wide. Where doors of equipment open or mobile equipment is rolled in, the latter measurement is usually required. Linear placement violates many principles of good work center arrangement. If linear arrangement must be used, breaks in frontal equipment every 12 ft (3.66 m) permit entry into the section. If four or more centers are planned in a linear section, the distance will be around 24 ft (7.32 m). This is a considerable travel distance. Linear placement works best in small facilities. If a linear section is placed at right angles to a service area, it is usually best to place hot top or grill, fryer, and broilers closest to service, and ovens last. Steam equipment may be in the center.

Face-to-face parallel arrangement may be used in areas where servers enter the kitchen and a traffic lane is required. Such an arrangement makes it possible to pick up soup, meat, or entrees from respective work centers. Parallel, face-to-face centers at right angles to a service area are often efficient. The volume of food processed must be sufficient to sustain the breakdown into several work centers. Traffic may become a problem along the parallel aisle into the service area.

The efficiency of face-to-face and back-to-back parallel sections is lessened by traffic through them, and this may be hard to prevent or supervise. It may be awkward for the sauce and vegetable cooks to work behind cooking units and coordinate production. Removal of walls between back-to-back arrangements improves communication. A chief advantage of this design is the minimizing of hood expanse over cooking equipment. The need for such grouping under one hood may be lessened by use of individual ventilators or hoods.

Arrangement of equipment in a square, or **L-shaped or U-shaped plan** is often difficult. The square section tends to invite traffic through it, and care must be taken to provide good aisle space at the back or front to avoid conflict with traffic in the section. The angle in the L-shaped plan tends to discourage traffic. This type section is best divided at the angle juncture between range, oven, broiler, and steam equipment. This will isolate respective work centers and allow for a more orderly procedure of work. U-shaped sections are efficient if not too large. With 4 ft (1.22 m) of aisle space between equipment, the workers can easily work from one area to another. U-shaped plans discourage traffic going through them.

Equipment Needs

The essential equipment for a production kitchen will be a worktable, sink, and cooking equipment. Depending on size and type of food facility, cooking equipment may include a hot top, such as a range or griddle, ovens, deep-fry kettle, steam kettles and cooker, and a broiler. Table 8–2 indicates how needs may vary.

TABLE 8–2   Survey of Equipment Used in Hotels Serving 300, and 1,500 to 3,000 per Day

	Meals Served per Day	
Type of Equipment	300	1,500–3,000
Range top, 12 × 24 in. (30 × 61 cm)	3 to 6	9
Ovens, sq ft or m area	9 sq ft (0.84 m^2)	18–27 sq ft (1.67–2.51 m^2)
Sinks, two-compartment	1	1 to 3
Mixer	1[a]	1[b]
Steamer sections	1	2 to 6
Steam kettles, 30–40 gal (114–115L)	1	3 to 5
Trunnion steam kettles 20 qt (19L)	1	3[c]
Broiler	0	0 to 2
Fryer	0 to 1	1 to 2

[a]20qt (19L) table model.

[b]60- to 80-qt (57-to 76-L) pedestal model with 30- and 40-qt (28- and 38-L) adapters.

[c]One to be 30 or 40 gal (114 or 151 L).

Note: Equipment in modern kitchens that utilize new fast means of cooking, have reduced menu variety, and/or use some partially or fully prepared items will vary considerably from these figures, especially for range top or griddle space.

Cooking Functions and Equipment Arrangement

What are the typical menu and volume requirements? Before planning the cooking work centers, study menus planned for the operation for typical treatment required in preparation and the kind of cooking equipment needed. Most cooking activities can be grouped into patterns that will serve as a basis for work center planning. Consider volume and transportation required, in addition to work.

Common functions in cooking include the following:

1. Preparation of mixtures, such as quick breads and casseroles may be done in a mixing center. Continued manipulation is required. Tables, scales, mixer, sink, utensil storage, and a supply cart will be needed.
2. Special treatment in chopping, mixing, shaping, breading, and panning may be done at the cook's table or on other working surface.
3. Browning may be done in a skillet on the range top, on a griddle, in a broiler, in a fry kettle, or in an oven.
4. Preparation of roux, sauces, soups, and gravy is done on range tops or steam kettles. Work will alternate between table and cooking equipment.
5. Roasting and baking in an oven may be timed and require little attention. Loading and unloading will be to table or cart. Slicing may be done.
6. Vegetable cooking by steaming or boiling may be in steam kettles, steam cooker, or on the range.
7. Broiling or deep frying may be required.

The **cook's table** is generally the core of the cooking section, because it provides a major working surface and is usually a storage place for ingredients for seasoning, thickening, and mixtures. Study work relationships from this area to points requiring repeated inspection or continuous manipulation.

The best arrangement of equipment in relation to the cook's table will depend on the items to be prepared and the quantity required. If roast meat accounts for the major amount of baking, and does not require frequent checking by the cook during the baking, the cook's oven will not need to be close to the worktable. If baking is required that calls for short processing time and needs frequent change of items or checking for doneness, it is well to have the oven opposite and parallel to the cook's table or adjacent to it. A table near roast ovens is convenient for resting items for insertion into or removal from the oven. In large sections, space in front of ovens should be sufficient for carts or rolling tables to be brought to ovens for loading and unloading. Roasts may be moved to the meat slicer for slicing and panning. A slicer on a mobile table possessing wheel locks may be used conveniently in more than one section or location and rolled out of the way when not needed.

Ranges for large facilities are best without ovens and the space below used for pan storage. In small units, compactness may require the oven to be below the range top. Where frequent reference to the oven by the cook is not required, the oven may be located with the steam equipment and the ranges and grill banked together. In some school lunch units with little need for range top cooking, it has been found adequate to have a small range top or hot plates placed in the steam section. Steamers are best located at the end of an equipment line because of plumbing needs, escaping steam, and for working from a cart. Water is needed for many of the cooking procedures and should be piped to the equipment, such as over steam kettles, ranges and mixing centers. A utility sink may be placed where it is accessible to several work centers. Figure 8.8 illustrates an arrangement that permits good traffic lanes in the progress of work and space for use of mobile items beside stationary equipment.

Dry ingredients for use in the cooking center are usually stored in the cook's table, which is used as a mixing or treatment center. Herbs, spices, and other seasonings are stored in small quantities on a shelf or in tilt bins above the table, and tilt or rolling bins

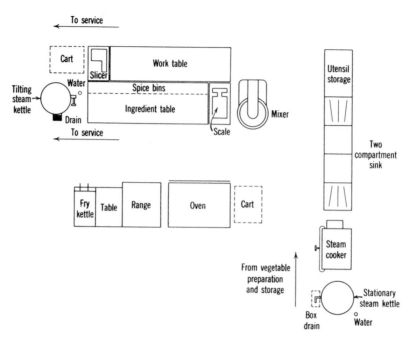

FIGURE 8.8   A suggested arrangement of equipment in a cooking section. Equipment is placed for interdepartmental use with a minimum of interference. The steam cookers and kettles may be arranged back to back with oven and range to permit use of a common hood.

below the table are used for flour, salt, sugar, and milk solids. Wet ingredients, such as eggs, milk, and fat, are brought from storage on a cart. Space must be allowed for foods arriving from storage or the **ingredient room.** Drawers directly under the tabletop and a rack above the space bins are used for small equipment needed for manipulations.

In a cooking center, scales for ingredient measurement and a mixer are needed and should be in proximity. Sink and utensil storage should be near the mixer. The work motions in mixing move from ingredient bins and cart onto the scale, then into the mixer. When mixing is finished, material is scaled into pans from the mixer and moved onto the table or a cart that transports the food to the oven. Where there is only one mixer in the cooking section, it should be placed where it is convenient to the steam cooker for mashing potatoes, unless dehydrated potatoes only are used. Rice and farinaceous products are often steamed and brought to the mixing center for the preparation of casserole dishes. The steam cookers are likely to be used by workers from more than one section and it is well to locate them with this in mind. Carts are commonly used for transporting loads to and from the cookers. Adequate space should be allowed for the maneuvering of the carts and the swing of the steam cooker door.

Steam kettles may be used for the preparation of bulky materials, such as cooking vegetables or meats for stock (Figure 8.9). This type of preparation requires little manipulation and requires a large amount of water. The average worker can easily cope with contents in a fairly large capacity kettle. Smaller kettles should be used for contents that require stirring or handling in a manner that may crush tender foods and that need an excess of energy. The preparation of puddings, sauces, and casserole dishes requires weighing of ingredients as well as stirring. Stationary kettles are satisfactory for fluid materials or materials from which it is desirable to draw off liquid. Trunnion or tilt kettles are preferable for thicker materials that are not to be drained and need to be poured from the container. Large quantity kettles may have power stirrers and may be emptied or filled mechanically.

Specialization in preparation and the fuller use of steam equipment reduces the need for range-top space. In some kitchens the hot top is divided and one unit approximately 12×24 in. $(30 \times 61$ cm) may be located near the steam equipment and another

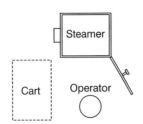

FIGURE 8.9 Equipment arrangement at the steam cooker.

near the cook's table and oven. In residences, griddles may be located in or behind the serving line for hot cakes, breakfast eggs, and hamburgers. The griddles may be in fixed location or mobile.

Foods removed from the oven are likely to be hot and heavy. They will be moved to a table for cutting into portions. Movement of the food may be by hand or on a cart and the table may be the cook's table, a slicing table, or other worktable. An oven located near a griddle, broiler, or fry kettle provides a good holding place for serving plates and foods that are ready for service.

Foods prepared by fast means of cooking have gained a great deal of popularity. Steamers, broilers, high-energy units, grills, fryers, toasters, waffle irons, and microwave, convection, combi, infrared ovens are used for this type of cooking. Bulk cooking may be done in another area and transported to this section to supplement the foods prepared by these means. A highly efficient center can be planned with proper arrangement. Maximum utilization of space vertically as well as horizontally is desirable. Speed calls for supplies and service dishes to be close at hand. Fryers should be arranged with work space nearby. End-of-line location to which a cart may be drawn is often used. A landing area at least 2 ft (61 cm) wide should be provided next to the fryer for supplies awaiting frying and for foods removed from the fryer. A small steam table may be used for soups, sauces, and other cooked foods.

Economical utilization of time is important in all areas of food production, but nowhere more than in final conditioning of precooked foods and in short-order preparation and service. Extreme freshness and sharp temperature essential to goodness, combined with time limitations make speed, for many diners, especially valuable. Menu plans and equipment arrangement should be evaluated for reduction of time and motion. If the volume of business requires only one worker to supply orders, the menu should be confined to equipment that can be located within easy reach of the worker and call for enough repetition of motion for the development of speed. Where the volume is large enough to employ several to prepare and set up orders, extra equipment and an assembly line with each worker performing specialized tasks can be used to advantage.

The equipment arrangement must permit two-handed work and free the right hand for performing those acts requiring greatest skill. The average worker will pick up and hold with the left hand and manipulate with the right. Deliveries of orders may be over a shelf-type hood over the grill and broiler or a shelf over a sandwich table. If china service is used, service to the plate will be most convenient with the plate located between the fryer and grill. If paper service is used, the fryer and grill may be adjacent and the paper supplies stored in the corner. Small plates should be located to the right of the sandwich table where they will be within reach of the grill for small orders. The sandwich maker, after cutting a sandwich, is likely to transfer it to a plate from the cutting board with both hands, so it is less significant to have the plate storage at the left hand rather than at the right.

Where counter service occurs in a dining area, the arrangement may have the cooking equipment located in the back counter and the sandwich preparation parallel with plate storage in the serving counter. Where plate levelers are situated between the fryer and griddle, it is advisable to have them mobile not only for easy transporting of plates from the dishwashing section, but also for thorough cleaning of the space. Fryers may be mobile also. The space below the supply table is usually blocked by other equipment and is therefore not usable, but the convenience of arrangement more than offsets this loss. Cantilevering tables permit movement of mobile equipment in and out under such tables. Utilization of the vertical space above is very important. Where paper supplies are necessary, the area above the supply table may be used for such supplies and for bread. Bread storage and a sink should be located near this section.

PANTRY SECTION

Production requirements of the **pantry section** dictate equipment needs and layout for efficiency. Wide diversity is common. In some facilities the requirements are relatively simple, dealing chiefly with salad preparation. In others, beverages, salads, sandwiches, relishes, fruit, fruit juices, cold plates, dessert dishing, tea and hors d'oeuvre, hot breads, ice, and breakfasts may be prepared and dispensed. Pantry responsibility for breakfasts will extend the load on its **short-order section** and reduce the early production load in the cooking section. Some food facilities have enlarged activities to encompass final conditioning of preprocessed foods so that pantry-type preparation constitutes the total food preparation done. The diversity emphasizes the need to identify activities to be performed and the order of their performance, plus indication of the number of workers required during peak hours of service and during slack periods. Equipment requirements will correspond with functions to be performed, and its layout should be one that will conserve motion, ensure speed, and reduce travel and prevent criss-crossing of service personnel.

The flow of raw materials will be from (1) central dry and refrigerated storage, (2) direct delivery, and (3) vegetable preparation. Some flow may be from the cooking section, where roast meat, poultry, and other foods may be prepared. It is often desirable to have access to steam equipment for cooking eggs, potatoes, and other foods for salads and salad dressings. A table-type mixer will be needed for such preparations as salad dressings and whipped cream (Figure 8.10). The mixer in the bakery or cooking sections is sometimes used. If desserts prepared in the bakery are to be dished in the pantry, this flow should be considered.

A characteristic of pantry foods delivered for service is their bulkiness. Individual salads, dessert portions, cold plates, and similar foods require considerable surface area. Plates will vary from 5.5 to 8 in. (17 to 20 cm) in width and the clearance of 5.5 in. (12 cm) between shelves is usually adequate for lettuce cups or sherbet glasses. If portioned and arranged on 18×26 in. (46×66 cm) trays and placed in mobile racks, they may be moved into refrigerated pass-through storage areas or other sections with a minimum of handling. Insulated carts with inserted chillers provide an efficient means of handling to distant points for service, as for special service dining rooms. Where vertical transportation is needed, attention should be given to easy access. The location of the pantry will be governed by best relationships to sources of supplies, production flow, and the intersectional operations (Figure 8.11). Production needs and flow of service will influence interrelationships of work centers within the section.

Multiplicity and repetition of motions characteristic of this section increase in terms of the variety of items required. Work centers can be planned to resemble closely a well-designed work center in a factory, using tier or vertical space. Assembly line preparation is possible where the volume is large. A moving belt can often be used to advantage for supplies and/or carrying the finished products to service. Table heights are important. Plans should include the possibility of workers sitting to do certain tasks.

Convenient storage is needed for a wide variety of food and equipment. Food will be in large bulk, as lettuce, bread, and ingredients for salads and sandwiches, and in small quantities for special garnishes. Large and small food containers and mixing bowls will be needed, and diverse sizes and shapes of plates and glasses may be used for service. Good vertical use of space and well-planned storage is needed to reduce lin-

FIGURE 8.10 A mixer such as this is helpful to cooks for mixing or whipping foods. It also is a useful piece for use in the pantry for making salad dressings and other products. Of course, it is an indispensable piece for use in the bakeshop. Where use is spasmotic in these sections, placing the mixer on lockable wheels makes it possible to quickly move it to where it is needed. (*Courtesy of Hobart Corporation, Troy, Ohio.*)

ear space. The vertical space may be in shelves above the table or in carts or mobile racks beside or under the table. A wide variety of serving dishes can be stored in bins under the table. Selection and reaching of items from the mobile bins is much easier than from low shelves. Prepositioning of many of the small tools and equipment used, gravity drops, and the elimination of search helps to promote fast work and is to be considered in designing these work centers. Pressure for speed is strong during peak periods when demands on this section are heavy.

The **salad and sandwich-making sections** have two work centers. The first includes assembling and such processing as slicing, chopping, dicing, and mixing of materials. The second division is the portioning or display arrangement after which the food will be sent to the serving station. In small operations, salad materials and other items may be cleaned and given preliminary handling here, especially if this section handles all of the preparation done. In the full production facilities, all washing, trimming, and even chopping of salad greens occur in the vegetable preparation section. Fruits and vegetables may be cut there also.

Salad operations require a sink, table, can opener, slicer, chopper, juice extractor, shredder, dicer, mixer, hot plate or steam equipment, and local storage. The equipment may be shared with other sections or located in the pantry. A garbage grinder or garbage cans will be needed. The disposal unit is especially desirable where the vegetables are cleaned in the pantry. Refrigerators should be planned to hold a variety of shapes and sizes of food containers. High humidity to discourage drying is needed in the refrigerators. Even-level floors into refrigerated areas are desirable to accommodate mobile bins or carts of salad greens or carts loaded with gelatin preparations to be cooled. This will help to reduce spillage and excess handling.

FIGURE 8.11 Tables are needed beside as well as across from cooking equipment for supplies and prepared foods. (*Courtesy of Hobart Corporation, Troy, Ohio.*)

If lettuce and other salad greens are to be washed and trimmed here, provide sufficient drainage space at the sink and sinks of suitable size for the volume to be handled. The flow of work in this preliminary center should move from a sink placed at one end of the center to a drain table, to a table for preparation, and thence into refrigerated storage, or bypass preparation temporarily and go to storage and thence to preparation. In small units, the refrigerator may be used both for storage of raw materials and for completed products. In larger sections where two or more workers may be working, it may be desirable to have a double-compartment sink in the center of the work area. This will give access to workers from both sides without their criss-crossing. Dry storage will be needed for gelatin, spices, oils, vinegars, and other ingredients.

The second center should be in close relationship to the first for the final makeup of the salads and sandwiches. Calculate carefully space needs in terms of the number of workers, amount of materials, and the number of items that must be within reach while the workers are working. If a person is to place the serving dish on a tray and arrange the food on the dish, the tray will be on the table in front of the worker while food is arranged. Trays commonly used measure 14 × 18 in. (36 × 46 cm) or 18 × 26 in. (46 × 66 cm). Plan convenient storage for the trays. If mobile racks are used, storage may be on the racks or from mobile dispensers. The trays may be on a shelf under the table or in a mobile dispenser at the end of the table. When arranging salads, lettuce may be at the left of worker and ingredients that require manipulation of scoop, fork, or tongs at the right. Dishes are convenient immediately in front of the tray or toward the back of the table or in bins immediately below the table top in front of the worker. A sufficient number of dishes should be exposed at one time to enable the worker to pick up several at a time for placing on the tray. Placing dished products on trays and then into mobile carts to be rolled into refrigerators having even-level floors provides for rapid, easy delivery of bulky items. A higher inside floor increases handling.

The arrangement area for sandwiches tends to differ from that for salads due to the volume and variety of fillings that are continually available to complete orders. The high perishability of the ingredients makes it necessary to keep fillings refrigerated. Bread should be kept enclosed, so that it will not be subjected to air currents or hot dry air that has a staling effect. Studies show that bread tends to stale more rapidly when refrigerated (not frozen) than when held at room temperature. If hot, toasted, or grilled sandwiches are featured, the appropriate equipment should be located in or adjacent to the sandwich section.

The salad and sandwich making may be done in a dual center or in separate centers. Fruits, fruit juices, and seafood or other cocktails may be prepared here also. In a continental-type operation, where a garde manger work center is planned, the pantry section may not make up salad dressings, relishes, and other appetizers, cold plates, and meat dishes; or the pantry section may come under the supervision of the garde manger or cold-meat chef. In that case, the two should be located close together.

Where the makeup center for salads and sandwiches is placed in the service section, local refrigeration in or under the counter should be planned. Bulk preparation for this frequently occurs in the preliminary work center and materials are sent to this area for final makeup.

If breakfasts are prepared in the pantry, a grill work area similar to that planned for snack bars or in-line counter operations should be planned. This would include a griddle, waffle irons, toasters, burners for egg preparation, egg boiler, and a small steam table for holding hot cereals, cooked meats, and other breakfast items. This steam table can be used later for hot sauces and hot desserts for lunch or dinner desserts. Because this work center may be closed part of the day, its location should not interfere with the flow of work in other work centers during the remainder of the day. If designed as a mobile unit, the equipment could be removed when not needed and the space used for other purposes.

Value-added foods sent to pantries for finishing differ in portion quantities and treatment required. Some are packaged with one portion of a single item, some with one portion of the main course hot foods, and others in multiple portions per package. The method of handling and equipment needed depends on treatment required and the volume handled. The food may arrive from an adjacent commissary kitchen and require no other treatment than to be kept at a palatable temperature and served. Frequently the food is frozen and requires low-temperature storage until needed, and may need refrigerated space for thawing plus completion of cooking before serving. The best equipment for this cooking depends on the foods and the volume to be handled at one time. The cooking equipment currently used includes deep fryers, convection ovens (Figure 8.12), steam equipment, and microwave ovens. The speed of microwave is often favored for units where foods can be prepared in one-portion quantities and the convection oven where large amounts must be prepared at one time. Deep fryers are often best suited to the requirements in a short-order facility that features deep-fried chicken, shrimp, and potatoes and other vegetables. The flow of work will move from storage area to table for panning or any other treatment required, thence to cooking equipment, and then to the serving table.

A beverage unit in the pantry area should be planned close to a place where a worker can supervise it and remake a supply as needed. In large facilities, beverages are often the responsibility of one person. The beverage unit should be close to the service exits. Roll warmers, ice cream storage, dessert storage units, and any other items needed for service should be installed here, if service is to be from this section. Storage for ice should be provided if it is to be dispensed here. Fountain installations are sometimes combined with the pantry section.

It is likely that several pieces of power equipment may be used, such as toasters, shake makers, and coffee servers, and an adequate number of sufficiently **ampered service outlets** should be provided. Arrange for a convenient location of small-tool or equipment storage, cutting boards, numerous containers for small quantities of fruits, vegetables, and various mixtures to be used, and for refrigerated drawers and hot roll

(a)

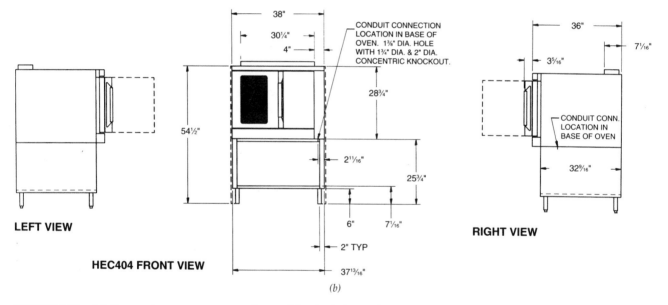

(b)

FIGURE 8.12   (a) Convection ovens are not only good for the baking of items, but also for gentle reheating. (b) Manufacturers of equipment will not only furnish planners with pictures of equipment but will also furnish drawings showing dimensions and setup specifications for the specific piece of equipment. *(Courtesy of Hobart Corporation, Troy, Ohio.)*

warmers under or near the work area. The floor should be a hard, moisture-proof, non-slip type. Light that reaches from 50 to 75 foot-candles is desirable on work surfaces.

BAKERY SECTION

The control of quality and cost of desserts and breads served by a food facility is very important to its successful operation. For short-order operations with limited kitchen equipment this is often a matter of careful purchasing of commercial products, but other establishments may prepare all or a part of their bakery items in a **bakery section.** There are economic advantages in many instances of having a suitably equipped **bakeshop** as a part of a foodservice facility. In small operations, the baking may be done in a small appendage of the cooking section. Where the demand is heavy, the bakery may be a separate, fully equipped department.

When locating this section, consider the relationships with other sections for use of equipment and flow of work. It may bear close relationship with the cooking section for shared use of ovens, mixers, sink, and certain other items. The flow of raw materials will be from dry storage, refrigerators, and frozen food storage. A refrigerator and frozen food cabinet may be located in the bakeshop, and dry stores for temporary supply stored in the table or a day-storage pantry. Prepared products will move to setup stations and service. The independent nature of the work in this section and the ease of transporting supplies and products make it possible for the bakery section to be remotely located in a large facility. There is sometimes a tendency to separate it from the main kitchen by walls that interfere with supervision and the sharing of equipment with other sections. The variety, complexity, and volume of items produced will influence space requirements and, to a certain extent, the most suitable location.

Production needs should be studied and the activities charted before planning the layout. Considerable traffic will occur to and from the section. Traffic aisles within the section should be planned with work aisles at right angles to them. Allow sufficient space for movement of mobile equipment to facilitate flexibility in work centers. The **dough roller** on a mobile table can be rolled out of the way when not in use. A mobile **proof box** can be moved from table to oven for easy transfer of items for baking. Arrange equipment so that it does not project into traffic lanes or work aisles, and so that workers will not have to cross main traffic aisles to reach commonly used equipment. At least 4 ft (1.22 m) should be provided in front of ovens so that workers will not be crowded when doors are open and hot items removed. If a **peel** is required, this distance should be proportionately increased for ease in handling and transporting items on the peel. (A peel is a long-handled, paddle-shaped implement for loading, moving, or removing items in a deep oven.)

Work centers develop in relation to the items to be prepared and the common functions to be performed. Typical sections include (1) formula weighing and mixing; (2) cooking of puddings, sauces, fillings, and frostings; (3) frying of doughnuts or other desserts; (4) folding, rolling, cutting, or shaping of Danish and French pastry; (5) pie and dough rolling, cutting, and panning; (6) proofing, baking, and removal to racks; (7) freezing of desserts; (8) landing, removal from pans, finishing, and dishing; and (9) pan washing and storage. Where a variety of spices, fats, extracts, garnishes, and other food items, and special tools and equipment are required, it is well to have a pantry storage area adjacent to the bakeshop.

The flow of work in the formula weighing and mixing center and for cooking of puddings and fillings is much the same as that described for the cooking section (Figure 8.13). A steam-jacketed kettle is desirable for this. Placement of ingredients, scale, and mixer is important for a motion-saving flow of work. Raw materials in the pantry or refrigerator should be near this area. Pans for scaling cakes or other mixed products for baking should be conveniently located. Materials from the mixing center may move to each of the other centers. Convenient refrigeration will be needed for work with pastries, and material from bread dough rolling and shaping will move to proofing equipment. If retarded yeast doughs are used, extra refrigeration must be provided. The largest number of pans will be needed at the mixing and dough rolling centers in the average bakeshop. The largest quantity of soiled equipment will come from mixing and finishing.

Plan facilities to minimize criss-crossing and backtracking in the flow of work. If ovens and baked storage units are located near the outer perimeter of the section, traffic into the section will be reduced. Linear travel should be eliminated as much as possible through effective utilization of vertical space. If premixes are used, water should be available at the mixer, measures within reach, or automatic measuring devices provided.

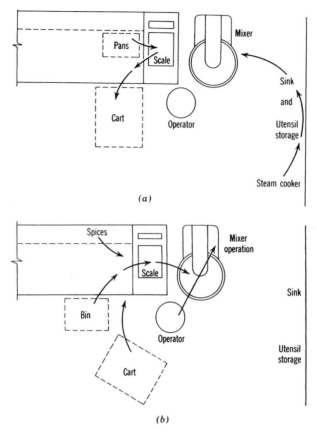

(a)

(b)

FIGURE 8.13   Equipment placement, with arrows showing work flow (a) for panning and (b) for mixing foods.

Plan under-table space for mobile bins and frequently used equipment. In planning space utilization, it is important to check for adequacy because cramping will lower productive efficiency. Adjust table heights in terms of work to be done. For example, where hand rolling of doughs is done, it is desirable to have the table slightly lower in height than that which is standard for other tables [approximately 2 in. (5 cm) lower].

A great deal of the work in a bakeshop may consist of rolling, shaping, and cutting, especially if Danish pastries, puff paste, and rolls are made that require a good bit of hand work (Figure 8.14). The table space or bench may be limited to the convenient reach of workers if tiered, mobile storage units are provided. If breads, rolls, and sweet dough are produced, the **bench** requirements will differ from that needed if yeast products are made. Hand rolling may be done either on wood or stainless steel tables or rolling may be done by machine, but where a great deal of cutting is to be done the wood-topped tables are favored. The tables should be 6 to 8 ft (1.83 to 2.44 m) in length and 2.5 to 3 ft (75 to 91 m) wide. Raised curbs of 6 in. (0.15 m) may be used around three sides to prevent flour and dough from dropping to the floor. Tables are best centrally located away from the wall. When this is done, curbs may be omitted so that the table may be approached from all sides. Baking pans should be stored at this table.

Provide adequate landing space for products as they come from the oven. A tiered cooling rack is usually best. Mobility is desirable so that products may be moved out of the way and taken later to the finishing or dish-up stations.

The oven selected may affect space requirements and work efficiency. Deep ovens in which a peel must be used for movement of items to the expanse of the deck and for inspection or adjustment during baking use extra time, motion, and space for handling over that required by **conveyor** (moving belt) or **reel** (revolving) **ovens** with shelves the depth of one-bun pan 18 × 26 in. (46 × 66 cm) or cabinet ovens that have decks of two-

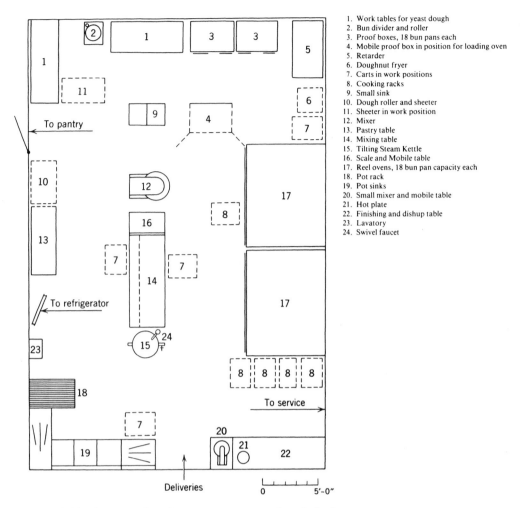

1. Work tables for yeast dough
2. Bun divider and roller
3. Proof boxes, 18 bun pans each
4. Mobile proof box in position for loading oven
5. Retarder
6. Doughnut fryer
7. Carts in work positions
8. Cooking racks
9. Small sink
10. Dough roller and sheeter
11. Sheeter in work position
12. Mixer
13. Pastry table
14. Mixing table
15. Tilting Steam Kettle
16. Scale and Mobile table
17. Reel ovens, 18 bun pan capacity each
18. Pot rack
19. Pot sinks
20. Small mixer and mobile table
21. Hot plate
22. Finishing and dishup table
23. Lavatory
24. Swivel faucet

FIGURE 8.14 Suggested equipment arrangement for a bakeshop.

bun pan capacity. Transportation time and oven space are saved by convection ovens into which a mobile rack of items for baking may be rolled from preparation table to oven and from oven to finishing table.

Variety in temperatures needed at one time is important. A reel or conveyor oven may have small or large capacity. The shelves move within a single compartment and are therefore subject to one temperature. This works well where large quantities of a single item are prepared at one time or several items having a common temperature requirement. In facilities requiring two or more temperatures simultaneously, smaller reel ovens or deck ovens may be desirable to operate separately. Steam should be provided in ovens where hard-surfaced breads are baked. Combi-ovens have the advantage of being able to be used with or without steam and are widely used for a variety of cooking and baking because of their flexibility.

The finishing center is combined with the dish-up center in many bakeshops. In large operations, the finishing center may be separated into several work centers for the various functions. Cookies and cakes to be iced and decorated may constitute one center. A marble-top table, a batch warmer, and other specialized equipment may be needed. A small-tool storage and a hand sink will be necessary and also, in convenient proximity, a baker's stove for sugar syrups, fondants, and icings.

The dish-up center may or may not be a part of the bakeshop. In any case, portion sizes are a concern of the bakeshop. The arrangement for dish-up should be similar to that described for salad making, with trays on which dishes are arranged and materials for arrangement in a semicircle around the tray. A mobile rack at a convenient location is desirable to receive the trays of portioned desserts. Dishes may be stored (1) at the back of the table, if the table is 36 in. (91 cm) wide; (2) under the front edge of the table on a shelf; (3) in plate levelers; or (4) in mobile bins under the table, depending on the type and variety of items needed. Refrigerated mobile racks for cold desserts or enclosed carts that provide tiered storage will give maximum utilization of space. The vertical height of desserts seldom exceeds 6 in. (15 cm) and when portioned will usually be from 3 to 4.5 in. (8 to 12 cm). The dish-up center may require a refrigerated storage space and this may be combined with that of the preparation center. If this occurs, proximity of the two centers is a factor to remember in layout planning.

A variety of storage conditions are required for bakery items. Breads, rolls, and sweet goods tend to be best at room temperature with some ventilation. Cakes and pies may be stored at room temperature unless they have custard fillings. Custard-filled desserts, puddings, whipped cream desserts, and similar perishable products should be refrigerated. Dishing and loading into mobile units that may be taken to various points where needed add greatly to efficiency. Storage areas may be pass-through cabinets between bakeshop and service area. Freezer space for frozen desserts and for holding items longer than normal periods is often needed.

Volume produced and variety of products to be made will govern equipment needs. Ice cream making calls for mixing equipment, a freezing unit, and a hardening unit. Where bread and rolls are to be produced in large quantity, power sifters, dough mixers, dough rollers or sheeters, cutters and rounders, overhead proofers, pan greasers, dough troughs, and other special equipment need to be evaluated for inclusion. Cookies in quantity may require special mixers, pan greasers, and machines to drop cookies automatically onto pans. An efficient operation will depend upon suitable provision for the specific needs.

CHAPTER SUMMARY

This chapter discusses many factors that should be considered in planning the production section. The preliminary preparation, fruit and vegetable, meat handling, cooking, pantry, and bakery sections are covered. The number of production sections and how they are planned depends on the type of production the facility uses—foods prepared from scratch, partially prepared foods, etc.

Preliminary preparation sections covered are fruit and vegetable and meat handling, which may or may not be in a facility depending on the size and production method. Fruits and vegetables carry a lot of soil and produce considerable waste and so the section should be located between the receiving and storage section and cooking section. The floor should be a hard, durable surface that can stand a lot of water and cleaning and wear from heavy loads—nonslip quarry tile is excellent. Equipment needed to pare, slice, chop, dice, and do other manipulations can often save time and money. Some facilities omit certain equipment and purchase these items already prepared. Safety in equipment handling should be sought. Much garbage can be eliminated by the use of heavy-duty garbage grinders.

Only very large facilities will have fully equipped meat handling sections with meat saws, cutting blocks, overhanging trolleys, meat grinders, and so forth. Planners should ascertain how meats, poultry, fish, and other products that may be handled in this section will be purchased and then plan space, equipment, and its arrangement based on this information. In most operations meat handling is done in the cook's section and, if so, the planner should provide for adequacy of table space and sink space plus other probable needs to facilitate their handling. Good refrigeration facilities are needed near the meat handling section. Governmental regulations recommend certain cooking procedures for meats because of sanitation problems. Planners should see that the facilities are designed to observe these recommendations.

For cooking sections planners need to consider the proper equipment to do the jobs expected, proper arrangement of them, a smooth flow of materials through the unit in processing, the ability to maintain high sanitation standards, and efficiently planned work centers. The number required will be set by the volume of cooking done and the type. Plan so that good supervision is possible, because it is here that some of the most important work is done. The type of service used in the operation will have a major influence on what the section includes and how it is planned. A drive-in cooking section, a counter-type operation, and a fast-food operation all require different cooking sections because of the type of service used and the kinds of meals produced. It takes a slightly different cooking section to prepare breakfast than a dinner, although many cooking sections can be set up so as to adequately handle both.

The cooking centers may be arranged in an L-shape, U-shape, square shape, parallel shape, or linear shape. The latter is best for small kitchens. In most other arrangements, foods that are prepared and served immediately should be produced next to where servers pick them up. Other foods that are prepared and stored awaiting service can be prepared in areas more distant from service work centers. In planning the bakery section eliminate, if possible, all through-traffic. A cooking section will usually require the following major equipment: ovens, ranges, fryers, broilers, sinks, mixers, steam and trunnion kettles, and other steam equipment. Some cooking sections may have special needs such as a salamander or infrared oven. The items requiring preparation will dictate the equipment. The method of preparation of the foods and their service will dictate the arrangement of this equipment.

The work in pantries varies. Some use them only for salad and cold plate making and perhaps beverage, hot bread, sandwich, and dessert handling. Others may be quite extensive with a food preparation and cooking center in it where breakfasts are prepared and perhaps short orders. In the continental kitchen the garde manger section will be located here. Some simple cooking units may be needed if the section is expected to prepare its cooked salad dressings, boiled eggs, potatoes for potato salads, etc., here. In smaller units the cook's section may serve this need. Its materials will come variously from dry, refrigerated, and frozen storage, from vegetable preparation, and from the bakery and cooking units. If catering is handled by the main kitchen, a considerable amount of refrigerated space is needed to handle appetizers, cocktails, and salads, unless such space is designated elsewhere. Some facilities use enclosed refrigerated mobile carts for this and move the carts out after loading to where they will be needed. Under-counter refrigeration may make it possible to store needed food items close to where they will be used. A good deal of dish and utensil storage space will also be required unless this is also stored elsewhere, but it should be close by. Again, having dishroom workers load clean and dry salad or pie plates, cocktail glasses, and other items used in this section into enclosed mobile carts may create efficiency and reduce storage problems. A place for the storage of such carts is necessary. Ensure that an adequate amount of worktable and sink space is provided. Often the pantry is planned too skimpily in this regard.

Many units today have no bakeshop but purchase already-prepared breads, desserts, and other bakery needs. If, however, a bakeshop is needed the equipment should be mixers, ovens, proof boxes, dough rollers, cooking units, etc., so a wide variety of items ranging from puddings, cakes, breads, sauces, and perhaps frozen desserts can be prepared. Some even have a candy-making section in them. Materials will come from direct delivery, frozen, refrigerated, fruit and vegetable preparation, and dry storage, so proximity to these units, if possible, promotes efficiency. However, because bakery products usually can be stored to await serving demand, the bakery need not be near the service areas. Often the pantry handles any last-minute preparation of these products, so storage may be there. If so, the planner should provide for adequate storage of the bakery items sent there.

A large bakery will have a number of work centers and the ovens may be large to produce the big loads that must be ready for service. Special mixers for breads are often installed where the demand is high. Sometimes the facility will retail its bakery products, increasing the production demands.

REVIEW QUESTIONS

1. Select a full production kitchen for observation. State system of operation and
   a. List the work centers in each of the food production areas.
   b. Enumerate the items of equipment in each center.
   c. Sketch the equipment layout in one section and trace the general flow of work in the section.

2. Select a fast-food production area. State foods processed and
   a. List the items of equipment used.
   b. Sketch the layout of the equipment and trace the flow of work.
   c. State average time required in filling orders.

3. Compare storage requirements of the two systems studied in Questions 1 and 2, in terms of common

and refrigerated, and in terms of central and unit location.
4. Evaluate the cooking sections studied in Questions 1 and 2 from the standpoint of
   a. Supervision.
   b. Interrelationships with other sections.
   c. Freedom from interruptions by outsiders.
   d. Labor-saving features.

5. List those features in the two kitchens from Questions 1 and 2 that promote
   a. Labor-saving features.
   b. Preservation of food quality.
   c. Sanitary food handling.

KEY WORDS AND CONCEPTS

ampered service outlets
bake shop
Bain marie
bakery section
basic functions of food production
bench
complete food processing
conveyor ovens
cooking section
cook's table
cutting board
disposal unit
dough roller
E. coli 0157:H7
fruit and vegetable preparation section
finishing
Hazard Analysis Critical Control Points (HACCP)
ingredient room
L-shaped plan
maximum work center length

meat block (meat saw)
meat sections
minimum work center width
pantry section
pass-through refrigerated cart
peel
portioning
preprocessed
production plan
proof box
ready-prepared foods
reel ovens
salad and sandwich-making sections
short-order section
"smell and poke" system
tilt kettles
U-shaped plan
value-added foods
wholesale cuts

CHAPTER
9

Serving Facilities

The goal of service is to see that foods of high appeal are delivered in a prompt, efficient, and pleasant manner. The facilities planned for service can do much to see that these goals are accomplished. The majority of foods are at their peak quality at production and deteriorate rapidly afterwards. Shortness of distance between the production and service speeds service. Thus, the placement of the kitchen in relation to service is important. It is better when the dining area is rectangular to have the kitchen located in the center of one of the sides rather than one of the ends. When on the end the distance to the other end is such that prompt delivery is not always achieved. Dissatisfaction with service complaints frequently exceed those of food quality in many operations.

Planners aware of the value preserving best quality use different methods of service in keeping with specific financial programs and the volume and characteristics of patrons requiring service. An example of the shortest route in the service of hot foods is counter service in which foods are cooked behind the counter and served directly to the patrons. The time lapse between preparation and service is almost as short in fine restaurants with sufficiently well-trained servers to deliver prepared foods with great promptness to patrons. Many of the foods for such service may be brought to the table in the cooking casserole and served to the plate at the table. Salad and dessert service provides excellent opportunity for skill and showmanship. Table service of these helps to preserve best temperature and freshness.

Planners of food facilities are forced to consider not only the protection essential for food quality but also the amount of funds that will be available for labor and facilities as well as the volume and characteristics of the persons to be served. Some of the specific requirements to be met through planning include the following:

1. Facilities that will help to preserve palatable qualities in the foods
2. Facilities that will provide fast, efficient service in keeping with the characteristics of those who are to be served
3. An atmosphere in the service areas that is hospitable and attractive
4. Conditions of service that will promote protection of health through sanitation and prevention of accidents
5. Traffic lanes for patrons and employees that are clear and trouble-free.

Suitable equipment for service and a good flow of traffic from service to patron are important. Major hazards to be overcome are time lapse, wrong temperature, unpleasant degree of moisture, and contamination.

The protection of quality requires limiting **holding time.** Equipment capacity needs to be planned on the basis of speed of quality deterioration of different foods. Many meats are best when served at the completion of their preparation. Coffee, on the other hand, can be held almost an hour. Mashed potatoes have a short life, not more than 20 minutes holding time. Vegetables under prolonged holding lose flavor, color, texture, and important nutrients. Flexibility in capacity is desirable since the same item may not be held in the serving unit each time. Another food with different quantity and holding time may be used. This is usually accommodated best by multiple pans sized to a basic 12- × 20-in. (30- × 50-cm) steam table pan.

Palatable quality requires proper temperature. A rare rib roast should be held just over 140°F (59°C). Soup should reach the consumer at a temperature of 180°F (81°C). Too high a temperature quickly destroys egg quality. Various means may be needed to supply the desired temperatures. Infrared heaters may be used for rare roasts, whereas soup may require a heating unit that will maintain a higher temperature. Here are some commonly recommended temperatures for holding foods for service:

Entrées, meats, roasts	140 to 160°F (59 to 64°C)
Soups, coffee, and other thin liquids	185 to 190°F (85 to 88°C)
Sauces, gravies, etc. (except hollandaise or other products high in egg or cheese and fat)	160 to 180°F (64 to 81°C)
Salads and other cold foods	35 to 40°F (2 to 4°C)
Frozen foods	8 to 15°F (−13 to −9°C)

Note that these temperatures also apply at the time the food is served. This may cause some problems since the holding temperature must be considerably higher to allow for the cooling that will take place during dishing, transporting, and service. The proper temperature of the plates on which food is served will be significant for ensuring proper temperature for service.

Food appeal calls for a fresh, good appearance. This requires sufficient humidity in serving equipment to prevent dehydration and to reduce discoloration. Meat slices should glisten from fresh slicing. Vegetables should have a bright, natural color. Equipment is needed, for some items, that will supply air moisture, and for other foods, such as french fried potatoes, the air must be dry because they lose their quality quickly if moist. Dry heat from an infrared lamp is best for these.

Enjoyment of food involves appealing texture. Production treatment as well as service will have an influence. Eggs are toughened by high temperature. Salads are wilted by improper temperature and a lack of humidity in the air. Ice cream that is dished between 8 to 15°F (−13 to −90°C) will not only lack texture, either being too hard or too soft, but will also lack bright flavor. Overcooking of many vegetables and other foods in the serving unit is one of the greatest hazards. The relationship of time to quality should not be missed, and speed of service is important to quality standards as well as to customer satisfaction.

Fast, efficient service is gained by planning good work centers in the serving section. To ensure fast service, every element influencing speed deserves analysis. Some of the most common causes of slowdown are (1) excess travel distance in supplying the section from production, and in serving and reaching the customer; (2) confusion of arrangement in the serving section that does not follow a logical order of pickup and does not provide a clear view of items available; (3) excess motion in serving because of the layout and menu selections; (4) delays caused by preparation-to-order; (5) numerous food choices that tend to delay judgment; (6) patrons serving themselves; (7) improper or inadequate equipment, such as wrong ladle sizes and ineffective serving tools or inadequate storage space; (8) information requests about choices, sizes, prices, and ingredients; and (9) accident hazards, such as obstructions in lines of travel, dangerously hot surfaces, blind corners, and sharp turns.

Planning a cafeteria counter that helps to speed decisions on where to go or what to select will do much to reduce costs and please customers. Customers should not be confused by the nature of the service. Thus in areas where customers are not familiar with the shopping center type of cafeteria service, considerable confusion may occur because customers do not know where to go to get their food. This does not happen when customers are frequent patrons and know the flow pattern.

In a hospital the speed of service may be influenced by comprehension of menu instructions on the dish-up line, the number and skill of serving personnel, the serving facilities, the speed of the tray line, the transfer to a cart, the waiting of a cart due to the number of trays placed on it or other reasons, the speed of the elevator or delivery service, speed of movement of the cart to the floor or ward, the distance of travel, and the promptness and method of presentation. Each facet needs to be followed and analyzed for speedup. It is important to keep systems simple.

There are certain essentials for a serving section regardless of the simplicity or elaborateness of the menu and service. Included in them are ready access to foods to be served, the dish-up tools, plates on which foods are to be placed, and a landing area for convenient placement and pickup. Eliminate any points of delay and provide for specific needs. Some serving sections prepare foods such as pancakes, hamburgers, french fries, waffles, and toast. Adequate storage and proper tool and equipment arrangement can speed such production and service. Some operations may restrict menus to fast foods, whereas others may utilize a hot serving table for additional foods or depend on a hot table with occasional use of mobile short-order equipment. Close relationship of the serving section with the production section is a step-saving aid toward freshly prepared food as shown in Figure 9.1.

Application of rules for good work center planning will help to speed service. Locate plates to be used with consideration for quick, logical, or natural hand motions in picking up a plate and placing food on it. It is natural for a right-handed person to hold with the left hand and manipulate with the right. Thus the server will grasp a serving tool with the right hand, and lift and place food on a plate held in the left hand. The more that motions, through practice, become automatic, the more quickly they can be

FIGURE 9.1 A serving area adjacent to preparation area.

made. Whenever judgments must be made as to size, pattern, condition, or location of the plate or the food, there is an instant slowdown. Search is a frequent slowdown factor. Length of reach causes delay in proportion to its length. Where a far reach is made frequently, an appreciable time and effort loss may result. Following the rules for storage cited previously, such as storing tools at point of use, will do much to speed work. Tools that reduce motion and aid skillful handling, such as dippers and ladles of full-portion capacity; pointed, offset spatulas for pie; slotted spoons for foods requiring draining; and many other tools that have specific use will be of benefit. Preportioning may be used also to speed service.

Choose the dish storage location that best fits into the serving system. Is it better to use a mobile, self-leveling storage unit beside the table, or to place plates on a ledge immediately under the counter top or in a heated compartment at the back of the serving counter with a landing ledge above? Various factors may cause the choice of one over another, such as space allowance, type of menu and service, and the volume. Servers in the restaurant sketched in Figure 9.2 serve the soup and beverages. The soup containers are set in line with heated cabinets for bowls and liners on the waitstaff side of the serving counter, with a landing shelf for served plates on top. This arrangement makes the hot

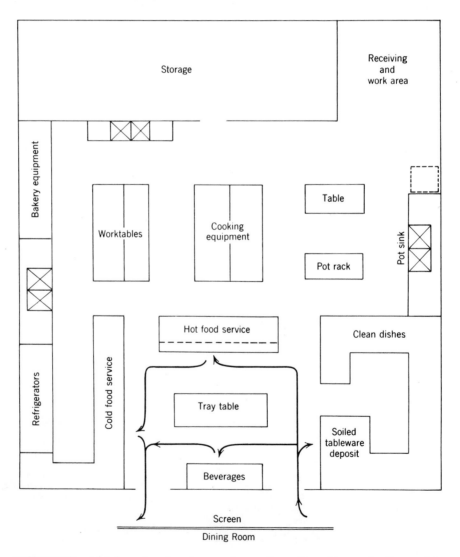

FIGURE 9.2   A kitchen plan showing serving section adjacent to production and the waitstaff's route of travel in picking up selective meals.

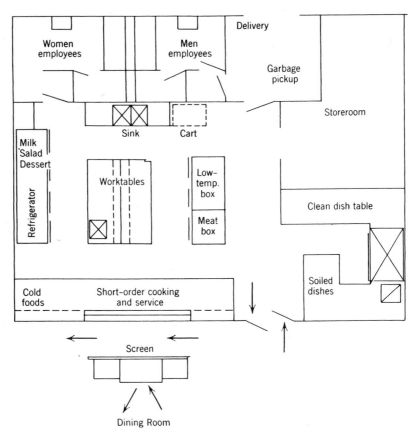

FIGURE 9.3 A simply arranged short-order facility showing close relationship between production, dish-up, and service to the dining room.

fluids available for easy, rapid service without rehandling. The coffee shop plan in Figure 9.3 permits servers to place and pick up orders from a window above the cooking section without going into the kitchen. This not only eliminates extra steps but also the slow-down hazard of going through swinging doors. The beverages, poured by the servers, are conveniently located in the dining room with the serving containers beside them.

Effective food merchandising calls for serving sections that are orderly, attractive, and possess patron appeal. This requirement has special importance for cafeterias, snack bars, food courts in malls, lunch counters, drive-in service windows, and for service carts and mobile catering units. Organization and neatness should be emphasized. The equipment and special units should fit well into the general decor. Colors and lighting should be pleasing. Food must be well displayed. The appearance should be planned to appeal to the taste of the specific group to be served. Students in a college union coffee shop may want far less in special decor than members of a club who may have to wait in a buffet line.

Opportunities for contamination of food and equipment during serving are many. Speed is too often granted precedence over meticulousness. Chances of contamination are increased in proportion to the number of food handlers, amount of time food is exposed for service, amount of hand contact with food and food handling equipment, and use of temperatures that favor the growth of bacteria. Every possible protection should be afforded that is reasonable and in keeping with good practice. Workers grouped and talking behind a cafeteria counter may contaminate food more than customers moving in front, where food is protected by a sneeze-guard. The strong possibilities for accidents in dining areas, due to handling hot foods, food spillage on slick floors, hurrying workers, and patrons strange to surroundings plus minds that are elsewhere, such as on making food selections or searching for a place to sit, are common and call for awareness and careful planning.

FIGURE 9.4   A well-planned, well-lit dining room. Note the wide aisle space, attractive simple decorations, and feeling of cleanliness. Guests upon entering should get a sense of warmth and feel easily able to get to their tables.

DINING ROOMS

The appearance of and the atmosphere in the area where consumers dine has much to do with their attitude of approval or disapproval of the food service (Figure 9.4). Even though hordes may be fed, the diner wants to feel that the service is personal. For a period of time, that spot takes the place of a home. An attractive surrounding will help to create a sense of well-being. In a home there are times when one is happy to snatch a bite at the kitchen table and other times when more leisurely dining in a well-ordered dining room is preferred. The locality in which the food facility is located will in large degree determine the type of dining room and service that will be most successful. There are times when satisfying hunger and nutritional needs is the major and perhaps the sole concern. At other times, sociability, entertainment, restfulness, sense of identity, change, and any other psychological factors may have an influence on selection and enjoyment of an eating place.

Size

Determine dining room size in light of preferences of the specific group. Diners in commercial establishments have shown preference for a certain amount of seclusion by gravitating to booths, wall locations, or other secluded areas of the rooms. In large operations managers have used various devices to divide rooms and to create the desired effect. One device is to center the serving sections and place the dining areas around it. Dividers, such as partitions, screens, furniture placement, planters, and other decorative arrangements, are used to create the desired feeling of intimacy.

Gregariousness will make people want to go where they believe the crowd goes. Those who possess this trait to a high degree, such as college students, would rather be crowded than patronize an excellent place that is sparsely filled. Sparsely filled dining areas spell lack of popularity to the average person and immediately raise a question of their desirability. This fact, in addition to limited investment, emphasizes the importance of choosing the probable capacity needs based on a close calculation of numbers to be served and speed of turnover.

Certain groups require control, and the dining room size may need to be adjusted to the amount and type of supervision required and available. Size adjustment may be desirable also for resident groups in order to promote acquaintanceship and a group spirit. Fewer close acquaintances are formed and a lower feeling of identity created when dining in a large, ever-changing group. Mealtime sociability has special significance in college residences and in retirement homes. Noise control and discipline are a frequent concern with young patrons and can best be handled with small groups. Banquet rooms where programs are presented may need to be large and have excellent acoustics.

Mealtime is a rest time for industrial workers. A change of pace and a change of atmosphere are helpful. If a person has been working somewhat alone, the activity in a large room with many individuals coming and going will add interest. If the person has been with many people and perhaps supplying their wants, a smaller area and a quiet atmosphere may be more restful. Those who have been employed in a bleak, drab plant are given a lift by a dining room that is bright and cheerful.

Traffic Flow

Plans should be made for a logical patronage flow to and from the various areas of the room. This will mean having main aisles and side aisles according to the size and shape of the room (Figure 9.5). Diners are not comfortable and find it confusing when they must thread their way through a maze of tables, dodging elbows of diners and servers carrying food or dishes. Aisles should be wide enough for the number of people who are likely to be moving along them at one time (approximately 3 to 4 ft or .91 to 1.22 m). Provide adequate waiting areas to avoid clogging of aisles with people waiting.

Plan according to the normal movement cycle of patrons and workers in the dining room. Those points of call likely to be made should be included on the path of the respective person. If self-bussing is to be done by patrons, for example, the deposit point for the soiled dishes should be located on the patron's path to the door. If candy and cigarette vending machines are to be used, the patron should not have to cross a server's path to get to them. All of the points of pickup for a server should be in orderly location according to need on the server's path. Distances of travel for both groups should be as short as possible, giving preference to routes in terms of frequency of travel. The need to provide wider aisles for individuals in wheel chairs has been mentioned.

Well-equipped service islands help to reduce travel by service personnel. Communication or signal systems, with lights, phone, or other means of communication, between production and serving sections, are valuable, especially when distances are great and traffic heavy. The use of conveyors for delivering food and removing soiled dishes will assist in speeding service and reducing labor. Ideas for reducing travel by using central supply stations are shown in Figure 9.6.

Safety and Sanitation

Safety and sanitation codes pertaining to dining areas should be carefully checked and followed. The number of entrances and exits to rooms must comply with fire ordinances. Toilet facilities for guests and employees should comply with codes as to location, entrances, and sanitary facilities. Floors and floor treatment should be reasonably nonslip and free from **surprise factors,** such as half-steps or obstructions, that might cause accidents. Follow a method of service and food handling that protects the sanitation of food and food service equipment.

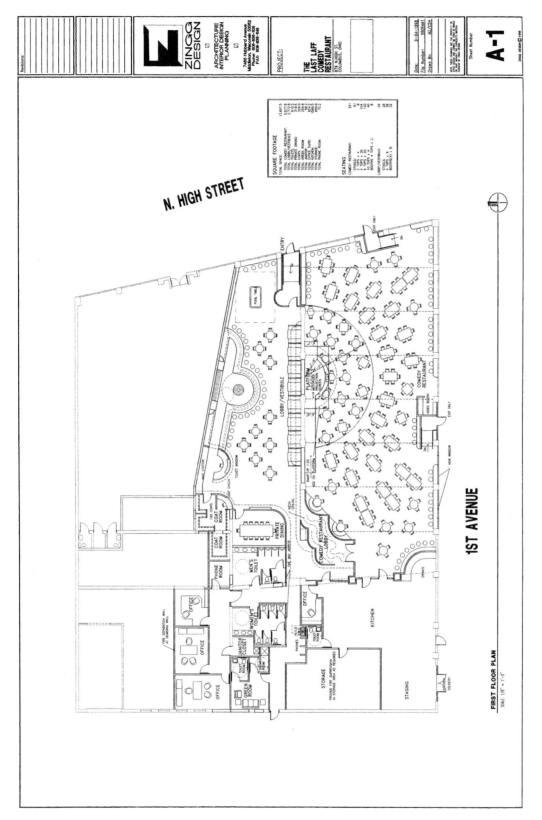

FIGURE 9.5 Special needs often dictate how a facility is planned. This dining room, shown in an AutoCAD floor plan, must be laid out such that diners can see the platform on the side of the dining room where the projection screen will be. Note how table arrangement is in an ever-widening semicircle with good aisle space around each table. A more favorable location for the kitchen would have been on the 1st Avenue side, but parking lot and building entrance requirements were such that the main entrance had to be from North High Street, forcing the kitchen location to one side of the dining room, which means servers travel a long distance to give service to the other side. (*Courtesy of Zingg Designs, Middleton, Wisconsin.*)

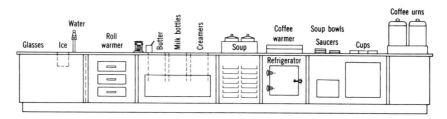

FIGURE 9.6 A central supply station can fill many service needs in dining area.

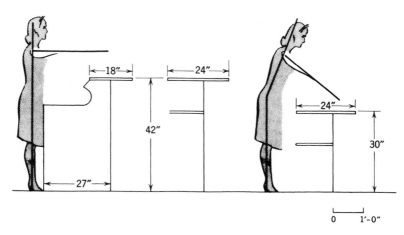

FIGURE 9.7 A server of average height and reach at counters of different height and width.

COUNTER SERVICE

Counter service is commonly considered one of the quickest types of service. The menu, the size, and the arrangement will to a large degree determine how well it competes for speed with other types of service. A simplified menu, short travel distances, and minimized motion help to ensure speed. Each station should be approximately 16 to 20 linear ft (5 to 6 linear m). When determining the height and width of counters, consider (1) the average height and reach of servers, (2) the best utilization of space for supply storage, and (3) the comfort of patrons. Counter heights usually vary from 30 to 43 in. (0.76 to 1.07 m) and widths vary from 18 to 30 in. (0.46 to 0.76 m)(Figure 9.7).

The high, wide counter allows for a ledge approximately 27 in. (68 cm) deep at the back for supplies, short-order equipment, dishes, and bus boxes. Table-height counters depend on the backbar for supplies and equipment. The wide counter is more generally favored for convenience and for hiding some of the normal clutter of service. It also allows more storage space. The seating at counters is usually on a pedestaled stool or chair. The seats should be 14 to 15 in. (36 to 38 cm) in diameter, a footrest 9 to 12 in. (23 to 30 cm) deep, knee space 8 to 10 in. (20 to 25 cm) from the edge of the seat to the counter pedestal, and 12 in. (30 cm) from the seat to the counter top. When stools are placed on step-ups, as required at high counters, accidents sometimes occur due to patrons forgetting to step down. This is one of the arguments for the table-height counter.

Plan this work center to have everything convenient, neat, and adequately equipped (Figure 9.8). In some operations food preparation may occur. Hot beverage-making equipment may be located at the counter or on the backbar. Cups and saucers should be within easy reach and a source for refrigerated dairy products provided for those who wish them. Bread dispensing will need to be considered in relation to the types served. Hamburger and hot dog buns to be reheated on the griddle need storage to retain freshness. If sandwiches with bread slices are to be made to order, a self-leveling dispenser is convenient. Hot rolls are better stored in a roll warmer that can be

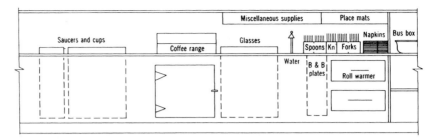

FIGURE 9.8   Counter serving station.

used also for made-ahead hamburgers prepared for peak periods. These keep satisfactorily if wrapped and held above 140 °F (59 °C). The small quality change tends to be more acceptable to the average patron than having to wait for service. A refrigerated water supply with a push faucet and storage for glasses is needed in this area.

Refrigerated display cases are sometimes located on the counter or in a central area partly for convenience and partly to promote impulse buying. They may contain salads, sandwiches, and desserts. A cabinet for ice cream and a refrigerated table for sandwich making should be considered in terms of menu requirements. A fountain may be advantageous if there is a demand for fountain items. It should be recalled that reduced variety will reduce space that must be allowed and will aid in reducing time and energy output. Sales potential should be very carefully calculated for each menu addition.

Arrange place-setting equipment to save motion. When serving across a counter a server places the service in a reverse position to his or her own. Forks and napkins will be placed with the right hand, and knives, spoons, glasses, and cups with the left. Blades and tines will be pointed toward the server and away from the patron. Plates, cups, glasses, and bowls should be at the left, if possible, of the items to be served in them. Salt, pepper, and sugar should be kept in a frame on the counter within reach of patrons.

The chief advantage of counter service—speed—is in a degree defeated by any factor that causes delay and handicaps the fast rate at which patrons receive service. When in operation, it is often beneficial to time service to ascertain whether speed is in keeping with the standard set, such as one or two minutes from the time the patron was seated until served. If the standard is not being met search for the reason. Common faults include menus that slow down choice or are complicated to serve, travel distance and excess motion, preparation-of-food delays, inadequate equipment, unavailable tools, awkward arrangement, overcrowded space, and nearest service location not given to the most frequently served item, such as beverages. Compactness in a serving station may call for limitation of supplies to that required for a meal. Automatic handling can be used to relieve server time, such as conveyors extending under the counter top to remove bus boxes or to deliver supplies. Convenience may be served through the use of mobile dispensing units rolled into position so that bulk storage is at hand behind the scenes.

TABLE SERVICE

There are three main types of table service: French, Russian, and American. Sometimes in clubs and other organizations a service called English, or butler, or family is used. Special types of service are used in ethnic restaurants, but these often are highly Americanized to suit the desires of patrons who are more comfortable with their own way of eating. Thus, one may request in a Chinese restaurant that they be given a pair of chopsticks to eat with, but normally the traditional knife, fork, and spoon are set on the table. We also have counter service, **cafeteria service** and **hospital bedside service** which have been previously discussed. **Self-service** is also used.

French service requires that much of the final preparation, all of the dishing up, and all of the serving be done at tableside. For this a cart outfitted with a heating unit and other required equipment, called a *gueridon* is used. Also food items are brought to the table such as a carving cart, a dessert cart, etc. These carts require that there be considerable space around tables, so even 20 sq ft per cover is not enough. Planners should also see that aisle spaces and space between tables are adequate for the movement of these. Such a service also requires that the kitchen be equipped somewhat differently than the regular kitchen so such table service is possible. A rather affluent clientele must support such service and the decor and furnishings must be in keeping with what they would expect in dining at a pricey, upscale operation. French service is usually the slowest type.

Russian service requires that food be dished onto platters or serving dishes and brought to the guests for service. This requires less table space and so 20 sq ft per cover is usually adequate. Again, this type of service demands that the serving dishes and table setting ware be suited to this type of service. If the planner is asked to select servers' jackets, they should be sure that their arms are roomy because servers often wrap a towel around the arm on which the platter is to be resting and these are often so hot they can result in burns unless such protection is given.

In **American service** the food is dished in the kitchen onto the dishes on which the patron will eat and so the dining area can be of normal space per cover. The equipping of the kitchen can also be normal. This type of service is used in most operations.

CHAPTER SUMMARY

Serving facilities should be planned to hold quality in food, and give fast, efficient, and pleasant service. The storage given foods before and after production can vitally affect their quality. The shortest distance possible between production and service should be planned. The type of service planned should be suited to the type of clientele. Decor and other factors that influence comfort and attractiveness should be sought. Provide for good sanitation and safety. Good work centers for the production of foods and their dish-up help the facility achieve its service goals. Similarly, well-planned service centers will also assist in meeting these goals. If some of the foods can be brought closer to where they are to be served, speed of service is promoted. Counter service with the product to be served right behind it usually results in the fastest service.

If the number eating in a dining area is too sparse, diners will feel uncomfortable in it. If the dining area must be large but will often be used by a relatively small number, planners should see that the room can be divided off by some means to give diners a feeling of intimacy and that the place serves food of good quality and gives good service. The space needs mentioned in the chapter are based on the number of square feet usually required per cover or person seated and should be observed in planning. Provide for good flow and see that there is sufficient aisle space to permit good traffic flow. The need to provide for individuals with wheelchair needs should not be forgotten. The service facilities should provide for good sanitation and sanitation practices.

There are three main types of service: French, Russian, and American. French service largely takes place at tableside and requires the most space and special equipment. The service is also the slowest. Russian service is next in time, space, and special equipment needs. American service, not surprisingly, is the most common in the United States, and is usually the fastest of the three. It requires the least special equipment and space. Other types of service are counter, cafeteria, bedside, and self-service. Ethnic restaurants may have their own specialized types of service.

REVIEW QUESTIONS

Compare the service requirements of the following from the standpoint of cost, speed of service, space, dining equipment, decor, upkeep, sanitation, and safety.

1. Management is planning to set up a very upscale restaurant near a very affluent residential area. What would be the advantages and

disadvantages of using French service? Russian service? American service?
2. What kinds of foods can be held awaiting service and what kinds cannot? For how long can some of the foods you listed be held and what kind of storage best preserves them?

3. What things should a planner do to see that good sanitation and safety are facilitated in a dining area? How about sanitation features that might be used in dish, glass, and flatware? Besides slipping on highly polished wax floors or accidents caused by aisles that are too narrow, what other safety needs must be covered? How about fire or other needs to rapidly exit the property? Do not cover things personnel should do; cover what a planner must do.

KEY WORDS AND CONCEPTS

American service
cafeteria service
counter service
French service
holding time
hospital bedside service

palatable quality
Russian service
self-service
surprise factors
table service

CHAPTER
10

Housekeeping Sections

Housekeeping refers to the care used in keeping a facility, its furnishings, equipment, and tools in good condition for use and enjoyment. A great deal of money and effort are afforded in many operations in creating an atmosphere that will be attractive to persons who dine there. Although attractive decorative schemes help, wise operators recognize the importance of setting the mood of diners and of reflecting the image of the restaurant. Favorable reactions are gained most readily through maintaining a hospitable atmosphere of cleanliness, orderliness, and a sense of being served by persons concerned about the diners' welfare. Even persons who are negligent in their own habits are repulsed by clutter, haphazard appearance, and musty, stale, greasy odors. Maintaining desirable qualities throughout the facility calls for conviction and discipline radiating from the management. The resulting standards permeate the operation pertaining to such things as immediate repair of items that are out of order, return of tools borrowed by fellow workers, leaving equipment in satisfactory condition after use, neatness and orderliness of work, and friendly, courteous behavior between workers and between workers and the public.

Facility planners can promote easy and satisfactory maintenance through selection of durable materials and finishes that will withstand the amount of wear that items are likely to receive. Avoid difficult-to-clean equipment designs in areas of the kitchen and dining rooms. The likelihood of excessive wear, breakage, spillage, accumulation of clutter and soil, and accident hazards is greater in some areas of the kitchens and dining rooms than in others. Special provision needs to be made for prevention and/or quick repair and cleanup in such areas.

Adequate cleaning around large pieces of heavy equipment can be difficult unless special provision is made. Even large ovens and ranges are now designed so that they can be raised by lever or moved to facilitate cleaning behind and beneath them. Drains should be placed in areas where there is likely to be spillage. They should be distributed in sufficient number for satisfactory drainage when scrubbing. Place storage for cleaning equipment where it can be readily reached for incidental cleanup when needed.

Proper sanitation requires selection of food machines that can be readily dismantled and reassembled for thorough cleaning and sanitizing. Food particles easily lodge in slicers and cutters and can cause food sanitation problems when not properly cleaned. Durable surfaces are required that can withstand repeated scrubbing and retain a bright new appearance. Even cutting boards, especially those used for meats, should be able to withstand scalding repeatedly.

Plan dining room cleanup equipment according to the care that will be required. A vacuum cleaner and attachments will be needed for rugs, draperies, and certain acoustic equipment. The floor finish may require waxers and polishers. Carts for handling pails, mops, brushes, and cleaning supplies help to save steps. A closet for these and also a location for small items needed in dining areas for quick cleanup should be a part of dining room plans. There are numerous aspects for which planners need to make provision in promoting safety, sanitation, and good housekeeping. Every area deserves questioning on this basis. The following is a suggested list of questions to stimulate thoughtful evaluation of housekeeping potential when making selections.

HOUSEKEEPING EVALUATION LIST

1. All items of major equipment: Will materials and finishes withstand necessary cleaning? Does the design or ease of disassembling permit thorough cleaning?
2. Acoustical treatment: Will the material and/or design permit adequate cleaning and periodic refinishing if necessary for good appearance?
3. Chairs, tables, stools, counters, tray rails, and other furniture: Is the structure sturdy, the surfaces smooth, and the materials cleanable?
4. China and glassware: Are they of a design and material that will withstand reasonable wear? Is there adequate stock for replacement? Are suitable facilities provided for handling and storage?
5. Conveyors: Is the operation smooth and reasonably hazard free? Are all parts readily cleanable?
6. Drains: Does the design permit free flow and prevent backsiphonage? Are location and number planned adequate?
7. Equipment attachments: Are they suitably sturdy, fully cleanable, and is storage provided for convenience and adequate protection?
8. Equipment bumpers: Do they provide adequate protection of walls and equipment?
9. Detergent dispensers: Can they be supplied easily? Do they give indication when supplies are needed? Do they function well?
10. Draperies, furniture, and decorative objects: Are they attractive, cleanable, durable, and suitable?
11. Electrical cords, outlets, and switches: Are they in keeping with safety codes, properly placed, in sufficient number, and in good condition?
12. Exposed pipes: Can they be placed in an inconspicuous location and covered for protection and a good appearance?
13. Flatware: Is it smooth, shapely, and attractive? Does it require burnishing to retain a bright appearance? Will the weight withstand normal wear? Are plans adequate for cleaning, storing, and dispensing?
14. Floors, ramps, platforms, and stairs: Are they of material that will withstand expected wear? Can the material be fully cleaned for good sanitation? Are they nonskid and designed for safety?
15. Floor mats or coverings: Does the floor design permit their use without hazard of tripping? Are they well placed, safety flat, and readily cleanable?
16. Hoods: Are they effective in removing smoke and fumes without causing a draft that is uncomfortable for workers? Can hoods and filters be fully and easily cleaned?
17. Ladders: Are they sturdy, safe, and of appropriate size to meet needs? Are they conveniently stored?
18. Linen supplies: Are uniforms, table linens, aprons, and towels to be owned by the establishment or supplied by a laundry? What number is adequate? What provision will be needed for storage, collection of soiled laundry, and issuing of supplies?

19. Lighting: Has provision been made for the amount of illumination needed in areas according to work done or display requirements. Are lighting fixtures and equipment well placed and readily cleanable and serviceable?
20. Safety valves on urns and steam equipment: Will the functioning provide adequate safety? Can adjustments be made with minimum hazard?
21. Scales: Do they retain accuracy? Are they placed for convenient use? Are they easily cleanable? Is there a sufficient number for good work?
22. Shelving: Is it sturdy, cleanable, well placed, suitably sized, and adequate?
23. Small equipment: Is it sufficiently sturdy for expected use, adequate in amount, and stored for convenience and cleanliness?
24. Sinks: Are they constructed of sturdy, easily cleanable, and bright material that will withstand expected wear? Does the design and location permit thorough cleaning and discourage lodging of insects? Will the supporting structure bear maximum weights likely to be in or on the sinks? Are sizes appropriate to uses? Are they well placed for convenience? Are they designed for complete drainage?
25. Storage equipment: Has suitable transportation equipment been supplied to meet expected need? Has adequate protection been supplied to prevent spoilage and theft and to preserve good sanitation? Is all equipment suitably sturdy and readily cleanable?
26. Ventilation fans, ducts, and grills: Will they function effectively in removing smoke and fumes? Can they be easily and adequately cleaned?
27. Walls and ceiling: Do they give adequate reflection of light? Are the surfaces cleanable and capable of withstanding repeated cleaning? Are the colors attractive, furnishing an appealing background for foodservice?
28. Water temperatures: Are appropriate temperatures supplied for dishwashing, kitchen use, drinking water, and steam cleaning?
29. Water: Is there an ample supply of safe water under suitable pressure that is good tasting for drinking and softened if necessary?
30. Wheels and casters on mobile equipment: Do they roll easily? Are they sufficiently sturdy to bear maximum loads required? Are they cleanable?
31. Windows and screens: Are they available where needed and clean?
32. Worktables, mobile and stationary: Are surfaces smooth and readily cleanable and constructed of noncorrosive, nontoxic materials? Are drawers removable for cleaning and shelving free of difficult-to-clean lodging spots for soil?
33. All areas of the food facility (work sections, dining rooms, lounge and toilet areas, office, storage rooms, garbage and trash areas): Are they well ventilated, properly lighted, orderly, adequately equipped, at suitable temperature, and clean?

WAREWASHING

Warewashing has a high rating of importance in foodservice facilities because of its significance in protecting sanitation; utilization of labor time; saving on operational costs for power, hot water, and detergent; and for prevention of loss and breakage of tableware. The pleasure of clientele is readily affected by the appearance and cleanliness of tableware. The sparkle of well-washed and fully rinsed dishes and the bright appearance and feel of properly cleansed flatware invite diners to enjoy their food.

The **dishwashing operation** includes removal of soiled tableware from dining areas; receiving, scraping, and stacking ready for washing; washing and drying of cups, glasses, dishes, flatware, and utensils; removal of tableware from baskets or a conveyor and stacking; and transfer to facilities for storage and dispensing or use. It is desirable that dishes be routed from the dining area in a manner that will create the least distance, noise, confusion, and unsightliness. Most persons dislike the sight and clatter of dish scraping and stacking in the dining area. The manner in which dishes are removed differs with the type of institution. In table-service restaurants they are usually cleared from tables by servers or buspersons to trays or baskets and carried to the dishroom. In schools and industrial plants patrons frequently return dishes to collection points or a conveyor (Figure 10.1). Although the majority dislike returning trays to a central point after their meal, they will do it in industrial and school dining rooms if the custom is established as a part of maintaining minimal costs. If patrons are to bus their dishes, the placement port should be in line with the exit and where the path of exit will not cross that of patrons going to or from the serving area. Screen the port to lessen noise and improve the appearance of the room. This is sometimes done by means of a conveyor that carries the trays through a small port and out of sight. Patient trays in hospitals are generally collected on carts or trucks and moved by elevator or conveyor to a central dishwashing area.

Dishwashing Operation

Significant goals for the dishwashing section include thorough cleansing and protection of the sanitation of tableware and utensils, prevention of loss and breakage, and economical use of supplies and labor time. Good results in dishwashing are brought about through: (1) completeness of scraping, washing, and rinsing actions; (2) water quality, quantity, and proper temperature; (3) effectiveness of **detergent** and **rinsing agent;** (4) type and quality of tableware; and (5) care in handling and proper procedures followed by the dishwashing personnel.

Thorough scraping lessens soil in the wash and directly influences bacterial count on the final result. A suitable force of water in the washing action must move soil from surfaces to be cleaned. The wash water and detergent are recycled, with a gradual flow

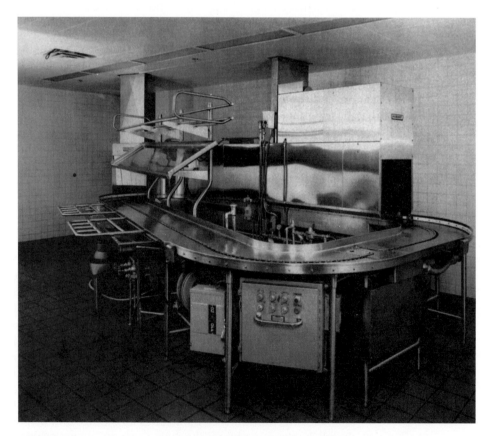

FIGURE 10.1   A compact, circular dishwashing arrangement that carries the dishes from scraping through prewash, wash, and rinsing sections to the clean-dish table *(Courtesy of Hobart Corporation, Troy, Ohio.)*

of fresh water from the rinse section to refresh the wash solution as it picks up soil in the washing process. Detergent must be added gradually also by dispenser in amounts sufficient to maintain an effective concentration. The dish is not clean nor fully sanitized until all of the washing solution has been removed by the higher temperature flood of fresh rinse water.

It is important that the detergent attack fatty substances, loosen soil, and rinse free from surfaces to be cleaned. To obtain a bright, sparkling surface, tableware must be thoroughly rinsed of soil residue and detergent. A rinsing solution that lowers the surface tension of water droplets will cause water to sheet away from surfaces in a manner that leaves the surfaces reasonably free of spots.

Three water temperatures are needed in the washing process. Prerinsing with warm water at 120°F (49°C) that will melt fat, but not cook foods firmly on the surface, is needed. The washing water should be 150–160°F (66–71°C). The sanitizing temperature should be at least 180°F (82°C). A lower temperature (75–120°F or 24–49°C) is permitted if an approved chemical sanitizing rinse is used. Manufacturers of dish machines warn planners that the use of sodium hypochlorite bleach will attack certain materials, including pewter, aluminum, and silver. Bacteria are also killed at 170°F (77°C) if held for 30 seconds or longer. This is the recommended temperature and time to use when washing items by hand. At temperatures higher than 195°F (91°C), water spray vaporizes sufficiently to interfere with the effectiveness of the rinsing action.

The type and quality of the tableware influence appearance gained through dishwashing. China surfaces from which the glaze has been removed through the hammering, rubbing action of wear will have a dull appearance that looks soiled. Plastic material does not absorb heat sufficiently during the washing process to quickly air dry and will remain wet unless some means such as a current of hot air or a good rinse solution is used to promote drying. Stained, tarnished, and worn flatware will require burnishing in addition to washing to produce a bright appearance.

Guard Sanitation.

Protection of sanitation requires concerted effort on the part of both planners and operators. Regardless of equipment and detergent used, good results depend on good judgment and on good procedures being regularly followed by dishwashing employees. Water temperatures are to be watched, detergent concentrations maintained, and sanitary handling practices faithfully followed. There are many examples in a one-person operation where the employee goes directly from scraping soiled dishes to handling clean dishes, taking them from baskets and stacking them, without benefit of handwashing. Some health authorities require that a wall close off the soiled-dish area from the clean-dish section to prevent possibilities for this method of contamination.

An organization of duties that provide separate workers for handling soiled and clean dishes is preferable for a one-person operation, but at times may not be practical. It is wise to take special precautions by placing a **hand-washing sink** in a convenient location so that employees will handle clean dishes with clean hands. Avoid hard-to-reach and difficult-to-clean areas and materials. Use special care in installing a conveyor so that all parts can be opened up for adequate cleaning. Select a dishwasher that can be opened up and dismantled where necessary for thorough cleaning. Choose a dishwasher, detergent dispensers, and other equipment for this section that meet National Sanitation Foundation standards.

Items important to good sanitation include adequate light, proper plumbing, good ventilation, and surfaces that are smooth, cleanable, and impervious to absorption of grease and moisture. The light should be well placed to avoid glare or shadow and be of 50 to 70 foot-candles. The floor should have a hard, nonslip surface. Floor mats, if used, should be removable, lie flat, and be of a type that can be thoroughly scrubbed or steam cleaned. **Coved corners** are required for hard-surfaced walls and floor. Acoustical material or noise control devices are needed to lessen noise and should be cleanable. Good ventilation is essential to remove steam and provide a good circulation of air.

Hose attachments should be provided on the **soiled-dish table** for flushing the table and cleaning the machine, and for use in flushing and cleaning the floor. Drains should be provided at points where spillage is most likely to occur, and the floor given a slight slope toward the drains. A hot water supply adequate in temperature and amount and at 20 to 25 lb pressure should be provided. Sewers and drains should be adequate to handle the large volume of water used in the section. Provide grease traps as needed and install these to prevent sewage from backing up into the dish machine. Have one large central trap, if possible. Install clean-out fittings in drain lines wherever they are needed. Plumbing, electrical, and other lines should be brought up through the legs of equipment or from overhead in a manner to minimize collection areas for grease and soil. All openings made for lines should be sealed in a manner to make the area **vermin proof.** Electrical wiring should be in concealed conduit.

Dish-Handling Equipment.

Conveyors provide quiet, inconspicuous help in moving dishes from dining areas to the dish room. When dishes are transported by hand, it is necessary for the dish room to be close to the dining room for step-saving. A conveyor can move the dishes to a remote area before scraping and stacking occur to avoid unpleasant noise. The speed of the conveyor belt should (1) be one with which customers feel comfortable in placing trays, (2) meet requirements for the number of items arriving at a time, and (3) enable clearance with sufficient speed in the dish room. The length of belt exposed to receive trays, plus speed of movement, should be determined in terms of the number of items that will arrive at one time. Breakage occurs and clearing is more difficult when space is inadequate and customers stack items on top of another, unless the conveyor has high sides that permit such stacking.

If service personnel move the soiled dishes to the dish room, routing should permit a smooth flow of traffic and eliminate worker delay, noise, and expensive collisions. "In" and "out" doors should be provided, and the doors should be wide enough to permit passage of workers with wide trays. Automatic opening doors are helpful; usually right-to-left flow is desirable.

Loss and breakage of tableware may be lessened by workers separating silver and glasses from soiled dishes when clearing tables (Figure 10.2). Those who are clearing cafeteria or patient trays should remove these items and any paper waste before sending the tray to the soiled-dish table for scraping. Plans for public schools should make it convenient for children to separate these items before placing the trays in the soiled-dish port. A wall opening next to the soiled-dish port, equipped with a slide on the dish room side that reaches to a sink of water, is a good plan for soaking flatware. Paper waste may be placed in a swing top container or through another port that is significantly different from the flatware port to discourage confusion.

Keep in mind when selecting equipment the 11 steps usually followed in the dishwashing process, the first three of which may have been performed as indicated in the dining area. The procedures include:

1. Removal of paper, cloth, or other items that are not to be included in the dishwashing process.
2. Removal of flatware to a soak bath.
3. Sorting of cups and glasses into their respective racks.
4. Diverting milk glasses or other glasses that require soaking or brushing.
5. Scraping, sorting, and stacking dishes and trays.
6. Racking or placing items on a conveyor belt of the dish machine.
7. Placing racks of cups, glasses, and/or china in the machine.
8. Washing of flatware by placing flat on a rack for the first run through the dish machine; sorting into cylinders with the eating portions up for the second run through the machine; followed by tipping the flatware into clean cylinders for storage so that the eating portions of the flatware are down and the handles are up.

FIGURE 10.2 Crowded dishtables mean excessive breakage, which can be avoided by adequate space and proper organization and flow of work.

9. Removal and storage of tableware.
10. Inspection and burnishing of flatware.
11. Drying and stacking of trays and other items.

Breakdown of the operation tends to happen when there is overloading of facilities, awkward motion, loss of work rhythm, interruptions, and lack of attention. These tend to happen when plans have not provided for sufficient space in relation to workload and a convenient area in which workers can work with normal rhythm, without unnecessary interruptions and according to proper sequence of operations. The point in the dishwashing procedure at which smooth flow is most likely to break down is in the receiving area of the soiled-dish table. Plans to prevent this must provide for a suitable balance between maximum soiled-dish arrival and space and labor to handle it.

Careful calculation of the probable load of dishes and their arrival schedule needs to be made to make plans to handle peak loads adequately. This should be based on the number served, the style of service, and the method of removal of dishes from dining areas. In establishments serving full-course dinners, approximately 15 to 20 pieces of china, glassware, and silver will be used per person served within a 45- to 60-minute turnover period. In a cafeteria, the quantity drops to about 3 to 10 pieces plus the tray, and the turnover period may average 30 minutes. Special service as well as regular service needs to be considered. In table service dining rooms and commercial cafeterias the tableware is cleared into trays or bus boxes for delivery to the soiled-dish tables. In hospitals, patient trays may be sent to the dish room by conveyor, dumb waiter, or on carts, each requiring its particular handling technique. The following are some of the questions to be answered in making a calculation of requirements:

1. What kind and how many items will arrive on the soiled-dish table per minute normally? As a maximum?
2. How many pieces can a worker, at normal pace, handle per minute?
3. How much space will be required for items on the soiled-dish table during peak periods?

4. How will dishes arrive—as unsorted items in waiters' bus boxes; as unsorted trays on dumb waiters; as unsorted trays or bus boxes wheeled to the dish room on tray carts, on which they can stand until time and space permits processing; or as a flood on self-bussed patron trays on a conveyor?
5. Can extra workers be available for peak period handling of dishes?
6. What size and type of dishwasher will be needed to wash the required load within desired time periods?
7. What dishtable space, machine capacity, and number of workers will be required for satisfactory balance of capacity in proportion to needs?

Careful planning to prevent dishroom pileups saves much expense and difficulty. A pileup on the soiled-dish table may result in loss and breakage, plus greater difficulty in scraping, sorting, and stacking. It may cause delay in dining room clearing that results in a slowdown in service. Peak period pileups can sometimes be solved by better separation at bussing stations or at dining room collection points. Even the removal of flatware and glasses from trays can save time and loss. This may be done either by patrons returning trays or by foodservice employees. Having dish carts on which extra loads, such as those from catering areas, may remain during peak periods can help to relieve congestion.

Soiled-dish tables should be adequate in size and support for the maximum number of dishes likely to arrive at one time (Figure 10.3). The gauge of the metal and the support must be sufficient to prevent sagging. Situations characterized by sudden and fluctuating masses of dishes require care in planning to prevent the temporary need from upsetting efficiency of normal operation. Providing extra workers for short periods is not always possible or practical. Excess dishtable space may be expensive to install and difficult for few workers to cover in normal operation. Racks or tray trucks may be used to handle a temporary overload.

Space and facility need to be provided for removal of coarse refuse and the sorting and stacking of dishes ready for filling baskets or placing these on the traveling belt of the dishwasher. How many dish baskets will be on the table at one time? Allow approximately 8 to 12 sq ft (0.74 to 1.12 m^2) for two or three racks. More space is needed if dishes are allowed to accumulate before going through the machine. The smallest amount of space is required when dishes arrive in a steady flow and a rackless machine is used. Allow space for scraped, sorted, and stacked dishes. Determine the plan of work and the largest number of items likely to be stacked before feeding the machine.

Prerinsing of dishes may be done in several ways. One is a continuous flow of water pumped over dishes as they are being scraped. In large facilities where several workers are required for this, the water may flow in a trough along the front of the table where flushing is done. Small units may use a single flood of water or flush by hose over a sink. The latter method is done by placing dishes in racks over a sink located in the soiled-dish table in front of the dishwasher (Figure 10.4). The hose used is equipped with a trigger-operated nozzle. The sink dimensions are slightly larger than those in the dish baskets (20 in. × 20 in. or 51 cm × 51 cm). The sink has slides across the top to ensure easy movement of the rack into the machine. Separate machines or a prerinse section of a large machine are commonly used for prerinsing.

The soiled-dish table should have drainage that will prevent water from the table going into the dishwasher. A slight pitch away from the machine, possibly toward the prerinse sink, or a drain approximately 3 in. (8 cm) wide extending the full width of the table near the entrance of the machine is desirable. The tables should be designed with a curb high enough to prevent overflow or spillage of water on the floor during the process of work or cleaning. A height of 3 in. (8 cm) is recommended. If a conveyor belt moves onto the table, it should be constructed for easy cleaning around and under it. It should be on a slightly raised area to prevent seepage of moisture under it. Scraping blocks, placed in convenient locations for workers, should be on raised coves to prevent liquids from running into garbage cans. Where disposal or pulper units are used, the block may be flush with the table or disposal cone.

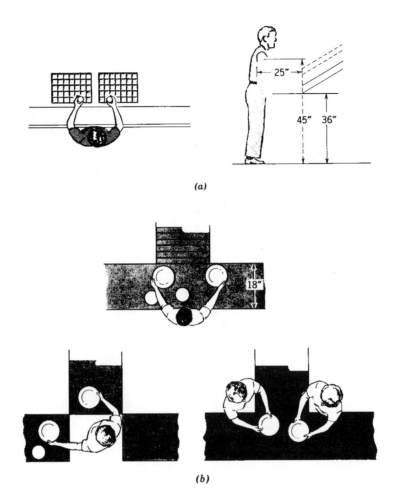

FIGURE 10.3   Arrangement of soiled-dish area. (a) Placement of shelf for dish racks. Position racks at height and distance convenient in terms of average human measurement. (b) Position of soiled-dish table in relation to feeding a continuous-belt-type dishwasher. Working beside or immediately in front of a machine is better than reaching across an expanse of table.

The selection of size and type of dishwasher needs to be based on load requirements, space for handling, time limitations, and economical use of labor and supplies. A large flood of dishes may come to the table at peak periods and require immediate handling to supply needs because space limitations prohibit gradual handling. Where gradual handling is possible, fewer workers and a smaller capacity machine may be adequate. Calculation of machine size needed and labor requirements necessitates knowing time required for loading, movement time in the machine, drying time outside the machine before stacking and removal, and the speed of workers performing at normal rate. It is necessary to seek a balance between probable load, performance rate, and machine capacity. It is wise to provide for 25% more capacity than normally necessary. Question whether the load is of right size and so distributed that labor is well utilized in using a manually operated machine. Determine if the load and distribution are such that assembly-line methods and a larger machine gives better satisfaction.

The economics of dishwasher selection involves not only the initial cost of the machine installed, but also the comparative costs of labor, power, hot water, detergent, and racks or other supplies required in the operation (Figure 10.5). Many designers estimate that dishwashers can be used to 70% of capacity. A major problem is keeping it loaded to capacity. To save energy dishes should be stacked until the dishwasher can be run fully loaded for at least 30 minutes at a time. In the meantime, heat should be shut off.

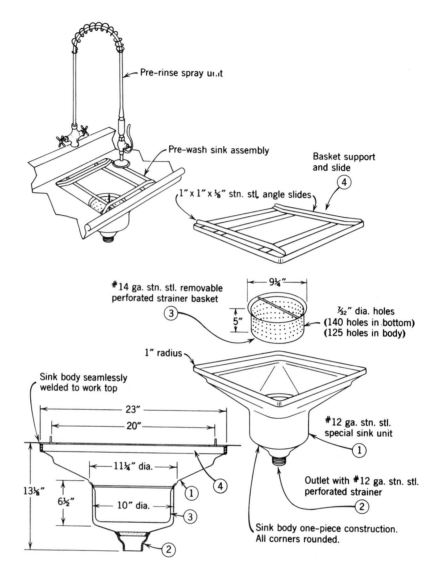

Pre-rinse spray unit

Pre-wash sink assembly

Basket support
and slide
4

1" x 1" x ⅛" stn. stl. angle slides

#14 ga. stn. stl. removable
perforated strainer basket
3

9¼"

5"

⅞₂" dia. holes
(140 holes in bottom)
(125 holes in body)

1" radius

Sink body seamlessly
welded to work top

23"

20"

11¼" dia.

13⅛"

6½"

10" dia.

1

4

#12 ga. stn. stl.
special sink unit
1

Outlet with #12 ga. stn. stl.
perforated strainer
2

3

2

Sink body one-piece construction.
All corners rounded.

SANITARY TYPE PRE-WASH SINK ASSEMBLY

FIGURE 10.4   Sanitary-type prewash sink assembly. (*Courtesy of S. Blickman, Inc., Weehawken, New Jersey.*)

An automatic feature that reduces labor time one hour per day may amount to a sizable sum per year. The time saved, for example, through elimination of rack handling with rackless machines has added to their economic popularity.

Small facilities using hand methods of dishwashing will follow a cleaning routine similar to that in machine washing but they will use sinks and not machines. The dishes are preflushed with a spray, washed, rinsed, and sanitized. The preflushing keeps much soil from the wash water and makes washing easier. The wash water should be a minimum of 110°F (43°C). The water in the second sink should be hotter and may be delivered against the dishes from a shower head spray with a trigger nozzle. If the dishes have been placed in a long-handled basket, they can be taken out (without the hands going into the water) into a third sink that contains 170°F (77°C) water or 75–120°F (24–49°C) water plus a **sanitizing** solution (check manufacturer's instructions for appropriate temperature to use with different sanitizers). A booster heater is required to raise water temperatures up to 170°F (77°C). Allow 30 seconds in this water to sanitize with hot water and 7 to 10 seconds when using sanitizers. Space should also be sufficient on the clean-dish table for the baskets of dishes to set and air dry.

FIGURE 10.5 A large double-tank dish machine—wash and final rinse—will process the dishware, silverware, glassware, and other items for a large foodservice operation meal in a few hours. *(Courtesy of Hobart Corporation, Troy, Ohio.)*

Mobile storage units to move clean dishes from the dish room to service areas save labor in handling and help to protect sanitation. Mobile storage units that accommodate specific items only require more floor space than carts used for transport of a variety of items to fixed storage. Plans should provide space for transport equipment to be drawn close to the clean-dish area for filling. If clean dishes are to be returned to serving pantries by conveyor or dumbwaiter, this relationship should be kept in mind.

Glasses and Flatware Washing. The glasses and flatware may be diverted for washing in separate machines than those used for dishes. This division is especially favored in large establishments. These items constitute the most intimate pieces of tableware. It is important not only that they be sanitary, but also that they be agreeable to touch. A roughness or greasiness is distasteful. Glassware should sparkle. Constant care should be exercised in sorting, cleansing, and sanitary handling of these items.

Procedures in dish rooms require immediate removal of flatware to a soak sink and glasses and cups to racks. Provision should be made near the beginning of the dishwashing line for this. Flatware may be washed in flat baskets or preferably held upright in wire baskets, or in perforated round containers of metal or plastic. These are then set in carrier baskets, which are then put through the dishwasher. The flatware when taken from the soak bath before washing should not be sorted before placing in racks for washing. The irregular shapes and sizes of knives, forks, and spoons hold the pieces apart for more thorough cleansing. When washing in the upright position, the handles should be placed down to permit the full force of the wash to strike tines, blades, and bowls. When washed, these containers are dumped into clean containers so the handles only are lifted out by customers.

Following removal from the machine, flatware may be dipped in a hot bath containing a solution to promote destaining and fast drying. A controlled method is needed for retaining sanitizing temperature for the dip. Another method for destaining and polishing is by machine, which tumbles it while going through an automatic cycle of washing, rinsing, and air-drying. Toweling should never be done. Flatware may be spread on clean cloth for sorting. Burnishers are desirable in facilities that use silver flatware and large quantities of hollowware, such as beverage pots, sugars and creamers, casserole cradles, trays, and punch bowls. Plan lockable storage for silver hollowware in convenient relationship to place of use, with suitable provision for heating or chilling. Mobile storage should be considered for items used in different locations.

Glasses used for milk drinks or other foods that adhere may be cleaned by brushing before placing in racks. **Brush machines** are available that brush one or two glasses at a time. **Brush-type glass washers** that provide approved sanitation in cleaning with detergent and sanitizing solutions are available for counter use. Due to possibilities for neglect in using the sanitizing solution, this procedure is not generally approved. When racks of glasses come from the dishwasher, they should be placed on carts or dollies for movement to the dispensing area. Glass and flatware washing are a normal part of dishwashing operations and should be kept in close relationship with it. Where separate machines are provided, allow at least 5 ft (1.52 m) for aisles between. In planning the equipment arrangement remember that the silver will be washed before burnishing. Soak sinks, dip sinks, and sorting tables must be placed where they will not interfere with the heavy flow of dishes.

Warewashing Layout.

Fact finding and analysis of many aspects are needed before planning the layout of the dishwashing section. Necessary information includes the following:

1. Type of tableware to be washed and treatments required
2. Volume of tableware to be processed within specified time limits
3. Mode for travel and speed of delivery to the dishwashing area
4. Methods used for scraping, washing, polishing, or other treatment
5. Normal time requirements for various stages of processing or handling
6. Space requirements equated to loads and processing methods
7. Equipment needs
8. Methods of transfer and types of storage
9. Sanitation standards and protection methods.

The type of tableware may vary from partitioned trays and stainless steel flatware in school food services to the silver and china of fine restaurants. Volume may require a one-person operation or a sizable crew performing assembly-line duties. There is more repetition of motion in the dishwashing operation than in any section of a food facility. Study should be made of typical motions and those made most easily in order to utilize effort to greatest advantage. Conditions that simplify dishwashing motions are (1) having materials delivered within easy reach, (2) having materials of similar character, and (3) having loads and treatment that are repetitive and uniform. The height and width of work levels and rack shelving are important to convenient reach. The principles governing motion and work center planning should be applied. (See Chapter 3, Operational Factors That Affect Plans.)

The layout of tables and machine should be adapted to the character of the operation in terms of load, flow, organization of work and personnel, and in a manner to minimize motion. **Load** refers to the maximum volume of dishes handled by the section in a given period of time. **Flow** is the path that the dishes follow and the rate at which they appear on the soiled-dish table—in even or in irregular quantities, fast or slow. If the work is organized like an assembly line where one worker does a specific task or where one or two workers perform a variety of functions, planning will be affected. Some operators may wish to shut down the dish machine during peak periods of receiving loads and scrape, sort, and stack only, so as to keep the soiled-dish area cleared for incoming dishes. If so, the size and sturdiness of the soiled-dish table and inventories of tableware must be planned for this.

The use of a conveyor serves to bring materials within reach and has the added advantage of promoting rhythm and stimulating continuous effort through the steady flow of material. When a conveyor is not used, table size and worker location should be spaced so as to ensure easy reach. Motion economy is better in large units where workers do classified tasks, such as racking glasses and cups only, scraping and stacking only, and feeding the machine only, than in cases where one persons changes frequently from one function to another. Where one worker works along doing several functions, motion economy is best if the flow of work permits performing one set of functions for a reasonable period, utilizing repetition of motion, and then shifting to another set of activities.

Plan of work and adequacy of space and supplies need to correspond. Specify a sufficient number of racks of different kinds (cup, glass, silver, and plate) to meet requirements if a rack type dishwasher is used. Plan a rack return from the clean-dish table to the soiled-dish area. It may be located across the face of the machine or along the back of the table behind the machine. Be sure that the reach of the worker will not be excessive in placing and taking the rack from the return, and that it is not in the way of operating the machine.

Tier or vertical use of space is important. Each worker should be allowed at least 2.5 ft. (0.76 m) linear space for working. Tables at which workers work at both sides may be 4 to 4.5 ft (1.22 to 1.37 m) wide; those where one worker works on one side only may be 3 ft (0.91 m) wide. In early planning, from 9 to 11 sq ft (0.84 to 1.02 m^2) may be used for estimating for each worker. The placement of overhead slanted shelves for glass and cup racks should be such as to permit free rhythmical motion to all parts of the racks with freedom from projections or posts that will interfere with the motion. It is better, if possible, to suspend them from overhead than from legs on the table. Motion should be minimized and not require excessive reaching up, stepping back, or stretching by the worker in the regular performance of the job. Plans for the work area should promote two-handed motion and reach and allow for a minimum of lifting of heavy racks loaded with dishes.

The layout of the dishwashing complex needs to provide for maximum loads and the largest number of workers required at peak periods, and it also must be convenient for one worker during slack periods. The hollow-square or U-shaped plan answers this need better than an L-shaped or straight-line plan, or one that requires the worker to go around the machine or table to attend to part of the functions. One employee working alone will scrape, sort, and stack dishes, load three or four baskets, and place them in the machine or feed the belt with a comparable number. Hand washing should follow, and then removal of the clean dishes, stacking, and placing them in storage carts. The worker will then return to scraping and basket filling. A manually operated machine will call for repeated placing and removing baskets in the machine and repeated operation of the machine. A fully automatic machine will only require shoving baskets to the opening of the machine.

It is desirable to have dishwashers located away from the wall far enough to permit cleaning and care. In large work sections where workers operate from both sides of the tables and mobile equipment will be used, it is desirable to have the dishwasher located centrally. In small operations where space is limited and few workers are employed, wall and corner locations may be used. Machines are available that can be operated from right to left. Designate in the specifications which direction is to be followed and where openings are to be for straight line or corner location.

Pot and Pan Washing

The **pot and pan washing area** should be located near areas of the food facility (1) where the largest number of soiled pots and pans originate and (2) where it will be convenient for users to have the general storage of pots and pans. Distribution by cart of many equipment items to specific production and serving sections for storage there provides time-saving convenience. The heaviest flow of soiled items comes from the cooking and baking sections in the kitchen and from the serving section. The largest number of pots from the production section arrives shortly before and during meal service as production is completed; those from serving areas will come during and immediately following meal service. Proper location of this work area can do much to minimize cross traffic, backtracking, and travel in the kitchen. Mobile collection carts in various work sections can reduce travel and promote one-motion storage.

Plan for adequate space for the number of carts, mixer bowls, roasting pans, and other large equipment, both soiled and clean, that will be in the section at one time. Traffic jams can be caused and accidents result when space is inadequate, and items brought to the area spill into traffic lanes. The space allowance and arrangement should promote satisfactory work flow (Figure 10.6). The process of cleaning includes scraping, soaking, washing, rinsing, sanitizing, and drying. Scraping is a hand process usually done in conjunction with the soaking process. Disposal of the soft refuse may be done by screening, draining, and emptying it into the garbage can or by putting it through a disposal or pulper unit. Where screening and draining are done, it is well to have a removable drain basket of sufficient capacity for normal loads extending across the soiled-pot table in front of the first sink. This will be convenient for handling swill garbage and will keep excess liquid from going into the garbage can.

The washing, rinsing, and sanitizing may be done by hand or by machine. In kitchens where there is a wide-belt conveyor-type dishwasher many of the kitchen trays, serving pans, and similar equipment may be washed in the dishwasher. Where **pot washing machines** are used, the pots and pans move through compartments where they are subjected to a strong force of hot water pumped through high-pressure pumps. After their removal from the machines, it is necessary to have sufficient space where the pots may remain for air-drying. Mechanical pot washers that operate in sinks are available also. Power-driven brushes may be used. In small kitchens the pot and pan sinks may be used for other purposes as well.

Equipment for the hand washing of pots consists of three-compartment sinks with a drainboard on one side for soiled pots and on the other for clean pots. Size of the drainboard for soiled pots will depend on the collection method and whether a cart is used or pots are brought by hand, and also the number and size of pots that will be in the area at one time. The clean pots drainboard will be governed by size and number of pots to be dried by standing and the nearness of storage. The size of the sink compartments should permit handling of the largest pots to be washed in the sink and allow convenient reach and comfortable working position of workers. The size of roast pans, baking sheets, and mixing bowls may help guide sizing, except for very large mixer bowls on dollies that require washing without placing in the sink. A convenient floor drain is needed for the wash water from these extra-large objects.

The height of drainboards and sink top should be considered in relation to comfortable working height and in relationship to adjoining table surfaces. It is important

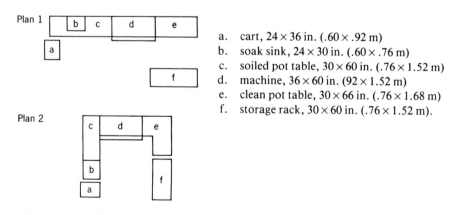

a. cart, 24 × 36 in. (.60 × .92 m)
b. soak sink, 24 × 30 in. (.60 × .76 m)
c. soiled pot table, 30 × 60 in. (.76 × 1.52 m)
d. machine, 36 × 60 in. (92 × 1.52 m)
e. clean pot table, 30 × 66 in. (.76 × 1.68 m)
f. storage rack, 30 × 60 in. (.76 × 1.52 m).

FIGURE 10.6 Suggested layouts in straight line and U-shape for pot washing, using a machine. Layouts may be reversed for flow from right to left. Carts may be drawn up to soak sink or to clean-pot table during progress of work.

for working comfort and for saving on hot water and detergent that sink compartments be no wider or deeper than required. Figure 10.7 illustrates posture positions of a worker 71 in. (1.80 m) tall working at a sink 38 in. (0.96 m) high and 28 in. (0.71 m) wide. The depth of pot sinks ranges from 12 to 16 in. (30 to 40 cm) (Figures 10.8 and 10.9). A depth of 12 in. (30 cm) is usually adequate, and the worker can work with a more comfortable posture than at the deeper sink. The bottom of the sink should be the thumb tip height of the average height worker when arms are straight by side, 27–29 in. (63–73 cm). Soak sinks may be 6 in. (15 cm) deeper.

Work progresses best from left to right. The worker who is right-handed will hold the pot with the left hand and scrape or wash with the right. It is desirable to have an overhead spray centrally located and with sufficient extension to permit its use for flushing refuse from scraped pots as well as rinsing those that have been washed. In large departments where many heavy pots are handled a movable holding rack facilitates work. A track on which the rack can move can be formed by the front edge of the sink and the rim of a gutter extending along the back of the three compartments between the drainboards. The gutter and drainboards should have sufficient pitch for good drainage. The drains from the sinks and gutter areas should come together and flow to the grease trap and sewer.

Pot sinks may be wall-mounted, leg-mounted against the wall, or leg-mounted and standing free in the open. It is sometimes desirable to have the sink in the open without splashbacks and with faucets centrally located so that workers may work from either side. Where the output of a section is large enough to require two sets of sinks, they may be mounted back to back as a single unit. When placed next to a wall or other equipment, they should be installed to prevent vermin from lodging between the equipment and the wall or other equipment. This will require sealing in or setting away from another

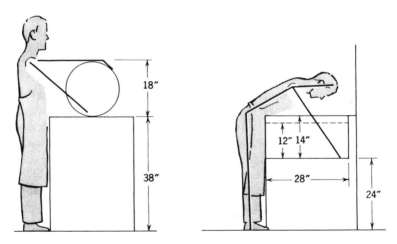

FIGURE 10.7 Posture positions of worker at pot sink.

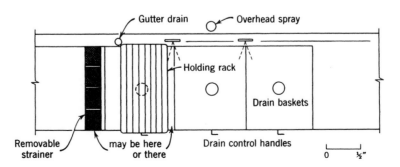

FIGURE 10.8 Suggested design for a pot sink.

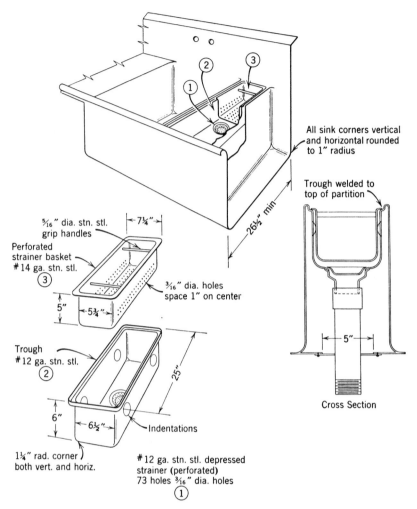

OVERFLOW COMPARTMENT FOR POT SINKS

FIGURE 10.9   Detail of overflow compartment for pot sinks. *(Courtesy of S. Blickman, Inc., Weehawken, New Jersey.)*

object. Mixing faucets preferably should be of the swinging type. Sanitation codes for the pot and pan washing section should be carefully followed.

Plans for the pot and pan section include facilities for storage. They may consist of one large rack adjacent to the sinks, plus work section storage of small tools and equipment, or an adjacent rack for storage of less used items and work section storage carts for the majority of utensils. Space allowance will need to be made appropriate to the system used. Mobile slatted or pipe constructed racks or carts are preferred to overhead or fixed shelves. Where hanging racks are used, such as those over the cook's tables, position them so that the point of grasp is approximately 6 ft (1.83 m) above the floor. Store utensils so that items can be readily seen and selected without having to move a stack in order to get items required. Store in relation to use, such as roasting pans near the cook's table and ovens, serving equipment handy to the dish-up area, and the pie pans, baking sheets, and cake pans where they are most likely to be filled.

GENERAL KITCHEN HOUSEKEEPING

Essential care and cleaning of major equipment and surfaces in the kitchen can be facilitated through careful selection of design and materials. High, black, overhead hoods supply an example. One may be selected that is fairly self-cleaning or has filters that can be easily removed and put through the dishwasher. Adequate light is important to display surfaces for cleaning. Ease of dismantling equipment for cleaning can promote equipment use as well as good sanitation practice. Workers avoid using equipment that does not save time and effort in proportion to that required for cleaning. Grinders, choppers, and peelers often fall into this category.

The following are typical points relating to material and structural features that will influence housekeeping care:

1. Durable, easy to clean, smooth surfaces, rounded corners or junctures, free from pits and crevices or other lodging spots for soil.
2. Adjustable, pear-shaped, round, or ball feet that permit leveling of equipment and will not catch mop cords.
3. Removable drawers and bins that may be cleaned in the dishwasher or sink.
4. Coved bases to eliminate legs and to enclose pipes for easier floor care.
5. Floor and wall materials or finishes that are durable and nonabsorbent.
6. Drains in sufficient number and located in areas where most needed, such as in dishwashing, pot washing, cooking, refrigerator, and vegetable preparation areas. Spillage is most likely in such areas.
7. Mop sink and hose connection located for convenient flushing or filling.
8. General storage and refrigerator shelving that is sturdy, cleanable, and removable.
9. Equipment that can be easily dismantled and reassembled for thorough cleaning, such as
   a. Meat saws and slicers
   b. Food grinders and cutters
   c. Oven and steam cooker shelves
   d. Range and broiler burners, grease pans, and shelves
   e. Potato peeler plate and peeling trap
   f. Milk shake equipment.
10. Floor drain covers and catch basins that can be opened for cleaning.
11. Cutting boards and equipment handles that are nonabsorbent and can be sanitized.
12. Shelving and condiment containers that are easy to reach and easy to clean. This is frequently a neglected, heterogenous, unsightly area. Small, removable bins with smooth, rounded surfaces located in high-shelf position are desirable.

TRUCK WASHING

Kitchen carts, dish storage units, and other mobile food handling equipment should be regularly washed to ensure satisfactory sanitation. The cleaning of such items is easiest if special provision is made for scrubbing and rinsing with a strong spray in an area where the water will be confined. This means having an area where there is space enough to work around the equipment. Hot and cold water with a hose connection that has a squeeze valve will be needed. A long-handled or irrigated brush is desirable. The area should have good floor drainage and splashproof walls. It is well to locate the section near that of dishwashing or pot washing, if possible. Carts used for soiled items are frequently used for return of clean ones and should be washed between uses.

GARBAGE DISPOSAL AND CAN WASHING

Foodservice refuse consists of swill garbage, paper, glass, plastics, wood crates, and tin cans. The bulk for disposal can be greatly reduced by mechanical means, such as disposal units, pulpers, and compactors. The largest quantities of swill garbage usually originate in dishwashing, vegetable preparation, pot washing, and cooking in normal order from greatest to least. The largest amount of paper waste comes from the serving section and the bakeshop. Certain egg, fruit, and vegetable crates, plastics, glass, and metal cans are salable or returnable to vendors. Storage space is required until they are picked up.

Some municipalities require that throwaway glass, paper, corrugated board, metal cans, and aluminum all be kept separate for pickup. This is often difficult because employees will not take the time and trouble to separate their trash this way. Some facilities hire a worker to separate it later.

Garbage cans can be washed by hand or by mechanical means (Figure 10.10). In hand washing the refuse adhering to the can is hosed off with cold water; the can is then scrubbed with a brush and hosed with hot water that is a mixture of cold water and steam. The hose should be equipped with a vacuum-breaker steam hose mounted 54 in. (1.37 m) above the floor and should have a squeeze valve. Cans may be laid in a trough, longer and deeper than the can, during cleaning. Cans cleaned mechanically may be inverted over a shallow bowl-like support 16 in. (41 cm) high and subjected first to the cold water flushing and then to hot water, steam wash, and sterilizing. The outside of the can should be manually washed and rinsed. Another type of washer is a cabinet into which the cans are placed, completely enclosed, and washed inside and outside with water and steam. Doorjambs to can washing areas should be of steel and the doors and walls bumpered.

Excellent floor drainage in this area is essential. The walls and floor should be tile or concrete and constructed for easy, thorough cleaning. A metal pipe rack should be provided on which cans may be inverted for drainage and airing. The rack should be of sufficient size to permit storage of cans until they are needed.

Volume and type of refuse, frequency of pickup, and climatic conditions will influence decisions relating to the best way of handling garbage. Included in considerations will be various means of reducing volume, refrigeration, and prevention of rodent attraction. Food garbage may be ground and flushed into the sewer by means of disposal units that are available in varying capacity and horsepower for grinding. The manufacturer's instructions for plumbing should be carefully followed. Difficulty may result if the drainage lines have insufficient drop and if machines are heavily fed with material that has a tendency to mat, such as paper and potato peelings.

FIGURE 10.10 Can washer and can storage rack. (*Courtesy of Institutions Magazine, Chicago, Illinois.*)

Some local municipalities do not, however, allow the use of food disposals in food services because of the load on the sewer system. In these operations, pulpers are a good alternative. Pulpers grind waste with water that is recycled and eventually pulled from the ground waste. The ground waste is then deposited in a waste container for removal from the food service. An added advantage of pulpers is that they also handle paper waste (such as napkins, paper dishes, etc.).

Where a refrigerated room is provided, the temperature should be kept at approximately 50°F (10°C). Garbage readily attracts rodents and vermin. Not only must it be kept tightly closed and in a carefully screened or enclosed area, but the surrounding building and landscape should be such as to prevent vermin lodging. Garbage odors will attract them to the area. Loose piles of wood or rockeries provide rats and mice with nesting spots from which they can slip into food areas whenever doors are opened.

JANITOR'S AREA

The **janitor's area** will include space for (1) storage of replacement supplies, (2) storage of cleaning equipment, and (3) a curbed mop sink for filling and emptying the mop truck, with (4) a place nearby where mops may be hung for airing. This area must have (5) a sink for washing mops and cloths or sponges used in cleaning. The size required for the storage areas depends on the equipment needed for care of the facility and the policy concerning amount of supplies carried in stock and/or issued at one time. The janitor may or may not be responsible for replacement supplies of tableware, utensils, and similar items. Cleaning supplies commonly stored include cleaning agents, brushes, brooms, mops, light bulbs, vacuum cleaner, waxer and polisher, and stepladder.

The most suitable place for filling, emptying, and cleaning the mop truck is in the can washing area, which is well equipped for this need. Provision for storage nearby would be desirable. Mops will require good air circulation of dry air, and should be hung elsewhere than in the humid can washing room. The location of the storage room should be adjacent to the kitchen or dining room, where it will be most convenient for repeated trips to get replacement supplies or equipment.

The mop sink may be an 8 in. (20 cm) deep, covered 18 to 24 in. (45 to 61 cm) square part of the tile door. The floor is usually sloped slightly to it. A good drain with removable strainer is necessary, and a mixing faucet that will permit hose attachment should be provided.

CHAPTER SUMMARY

The housekeeping functions of keeping a foodservice facility, clean, sanitary, and orderly are extremely important because patrons will not go to places they think do not meet desirable standards. A planner can do much to see that high standards are met in this area. Easily cleanable walls and ceilings and floors durable enough to withstand the wear they get should be planned. Equipment that is easy to clean and is easy to assemble and disassemble should be selected, and equipment placement should be such that cleaning is possible all around it. Even heavy ovens are now mounted on wheels so they can be moved out from the wall for cleaning in back of and under. A housekeeping evaluation list is presented to help planners check for details.

Warewashing in this text covers dishwashing, glass washing, and flatware washing. It is most important to see that these items are sparkling clean and in a sanitary condition because they are the items that come in personal contact with patrons. The operation requires the manipulations of table removal, transport to the cleaning and sanitizing area, scraping, rinsing, washing, drying, and storing. After scraping off the major soil, items should be rinsed either by hand flush units or have water pumped onto them. Good drainage of this flushing water and soil collection is needed. The collection of garbage is usually through a hole in the soiled-dish table with a garbage can under to collect the scrapings. Some install garbage grinders or pulpers.

Detergents and sanitizers should be selected to aid in cleaning, and should be able to attack fats and other soil and help remove it from the ware. For hot water dish machines, warm water at about 150–160°F (66–71°C) is needed for washing and water at least 180°F for rinsing. If temperatures are not high enough, booster heaters are used at the point where the hotter water will be needed. Dishes may also be washed in machines using chemical sanitizers. The temperature for the chemical rinse should be about 75–120°F (24–49°C). Manufacturer's directions should be followed for specific guidelines. It is desirable that a small hand-washing sink be placed between the soiled-dish handling and the clean-dish handling areas, so clean dishes are not soiled by workers' hands that have touched soil.

Dishes may be transported from the dining to cleaning area in what are called the tote boxes, mobile carts, or conveyors. Where self-bussing of dishes is used, an arrangement where glasses and flatware are left at one point, soiled dishes at another, and trays at another facilitates the cleaning task. This also is desirable when employees bus items in. Such an arrangement also reduces breakage. The soiled-dish table should be sufficiently large and built strongly enough to take the heavy loads they must bear. Dishwashers need to be sized to the loads they are expected to handle and clean-dish tables should be similarly planned. Conveyor belt (non-basket-type) dishwashers are often preferred to the basket type.

Hand washing of ware requires three sinks: one for washing, one for rinsing, and the third for sanitizing. Glasses and flatware may be washed in their own separate machines. Glass washers are equipped with fast rotating brushes through which water with detergent is pumped so that glasses placed over the brushes are given a thorough cleaning. Outer washing is done, then sanitizing, and rinsing. Glasses are then inverted for drying. Flatware machines are available that tumble the ware with a detergent and wash it. Some cleaning and rinsing water by spray is also used. Silver flatware polishers often have small stainless steel balls in them to tumble with the ware and polish it.

The planner should devote considerable attention to the layout of the warewashing section because a lot of hand work occurs here. Convenient work centers are important so that the speed of motions is maximized and work is accomplished in a shorter time with greater ease. Do not forget to supply storage. There will be four major work centers for washing dishes:

(1) soiled-dish area, (2) machine loading area, (3) clean-dish area, and (4) storage for transport out of the section.

Pots and pans in small operations are often washed in the cook's or dishwashing sink or run through the dishwasher, but usually a separate location will be used for this purpose. Its location should be close to the cooking, serving, and baking sections, where the largest number of items are soiled, and close to where pots and pans are stored. Some facilities store pots and pans on mobile racks for delivery to using areas where they remain on these racks until needed. This saves the work of removing and storing elsewhere.

The area where items await cleaning should be sufficient for their storage. A clean unit area where they can dry should also be allowed. Space for carts and other mobile equipment on which items are moved is desirable. Besides a three-compartment sink, a soak sink is sometimes needed. Some units use heavy-duty pot and pan washers. Some hand scraping and soaking are also required with these.

Plan also for care, maintenance, and cleaning of equipment. The walls and ceilings of the operation also will need care. Durability of surfaces under constant cleaning demand that the planner provide for this. A truck washing area may also have to be set up if a lot of such equipment is used.

Garbage disposal and can washing are also important factors in the cleaning and sanitation area. Some areas need refrigerated garbage storage areas. All garbage storage areas should be capable of being maintained properly and be free of rodents and vermin. Some units use garbage disposals or grinders. These should be connected to the sewage lines *after* the grease trap and not before it. Dry trash must also be cared for. Some municipalities require that various types of trash be kept separate.

Garbage cans can be washed by hand using a long-handled brush, and hot and cold water shot forcefully from a hose. Others use a mechanical device that is on the floor and sends a forceful spray up into the can. The outsides of cans are hand cleaned usually and then hosed down for rinsing. A good drainage rack should be provided.

The janitor's area should provide for storage of the supplies equipment and other items used by the janitor. Usually a janitor's sink is provided. A storage space for light bulbs and other equipment may be required.

REVIEW QUESTIONS

Observe and note the following in a food facility, and state the housekeeping care given to each:

1. Floor material. Is a covering used? If so, state kind.
2. Material of wall finish.
3. Is an acoustical treatment used? If so state kind.
4. Dishes and flatware.
5. Material and finish of chairs and tables and other furnishings (state kind).
6. Ventilation type and material.
7. Are floor mats used? If so, state location.
8. Kind and amount of mobile equipment used.
9. Number and kind of scales used. State section where located.
10. Dishwashing and pot washing equipment.
11. Floor drains—number and location.
12. Shelving for utensils, refrigerators, dry stores—material, measurements, adequacy.
13. Sinks and worktables—materials, design, and measurements. Give size and depth of sink compartments.
14. Facilities for garbage removal and can washing.
15. Kind and location of housekeeping equipment and cleaning materials. Evaluate the condition of each of the above items on the basis of
    a. Condition of wear
    b. Appearance
    c. Adequacy and convenience
    d. Sanitation and safety
    e. Appropriateness to use.

Make recommendations that you believe would improve conditions, with reasons for the recommendations.

KEY WORDS AND CONCEPTS

brush machines
brush-type glass washers
compacters
coved corners
detergent
Dishwashing operation
flow
hand-washing sink
housekeeping
janitor's area
load
pot and pan washing area
pre-rinsing
pulper
rinsing agent
sanitizing
soak sink
soiled-dish table
warewashing
vermin proof

CHAPTER

11

Management Office and Guest and Employee Facilities

MANAGEMENT (CONTROL) FACILITIES

Management of a food facility involves planning; maintaining records of many aspects of operation; interviewing personnel, tradespeople, and the public; performing such business operations as placing orders, keeping records, calculating payrolls, handling cash, and paying accounts; training, supervising, and instructing staff; and observing and directing operations. Performance of these management functions calls for an office area that is suitably located and adequately equipped. In a small facility the functions may be simplified so that one individual can cope with them. In a large operation each of the aspects of the operation may have sufficient magnitude to require separation into departments. Regardless of size, omission of a suitable place for the functions of management may ultimately be very expensive for the organization. The office is an important work section that should be planned in relationship to the food operation, even if it includes little more than a shelf and a desk.

Criteria for locating **management offices** (control centers) should be based on functions to be performed. These functions include the following **location factors:**

1. **Proximity** for continual awareness and ease of supervision in specific areas of responsibility. Convenient location can promote better control and utilization of management time and effort. Just as in driving on the highway, the person at the wheel must know direction, observe obstacles, and guide action. A manager needs to know what is happening and give timely instructions. Lack of awareness tends to result when a manager becomes absorbed with office activities in a remotely located office.
2. Ready **visibility** of areas to be supervised can save many steps in keeping aware of work progress. There are many times when office functions can be performed if things are able to be seen as progressing well in the various work sections.
3. **Accessibility,** through location of the office, is valuable for business contacts with personnel, tradespeople, patrons, and persons seeking information or service. Where reasonably possible the office should have direct entry from public areas as well as a close relationship with food sections. The public should not go through the kitchen to reach the office.

4. **Privacy** should be sufficient for carrying on business operations or counseling sessions that are of a confidential nature.
5. **Adequacy.** The office should have enough space in which to work, be comfortable, and be equipped for efficient work. Many of the office activities require concentration for doing accurate work with reasonable speed. Freedom from needless distraction helps to save time and ensure good results. Good light is essential. Proper ventilation and heat are necessary for health and comfort. Best economy calls for providing those items of equipment needed in performing essential functions with accuracy, speed, and convenience.

Food operations are characterized by variety. Many significant differences are true of management in terms of training background, standards and method of operation, relationship to ownership or those in authority, extent of responsibility, and specific preparation for the duties to be performed. Where there is one office for the food department, it is not unusual to find it next to an accounting office for ease in recording, approving, and paying accounts or tucked away in a storeroom where the manager can stand guard on supplies, instead of being close to the most significant area of action, that of production and service of food. The choice of the office site should be at that point that gives the most effective control over responsibilities for which the specific office personnel are responsible.

Where it is not possible to select a location that affords a view of all areas for which management may be responsible, it is wise to choose nearness to those having major significance. The basis for choosing needs should be in terms of major values to be protected, such as quality of products, cost of labor and materials, service quality, patron satisfaction, and counseling services. Supervisory observation can often supply the "stitch in time" that guards utilization of labor and materials and ensures the use of approved techniques that may spell the difference between success and failure of the operation. "Merchandise for sale" calls for protection from the time that supplies enter the facility and are processed until the time that patrons' needs are served.

A peak period calling for close supervision is the time when food is being served. The tempo of activities increases, more personnel are actively supplying orders, distractions are numerous, and the food qualities that have been carefully created are at their highest and most fragile point. Supplying qualities of gracious service and regulating portions may mean gain or loss for the food operation. Alert supervision may prevent accidents that injure persons, waste food, destroy serving equipment, and impair the quality of service or food.

Food managers commonly carry numerous and varied responsibilities, some of which call for desk work and others observation or checking of work progress. A kitchen supervisor should be aware of what is happening throughout the day. A view of the area where workers check in or out aids control and adds convenience in getting records for calculation of payroll. Entrances for receiving and storing within office view may safeguard the receipt of goods by the authorized agent and instruction of delivery people as to the location where material is to be placed. This can prevent error and save time and effort. A view of production sections may help to ensure proper procedures being followed and give assurance that foods are being prepared on schedule (Figure 11.1). The view of the various areas may be through a window or an open door.

There are numerous occasions in the operation of a food business when it is desirable to have private conferences. Typical of these situations are hiring, correcting, or counseling employees; discussing purchases with salespeople; discussing food or catering plans with patrons; and conferring about problems or complaints that may have arisen. Information overheard and half understood may be broadcast so as to be harmful.

The office, like other work sections, should be equipped for quick, easy, efficient performance of necessary functions. Work requiring mental concentration is usually done most efficiently when there is reasonable freedom from distraction. An office for the routine checking of performance can be in the midst of activity, but where planning and mathematical calculations are done the office workers should be protected from

FIGURE 11.1 Production areas are readily viewed from this office window. *(Courtesy of University of Washington, Seattle.)*

needless disturbance. The size of the facility and the type of activities required will govern whether a table and shelf of books and records will suffice or whether the office should be separately enclosed and more fully equipped.

Management functions in large organizations are likely to be departmentalized. The buyer will hold buying conferences, receive and check samples, place orders, and send copies of orders to a receiving clerk and an accounting department. Suitable space is needed for conferences and for salespeople to sit while waiting. Equipment should be available for cutting and testing samples. This may be done in a kitchenette adjacent to the office or in the main kitchen.

The receiving clerk or storekeeper will need a desk or office area for instructions and records near the receiving dock or storage area. Supplies will be checked in and approved on the basis of the orders placed. The order lists when received and the delivery slips or invoices will then be sent to the accounting department with acknowledgement for payment.

The accounting department may be responsible for recordkeeping and accounting. This activity will involve training and supervision of cashiers; receiving, counting, and depositing cash; preparation of payrolls; and drawing checks for payment of payrolls and accounts. The use of computers, scanners, and calculators has prompted accuracy and saved time. A copy machine is useful for record duplicating. A safe should be provided for cash and costly items requiring protection. It should be heavy enough or so placed that it cannot be easily removed.

The employment officer, like the buyer, will have numerous conferences. If offices are adjacent, a common room may be used by those waiting for an interview. The equipment can be simple. If training is a responsibility of this department, an area for group meetings may be needed.

Functions covered by many foodservice operations vary widely, and special office facilities may be needed in terms of the specialized responsibilities. In hospitals, it is desirable for the chief dietitian's and the therapeutic dietitian's office to be located near other administrative offices for convenient consultation with the medical staff and exchange of information with other administrative departments. The office of the production dietitian should be adjacent to the production and service departments. An outpatient dietitian consults with and instructs patients who are not in the hospital, and the office should be easily accessible from the street. A close relationship with other members of the dietary department is usually not necessary. Equipment will be needed for simple food demonstrations. Floor and ward dietitians who are responsible for individual needs of hospital patients may need an office in their respective areas. An efficient communication system is needed between offices and the main production and serving area.

The dietary department staff is frequently responsible for instruction in nutrition and diet therapy for dietetic interns, medical interns, nurses, and patients. The size and nature of the group will govern needs for space and equipment. It is a time-saving convenience for the classroom to be near the office.

The manager of food service in hotels requires an office that is easily accessible to patrons and frequently may be near the main lobby. Good communication between patrons and this office and between the office and the kitchen is essential. The office should be equipped for planning, interviewing, recording, filing, and billing. It is desirable, where possible, for the office to be close to the special service areas for adequate supervision and step saving.

All offices should have sufficient electrical outlets for attaching computers, lights, fans, typewriters, and other equipment likely to be used. The foot-candles of light supplied should be appropriate for the amount of detailed work to be done (50 to 70 footcandles). Temperature controls and good ventilation are important for comfort and wellbeing and should be given special attention for small or crowded office areas. Acoustical treatment should be provided to muffle excess noise. Where several persons occupy one office, the noise of business machines, phones, and voices in conference may cause distractions that interfere with work. Valuable records and miscellaneous office supplies require appropriate storage. The office, like a well-designed tool, should satisfy significant functions and be a pleasure to use.

GUEST FACILITIES

Planning should give strong consideration to **guest needs.** The entrance to a dining room, the waiting area, and the facilities provided for guests create a lasting impression. The adequacy, cleanliness, and attractiveness that patrons view on entering have an influence on their enjoyment of food served. The entrance should be easy to find and inviting in appearance. The doors for entrance and exit should be placed so as to prevent accidents between those entering and leaving. A waiting area should be provided that will accommodate the number who will be likely to arrive ahead of time, during a peak period when the dining room is filled, or who may wish to wait for a friend. The area should be comfortable and attractive and make patrons feel that they are in line for service. Coat, parcel, and umbrella storage should be provided where it can be readily seen and supervised either by management or the patrons. In college food units, students are likely to arrive for meals with books, supplies, and coats for which cloakroom storage will be required. The dining room entrance in residence halls should be from a hall or vestibule rather than from the lounge to lessen excess wear through the lounge.

Use of a telephone is frequently requested by patrons, and a paging system may be needed also. It is better to have a conveniently placed public telephone for patron use than to have business phones tied up by patron calls. A booth or location that will provide reasonable privacy for calls is desirable. The location should be where it is convenient for the patron and where the calls will not disturb office workers or the cashier.

Toilet rooms should be provided for women and men. Locate these, if possible, adjacent or convenient to the waiting area. Attractive housekeeping and good sanitation is important for patron comfort and for creating a favorable impression of the food establishment.

EMPLOYEE FACILITIES

The type of locker room, toilet, lounge, and dining facility provided for employees tends to express management's respect for personnel standards and the dignity of workers. Good standards for **employee facilities** can do much to create goodwill and promote good health and sanitation practices. Toilet, locker, and dressing rooms that are bright, clean, and cheerful help to set the right note with workers who are instructed to create good standards in food production and service. Remember that the personal habits of personnel handling food are one of the strongest single factors in food safety and sanitation.

The employee entrance to dressing rooms should be convenient from the street and, if possible, observable from the office. Workers should not have to go through the kitchen work areas or the dining room in order to reach their dressing room. The time clock and instruction board should be located on the path that workers take from dressing room to work sections. Supervision of workers as they come on duty is desirable, and the time clock should be near and within view of the office.

When toilets are remote from work areas, busy workers tend to neglect good health practice and lazy workers use remoteness as an excuse for not being at work. Location adjacent to work areas is desirable and permits easy supervision. Toilets should be separated from all food areas by a hall or double entrance. Building codes often specify type and amount of fixtures to be furnished. Usually one toilet stool is provided for each 12 to 15 employees and a lavatory for every 8 to 10 persons. In men's toilets a urinal is provided for each 12 to 15 men. Toilet stalls should be enclosed by doors. Knee, foot-action or automatic flushing controls are recommended. The double-entry doors to toilet rooms should be self-closing.

Suitable safety should be provided for employees' personal possessions while they are at work. It is an unsanitary practice for purses or other personal possessions to be carried and stored in work sections, and worry over their safety can interfere with work. Lockers that can be locked may be large enough for clothing on hangers or a small size appropriate for purses and packages. The place where clothing is hung, whether for individuals or a group, should be long, deep, and wide enough for the clothing to hang without crowding. Proper sanitation requires that street clothing and uniforms be hung in separate compartments of the locker.

The appearance of the locker section is attractive when sealed in as a part of the wall. Where this is not possible, the lockers should have a slanted top that prevents unsightly clutter and dust collection. An enclosed base improves appearance and makes cleaning easier.

Allow ample dressing space and benches or chairs on which workers may sit when changing clothing. Unless there are broken shifts, lounge facilities may be restricted to the dining area. Loafing and congregation in the dressing and toilet areas should be discouraged. Promote good grooming by having adequate light and good mirrors. A full-length mirror will be an effective reminder if placed where the employees can note personal appearance before leaving the dressing rooms. A mirror and cosmetic shelf can be used by more people if placed at one side of the lavatories where it can be used by individuals while others are washing their hands.

Shower equipment may not be practical on the basis of amount of use. Specific working conditions, kind of work, and the class of employees will influence the extent of use. Where ventilation is poor and the temperature and humidity high in work areas, showers will be especially appreciated. Employees from poor residence areas may not have convenient access to bath facilities. Showers in dressing rooms can help to ensure good standards of personal cleanliness of food workers.

Clean hands are essential in sanitary food handling. Production and service employees must often handle unsanitary objects as well as food in the normal course of their work. The objects may be as common as a food crate or parcel, a door knob, or a personal handkerchief. Therefore, lavatories need to be located in sufficient number and in convenient relationship to all food handling areas in order to promote sanitary food handling. The need is especially acute where there are large numbers of temporary employees (as in college food units) who arrive for work in street jackets which they quickly shed for server's coats and tend to go on duty without washing their hands. Hand washing in sinks used for food is not allowed. Hand sinks should be conveniently located to encourage frequent hand washing by all who handle food and food equipment.

A work section in which there is strong likelihood of inadequate hand washing is dishwashing. Employees often scrape dirty dishes, fill baskets, then go directly to the clean-dish table and handle clean dishes without washing their hands. This tends to happen most often where the unit is too small to employ separate individuals for the different activities. Prevention of this kind of contamination calls for a conveniently placed hand-washing facility. Time loss and ignoring of proper practice result when the lavatory is inconveniently or remotely located.

Encourage the use of soap by supplying a suitable dispenser and a mild odorless soap. In addition to a paper towel dispenser, also provide a paper cup dispenser so that workers may get a drink of water when they wish. A bubbler fountain may be used if preferred.

It is valuable to foster friendly relationships in an employee group. Pride in the belonging to the group, cooperation with each other on the job, understanding and liking that discourage turnover, and many other values may grow out of pleasantly dining together. An appropriate dining area can be one of the very important facilities for employees. It should promote rest, relaxation, and enjoyment during meals and coffee breaks. It may be a special room or a section of the main dining area. Although the furnishings in a special room may be simple, the room should be bright, cheerful, and homelike. Where space is limited, crowding can be prevented through the scheduling of meal periods. Good morale and restful dining are not likely to result when workers are required to dine alone or in a public dining room wearing uniforms that bear traces of their activities.

Employee instruction boards may vary in size, shape, use, and placement. The "general interest" bulletin board is often a framed cork board. Boards with removable letters or sections, as for menu boards, may be used effectively in production and serving sections for stating portion sizes. Permanent instructions, such as those for operating major equipment, may be framed under glass or glued to the wall and lacquered for waterproofing. These should be located near the equipment and in a position where they are easy to read. Avoid a clutter of material on bulletin boards or walls. Items that are too numerous in number or remain too long in one position tend to be ignored. Therefore they are worthless and create an unattractive appearance. If only recent and significant information is supplied in this way, the workers will give it more careful attention. Instructions supplied in this manner should be brief, adequate, clear, readily seen, up-to-date, and meaningful.

CHAPTER SUMMARY

Management offices act as locations where control of the operation occurs. To adequately fill the requirements of control, certain factors in planning should be considered:

1. Proximity to where control is needed such as near the receiving and production areas, and near the service areas.
2. Location and construction so that management has good visibility of these two areas and others that might need management supervision or observation.
3. Good accessibility for those who will be using the offices.
4. Adequate privacy so matters that management should keep confidential and private are not endangered.
5. Adequate lighting, heat and ventilation, and equipment needed to meet all needs for adequate control.

In large operations control offices might be planned to be separate. There might be a management office, an accounting office, a receiving clerk office, and health facility offices for the various members of the dietary staff.

Guest facility needs include a safe and attractive entrance area, an adequate receiving and waiting area, a pleasing dining area, good tables and chairs, adequate provision for the storage of coats and hats and other paraphernalia, a place where guests may use a telephone in private, and clean, pleasant toilet rooms.

Good employee facilities can contribute much to encouraging the growth of good morale. Locker room and toilet areas should be located near where employees enter the premises and close to where workers go to work. A time clock should be located near where the employees pass after dressing for work. Lockers should provide enough space to give employees a chance to keep work and street clothes separate. A slanting locker roof helps to keep employees from piling things on top. Dining facilities should be in a pleasant place, adequately lighted, heated, ventilated, and appropriately furnished and appointed. Good handwashing facilities should be provided in locker rooms and in the work areas. These should be separate from food preparation sinks.

REVIEW QUESTIONS

1. Choose office facilities in three different types of food operations, such as a school, commercial, hospital, or industrial food department, and observe and enumerate the specific management activities performed.
2. List all of the office equipment in each, and state the location of the office in relation to the food department.
3. List all staff members, areas of responsibility, hours on duty, time spent in the office, and duty-time spent elsewhere (state where spent).
4. Indicate how much of the office space and equipment are utilized during parts of the day by more than one staff member (state approximately how long).
5. Evaluate adequacy and suitability of space, location, and equipment. Recommend changes that you believe would be advantageous. (Find out probable cost.)
6. Describe guest facilities in three public eating places, and give your evaluation of them on the basis of convenient location, adequacy, and appeal.
7. What employee facilities are provided in the food facilities that you chose for analysis (under Question 1)?
8. Plan a layout for an office and for employee facilities, and describe their location in relation to work sections.
9. Prepare specifications for the equipment shown in the office and employee facility plans.

KEY WORDS AND CONCEPTS

employee facilities
guest needs
location factors:
   accessibility
   adequacy

privacy
proximity
 visibility
Management offices

3

SUPPORTING FACTORS AND PHYSICAL CONDITIONS

PART

3

SUPPORTING FACTORS AND
PHYSICAL CONSTRAINTS

CHAPTER

12

Energy

Well-made equipment of excellent value is useless until it is properly "hooked up" to the correct energy source. The important connection may be power, water, steam, or plumbing. Clearly, not all planners or members of a design team will have enough knowledge of engineering to design the utilities for an operation. They will, however, have essential information about operational requirements. A clear statement of requirements from the team member representing operations must be provided to the engineers to see that adequate standards are met.

Team members who lack engineering or mechanical backgrounds must know how to communicate needs so that they will not be misunderstood by the engineers and specialists. For example, an engineer told to provide a minimum of 50 foot-candles of light on a work surface will understand the exact requirement. On the other hand, if told to provide enough light to see well, the amount of light provided may depend on the engineer's sight and personal judgment.

Team members lacking engineering knowledge can better appreciate why engineers or specialists set up specific requirements if they know some of the technicalities involved. This chapter discusses energy and factors related to planning for energy use in food services so that foodservice team members may feel competent enough to work well with engineers and architects in securing the best possible plans.

Coordination and planning for energy needs has not always been done well. The need for more careful energy planning is clearly a concern today. The energy shortage has aroused awareness of the need to utilize our energy more fully and to prevent its waste. Energy has often been used carelessly in the past due to its low cost. Energy has been cheap compared with human effort. A **kilowatt** of electricity does the same work as 30 men in climbing the stairs of the Washington Monument. Even further, heat, light, power, ventilation, air conditioning, heating, and humidity control have often been overprovided just to be sure that there is enough. Prevention of energy waste in the future may be encouraged by its high cost or mandated by government regulation. A better method of control, however, results from an accurate prediction of needs with suitable provision for meeting them.

A knowledge of what energy is and how it works can help conserve and maximize its use. Planners should know (1) the types of energy available, (2) which one is most suited to a particular need, (3) how much is required, (4) alternative ways of achieving the same results, (5) costs, and (6) when proper standards in energy use are met. Some of the significant aspects of energy use are presented in the next section.

ENERGY AND ITS SOURCES

Energy is a force capable of exerting power or performing work. Aristotle coined the word "energy" from two Greek words: *en* meaning "at" and *ergon* meaning "work." Energy comes in many forms. One form can be converted to another. It can also be lost by becoming energy that is not used. Unfortunately, most systems are not 100% efficient. The energy efficiency of electrical motors varies from about 50% to 90%. A pot on a hot plate may absorb only about 14% of its heat.

The main source of the earth's energy came from the sun many millions of years ago. Through a process of photosynthesis, the sun's energy was fixed in living earth substances containing carbon, hydrogen, and oxygen. This was then stored largely as coal, oil, and gas (fossil fuels). This captured energy can today be released from these fuels by the process of *combustion*.

Fossil fuel supplies are limited. It is estimated that only enough **fossil fuels** remain, at present usage rates, to last about 1,000 years. Critical shortages in some fuels are now appearing.

The United States is heavily dependent on the use of oil although it has very little of the known world oil reserves. Forty percent of the total energy consumption in the United States is from oil. Oil is used for heating, as well as the production of gasoline, natural gas, solvents, kerosene, and lubricating oil.

Coal is one of the most abundant fossil fuels in the United States. It is used mostly in the production of electricity. Coal can also be used to produce synthetic oil, but the process is not very energy efficient. One problem with coal is that some sources contain sulfur, which becomes a pollutant when coal is burned.

Gas energy sources include natural gas, liquid natural gas, liquefied petroleum gas, and synthetic natural gas. Natural gas in the United States is largely used to produce heat. Liquid natural gas is produced when natural gas is placed under high pressure for storage and converts back to natural gas when the pressure is released. Liquefied petroleum gases, such as propane and butane, are produced from natural gas. They are used for a variety of purposes as "bottled gas" or "tank gas" or LP gas service through utility lines. Synthetic natural gas may be made either from petroleum or coal, but the conversion process is not very efficient and is expensive.

The sun is constantly creating energy by a process of atomic fusion in which hydrogen is merging into helium. This is largely the source of the energy it sends out. Every day the sun radiates tons of its mass as energy. At the rate it does this, it will do it for more than a billion years. Although only one part in 120 million of the sun's energy reaches its planets, the amount received by the earth alone in five hours is more energy than is locked in the earth in its fossil fuels. The problem is capturing this energy. Today, the earth uses only a very small portion of all it receives. The remainder radiates back into outer space.

Direct **solar energy** may be more fully used in the future for meeting energy needs. Major problems still need to be resolved, however. For example, ways need to be devised to more efficiently store daytime amounts to last until the next sunrise; store energy from a season with more sunlight (summer) for use in another season with less sunlight (winter); create smaller, more efficient photoelectric plants; improve the heat conversion efficiency (related to this is the fact that current solar collectors only provide temperatures up to 120–200°F or 43–93°C, which is not high enough for most building heating systems); and decrease the cost of conversion to solar energy. (An added problem is that most solar systems still require other energy systems as backups.)

Energy from **atomic fission** is also possible. It requires the splitting of the uranium atomic nucleus, with the subsequent release of large amounts of energy. This energy is used to produce electric energy. In some parts of this country nuclear energy is an important source of electricity. Some potential problems with nuclear energy include environmental pollution and disposal of radioactive materials.

Energy from the warmth of the sun carried in seawater may also be used in the future to operate electrical plants. Other alternatives include wind energy, tidal energy (using the movement of water in tides), geothermal energy (using hot water or steam trapped within the earth), and hydroelectric systems (using water from dams which flows through hydroelectric generators). So far, these alternatives have proven to be expensive and geographically limited.

Because energy sources are limited and costly, it is important that food services make maximum use of minimal energy amounts. Our national problem of energy is not a small one and every person is challenged to use it wisely. Energy sources will continue to be a major concern into the 21st century.

ELECTRICITY

Electrons are tiny particles of matter. They are substances that form the outer shell around the nucleus of an atom. There are tremendous numbers of free electrons in the air and in the earth. They move about pretty much in a random fashion, but when they are gathered together in countless billions and directed along a path, they exert tremendous power. Moving as a mass, they become an **electrical current.**

Electrons carry a negative charge. A positive charge has a terrific attraction to these negative charges and they will seek to join with them. A battery, for example, has an area with a large number of negative electrons in it and another part with a large number of positive charges in it. When a wire connection is made between the two bodies, the negative electrons flow to the positive side. This flow has power to do work such as light a flashlight or start an automobile. When a battery is "dead," there are no more positive charges or negative electrons to create the electrical flow. A battery can be recharged by reversing the current flow so it can start all over again.

The flow of electrons as an electrical current can be compared to the flow of a stream of water. It can exert force. The larger the stream, the greater the force. Thus a stream of water flowing as rapids or over a waterfall has more power than the same quantity of water moving through a meadow.

The amount of electricity or water in a current can also be measured. Water flowing through a pipe can be measured by the gallons (or liters) per minute flowing through a pipe. Electricity can be measured by measuring the number of electrons that flow by a given point per second. If 6,242,800,000,000,000,000 electrons go by in a second, this is one ampere (amp or its symbol, I) of electricity. An **amp** is the basic unit of measure for the flow of current.

Water force is measured in pounds per square inch (psi), whereas the force behind electricity is measured in **volts** (V). A volt is the force required to push one amp of electricity by a given point in a second. The amount of power in electricity is stated in **watts** (W). The number of watts used is equal to the force (volts) behind the flow times the amps (or I) flowing, thus:

$$W = V \times I \tag{12.1}$$

or

$$I = W/V \tag{12.2}$$

or

$$V = W/I \tag{12.3}$$

Equations (12.1) through (12.3) are used for **single-phase systems.** For a **three-phase system,** the equation would be the following:

$$w = \sqrt{3}V \times I \tag{12.4}$$

Such formulas are helpful in planning electrical requirements. For example, if 1,500 W of electricity will be used by one electric light circuit (single phase) and the voltage is 120 V, the amperage carried will be 12.5 I. This would mean that the circuit should be fused for at least 15 amps and perhaps more since a circuit should have a 25% safety factor. See the following equation:

$$1,500 \text{ W} = 120 \text{ V} \times 12.5 \text{ I} \tag{12.5}$$

Note that if the voltage increases, the amperage decreases. For instance, if the 1,500-W requirement were on a 240-V line, the amperage required would be 1,500/240 = 6.3. The equation would be:

$$1,500 \text{ W} = 240 \text{ V} \times 6.3 \text{ I} \tag{12.6}$$

If a three-phase system with 208 V is used for a 15-kW heater (15,000 W), the following equation would be used:

$$15,000 \text{ W} = \sqrt{3} \times 208 \text{ V} \times 42 \text{ I} \tag{12.7}$$

Often in planning circuits, electricity is carried in main lines at higher voltages. The voltage is then reduced at branch circuits or at the usage point. This saves on wire size, amperage, and also prevents power loss when transmitting the electricity.

We can use electricity to develop either heat or power. Both are forms of energy coming from electricity. Resistance against the flow of electricity creates energy in the form of heat. One example would be a copper electrical wire, which warms slightly when electricity passes through it. Even though a good conductor, there is still some resistance against the flow. Another example would be a heating element in a stove. If the flow of electricity is partially stopped, as in a nickel-chrome electrical element, the friction causes heat to develop. Electricity also has magnetic power, and this power can be used to run a motor or do other useful things.

Electrical Currents

Electricity may flow as a **direct current** (DC) or as an **alternating current** (AC). When the current flows evenly in one direction, it is DC. AC flows with an alternating pulse between a positive and negative flow, causing the current to alternate in its direction. It pulses back and forth.

One limitation of DC is that it can only be transmitted about 20 to 30 miles. After this, the R or friction from **conductors** drops the voltage force (potential) to a point at which the current is too weak to be very useful. Because AC can be stepped up to extremely high voltage by transformers, it can be given terrific force for transmission. AC, therefore, can be transferred easily up to 300 or more miles. If the voltage should drop, it can be run again through a transformer and the voltage increased for further transmission. When AC reaches its destination, transformers can then step the voltage down to the levels desired.

A generator of electricity called an **alternator** creates AC. A generator works by sweeping up masses of electrons out of a magnetic field and sending them on their way as an electric current. Most alternators revolve 3,600 times per minute. This sets up 60 alternating pulses per second called **cycles** (c) or **hertz** (Hz). A cycle in AC is a complete pulse from positive to negative back to positive. The number of cycles per second is called a *frequency*.

Most equipment in this country uses 60-cycle power, except for equipment such as microwave ovens, X-ray machines, and televisions, which use much higher frequencies. Equipment must be operated on the proper cycle. Name plates on equipment, information on the electrical units, and so forth will indicate the cycle required.

AC flowing only as one cycle or pulse has an uneven up and down flow since the current is pulsing between a negative and positive flow. Such single-cycle flow is suitable for most heating and lighting needs, but for power equipment a more steady current is needed. Adding a second current carrying wire will even out the pulse of flow of electricity. The pulse is further smoothed out by using three current carrying wires. This is commonly referred to as a three-phase system. Three phase has three single phases flowing one closely after the other.

For motors operating elevators and some other equipment, a more even flow than this is required. An MGM set (which uses an AC motor to drive a DC generator, which drives a DC motor, which moves the elevator) may then have to be used to change AC to DC so that a steady flow of electricity is obtained. If an operation has DC, the changeover would not be required for elevator use.

The alternator making three-phase AC has three poles in a cycle so in one revolution three separate AC pulses are created. Usually each pulse is 120 V. Having three pulses in a cycle results in one pulse being close to maximum when another of the three is dropping and another is at low ebb. This gives a steadier current flow. See Figure 12.1. Either a delta (d) or wye (Y) arrangement is used for locking the three poles on the alternator, the outer points of either being the pole location. Figure 12.2 shows graphically how these arrangements are made and the 120-V lines that run from each of the three-pole connections. The delta arrangement is more commonly used. A ground or neutral wire is always provided for either a wye or delta setup.

Three-phase electricity can be manipulated so as to give a wide number of different voltages. Some equipment manufacturers do not like to manufacture equipment that

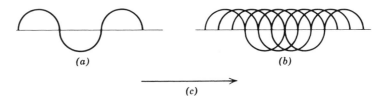

(a) (b)

(c)

FIGURE 12.1 (a) AC, single-phase, with top of line positive and below the line negative surges. (b) AC, three-phase; note how positive and negative variations level off when three surges occur in a cycle rather than one. (c) DC current flowing constantly in one direction from negative to positive.

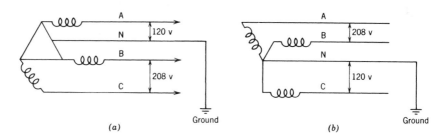

(a) (b)

FIGURE 12.2 (a) The delta arrangement of poles on an alternator and (b) a wye arrangement. Note in (a) joining "hot" or "live" line A with neutral line N gives a 120-V current, while joining two "hot" or "live" lines B and C gives a 208-V current. Also, when two "hot" or "live" lines A and B are joined on the wye (b) arrangement a 208-V current is obtained, while joining neutral line N with the "hot" or "live" line C gives a 120-V current. A two-wire, single-phase 120-V AC circuit results when one "hot" line is joined with N line, while a single-phase two-wire 208-V AC circuit results when two "hot" lines are jointed. A three-wire 120-V single phase is obtained by joining A, B, or C with N, while three-wire 208-V is obtained in this manner by N to joining two "hot" lines. Such a three-wire circuit is suitable for light loads and small motors, the latter on 208-V. A three-phase, four-wire 120/208-V circuit is the same as the three-wire, but the N is used. A 120-V circuit can yet be obtained by using any one of the three "hot" lines. A three-phase, four-wire arrangement of this kind is suitable for heavy or light load circuits and is usually the most flexible. Sometimes an additional N line is used that is grounded. In this case, the wire used is green and this gives rise to the term "green grounding system."

will satisfy the possible variations; instead they market equipment set only for a limited number of voltages. Equipment should be checked therefore to see that it meets the voltage requirements of the facility before selecting it for purchase.

Different voltages can be obtained from an alternator depending on how electricity from the various poles is combined. If current is taken from any two poles or "hot" or "live" wires, the voltage is 120 V + 120 V or 240 V (which actually comes out as 208 V). If only one pole plus the neutral wire is used, the voltage is 120 V. If different voltages are required, transformers must change these voltages. (Although a transformer changes voltages, it will not change the phase.)

Most electrical companies transmit AC for short distances at 480/277 V. At the using point a transformer steps it back to 208/120 V. At the panel box, different combinations of wires then give either 208-V or 120-V circuits. If two hot wires are combined either with or without a neutral as a third wire, 208-V is obtained. If only one live wire is combined with the neutral, a 120-V circuit results. Heavy-duty equipment such as ranges, heavy motors, and heating units usually takes 208 V, whereas light circuits and normal wall plugs use 120 V.

There may be good reason also for using heavier voltages than 208 V and, if so, 480 V or other circuits may be set up. If these heavier voltages are not available, transformers in the facility can be set up to give them. All circuits should have a ground system to pull off any hazard electricity.

Use of a higher voltage permits use of smaller wiring, smaller conduits, and so forth, thus saving on cost. Smaller wire and other units are possible because as voltage increases, amperage drops for the same amount of wattage. For example, a 15-kW load on a three-phase 208-V unit pulls 42 amps, which requires a No. 8 size copper wire. The same load on a 480-V line pulls only 18 amps and requires a No. 12 copper wire, which is smaller.

It is sometimes more economical to operate some equipment on higher rather than lower voltage, providing it is built for the higher voltage. Fluorescent lighting works better on higher voltages such as 277 V and also on frequencies higher than 60 cycles. While voltage is not a problem, the frequency may be because it cannot be changed. If 277 V is run through the circuits, small 3- to 25-kVa (kilowatt-volt-ampere) dry-type closet transformers can be installed at strategic spots to lower the voltage for other voltage needs.

Equipment specifications should require electrical equipment to meet exact electrical voltages. An undervoltage or overvoltage may be harmful to equipment or lead to a waste of energy. Although manufacturers will indicate that motors or other equipment operate at either a 10% plus or minus voltage without harm, a motor on a 10% undervoltage will have a 20% loss in efficiency, hotter operation, and a shorter life and lower torque (twisting force). An underload of 10% on a light bulb, for example, may cause a 30% drop in light power. A 30% drop in voltage for an oven or range top may cause a 20% drop in its efficiency.

Similar undesirable results can be seen with overvoltage. Ovens and heating elements do not function properly. An overload of 10% in an oven or range top may cause overheating and a much shorter operating life. Similarly, phasing and cycles should agree with the facility requirements, and these should be clearly stated in the specifications for equipment.

Motors, radios, televisions, and some other electrical equipment may be very susceptible to changes in current load or voltages. Damage can easily result, and it is advisable to set up equipment specifications that specify the equipment is to carry a small fuse in the housing through which the electric current going into the equipment must pass. Thus, if an oversurge occurs in the line, the equipment will not be burned out. Larger fuses or breakers, such as 30 amp, would let 30 amps through a circuit. This may be too much for a small or delicate piece of equipment. Fusing should be set to carry enough to operate the equipment but not much more. If equipment companies will not do this, installation specifications can require it to be done on site.

Conductors and Nonconductors

Silver, gold, platinum, copper, aluminum, and some other metals conduct electricity. Some conduct it more readily than others. Silver is the best conductor, whereas aluminum is about half as good a conductor as silver. The others are closer to silver than to aluminum in conductivity.

Other materials do not conduct electricity as well, and are said to have high resistance. Planners may sometimes hear the term **impedance** used instead of resistance. Impedance is used to indicate resistance when AC (alternating current) is used.

Because of cost, the best conductors are not used except for special purposes. Copper is a good conductor and it is also less expensive, so it is used extensively. Because aluminum is light and low in cost compared with the others, it is often used, especially in heavy wires.

Diameter of the wire is also a factor. Wire sizes go either by the American Wire Gauge (**AWG**) or by the **MCM** (thousand circuit mils) standards. The larger the **gauge** number, the smaller the diameter of the wire. Small wires go by the AWG sizes. Wires that are 0.5 in. or more are in MCM sizes. As examples, No. 10 and No. 12 are 0.102 and 0.081 in. in diameter, respectively. These are usually used for electric light circuits and light-duty load circuits. A No. 0 AWG wire is 0.325 in. in diameter and a No. 0000 AWG wire, the largest size in this standard, is 0.460 in. in diameter. MCM wires carry heavy loads in electrical transmission lines. A 250 MCM is 0.500 in. in diameter and a 500 MCM is 0.775 in. in diameter.

The reason why the diameter of the wire is important is that the greater the resistance of the conductor, the larger it must be to carry the same quantity of electricity with no increase in resistance to the flow. As an example, aluminum is not quite as good a conductor as copper, but by using an aluminum No. 4 wire (0.2 in. in diameter), the same amount of electricity can be carried with the same amount of resistance as is carried in a No. 6 copper wire (0.16 in. in diameter).

Note that aluminum wiring has been known to cause 2 million home fires because of undersized wiring and improper installation. At this time, aluminum wiring can be used in both commercial and residential installations, but must follow all code requirements.

Some substances will carry almost no electrical current. These are called **nonconductors.** Examples are plastic, rubber, glass, and wood. These materials are useful because they may also be used as insulators.

Wires are generally wrapped in **insulation** to keep the flow of electricity where it should be. Generally the insulation is color coded to help identify the conductor. Grounded conductors (which are discussed later) are often colored white or gray, for example. Insulation materials should not only not conduct electric current, they should also be heat resistant, resistant to damage from chemicals, and not allow passage of water. Most common insulation materials for buildings are rubber, plastic, or mineral fiber. Electrical building codes will specify which type may be used in specific areas.

Resistance and Ohms

When **resistance** (R) is set up against the flow of electricity, heat is formed. Nickel, chromium, and their alloys resist the flow of electricity and can also rise to considerable temperatures before they melt. For this reason they make good heating elements. Thus, when a chromolux, nickel-chrome (part nickel and part chromium), or other heating element is attached to a good electrical conductor and a current is run through both, the electricity flows readily through the conductor, but when it reaches the element it is blocked and the resistance creates a large quantity of heat that may become so great that the element has a red or almost white glow.

The development of heat may be desirable in an element, but is not in motors or electric wires. Heat may become so intense in a motor that the motor "burns out". Wires that become warm when electricity flows through them indicate an undersizing problem. A loss of power results. Wires may also become so hot that they start a fire.

In addition, R increases as temperature does. Therefore as a motor or wire heats up, resistance becomes greater and there is a loss of power. Resistance is measured in **ohms.** One ohm equals 1 amperage at 1 volt. The formula is

$$R \text{ (ohms)} = V/I \tag{12.8}$$

Thus, a heating element drawing 8.7 amps on a 115-V circuit has an R of 13.2 ohms or

$$13.2 \text{ ohms} = 115 \text{ V}/8.7 \text{ I} \tag{12.9}$$

It also follows that:

$$I = V/R \tag{12.10}$$

or

$$V = IR \tag{12.11}$$

The amount of power or electrical energy used (watts) also can be determined if I and R are known because:

$$W = I^2R \tag{12.12}$$

Thus, an element using 115 V at 8.7 I would require 1000 Wh (watt hours) using Eq. (12.1):

$$115 \times 8.7 = 1000.5 \tag{12.13}$$

The same result can be obtained using Eq. (12.12):

$$8.7^2 \times 13.2 \quad \text{or} \quad 75.7 \times 13.2 = 999.1 \tag{12.14}$$

Circuits

When electricity starts out from an electric panel to give power, heat, or light to equipment, the wiring returns to the panel, completing what is called a *circuit.* In an **open circuit,** no current flows because the connection at some point in the circuit is "broken." In a **closed circuit,** electricity is free to flow.

An electrical current can also flow in a direction that is not desired. A **short circuit** occurs when the circuit is shortened by a break in the wire or for some other reason. This is called a "short" because the flow path is shortened. An exposed wire that is touched causes a short that gives an individual a heavy shock; death can even result. Sometimes in equipment, electricity becomes free and does not flow where it should. Again there is danger of shock or the equipment may be damaged. For these reasons, electrical systems and equipment are frequently *grounded.* To do this, a wire leading to a **ground** is set up. When the negative electrons arrive at a positive body, they are neutralized and they become at rest or locked to the positive charge. In other words, they are "grounded." The ground may be a water pipe, a copper rod buried deep in the ground, or some other device that will attract the free electricity. Three-pronged plugs contain one plug that acts as a ground.

A panel box receives electricity from the main circuit and distributes it over branch circuits. The branches carry the electricity to the point where it is used. The voltages and the number of circuits needed in an electrical system will dictate the size of the panel box. Sometimes supplemental panel boxes are installed after the main panel. In this case, higher voltages are run from the main panel to the supplemental panel where the voltages are broken down to those desired.

Panel boxes are equipped with fuses or circuit breakers that stop an overload of electricity from flowing into a circuit. Such an overload could cause a fire or do damage to the equipment.

A **fuse** is a device that has a wire thread that melts when a current over a specified amount flows through it. Fuses come in a variety of sizes (rated in amperes). One disadvantage of fuses is that they are destroyed after they have protected a circuit and must be replaced with the same ampere rating.

A **circuit breaker** trips open if an excessive quantity of electricity flows through it either because of the development of heat or because magnetic forces act to trip it. Circuit breakers can be reset if the overload condition does not persist. This is generally done by flipping a toggle switch or a handle and may be done automatically or manually. The disadvantages of circuit breakers are that they are not available with as high an interrupting capacity as fuses and they are more expensive.

The maximum temperature around a panel should be 90°F (32°C). Higher temperatures may cause malfunctioning or even cause breakers to trip. Panels should have disconnect switches on the power side so electricity can be cut off in the panel in case of emergency. It may also be desirable to have disconnect switches that turn off special circuits in an emergency, leaving others on. Panels should be located where they can be quickly and easily reached. If locked, keys should be available in a secure place nearby.

An electric meter is usually installed just before the main panel. This meter measures the electrical flow from the company's lines. The reading on such a meter is usually in kilowatt-hours (kWh) and is the basis for charges for current used. As noted, the charge may also be based on peak consumption. Peak consumption is generally tracked on a second meter. Charges may also be based on a combination of both total consumption and peak consumption.

Designing Circuits and Circuit Loads

When electricity flows through a circuit operating a motor or other equipment, some voltage or power potential is lost. To design circuits correctly, this loss must be known in order to plan for the correct voltage, amperage, and wattage. The calculation is somewhat complex but is derived basically from a calculation of the loss potential in the conductor and various pieces of equipment. It is necessary at times to ascertain if additional loads can be put onto a circuit. Again a calculation for the addition to the circuit must be made to know if the circuit will be overloaded.

Almost all equipment on circuits will be connected in what is termed a **parallel circuit.** In doing this every unit drawing electricity receives its energy from the main conductor line and not through any other piece of equipment. In this way, no other piece of equipment is dependent on its energy coming through another piece and all pieces on the circuit are guaranteed the same uniform amount and voltage of electricity.

If the connection were a **circuit connected in series,** the electrical current would flow from one piece of equipment to another. The voltage and amount of electricity received would decrease from the beginning to end of the series. When small Christmas tree lights are connected in series, the first light is usually brighter than the last one, especially if several strings are put together. Also, if one light burns out, all lights go out. No current goes through because the burned out light will not conduct electricity through it.

A circuit should have on it items that require the same cycle, phase, and voltage. Wattage, however, can vary. Before connecting a piece of equipment to a particular circuit, these should be checked. Every piece of electrical equipment should have a plate that lists the cycle, phase, voltage, and wattage it requires.

For example, a 120-V single-phase, 60-c circuit could carry three 100-W light fixtures, a wall plug to which might be attached a small 840-W blender, and a clock and radio pulling 40 W. All require single-phase, 60 c, 120 V. The total wattage would be 1180, which would be about 10 amp using Eq. (12.1) (1180 W/120 V = 9.83 I). Since all circuits should be fused 25% above maximum demand, a 15-amp circuit breaker or fuse would be ample for this circuit. However, it would not be suitable to add a 1.5-hp electrical motor onto such a circuit. Such a motor requires three-phase power and would do better on 208 V rather than 120 V. Also, 1 hp is equal to 746 W and so about another 1100 W (1.5 hp × 746 W = 1,119) would be required on this circuit, which would mean that the amperage needed would be 19 (2280 W/120 V= 19 I), which would considerably exceed the 15-amp breaker.

Some heavy-duty equipment requires that it be the only unit on a circuit. Branch circuits should not run over 100 ft, and this may mean in a large facility that supplemental panels will need to be placed distant from the main panel.

Most electrical companies deliver three-phase, 120/280-V, four-wire service but larger food services may ask for three-phase, 277/480-V, four-wire service. This can be obtained by stepping up the voltage using a transformer. Normally, 120 V is about a third of the total load used in food service, but this varies.

Preliminary load requirements for food services can be taken from architectural tables that indicate broadly what is needed. Normally, a facility under 5,000 sq ft takes a total of 200 amps or less at the main panel and a facility under 10,000 sq ft takes 400 amps or less. Total requirements depend, of course, on whether heating, air conditioning, and other high-demand units are used. It is usual to estimate kitchen requirements on the basis of individual demand and not from general tables since the requirements can vary so much depending on whether gas or other energy sources are used instead of electricity. The lighting load is usually estimated on the basis of 2 to 3 W/sq ft and storage and other low demand areas at 0.5 W/sq ft.

The National Electrical Council and the National Fire Protection Association have established standards for circuit loads and these should be followed. For instance, outlets for floors plugs are usually calculated as requiring 1.5 amp each (180 W) and a circuit on which they are placed should not carry over 60% of its total rated capacity. Using this information for example, a 15-amp circuit should not have more than six outlets of this type (15 × 60%/1.5 = 6). However, this guide applies to small equipment only. If heavy equipment is used, this guide should not be used. Codes should be referenced to provide other helpful information in planning circuits.

Circuits should carry the proper size wire. A range top pulling 12,000 W at 208 V will use 57.7 amp and require a 70-amp or larger breaker and a three-wire No. 6 AWG line not including grounding wires. A small deep fryer pulls 1,300 W on a 120-V line and needs a 20-amp breaker and two No. 10 wires. Standard tables in architectural materials indicate desirable wire sizes for different electrical equipment and loads. These are based on the standards of the National Fire Protection Association.

The Electrical Plan

The electrical plan for lighting is usually separate from that for equipment and other units. This allows presentation of each without confusing detail. After electrical equipment has been located properly and the circuits planned, it is possible then to set up the plan. Programs have been developed for computers that take much of the detail work out of such planning. All electrical units, switches, receptacles, motors, and other electrical details should be properly identified on the plan. Symbols are often used and reference to an architectural handbook can be helpful with their identification. An electrical schedule may be set up that resembles an equipment schedule for a regular plan. After this, panel loads can be calculated and the location established. Panels usually carry about 75% of their maximum load, so should additional circuits be needed the addition is not a problem. It is important to check plans to see that space for panels, feeder lines, conduit lines, and so forth is provided.

Price of Electricity

The price of electricity is often calculated on the amount used per hour. A watt-hour (Wh) is a watt flowing steadily for an hour. A kilowatt-hour (kWh) is 1,000 W flowing steadily for an hour.

For most industrial users the price of electricity is based on the amount used plus a maximum demand charge. The maximum demand is based on the highest quantity of electricity used at any one specific point of time. This is important because high-demand loads increase the need for construction of new electrical generating facilities. Highest demand loads tend to occur during the cooling season when electricity is needed for air conditioning.

The price of electricity will also vary with the time of day. Utility companies will charge more for electricity during on-peak hours than they will for off-peak hours. On-peak hours may vary with the season and the geographic area, but are generally between 8 to 13 hours a day, typically 10 A.M. to 8 P.M.

If maximum demand can be reduced (particularly during the day), electrical costs can be reduced. If it is possible to plan for some of the energy use at night, for example, to heat water or bake items, the food service may be able to reduce energy costs.

Electrical Heat

Heat develops in an element due to friction created by resistance to electrical flow. If all flow stops, no heat develops. Some electricity must be allowed to reach the end of the element and flow back to the source. When an element has a reddish glow, infrared heat waves are produced. When the color becomes an almost white-red glow, greater radiation of heat is occurring. Infrared heat is suitable for many purposes, but for toasting or broiling, heat radiation is required. One of the best resistance wires that can be specified for heating elements is nickel-chrome (ni-chrome) of Navy Grade E, centered in a tubular sheath of authentic stainless steel.

The forms of radiant energy have been grouped by scientists into an electromagnetic spectrum. The forms are characterized by wavelength and frequency of vibration (number of complete cycles per second). They are grouped in the spectrum from the shortest to the longest wavelength. Their length varies from miles to thousandths of an inch. These, grouped from the shortest to the longest, are

- Cosmic rays
- Gamma rays
- X-rays
- Ultraviolet
- Visible light
- Infrared (heat) waves
- Radar waves
- Microwaves
- FM
- TV
- Short (wireless) waves
- Radio
- Sound waves.

Light waves are measured in nanometers (nm) or billionths of a meter. The light band waves run from 400 to over 700 nm in length. Radio and some of the other larger waves are measured in centimeters or meters and are about 1000 cm or 10 m (3 yd) long or longer. Much of the heat developed for cooking is in the infrared zone or in the radiation zone.

The shorter the waves, the higher the frequency of vibration. Microwaves are not hot but create heat in material that is capable of absorbing them by agitating molecules

FIGURE 12.3 Basic parts of a microwave oven include (1) door with window, (2) stirrer that distributes microwaves more evenly as they are reflected back from metal sides of the oven, (3) waveguide that channels microwaves from the magnetron tube, (4) magnetron tube, (5) power supply, (6) and electric connection.

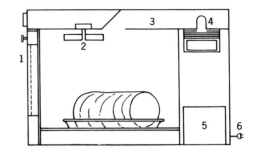

that try to line up in the electrical field, thus developing friction that creates heat. The depth of penetration of microwaves varies from 1.5 in. (3.7 cm) to 3 in. (7.8 cm) as influenced by the nature of the material and the wave frequency. Two microwave frequencies have been allocated by the Federal Communications Commission for industrial, scientific, and medical use. These are 2,450 MHz (megahertz or millions of cycles per second) with a wavelength of 5 in. (12 cm) and 915 MHz with a wavelength of 12.5 in. (32 cm).

Three characteristics of materials are of special interest in utilizing microwave-created heat. These are ability to reflect, absorb, and transmit the microwaves. Metals reflect the waves and do not absorb or transmit them. Metal in an oven lining reflects the waves into the food and keeps them from escaping into the room. Glass, china, paper, and plastics transmit microwaves but do not absorb them and therefore are suitable for cooking containers. Food or other materials containing moisture absorb microwaves, and the molecules are agitated to a degree that the friction creates heat.

Microwave ovens consist of two basic parts: a low-voltage line connected to a power supply (the line converts the low voltage to the high voltage required by the microwave energy generator) and an electronic vacuum tube called a *magnetron*. Microwaves issuing from the magnetron flow through a waveguide and are stirred by a rotating paddle so as to disperse them more evenly throughout the oven cavity. The switch or lock that activates the microwave operation is connected to the door closure. A federal ruling calls for two safety interlocks or switches, either of which will prevent open-door operation. It requires that one of the locks or switches be hidden so it cannot be activated by any part of the body or by inserting a 4-in. (10-cm) rod. A diagram of a microwave is shown in Figure 12.3.

Radiation leakage from microwave ovens presents certain health hazards. The Department of Health, Education, and Welfare has set standards for manufacturers of ovens to follow. The allowable emission is $1\ mW/cm^2$, measured about 2 in. (5 cm) from the oven surface. Although specifications may be carefully written and regulations well followed, safety depends on proper care and use of the oven. If it is improperly cleaned and has food particles clinging to edges of the door closure, or if a paper towel is caught in the door so that the door does not close securely, they can leak. There is sometimes leakage around the window and as eyes are particularly susceptible to damage, users are cautioned not to peer into the window closely while the oven is operating.

GAS

Gas is another important source of energy used by food services. Most of the gas used is natural gas, which is largely methane (CH_4). It produces from 960 to 1,150 Btu of heat per cubic foot but the amount is usually calculated as being 1,000. Some manufactured gas (called water gas) is used. It has from 500 to 550 Btu/cu ft. Another kind of gas used is liquefied petroleum gas (LP), which is either propane or butane. These have 21,600 Btu/lb or 91,900 Btu/gal or 3,200 Btu/cu ft. Actually, butane usually has about an 11% higher Btu yield than propane.

Gas produces heat by burning, and for this, air containing oxygen must be introduced. Old-fashioned type burners such as the Bunsen and others allowed air to enter the bottom of the burner, mix with the gas, and then flow out of the burner where the flame developed. These burners were not too efficient and some gas was not properly mixed and did not burn. Newer burners have now been developed that do a much better job of mixing the air and gas, therefore increasing efficiency. Some large units have special air and gas mixers that do the mixing and then feed the gas into the burner. Other pieces of equipment do a better job of bringing air where the burners must pick it up. Pipe-type or ribbon burners are usually considered to be the most efficient.

Some kinds of burners are used to develop radiant heat for toasters, broilers, and other equipment. These burn the gas using porous ceramic plates that have up to 200 openings per inch. The ceramic heats up to a temperature around 1,650°F (900°C), which develops into about 50% infrared or radiant heat. These units are fed air in such a manner that they can be operated in almost any position and give good results.

The efficiency of gas equipment, as for other heating equipment, is judged on the basis of heat developed in the burning of the gas that gets into the cooking pot or cooking unit. Thus, if a unit has an input of 40,000 Btu and 24,000 get into the pots on the stove, there is an efficiency of 60% (24,000/40,000 = 60%). Normally, gas equipment is considered to have an efficiency of 60%. However, this can vary. A griddle with burners directly underneath a plate may have a better efficiency than this , while a salamander may be below the average. The efficiency of gas equipment has been improving with systems that recirculate heat and have better heat capture and other improvements.

It takes 1.6 more gas Btus to equal the Btus developed by electricity. This is because when gas burns it develops combustion products that must be exhausted. In exhausting this some heat is also lost. In some cases, electricity may have an efficiency of 100% since all of the heat developed is captured as in the case of heating coils in a hot water tank completely surrounded by water. Electric equipment of other kinds, however, may have only slightly better efficiency than gas.

Whether gas or electricity is less expensive to use depends largely on the cost of these substances in local areas. In some areas, such as in Texas and Oklahoma where there is much natural gas, gas will normally be less expensive than electricity. But, in the West where there is good water power to develop electricity and the source of gas is distant, electricity may be less expensive.

An example illustrates the relationship of efficiency and cost. Assume that 1,000 Btus is the amount of heat produced per cubic foot of gas and that 1.6 is the efficiency correction factor of gas as compared to electricity. If in an area, electricity sells for $0.05 per kilowatt and gas is selling for $6.30 per 1,000 cu ft, the calculation to see which is lowest in cost would be:

$$\frac{1,000 \text{ cu ft} \times 1,000 \text{ Btu/cu ft}}{1.6} = 625,000 \text{ Btu} \tag{12.15}$$

The cost per Btu for gas is:

$$\$6.30/625,000 = \$0.0000101 \tag{12.16}$$

The cost per Btu for electricity is (assume that 3,412 Btus are produced by 1 kW of electricity):

$$\$0.05/3412 \text{ Btu/kW of electricity} = \$0.0000146 \tag{12.17}$$

Thus, gas would be slightly less expensive on an equivalent Btu basis.

Gas is pushed through large mains to the food service under pressures of 600 to 1,000 psi. This is then reduced by pressure reducers to about 25 psi after it goes through the facility meter—the last reducer is usually just before the meter.

The proper size pipe must be used to allow sufficient gas to flow to the equipment. By totaling the Btus required when all gas equipment on the line is on, the total amount of gas required can be estimated and the size of the pipe calculated. Gas companies can furnish information on pipe sizing to meet needs.

Gas fumes must be exhausted. Some gas equipment may be connected to pipes and flues that carry these combustion products away through vented chimneys up to the top of the roof where they go out into the atmosphere. Other gas equipment exhausts their fumes under a hood that picks them up and exhausts them with the outgoing air. To properly exhaust such fumes, about 100 fpm should flow out of the hood or about 30 air changes an hour should take place in the area.

SAVING ENERGY

The cost of electricity and gas has risen dramatically in the last 25 years and will continue to increase. The day of low-cost energy has passed. Food services can expect to see continuously rising costs. It is thus important that maximum results be obtained from the energy used. When energy was relatively cheap, food services were not concerned about saving it. The extra cost in better insulation, better construction, better thermostats, etc., was not worth the cost. It was cheaper to waste energy. That situation has now changed and equipment manufacturers are being asked to produce equipment that gives a higher yield of energy for the work to be done. Improved thermostat control through the use of the solid-state thermostat, the elimination of gas pilot lights through the use of electronic ignition devices, better insulation, the recirculation of heat, automatic on and off switches (see Figure 12.4), heat recapture, and many other developments are being used to reduce the amount of energy required to do the various jobs.

About 20 years ago when labor costs started to rise appreciably, it began to be important to not only ask about the cost of the equipment and its installation but how much labor it would save. Today this question of labor saving is even more important. Still, the question must be asked "How efficient is it in saving energy?" The federal government requires that equipment manufacturers indicate the amount of energy that equipment uses. It is thus possible for equipment buyers to compare equipment and see which types are the most energy efficient.

Heat recapture is becoming important. Some units on the market today capture the heat developed when refrigeration equipment condenses refrigeration gas into a liquid.

FIGURE 12.4 Automatic turn-off or turn-on equipment is being designed to reduce energy needs. Some units stay only on stand-by heat while others are completely shut off. This salamander-type unit activates only when weight is put onto the grid. (*Courtesy of Lang Mfg. Co., Redmond, Washington.*)

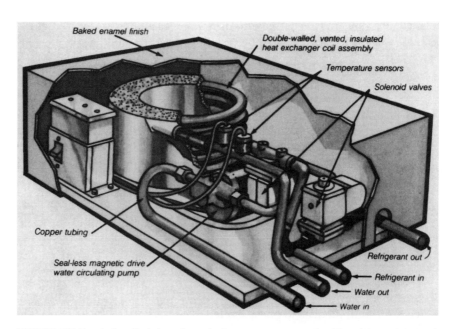

FIGURE 12.5   A detailed drawing of a heat extractor used with refrigeration equipment. The hot refrigerant liquid (after condensation into gas) is brought into the unit where water in coils extracts the heat in the insulated heat exchanger. The warmed water is then sent to heat units that raise the temperature of the water further, if desired. Thus, heat that otherwise would be lost is retained. *(Courtesy of Energy Products Division, Schneider Metal Mfg. Co., Inc., Mason City, Iowa.)*

Usually water or some other fluid is used to capture this heat. A drawing of the heat extractor system is shown in Figure 12.5.

Large refrigeration units may produce enough heat to heat swimming pools or bring cold water up to a tepid temperature so much less energy is needed to make it into hot water. Other types of energy recapture are being tried and it is expected that as energy costs increase, ways will be found to reduce the use of energy so as to hold down energy costs. This happened with gasoline. As gasoline grew more and more expensive, car manufacturers produced more fuel-efficient cars.

CHAPTER SUMMARY

Proper energy design is an economic necessity today. The cost of energy has risen tremendously in the last 25 years as the supply of fossil fuels has become more limited. In addition, under- or overpowering equipment can lead to inefficiency or safety hazards. Detailed engineering knowledge is not required by all foodservice planning team members. They will need to know, however, how to communicate so that operational needs will not be misunderstood when energy installations are planned.

Selection of the energy source and design of the food service is complex. Electricity is often selected as the energy source to give power, heat, and light to equipment. It starts out from an electric panel, which receives electricity from a main circuit. From there branches carry the electricity to the point where it is used. Fuses and circuit breakers are used to stop overloads in the system. Equipment and the electrical current must be matched carefully for voltages and phase requirements. Wiring must also be the appropriate type and diameter and be properly insulated. Electrical usage is measured by meters. Charges for electrical use are based on total demand, peak demand, or a combination of these two.

Gas may also be selected as one of the energy sources. The efficiency of gas is less than electricity, but the lower price of gas often makes it a more economical choice. Calculations can be done to determine if the choice of a gas or electric piece of equipment is more economical.

The days of low-cost energy are gone. Food services can expect to see continuously rising costs. It is even more important today to achieve maximum results from the energy used. The extra cost of better design, construction, and insulation in the energy system, as well as the cost of more energy efficient equipment, is generally worth the extra effort and expense.

REVIEW QUESTIONS

1. Read a recent article on energy and report its message to the class.
2. Form a panel with two or three other members of the class and discuss ways in which food services can reduce energy consumption. (Review National Restaurant Association reports and materials for information on the subject.)
3. Visit an electrical plant to observe how electricity is generated, transformed, and transmitted.
4. Visit a production kitchen and note the information on the equipment as to phase, cycle, voltage, and wattage.
5. Add wattage on various circuits and calculate amperage, checking to see that it is within limits established by the breakers or fuses on the circuit.
6. Study an electrical plan for a facility and identify the various symbols and interpret the details of the plan.
7. Draw a simplified electrical plan for a circuit that carries a light load and another that carries a heavy load.
8. Answer problems utilizing various formulas such as $I \times V = W$, $W/V = I$, $I = V/R$, and $W = I^2R$. What is the wattage if the amperage is 1.5 and the voltage on the line is 120 V? If a circuit for a range pulls 12.5 kW on a 208-V line, what is the amperage and what should the breaker be in the panel? (See answers to selected problems at end of text.)

KEY WORDS AND CONCEPTS

alternating current (AC)
alternator
amp (I)
atomic fission
AWG
circuit breaker
circuit connected in series
closed circuit
conductor
cycle
direct current (DC)
electrical current
electrons
fossil fuels
fuse
gauge
ground

Hertz (Hz)
impedance
insulation
kilowatt (kW)
MCM
nonconductors
Ohm
open circuit
parallel circuit
resistance (R)
short circuit
single-phase system
solar energy
three-phase system
volts (V)
watts (W)

CHAPTER

13

Lighting

Lighting serves both utilitarian and aesthetic needs in a food facility. Definition of requirements will involve amount, direction, and such qualities as color, steadiness, and diffusion. Adequate lighting provides clear vision in a manner and to a degree that will not cause eye discomfort. Needs differ in given areas of the kitchen and dining room. Artistic requirements will also vary.

There are numerous economic aspects. They involve the cost of electrical power to create light as compared to the utilization of natural light. In addition, lighting influences work efficiency, safety, and even patron reactions. Work proceeds best when workers can see clearly and comprehend quickly. They tend to feel less fatigue if they are free from eye strain and feel buoyant. The amount and quality of light also tend to affect individuals psychologically in terms of lightness of spirit, calmness, or despondency.

Members of the planning team must carefully analyze lighting requirements for the various areas of the food facility and set up standards to be met. Adequacy in lighting cannot be achieved by merely inserting extra lights to give the required candlepower.

A unit of light quantity is called a **lumen** and abbreviated lm. Because light intensity decreases with distance, a more practical measure, however, is a foot-candle. A **foot-candle** is light intensity per unit area. Lighting requirements vary from 100 foot-candles (ft-c) in offices and kitchen work surface areas to the subdued light in dining and cocktail areas. Light must have quality as well as quantity. Achievement of desirable lighting patterns, variations, and contrasts is an art requiring considerable knowledge about light. Standards that have been set up by the Illuminating Engineering Society are helpful in establishing many of the requirements. In addition, minimum guidelines are also suggested by the Food and Drug Administration and the Americans with Disabilities Act. Standards vary with each area of the food service.

CHARACTERISTICS OF LIGHT

Visible light is one part of the electromagnetic spectrum of radiant energy (see Chapter 12). It moves in undulating waves. The light waves energize the optic nerve, causing us to see. They strike an object and then bounce from it to our eyes. Whatever light waves are reflected by the object is what we see. Thus, a leaf of a tree will have white light strike it. It absorbs all of the various waves except green. These green light waves will then be reflected and only green color will be seen. The various lengths of light waves excite the optic nerves differently, causing the eye to see different colors. Thus light waves in the 400-nanometer (nm) range are indigo; those in the 700-nm range are red. Combining different wavelengths gives different shades. White light contains light of all wavelengths. However, if white light is filtered through a glass prism, a rainbow, or a mist, it is broken up into various colors. If an object, such as white paper, reflects white light, no light waves are being absorbed by it. If colors are reflected, the various bands making up the color are being reflected, while the others are being absorbed by the object. Black is the complete absence of light.

Light is energy and creates heat when it strikes an object. A white object reflects almost all of the energy striking it, but a black object absorbs most of it. The white object becomes less warm in the sunlight than a dark one. If a white and a black cloth of the same kind and weight are laid over snow in the sunlight, the snow under the black cloth will melt much faster than the snow under the white cloth because of the difference in the amount of energy absorbed.

Some artificial light appears white but actually is not white. It may lack certain red waves or others. Objects under such lights will not appear natural. For instance, some types of fluorescent lights do not give off waves in the red band. Thus a woman's lipstick under such light may appear purple or almost black. A cherry pie will have an unappetizing color. It is important, therefore, to have the right type of light where color reflection is important.

SOURCES OF LIGHT

Incandescent Light

The modern **incandescent light** globe has a tungsten filament set within a glass globe (quartz globes are used to withstand high heat). If electricity is conducted through tungsten exposed to the air, the tungsten quickly oxidizes in the air and the filament burns up. If this occurs where oxygen is not present, such oxidation does not occur and the light will last a long time. An inert gas, such as a mixture of argon and nitrogen, fills the globe. The standard life of a good globe is 1,000 hours. Tungsten lights decline in efficiency due to heat gradually evaporating the tungsten. This then deposits on the globe, darkening it, causing some of the light to be absorbed. Finally, so much of the tungsten evaporates that the filament ruptures and the current is stopped.

Special incandescent lights are available. The tungsten-halogen lamp (a lamp in engineering terminology refers to the bulb from a fixture) is filled with iodine in combination with other inert gases. The iodine vaporizes when the lamp becomes hot, and the hot iodine has the ability to pick up the vaporized tungsten and return it to the filament when it cools. This light does not have a lowered light output due to tungsten darkening. It also has a longer life (about twice as long). It is more expensive than regular tungsten lights because of the manner in which it must be made and also because it is made of quartz and not glass. It has an expected life of about 2,000 hours. Krypton gas or other rare gases may be used to give lights longer operating life.

Most of the light produced by incandescents is in the yellow to red portion of the spectrum, although it depends on the wattage. Generally, the higher the wattage, the whiter the light, and the lower the wattage, the more yellow the light.

Lamps should be operated at the voltage for which they were intended. If lamps are operated at higher voltages, they are brighter, but lamp life is shortened. If they are operated at lower voltages, their lamp life is lengthened, but they are dimmer. In special areas, however, dimmers are sometimes used to vary the voltage to be able to decrease brightness from normal depending on the lighting needs.

Frosting may also be done on incandescents to achieve special effects. Frosting on the inside of the bulb produces softer illumination than clear bulbs, but silica-coated (white) bulbs produce even softer illumination.

There are also rough service or vibration lights that can be placed in areas where movement might quickly destroy other types of lights. In addition, special lights are made that carry away heat that develops from the bulb. These can be used in refrigerated display cases and other areas where the heat buildup would be undesirable.

Fluorescent Light

Energy can be saved by using **fluorescent lighting** rather than incandescent. Nearly five times as much light is given off by fluorescent lights per watt than by incandescent lights. In addition, fluorescent lights generally produce less glare. The lumens (lm) produced per watt by different lights usually average as follows:

Tungsten-halogen light	16 to 20 lm
Fluorescent light	50 to 85 lm
Metal-halide	60 to 80 lm
High-pressure sodium	90 to 100 lm

The operating life of a fluorescent light is also longer. Flourescents generally last about 10 times as long as incandescent lamps. Because the life of a fluorescent light is shortened by turning it off and on, however, some operations never turn off the lamp. The energy required to start a fluorescent light is considerable also and so energy can be saved if the light is left on in areas where it might be turned on and off many times during a day. The life spans of fluorescent lights are calculated on the basis of a 3-hour continuous burning time before being turned off. Light production declines considerably in fluorescents in the first 100-hours of burning and so light production is calculated on the basis of 80-hours of burning and not from the start. After 100 hours the light production is fairly steady.

Fluorescent lights operate with two cathodes inside a tube, one on each end. When electricity flows into one, it becomes excited and starts a flow of electrons to the other cathode. These electrons in passing down the tube develop ultraviolet light, which in turn activates phosphors on the inside lining of the tube. Energy is then produced in the form of light. This is cool light and is the same kind of light that is present in glow worms or fireflies.

Fluorescent lights do not function well under cooler conditions (refrigerators and outdoor use). All-weather and jacketed bulbs are available that will maintain lumen output over a wider temperature range. For temperatures below 50°F (10°C), rapid start lamps with low-temperature ballasts are also available.

Fluorescent lights operate better on higher voltages, and some systems may require special devices, such as a **ballast,** to push up voltages. A slow start and flickering are undesirable factors in such lights and may be corrected by using such special devices. Normally, the cost of fluorescent lights and their installation is more than for incandescent lights. The cost of operation for fluorescents, however, is less. Bulb replacement cost should also be considered when making cost comparisons for different lighting systems.

In addition, operating the system on a frequency higher than 60 cycles may increase lighting efficiency, and decrease light size, weight, and heat output. Maintenance may also be less.

The type of frost may also make a difference. An outside frost on a fluorescent light may cause a 20% loss of light, whereas an inside one may cause only a 2% or 3% loss. Incandescent lights also have a higher efficiency if given an inside, rather than outside, frost. Clear lights have the lowest light loss but may contribute to glare.

Some fluorescent lights do not give off light equal to the colors in daylight. They frequently lack waves in the red color range and give off light in the blue-green area. As noted, red objects under such light do not have a natural color. By adding substances to the phosphors, red light waves can be produced to correct the deficiency. Generally, fluorescents are rated as follows in comparison to sunlight (which is rated at 100):

Deluxe cool white	89
Sign white	86
Daylight	79
Deluxe warm white	73
Cool white	66
White	60
Warm white	50

Thus, deluxe cool white would give 89% of the kind of light that sunlight gives. (Light from an incandescent light approximates daylight but gives off more waves in the yellow-orange range than is found in daylight, probably due to the heat produced.) This type of light produces the best overall color of fluorescents, but lamp types should be tested for the one that best fits in with surroundings.

Mercury Lights

When electricity flows through mercury, ultraviolet light waves are produced. **Mercury lamps** filled with high-pressure mercury gas have a long operating life and high efficiency. The light has a large quantity of blue-green waves and, unless corrected, lacks red waves. They are used at times in refrigerators and other areas to destroy bacteria. The ultraviolet light is lethal to many microorganisms. The light is not effective against bacteria over great distances, so such lights may be worthless if they are not close enough to the items requiring protection.

Mercury lights are also often used in parking lots and warehouses where high-intensity illumination is needed, but the color of the light is not as critical (mercury lights tend to have more green color). Newer mercury lamps have also been developed to simulate the color characteristics of cool-white fluorescent lamps. These are being used in large interior areas where color is somewhat more critical, such as sporting arenas or large exhibition areas.

A special sodium-mercury lamp is used where a long operating life is desired. This light has a very high lumen output.

Mercury lights (as well as fluorescents, particularly those with a ballast) may create noise (similar to a hum) while operating. This is especially true if incorrect installation methods are used or the proper electrical current is not used. Noise ratings may be obtained by manufacturers if this is thought to be a possible problem.

Another possible problem is that these lights may interfere with radio and other communication signals. In addition, some mercury lights may require a 5- to 10-minute cooling period before they will go on again. If this is a problem, a few incandescent lights can be installed to maintain a particular light level when this happens. Fluorescent and mercury lights should be specified as the instant-start type unless there is some reason not to do so.

High-Pressure Sodium Lights

One of the highest efficiency lights is the high-pressure **sodium light.** As a result, it is extremely energy efficient. High-pressure sodium lights are used in parking lots, warehouses, and other large lighted areas.

High-pressure sodium lights operate as an arc discharge unit with a ballast. The light that is produced has a definite yellow tint. They are frequently used in areas where high-intensity illumination is necessary, but color is not critical.

In comparison to other high-intensity lighting, high-pressure sodium lights are generally less expensive than mercury lights and have lower operating costs. On the other hand, mercury lights generally have a longer life. Restart time for sodium lights is also generally less than that for mercury lights.

LIGHTING REQUIREMENTS

Light quality is made up of many factors. Manipulating these gives many useful and artistic effects. The quantity of light, its color, brightness, amount of diffusion, source, shadows, reflection, and its absorption play a part in giving quality to light.

The characteristics of the floor, walls, and ceiling, as well as the objects to be viewed, affect lighting requirements. For example, light colored walls will decrease lighting requirements. In addition, smooth surfaces require less light than textured surfaces.

Lighting needs are based on several factors, including the following:

- The difficulty of the task (more difficult tasks require more light; for example, reading fine print as compared to large print on a menu)
- Time (tasks that must be done more rapidly require more light)
- Employees (standard factors are usually used, but older employees may require more light)
- Cost of errors (economic trade-offs are considered, but standard lighting should allow for about 90% accuracy)
- Special needs (examples include the use of special tools, three-dimensional tasks where one must see into smaller openings, or tasks where shadows are a problem).

Quantity of Light

A large quantity of foot-candles may be required in certain work areas, while in others a much more subdued lighting effect might be desired. Table 13–1 summarizes some of the recommended foot-candles for various areas in a facility. In general, more light is needed for small details, dark colors (or when there is poor contrast with the background), and tasks that last longer (for example, several hours).

The quantity of light on a surface is a very important factor in determining light quality. The quantity depends on (1) the lumens emitted by the lamp, (2) the number of lamps per fixture, and (3) the number of fixtures. Not all of the light from a luminaire or source reaches the surface being considered. Lighting engineers call the percentage produced as compared to that reaching the surface the **coefficient of utilization** (CU). This is never 100% because of blackening from soil on lamp globes, tungsten destruction, distance of travel, reflective value, and so forth. The two most important factors, soil on the lamp globes and blackening, are often called the **maintenance factor** (MF). This is usually considered to be 70%. The total CU contains the MF factor plus the other light-destroying factors. This can be calculated, but engineers frequently use tables for different fixtures and different work area levels.

CU factors can vary anywhere from 15% to 90%. Much depends on the light-destroying factors involved, which may include the fixture; the quantity of light produced; the amount reflected from the ceiling and other surfaces; whether the light is direct, semidirect, or indirect; and whether or not the light is diffused.

Lighting requirements are dictated by the area and the activity that occurs there. The number of luminaires (a **luminaire** is a light fixture with a bulb), the amount of light each produces, the amount of area to be lighted, and the CU factor (obtained from a table) dictate how much light must come from the source. The formula used to determine the number of units that must be installed is as follows:

$$\text{No. of lamps or fixtures} = \frac{\text{ft-c needed} \times \text{area in sq ft}}{\text{lamps in the fixture} \times \text{lm-lamp} \times \text{CU} \times \text{MF}} \quad (13.1)$$

TABLE 13-1   *Minimum Footcandles of Light for Various Areas*

Type area	Minimum ft-c	Type area	Minimum ft-c
Cashier	50	Building surroundings	1–5
Fast service unit	50–100	Auditorium	15–30
Intimate dining, cocktail		Auditorium exhibits	30–50
lounge		Dancing area	5
Light environment	10	Bathrooms, general	10
Subdued environment	5	Bathrooms, at mirror	30
Luxury food service		Bedrooms, general	10–15
Light environment	30	Corridors, elevators, stairs	10
Subdued environment	15	Hotel or motel entrance	20
Food counters and displays	50	Reading or work areas	30
Food checker	70	Linen room, general	10
Detail work area	70–100	Linen room, sewing, etc.	100
Other kitchen areas	30	Hotel or motel lobby, general	10
Storerooms	10	Offices, accounting, etc.	100–150
Baking mixing room	50	Offices, general	100
Oven area	30	Mechanical rooms, general	10
Decorator's bench	100	Mechanical rooms, worktable	50–100
Fillings and other		Parking lot, self-parking	5
preparations	30–50	Parking lot, attendant	2
Loading platform	20	Laundry, washing area	30
Storage area, active	20	Laundry, pressing, etc.	50–70
Storage area, inactive	1–5	Outdoor signs, light surfaces	20–50
Building entrances	5–20	Outdoor signs, dark surfaces	50–100

To discover the area each fixture must cover the formula is

$$\text{Area/luminaires} = \frac{\text{lamps in fixture} \times \text{lm/lamp} \times \text{CU} \times \text{MF}}{\text{ft-c}} \tag{13.2}$$

As an example, if 70 ft-c is desired on the work surface 36 in. above the floor in a room 45×75 ft with a fixture with four lamps, each of which produces 3000 lm with a CU of 0.675, and the standard MF of .7 is used, the number of fixtures will be

$$\frac{70 \text{ ft-c} \times 45 \text{ ft} \times 75 \text{ ft}}{4 \text{ lamps} \times 3000 \text{ lm} \times .675 \text{ CU} \times 0.7 \text{ MF}} = \frac{236,250}{5670} = 41.66. \tag{13.3}$$

The spacing for these fixtures is obtained as follows:

$$\frac{4 \text{ lamps} \times 3,000 \text{ lm} \times 0.675 \text{ CU} \times 0.7 \text{ MF}}{70 \text{ ft-c}} = 81 \text{ sq ft} \tag{13.4}$$

This suggests that each fixture will cover 81 square feet. The engineer would then draw a grid for the area showing approximately 9-ft squares ($9 \times 9 = 81$).

Light Direction

Light quality is also affected by the direction of the light and how it is reflected. In certain places, shadows are desired to give pattern and variety. A hotel lobby lighted by a considerable quantity of diffused light appears stark and has a sort of "bled" appearance. If shadows are made on wall surfaces and other areas, the lobby becomes a much more interesting place. In work areas where close inspection occurs, especially on surfaces, shadows are helpful in delineating defects, edges, and so on. If the light strikes from all angles (is diffused), the worker has more difficulty seeing varied levels on the objects and other surface variations.

Direct lighting gives the most shadows and the highest efficiency from the light produced. If direct lighting is used, shielding may be needed to prevent glare at certain angles.

If undesirable features, such as pipes or ducts, must be hidden or if ceiling height should be made to appear lower, the ceiling can be painted a dark color so it will not reflect light, show the undesirable objects, or indicate the ceiling height. The light then can be focused down so that the nonlighted area above is hidden in darkness.

On the other hand, if direct light is spread out so that it is well diffused by the walls and floor, the attention of viewers will move toward furniture and other features in the room rather than to the walls because the walls darken slightly. By contrast, if light concentration is desired, direct light is the best way to obtain it. Too much direct light, however, should be avoided in a work area because it gives an uncomfortable feeling to those working there.

Semidirect lighting is obtained when 60% to 90% of the light produced is directed downward and the remainder goes to the ceiling where reflection occurs. Ceilings should have a good reflective value since the direct light can create a glare unless sufficient additional light comes from above. If done well, good diffusion occurs and at the same time some shadowing is possible. It is fairly efficient in energy use also.

If from 60% to 90% of the light is sent up and then reflected downward from the ceiling, a **semi-indirect lighting** system results. The distribution of light appears similar to the semidirect, except that it is somewhat more efficient. To do this, the ceiling must have a fairly high reflectance. Paints and colors with satisfactory reflectance values may be used for this. The lights themselves are less apt to stand out in such lighting because there is less contrast between the fixture and the ceiling brightness. This may or may not be desirable. Semi-indirect and indirect lighting create a monotony in light tone unless care is taken to see that variations in light brightness and contrast occur.

Indirect lighting results when 90% to 100% of the light goes to the ceiling and upper walls. It cannot be used in a ceiling lower than 9 ft 6 in. since the lights must be at least 18 in. from the ceiling to give proper light spread. If cove lighting is used, the ceiling can be lower. Cove lighting has a sort of skylight quality to it. Local lighting from tables or other lamps at a lower level can also add texture to vertical surfaces. Otherwise, the high amount of diffusion leaves little variety in light pattern and considerable monotony. Indirect lighting gives the lowest efficiency in light use. It does, however, create the least amount of glare. Lighting over 75 ft-c is usually not possible with indirect lighting since a ceiling brightness over 400 ft-c is required for this. A ceiling this bright could contribute a high amount of glare.

Direct-indirect lighting provides about equal distribution of light upward and downward. The result is that the ceiling and upper walls appear brighter. **Diffuse lighting** fixtures provide light in all directions, including horizontally. These both require that fixtures be placed at least 12 in. from the ceiling to avoid excessive ceiling brightness. Diffuse lighting will appear lighter than direct-indirect because more light is directed horizontally to wall surfaces. The efficiency of both of these systems is good. Because a great deal of light is directed downward, care must be taken, however, to ensure that eyes are not disturbed by overly bright fixtures.

To achieve a desirable light quality, the use of general and localized lighting must be done carefully. **General lighting** is that which flows over the whole area. **Localized lighting** is that which comes from a set fixture in a given area. A room may need only a limited quantity of general lighting with special lighting required at different areas. A lounge appears much more interesting if the general light is sufficient for ordinary movement and concentrated light appears from table lamps and other units. Different kinds of light also add interest. In addition, light variation may be used to call attention to certain features and not to others in a room. Examples of the different types of lighting are shown in Figure 13.1.

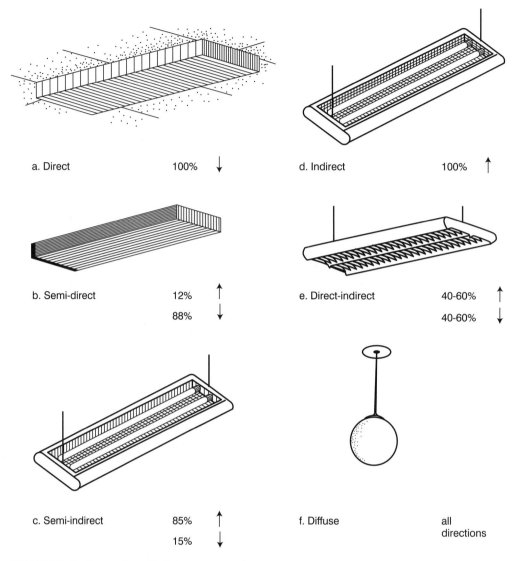

FIGURE 13.1   Examples of lighting types.

Light Color

Color contributes to light quality. A green wall makes red foods appear more attractive because the eye sees the opposite complementary color when the eye shifts from the wall to the food. Thus the eye sees the food as redder than it really is. After looking at a blue wall one is likely to see more yellow in a yellow object.

Pink, pale blue, ivory, and other light colors have the highest amount of reflectance with white the highest. Red, orange, brown, gray, and other dark colors reflect about one-fourth of the light that white and light colors do. Examples of some reflection factors from different colors (in a medium value) are shown in Table 13–2. Studies have shown that the makeup of the light reflecting on food can affect its acceptance or rejection.

Glare and Contrast

Glare is a disproportionate amount of light coming into the eye. Glare is annoying and can reduce workers' production. It also can create blind spots that may lead to accidents. It may come directly from the source or it may be reflected from some surface. A bright

TABLE 13-2 *Reflection Factors of Common Colors*

Color	Reflection Factor
White	80–85
Ivory	60–70
Light gray	45–70
Dark gray	20–25
Tan	30–50
Brown	20–40
Green	25–50
Sky blue	35–40
Pink	50–70
Red	20–40

stainless steel surface or a high sheen in a white tile wall may cause glare in the area because of the reflectance. Normally, the recommended reflectance of room surfaces is as follows:

Ceilings	80% to 90% (best reflectance is usually about 80%)
Walls	40% to 60% (best reflectance is usually about 50%)
Floors	21% to 39% (best reflectance is usually about 30%)
Furniture and equipment	26% to 44% (best reflectance is usually about 35%)

These reflectance values should be used only as broad guides, because they may not be advisable in every instance nor give the best lighting quality in particular circumstances.

Glare is also much more apt to occur if the flow of light is more than a 45° angle from the light source, because such light can fall on a desk, table, or other object and be reflected back to create glare. The positioning of a light fixture, therefore, should be done carefully to prevent glare. Lamps giving a high amount of diffusion usually require less attention in preventing glare than those with little diffusion. Ceilings, walls, and other objects assisting in diffusion can reduce the potential also.

Contrast is an important factor in obtaining adequate light quality. It is easier to discern items if there is some contrast of light on them and on their backgrounds. Too much contrast between an object and its background, however, may be distasteful, and if the background is too bright, glare may result. Direct glare can be reduced by increasing the brightness behind the light. The lights of a car in daylight are less blinding than at night because of background light.

The Illuminating Engineering Society (IES) says that to achieve a desirable balance of contrast at a workplace, the maximum contrast desired is usually as follows:

1 to ⅓ contrast between the work and adjacent surroundings,

1 to ⅒ contrast between the work and more remote darker surfaces, and

1 to 10 contrast between the work and more remote lighter surfaces.

LIGHT SELECTION

A lighting engineer or specialist, if given adequate instruction on the quantity and quality of light desired, can develop a satisfactory lighting system and a very good lighting pattern. Team planners need to establish lists indicating the amount of light desired in the various areas. Reference to illuminating standards can be helpful, but remember that light tends to be overprovided. Lights that are capable of being turned off in halls and special areas can conserve energy without loss of lighting efficiency. Team planners and the person in charge of lighting decisions need to thoroughly discuss desired lighting effects in the various areas. Pictures showing desired effects can be useful. Construction factors and other features of the facility should be studied in terms of what should be emphasized by lighting and what should be hidden. Care taken in developing a suitable lighting plan is well worth the time and effort required.

Building and sanitation codes should also be checked for minimum lighting requirements. Adequate and proper lighting is required for employee safety while working, for adequate cleaning, for customer comfort, and for emergency exits. Codes may also require shielding on lights in certain areas for employee or customer safety and protection of food.

When selecting lights, temperatures will make a difference in the lamp life. High temperatures will reduce lamp life considerably. This might include high ambient temperatures, poorly designed fixtures that do not allow for heat dissipation, or use of a lamp at a wattage greater than that recommended by the manufacturer. As an example, operation of a lamp at 18°F (10°C) over its rated temperature may reduce its life by about 50%. Conversely, operation at temperatures below the rated maximum will increase its life. Because of this, the best lighting fixture provides for dissipation of heat produced by bulbs.

Efficiency in light output should also be kept in mind. High wattage incandescents and fluorescents are generally more efficient in light output than low wattage. For example, a 100-watt lamp may generate 1,750 lumens, whereas two 50-watt lamps generate a total of 1,280 lumens. Operating costs, therefore, may be reduced by using fixtures with fewer but higher wattage lamps.

Size of fixture should also be considered. Fluorescent lamps will require larger fixtures than incandescents and may require ballasts or transformers.

Special needs should also be considered. Some bulbs are coated with a material so that they may be used in the high heat temperatures of ovens. For areas where bulb breakage is a problem, bulbs are available that are covered with a shatter-resistant coating. If the bulb is damaged, the bulb may break, but the coating will keep the bulb from shattering into pieces.

ENERGY EFFICIENCY

Adequate lighting is essential, but it has been inefficiently used in the past. Good lighting is essential for safety, efficiency, cleaning, comfort, or creating a mood for a building's occupants. Although lighting requires a significant initial investment, it should really be considered on a life-cycle cost analysis basis. Maintenance, energy, and replacement costs should also be considered because they represent significant amounts of money.

As an example, some operations have a program of planned light replacement because of loss of efficiency. It is a system in which all globes are replaced at a specified time regardless of whether they are functioning or not. This is done to maintain a high light level and to reduce cost. The labor to replace a burned out individual light can cost more than the new light. Replacing all at one time considerably reduces such labor cost. This is especially true when an area has lights that are difficult to reach. A stadium, for instance, may replace lights once a year on such a system. To obtain the necessary operating life, which may be over 1,000 hr, it may use lights of a higher wattage than required but operate them on a lower voltage. The lower voltage will give about the right amount of light or wattage but, because the lights are being operated on a lower voltage, they will have a longer life, thus achieving the desired time and amount of light. Such lights burned three hours per night, 365 days a year will perform satisfactorily.

One of the ways to minimize energy use may be to take advantage of daylight, rather than to rely solely on artificial light. Thermal cost will have to be considered because window openings generally increase heating and cooling costs, but they may also dramatically decrease lighting requirements if they are well designed. For example, in rooms that extend a long distance from the windows, the top of the windows should be placed as close to the ceiling as possible to permit deep penetration of daylight into the room. To prevent glare, windows should be shielded from direct sunlight. Preferably, light is actually reflected into the window from the ground instead of from the sky. Finally, rooms with windows on two sides allow greater light penetration as well.

Computer technology has advanced in recent years so that lighting controls may now be set up in buildings to help control energy costs. These lighting controls may be set to automatically adjust lighting levels throughout preprogrammed schedules with the time of day. They may also be set up to use photocontrols, which adjust illumination based on the combination of artificial light and daylight. Motion sensors may also be used to turn lights on only when a room is occupied or to activate night security systems.

CHAPTER SUMMARY

Lighting is important for its impact on utilitarian needs such as work efficiency, safety, and cleaning. It is also important for its aesthetic effects on the mood of the food service and customer reactions. Members of the planning team must carefully balance the economic aspects of lighting with the psychological affects of lighting.

Selection of which lamp to use (incandescent, fluorescent, mercury, etc.) and which style of lighting (direct, indirect, semi-direct, etc.) depends on the type of activity planned for that area. Both quality and quantity of lighting are important considerations.

The choice of which lamp to use depends on several factors. Such considerations might include the fact that fluorescent lights are less expensive to operate and last longer, but the quality of light may not be as good as incandescents, and the bulbs cost more. The quality of mercury lighting is not as good, but they may be useful in producing more light in large areas (such as parking lots, convention centers, and sporting arenas).

The amount of lighting required will also depend on the environment. The color and reflective characteristics of floors, walls, and the ceiling affect lighting requirements. Positioning of lights should be done to achieve the desired effect without creating glare. Often, to achieve the desired effect, a combination of general and localized lighting is used.

Efficiency in lighting is also important. Some of the ways to minimize energy usage may be to take advantage of artificial light, use computer technology to control energy costs by programming the light levels throughout the day, use photocontrols to adjust light levels, or use motion sensors to turn on lights only when a room is occupied.

Lighting is a very basic need in a food service. In the past, it has not been done efficiently. With today's technology and careful choices from the planning team, it can enhance an operation at an economical cost.

REVIEW QUESTIONS

1. Use a prism to discover how white light can be broken into different wavelengths, resulting in different colors.
2. Examine an incandescent and a fluorescent light and make a drawing to show major components and how they work.
3. Locate for observation as many different types of light as possible, such as mercury, sodium-mercury, and tungsten-halogen lamps. Note the color qualities of these and also those of fluorescent lights that lack reds and others that have them. State where each of the lights is used and evaluate the degree of satisfaction with color in the situation.
4. Select a given area to be lighted and secure the square footage covered; then calculate the number of lamps or fixtures required to light it.
5. Choose a facility plan and indicate the quantity of light to be given in the various areas.
6. Calculate the number of fixtures required if each fixture has four 100-W light globes producing 1,400 lm/globe if the CU is 65% and the MF is 70% and 50 ft-c are desired per square foot in a room having 700 sq ft. How many square feet of space will each fixture need to cover? (See answers to selected problems at end of text.)

KEY WORDS AND CONCEPTS

ballast
coefficient of utilization (CU)
contrast
diffuse lighting
direct lighting
direct-indirect lighting
fluorescent light
foot-candle (ft-c)
general lighting
glare

incandescent light
indirect lighting
localized lighting
lumen (lm)
luminaire
maintenance factor (MF)
mercury lamps
semidirect lighting
semi-indirect lighting
Sodium light

CHAPTER
14

Water, Steam, and Plumbing

The amount and quality of water available are two of the most important concerns for those planning a food facility. Unfortunately, they are often taken for granted and not given the attention they deserve. Water coming into the food service must be drinkable (that is, **potable water**). Not only is it used as a beverage, it is used in ice, food (as an ingredient), hand washing, restrooms, cleaning, laundry, waste removal, and showers.

Unsafe water can carry bacteria, viruses, and parasites. Ordinarily, the public water supply in the United States is safe to consume because of public health regulations and inspections. Chlorination systems are widely used to destroy harmful pathogens.

WATER QUALITY

Water supplies in some areas also have to be treated to remove sediment or coloring matter. Algicides, gelatinous compounds, or filters are used for this. Iron is seldom found in sufficient quantity to cause problems. However, water flowing through rusty pipes may pick up enough iron to require removal.

Frequently, water coming from lakes or streams where there are decomposing organic materials, such as leaves, is dark and needs to be decolored. Water from lakes and streams may also contain enough acid to attack metal. This water must be treated to bring it above a pH of 7.0. If the pH is not corrected, copper piping must be used, which is resistant to attack from such water. Plastic piping may be used if codes permit.

Most food facilities obtain their water from municipal sources. This water will have been treated, except for softening (which may be necessary if the water is extremely hard). Figure 14.1 shows areas in the United States where **hardwater** is a problem.

Where a treated public water system is not available, a facility may have to install its own water system. In addition to a chlorination system and any other necessary treatment, the planners must consider pump capacities, storage tanks, potability, water pressure, and other aspects. Regular testing should be done to determine potability. Generally, nonpublic water systems should be tested at least quarterly, if not monthly. Water testing reports should be kept on file in the food service in case of questions from health inspectors.

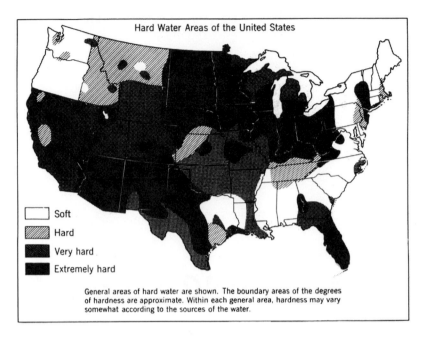

FIGURE 14.1   Hard-water areas of the United States. (*Courtesy of Volume Feeding Management, New York.*)

Hard water contains a quantity of **alkaline salts** that may interfere with its ability to clean items well or that may not give good results in cooking. Hard water also interferes with equipment's ability to function effectively. The buildup of just 1/40 of an inch of lime on the evaporator in an ice machine increases energy costs by as much as 30%. Dish machines and steamers with hard-water buildup also perform poorly or may even break down with lime buildup. Such water must be softened.

The hardness of water is judged either on the basis of parts per million (ppm) of calcium carbonate in the water or on the basis of grains of hardness. One grain of hardness is equivalent to 17.1 ppm. If water contains over 65 ppm or 4 grains hardness, it usually must be softened. Hot water over 5 grains hardness will deposit hard-water salts called **scale** or **lime** in pipes and equipment. This can eventually clog pipes or cause equipment to malfunction. Hard-water salts will combine with detergents or soaps to make an insoluble precipitate that spots glassware, dishes, and flatware. It also makes it necessary to use more detergent or soap since this bonding with the hard-water salts removes detergent or soap as a cleaning agent.

One of the simplest and most economical methods of softening water is with the sodium-exchange system. This is a process in which sodium chloride (ordinary table salt but usually unrefined) is exchanged by a zeolite process for the magnesium, calcium, and other hard-water substances. Thus water high in calcium carbonate will come out of the zeolite softener high in sodium bicarbonate (which does not contribute to water hardness). The calcium carbonate is captured in the softener and from time to time the exchanger must be regenerated and the supply of sodium chloride renewed. In some hospitals, an additional supply of water other than that softened by sodium must be available for patients who are on low-sodium diets.

Water can be treated with other filters as well. Activated carbon filters remove chlorine, organic chemicals, and some pesticides and improve taste and odor problems. A carbon block filter does the same job as activated carbon filters, but it has a shorter life span. Reverse osmosis filters out more, but it is slower and more expensive. Reverse osmosis reduces suspended solids, metals, chlorine, pesticides, nitrates, and some viruses and bacteria.

WATER QUANTITY AND PRESSURE

The quantity of water used in a facility is substantial. A hotel may use 40 gal (151 L) or more per guest per day, 40% to 60% of which is hot water at 160°F (71°C). A food service may use 5 gal (18.9 L) or more per person served. A dishwasher uses an average of 1.8 gal (6.8 L) per person served and this may vary from 2.1 gal (7.9 L) per person for large banquets to 1.3 gal (4.9 L) for light lunches. Hand washing of dishes requires less water than by machine.

The demand for water may vary considerably with the time of day. A hotel may find that 75% of its room demand for hot water comes from 7 to 10 A.M. Adequate capacity for heating and storage of water must be planned to meet these peak demands. The need for hot water for a kitchen must also be carefully calculated.

The water pressure coming from large municipal mains is usually 50 to 80 psi. Most water pressure in a facility will be around 20 to 30 psi. For equipment such as lavatories, toilets, and dishwashers, it will need to be around 10 to 15 psi. Open tap pressure is usually specified as 4 to 5 psi.

For every psi, water can be lifted 2.3 ft. Thus if water is in the main at ground level at 50 psi, there is enough pressure to raise the water 115 ft or

$$\frac{2.3 \text{ ft}}{\text{psi}} \times 50 \text{ psi} = 115 \text{ ft} \qquad (14.1)$$

This is generally adequate pressure to raise the water to high enough levels for a four- to six-story building and still have enough pressure at plumbing fixtures. (In addition to lifting the water, additional pressure must be available so open tap pressure will be at 4 to 5 psi.) If the facility is 200 ft high, a supplemental tank and pumping system must be installed to get it up to the 200-ft level. An alternative system for tall buildings is to pump water to tanks on top of the facility and then let it feed by gravity to lower levels. Enough pressure is usually built by the drop to provide the pressure required.

If a vacuum is made in a tube that is sealed on one end with the other open end in water, water flows up into the tube. This is due to atmospheric pressure on the water surface, which pushes the water up into the tube where vacuum existed. Often the statement is made that "water is pulled up" by suction from a pump, but this is not true. The water is *pushed* up by the atmospheric pressure. The normal pressure of the atmosphere at sea level is 14.7 psi, which gives it a theoretical lift with a perfect vacuum of 34 ft or

$$\frac{2.3 \text{ ft}}{\text{psi}} \times 14.7 \text{ psi} = 34 \text{ ft} \qquad (14.2)$$

It is not possible, however, to have 100% efficient equipment, and so the limit a suction pump can "pull" water up is about 25 ft. If the distance of the lift is greater than 25 ft, additional suction pumps must be put at higher levels. Frequently pumps that force the water up are used. This permits the water to be forced a longer distance with only one pump. Air pressure can also force water up. The size of the pump and the quantity of pressure required must be calculated carefully.

HEATING OF WATER

Water may be heated in various ways. The efficiencies of fuels listed in Chapter 15 can be used to calculate the cost of heating water. Only about 60% of the Btus produced by burning gas or other fuels is utilized. Electricity may have 90% or more efficiency, especially if the elements are buried in the water so that all of the heat produced goes into the water.

Heat is lost when water is transported. Water may have to be heated to 160°F (71°C) or higher to reach a guest room in a hotel at 130°F (55°C). When water higher than 160°F

(71°C) is needed at a using point, **booster heaters** are usually installed to raise the temperature. Examples would include sinks used for hot water sanitizing of dishes and dish machines that use hot water sanitizing. Water for guest use should not be much over 130°F (55°C). Some facilities heat water to 180°F (82°C) and then lower it to the temperatures required by means of mixing valves at the using point. About 40% of the total hot water load in food services is at 180°F (82°C) and 60% at 140°F (60°C).

Approximately 55% of the total hot water use comes at peak periods of relatively short duration, closely coinciding with serving periods. About 28% of the remaining total comes before service and about 17% later. Hotels may need a 20% to 25% head start with a heating capacity of 15% to 20% per hour thereafter of the total need. Thus, if a hotel has guest needs of 8,000 gal (30,280 L) per day of 130°F (55°C) water, it should start with 2,000 gal or 7,570 L (25%) and be able each hour thereafter to heat an additional 1,600 gal or 6,056 L (20%) to meet needs. Better hotels have a lower peak demand than commercial hotels but have a higher total hot water requirement per guest.

Heaters and tanks should be sized to give sufficient lead time to cover peak demands and recovery needs for hot water. Usually the quantity stored ahead is 15% to 25% of peak requirements. Improved instant-type heating units may lessen lead time requirements. Circulators should be installed so water is instantly at the required temperature. This eliminates the need to run the water until proper temperature of water is obtained. Tanks and lines should be insulated to minimize heat loss.

STEAM[1]

Steam can be generated in a central boiler and then distributed; it may be produced in the equipment using it; or it may be produced by an outside supplier in the local area. A unit in which the steam is generated for its own operation is called a **self-contained steam unit.** The amount of steam generated in the individual piece may be sufficient for its operation only or sufficient for the operation of an additional item or items of equipment.

Steam generated in a boiler is measured in **boiler horsepower (Bhp).** One Bhp equals the production of 34.5 lb of steam per hour. Thus a boiler rated at 5 Bhp produces 172.5 lb of steam per hour. Ratings are controlled and must meet certain standard approved ratings. Chimney sizes must meet specified standards also.

Steam may be measured by **pounds per square inch (psi).** A steamer cooking food may be said to operate on 5 or 6 psi of steam. Another measure used for steam is the amount of steam flow/hour. This is the quantity of steam in pounds used or flowing to a piece of equipment in an hour. Calculation of the quantity of steam required for a kitchen is done by totaling the quantity of steam flow required by the individual items of equipment. Thus if six pieces of equipment use a total of 163.9 lb of steam per hour, 5 Bhp is required to supply it (assuming 1 Bhp produces 34.5 lb of steam per hour) or

$$\frac{163.9 \text{ lb of steam per hour}}{34.5 \text{ lb of steam per hour/Bhp}} = 4.8 \text{ Bhp} \tag{14.3}$$

However, the boiler must have a greater generating capacity because there is always a loss of steam from the boiler to the equipment. In making quick calculations, engineers use rounded values to calculate heat needs for boiler production; a Bhp on this basis is considered to require 10 kWh of electricity or 34,000 Btus (British thermal units)[2] of heat.

---

[1] A translation of values into metric values is not made here for the values used in the British system. Eventually, psi will probably be translated into grams per centimeter, Bhp into kilograms of pressure, Btus into calories, etc. When the change to the metric system occurs, these translation values will be established and then can be used.

[2] See definition in Chapter 15.

TABLE 14-1   *Steam Flow per Hour for Equipment Needs*

	Delivered Bhp	Steam flow, lb/hr
Large steamer (per compartment)	¾	25.90
Steam-jackted kettle (per 20 gal)	1	34.50
Direct-connected steamers[a]	½	17.25
Direct-connected jet-cookers[a]	2½	86.25
Coffee urn (per 10 gal)	⅒	3.45
Steam table (per sq ft)	⅟₂₀	1.72
Bain marie (per sq ft)	⅒	3.45
Warming oven (per sq ft)	⅟₂₀	1.72

[a]Requirements abstracted from Market Forge catalog for the manufacturer's specific equipment. Check requirements on equipment selected from other manufacturers.

The efficiency rating of a boiler also governs the quantity of heat that must be furnished to supply the required steam. Thus a boiler that requires 136,000 Btus/hour with a 50% efficiency will deliver 68,000 Btus of heat into the water to make steam. This means that it will produce 2 Bhp/hour or

$$\frac{68,000 \text{ Btus/hour}}{34,000 \text{ Btus/Bhp}} = 2 \text{ Bhp per hour} \qquad (14.4)$$

Boilers in which coils are installed are commonly used to produce steam for kitchens and to heat water. This provides steam that can come in contact with food (that is, clean steam).

On the other hand, in boilers where toxic descaling compounds are needed, steam cannot be used on food. Descaling compounds are used because solids from the water remain in the boiler when water changes to steam. When water is hard, a large quantity of residue occurs. If descaling compounds are not used, coils will need to be replaced more frequently because of the residue buildup.

Food frequently comes in contact with steam that is delivered into compartments. Reducers, regulators, or other units are often used to bring steam into the compartment at the proper psi. When steam does not flow freely but is contained (as in coils or in the jacket of a steam kettle), reducers and regulators are not required.

The quantity of steam required of equipment is measured in pounds of steam flow per hour. Examples of equipment steam requirements are shown in Table 14–1.

The quantity of steam delivered depends on the psi and the pipe size (see Table 4–2). Manufacturers provide instructions for connecting their equipment to steam lines and these should be closely followed. Normally, a globe valve to turn steam on or off, a ball float trap with a connection to drain, the pressure gauge, and the pressure-reducing valve follow in that order into the equipment. The size of these units varies with the pipe size and steam requirements.

Floor drains are usually 1.5 or 2 in. (3.75 to 5.0 cm) IPS (inside pipe size). Solid or direct connections from equipment drains to building drains should not be made.

Due to a large temperature difference between steam pipes when they are hot and cold, elongation may be a problem. In most facilities, an elongation device is added for every 100 ft (30 m) of pipeline run. Proper sloping must occur also. The slope usually given for every 10 ft (3 m) of line is ⅛ to ½ in. (0.3 to 1.3 cm). Good strapping is required also. Steam traps, reducing valves, return condensate lines, and other specialized equipment must be installed at proper locations. A capable heating engineer should be consulted on all requirements.

TABLE 14–2 *Equivalent Length Values of Pipe Fittings in Feet*

Fittings	Pipe Size in Inches[a]					
	½	¾	1	1¼	1½	2
Standard elbow	1.3	1.8	2.2	3.0	3.5	4.8
Side outlet tee	3.0	4.0	5.0	6.0	7.0	8.0
Gate valve	0.3	0.4	0.5	0.6	0.8	1.1
Globe valve	14.0	18.0	23.0	29.0	34.0	46.0
Angle valve	7.0	10.0	12.0	15.0	18.0	22.0

[a]To get centimeter values in this table, multiply the inch values by 2.5.

PLUMBING

All plumbing should be designed to meet local building codes, the National Standard Plumbing Code, and health codes, such as the FDA Food Code. Well-designed plumbing installations coordinate plumbing needs with other structural and architectural elements (including electricity) because they often share shafts intended to house piping. Usually the other systems are given higher priority in that changes to the other systems to accommodate plumbing are more expensive. On the other hand, well-designed plumbing systems minimize the length of piping necessary to keep plumbing costs low. The best plumbing installations will closely group similar fixtures whenever possible. For example, bathrooms located on the same floor may be placed back to back. Multistory buildings may group bathrooms above each other.

In addition to good design, good workmanship is essential to proper installation of plumbing. **Fittings** (those parts of the pipe that are used to change the direction of flow, make connections, plug openings, or close off ends of pipe) should be capable of containing the pressurized flow. These should be of equal quality to the surrounding pipes. Fittings may be threaded or compression type (compression fittings include soldered fittings). Threaded fittings are usually stronger than compression fittings and are generally recommended for higher psi. Joints should be tight fitting. Solder points should be strong, neat, and wiped clean.

Allowances should be made for expansion and contraction of the pipe with temperature change. An iron pipe 100 ft (30.5 m) long changes three-quarters of an inch (1.9 cm) in length for every 100°F (56°C) change in temperature. Copper and plastic pipes will change even more in length than iron pipe.

Plumbing should not come through the floor; instead it should be placed through the wall. Overhead plumbing should be strapped. Faucets and fittings should be of high quality and of heavy weight to withstand wear.

Air gaps must be provided to prevent backflow from waste water into the water system at plumbing fixtures. An air gap should be provided between the outlet fixture of the water supply and the flood level rim of the waste water receptacle (see example of an above-sink air gap in Figure 14.2). Building codes usually require that the minimum size of gap be 1 to 3 in. (2.5 to 7.6 cm) depending on the location. Plumbing fixtures to which hoses will be attached must have a backflow device attached before the hose to prevent backflow of waste water.

Air gaps may also be used to prevent waste water from "backing up" into preparation sinks. Indirect drains have an air gap between the sink drain and the water trap (see example of a below-sink air gap in Figure 14.2). If the drain clogs and backs up, the water will therefore spill out onto the floor and not into the food preparation sink.

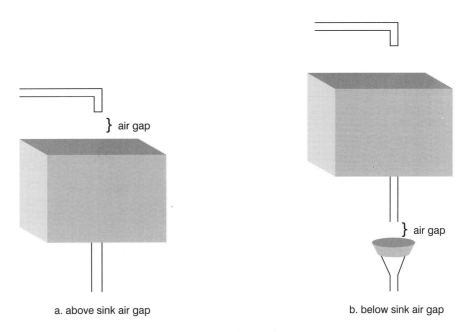

a. above sink air gap   b. below sink air gap

FIGURE 14.2   Examples of above- and below-sink air gaps.

Underground sewer pipes may be glazed vitrified clay, cast iron, or cement. Sewage pipes within buildings should be copper, plastic, extra-heavy cast iron, or plastics. Other materials may be approved in local codes.

Drain pipes should quickly run into large pipe sizes: 6 in. or 15 cm **ID, inside diameter**. If the volume of flow is heavy, a larger size may be needed. Sewer pipe sizes run up to 15 in. (38 cm) ID.

Joints should be made perfectly tight by calking. Horizontal line slope should be ⅛ to ¼ in. (0.3 to 0.6 cm) per ft (30 cm). Inside sewer lines should have cleanouts every 50 ft (15 m). All drains and sewage lines should be trapped.

Venting is required in plumbing systems. A **vent** is a waste stack that is connected to a sewer line and then extends through the roof to permit the sewer gas that rises to escape into the atmosphere instead of forcing its way through a trap. **Traps** provide resistance for the flow of such gas and also for the passage of vermin. Venting also prevents the downrush of water in drain and sewer lines from creating a suction that draws the water from the traps. The free flow of air allows pressures inside such lines to quickly adjust. See Figure 14.3 for an example of a sink trap and vent stack. Most codes allow for loop venting, which permits one venting system for a group of equipment instead of requiring that each piece of equipment be separately vented. The number of pieces that can be loop vented and their size are regulated by local codes. The National Plumbing Code also provides standards. In some areas, devices that remove the need for venting are permitted.

All waste water leaving a commercial kitchen should first pass through a grease trap to reduce the grease being discharged into the sanitary sewer system. Most grease traps remove grease by allowing the grease and water to separate. The heavier water is then allowed to drain away from an outlet in the bottom of the grease trap. Grease traps must be emptied regularly to prevent grease from filling the first compartment to the point that it passes under the dividing wall with the water. See Figure 14.4.

A facility may have a need to remove storm or other outside water. A check should be made that the drainage provided is adequate. Pumps may have to be installed to remove water from drainage into basements or other low areas. Drain connections for these

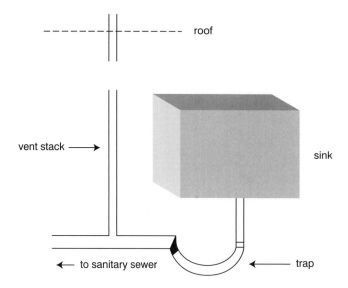

FIGURE 14.3   Plumbing sink trap and vent stack.

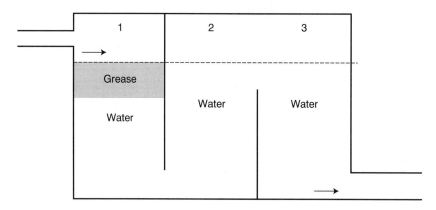

1 – Grease is trapped here, water flows under the divide into the
    second compartment
2 – water fills the compartment and flows into the third compartment,
    second compartment acts like the water trap on a drain
3 – water (without grease) flows into the sanitary sewer system

FIGURE 14.4   Example of a grease trap.

must be set up appropriately. Most building codes require that storm water drain into storm sewers (which carry only water runoff from the outside of the building) and not into sanitary sewer systems (which carry so-called domestic waste water, which is water from the building water supply, to which is added wastes from bathrooms, kitchens, and laundries). If storm water is allowed to run into the sanitary sewer system, sewage treatment becomes very difficult and costly because of the greatly increased volume.

Most municipalities have sewage disposal systems and a facility that will connect to sewer lines leading to these for sewage disposal. Most communities must now have systems that completely digest sewage and reduce it to harmless material. About 0.2% of the sewage is solid material. This can be digested by bacteria except for a small quantity of sludge that must be removed from the system from time to time. Most systems use a preliminary settling tank in which excess liquid is drawn off. The remaining sewage is put through aeration tanks for about a three-hour trip during which time bacteria digest the sewage to a point where it is 95% pure. Chlorination may be used to purify the remaining 5% before it is allowed to flow into drainage systems. See Figure 14.5.

FIGURE 14.5 Swivel faucets and box type drains provide convenience at stock kettles. The drain box is high enough to prevent splashing and rotates so that it can be pushed aside for a container to be placed under the faucet. The box and strainer can be removed for washing at the pot sink. (*Courtesy, University of Washington, Seattle.*)

In some instances a facility may not be able to connect to a municipal sewage system and may have to build one to take care of the facility's needs. Local codes and U.S. Public Health Service authorities should be consulted and their requirements carefully followed. Usually a **septic tank** large enough to hold a day's sewage is required. Tees and baffles in the tank force the sewage to circulate and improve bacterial digestion. A seepage pit or drain field receives the digested sewage and allows it to flow into the soil. Soil requirements are strict as well as the manner in which the drainage field is installed. A septic tank usually eliminates about 70% of the solid waste and the remaining 30% is digested in the drainage field.

WATER MANAGEMENT

Just as with the other utilities, water and plumbing systems need to be managed carefully for cost-effective use and maintenance. Appropriate insulation around hot water storage tanks and pipes helps to minimize heat loss and hot water needs. Leaking valves (such as dripping faucets) result in unnecessary water loss. Unnecessary use of water should also be avoided. For example, plumbing fixtures have been designed that minimize water use. Low flush toilets empty the bowl with as little as 0.5 to 1.5 gal (1.9 to 5.7 L) of water (compared to standard toilets, which require 5 to 7 gal or 18.9 to 26.5 L). Another example would be faucets and shower heads, which mix the stream of water with air to produce the same function and sensation of a larger volume of water. Standard shower heads, for example, use about 8 gal (30.3 L) of water per minute, whereas water conserving shower heads may only use 2.5 gal (9.5 L) per minute.

With very little maintenance, plumbing should work well for long periods of time with no breakdowns. If problems occur in one part of the system, it should be possible to isolate that portion of the system for maintenance while the other portions of the system continue to operate.

CHAPTER SUMMARY

Well-designed plumbing systems should provide a safe, sufficient, and reliable supply of hot and cold water. The amount and quality of water available are basic to a food service's operation and clearly require careful design and construction.

The public water supply is first treated to destroy harmful pathogens. Private water sources must also be similarly treated and tested regularly to make certain that the water is potable. Other water treatments may include water softening, removal of sediment or coloring matter, iron removal, pH correction, or filtration to remove chlorine, pesticides, or other organic chemicals.

Large quantities of water are used in food services. Demand for both hot and cold water will vary considerably with the time of day. Heaters and tanks should be sized to provide sufficient hot water at peak demand times. In addition, adequate water pressure must be available in order to supply needs.

Steam may be generated in a central boiler and distributed, produced in the equipment using it, or produced by an outside supplier. Manufacturers provide instructions for connecting their equipment to steam lines and these should be carefully followed.

All plumbing should be designed to meet building and health codes. Proper installation will include the use of appropriate fittings, allowances for expansion and contraction of pipes with temperature, suitable location for pipes with appropriate supports, the use of proper materials, correctly sized pipes, air gaps, and venting. Well-designed plumbing is worth the effort involved in its planning and construction.

REVIEW QUESTIONS

1. Visit a local municipal water and sewage department and inquire of officials what problems are encountered and how they are solved.
2. Compare the amount of detergent required to create comparable suds in 1 qt of hard water and 1 qt of softened water. (Use a carefully measured amount of common liquid household detergent for the test.)
3. Select a food service unit for study and calculate the amount of water and the temperatures required by the operation.
4. Calculate the amount of pressure required to supply water at 20 psi at a 250-ft level if the water is at 35 psi at the main line on ground level. (See answers to selected problems at end of text.)
5. Study the plumbing plan for a building. Read the different specifications for equipment to be connected to the plumbing established by the plan.

KEY WORDS AND CONCEPTS

air gap
alkaline salts
boiler horsepower (Bhp)
booster heater
fittings
hard water
inside diameter (ID)

potable water
pounds per square inch (psi)
scale (lime)
self-container steam unit
septic tank
trap
vent

CHAPTER
15

Environmental Planning

The comfort and well-being of people call for an environment in which the air is clean, maintained at suitable temperature and humidity, and kept free of obnoxious odors and other objectionable or injurious elements. Achieving this in food service and hotels, where heat, odors, and excess air moisture are commonly created, presents special problems. The continual change in the level of objectionable factors, such as high and low temperatures, strong odors, and air drafts, calls for a flexible environmental system of control. Planning members who are aware of problems need to participate actively in planning with heating and other specialists to achieve desirable results.

The goal is to obtain precisely controlled conditions that are highly flexible, quickly responsive, automatically controlled, and will operate at a minimum cost. Rule-of-thumb guides are likely to lead to serious errors and much higher costs. Exact definition of requirements is needed to produce the right conditions. The system should be as maintenance free as possible and contribute far less to pollution of the air and environment than those of the past. Standards that will provide helpful guidance in planning have been set up by the **American Society of Heating, Refrigerating, and Air Conditioning Engineers (ASHRAE),** 1791 Tullie Circle N.W., Atlanta, Georgia 30329. A useful reference is the *1997 ASHRAE Handbook—Fundamentals.*

AIR CONDITIONING

As the name implies, air conditioning is the process of changing one or more of the air properties. Properties that are usually conditioned include temperature, humidity, floating particulates, and gas composition. Air is either heated or cooled and the humidity adjusted to create a comfortable environment.

Humidity level is important because it affects health as well as comfort. Both high humidity and low humidity are undesirable. Floating particulates and certain gases can also affect health. Particulates are generally removed by filters as are some of the undesirable gases. Undesirable gases, however, are usually removed through the ventilation process of removing stale air and introducing fresh air (Figure 15.1).

FIGURE 15.1   A removal of excess steam and grease fumes arising from cooking equipment may require a variety of ventilating equipment. (*Courtesy of George Bundy & Associates, Seattle, Washington.*)

VENTILATION

Proper air velocities need to be maintained. Wide fluctuation is undesirable, and on and off cycles of air conditioning equipment need to be set to give small variation. Temperature rises as rooms fill with people because every human body gives off approximately 300 Btu[1] per hour or heat equivalent to that of a 100-watt incandescent light globe. About ⅒ of a pound of moisture is expired by one room-occupant in an hour. Air conditioning has the task of providing for changing conditions and changing load requirements.

About 15 **cubic feet per minute (cfm)** per person of fresh air input is a good standard for a dining room. This air should be clean, fresh, and move at a velocity that is not noticeable. Local codes usually specify ventilating requirements for dining areas. See Table 15–1 for examples of ASHRAE and OSHA-recommended ventilation rates for different areas. An even distribution should be obtained to prevent noticeable air currents; usually 40 to 50 **feet per minute (fpm)** air velocity is sufficient to give satisfactory air movement.

Buildings can be sealed so tightly that the loss of heat from the inside to outside or the flow of air from the outside to inside is reduced considerably. When a building is properly constructed, the amount of air change resulting from seepage or infiltration from the outside is reduced from one to two air changes an hour to one-half to three-quarters. This difference means a considerable saving in heating and air conditioning cost, which often more than pays for the extra cost in constructing a tighter building. Vapor buildup that can cause blemishes, rot, paint peeling, or create other undesirable conditions within the building is also reduced. When tightly sealed, the building's environment is much easier to control. Special problems occur when a large number of

---

[1]Btu = British thermal units; Btuh = British thermal units per hour. A Btu is the heat needed to raise a pound of water 1°F.

TABLE 15-1   *Recommended Ventilation Rates*

Room	Minimum (cfm)	Recommended (cfm)
General office	15	15–25
Smoking lounges	60 (no recirculation)	
Dining rooms	10	15–20
Kitchens	30	35
Bars	30	40–50
Bedrooms	7	10–15
Living rooms	10	15–20
Bathroom	20	30–50
Lobbies	7	10–15

Source: 1997 ASHRAE Handbook—Fundamentals, *American Society of Heating, Refrigerating, and Air Conditioning Engineers, Atlanta, GA, 1997.*

people go in and out of a building or when there must be a large number of doors, windows, and other openings. Much can be done, however, to reduce the influx of air one way or another. Just putting an air-flow vapor barrier on a revolving door or other entrance may save considerable heat loss or gain.

Ventilation requirements should be based on the quantity of vapor and hot air to be exhausted. Heat and vapor buildup can be reduced by proper equipment selection and operation (Figure 15.2). Good insulation on ovens, bain maries, steam tables, and other equipment will prevent heat loss. Selecting equipment to give maximum input of heat into products and minimum heat loss will reduce heat buildup. It has been estimated that from 30% to 50% of the heat generated for cooking foods is lost.

Structural features can be used to help prevent an undesirable spread of heat and vapors. Walls and partitions are used, for instance, around the dishwashing area. Partial partitions on standard components that drop from ceilings capture undesirable air and hold it until it can be eliminated. Double doors for pass-through areas or halls retard air speed. Lights hanging from ceilings can contribute to heat buildup. If lights are placed into ceilings so that the warmed air flows up into dead air spaces, heat will be captured there.

Air input must be balanced against air exhaust. If this is not done, negative or positive pressures will develop. The intake air for kitchens can frequently be taken from other areas; if brought from air conditioned spaces, this reduces cooling requirements. Local codes usually provide regulations covering recirculated air in buildings. If air is taken from the dining area, only about 50% of total requirements should be drawn from there to prevent too heavy a drain from the dining area. In planning input and output locations, avoid having them so close together that fresh air coming in is exhausted as it comes in instead of hot or vapor-laden air. Slight negative pressures in the kitchen prevent odors, heat, and humidity from flowing into other areas.

Air ducts should be properly sized to allow free air passage. If ducts are not properly sized or have many turns, static pressure builds up, which increases fan requirements. Air should be moved 1,500 to 2,100 fpm (average 1,800 fpm); air at 2,000 fpm will carry away most of the dirt and grease so that they do not settle in the ducts. If it moves faster than 2,100 fpm, a rumbling noise is created.

It is frequently desirable to insulate ducts that run through areas where they can lose their heat into working spaces. Ducts should be airtight. Where there is vapor condensation, ducts should be watertight, equipped with drains, and lead back to sewer lines to carry away condensate. Weather caps may be required over ducts where they come out of buildings.

Filters and baffles should be used to change air flow, and remove pollen, dust, smoke, odors, gases, bacteria, spores, and other living microorganisms. Several types are

FIGURE 15.2   Note equipment showing good adjustment of hoods to height of equipment and area requiring ventilation. (*Courtesy of George Bundy & Associates, Seattle, Washington.*)

available and these are listed in Table 15–2. Screening filters should be able to remove particles 10 to 150 microns in size. Electrostatic precipitators are able to remove particles down to 0.25 microns in size. Activated charcoal is sometimes used to remove gases and odors. Ultraviolet lights may be used to kill bacteria.

A single-entry-type fan with reversed blades will move grease and dirt through filters and baffles without allowing them to collect on the fan. Select the centrifugal type with forward or backward curved blades and either belt or direct drive. Some authorities recommend squirrel cage blowers because they have more power and capacity to expel air. Propeller fans are considered undesirable because they do not operate well against duct resistances.

Once an installation is properly balanced in input and output air requirements, it is not advisable to deduct or add to ventilating requirements without changing the ventilating equipment. It is frequently desirable to have fans equipped to run at two speeds so that high speeds can be used at peak loads or summer operation and low speeds at nonpeak loads or winter operation.

KITCHEN VENTILATION NEEDS

Ventilation hoods are a special type of air filtration system used in kitchens. They are designed to remove excess steam, heat, grease, smoke, odor and gas. Kitchen ventilation hoods are divided into Type I and Type II hoods. Type I hoods are used to collect and remove smoke and grease from cooking equipment. Grease filters and baffles are installed

---

TABLE 15-2   *Types of Air Filters*

Dry Screen
- Depend on a fine mesh to prevent passage of airborne particles
- Often made of fiberglass
- Filter is disposed of when dirty, reusable types are now available
- Popular for public space filtration needs and protection of HVAC equipment from excessive dust
- Resistance to flow is low
- Traps large airborne particles only
- Ineffective for odors, smoke, and some small particles (pollen, spores, bacteria, etc.)

Oil Treated
- Dry filter sprayed with oil or chemicals to catch more airborne particles
- Only slightly more effective than dry filter
- Filter is washed and reused, disposable types also available

Water-spray
- Energy requirements are higher than dry or oil-treated filters due to the need for a pump to spray water, the need for water itself, moderate resistance to air flow
- More effective at removing smoke, dust, and pollen than dry filters
- Raises humidity level of air

Electrostatic Precipitator
- Air supply passes between electrically charged plates, which give particles an electric charge; they then pass between collector plates which have the opposite electric charge where they are attracted to the plates and trapped
- Removes most air pollutants including dust, pollen, and smoke
- May not remove some chemical pollutants
- High installation cost, low operating cost
- Cleaned by washing
- Low resistance to air flow

HEPA Filter
- HEPA stands for high-efficiency particulate arrestance
- Filters almost all particles that are 0.3 microns or larger
- Examples of particles that are filtered includes pet dander, pollen, spores, many molds, dust mites, dust, many bacteria (will not filter viruses)
- Will not kill microorganisms unless has been treated to kill bacteria or there is a germicidal ultraviolet light

---

in these hoods. This type of hood is placed over fryers, ranges, grills, broilers, skillets and other grease-producing equipment. Grease removal systems generally work by passing air through a series of baffles. The air is forced to move through these baffles at high speed while making a series of turns. The high speed causes the grease to be thrown out of the airstream by centrifugal force. Type II hoods are designed to remove steam, heat, and odors, but not grease. They may be used over such equipment as dishwashers and steam tables. The three types of grease filter systems are shown in Table 15–3.

Six types of hood systems are used. Wall-mounted hoods are used for all types of cooking equipment that might be set against a wall. The single island canopy is used for single lines of cooking equipment, whereas the double island is used for back-to-back arrangements. The backshelf is another option for equipment against a wall, but is also found with free-standing units. The eyebrow hood is mounted directly onto equipment such as ovens and dishwashers and the pass-over style is used over counter-height equipment when a pass-through from the cooking side to serving side is needed.

TABLE 15-3   *Grease Filter Systems*

Baffle Filters
- Vertical baffles of aluminum, steel, or stainless steel
- Gives grease extraction between 40% and 65%
- Cleaned by dishwasher or by hand washing

Removable Extractor
- Horizontal baffles of stainless steel
- Gives grease extraction between 90% and 95%
- Cleaned by dishwasher or by hand washing

Stationary Extractor or "Water-Wash Hoods"
- Horizontal baffles of stainless steel
- Gives grease extraction between 90% and 95%
- Baffles are not removable for cleaning, some systems use spray nozzles in the hood to clean with hot water and detergent (typically done at the end of the day after cooking equipment and fans are turned off); other systems use a continuous cold water mist system to continuously extract grease during cooking

---

TABLE 15-4   *Examples of Overhang Requirements for Different Hoods*

Type of Hood	End Overhang (in.)	Front Overhang (in.)	Rear Overhang (in.)
Wall mounted	6	12	N/A
Single island	12	12	12
Double island	6	12	12
Eyebrow	0	12	N/A
Backshelf/passover	6	Front setback ½ over equipment	

Source: North American Association of Food Equipment Manufacturers, An Introduction to the Foodservice Industry, *NAFEM, Chicago, IL, 1997.*

The size of the hood is important as well. The hood must extend beyond the edges of the cooking equipment in order to collect exhaust and heat coming up from the top and sides of the equipment. Typical overhang requirements are shown in Table 15–4.

Exhaust flow rates depend on the style of hood, the amount of overhang, the distance from the equipment to the hood, whether end panels are present, and the type of cooking equipment. The type of cooking equipment is particularly important. The velocity will vary from 15 fpm for steam jacketed kettles to 150 fpm for charcoal broilers. Equipment is generally grouped into four groups based on ventilation needs. These are shown in Table 15–5. Exhaust flow rate is based on the heaviest group requirement (see Table 15–6). For example, a bank of equipment that includes steam jacketed kettles, a range, a combi-oven, and a charbroiler will require heavy-duty ventilation because of the charbroiler. In addition, a safety allowance to absorb cross-drafts and flare-ups as well as a safety factor for the style of hood is generally added in.

Ductless hoods are sometimes used for specific pieces of equipment. Local regulations should be consulted to determine if they may be used. The advantage is that equipment does not need to be placed under the hood. The disadvantages are that it cannot be used on gas equipment and typically does not remove heat.

TABLE 15-5 *Ventilation Requirements Based on Type of Equipment*

Group	Type of Equipment	Maximum Temperature
Light duty	Ovens, steamer, small kettles	400°F (204°C)
Medium duty	Large kettles, ranges, griddles, fryers	400°F (204°C)
Heavy duty	Upright broilers, charbroilers, woks	600°F (316°C)
Extra heavy duty	Solid fuel-burning equipment	700°F (371°C)

Source: North American Association of Food Equipment Manufacturers, An Introduction to the Foodservice Industry, *NAFEM. Chicago, IL, 1997.*

TABLE 15-6 *Minimum Exhaust Flow Rate Based on Cooking Equipment Type*

Type of Hood	Light	Medium	Heavy	Extra Heavy
		cfm per linear foot of hood)		
Wall mounted	150–200	200–300	200–400	350 +
Single island	250–300	300–400	300–600	550 +
Double island	150–200	200–300	250–400	500 +
Eyebrow	150–250	150–250	N/A	N/A
Backshelf/Passover	100–200	200–300	300–400	Not recommended

Source: North American Association of Food Equipment Manufacturers, An Introduction to the Foodservice Industry, *NAFEM, Chicago, IL, 1997.*

HEATING

Heating Measurement

Heat is measured in two ways: by degree (level or intensity) and by amount. The degree or level is indicated by temperature, while the amount is indicated by British thermal units (Btu) or calories. A Btu is the quantity of heat required to raise a pound of water 1°F, while a calorie (cal) is the amount of heat required to raise a gram of water 1°C. A kilocalorie (or Calorie with a capital "C", or kcal), which is the equivalent of 1,000 calories, is the quantity of heat required to raise a kilogram of water 1°C. The calorie value of food is generally indicated in kcal or Calories, while the caloric value of a fuel is generally indicated in calories. A calorie equals 3.968×10^{-6} Btu, and a Btu equals 252 Calories or kcal. The amount of Btus released in burning specific fuels varies. For instance, crude petroleum has a Btu-lb value of 20,000; the best coals, 17,000 to 18,000; poor coal, 10,000; dried wood, 10,000; and straw, 8,000.

Three scales are used to measure the temperature or intensity (level) of heat: (1) Fahrenheit, F; (2) Celsius, C; and (3) the kelvin or absolute (K or A) scales. The Fahrenheit scale was developed in 1724 by a German instrument worker, Gabriel Fahrenheit. On it, the melting point of ice is 32° and the boiling point of water is 212°. A Swedish professor of astronomy, Anders Celsius, developed a more logical scale in 1742. He made zero the melting point of ice, 100 the boiling point of water, and divided the interval into 100 equal degrees. This Celsius scale is universally used in scientific work.

The absolute, or kelvin, scale, named for Lord Kelvin for his share in its development, places 0 as the total absence of heat. The points between the freezing and boiling of water are divided into 100 degrees, and all other units of temperature are based on one of these. Thus **absolute zero** is 0 K, the melting point of ice is 273 K, and the boiling point of water is 373 K. If water in a scientific laboratory is at 50°C, it is 323 K (50 + 273 = 323). The kelvin scale is used when extremely high or low temperatures are used. Thus, the temperature of the northern lights is said to be around 8000 K.

In the Celsius scale there are 100° between the melting point of ice and the boiling point of water, while in the Fahrenheit scale there are 180° (212 − 32). Each Celsius degree equals $^{180}/_{100}$, or $\%$ Fahrenheit degrees. To convert Celsius to Fahrenheit, the Celsius temperature is multiplied by $\%$ or 1.8 and then 32 is added:

$$\frac{(°C \times 9)}{5} + 32 = °F \tag{15.1}$$

Thus, if the temperature is 50°C, the equation is

$$(50°C \times 1.8) + 32 = 122 \text{ or } 122°F \tag{15.2}$$

To convert Fahrenheit to Celsius, 32 degrees is deducted from the Fahrenheit temperature and the remainder is multiplied by $\%$ or 0.555:

$$(°F − 32) \times 0.555 = °C \tag{15.3}$$

For instance, 212°F in the equation reduces to:

$$(212°F − 32) \times 0.555 = 99.9°C \text{ or } 100°C \tag{15.4}$$

To change temperatures to the A or K scale, a Celsius temperature merely needs to have 273 added to it.

$$°C + 273 = \text{kelvin or A} \tag{15.5}$$

Thus, 58°C becomes 331 A; −25°C becomes 248 K. The easiest way to convert Fahrenheit to A or K would be to convert to Celsius and then to the A (K) scale.

$$[(°F − 32) \times 0.555] + 273 = \text{kelvin or A} \tag{15.6}$$

To convert the A (K) scale to either Celsius or Fahrenheit, use the inverse of converting the A (K) scale to Celsius and then to Fahrenheit:

$$\text{kelvin} − 273 = °C \tag{15.7}$$

$$(\text{kelvin} − 273) \times 1.8 + 32 = °F \tag{15.8}$$

Many liquids or solids expand or contract at a constant rate when heated or cooled. By using a liquid such as mercury or alcohol, Celsius and Fahrenheit were able to make a thermometer that would show the temperature as the liquid climbed or fell in a column on which the temperature scale was marked. Metals can also be used to measure the intensity of heat because they expand or contract similarly at a constant rate. A thermostat or meat thermometer operates on this principle. A **thermostat** can cause a current of electricity to flow when metal cools to a point at which contact is made. As the temperature increases, the metal expands, breaking the contact and stopping the electrical current. A meat thermometer has a tiny spring inside the part inserted into the meat. This expands or twists as it warms up, turning a needle that is set in the head.

A **thermocouple** is a very accurate type of thermometer. If two different metal wires are joined in a wire with one part being all nickel and the rest copper, and the copper end is heated, an electrical current will flow from the copper into the nickel wire. The amount of electricity flowing from one metal to another is always in an exact ratio to the amount of heat in the substance. By measuring the quantity of this electrical flow, the temperature can be ascertained; instruments on a thermocouple do this automatically, so the reading comes in either Fahrenheit or Celsius, depending on the scale. It is of interest that while one end of a metal wire such as this receives heat, the other end of different metal gets cold. By reversing the metals, the end that got cold now gets hot while the other now gets cold. (That heat and electricity are closely related, as formerly indicated, is again emphasized.)

Temperature indicates the heat intensity of a substance and only indirectly the amount of heat in it. Heat quantity is measured in Btus or calories and not by degrees of K, C, or F. This difference between temperature and the amount of heat in a substance may be compared to water in a well. If the water level is 20 ft in the well, we know only how high the water is, not the amount. Likewise, knowing that the temperature of water is 80°F (27°C) does not tell us how much heat is in the water. However, if the radius of the well is known in addition to its depth, the amount of water there can be calculated. Similarly, the amount of heat in this water can be ascertained if the amount of water and the temperature are known.

Specific Heat

The quantity of heat in a substance can also be calculated if the substance, its mass, temperature, and specific heat are known. **Specific heat** is the quantity of heat in calories required to raise a gram of the substance 1°C. All substances do not have the ability to hold the same quality of heat at the same temperature. A gram of water at 100°F (38°C) holds more heat in it than a gram of brass at 100°F (38°C). If 100 cal are put into 100 g of water, the temperature rises 100°C. But only about 9 cal need to be put into 100 g of brass to raise it to the same temperature; this is because water can hold more heat than brass without increasing the temperature. Thus, water has a specific heat of 1.0 while brass has one of 0.09.

Water, compared with many substances (especially metals), holds a fairly substantial amount of heat before rising in temperature. For this reason, the amount it could hold before a gram rose 1°C was given a value of 1, and all other substances were given values in relation to this. In comparison with the specific heat of water at 1, that of other substances is shown in Table 15–7.

Hydrogen, with a specific heat of 2.41, holds more heat per gram than any other substance. For this reason, hydrogen is sealed in electrical turbines to absorb heat and

---

TABLE 15-7 *Specific Heats of Some Common Substances**

Substance	Specific Heat
Air at 80°F	0.24
Water vapor	0.49
Aluminum	0.23
Brick	0.20
Brass	0.09
Bronze	0.10
Copper	0.09
Hydrogen	2.41
Ice	0.48
Iron	0.11
Limestone	0.22
Marble	0.21
Nickel	0.11
Steel	0.12

*Source: *Adapted from Frederick S. Merritt and James Ambrose,* Building Engineering and Systems Design *(2nd ed.), Van Nostrand Reinhold, New York, 1990; and Robert H. Perry and Cecil H. Chilton,* Chemical Engineers' Handbook *(5th ed.), McGraw-Hill Book Company, New York, 1973.*

carry it away so the turbine does not get too hot. Ice and steam are about one-half the specific heat of the parent water. Brass, having ⅟₁₁ the specific heat of water, rises 11°C for every 1°C water rise. (Moist foods, such as fresh fruits and vegetables, have specific heats that are extremely close to water, in the range of 0.80 to 0.95).

Raising the temperature of a 15-lb (6.8-kg) aluminum kettle plus 50 lb (22.7 kg) of water and potatoes from 40°F (4.4°C) to 212°F (100°C) takes 9,152 Btus or 2,309,442 cal without considering heat loss in the process. The calculation is as follows (note that there are 454 g in a pound):

$$50 \text{ lb} \times 1 \text{ (specific heat} + 15 \text{ lb aluminum} \times 0.23 \text{ (specific heat} = 53.45$$
$$\text{of water/potatoes)} \qquad \text{of aluminum)} \qquad (15.9)$$

$$53.45 \times (212 - 40°F) = 9193 \text{ Btu} \qquad (15.10)$$

The calories needed are as follows:

Water and potatoes:
$$50 \text{ lb} \times 454 \text{ g/lb} \times 1 \times (100 - 4.4°C) = 2,170,120 \text{ cal} \qquad (15.11)$$

Aluminum kettle:
$$15 \text{ lb} \times 454 \text{ g/lb} \times 0.23 \times (100 - 4.4°C) = 149,738 \text{ cal} \qquad (15.12)$$

Total calories (food, water, and kettle):
$$2,170,120 + 149,738 = 2,319,858 \text{ cal} \qquad (15.13)$$

These calculations may seem rather involved, complex, and not relative to planning and operating a food facility. They have been included with the hope that a fuller understanding will sharpen awareness of energy uses and utilization. Although the essential cooking may require only 2 million calories in a specific situation, through the use of inappropriate methods or carelessness, 6 million calories may be wasted. It is a good idea to challenge plans and methods with questions such as these: Is there a better way? Can acceptable values be secured by means that reduce required heat input? Do some of the modern techniques increase or reduce energy requirements? For example, the choice of metal for a cooking pan may increase or decrease calories required for heating based on their specific heats (see Table 15–7).

Latent and Sensible Heat

Sensible heat is defined as heat associated with a change in temperature. By contrast, **latent heat** is heat related to a change in state of a substance (for example, from a solid to a liquid or from a liquid to a gas). These changes in state cannot occur without heat. Because there is no change in temperature as the solid changes state into a liquid or from a liquid to a gas, this heat is referred to as latent or hidden. Latent heat is important because it must be taken into account in calculations of total heat content. Air, for example, almost always contains some water in the form of vapor and this must be calculated into heating and air conditioning requirements.

Air at 72°F (22°C) and 35% **relative humidity (RH)** holds about 0.0004 lb of moisture per pound of air. If this moisture is condensed and its heat goes into the air, the temperature of the air rises 4.25°F (-15.4°C). The air then becomes 76°F (24°C). If air is 87°F (31°C) and the RH is 50%, the air holds 0.014 lb of moisture per pound of air. If all this moisture condenses, a temperature rise of 15°F (-9.4°C) occurs; the air temperature then goes to 102°F (39°C), which is quite warm. Thus latent heat can be a problem in cooling. A fairly high latent factor is desired in winter because moist air feels warmer.

Environmental engineers normally use a value of two-thirds sensible and one-third latent heat in estimating the total heat potential of air when calculating the quantity of sensible heat resulting from the latent heat in air. This total heat potential is called **enthalpy.** This division of two-thirds sensible and one-third latent heat is, however, for living spaces holding only a normal number of people. If a dining room is filled with diners and a lot of personnel are working there, the ratio of latent heat to sensible heat will rise considerably. Also, the amount of latent heat rises to sensible heat if human activity increases. An individual doing light work or being moderately active loses about 255 Btuh of sensible heat and 145 Btuh of latent heat. However, when dancing, the same individual will lose 305 Btuh of sensible heat and 545 Btuh of latent heat. The moisture buildup and latent heat potential in a room (either because a large number of people are in the room or because of greater activity) can be a problem in air conditioning.

Additional moisture buildup can occur because of moisture coming from steam, cleaning, or other reasons. For instance, an individual showering can put 0.5 lb of very warm moisture into the air. Cooking three meals for one person in a day can add almost 5 lb of moisture. Washing dishes for these meals adds another pound. One house plant can put a pound of moisture in the air in a day. Mopping an 8 × 10-ft area adds nearly 2.5 lb of moisture to the air.

Heat from lights is mostly sensible heat and must be calculated in air conditioning. If lights use more than 5 W/sq ft of floor space, enough heat is generated to heat the building in a mild winter. Cooking equipment in commercial kitchens is considered to give off 65% of its heat in sensible heat and 35% in latent heat.

If an efficient hood with good ventilation is placed over the equipment, most of the latent heat is removed. When such a hood is installed, the environmental engineer will eliminate latent heat from consideration and merely increase sensible heat by 10% to make up for the omission. Thus a 200 sq in. griddle rated at 6 kW and developing 20,400 Btuh produces about 6,600 Btuh of sensible heat and 3,600 Btuh of latent heat, or a total of more than 10,000 Btuh. However, under a good hood, the total would be 7,260 Btuh (6,600 + 660 = 7,260). Most manufacturers give information on the Btuh output of their equipment both in sensible and latent heat. If they do not, an environmental engineer will take the total Btuh output as rated by the manufacturer and divide this by half and then consider the remainder two-thirds sensible heat and one-third latent heat, except when under a good hood with good air draft. In the latter case, the sensible two-thirds value is multiplied by 10%; this is added as sensible heat and no value is added for latent heat.

Change of State from Heat

Most matter at low temperatures is a solid. The molecules are bound close together and their movement is limited. As heat increases, molecules move away from each other and expansion results. Liquid also expands because its molecules move farther apart. A pot full of water spills over when it heats up; the coil in the meat thermometer expands and turns an arrow indicator that tells us the temperature. When the molecules in a solid move far enough from each other, the solid turns into a liquid, and when the molecules in a liquid move far enough apart, they vaporize. This change of matter from one state to another is called a **change of state.** Heat is responsible for a change in state because it generates a **kinetic action** that causes molecules to move. When gas loses its heat, it condenses into a liquid, and when a liquid gets cold enough, it turns into a solid. We see this circle occur when steam turns into water, water into ice, and then ice back to water and water back to steam. It takes energy to cause a change of state from a solid to a liquid and a liquid to a vapor, and when a vapor condenses back to a liquid or a liquid changes to solid, heat is given off.

The quantity of heat required to induce a change of state varies with different kinds of matter. Experiments show that it takes 144 Btus to change a pound of ice at 32°F (0°C) to a pound of water at 32°F (0°C). (The energy requirement in calories to do this can be found by multiplying the Btus by 252). Experiments also show that it takes 970 Btus to change a pound of water to a pound of steam at 212°F (100°C). The heat needed to change a solid to a liquid is called the *latent heat of fusion* and the heat required to change a liquid to a vapor is called the *latent heat of vaporization.*

When vapor changes to a liquid and when a liquid changes to a solid, both changes give off heat, but when a liquid changes to a vapor or a solid to a liquid, heat is absorbed. The phenomenon of requiring heat or giving off heat in making a change of state is important in calculating humidity, refrigeration, and other needs in a facility. Planners need to understand the basic principles and how to do some of the rudimentary calculations to contribute adequately to planning.

Steam contains much more heat than water. At 212°F (100°C) a pound of steam has much more heat than a pound of water at the same temperature because it has absorbed 970 more Btus (latent heat of vaporization for a pound of water). By the time a pound of steam has been raised to 240°F (115.5°C) the Btus in the pound total 1,040. When such steam condenses on food, it gives off its heat of vaporization plus the other heat that was in it. This is why steam cooks faster than water.

Heat and Color

When a flame is white or a bluish white, it is about 6,000°F (3333°C). A yellow or orange flame will have a lower temperature. Heat around 2,000°F (1,110°C) is bright red to a deep, dark, or cherry red. However, even below the point where matter takes on a change of color due to heat, the hotter substance will radiate heat to a cooler one.

Heat Movement

Heat travels either by (1) conduction, (2) convection, or (3) radiation. Each works in a different manner to transport heat, and some of the heat transported may differ from others. Radiated heat is different from heat transported by conduction and convection.

Conduction is the transfer of heat from one piece of matter to another. When heat is developed under a griddle, it is conducted through the griddle plate into material placed on top of it. The heat may be conducted through a pan and into food to be cooked. The food is cooked as the temperature rises from the heat conducted into the food. Conduction works because one particle of matter picks up heat, passing it on to another particle through kinetic action. Thus particles must be in contact with each other. Some substances transfer heat better than others. Silver, gold, platinum, copper, aluminum, and iron, in that order, are good heat conductors. These are good electrical conductors also. Stainless steel conducts heat poorly. Food in a stainless steel pan over direct heat scorches easily because the metal fails to spread the heat evenly and quickly. The use of metals that conduct heat quickly and evenly (e.g., copper, aluminum, or iron) as the bottom of a pot or as a core between layers of stainless steel helps spread and transfer the heat more evenly through the stainless steel.

Convection is the movement of heat transported by air, liquid, or some other medium of flow. A convection oven causes heat to flow by using a fan to push the air around. Rooms are heated by the natural convection of air. Warm air tends to rise and cooler air descends. This results in air movement from a heated surface upward over a cooler area, and as it loses its heat, the air descends. It moves back into the heated area and again rises as it warms, and the cycle is repeated. Because of this, it is best to put a heating unit under a cooling surface such as a window. The cool air then drops down into the heater, where it is warmed. It moves out and up and back down so that a complete circle is made. Air that does not move, called *dead air,* conducts heat poorly. Air must move, or convect, to transfer heat. The conduction value of air is 0.00005 compared with 0.001 for water and 0.210 for iron. Thus, dead air space is a good insulator.

Radiation is energy that moves with the speed of light. It is matter, just like light. When radiated particles strike matter, they collide with a tremendous force even though the radiated particle is small. This causes vibration that develops heat. Any warmer body radiates heat to a cooler one. Heat flows in radiation because bodies have different temperatures. The hotter the one body and the colder the other, the faster and greater the radiation. A glowing substance with white heat emits a considerable quantity of radiated material. Broilers and toasters cook largely by radiated heat or infrared heat.

Dark surfaces absorb more radiation than light ones. Aluminum containers in which frozen food is to be baked may be painted with a dull, black paint on the outside. This improves heat absorption, thus shortening cooking time. If heat is to be kept inside an alumninum foil, the bright side should be inside and the dull side out. If bright foil faces an air space, it radiates heat back and will let only a small quantity pass. Thus reflective surfaces in buildings can send back much heat that otherwise would escape to the outside. The reflective surface should be on the side facing the area in which the heat is to be returned.

Radiated particles, like light, move in a straight line. They do not go around corners but, like light, can be reflected around them. *Heat shadows* are thus possible. Radiation passes through transparent objects just as light does. No heat is created in its passage. Heat is produced only when the radiated particle is stopped. However, when radiated particles and light go through a window and strike opaque or solid matter inside, heat develops usually in the form of infrared waves. These waves cannot be transferred through transparent substances, but are stopped by them. Thus, in a room into which solar energy flows, a rapid buildup of heat can occur from the trapped infrared waves inside.

Heat and Humidity

Warm air can hold more heat and moisture than cold air. When moist air becomes cooler, it frequently not only loses heat but will also lose some of its moisture because it cannot hold as much moisture. When moist air rises into the upper atmosphere and cools, clouds form, indicating the presence of water vapor, which condenses and causes rain. Warm air striking a glass filled with ice water loses moisture on the glass, and gradually small beads of moisture gather on the glass. Refrigeration coils ice up because of moisture condensing on them as moisture-laden air strikes them and cools. The temperature at which air loses moisture as it cools is called the **dew point.**

Moisture in air is often called **humidity.**[2] Relative humidity (RH) is the amount of moisture in air as compared to the maximum amount it could hold at that temperature. Air at 50% RH holds only 50% of what it could hold at that temperature before it reaches the dew point. Air at 100% RH has reached a saturation point, and any more moisture picked up by it would cause condensation at that temperature. A slight cooling of the air would mean that it would lose some of the moisture because it no longer could hold the same quantity at the lower temperature. That is why clouds as they cool in the higher atmosphere condense and cause rain. Air that has reached 100% RH, or dew point, can pick up more moisture if its temperature rises (which explains the drying effect in a refrigerator with the opening and closing of doors). One pound of air at 70°F (21°C) and 50% RH contains 0.008 lb of moisture, while a pound of air at 80°F (27°C) holding 0.008 lb of moisture will be 35% RH. At 60°F (16°C) the RH is nearly 70%. At about 50°F (10°C), this air reaches dew point or 100% RH.

Air that is dry will feel cooler than air of the same temperature carrying more moisture because dry air evaporates moisture from the skin and such evaporation requires some heat, which it takes from the body. When air is quite moist, such evaporation is much slower, therefore one feels warmer, even though the two air samples may be at the

---

[2]Absolute humidity (AH) is the percent or quantity of moisture in a given volume of air, usually per cubic foot. If AH is 2%, the air contains 2% moisture. AH in air can vary; the air volume is dependent on its temperature because warm air expands and cooler air contracts. The cubic feet of warm air with a 2% AH will have a higher AH per cubic foot if it cools. Mixing ratio humidity (MRH) and specific humidity (SH) doesn't matter because they are based on the mass of weight of water vapor per pound of air, as noted in the text for the 0.008-lb value. Both MRH and SH are usually the same, so they are frequently used interchangeably by heating and air conditioning engineers.

same temperature. Normally, a RH of 50% is most desirable in summer. A lower RH of, say, 30% to 35% may be desirable in winter to prevent condensation on windows. In general however, a range of 20% to 60% RH is acceptable.

The quantity of humidity in air may be measured in several ways. Normally, the RH can be measured by taking the temperature of a dry bulb and the temperature of a wet bulb. The moistened bulb will show a lower temperature depending on how much moisture is in the air because, when the moisture evaporates, heat is needed for the evaporation—which it draws from the bulb. If the air is saturated with moisture, little difference in temperature occurs between the dry and wet bulbs. If the air is very dry, a considerable temperature difference is found. By referring to tables, the RH can be found based on the temperature difference. As an example, a 90°F (32°C) dry bulb temperature and a 76°F (25°C) **wet bulb temperature** indicate an RH of 54%.

Heating of Spaces

The inside environment must be defined to calculate the heating needs of a building. Normally, living spaces should be around 70°F (21°C) in winter and not higher than 78°F (26°C) in summer with an RH of around 50%. This can vary. Active workers prefer an slightly cooler atmosphere. The temperature outside in summer can affect the temperature needed inside.

Local codes may vary on the ratio of air that must be brought in from the outside to air that is reused in the building. In very cold weather, a lot of cold air brought in and warmed increases the cost of heating considerably. Air at −30°F (−34°C) that is to be raised to 70°F (21°C) is often heated to over 100°F (38°C) and then allowed to pick up moisture to be comfortable after it has cooled down to room temperature. Building codes may require that fresh air be at least one-third of the total, but not less than 5 cfm per person, with the remainder being reused air. Air may not be recirculated from certain areas, bathrooms or toilet rooms, for example. Often, a portion of the kitchen supply air is taken from dining areas. On the other hand, generally the attempt is made to keep kitchen smoke and odors confined to the kitchen by maintaining a slightly negative atmospheric pressure. The negative air pressure is designed by exhausting slightly more air than the amount being supplied. Normally, the cubic feet per minute of air intake per person is between 10 and 40 in food and housing facilities.

Minimum ventilation may also be specified as the minimum number of air changes required per hour. Usually, five air changes per hour is considered a minimum. Large changes are not desirable because of high air velocities so that a maximum is considered to be 60 air changes per hour.

In preliminary planning, the building should be studied to see if its basic design is one that can be efficiently heated and cooled. Some buildings that are beautiful in design are impractical to heat or cool at low cost. The type of central well in a building such as is seen in the Brown Palace Hotel in Denver or in the Student Union Building at the University of Montana, or as seen in moving stairs and other openings between floors, complicates the problem of heat control.

Heat Loss and Insulation

Heating engineers in setting up a heating system carefully calculate the amount of heat a building will lose through walls, ceilings, and floors. Most building materials have known heat transfer values. Engineers will speak of U, k, or R values. The U value indicates the number of Btuh that go through a square foot of space of building material 1 in. thick when there is a 1°F difference between the outside and inside temperature of the building. If there is a 40°F (22°C) difference, the U coefficient must be multiplied by 40. A k value is the amount of heat conducted through a square foot of homogeneous material 1 in. (2.5 cm) thick when there is a 1°F temperature difference between the inside and outside. Thus the only difference between U value and k values is that the U material may be more or less than 1 in. (2.5 cm) thick, and may be on a mixture of materials, but the k value is always based on a 1-in. (2.5-cm) thickness and on one kind of material. If the surface with the k value is more than 1 in. (2.5 cm) thick, the amount of heat lost through the surface must be multiplied by the true width. This then gives the U value. Engineers may speak of a U value or k value as conductance values, written "C."

An R value is the reciprocal of a U value, or 1/U. It indicates the number of hours it takes a Btu to go through the material. If, for instance, an 8-in. (20-cm) concrete block wall has a U value of 2 (2 Btuh going through when only a 1°F temperature difference exists between the inside and outside), the R value is ½, meaning that it takes a Btu a half hour to go through the material. The k value of this wall is 0.25 (¼) or ¼.

A heating engineer will calculate the total R, or **thermal resistance** (written **RT**), of walls, ceilings, floors, roofs, and so on. This is helpful in indicating how much heat will be lost from the building at the desired temperature since there is now a total heat loss per hour. If too small a heating unit is added, the building will be too cold in the coldest weather. If a unit is too large, excess cost and perhaps poor heating results will occur.

For 550 sq ft (51.1 m^2) of wall made of 4-in. (10-cm) brick, 6-in. (15-cm) concrete block, 0.75-in. (1.8-cm) air space, and 0.75-in. (1.8-cm) plaster, the engineer—by consulting tables and making necessary calculations—will find that the RT is 3.33 (the U value is 0.3). This may be too high and the engineer may then ascertain what effect 3 in. (7.5 cm) of insulation with a U value of 0.087 would have. The engineer will now find that the RT value is 14.9, with a U value of 0.067, which means that 1 Btu is being lost every 14.9 hours, which is sufficiently low to give satisfactory results. This is shown by the fact that the wall, with a 60°F (16°C) temperature difference in midwinter, would have a heat transfer of 9,900 Btuh:

$$0.3 \text{ U value} \times 550 \text{ sq ft} \times 60°F = 9,900 \text{ Btuh} \qquad (15.14)$$

In the wall with added insulation, it would have a 2,211 Btu transfer, over a fourth less:

$$0.067 \text{ U value} \times 550 \text{ sq ft} \times 60°F = 2,211 \text{ Btuh} \qquad (15.15)$$

Over a period of years, this additional cost of the insulation may be returned many times and may yield a building with more even heat.

Glass has high heat loss. A single pane has an R of 1.13; a double pane, 1.64; and a triple pane, 2.5. The U values are 0.9, 0.6, and 0.4, respectively. Thus a 550 sq ft (49.5 m) surface of single-pane glass with a temperature difference of 60°F (16°C) would have a heat loss of 29,700 Btuh:

$$0.9 \text{ U value} \times 550 \text{ sq ft} \times 60°F = 29,700 \text{ Btuh} \qquad (15.16)$$

Double- and triple-pane glass would have higher R values and less heat loss because dead air space is a good insulator. If reflective paper, such as bright aluminum foil, is put on the inside of a dead air space pointing toward the space from which heat will come, a much more effective heat barrier is achieved. Thus, to prevent heat loss from inside a building, the reflective material should be on the outside wall of the dead air space. If it is to prevent entry of heat into the building, it would be on the opposite or inside wall. Putting reflective paper where there is no dead air space does little to insulate.

Much heat can be lost where slabs or floors are near grade level. Having insulation below, dead air space, reflective material, and a warm basement underneath can do much to reduce heat loss. Much heat is lost where floors and ceilings join outer walls. If insulation is provided at this point, much heat loss can be reduced. The heat loss of a floor at this point can be around 30 Btuh/linear ft.

Calculating Heating Needs

The heat loss of a building will also be influenced by the outside design. Architects design buildings to meet a specific outside winter temperature. This may go as low as −30°F (−34°C) or lower and up to 20°F (−7°C) or more. The lowest temperature is not used for this; an average of the coldest days in the area is used. Special tables give information on what the outside design requirements are. For instance, St. Paul, Minnesota, will have an outside design requirement of −30°F (−34°C); Portland, Oregon, +10°F (−12°C), and Denver, Colorado, −10°F (−23°C). Normally, a winter wind of 15 mph is used, which gives an R of 0.17 for outside surface loss. Walls below grade are usually considered to lose 4 Btuh (R = 0.25), and basement floors, 2 Btuh (R = 0.5).

A heating engineer might present a planning team with the following calculations of heat loss from a motel that has 89,600 sq ft (8324 m^2) of space or 1,075,000 cu ft (30,440 m^3) designed for 2°F (−17°C) outside and 72°F (22°C) inside.[3] The building will be well constructed and have a calculated half air change per hour from seepage, transfer, and so forth. Local codes require that 20% of the air provided per hour be from the outside and that this must be based on the total capacity of the building. Extra outside air providing from 10 to 30 cfm must be provided for meeting rooms, dining areas, and other areas where smoke and other factors would require a greater input and output of air. This increases the total air requirements by 34,270 cfm.

Btuh to provide heat loss from building surfaces	= 2,268,700 Btuh
One-half air change/hr of 1,075,000 cu ft =537,500 cu ft	
and 537,500 × 0.018* × (72 −2°F)	= 677,250 Btuh
20% outside air × 1,075,000 cu ft × 0.018 × (72 −2°F)	= 270,900 Btuh
34,270 cfm extra air × 1.08 × (72 − 2°F)	= 2,590,812 Btuh
Total Btuh needs (heat loss)	5,807,662 Btuh

---

*This is a factor used by heating engineers to indicte the number of Btus required to heat 1 lb of air 1°F. This is obtained as follows: 0.241 (specific heat of air) × 0.075 (weight of a cubic foot air) = 0.018. If cfm is used for air flow and not cfh, the factor 0.018 is multiplied by 60 minutes to get a factor of 1.08.

Based on this requirement, the engineer would have to provide a heating plant that would produce around 6 million Btuh.

Different fuels might be available and the engineer might be requested to give the planning team information on costs plus recommendations. Normally, gas and oil have about 70% to 75% efficiency. This refers to the quantity of heat available for heating from the total Btu obtained by burning that particular fuel. Coal has about 70%, and electricity (when elements are immersed in water) has 95% to 100% efficiency. Table 15–8 indicates the cost of different fuels based on a 5,700,000-Btuh requirement at a cost of $0.008/cu ft for gas, $0.50/gal for fuel oil, $20.00/ton for coal, and $0.04/kWh for electricity. The Btus from the various fuels are based on standard values. The Btu per unit for gas is for natural gas, for No. 1 or No. 2 fuel oil, and for anthracite (high heat value coal).

Coal is much lower in cost than any other fuel but it is dirty and causes other problems such as storage and labor needs. Gas is twice as costly as oil but it is clean and does not have to be stored. Electricity is often more costly but, like gas, is clean and does not present storage problems.

The team planners may recommend also that the heating engineer and other experts investigate the advisability of a total energy system that utilizes waste heat to heat spaces, to provide heat for absorptive refrigeration, or to meet other energy needs.

---

[3]This is the simplest type of calculation made. If the degree day method is used, based on number of degree days in cold weather, the calculation is more complex.

TABLE 15-8   *Heating Efficiencies of Different Fuels*

The Btus of Heat Contributed by Various Fuels Is Usually Stated As:

No. 2 fuel oil	140,000 Btu/gal	Natural gas	1000 Btu/sq ft
Electricity	3412 Btu/kWh	Coal	950 to 15,000 Btu/lb[a]
Propane	91,686 Btu/gal	Wood	8500 Btu/lb
Propane	21,089 Btu/lb	Alcohol	11,000 Btu/lb
Coke	12,400 Btu/lb	Kerosene	19,800 Btu/lb

[a]The values are for the poorest quality lignite to the best anthracite.

Planners should inspect the heating system after installation and prior to acceptance. The inspection should cover the Btuh capacity of the system, adequacy of distribution, and efficiency of fuel use. Fossil fuels must have their waste products exhausted. The system should provide for maximum combustion of these fuels, which allows all the air needed to do this plus that needed to move away combustion products, but no more. An excess of air would mean that warm air is exhausted. A check can be made of fuel gases to ascertain if efficient combustion is occurring and air flow is correct. For instance, if No. 2 fuel oil is used, the carbon dioxide content of the fuel gas should not be more than 12.3% of total gases if the excess air introduced is 20%. Engineers can make these calculations and refer to tables that give desirable levels. For such fuels, the stack temperature should not be over 600°F (316°C). If it is, a loss of heat is occurring.

The smoke readings should not be greater than the standards established by the Environmental Protection Agency. If systems are checked in this manner and also checked frequently during subsequent operation, much air pollution from combustion products will be eliminated and savings on energy and cost will be made. Too frequently in the past, the planning for heating has been done on a loose, haphazard basis. Buildings having a high heat loss, with just a bit more insulation or construction or design treatment, could have been built to save much energy. Unfortunately, heating systems that overprovide heat or distribute it poorly have often been built. Planning team members who acquaint themselves with basic needs in heating and how calculations are made for providing adequately can be effective in seeing that the best job is done and a minimum of energy used.

COOLING

In some climates, the inside of a building may need to be cooled every day of the year, while in others it may be required for a short time only. Cooling may be needed for the entire day or only a part of a day. The eastern United States requires air conditioning 24 hours per day for 15 to 21 weeks of the year; the southern United States, for 4 to 8 weeks longer. Other areas may require it only for summer months. Even in cold weather, cooling may be needed. A dining room with a large amount of sun exposure on the west-facing side may build up enough heat in the afternoon to need cooling, even though the temperature outside is cold. Heat from lights and occupants may be sufficient to create cooling needs in a building center even though the outside rooms require heating.

Cooling requirements are calculated on the basis of the hottest part of the day, while heating needs are calculated for night when the weather is coldest. Although heat given off by lights, individuals, latent heat, and equipment is not considered in heating, it is in cooling. U values and others may be used, but most often **heat transfer values (HTM)** are used to calculate cooling needs. The quality of latent to sensible heat, as pointed out earlier, is also important.

In many areas, a 15°F (8°C) temperature difference between the high outside temperature and the desired inside temperature is planned. Individuals coming into a 70°F (21°C) room when the temperature is 90°F (32°C) outside may find the temperature cold. The federal government recommends that 78°F (25°C) be a standard for living space in the summer. The humidity of the air should also be considered. Thus, in areas of high humidity, the temperature may be lower, but in very dry areas, such as Las Vegas, Nevada, the temperature can be higher because of the cooling effect of very dry air. Engineers calculate the effect of wind velocities in the summer to be lower than in the winter, so a smaller correction is made for this factor.

Building design is important. A roof overhang allows the sun to enter through glass in some areas in winter when the sun is low on the horizon, but the overhang stops heat in summer when the sun is high. The use of louvres outside the building can also help provide shade in summer and allow solar heat to enter in winter, if adjustable. Trees and plants can do the same. Deciduous trees that shade a building from heat buildup in summer lose leaves in winter, allowing the sun to provide heat in the winter. Full outdoor shade reduces heat by 80%; shading from inside is far less efficient.

Engineers must vary the HTM values according to the type of climate—which may be classified as cool, medium, or hot. The hottest usual outside temperature is used instead of an average of the coldest days, as is used in heating. Heat transfer values will depend on the type of climate, material, and wind velocities, in some instances. In normal living spaces, individuals are calculated as giving off 300 Btuh, but in foodservices, a value of 400 Btuh are used, 255 being considered sensible heat and 145 being considered latent heat. An engineer may calculate only sensible heat and multiply it by 1.3 to get enthalpy. Equipment giving off considerable heat is calculated separately for the heat it gives off. Normally, planners can expect that the cooling Btuh required in northern climates is about half of the heating Btuh in winter. (Consult ASHRAE standards.)

The humidity or moisture in the air is a factor to consider in cooling. High RH values push up cooling requirements because moisture has to be extracted from the air as it cools down.

Cooling Systems

Cooling systems operate either by a chilling process called *refrigeration* or by a heating process called *absorption*. Both operate on the basis of the change of state that turns a liquid into a gas. This requires heat that is taken from the area to be cooled and the condensation of the gas back to a liquid in which the absorbed heat is given off and exhausted. Figure 15.3 shows how a heat absorption system works. In refrigeration, a compressor turns the gas back into a liquid. In refrigeration, this liquid expands into a gas in what is called *expansion coils*. When this gas expands in the coils, it needs heat that it takes from the items and the area to be cooled.

Absorptive cooling is growing in use. It uses a liquid that turns into a gas in an evaporator. Again, this expansion or change of state requires heat, and it is taken from the surrounding area—the cooling area. The warmed gas is then carried to an absorber that reconverts the gas into a liquid releasing the heat. To do this, the absorber usually contains a liquid that has a high affinity for the gas. When this is sprayed in the chamber, the gas is absorbed. Many use saturated lithium chloride solutions that pull the gas back into the solution. When the solution absorbs as much gas as it can, it is taken to another area where it is heated under pressure to concentrate the salt solution. This prepares it so it can absorb gas again. Figure 15.3 shows the process commonly used.

The heat developed in a refrigeration compressor or an absorber can become a problem. It may cause heat buildup in machine or evaporating rooms, thus lessening the efficiency of the system and of motors and requiring it to be moved out at some cost. Engineers today often design systems in which such heat is captured and concentrated in a heat exchange. This heat is then used to heat water or other things.

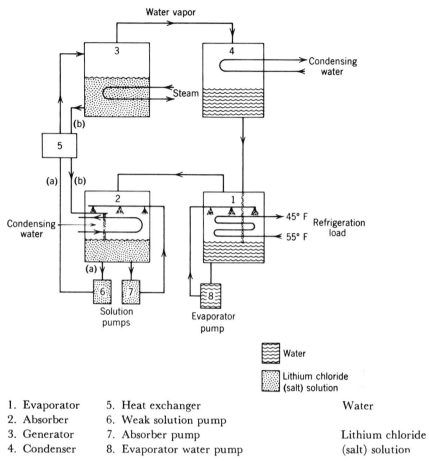

FIGURE 15.3 An absorptive system. Water pumped by the evaporator pump (8) is forced through sprays and as it falls it evaporates, cooling the interior of the evaporator (1). Water for cooling the building comes into coils in (1) at 55°F (12°C), is cooled and leaves at 45°F (7°C). Moist air in (1) is conducted over to (2), the absorber. A concentrated salt (lithium chloride) solution pumped up and sprayed takes this moisture from the air; the air is exhausted. The absorption of this moisture in the absorber (2) creates warmth, which is carried away by the condensing water flowing through coils. Moisture absorbed by the salt solution is carried down to the salt solution at the bottom where it weakens the solution. A continuous pickup of the weakened solution occurs with a pump (6); the weak solution (a) travels up through the heat exchanger (5) that warms the weak solution as it goes through. The weak solution (a) now moves up to (3) the generator. Here steam warms the solution to boiling, causing water vapor to be driven off and causing the salt solution to become concentrated again. Hot concentrated solution (b) now flows down through the heat exchanger where it gives up heat to warm the weak solution (a) flowing upward. The concentrated solution (b) then flows back into the absorber (2) where it is ready once more to pick up water vapor. The steam from the generator (3) now is carried over into the condensor (4). Here coils of cool water condense the steam back into water and this water flows back into (1) the evaporator where it can be evaporated and once more be sent through its cycle. (*Source: Mechanical and Electrical Equipment for Buildings,* William J. McGuinness and Benjamin Stein, 5th ed., John Wiley, p. 235. Reprinted by permission.)

In many modern buildings, air conditioning units and heating units are now the same machine, known as a heat pump. These are through-the-wall cabinets that cool in the summer and heat in the winter. In the summer, the compressor coil is vented to the outside so the heat from the compressor is dissipated outside and does not warm the room. In the winter, the compressor heat is turned inside. It is also possible to have large heat pumps in hotels or other buildings. The heat pump extracts heat from the refrigeration compressors and uses this to heat water, warm water for bathing pools, create steam, or even heat spaces.

Whenever possible, planners should be alert to ways to utilize wasted heat. Too frequently in the past, heat from refrigeration compressors built up in the machine rooms, where it reduced motor efficiency and created extra cost. Instead, to be efficient, water flowing around such compressors could be heated or warmed and then carried to booster heaters, where additional warming could occur, or it could be used for creating steam if required. The Kahala Hilton Hotel in Honolulu uses the heat from the compressors on its air conditioning units to warm water for bathing pools and for other hotel needs. Such water flowing through heat exchangers can pick up heat carried to the exchangers from the compressors. These heat exchangers are inexpensive and are not difficult to operate. They pay for their installation in a short time.

Cooling Requirements

The hypothetical motel used previously in the section titled "Calculating Heating Needs" as an example of heating requirements can also be used to illustrate the calculation of cooling requirements. An engineer would probably use the HTM method of calculation. By this method the engineer might find out how much heat is transferred into the building when the temperature is 90°F (32°C) outside and 75°F (24°C) inside, these parameters being set by local summer conditions. The figures would be as follows:

Infiltration through building (by HTM method)	490,000	Btuh

Outside air drawn in for ventilation, air conditioning, and so on:

One-half air change/hr	537,500	cfh
Outside air	215,040	cfh
34,270 cfm × 60	2,056,200	cfh
2,808,740 cfh × 0.018 × 1.3 × 15*	985,868	Btuh

Heat from lighting

(89,600 sq ft × 2 W/sq ft × 3.41 Btuh[†])	611,072	Btuh

Heat from people

(2,000 individuals × 400 Btuh/person × 1.3)	1,040,000	Btuh

Heat from equipment, machinery, and so on

	200,000	Btuh
	2,836,940	Btuh

---

*There will be 2,808,740 cfh of air from the outside coming into the building; 537,500 cfh from infiltration, doors, windows, etc.; 215,040 cfh because of a local requirement that 20% of the air used must come from the outside; and 34,270 cfm (multiplied by 60 to make it cfh) that must be brought into meeting rooms, etc. The factor 0.018 is the number of Btus that must be extracted from 1 cu ft of air to lower it 1°F, which was explained earlier in the Heating section. The 1.3 factor is the correction factor for latent heat in this air, and the factor of 15 is the temperature difference between 90°F (32°C) and 75°F (24°C).

[†]The lighting engineer states that the average amount of light in the building will be 2 W for every square foot of space. This is about normal for a hotel or motel. For each watt of electricity used for lighting, 3.41 Btuh are produced, so this factor is used to get the total Btuh from lights.

Note that in heat from people the 400 Btuh given off by one person is multiplied by 1.3, which corrects for the latent heat in the Btus.

Normally, cooling needs are never quite as great as environmental engineers might calculate using this method because buildings do not heat up as fast as the outside. Thus, while it may be 86°F (30°C) outside, the building is only about 75°F (24°C) inside. Later, however, when the atmosphere begins to cool off, the building, having absorbed heat, will warm up inside. The total amount absorbed, however, even with such a temperature swing, is not as great as the temperature rise outside. Therefore, an engineer will often use a **swing correction factor** of 71% of total needs to arrive at the final cooling needs. Thus, in this motel, the total 2,836,940 Btuh for cooling needs times 71% results in a final requirement of 2,014,227, which the engineer would probably round off to 2,000,000 Btuh.[4] He would then have to calculate the quantity of ice melt or cooling power in equipment required to give the amount of cooling. Note that the total load would seldom be required, thus the engineer will perhaps introduce several cooling units, so only those required to give the cooling desired would need to be operated.

Most cooling systems are planned to meet a cooling requirement of a specific number of Btuh. However, some engineers and others may still speak of the requirement measured by *ice melt*. One ton of ice melt is equal to 12,000 Btuh, which is the quantity of heat required to melt a ton of ice at 32°F (0°C) to water at 32°F (0°C). If an environmental engineer established the cooling requirement in ice melt, the system under discussion would require slightly less than 200 tons of cooling.

When air is used as a cooling medium, it is usually delivered in the room at 60°F (16°C). If air is at 90°F (32°C) and is cooled to 60°F (16°C), the difference is 30°F (17°C), which would require 0.54 of a Btuh for every cfh of air used (30 × 0.018 = 0.54). If water is used as the coolant, it is usually cooled to 45°F (7°C) from 55°F (13°C) and then piped to various areas, where this cooled water in coils reduces the air temperature of the area. If the room air is partially used, say, 80%, and only 20% is brought from the outside, the Btuh requirement is less because much of the air is at 75°F (24°C) in the room, instead of 90°F (32°C) on the outside. The cooling of a local area therefore depends on the quantity of outside air brought in. It is usually considered preferable to cool with water than with air because the duct work alone for air flow can be a problem.

Conditioned air can be expensive for a kitchen. Many codes require 20 air changes per hour. An area 20 × 40 × 10 ft (6.15 × 12.30 × 3.07 m) with an air change of 20 times per hour will require 160,000 cu ft of air per hour. Many installations using conditioned air bring in 75% from outside and the other 25% from cooled air from dining rooms or other adjacent areas. It is best for incoming air to be at ceiling height and as far as possible from the exhaust area.

CHAPTER SUMMARY

Ventilation systems should be set up to precisely control air quality, temperature, humidity, and movement with a system that is highly flexible, quickly responsive, and automatically controlled at minimum cost. Ventilation requirements will depend on the building and the equipment inside. They are based on the quantity of vapor and hot air to be exhausted. Air input must be balanced by air exhaust. If remodeling is done or equipment is changed, ventilation equipment may also need to be changed.

Heat is measured by its degree (temperature) and by its amount (Btu). Temperature may be measured on

---

[4] The statement was made previously that cooling Btuh are often half of the Btus needed in northern climates for heating in winter. Without previously adjusting figures, this indeed is the case in the example where about 5,800,000 Btuh were needed to heat the motel and about 2,000,000 Btuh were needed to cool it.

the Fahrenheit, Celsius, or kelvin scales. All substances do not have the ability to hold the same quantity of heat at a given temperature. This characteristic is referred to as specific heat, which is the quantity of heat required to raise a gram of a substance 1°C. Latent heat is the energy required to change matter from one state to another (a liquid to a gas, a solid to a liquid, etc.). Sensible heat is heat associated with a change of temperature. These concepts are important in calculating humidity, refrigeration, and other needs in a facility.

Air conditioning is more complicated than simple cooling of air. Both heat and moisture are important to comfort. Air that is dry will feel cooler than air of the same temperature and a higher relative humidity. Moisture buildup can occur for a variety of reasons, including equipment, steam, cleaning, or individuals within the building. Relative humidity is the amount of moisture in air compared to the maximum amount that it could hold. Recommendations include a temperature of 70°F (21°C) in winter and no higher than 78°F (26°C) in summer and a relative humidity of 50%.

Building codes regulate the quantity of air that must be brought into the building compared to air that is reused in the building. Some local codes may require, for example, that 20% of the air provided per hour be from the outside. A minimum number of air changes per hour may also be specified. Usually 5 air changes per hour is considered a minimum and 60 air changes per hour is considered a maximum.

Heating and cooling efficiency should also be considered. Factors that affect efficiency include general building design, building materials, insulation, the use of double- or triple-pane glass, and the air change rate, among others. Efficiency of different fuels may also affect selection of heating, ventilating, and air conditioning systems.

REVIEW QUESTIONS

Arrange to have as class speakers:

- A construction engineer to discuss building construction that prevents heat loss and infiltration and permits successful climate control.
- An environmental engineer to discuss the problems of heating and cooling large buildings.

Arrange demonstrations:

- Strike quartz and steel together, noting the sparks, which can start a fire. Examine the action of a cigarette lighter.
- Using a Bunsen burner in which air input can be regulated, demonstrate the temperature differences of different color flames—-white tip, yellow flame, and blue core—noting the speed with which each will ignite a piece of wood and, also, the difference in soot deposited on a pan bottom.
- Combine chemicals that react to generate heat.

1. Prepare a table showing temperatures from freezing to boiling, converting Fahrenheit to Celsius, at 10-degree intervals. Continue the table by converting Celsius temperatures to Fahrenheit.
2. Calculate the quantity of heat required to bring to 212°F 5 lb of presoaked beans in 10 gal of water if both are at 72°F. They are cooked in an 8-lb iron pot at 72°F. How much heat is needed to bring 2 lb of noodles in 1.5 gal of water in a 4-lb aluminum pot from 72°F to 212°F? (See answers to selected problems at end of text.)
3. Calculate the quantity of heat, in Btu and calories, required to raise the following 50°F: (a) 1 lb of water, (b) 1 lb of ice, and (c) 1 lb of steam. (See answers to selected problems at end of text.)
4. Draw a diagram illustrating how a refrigeration system works.
5. Explain the atmospheric condition that exists when it rains and how it develops. How is it possible for a person to feel the latent heat in moist air?

KEY WORDS AND CONCEPTS

absolute humidity (AH)

absolute zero

ASHRAE (American Society of Heating, Refrigerating, and Air Conditioning Engineers)

Btu (British thermal unit)

cfm (cubic feet per minute)

change of state

conduction

convection

dew point

enthalpy

fpm (feet per minute)

Heat transfer values (HTM)

humidity

insulation values U, K, or R

kinetic action

latent heat

radiation

relative humidity (RH)

sensible heat

specific heat

swing correction factor

thermal resistance (RT)

thermocouple

thermostat

wet bulb temperature

CHAPTER
16

Sound Control

IMPORTANCE OF SOUND CONTROL

The type of material, the amount of activity, and the specific conditions normally found in foodservice facilities result in noise conditions that call for control. The clanging of hard metal equipment, the bell-like ring of vitrified tableware, the reverberations from hard, slick surfaces, an occasional crash against a resistant floor, the sound of many voices, plus the hustle of activity are characteristic and commonly create a noise level of 60 to 75 decibels. (Decibels are a measure of sound intensity.)

Reverberation of sound waves tends to jumble speech so that words are not clearly understood. Hard surfaces reverberate (transfer) sound. Repetition of words in louder tones usually results in understanding but compounds hearing problems. Persons in a food facility need to be able to hear clearly and be understood when speaking at normal voice levels. Good acoustics can help prevent the irritations resulting from having to repeat orders and from having orders misunderstood. As stated in Chapter 3, noise can interfere with employee efficiency and increase fatigue. It can affect the pleasure and comfort of both workers and clientele.

PRINCIPLES OF SOUND

Sound waves are among the larger waves in the energy spectrum. Sound travels at the speed of 1,100 ft/sec. The energy in sound can be changed into other energy forms, such as heat or electricity. When sound is absorbed by an object, it can even cause vibration from the energy imparted.

Sound has different qualities. One is the frequency of sound vibrations, or the number of times per second the sound vibrations occur. Such sound **frequency** is measured in **cycles per second (cps)** or **hertz (Hz).** The normal human ear hears vibrations from 20 to 20,000 Hz although the upper limit decreases with age. Speech occurs in the range of 600 to 4,000 Hz. High-frequency sound travels by short waves, whereas low-frequency sound travels by longer waves. Frequency is often referred to as the *pitch,* a term that is used in music. The higher the frequency, the higher the pitch, and vice versa.

Another factor in sound measurement and treatment is the magnitude of the sound. **Magnitude** is the energy or power behind the sound. It is more difficult to define, because several similar terms are used to describe it, including sound power, sound pressure, and sound intensity. These calculations take into account distance from the sound source.

Sound intensity and loudness are not the same. Intensity relates to the amount of sound and is inversely proportional to the square of the distance from the sound source. In this respect, the intensity is like a Btu or calorie. It indicates the quantity and not the level. Loudness is the level of intensity. It is to sound as temperature is to heat. It does not state the amount, but only how high the sound level is.

Loudness is measured in **decibels (dB).** Sound ranges from 0 dB, which is the lowest detectable by the human ear, to about 130 dB. The sounds of ordinary office activity register at about 50 dB; normal speech, about 60 to 70 dB at 3 ft; shouting about 90 dB at 5 ft; and a large orchestra in a crescendo, about 130 dB. Sound above 130 dB is painful to the human ear.

Continuous exposure to high noise levels for long time periods can cause permanent hearing loss. The **Occupational Safety and Health Administration (OSHA)** limits exposure of employees to excessive noise levels. Because employees rarely remain in a single acoustical area for all eight hours, permitted exposure is based on a **total weighted average (TWA)** using formulas and tables given in the OSHA code. Another method used to measure noise exposure is a dose meter, which can be worn by the employee. The dose meter measures TWA level directly. Generally speaking, permissible noise exposure is 90 dB for eight hours, but many experts suggest a limit of 85 dB, and perhaps 75 dB. Many people have suffered ear damage from continual noise without realizing that the damage was occurring. In addition, noise at levels as low as 75 to 85 dB have been found to contribute to several physical and psychological illnesses, including headaches, digestive problems, high blood pressure, anxiety, and nervousness. See Table 16–1 for common noise levels.

Decibels are not additive. They actually combine to give a lower decibel rating than their combined sum. Thus 40 dB added to 50 dB gives 50.5 dB and not 90; 50 dB plus 50 dB gives 54 dB. The reason is that some of the sound waves combine so that they become the same thing.

Sound waves resemble light waves in that they can be diffused, absorbed, or reflected. The different building materials vary in their ability to reflect, diffuse, or absorb sound. When too much is reflected, objectionable sound can be projected into an area. **Reverberation** is a mixture of reflected sound. In some instances it is desirable, and in others it is highly objectionable and interferes with hearing distinctly. **Echoes** are re-

TABLE 16–1 *Common Noise Levels*

Sound Level (dBA)	Typical Sound	Subjective Impression
140	Jet plane takeoff	Can cause hearing loss
130	Artillery fire	Deafening (pain threshold)
110	Accelerating motorcycle	Sound can be felt
70–100	Street noise	Must raise voice to be understood
80–90	Factory	Must raise voice to be understood
60	Hotel lobby, restaurant	Normal conversation easily understood
40–50	Offices	Noticeably quiet

Source: Adapted from: Benjamin Stein and John S. Reynolds, Mechanical and Electrical Equipment for Buildings *(8th ed.), John Wiley & Sons, New York, 1992.*

TABLE 16-2 *Sound Absorption Qualities of Some Materials*

Material	Coefficient of Absorption		Percent Sound Reflected	
	High Frequency	Low Frequency	High Frequency	Low Frequency
Glass	0.35	0.04	65	96
Carpet or foam rubber	0.08	0.63	92	37
Heavy drapery	0.14	0.65	86	35
Marble, glazed tile, concrete, terrazzo, and painted brick	0.01	0.03	99	97

TABLE 16-3 *Recommended Noise Ranges*

Type of Space	dBA
Concert halls	20–30
Large auditoriums	30–35
Small auditoriums and theaters, large meeting and conference rooms	35–40
Hospitals, residences, apartments	35–45
Hotels, motels	35–45
Private offices, libraries	40–45
Large offices, reception areas	45–60
Restaurants	45–60

Source: Adapted from: Benjamin Stein and John S. Reynolds, Mechanical and Electrical Equipment for Buildings *(8th ed.), John Wiley & Sons, New York, 1992.*

flected sound that is delayed in travel to the reflector and back to the spot where it originally occurred.

The ability of building materials to reflect or absorb different frequencies of sound is referred to by sound engineers as the **coefficient of absorption.** This is the ratio of sound absorbed to the total quantity of sound striking a substance. Table 16–2 shows some of the absorption factors of some substances. The amounts reflected for both high- and low-frequency sounds are also given.

These data indicate that glass has a high transmission of sound at high frequencies and that hard surfaces, such as marble, will transfer both high and low frequencies with little absorption. Heavy textiles and carpets do a better job of absorbing high frequencies than they do low ones. A sound engineer looks at these records of sound-absorbing qualities of materials and uses them to absorb or reflect sound as required. Table 16–3 gives some examples of recommended noise ranges.

Some sounds may not register in high decibels, but may still be objectionable and even do harm to individuals. For example, the high frequency of the sound created by a jet engine of an airplane can be so annoying and painful as to make one ill. Other sounds may be objectionable because they are so loud (high decibels). Those who are around either of these types of sound a great deal need to wear ear protectors. Generally speaking, noise becomes more annoying to both employees and customers when it is louder, of higher frequency, intermittent rather than continuous (for example, sharp clanging sounds from a dishroom), moving from one location to another (rather than from one stationary location), and information bearing (radio) as compared to non-information bearing noise (background music). Some locations may wish to control and amplify sounds (auditioriums), but restaurants generally seek to minimize sound levels. Different types of sounds will require different treatments.

METHODS OF CONTROL

Sound control is needed in almost every space in a food facility. In meeting rooms and auditoriums, it may be important to move or project sound, direct it to certain areas, and prevent or encourage its absorption. In other areas, sound may have to be stopped or deadened. Sound can be controlled in several different ways.

The best way to reduce sound is to stop it at its source. This can be done by quieting equipment and by instructing personnel to speak in moderate tones. The **sound level** of equipment is often not considered in the purchase selection, but may be an important factor if the equipment will be located in or near the dining room. Some equipment is noisy because it is poorly mounted or fastened. Other equipment makes noise because it is not maintained properly. A fan in a room can emit low-frequency sounds that may not be too undesirable, but the resulting air flow rushing out from the vent can give off medium-frequency sound plus high-frequency sounds that come from the air diffuser and damper, which results in objectionable noise. This could be stopped by proper insulation of the inside of the duct before noise from the fan gets out of the duct. It might be stopped also by better mounting of the fan and duct.

Locating noisy equipment in separate areas may be another solution. Dish machines can be located away from the dining room. Ice machines can produce a fair amount of noise as well. For this reason some operations locate these in the kitchen and simply refill ice dispensers in the service area. Similarly, doors between the kitchen and dining room help to block the sounds of a busy kitchen.

Sound deadening can be done by using soft absorptive materials. Sound will enter these and be captured in the air spaces so that the waves are not reflected. The effectiveness of such absorptive materials depends on the porosity and kind of material. Thickness is also a factor. It is desirable to have some air space behind absorbing materials. Thus a ceiling of absorptive materials is more effective if it does not adhere directly to the ceiling surface but is affixed at a level somewhat below it. Sound can be deadened also by using a panel resonator, a thin membrane of material such as thin plywood placed before an air space. Sound strikes it and it vibrates slowly, capturing sound.

Carpeting, draperies, furniture, and people absorb sound. The sound created by footsteps across a bare floor of a room that has nothing in it is strikingly different from footsteps in the same room if carpeted and furnished. Carpeting with padding underneath is even more effective at absorbing sound.

Sound can also be deadened by a **series isolator.** This type holds and absorbs sound. For example, an inverted box can be built, lined with sound-absorbing material, and attached to the ceiling over a machine. The machine noise rises, goes into the hollow area, and dies there. Such a device over a dish machine should have moisture-proof absorptive materials and a vent installed so moist hot air is pulled out. Sound barriers around noisy areas can be effective. A lattice of wood will absorb sound. A waffle-type lattice with 3-in. (7.5-cm) squares will stop most sound waves over 3 in. (7.5 cm). Height barriers up to 4 or 5 ft (1.2 to 1.5 m) can lower sound levels 8 to 10 dB.

Sealing buildings to prevent sound from getting through holes and cracks in walls can also help. A hole 1 sq. in. can let more sound through than 100 sq ft of wall space. Sound can travel along pipes, ducts, and other connectors between spaces, especially if the connectors are metal. Cracks around windows may also allow sound to pass through.

If sound is dropped below that of the ambient noise level, it is not heard. Thus an individual in an office next to a busy street may not hear sounds from the next office; but those in the next office on the other side where the noise level is much less will hear the sounds in spite of the traffic. Sound-deadening materials between walls are one way to cover up ambient noise. Another way would be to introduce other ambient noise. Music may be used for atmosphere in a restaurant and can also cover up the sounds from a busy street.

Sound can be concentrated and then directed to a specific area by using a hard concave surface. The original sound comes into the concave surface, where it concentrates, and then the hard surface sends it back in the desired direction. Thus a speaker can be on a stage and the voice lifted to a concave surface somewhat ahead of and above, and then the voice sounds can be transferred down to an audience. By contrast, in a dining room, a concave ceiling might cause sound concentration problems because sounds might be directed down to areas where a high noise value would occur.

One way that sound can be diffused, therefore, is with a convex soft surface. This is just the opposite of using a concave hard surface to concentrate and direct sound. A convex soft surface makes a good sound deadener.

The problem of reverberations and echoes may be stopped by shortening the sound paths. Hollow drop ceilings, objects, and other units may be used to do this. Sound may also be captured in space and prevented from echoing or reverberating.

Sound can transfer itself by a process called **creep.** This happens when sound travels along a wall or some other object. It may not be heard a short distance from the wall or object, but can be heard by anyone standing close to the wall or object. Thus, among an audience listening to a singer on the stage, those in the center of the auditorium will hear the singing well while those seated along the aisle near the wall might hear both the singing directly and hear it transferred later from the wall. Soft, absorbing materials can prevent creep.

SELECTION OF ACOUSTICAL TREATMENT

When selecting an acoustical material for a food service, not only must its sound-absorbing quality be considered, but also its fire rating, sanitary qualities, appearance, and maintenance requirements. Kitchen areas, where acoustical material is likely to be used, are usually humid, so the material selected should be moisture resistant. Materials that are less resistant to moisture will not hold up well and are likely to crack, buckle, mold, and mildew.

Codes should be checked in determining the acceptability of a specific material in relation to fire resistance. Many materials are fire resistant; others that may be combustible are slow burning. Fires in hotels and motels have shown that even though materials are slow burning or noncombustible, a high loss of life can occur from materials that smoke. It is advisable to check with local fire codes to ascertain what materials are allowed and which ones are not. If codes have not been updated, they should be exceeded.

Sanitation codes should be checked regarding the use of sound-deadening materials. Materials that absorb water (as well as sound) are not allowed in food preparation or storage areas, although they are generally allowed in the dining room. For example, carpeting, draperies, and fabric-covered furniture are useful for sound deadening, but cannot be used in food preparation, storage, dishwashing, or restroom areas. They are extensively used in dining rooms, however, to lower sound levels.

Appearance is also important because of its effect on the decor. Most of the noise control materials are in the form of tiles or panels. Some of these are perforated in a straight-row design and others are in a random pattern. They may be textured, fissured, or slotted. Sprayed-on and troweled-on cellulose fiber, mineral fiber, and plastic plaster are also available. The wide variety facilitates the selection of a material that will harmonize with a specific decoration plan.

Maintenance may require frequent washing or repainting for sanitation and a good appearance. Vacuuming, washing with a damp cloth, or scrubbing with a brush may be necessary. None of the porous or fibrous tiles should be subjected to a large amount of water because it will cause discoloration and buckling. Most of the materials can be painted by brush or spray, using a thin paint that will not clog the holes or crevices. Sealing the surface, however, will generally greatly lessen or destroy the acoustical efficiency.

CHAPTER SUMMARY

Sound control is important because unwanted noise can interfere with employee efficiency, increase fatigue, and affect the pleasure and comfort of both workers and clientele. Sound has different qualities, including frequency, magnitude, intensity, and loudness. If the comfort levels of these qualities are exceeded, the sound is perceived as annoying. Continuous exposure to high noise levels for long periods of time can also cause hearing loss. Because of this, the Occupational Safety and Health Administration limits employee exposure to high noise levels.

In a restaurant, a great deal of sound may be produced by employees, equipment, and ventilation systems. Sound levels generally need to be minimized through a variety of different treatments. The best method of sound control is to stop sound at its source. Isolating noisy pieces of equipment away from quiet areas, such as the dining room, may be another method. Sound deadening may be done in a variety of ways. These include using absorptive materials (such as carpets and draperies), series isolators, dropped ceilings, convex surfaces, and background music.

Selection of the most appropriate acoustical materials should be based on more than just its sound reduction ability. Consideration should also be made of its fire rating, sanitary qualities, appearance, and ease of maintenance.

REVIEW QUESTIONS

1. Arrange for a sound engineer to discuss current techniques used to increase, direct, and deaden sound, and the problems commonly encountered.
2. Arrange for students to experience sound at different levels: 30, 60, 70, 90, and 130 dB. (The physics department or an engineer may have equipment and records or tapes that might be borrowed for this purpose.)
3. Note and evaluate sound conditions in various sections of a food facility from the standpoints of (a) interference with understanding words uttered at normal speaking levels, (b) a pleasant noise level, (c) a distracting noise level, (d) the source of sounds, and (e) the quality of sounds heard.
4. Analyze the sounds heard from the standpoints of (a) acceptability, (b) likelihood of repetition, and (c) need for correction.
5. Recommend a method for the correction of objectionable sounds in a facility.
6. Locate and identify the sound control methods used in five modern buildings. Evaluate them from the standpoints of (a) effectiveness, (b) appearance, (c) maintenance, and (d) fire safety.

KEY WORDS AND CONCEPTS

coefficient of absorption
creep
cycles per second (cps)
decibel (dB)
echoes
frequency
hertz (Hz)
magnitude

Occupational Safety and Health Administration (OSHA)
reverberation
series isolator
sound intensity
sound level
total weighted average (TWA)

CHAPTER

17

Floors, Walls, and Ceilings

The possible choices for floors, walls, and ceilings are almost endless. Proper selection relies on several factors that can change in priority with the location. These factors include (1) cleanability, (2) safety, (3) durability, (4) cost, (5) absorbency (floors, walls, and ceilings must be made of nonabsorbent materials in the kitchen), (6) comfort and quietness, (7) color (light colors reflect more light and make soil more obvious) and attractiveness.

The needs of specific areas within a food facility should be kept in mind when selecting floor, wall, and ceiling materials. Differences may be found in relation to wear (special materials may be required where heat or splashing of grease or water is a problem), maintenance that will be required and likely to be given, length of time the installation will be used, and plans for decoration.

CLEANABILITY

Floors, walls, and ceilings should have easily cleanable surfaces and be reasonably impervious to the absorption of grease and moisture. They should be free from gaps or crevices where soil or moisture may gather. Broken or cracked flooring and materials will need to be replaced to avoid giving soil a place to collect, as well as to prevent accidents. Floor and wall surfaces should be resistant to attack or damage from hot water, cleaning agents normally used, and the repeated scrubbing necessary to keep them in good condition.

Light-colored walls and ceilings are best because they reflect more light and show soil more easily. Coverings that also absorb sound are good choices. Smooth sealed plaster, **plastic coated tiles,** and **plastic laminated panels** are often used.

Supplemental flooring such as mats and slatted floor boards should conform to local sanitation codes. Such flooring should be durable, readily cleanable, and allow comfort when workers stand on it.

Coving is a trimmed, curved base between walls and floors. It is required by sanitation codes because it makes the edges and corners of the floor easier to clean. Rubber coves are available for use with resilient flooring. Ceramic tiles in cove form may also be obtained. Rounded corners and edges on equipment bases (similar to coving used on floors) are also available and eliminate the need for cleaning under low equipment. For ease of cleaning, any seams or junctures should be closed to no larger than 1 mm (1/32 of an inch).

SAFETY

An important safety factor in relation to floors is the degree to which they provide sure footing. Slippery surfaces are a common cause of falls, which result in physical injury and equipment breakage. Tests show that the most slippery floors include waxed maple, concrete, and pressed wood. The least slippery include rubber, cork, and asphalt tile. Linoleum, ceramic tile, and quarry tile are one and a half times less slippery than maple. Marble is one of the most slippery of floors, especially when greasy and wet. **Terrazzo,** because it has marble chips in it, tends to be somewhat slippery. Quarry tile can be purchased with varying abrasive qualities to reduce slippage.

DURABILITY AND COST

Expected use should be equated to durability and cost. The price range of floor coverings, for example, is almost unlimited. Where there is likely to be heavy wear, the most economical floor in terms of total investment plus maintenance will be a floor such as **quarry tile,** which will withstand hard wear and require a minimum of maintenance. **Ceramic tile,** on the other hand, is not recommended in food preparation areas because it is nonresilient and can break if something heavy were dropped on it (such as a No. 10 can). The same degree of sturdiness is rarely required throughout a food facility. Conditions calling for durable and resistant flooring are areas with heavy traffic (especially mobile equipment), excess moisture and grease (they may soften or damage flooring materials), and rapid accumulation of soil (more frequent scrubbing and stronger detergents are required). Such conditions are characteristic of receiving, preparation, dishwashing, pot washing, and garbage removal areas (Figure 17.1). Dining rooms usually require less vigorous wear or cleaning and may be covered with less costly, lighter, and more decorative materials.

The workmanship applied when laying floors will influence their durability and satisfactory use. Smooth junctures and close abutments are required. The binding cement or mortar should be water and grease proof and resist erosion. The type or nature of the subfloor may determine the life, appearance, and cost. Alkaline and moisture-resistant floorings should be used on concrete below grade. Special treatment is necessary, depending on the subfloor used, and operation team members should carefully consider all factors when setting up specifications.

The installation cost of wood floors is usually high in relation to material cost. Quarry tile, mosaic floors, and other types of hard materials laid in cement or **mastics** have a high installation cost. Ceramics should be laid so that there is not more than 3/16 in. between joints (Figure 17.2). Because mosaics are usually shipped premounted on paper, this helps somewhat to reduce installation costs.

Floor thickness will also affect durability. All floorings should have color and design throughout the thickness of the material so that, as wear occurs, appearance will not be marred. With the development of the tough plastics, the use of battleship linoleum about 1/4 in. thick and 10.5 lb per square yard has declined. The recommended gauge for plastics is 3/16 in.; rubber and cork, 3/8 in. (especially for heavy traffic areas, such as on stairs); terrazzo topping, 1/2 to 3/4 in. thick on top of a 2- to 3-in. bed of cement; quarry tiles, 1 1/4 to 1 1/2 in.; ceramic tiles, a minimum of 1/4 in. Wood floors should normally be maximum thickness because of the frequent need in facilities for resanding, plus traffic wear. Concrete floors should be poured 3 to 4 in. on or below grade and slightly less above grade.

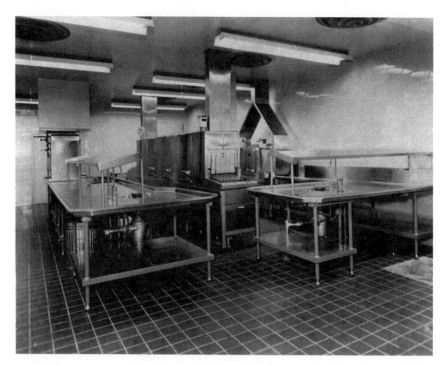

FIGURE 17.1   A well-lighted, easy-to-clean dishwashing area that has a quarry tile floor, glazed tile walls, and good ventilation treatment.

FIGURE 17.2   Well-laid ceramic tile makes an attractive, easy-to-clean floor.

Wall surfaces in work areas should be hard and smooth. In kitchens and serving areas, glazed tiles are popular as a wall surface because of their ease of cleaning and durability. They may be used as a covering for the entire wall or for only the lower section to a height of 6 to 8 ft (5.5 to 7.4 m) if costs are to be kept low. The remainder of the wall is generally plaster, which is painted with a washable paint. Toxic paints, such as those that have a lead base, cannot be used. New paints do not contain lead, but this may be a problem when remodeling older food services and removal of previous paint is necessary. Painted surfaces are generally not recommended in areas where food or grease splash. In kitchens and travel areas where equipment is used, hardwood, plastic, or metal corner guards are usually required.

Stainless steel is an extremely durable wall covering, although it is more expensive. It has good resistance to moisture and is often used in food preparation areas where the humidity is high, where grease may splash, and where there is much wear and tear.

In dining areas, decorative effects and the desire to cushion noise may make it desirable to use different surfaces. Smooth, hard, plastic-coated plywood may be used in both the serving and dining areas. Textured plastic coverings in colored patterns provide good durability and are also decorative. Hardwood molding or metal guards can be used to protect walls. Metal corners may also be required. Wallpaper may be used as long as it can be cleaned.

Paints are often used for a low-cost wall covering. **Acrylic paints** have a water base. They will not peel and are used in areas having a high humidity. **Lacquer-based paints** are made of synthetic resins dissolved in an organic solvent other than turpentine or mineral spirits. They dry and harden quickly. They may be used on concrete because they have a high resistance to the alkali of concrete. Paints containing chlorinated rubber of a styrene-butadiene resin may be used with success on concrete floors resting on subgrade. Vinyl-resin paints are used mostly on walls. These paints may be used in washrooms, laundries, or other highly humid areas. Paints with mold-resistant qualities are available for use in storage areas or fermentation rooms where mold is a problem.

Cinder block walls are relatively inexpensive and may be used in relatively dry areas. They must be sealed, however, with washable paint. They are generally not considered attractive and are more typically seen in storage areas.

ABSORBENCY

Acceptable floor, wall, and ceiling materials differ according to location because of absorption requirements. Because of sanitation codes, nonabsorptive materials must be used for floors, walls, and ceilings in food preparation, storage, dishwashing, and restroom areas. In addition, because of absorption, **structural elements** (studs, joists, rafters, etc.) may not be exposed in these areas unless they are sealed for easy cleaning (Figure 17.3). By contrast, in the dining room, the use of wallpaper, fabric, wood panels, and other absorptive materials is allowed, although they must still be periodically cleaned.

COMFORT AND QUIETNESS

A **resilient** floor is quiet and reduces fatigue (Figure 17.4). Before installing floors, these factors should be checked and balanced against durability and use requirements. The force of the blow of a leather heel was found to vary from 7 lb on high-density cork to 9.1 lb on quarry tile. Below 8.5 lb were rubber tile, linoleum, beech wood, pressed wood, and maple; above 8.5 lb were asphalt tile, cement, ceramic tile, terrazzo, and quarry tile.[1] Table 17–1 gives the loudness of various noises, expressed in decibels, resulting from impacts with various floor types.

---

[1]Dorothy Goodrich, *Floor Materials, Qualities Desirable for the Institution Food Service Unit,* Master's thesis, University of Washington, 1940.

FIGURE 17.3   Good floors, good light, hard-surfaced walls, and acoustical ceilings provide fine supporting facilities. (*Courtesy of Michael Reese Hospital, Chicago.*)

FIGURE 17.4   Washable carpeting furnishes a resilient, non-skid floor surface in a waiter pick-up-area. (*Courtesy of George Bundy & Associates, Seattle, Washington.*)

TABLE 17-1   *Loudness Level (in Decibels)[a] Produced from Falling Plates and Impact of Heels[b]*

	4.5-in. Plate Dropped 30 in. to Floor	Impact of Leather Heel	Impact of Rubber Heel
Cork tile	62	38	37
Rubber tile	62	40	36
Linoleum	64	39	36
Linotile	66	40	37
Asphalt tile	68	43	37
Maple flooring	68	43	38
Magnesite	68	39	36
Cement	77	39	35
Ceramic tile	79	39	36
Terrazzo	79	39	35
Quarry tile	80	39	36

[a]Zero decibel is taken as the threshold of audibility.
[b]Dorothy Goodrich, *Floor Materials, Qualities Desirable for the Institution Food Service Unit,* Master's thesis, University of Washington, 1940.

COLOR AND ATTRACTIVENESS

Decor, which is important, may vary widely. Ceilings, floors, and walls can be an important and harmonious part of the decorative scheme. Warmth and good taste are components of attractiveness and patron appeal. Creating a pleasant atmosphere for both patrons and workers is essential.

White, for example, is depressing to many workers. Light green, soft yellow, or peach wall colors increase productivity and worker satisfaction with the environment. Light-colored floors increase light efficiency by reflecting the light upward. Psychological reactions to color and physical eye comfort should be considered. The use of expert assistance in planning the decor may be money well spent in terms of resulting satisfaction.

The beauty and appeal of floors and wall finishes can be spoiled by soil, abrasion, or scarring. Selecting for attractiveness is, therefore, closely tied to ease of cleaning and durability. Costly maintenance or replacement tends to increase unsightly neglect. The easiest floors and walls to maintain are those that are simply cleaned and that do not require special treatment, such as waxing and polishing. Discoloration, staining, chipping, and rapid soil buildup spoil appearance. Fibrous or porous materials are more susceptible to staining than hard surfaces and hold soil, thus requiring more vigorous cleaning.

An appealing custom appearance can be created by using tiles of different colors. Patterns may be incorporated in floors to mark off areas, guide patrons, or indicate table and chair placement.

Table 17–2 indicates ratings of floors (excellent, good, fair, or poor) in relation to desirable qualities. Some of the characteristic factors of the most commonly used floors are as follows:

Asphalt tile: Should specify grease proof; not very resilient for heavy traffic areas; nonslippery; good for below-grade areas; should use only nonorganic cleaners and waxes.

TABLE 17-2   Qualities of Common Floor Materials

	Comfort Underfoot	Quietness	Cleanability	Maintenance	Slipperiness with Grease or Wax	Resistance to: Abrasion	Dents or Cracks	Grease	Alkali Cleaners	Color Change
Resilient Floor Materials										
Asphalt tile, dark colors	F	F	G	F	F	F	P	P	G	G
Asphalt tile, light colors	F	F	G	F	F	F	P	F	G	G
Asphalt tile, grease-proof	F	F	G	F	G	F	P	E	G	G
Rubber tile	E		G	P	P	F	E	P	G	G
Linoleum tile	F	E	G	P	F	E	G	E	P	F
Cork tile	E	G	F-G	P	F-E	F-P	G-P	F	G-P	P
Vinyl plastic tile	G	E	G	E	E	P	E	E	E	E
Linoleum sheet (inlaid)	G	G	G	P	F	G	G	E	P	F
Vinyl sheet	G	G	F	F	E	G	G	E	E	E
Hard Floor Materials										
Quarry tile	P	P	G	E	E	G	G-E	E	E	E
Concrete	P	P	F	F	P	F	F	E	G	E
Terrazzo	P	P	E	G	P	E	G	E	P	E
Wood	F	P	F	F	F	P	G	P	F	P

Source: Adapted from Volume Feeding Management, *March 1958, p. 54.*
Key: E, excellent; F, fair; G, good; P, poor.

Carpeting: Cannot be used in food preparation, storage, dish room, or restroom areas because of absorbency; is resilient; absorbs sound; gives nice appearance in dining room; needs much maintenance.

Ceramic tile: Shows footprints; is not resilient; may crack if heavy objects are dropped on it; can be used around steam equipment basins and so forth, where close fit is desired; for flooring, should specify 1% to 10% abrasive (or it becomes too slippery when wet); may be used for walls.

Concrete: Low cost; must be adequately sealed to make it nonabsorbent (paint is not acceptable as a sealant because it wears off too easily); not resilient; is slippery; erodes easily; not considered very attractive; best used for storage and restroom areas (if sealed).

Hardwood: Attractive; resilient; requires significant maintenance, including waxing and polishing; all grades give good wear but vary in appearance; expensive; must be sealed (made nonabsorbent) if used in areas other than the dining room; generally only used in dining areas because of cost.

Linoleum: Resilient flooring made from powdered cork, oxidized linseed oil, gums, fillers, and pigments on burlap backing; poorer quality; dents easily from dropped objects or concentrated weight; higher quality pieces are more resilient; attacked by fat solvents.

Marble: Natural, polished stone; not resilient; slippery; very expensive, but beautiful appearance; sometimes used in an entry area.

Quarry tile: Natural stone; durable, cleanable, stain resistant, good footing (if an abrasive is added); available in ceramic or dairy paver tile thickness; initial expense high but gives long-time service; not resilient; tends to be noisy; best use is for heavy wear and traffic areas.

Rubber: Comes in rolls, sheets, and tiles; is anti-slip; very resilient; is affected by oil, strong soaps and detergents, and solvents.

Terrazzo: Marble chips in a cement binder; not impervious to attack from grease or other materials; is slippery when wet; has tendency to crack or separate along metal strips, which creates cleaning problems; not suitable for kitchens; attractive and durable for entrance and dining areas.

Vinyl tile: Resilient; nonslippery; easy to maintain; water and grease resistant; tough and durable, although it may dent when heavy objects are dropped on it; has beauty, comfort, and quietness; fairly high in cost.

CHAPTER SUMMARY

Choices and price ranges for floors, walls, and ceilings are limitless. The best selection depends on the location. Factors that are used to determine the best choice include cleanability, safety, durability, cost, absorbency, comfort and quietness, and color and attractiveness. Other considerations include the type of wear that the surface will be exposed to, the maintenance that it will receive, the length of time before it is replaced, and its decorative function.

In general, all materials should be easily cleanable. Surfaces must be nonabsorbent, however, in food preparation, storage, dishwashing, and restroom areas. More materials are allowed in the dining room area, including wallpaper, cloth furniture, draperies, etc.

In addition to cleanability and absorbency, two very important concerns are durability and cost. The most economical investment considers original cost, maintenance requirements, and the expected lifetime based on durability. Extreme durability is a prime consideration in areas with heavy traffic, moisture and grease, and rapid soil accumulation. Decorative appearance may be more important in dining rooms with less vigorous wear.

Safety is also an important factor as slippery floor surfaces are a common cause of falls. Some of the most slippery floors are waxed maple, concrete, and asphalt tile. They are particularly slippery when they are wet.

Resilient floors are often selected because they are more comfortable to walk on and are often more quiet. Color and attractiveness of floors, walls, and ceilings is also considered carefully in the design scheme because of their contribution to a pleasant atmosphere for both employees and customers.

Based on these considerations, typical floor materials for the kitchen include quarry tile, linoleum, or vinyl tile, and perhaps sealed concrete for storage areas. Carpeting, decorative linoleum, vinyl tile, sealed wood, or terrazzo are used for dining room floors. Popular wall materials for the kitchen include painted plaster, ceramic tile, stainless steel, and perhaps sealed concrete or cinder blocks for storage areas. For dining rooms, painted plaster, wallpaper, or wood panels are often used. For ceilings, smooth sealed plaster is generally used.

REVIEW QUESTIONS

1. Observe the flooring materials used in different sections of three foodservice establishments. Find out, if possible, how long they have been in use and evaluate them from the standpoints of appearance, kind of care required, degree of wear apparent, slipperiness, and suitability.
2. Visit flooring companies and observe the flooring materials available and comparative prices per square foot. Inquire where installation of the chosen flooring materials may be observed. Visit the location to study appearance, amount of care required, and degree of wear.
3. Evaluate various types of wall coverings from the standpoint of cost, appearance, durability, cleanability, etc.

KEY WORDS AND CONCEPTS

absorbency

acrylic paints

ceramic tile

cinder blocks

coving

lacquer-based paints

mastic

plastic coated/laminated tiles and panels

quarry tile

resilient

structural elements

terrazzo

PART
4

EQUIPMENT SELECTION

CHAPTER
18

General Principles for Equipment Selection

Equipment purchase can be necessitated by expansion (in either facility size or in menu), a change in menu, the need for replacement (because of high maintenance, obsolescence, automation needs, or over- or undercapacity), and, of course, the construction of a new operation. Equipment values are based on the degree to which the equipment is needed and how well it performs. A food facility's standards, volume, and financial success may be directly affected by its equipment. Needs will vary according to the specific operation. They will be influenced by menu, volume, peak loads, type of service, utilities and services available, layout, and many other factors. Many aspects must be carefully weighed when making selections.

GENERAL TYPES

Food facility equipment may be (1) custom built for a specific installation or (2) chosen from the standard stock of manufacturers. **Stock equipment** produced in large quantity from a standard pattern is lower in cost than equipment built to a specific design. Adjustment to a particular need, however, may give the **custom-built equipment** greater economic value. Detailed drawings and exact specifications are needed when ordering custom-built equipment. By contrast, a manufacturer's number or catalog description may be used when ordering stock equipment.

Many pieces of specialized equipment have been developed by manufacturers to improve operating efficiency. One need not depend on one range surface and a variety of pots and skillets today. It is now possible to obtain temperature-controlled grills or deep-fat fryers of a size or type to fit specific needs. Cooking may be done in a steam kettle, steamer, char-broiler, infrared oven, combi-oven, or rotisserie. Specialized equipment can be used to improve quality, increase handling of volume, or provide operating efficiency.

SELECTION POINTS

The selection of equipment to yield the best values for a food operation will be based on (1) need, (2) cost, (3) performance, (4) satisfaction of specific needs, (5) safety and sanitation, (6) appearance and design, and (7) general utility values.

Need

Need should be evaluated in terms of whether the equipment is required to enhance quality, handle quantity, or reduce cost and time of operation. A range may not be needed in a school kitchen where the bulk of the food is prepared in steam cookers and ovens. A dishwasher might be advisable in certain units in terms of labor saving. Needs should be prioritized in planning as (1) essential or basic, (2) high utility, and (3) useful. If purchases are not all made at one time, this list will guide planning for future additions.

Equipment that furnishes the most practical means of securing the quantity and quality of food or services required is essential. On such a basis the purchase of expensive equipment may be challenged if processed products are available that eliminate the need for the equipment. Analysis should determine whether market prices and quality of processed products compare favorably with the costs of equipment plus labor plus raw materials to produce the equivalent supplies or services. Calculation should be made, for example, as to whether it is better to equip a meat shop or buy prefabricated meat, to have a vegetable peeler or use preprocessed vegetables, or to operate a bakeshop or buy commercial products. Where standards are high, quality may easily be the determining factor. On the other hand, many food services today purchase more convenience food products to minimize equipment needs and reduce high labor costs.

It is rarely wise to purchase more or larger equipment than required for immediate needs. One may be oversold and overequipped in certain areas and have an inadequate amount for satisfactory work in others. This often happens when plans are made by persons unfamiliar with production and service needs. Investment costs, loss through obsolescence, labor cost for cleaning and maintenance, and changes that mean the equipment is no longer used should discourage purchasing beyond requirements.

On the other hand, probable growth or change affecting future needs may cause certain service and utility installations to be listed as essential. Installations done during the original construction are often a great deal cheaper and more easily accomplished than adding them at a later time. It may be difficult and expensive, for example, to put in electrical conduit or dig and install larger sewer lines later after the original construction if you find out more or larger equipment is required.

Cost

There are many points to consider when evaluating the immediate and ultimate cost of equipment. The expected cost of equipment should be evaluated over the course of its lifetime. This is called **life cycle cost analysis.** Costs included in life cycle cost analysis are (1) initial price, (2) installation expense, (3) maintenance and repair, (4) depreciation, (5) insurance, (6) financing expense, (7) operating cost, and (8) values lost versus those created.

In practice, this is not easy to do because the variables are based on estimates of labor rates, energy costs, food costs, maintenance/repairs, and equipment lifetimes. Where large-scale equipment purchasing is done, however, the effort produces significant savings. It is particularly worthwhile for chain operations. A comparison of market prices and selection of specific makes is a beginning for such a study. Records of performance that will aid evaluation should be sought. Is the item durable and inexpensive to use or are frequent repairs needed? The future cost of repairs is often the biggest unknown. If repairs are needed, is the manufacturer reliable and prompt in supplying repairs and parts?

Installation may add a sizable percentage to the cost of the equipment. Bid prices may or may not include installation. Special conditions, such as utility piping, wiring, hoods, ducts, or fire proofing will also add expense.

Repair, maintenance, insurance, and the lifetime/depreciation of the equipment are important factors to consider when evaluating costs. Equipment that is too light or poorly constructed is likely to need frequent repair and adjustment. The lifetime of equipment depends on a number of factors. Most important are the amount of preventive maintenance, employees' use (or abuse) of machines, the volume of operation, and the quality of the equipment. The accepted durability of equipment for accounting purposes is 10 years, or a depreciation of 10%. Well-constructed equipment that receives regular maintenance and is not mistreated will often last 15 to 20 years or longer. Stainless steel equipment, in particular, will generally last 5 years longer than equipment made from less expensive materials.

Certain pieces of equipment may be too complicated to be repaired or conditioned by local mechanics. If company service is not readily available, such equipment may be a bad investment. A breakdown of key pieces of equipment can seriously impair quality of the operation and add to labor costs. Significant value is added to specific equipment in terms of a company's reliability, promptness in parts delivery and servicing, and gratuitous inspection and periodic adjustment of equipment.

The future value of money must be considered in any cost evaluation. Experience has shown that the capital plus its interest paid in the future is not the only test to apply. Inflationary trends decrease the value of money and make it much more valuable now than in the future. Management must also ask if the funds to be expended would yield more if they were invested otherwise or if the contribution of the equipment will be equal to the future value of the money. Can the borrowed funds be paid back from savings or other value contributions?

An evaluation of operating cost will include labor savings plus other factors. Utilities to operate equipment may affect choice. A comparison between dishwashers, for example, may show a pronounced difference in the amount of water required, the fuel to heat the water, and the power to operate the motors. Its operation may mean an efficient or poor utilization of detergent and sanitizer. Gas, steam, and electricity are the most often used fuels for heating water and cooking. Gas equipment is generally less expensive to operate, but the cost of the different fuels varies across the country. It is a good idea to obtain estimates of local costs before deciding on equipment that uses a specific fuel. Fuel efficiency also varies. In the calculation of an energy efficiency ratio between electricity and gas, the energy efficiency ratio of gas to electricity was found to average 1.6 to 1. In most operations where all-electric units are used for cooking, 40% to 60% of the total electrical connected load is used for cooking. A rough estimate of fuel required per meal served on an average is 0.33 kW of electricity or 1,800 Btus of gas with smaller operations requiring more heat energy per meal.

Equipment should be selected that is energy efficient. Ovens, for example, may have specific features that help to ensure maximum use of heat. These include insulation for heat retention, windows for visibility so that doors will not be opened as often, causing heat loss, thermostats and timers to control heat, and automatic shutoffs to save heat. Automatic recorders of temperature (the so-called "smart machines," which track and record temperatures by computer) indicate when temperatures have been allowed to vary from desired standards.

Based on all of the life cycle cost analysis factors, some operators use the following formula in judging new equipment needs:

$$\frac{A + B}{C + D + E + F - G} \qquad\qquad (18.1)$$

where

A = Savings in labor over the lifetime of equipment
B = Savings in material over the lifetime of equipment
C = Cost plus installation
D = Utilities over the equipment lifetime
E = Maintenance and repair over the equipment lifetime
F = Interest on money in C if left in a savings bank over the equipment lifetime
G = Turn in value of the equipment (salvage price).

If the result is 1.0 or more, the equipment should more than pay for itself in savings in labor and material. If it is 1.5 or more, the purchase is highly advisable. Situations exist where budgetary limitations forbid purchase even under circumstances where the result might be large. Overextension of capital for equipment is not advisable if it means the business must be severely hampered in operation because of it. Equipment that will require a minimum of labor and energy should be selected.

If the equipment budget is severely limited, it is a good idea to study the various ways of reducing costs. Among these may be possibilities of buying good, used equipment, renting equipment, or reducing the need for equipment through use of processed food or menu simplification.

Used equipment may become available for a variety of reasons. The equipment may have become obsolete to the previous owner's needs, the previous owner's menu or size needs may have changed, or the previous owner may have gone out of business (the foodservices industry is one of high turnover).

Occasionally, equipment may become available for purchase from the previous owner/operator. The disadvantage of buying directly from a previous owner is that there is no warranty. The advantages are that you may be able to see the equipment in operation and learn about its history.

It is becoming more common to purchase equipment from used equipment dealers. Two kinds of used equipment may be sold. **Reconditioned machines** are cleaned and the broken or worn parts are replaced. A minimal dealer warranty is offered and the price is generally 40% to 50% of the new equipment price. **Rebuilt machines** are dismantled and rebuilt. Parts are replaced, realigned, etc. When rebuilt, the equipment should hold to the original tolerances when tested. Dealer warranties are more inclusive than those for reconditioned machines and the price is generally 50% to 70% of the price of a new machine. If there is a question about the history of the equipment, it may be possible to find out more about the age and usage history of the equipment by tracing serial numbers through the manufacturer. Caution should be used, however, in the purchase of any used equipment or "**caveat emptor**," let the buyer beware.

Rental of equipment is also becoming more common. About 20% of office and industrial equipment is rented. Rentals may be done more often for certain pieces of kitchen equipment as well, such as dish machines, soft drink dispensers, or banquet supplies, such as tables and chairs.

Performance

Equipment is selected to fulfill specific functions. Comparisons of market offerings should be based on performance and how long the equipment is likely to maintain that performance. If the equipment is to slice or chop, will it make a clean cut or bruise and tear the food? If it is to transport, will it move easily and safely or break down under a normal load? Is the machine easy to operate or must one follow a complicated book of instructions? It should be easy to assemble and disassemble and to clean thoroughly. Workers will avoid using equipment that is complicated to clean.

Cost should be equated to performance. Several makes and models are usually available. Some may have special features that ensure better performance. Many times, for a small difference in cost, a considerable upgrading in performance can be obtained. Evaluations should be based on performance records if available; for this, users are the best source. If possible, see the equipment in operation and inspect the quality and quantity of work done. Actual tests will provide a good basis for judgment. Manufacturers and dealers are often willing to loan equipment for tests if handling and installation costs are not prohibitive. Examine equipment at shows or showrooms and collect information from equipment companies.

How long is the equipment likely to serve reliably in its functioning? The value of its performance is closely related to its remaining in good working order. Equipment that gets out of adjustment easily may give poor service and be costly to maintain.

Satisfaction of Specific Needs

The selection of equipment for the various sections of a specific food facility calls for careful calculation if investment is to be wisely made and successful operation assured. A detailed analysis of needs is necessary. Don't use the shortcut of trying to get by with the equipment lists of other operations. Being over- and underequipped for a specific operation is a common hazard resulting from blindly following someone else's plan. The experience of others may give valuable information, but it must be evaluated in the light of specific needs.

Manufacturer's statements must also be considered cautiously. A mixer, for example, can be operated under normal conditions at only 40% to 50% of total capacity. Only rarely and only at slow speed can 65% capacity be reached. Steam-jacketed kettles vary in working capacity by 75% to 85% depending on the solidity of the food and the manipulation required. For cooking equipment, loading and unloading time are generally not included when capacities are stated by the manufacturer. Capacities are often stated without recognition of operational requirements by those who manufacture rather than by those who use the equipment.

Safety and Sanitation

The National Sanitation Foundation, International, has become a strong force in establishing high standards for equipment and its installation. Anyone planning a food service and/or selecting equipment should be aware of the published standards of this organization and see that they are followed during selection and installation of equipment. The seal of approval of this body should be on all equipment purchased.[1] The **FDA Food Code**[2] is also a source of information on equipment sanitation. These are the standards that states use to make regulations, which are then used in local health department inspections.

When selecting equipment, consideration should be given to its freedom from hazards to safety and sanitation and the extent to which it protects against injury or contamination. For equipment to be safe, it must be made of nontoxic materials that will withstand normal wear and be thoroughly cleanable. All sharp edges and moving parts that are hazardous should be guarded and be free from "surprise features" that may be the cause of injury.

Self-service equipment should be carefully checked for safety. Gooseneck venting should be provided on self-service coffee urns so that hot water overflows will not burn

---

[1] National Sanitation Foundation, 3475 Plymouth Road, P.O. Box 130140, Ann Arbor, MI 48113-0140. NSF, International, can also be reached via a web site, www.nsf.org.

[2] The FDA Food Code is available on the Internet (vm.cfsan.fda.gov) along with a great deal of other food safety information.

customers. Moving belts or conveyors on which customers deposit dishes should be entirely safe. Fabricated equipment should be constructed such that there are no sharp or rough edges that can catch, tear, or cut. Safety-type pilot lights and adequate venting should be on all gas equipment. Overloads on electrical equipment should be avoided and all electrical (even 110 to 120 single-phase) equipment should be grounded. Wiring should not be open or liable to wearing or fraying. Steam kettles should be equipped with side lift handles or with automatic condensation control devices to avert burns. Equipment requiring extended reach into dangerous areas should be avoided. Pressure steamer doors should have safety catches so that opening is not possible without exhausting of steam. Mobile equipment should be equipped with wheel locks where necessary.

Sanitary features of equipment will affect customer reaction and influence food quality and production costs. Keeping foods at proper temperatures to avoid bacterial growth is important. Equipment should help to eliminate chances of food contamination. Avoid equipment with rough surfaces and inaccessible areas that require cleaning. Food cutters, slicers, and similar equipment that require thorough cleaning should be easy to take apart and reassemble. Metal mesh safety gloves may be provided for employees to use to increase their safety. Stainless, durable surfaces, coved corners, and filters that can be washed in the dish machine promote easy cleaning.

Appearance and Design

Equipment should be attractive in design and workmanship. It should be in harmony with the standards of the facility, the building, its purpose, and the other items of equipment. In many dining rooms, the impression of speed and economy is undesirable, even though speed and economy may be, in fact, essential for the operation. Equipment that creates a spirit of quiet refinement, ease, and luxury may be selected for some rooms, and in others the open display of the operation is acceptable or even desirable (display cooking, for example).

Design of foodservice equipment should stress function, simplicity, and maximum utilization of space. Smooth flowing lines permit ease of cleaning. Designs that give strength and utility as well as beauty should be sought. Designs that permit multiplicity of use are very desirable and commonly used. Color harmony and an attractive blending of materials can be attained. The mixing of equipment made of different metals may be satisfactory or unsatisfactory. Black iron may go well with some metals or enamel-covered equipment and poorly with others. It is not necessary for a kitchen to have all stainless steel equipment. Scale of equipment should be considered in its selection, and a similarity of design between pieces of equipment should be achieved. Food facility planners add expense when they ask for custom-designed equipment that is expensive to make and poorly designed. Equipment manufacturers frequently complain that they are called on to construct equipment designed by those who lack a knowledge of good equipment construction and design. More standardization in design and more emphasis on economy in designing equipment will reduce costs.

General Utility Values

Quietness of operation should not be forgotten when selecting mechanical equipment. At times, space relationships may be important in order to save labor and because only a given space exists. Space in such instances is a major consideration. Mobility may also be a factor. Distance relationships for certain installations and special features of a building may make it necessary to select one piece of equipment rather than another. Remote motors and condensers for refrigeration may have to be so far from the refrigerated area that self-contained units must be purchased for good efficiency.

The selection of equipment from reliable dealers and reliable equipment manufacturers is important. Equipment should bear the approval of associations that establish construction, performance, and sanitary standards. It is important that equipment meet local code requirements of the area in which it is installed. Equipment should have the approval of certifying agencies such as **UL** (United Laboratories), **AGA** (American Gas Association), **NSF, International** (National Sanitation Foundation, International), **ASME** (American Society of Mechanical Engineers), and others. See other abbreviations in the Appendix.

ESTIMATION OF EQUIPMENT NEEDS

Three reliable methods are used by layout planners when estimating equipment needs:

1. A detailed analysis of work needs may be made through the use of industrial engineering techniques, as described in Chapter 3.
2. A production chart and a production summary can serve as a basis for judging equipment requirements.
3. Calculation of functional requirements in relation to equipment specifications can be done, such as the number and size of portions needed in relation to equipment capacity.

The production charts (method 2), which are used for estimating equipment needs, should list menu items, total quantities required, type and size of equipment needed, time required for batch preparation, and other pertinent factors. Serving periods for estimating adequacy of production in relation to serving demands should be indicated. From this chart a production summary is made indicating utilization of equipment and ability of equipment to meet production demands.

Table 18–1 shows a typical menu used in an institution serving 300 patrons three meals a day. The portion sizes and total quantity required are given. Table 18–2 is a production time chart showing equipment required to prepare these foods. Table 18–3 is the

TABLE 18-1 *Menu, Portion, and Total Production Required to Serve 300 Patrons Three Meals a Day*[a]

Menu	Portion	Total Quantity Required
Orange juice		
Oatmeal	6 oz (¾ c)	13 gal
Milk		
Fried eggs	2	50 doz
Hot biscuits	2 (¾ oz dough each)	32 lb
Butter or margarine		
Coffee or milk		
Fresh fruit cup		
Grilled loin steaks	8 oz, ½ in.	150 lb
Mushroom gravy	2½ oz	6 gal
Hash brown potatoes	6 oz (1 c)	100 lb
Peas	4 oz (½ c)	24 2½-lb pkg (60 lb)
Bread	ad lib	40 lb bread dough
Butter or margarine		
Blueberry pie	⅙ pie	50 pies
Coffee or milk		
Chicken casserole	8 oz (1 c)	6½ gal sauce, 35 lb net chicken
Steamed rice	4 oz (½ c)	9½ gal
Green beans	4 oz (¾ c)	29 2½-lb pkg (72½ lb)
Tossed vegetable salad		
Ranch dressing	1¼ T	6 qt
Bread	ad lib	43½ lb bread dough
Butterscotch bars	2 (1 oz dough each)	34 lb

[a]Only portions and total production required, as shown on production chart, are listed here.

TABLE 18–2 *The Production Time Chart Hours of Preparation and Service*

Mean Items	Total	A.M. 5:30	6:00	6:30	7:00	7:30	8:00	8:30	9:00	9:30	10:00
Steam-jacketed kettles (10 gal)											
Mushroom gravy	6 gal										
Oatmeal	13 gal	—	—								
Steamer (2 compartment)											
Peas	24 2½-lb pkg										
String beans	29 2½-lb pkg										
Rice	9½ gal										
Tilt skillets (2)											
Eggs, fried	600			—	—						
Sauce with frozen diced chicken for casserole	29½ gal										
8-oz steaks, grilled	300										
Mixers (60 qt)					½	½					
Bread dough	59 qt (83½ lb)			—	—						
Butterscotch bar dough	36 qt.						—				
Biscuit dough	35 qt	—									
Ovens (Type 125—3 deck)						30 tins	20 tins				
Frozen 10" blueberry pies	50				—	—					
Bread (1# 14 oz each, 11"×3")	40 pans									—	—
Butterscotch bars (16"×25")	6 pans		3 pans	3 pans					—	—	
Biscuits (16"×25")	6 pans		—	—							
Hash browns (16" × 26")	6 pans										
Chicken casserole (16"×26")	6 pans										

production summary based on the findings obtained in Table 18–2. The data required to estimate the adequacy of the equipment are listed. Percent utilization of capacity is the result of dividing maximum usable capacity into maximum production at one time. Any utilization of capacity of 80% or over is considered satisfactory, but this factor considered alone may be misleading. Usage time is an important factor and the usage times listed here are typical, but not very efficient. More efficient use of equipment could be obtained with multiuse equipment such as combi-ovens or other combined technology cooking equipment. Average production rate per minute is derived by dividing the total production by usage time. A study of the data obtained in Table 18–3 indicates that the tilt skillet is not used as efficiently as it could be. Elimination of the steamer and preparation of these products in the tilt skillet using steam may be one alternative.

The simplest method used to calculate the adequacy of equipment is a calculation of functional requirements in relation to equipment specifications (method 3). This determines the actual productive capacity of equipment and evaluates it in terms of production demands. The six steps used in method 3 are shown next. An example is given to the right using a high-pressure steamer to produce 800 five-ounce portions of steamed whole potatoes.

1. Anticipate number of portions required and portion size either in weight or volume, depending on the method used for portioning.

Example
1. 800 5-oz portions of potatoes.

10:30	11:00	11:30	12:00	1:00	1:30	2:00	2:30	3:00	3:30	4:00	4:30	5:00	5:30	6:00	P.M. 6:30
	1 pan	3 pans	2 pans								3 pans	4 pans	2 pans		
										3 pans					
2 pans	3 pans	1 pan													
											4 pans	2 pans			

2. Multiply the anticipated number of portions by portion size to obtain total quantity required. Translate if necessary into state in which food item is to be processed through equipment, that is, as-purchased, ready-to-cook, and so forth.

3. Calculate food demand (especially peak demands) in portions and in weight or volume. Calculate maximum demand per minute.

4. Obtain accurate information on quantities and time required for processing the food item through equipment. Information on different models of equipment may be required. This information should give productive capacity per minute of the equipment in quantity produced per batch and number of portions.

2. 800×5 oz $= 250$ lb pared potatoes (purchase pared potatoes 5 oz each).

3. Serving time 1½ hr, demand loads are 500 portions (156 lb) first 45 min, 150 portions (46 lb) next 20 min, 150 (46 lb) next 25 min. Peak demand is about 12 (3½ lb)/min.

4. 30-lb electric pressure cooker is used, capacity is 20 lb whole potatoes or 64 portions/12 min or 1⅔ lb/min (includes loading/unloading time).

TABLE 18-3 PRODUCTION SUMMARY

	A	B	C	D	E	F	G (C/B)	H (E/F)
Equipment	Capacity	Usage Time	Total Production	Batches	Max. Production at One Time	Max. Usable Capacity	Aver. Prod. per Minute	Percent of Working Capacity
Steam kettle	10 gal (6 12"×20"pans)	1½ hr	19	3	6½ gal	6½ gal	0.22 gal	100
Steamer		3½ hr	200.5	7	4 pans	4 pans	0.95 gal	100
Tilt skillet								
Eggs	43"×23"	1 hr	600 eggs (9,000 sq in.)	12½	48 eggs (720 sq in.)	1,978 sq in.	16 eggs	36
Sauce/chicken	33 gal	½ hr	29½ gal	1	29½ gal	33 gal	0.98 gal	89
Steaks	43"×23"	1½ hr	300 steaks (8,415 sq in.)	7½	46 steaks (1,122 sq in.)	1978 sq in.	3.14 steaks	57
Mixer	60 qt	2 hr	130 qt	4	36 qt	40 qt	1.08 qt	90
Oven (3 deck)								
Pies	30 tins (105 lb)	1½ hr	50 tins (175 lb)	2	30 tins (105 lb)	30 tins (105 lb)	0.40 tins (1.4 lb)	100
Bread	45 pans (83½ lb)	1 hr	40 pans (72 lb)	1	40 pans (72 lb)	45 pans (83½ lb)	0.67 pans (1.2 lb)	89
Butterscotch bars	6 pans (34½ lb)	1 hr	6 pans (34½ lb)	1	6 pans (34½ lb)	6 pans (34½ lb)	0.1 pan 0(.58 lb)	100
Biscuits	6 pans (32 lb)	1 hr	6 pans (32 lb)	2	3 pans (16 lb)	6 pans (32 lb)	0.1 pan (0.53lb)	50
Hash brown potatoes	6 pans (106 lb)	1½ hr	6 pans (106 lb)	3	3 pans (53 lb)	6 pans (106 lb)	0.07 pan (1.18 lb)	50
Chicken casserole	6 pans (102 lb)	1½ hr	6 pans (102 lb)	2	4 pans (68 lb)	6 pans (102 lb)	0.07 pan (1.13 lb)	67

5. From steps 3 and 4 calculate size or number of pieces of equipment required to produce the quantity of food per minute to meet maximum serving demands per minute. Take into consideration the following:

   a. Certain foods lose quality soon after they are prepared and batch times should be such that, during the required holding and serving, quality is retained.

   b. Quality of the product is often affected by the quantity processed. Quantities prepared should be limited to producing high-quality products.

   c. Ability of employees to handle and use equipment with ease and safety should be considered.

6. Make a table listing types of equipment and sizes or capacities required to meet production needs.

5. Two steamers will cook 40 lb (128 portions)/12 min or 3⅓ lb/min (10½ portions). Prepare 40 lb (128 portions) at beginning of service, peak demand can be met by three batches in the next 36 min (120 lb or 384 portions). Since new batches will arrive every 12 min and potatoes can be held 20 min without loss of quality, the two steamers will satisfy production requirements and retain product quality.

CONSTRUCTION PRINCIPLES

Principles of construction of food facility equipment pertain to (1) design, (2) material, and (3) construction standards. These factors influence satisfactory functioning and economical operation. Major goals are to produce simple, functional designs in equipment that will yield maximum utility and durability at reasonable cost and be in keeping with high sanitation and safety standards. The design of equipment should be aimed toward quality production and minimal labor.

Much progress has been made in adapting equipment to meet modern needs, but further development is greatly needed in many areas. Technology has advanced tremendously in certain industries, particularly with the advent of smaller and smaller computer chips which have been incorporated into numerous control functions. The foodservice equipment industry, until recently however, has been relatively slow to implement the newer technologies. Some pieces of kitchen equipment have remained relatively unchanged in the last 30 to 40 years. Thermostats permit too wide a variation in temperature. Grills may heat unevenly and ovens may have "dead" spots. More precision is needed.

Needs have also changed. Labor costs have risen tremendously so that faster cooking is desirable, as well as cook and hold features. Also extremely valuable are automated features (to save labor costs), flexibility in use (multiple cooking modes, for example), and mobility (so that it may be used in more than one location). Building costs, particularly real estate prices, have also increased. As a result, more efficient use of space is important to keep the kitchen "footprint" as small as possible. Better use of space, especially vertical, also allows for more efficient placement with a decrease in labor costs. Outside appearance and good sanitation are important considerations but the majority of emphasis is generally placed on the functioning of equipment, labor requirements, and energy utilization.

Construction costs should be minimized when it is possible to do so without lowering standards. Labor and material costs can sometimes be saved by using materials that are less expensive and easier to fabricate. Labor in providing certain forms and finishes should be evaluated. Examples of this include the use of aluminum or chrome-plated steel instead of stainless steel for legs, galvaneal (galvanized iron) on interiors and nonfacing exteriors, No. 2 or 100 grit finish for stainless steel instead of No. 4, angle edges instead of curved edges, plastic drawers instead of stainless steel drawers or brake-bent or pressed sinks instead of all-welded sinks. Standard equipment should be used whenever possible. It is difficult to justify the price of a custom-built sink or a simple roast beef cart that is as high in price as a moderate-priced automobile.

Equipment should be sufficiently durable to give good service during its operational life. Balance of durability is often neglected. Frames are built to last forever, while the functional parts last only a short time. Easy replacement of the worn parts should be designed into equipment. Why should it be necessary to discard good frames on ovens and stoves and purchase new ones because linings and insulation cannot be easily replaced? Why should good stainless steel equipment built for a 20-year life span have to be discarded because of a failure of elements or other functional parts? Excess durability built into equipment may be undesirable. New or improved models may make it desirable to replace equipment at established time intervals. The storerooms of food facilities are sometimes filled with the mistakes of equipment manufacturers who have not properly assessed durability factors in their equipment.

MATERIALS

Labor cost represents a significant portion of the manufacturing cost. The labor cost for making a piece of equipment from either less desirable or better materials, however, is approximately the same. Purchase of equipment made of more durable materials may be worth the somewhat higher cost. Proper selection of materials should be made consistent with expected life, use, and budgetary limitations. Additional strength can be achieved by proper use of angle construction or channeling. The recommendations of the National Sanitation Foundation should be followed for materials.[3]

Wood

Wood has the advantage of being light in weight and economical, but its permeability to bacteria and moisture, absorption of food odors and stains, and its low resistance to wear make it a material with low utility and sanitation value. Its use in kitchens is usually restricted to cutting boards, butcher blocks, and a few utensils. Although the use of wood is allowed in the FDA Food Code, local food codes should still be consulted as some of these may be more restrictive.

If wood is used, it must be a hard wood (such as oak or maple) and must be in good condition with no open seams, cracks, or gouges. Wood cutting boards and wood tops are sometimes specified, but plastics and other materials may be more satisfactory because they can be cleaned and sanitized in the dish machine. Pastry table tops are often made from wood, however, since this seems to give best durability. All cutting boards should be readily removable but table tops need not be. All should be readily cleaned and sanitized and give no odor or flavor to food.

Because it cushions noise, has beauty, and can furnish variety in color and texture, wood *is* often used for dining room equipment. Moisture-proof plywood, pressed wood, and plywood covered or impregnated with plastics have been satisfactorily used as facing materials or for surfaces that receive only light wear.

Metal

Metal sheets and plates are usually specified according to a **standard gauge** indicating the weight of the material per square foot. The larger the number, the thinner the metal.

---

[3]See NSF Standards 1 through 52.

TABLE 18-4 *Standard Finishes on Stainless Steel*

Finish	Description
No. 1	Hot-rolled, annealed and pickled; a dull rough finish
No. 2B	Full finish—bright, smooth—cold-rolled
No. 2D	Full finish—dull and smooth—cold-rolled
No. 4	Standard finish for foodservice equipment; may be obtained on one or both sides of a sheet—bright satin finish produced with abrasives.
No. 6	High tampico-brushed finish with soft, velvety luster used primarily as a finish for tableware, etc. This finish highly buffed in 2B.
No. 7	High glossy polish with mirror or highly reflective finish from fine grinding and high buffing.
No. 100 grit	A polish that is more durable and cheaper for foodservice use than No. 4. It does not have as high a polish and this gives it more durability since under heavy wear No. 4 finish dulls. Obtained by first grinding down with No. 60 grit paper and then with No. 100 grit.

A 20-gauge stainless steel sheet weighs 1.5 lb/sq ft and is $\frac{1}{32}$ in. Fabricated equipment is seldom made of plates thicker than $\frac{3}{8}$ in. (000 gauge). Cast materials may be heavier.

The type of finish or polish given metals is frequently referred to in equipment construction. Table 18–4 indicates some of the finishes used. High finishes require more labor and add cost to the equipment, and should be used only when there is a distinct advantage. Where the surface is not seen, dull finishes are adequate and save money. An inexpensive brilliant mirror finish for stainless steel can be obtained by electropolishing, but this finish has not been too successful when used for foodservice equipment. Too bright a finish can cause excessive glare and hinder production. For this reason, No. 4 satin finish is generally used as a **standard finish.**

Covered Metals

Plated metals are usually specified according to the weight per square foot of the metal. A 32-oz sheet is called heavy, while a 24-oz one is called medium. Electroplating is the most common method used for plating and the most satisfactory. The thickness of the plating is specified as so many ounces of plating material per square foot. Preparation of the base metal for plating is called **pickling,** which is usually treatment with acid. Plating metals are chromium, nickel, and tin over base metals of steel, copper, or brass. Chromium over steel gives a beautiful, easily cleanable, silvery, high-luster finish and is frequently used for toasters, waffle irons, trim, and areas where high luster is desired. Copper is usually plated to make it corrosion resistant. Nickel or chromium-plated copper is used where high heat conductivity is desired. A bright, high-quality corrosion-resistant plate is obtained over copper if three coats of nickel plate are covered by a final chrome plating. Brass plated with chrome or nickel is used extensively for fittings; tinned brass or whitened brass fittings are not as acceptable.

Wrought iron covered with two coats of lacquer has been used in kitchen equipment in the past, but **aluminum alloys** have largely replaced iron because of their lighter weight. Aluminum is widely used for legs, supporting materials, wall brackets, and equipment such as racks, hoods, or baffles.

Cold-rolled steel may be covered with vitreous enamel and used for wall linings of equipment. It may be known either as **vitreous enamel steel** or **porcelainized steel.** The steel is first **bonderized,** a pickling process used to give adherence and anticorrosion qualities to the base metal. It is then coated with a silicon or a glasslike type material and baked at temperatures of 1400 to 1600°F (760 to 870°C). The first or ground coat is generally blueblack in color and provides the bond to the metal. Additional coats are applied and fired to obtain white or colored surfaces. The specifications for this material should state that not less than three coats will be accepted without runs, checks, or other imperfections. Vitreous enamel steel is used on refrigerators, ovens, and other large pieces of equipment where surfaces are large, and where economy, durability, cleanability, and a noncorrosive surface are desired. It has the disadvantage of chipping or crazing. Cast iron is sometimes covered with a heavy coating of vitreous enamel and used for plumbing fixtures.

Full pickled sheet steel is sometimes covered with zinc and used for making sinks, tables, and other equipment. **Galvaneal** or galvanized iron, as it is called, may not however be used as a food contact surface for acidic food because the zinc may come out into the food and be potentially toxic. The electrogalvanizing process is preferred, but some pieces may be dipped in two coats of hot galvanizing compounds. The compound should be approximately 98% zinc, but a small quantity of copper may be added to retard the rusting of the iron base. A total coating of about 2 oz of compound per square foot is usually satisfactory. All surfaces should be completely covered with the coating. Sheets of galvanized material may be used for equipment fabrication, but this is not as satisfactory as equipment that is made from full pickled steel and then galvanized. If sheet galvaneal is used, it should be open-hearth, copper bearing, heavy hot galvanized material, and the welds should be brushed and recoated with two coats of zinc or aluminum bronze lacquer.

Although galvaneal steel is not as workable as stainless steel, it can be rolled and will take a good weld that can be ground down. The coating is subject to wear, exposing the steel, which will rust, pit, and corrode. Galvanized sinks have a life expectancy of five to seven years, while tables will last longer and shelving a long time. One disadvantage is that china and crockery are given black markings from the zinc. Gauges slightly heavier than those used for stainless steel are usually specified for galvaneal equipment.

Aluminized steel is now being used for baffles, linings, flues, combustion chambers, reflector plates, and element retainers in electric and gas equipment. It has the ability to return about 80% of the heat as radiant heat. Used as reflector material it is as adequate as stainless steel, lighter in weight, and less expensive. It is also being used as a heat reflector where heat must be turned away. It has high heat resistance and structural strength.

Plain or Mixed Metals

Stainless steel is an alloy with good appearance, easy cleanability, and high resistance to corrosion. Stainless steel is a family of more than 60 different iron-based alloys that must contain at least 10.5% chromium. The chromium creates an invisible surface film that resists oxidation (rusting) and makes the material corrosion resistant or "stainless." It is inert chemically, stainproof, ductile, strong, easily welded, and durable. Most of the stainless steels used in foodservice equipment have fairly low carbon and fairly high chromium and nickel content. Stainless steel most often used in foodservices is No. 304 and contains:

- 18% to 20% chromium,
- 8% to 10.5% nickel,
- 0.08% carbon,
- 2% manganese,
- 0.04% phosphorous,
- 0.03% sulfur, and
- 1% silicon.

Because of its 18% chromium and 8% nickel content it is called "18-8" stainless steel. It is more expensive than some other metals, but its durability and other service factors make it desirable in spite of cost.

Stainless steel takes special skill and powerful equipment to fashion because its strength is twice that of **mild steel** (which contains less chromium and more carbon). The high ductility or bendability of stainless steel allows it, however, to shape well in fabrication. It will take a strong weld (where two pieces of metal are joined by melting them together to form a seamless joint), but because of its poor heat conductivity it will warp, bend, or discolor unless a skilled operator makes the weld. Traces of welds should be removed by grinding and polishing.

Oxyacetylene welding is used for 20-gauge or lighter stainless steel. **Acetylene welding** must be done carefully. If it is not, it will cause carburization. **Carburization** is an increase in the carbon content at the surface of the metal. This results in the formation of a very hard top layer that is more brittle than the material underneath. The resulting weld is of poor strength and has low corrosion resistance.

For heavier gauges the arc-type weld is recommended. It is generally not used for metals lighter than 20 gauge because it may cause holes in the metal. **Heliarc welds** (also called "heliweld" or "inert arc" welds) are made with a torch that dispenses helium or argon gas around a single tungsten electrode, eliminating oxygen and thus carburization. This weld leaves only a small bead that saves labor in grinding down.

Welds should be free from pitting, cracking, or other mechanical imperfections. Tack or spot welding or riveting straps under seams and filling with solder should not be permitted. Riveting may be permitted, if necessary, to join equipment by **field joints,** a joint made at the point of installation, although it is sometimes possible to do heliarc welds on the job and thus avoid field joints.

In some pieces of equipment, soldering may be done (in soldering, two metals are joined by melting a softer metal to bond them together). In some areas, **soft solder** (with a melting point under 800°F or 427°C) may be permissible. Traditionally, soft solder used to contain lead and tin, but since the Environmental Protection Agency banned the use of lead containing solder in water supply systems, lead-free solder must be used. **Hard solder** (with a melting point over 1,100°F or 593°C) or what is called "silver" solder is an alloy of silver (or sometimes brass). Hard solder is generally preferable to soft solder because of its higher melting point, which creates a stronger bond. Hard solder cannot be used with metals that have low melting points, however. Hard solder also should contain no toxic substances such as cadmium, bismuth, or antimony. All soldering should be securely bonded so it does not crack or chip and should have a smooth surface. **Flux** (used to prevent oxidation and help the solder flow so that the solder will bond properly) should be neutralized and removed because most fluxes are corrosive (see NSF C-2, 3.7.1, and 4.10). It is wise to restrict soft solder to joining only metal or sealing seams between abutting metal surfaces. Whenever possible, equipment surfaces should be one continuous piece obtained by either stamping, extruding, forming, or casting.

No bolt, screw, rivet, stud heads, or nuts should be permitted on food contact surfaces. If absolutely necessary, exposed threads may be used if they are American Standard 60 degrees stub or equal with not more than eight threads per inch and having a major diameter of not less than 5/8 in. (15.88 mm). If the threads are unexposed, they should be American Standard 60 degrees stub or equal.

Monel metal is composed of two-thirds nickel and one-third copper and has the appearance and sheen of stainless steel, although when stainless steel is placed side by side, the monel is readily distinguishable by its coppery color. A small amount of iron may be used to give the monel more strength and durability. Monel takes a high polish like stainless steel. Monel is more susceptible to attack from foods than stainless steel but less so than aluminum. Stainless steel has largely replaced the use of monel today.

Aluminum alloys are inexpensive metals that are commonly used in foodservice equipment. Their light weight and strength make them desirable for mobile equipment. They conduct heat well and are often used for griddles, pots and pans, and other cooking equipment. More than half of all cookware sold today is made from aluminum.

Aluminum sheet is seldom used for tabletops or sinks because it abrades easily. It cleans easily, but it may be attacked by mild alkalis and strong acids and may discolor, especially if iron is present. Aluminum castings are also used for equipment today instead of cast iron castings.

Aluminum can be given a dull, plain, or highly polished finish. Cold-rolling gives a hard, durable finish. One reason that cookware manufacturers have turned so extensively to the use of aluminum is the development of **anodized aluminum.** Anodized aluminum has been treated by electrochemical baths to thicken the oxide film that forms naturally on aluminum. The thickened coating makes the metal harder, more scratch resistant, less likely to have food stick on it, and less reactive with acid foods.

Special treatment is sometimes used to give color to aluminum surfaces. Penetration, however, is only slight, and scratching will show the original aluminum color underneath. The gauge for aluminum and other nonferrous sheet and plate metals is not given in U.S. gauges as listed in Table 18–5 but are listed according to the Brown and Sharpe gauge.

Copper is used when high heat conductivity is desired. At one time it was much used for utensils, but because of its cost, weight, frequent need for relining with tin or stainless steel, and its reaction with foods, it is not used very often. Copper also destroys ascorbic acid. Some copper may still be used for sugar-cooking kettles or where it is desirable for heat to be captured and spread quickly to the food. General cooking with unlined copper is not recommended, however, because the metal dissolves relatively easily in contact with some foods and can cause nausea, vomiting, and diarrhea. Its thickness is specified by ounces per square foot in the same manner as plated metals. A 32-oz copper sheet is 0.0403 in. thick.

Cold-rolled polished steel is a highly durable metal used for tabletops and other equipment. It is not as workable as stainless steel but edges can be rolled down to a 2-in. radius. It rusts and must be oiled or greased when not in use. It is used in inexpensive

TABLE 18–5   *U.S. Standard Gauges for Sheet and Plate Metal and Their Thickness*

U.S. Standard Gauge Number	Decimal (in.)	Sheet Steel (fractions of an inch)	Stainless Steel and Monel (fractions of an inch)
		Plate	
000	0.3750	⅜	⅜
0	0.3215	⁵⁄₁₆	⁵⁄₁₆
1	0.2812	⁹⁄₃₂	⁹⁄₃₂
2	0.2656	¹⁷⁄₆₄	¹⁷⁄₆₄
3		¹⁵⁄₆₄	¼
4		⁷⁄₃₂	¹⁵⁄₆₄
5		¹³⁄₆₄	⁷⁄₃₂
6		³⁄₁₆	¹³⁄₆₄
7		¹¹⁄₆₄	³⁄₁₆
		Sheet	
8	0.1644	¹¹⁄₆₄	¹¹⁄₆₄
10	0.1345	⁹⁄₆₄	⁹⁄₆₄
12	0.1046	⁷⁄₆₄	⁷⁄₆₄
14	0.0747	⁵⁄₆₄	⁵⁄₆₄
16	0.0598	¹⁄₁₆	¹⁄₁₆
18	0.0478	³⁄₆₄	³⁄₆₄
20	0/0359	¹⁄₃₂ [a]	¹⁄₃₂ [a]
24	0.0239	¹⁄₄₀	¹⁄₄₀

[a]This thickness is usually slightly over ½ in.

or temporary equipment. It may be used for supports or areas not subject to friction and covered with two coats of aluminum paint. Steel channels and angles are placed under much stainless steel equipment to give additional support and to reduce the gauge of the stainless steel required.

Black iron is used in some equipment for facings and linings but is mostly used for baking sheets and roasting pans. It may be treated to be rust resistant. It has good heat absorption.

Cast iron is sometimes used for bracings and for supporting stands for heavy equipment. Castings are also used for heavy-duty range tops and griddles. Cast iron is made by pouring the molten metal into molds. It is more porous, less ductile, and breaks more easily than rolled iron. At one time it was widely used for cast iron skillets, Dutch ovens, griddles, and other cooking or baking utensils but stainless steel and aluminum are now used more commonly.

Nonmetallic Compounds

Glass or ceramic equipment is used for food containers especially where metals may give off-flavors. Glass or ceramic equipment is highly resistant to acids and alkalies. Plate glass is used for doors in equipment. Its primary utility is its smooth, impervious surface, low cost, easy cleanability, and visibility. But it does shatter easily. Plate and edges should be protected to prevent chipping, and exposed edges should be ground smooth.

Plastics and fiberglass are being used more and more in foodservice equipment. Heavy, tough, molded drawers have been found satisfactory for some equipment. Plastic is durable, inexpensive, and light in weight. The use of plastics will continue to increase in equipment as they are made more durable.

Plastic can also be laminated or strongly adhered to metals or other hard, durable materials to give a nontoxic, sealed, durable, smooth, nonabsorbent, easily cleanable, sanitizable, nonrusting, and corrosive surface. The advantage of using such **laminated materials** is lower cost. The bottom material gives rigidity and strength to the less expensive laminated materials, such as plastic or enamels. However, where heavy wear occurs, such materials are not suitable. Standard Nos. 35 and 51 of the National Sanitation Foundation should be followed in the specification for such plastic coverings.

Plastic materials intended for use in plumbing should comply with NSF Standards Nos. 14 and 15 as well as with local codes. Plastic materials used for plumbing should be given better support than the more rigid materials formerly used. Their flammability should also be checked.

A wide number of different plastics have been found to be useful in foodservice equipment. Some of these are somewhat flexible and are used for tote boxes, bins, and other containers. More rigid plastics are used for equipment paneling, trays, shelving, and so forth. All plastics should meet the NSF requirements for odor and taste transfer, toxicity, shatter strength, heat, durability, and wear and tear. Additional strength can be gained in some plastic materials by the use of cotton, linen, glass wool, or other fibers.

DESIGN AND CONSTRUCTION STANDARDS

The design and construction of equipment should provide adequate durability and easy cleanability. Where necessary, removal of parts and reassembly should be done with ease. The design and construction should be such as to exclude all vermin, dust, dirt, splash, or spillage. Removable panels can be installed on sealed-off interiors to permit entry for cleaning or repair. Otherwise, panels should be fitted tightly so that vermin and soil cannot enter. Steps, bases, and other substructures should be sealed off against penetration of soil and vermin. Construction requirements vary according to whether food touches a surface or area or is liable to receive splash, drain, or drip from food (food contact surface), or whether the surface or area is a nonfood contact surface. Equipment construction should also permit easy operation, maintenance, and servicing.

Where moisture or condensation is apt to accumulate, care must be taken that drip pans are properly placed to catch this. The pans should be easily removable and cleanable. All drainage devices should be pitched to give good runoff. Strainers should be removable. Where needed, gutters should be installed to carry off grease and moisture. The gutters should be easily cleanable.

Standards of workmanship are an important part of good construction and can only be done by manufacturers who possess good standards and have well-equipped plants and skilled workers. Good construction standards have been established by the National Sanitation Foundation. These should be closely followed in equipment construction. The better equipment manufacturers usually exceed NSF requirements. Equipment brochures and catalogs published by reputable equipment manufacturers can also be used in establishing reliable standards.

Specifications for equipment should state that all corners or angles of 135 degrees or less should be rounded. The intersection of two planes should never have less than a ⅛-in. (3.18-mm) radius. Where three planes meet as in a corner, two can have a ⅛-in. radius but the third must have a ¼-in. (6.36-mm) radius or more. It is not acceptable to use solder to fill in areas (see NSF Standard No. 2, 4.03, p. 2).

Square corners on tables or other similar equipment should not be permitted and all external corners should be rounded, closed, and smooth with all joints and seams smooth and sealed. Raised edges of 3/16 in. (4.8 mm) or more are used where drip or seepage might occur. Other edges are used to give utility, finish, or strength to equipment. Exposed edges and nosing should be rounded on a ¾-in. (19-mm) diameter with the bottom edge of the rounded edge not less than ¾ in. (19 mm) from the edge of the body. This makes cleaning beneath easier and discourages the harboring of vermin. Where edges are turned down so they touch the body, they should be closed against the body.

Edges turned down away from the body should be at least ¾ in. (19 mm) away at their nearest point. Rounded edges should not be less than 1½ in. (38 mm) in diameter. Where openings are made in tops, the edge should be turned down, and if seepage may occur, the edge should be raised at least 3/16 in. (4.8 mm). Usually edges of sink drainboards and other tables where splash occurs are raised 3 in. (76 mm) and then turned down on a rounded edge. Backsplashes that fit against a wall must tightly adhere to the wall about 10 or 12 in. (254 or 274 mm) up. The way surfaces fit or overlap each other should conform to the NSF standard for surface joining. All gaskets and gussets should be sealed (see Standard No. C-2, 4.12, 4.15, and 4.22.1). Figures 18.1 and 18.2 show some acceptable workmanship on gussets and other junctures in equipment.

Channeling or bracing used to give added strength is usually made of iron or steel if not exposed. Body frames may be constructed of angles, pipe, or tubing and then covered with sheet materials. When good channel or bracing is provided, lighter covering materials may be used. Shelving, turned down edges, pipe supports, and so forth give added strength to equipment. Strong welds and sufficient bracing to hold heavy loads are required. Channeling or open angles that offer places for harboring of vermin should be avoided. All tubing should be the welded or the seamless type and easily cleanable, with no crevices at welds. Concealed bolt construction where iron bolts are solidly welded into stainless steel should be specified. Avoid, if possible, bolts and screws on fixtures, specifying, if they must be used, acorn nut type with round heads. "V" type threads on screws used on food contact surfaces are not allowed, except for hot oil cooking or filtering equipment. Counter sink bolt or screw heads, if they must be used, fill and solder, grinding down to a smooth finish. Avoid trim for doors, bodies, and cabinet corners. Use heavier gauge metals instead. Reduce inside framework if possible by using heavier gauge metals.

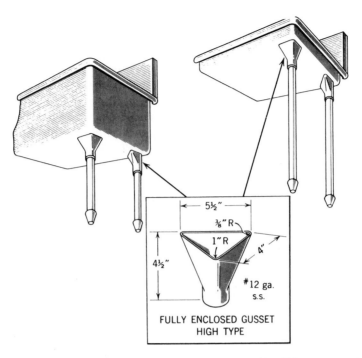

FIGURE 18.1 Fully enclosed gusset.(*Courtesy of S. Blickman, Inc., Weehawken, New Jersey.*)

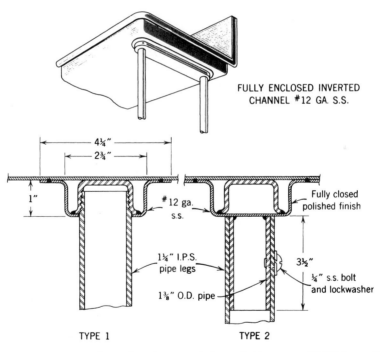

FIGURE 18.2 Fully enclosed inverted channel. (*Courtesy of S. Blickman, Inc., Weekawken, New Jersey.*)

Fixed paneling or sides on equipment should be attached so projections and openings are minimized. Where necessary for inspection and maintenance, easily removable panels may be required. These panels should be of a size and weight appropriate for one person to handle them. All joints and seams in the food contact area should be sealed. Overlapping may be permitted in vertical planes if dirt-catching ledges are eliminated.

Where seepage or condensation might occur, all joints and seams should be sealed and made smooth by welding or soldering. Only when absolutely necessary should exposed threads, projecting screw heads or studs be permitted in nonfood contact areas. Exposed rivet, screw, or bolt heads should be of the low profile type or countersunk with smooth soldering covering. Brazier or modified brazier rivets or pan or oval screws or bolt heads should be used (see NSF Standard No. C-2, 4.13).

The strength of the material depends on the loads the equipment must bear. In general, the gauge and strength of the supporting structure must be suited to the weight of loads and the extent of surface area. Table 18–6 lists some gauges generally recommended for standard pieces of equipment.

Doors and covers should be properly sized and should fit tightly. Doors, except heavy ones, should be removable and, if sliding, should move freely and be hung from the top, rolling on either ball-bearing or nylon glides. Tracks or guides to stop the door should be provided ½ in. (12.7 mm) from either end. Bottom guides should be open, shallow, and wide for ease in cleaning and should be open-slotted so soil will drop through. If not open-slotted, then cleanout holes should be provided. All gaskets should be cleanable and removable. Piano type hinges should not be used in food contact areas. Hinges used in these areas should be easy to clean and simple to take apart. Door vibration or jarring should be eliminated. Protective channels for glass doors should fit tightly and the glass should be at least ¼-in. (6.3-mm) plate fitted into strong channel frames. Single-panel doors have only one thickness of metal and usually need additional brace support. Better construction occurs when double-panel doors are framed into channel-shaped sections, reinforced and the corners welded so that the door is tightly sealed.

TABLE 18–6 *Gauges Commonly Recommended for Equipment*

Item	Recommended Gauge for Top[a]	Framework or Bracing if Required[b]
Bain marie	14	1¼″ × 1¼″ × ⅛″
Canopies or hoods	20	2″ × 2″ × 10–14 gauge
Drainboards	12–14	12-gauge angle, 3″ wide
Sinks	12–14	
Steam tables and counters	12–14	1½″ × 1½″ × ⅛″–3/16″
Tables	12–14	1½″ × 1½″ × ⅛″–3/16″
Urn stand	14	1½″ × 1½″ × ⅛″–3/16″
Wall backings	20–22	1½″ × 1½″ × ⅛″
Trucks	16 (shelving)	
Bodies	20	
Bottoms	18	
Doors	18–20	(may require some)
Shelving	16–18	
Sides	16–18–20	
Legs	10–12 (1⅝″ OD or 2″ × 2″ × ⅛″ or 1½″ × 1½″ × ⅛″	

[a]These gauge listed are recommended for stainless steel. Galvanized steel or steel might take one gauge heavier, that is, if 12-guage stainless steel is recommended, 10 gauge would be required for the other metals.
[b]Framework or bracing may vary according to size of the equipment. Thus for small hoods or canopies no bracing is required and the trim is made slightly heavier than the remainder of the structure, giving sufficient strength. Wall or ceiling supports would also tend to reduce the need for angle support. Sometimes a lighter gauge top is used on equipment with a heavier galvanized metal underneath, such as 20-gauge stainless steel might be put over a 14-gauge galvanized top for an urn stand. Shelving, trim, edging turndowns, and so forth, all affect required amount of support. Integral construction also adds strength. Metal cross bars between the legs of equipment, and so forth give strength. All these factors should be considered in an estimate of required supports.

Avoid trim on doors to make for easier cleaning. If necessary, doors can be insulated against heat loss or heat penetration. Metal doors should usually be 16 gauge, with inside doors braced full length with channel-shaped sections for stiffening and for fastening recessed handles. Limit stops should be provided. Dust-proof racks overhead should be fastened in such a way as to prevent vibration or jarring. Depressed openings in place of handles on doors should be easily cleanable. Swinging doors should be mounted on hinges sufficiently strong to carry the weight of the door and the use it will receive. If possible, doors should be eliminated since their opening and closing is a work motion that contributes little to production time.

If allowed, louvers and openings in the food contact area should be of the drip-deflecting type. They are best located where they will not be subject to splash, splatter, spillage, or overhead drippage. They should be readily accessible and the space behind easily cleanable. Any screen openings should be closed off by 16 mesh or smaller and be removable to facilitate cleaning. A canopied cover should be placed over openings to deflect spillage, splash, or drip. Louvers should be large enough or spaced so they are easily cleanable. All workmanship should leave no burs or sharp edges on openings or louvers.

Drawers and bins should be readily removable and easily cleanable (Figure 18.3). The drawer should be an insert setting on the drawer frame so it can be lifted out and be completely free of the frame. No recesses should be found in the frame that can harbor soil or vermin. The drawer insert should have properly rounded corners and angle junctures (see NSF Standard No. 2, 4.38, and Figure 18.4). Drawers and bins should be removable and easily cleanable. They should be made of galvaneal, plastics, or better. Limit stops or safety-catches, roller-bearing glides or nylon glides, and self-closing drawers are desirable. Bins should be balanced properly so that they are not hazards when closed too quickly. The fronts of drawers and bins are usually 16 gauge or better, with 20-gauge bodies. They should be flanged back approximately ½ in. (12.7 mm). Standard depths are usually 5 in. (127 mm), but others are acceptable. Specify depth to suit the storage required. Some cases have removable bottoms so that they can be hung during work hours where workers can quickly select tools hanging from them. Good construction for bins calls for rounded fronts and fully rounded bottoms. Bodies should be 18 gauge, with 14- to 16-gauge fronts. Tops should be removable.

The use of aluminum alloys, anodized aluminum, covered steel or other metals may be permitted to reduce cost of equipment legs provided they meet strength and sanitation standards. Adjustable pear-shaped feet should be used. These should be 6 in. (152.4 mm) high or more and designed to prevent the accumulation of dirt and the

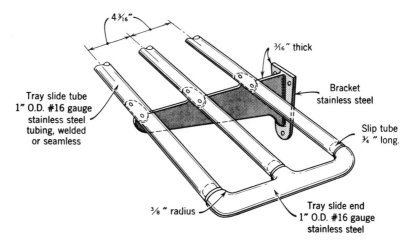

FIGURE 18.3 Specify for tray slide assembly: (1) 16 gauge or better stainless steel tubing not nickel silver tubing, and (2) 30% nickel silver or stainless steel brackets, ground and highly polished. (*Courtesy of S. Blickman, Inc., Weekawken, New Jersey.*)

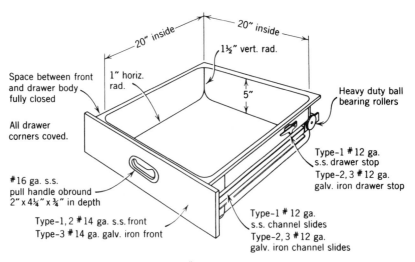

Type-1 All s.s. construction, #18 ga. stn. stl. body
Type-2 Galv. iron, with s.s. front only #18 ga. galv. iron body
Type-3 All galv. iron construction #18 ga. galv. iron body

ROUNDED CORNER WORK DRAWERS

FIGURE 18.4   Rounded corner work drawers. (*Courtesy of S. Blickman, Inc., Weekawken, New Jersey.*)

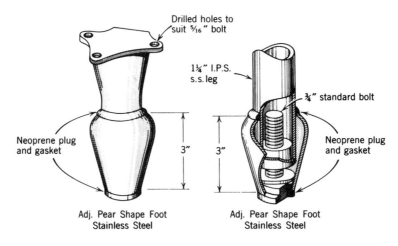

FIGURE 18.5   Adjustable pear-shaped foot. (*Courtesy of S. Blickmen, Inc., Weehawken, New Jersey.*)

harboring of vermin (see Figure 18.5). Any hollow sections on legs should be completely sealed. Legs should be sufficiently strong to permit a minimum of cross bracing. Legs should be strongly bonded to equipment with sealed gussets giving added support (see Fig. 18.1). Legs with an outside dimension greater than a ½ in. (12.7 mm) more than the foot should have a foot that extends at least 1 in. (25.4 mm) below the leg at minimum adjustment. No opening greater than ½₂ in. (0.79 mm) should be permitted between openings of legs and feet.

Whenever possible shelving should be removable and adjustable. It should exclude vermin. Size of the shelving should be such that in closed interiors it can be easily removed and handled. Where shelving must bear heavy loads, bracing, with turned-down edging, is recommended. Undershelves should be 14 to 16 gauge and edges should be turned down 1 to 1½ in. (25 to 38 mm). If the shelving is slatted (which is often preferable for better air circulation), slats should not be more than 1½ in. (38mm) apart.

Mobile shelving is much more desirable than fixed in many instances. If fixed, the back and ends against the wall or panel should be either turned up a minimum of 1 in.

(25.4 mm) and be completely closed along the length, or an open space should be provided between the shelf and wall or side panels wide enough to discourage the lodging of vermin (see NSF Standard No. 2, 4.303 and 4.304). Another alternative is to completely seal the back of the shelving to the area to which it is attached. Mobile shelving is more readily cleanable if slides and shelves are easily removed so they can be taken to a sink for cleaning.

Where wall shelving is used, white metal streamlined brackets with single slotless head tie-in bolts have been found satisfactory. Slatted type shelving is usually constructed of 12-gauge metal with lateral bands at least 1½ in. (38 mm) wide and not more than 1½ in. (38 mm) apart. Additional strength is gained if longitudinal bands are used. It is recommended that in tables 30 in. (762 mm) wide, at least two longitudinal angle braces be welded in. Pipe frame shelving would be 1 in. (25.4 mm) OD (outside diameter), 12 gauge. It should be all-welded construction with welds ground smooth and rounded so that all corners are coved. Flanged corners should be closed tightly to prevent soil accumulation. Diverting shelves placed to catch seepage should be turned up a minimum of 2 in. (51 mm) and made with closed angles and corners. The angles or cleats holding shelving should be removable and easily cleaned. See Figures 18.6, 18.7, and 18.8.

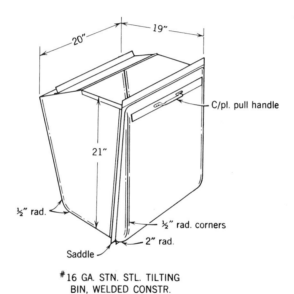

FIGURE 18.6 Tilting bin. (*Courtesy of S. Blickman, Inc., Weehawken, New Jersey.*)

FIGURE 18.7 Intersections of tubular members have generous fillets, are polished smooth, are free of pits or crevices, and are easy to clean. (*Courtesy of S. Blickman, Inc., Weehawken, New Jersey.*)

FIGURE 18.8 Well-formed edge and corner construction. (*Courtesy of S. Blickman, Inc., Weehawken, New Jersey.*)

When shelf brackets are removable and/or adjustable, the support brackets should be readily removable or easily cleanable. Shelving in these should also be easily removable. When shelves act as false bottoms, they should be readily removable and have flanged corners that are closed or are flanged sufficiently to make cleaning easy. All shelving should have either rolled or flanged edges (See NSF Standard No. C-2, 4.24).

Heating strips in enclosed interiors or in equipment should be baffled and guarded against spillage of food. Immersion electric heaters in bain maries and steam tables should be protected. Electrical equipment put into water for cleaning should be tightly sealed so that water penetration does not occur. Insulated areas should be sealed against moisture damage. Equipment that must be immersed in water for cleaning should be able to stand hot water temperatures.

Thermostats on equipment should be accurate to within 3°F (2°C). All thermometers or temperature controls should be easily cleanable and easily visible. Thermometers in cold holding units should be located in the warmest part; in warm holding units they should be located in the coldest part. The reason is that thermometers located in these areas will show that all foods will be at these temperatures or better.

SPECIFICATION STANDARDS[4]

Equipment specifications should define exactly what is desired and the condition for its purchase. Written specifications become an established record, prevent misunderstandings and dissatisfaction, and make it possible upon delivery to determine performance. Precise, clear, and tightly written specifications are desirable. They leave little doubt as to what is desired. Contractors can precisely calculate costs and often give lower prices. Disagreements will be avoided because both parties know what is expected. The terms and language should be common in the trade.

Specifications usually have a section devoted to general provisions and another delineating specific factors desired in individual pieces of equipment. General conditions or general provisions are fairly standard and the American Institute of Architects has forms that usually cover most of the provisions needed.

Specifications should be written simply and concisely. It should give only those details necessary to assure delivery of the equipment desired. Certain words and terms have well-defined meanings in equipment construction; using these can give precision in defining what is desired. Thus, if the word *closed* is used, it means the opening cannot be over ½₂ in. (0.79 mm) but if the word *sealed* is used, no opening at all can exist. In fact, the area may have to be filled in so it is solid. Those who write specifications will find the NSF definitions of equipment terms useful. These terms are also generally understood by the foodservice industry and equipment manufacturers.

---

[4]See Appendix for one example of equipment specifications.

Specifications should represent the minimum quality acceptable and set up exact performance. Under competitive conditions the specifications will represent a close approximation to the maximum performance contractors will deliver, for few can afford to deliver more than specified. Assistance in writing specifications can be obtained from reliable equipment firms, but care should be taken in using such sources to leave bidding free and open and not restricted to one or a few bidders.

In some formal bidding situations, policy prevents the use of proprietary or trade names. Under others, a proprietary or trade name can be used, provided the clause "or equal" is used. The use of the **"or equal" clause** should be avoided. It is recommended that, instead, a list of acceptable products be named and allowance made also for **base bid alternates.** It is difficult to keep up with all the equipment changes and frequently manufacturers are aware of new equipment superior to that named in the specifications. Allowing for base bid alternates gives an opportunity to offer other items that may be as satisfactory as the equipment named. The burden of proof of what is equal is placed on the bidder and the operating member of the team who has the final decision.

If the clause "or equal" must be used, it is recommended that bids be requested from three or more responsible bidders. The following information, taken from the 1973 revision of Specification No. 2215 of the Federal Department of Justice, Bureau of Prisons, should be added:

> Bidders must state clearly in their bid any exceptions or deviations to these specifications and shall submit for evaluation evidence that the exception or deviation is equal or superior to the specifications. Requests for deviations after award has been made will be denied. Should the equipment furnished under the specification be found not to comply with the specifications at the time of final inspection, the contractor shall be notified and shall be given 10 days in which to bring the equipment into full compliance. Payment will therefore be withheld even though the equipment may of necessity be put into operation until compliance is achieved.

In regards to deviations from manufacturer's standard products, the following should be added to the specifications: "The naming of acceptable manufacturers shall not waive necessity for compliance with these specifications. When compliance with these specifications shall require deviations from manufacturer's standard practice, the manufacturer shall deviate from their own standards accordingly."[5]

In the formal bidding system, general conditions are the instructions given to bidders setting forth the conditions under which bids will be received. They should establish the form of the proposal for a bid, which is usually an itemized schedule of equipment listing the unit price of each item, identifying the item by name and number as given on the plan and specifications. If provision is made in the general conditions to accept individual bid items, aggregate bids, or a total bid for all the equipment, it should be so stated. Proposals should be delivered, sealed on or before a specified date, and addressed to the individual or agency as given in the general conditions. Each proposal should be accompanied by a bid bond or certified check; this may be from 5% to 10% of the total bid. Conditions vary and practices and policies common to the area should be ascertained. After the contract is awarded the successful bidder is required to furnish a satisfactory surety bond to guarantee fulfillment of conditions. The bond is then returned when satisfactory delivery occurs.

General conditions should also clarify the relationship of the owner, architect, contractor, and subcontractors to each other. Responsibility should be clarified with regard to the owner's authority, architect's supervision, the obtaining and returning of drawings and specifications, schedule for commencement of work and completion of it, when and how payments will be made as work progresses, working conditions at site, storage

---

[5]These precautions in writing specifications are largely taken from "Or Equal—How to Protect Yourself," No. 9, Middleby Marshall Oven Company.

limits, removal of rubbish, insurance that must be held by the successful bidder (fire, liability, and property damage), general information, and final approval and acceptance. The scope of the work should be established. Contractors usually furnish the utilities used to install equipment. Some public institutions do not pay taxes. If so, this should be stated. Installation may or may not be separate. If it is a part of the contract, then installation standards should be specified and acceptable workmanship described. Connection to utilities should be specified if such installation is required.

Delivery and shipment conditions should be stated. Dates of arrival, method of shipping, and other conditions should be listed. Bid prices should include shipping charges. Exact destination should be stated. Shipment to a central freight depot in a locality may result in additional shipping costs.

Bids for equipment are frequently separated from the general building contract. General conditions should cover only provisions required to obtain and perhaps install the equipment and should not repeat or cover other contingencies. Provision should be made to eliminate from consideration bidders who are not capable of fulfilling the contract. A general condition statement should be made that price alone will not be the sole criterion for awarding bids.

Specific factors for individual items make up the second section of specifications. They may be for custom-built or for standard stock items. They will differ somewhat in the amount of detail required. Specifications for standard stock items are usually quite simple but since nothing is preestablished for custom-built equipment, all factors must be covered and the need for accuracy and detail make the specifications for this equipment longer and more difficult to write.

Specifications for equipment are frequently accompanied by a blueprint of the layout (¼ in. to 1 ft). Electrical and plumbing plans are usually included. These drawings should locate each item and identify it by an item number in the specifications and the proposal for bid. The name or identity of both standard stock and custom-built items should be clearly established. The use of federal specifications and standards as published by the General Services Administration Federal Supply Service may be helpful in establishing identity and details required. The quantities of equipment required should be clearly stated. If custom-built equipment is purchased, quality of workmanship, standards of construction, materials, fittings, and fastenings, should be covered in the general conditions. Samples of work to be done should be required from successful bidders and held for comparison when equipment is delivered. Shop drawings (¾ in. to 1 ft) should be submitted within a specified time after the bid is awarded. These should be approved by the members of the planning team with desired changes noted in red pencil and one copy approved as changed and returned to the bidder. These drawings establish final construction details and should be given careful scrutiny before return.

When specifications for custom-built equipment are submitted, it may also be desirable to submit clear, accurate, two-dimensional perspective drawings of all such equipment. Rough drawings giving essential construction and design characteristics should be made by operation members of the planning team. If necessary, this rough drawing can be smoothed using an AutoCAD computer system or by a professional draftsman. Good drawings tighten specifications and correct omissions and errors. Experience has shown that if sharp, accurate drawings accompany precise, tightly written specifications, better equipment is obtained at a lower cost. See Figures 18.9, 18.10, 18.11, and 18.12.

Standard stock items are usually in storage awaiting demand. Manufacturers publish brochures or catalogs listing essential details of the construction, performance, and so forth, reducing the need to repeat this in specifications. Usually the name of the item and the model number are sufficient to establish the identity of the item desired.

Specifications for standard stock equipment should specify, if applicable, the correct name of the equipment, catalog number, model number, the type of heating or power source to be used (if steam, psi; if gas, type and approximate Btus per cubic foot; if electricity, voltage, phase, AC or DC, and cycles if AC and wattage), plus other required details so that the equipment will satisfy requirements upon delivery. All points

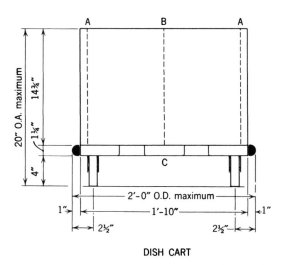

DISH CART

FIGURE 18.9 Rough sketch of mobile dish cart.

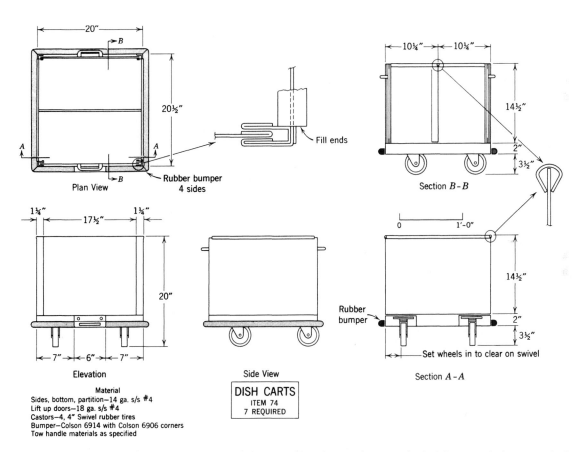

Plan View

Rubber bumper
4 sides

Fill ends

Section *B-B*

Elevation

Side View

DISH CARTS
ITEM 74
7 REQUIRED

Rubber
bumper

Set wheels in to clear on swivel

Section *A-A*

Material
Sides, bottom, partition—14 ga. s/s #4
Lift up doors—18 ga. s/s #4
Castors—4, 4" Swivel rubber tires
Bumper—Colson 6914 with Colson 6906 corners
Tow handle materials as specified

FIGURE 18.10 Smooth drawing of dish cart presented with specifications for bidding. Made from rough drawing shown in Figure 18.9.

affording choice or variation must be covered. Precision is sometimes attempted by using proprietary or trade names.

The specifications for standard stock equipment should contain a request for at least three operating manuals and a spare parts list of the equipment delivered. One of each of these should be kept in the foodservice office, in the maintenance and repair manual where foodservice employees may refer to it, and in the maintenance engineer's department or whomever is responsible for the maintenance of the equipment.

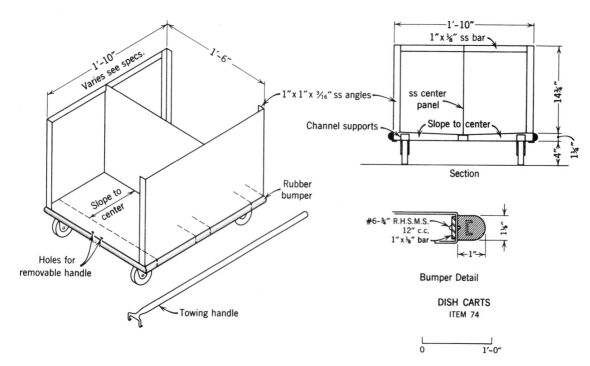

FIGURE 18.11   Shop plans of drawings shown in Figures 18.9 and 18.10.

FIGURE 18.12   Actual dish cart from drawing in Figures 18.9, 18.10, and 18.11. Note that the cart was designed to roll into an undercounter heated area.

CHAPTER SUMMARY

Equipment that has been wisely chosen and well constructed faces the additional requirement of functioning satisfactorily to produce both the desired quantity and quality of food. It must also minimize labor and other operational costs. To function properly, it must be properly installed and supplied with the essential utilities.

Custom-built equipment is generally more expensive than stock equipment, but may be necessary to fulfill unique operational needs. Selection of equipment should be based on need, cost, performance, safety, and sanitation, appearance and design, and general utility values. Best selection is based on the lifetime cost of the equipment. This is called life cycle cost analysis. Other alternatives to the purchase of new equipment include purchase of used equipment, equipment rental, or reducing the need to purchase equipment through the use of processed foods or menu modification.

Equipment needs can be estimated in three ways: industrial engineering analysis of work needs, use of production charts, or calculation based on equipment capacities and menu needs. The simplest method to use is the calculation based on equipment capacities.

Foodservice equipment should be purchased that meets the principles of construction related to design, materials, and construction standards. Equipment should be designed to minimize labor costs. Valuable features to keep labor costs minimal include faster cooking, cook and hold, automated features, flexibility in use, and mobility.

Building costs have also increased. To keep these low, more efficient, compact equipment design, including better use of vertical space, is valuable. Construction costs of the equipment should be kept as low as possible without sacrificing standards or durability. Equipment materials and design should be selected that are easy to clean, strong, and safe to use. Specifications should define exactly what is desired for design, materials, and construction standards.

REVIEW QUESTIONS

Select a foodservice facility for study and analyze each of the aspects pertaining to equipment selection for each item of its equipment from the standpoints presented in this chapter.

KEY WORDS AND CONCEPTS

acetylene welding
AGA
aluminized steel
aluminum alloys
anodized aluminum
ASME
base bid alternates
bonderized
carburization
cast iron
caveat emptor
custom-built equipment
FDA Food Code
field joints
flux
galvaneal
heliarc weld
laminated material

life cycle cost analysis
mild steel
monel metal
NSF, International
"or equal" clause
pickling
plated metals
rebuilt machines
reconditioned machines
soft/hard solder
stainless steel
standard finish
standard gauge
stock equipment
UL
vitreous enamel steel (porcelainized steel)
welds

19

Food Preparation Equipment

This chapter includes information about electric equipment that is used in food preparation. Many of these pieces of equipment have been used for 40 years or more with relatively few changes. Other pieces of equipment have added computerized, automated, and/or programmable controls. The newer technology may improve the quality or quantity of food prepared, increase employee safety, or decrease labor requirements. Some of these factors add significantly to the price of the equipment. Other options may be useful, particularly given the long life of equipment.

In addition, new types of equipment have been developed to accommodate some of the specialty food trends. Good examples would include bagel and pizza dough mixers (which have a motor powerful enough to handle the stiffer bagel and pizza dough) and bagel slicers.

In this chapter, the following pieces of equipment are covered:

- Mixers
- Cutter/mixers
- Spiral mixers
- Food cutters and choppers
- Food processors
- Slicers
- Vegetable peelers
- Meat unit equipment
- Extruders
- Ice cream freezers
- Bakeshop equipment.

MIXERS

Mixers are some of the most important machines used in food services. They are used extensively in bakeshops and the cooking and preparation sections. They can be used to stir, beat, knead, whip, and emulsify. Attachments can be used to operate the mixer motor for chopping, grinding, shredding, dicing, and slicing. Small kitchens may have only one mixer, and if it is mobile, it may be used in various kitchen sections. Small mixers mounted on mobile platforms often have high utility.

Specifications for mixers should be stated as to make, model, size, type of material, and finish of machine and parts. The model number given should refer to a specific manufacturer's design. An itemized list of attachments should also be prepared.

Food mixers can be broken down into three types: the vertical mixer, the vertical cutter/mixer, and the spiral mixer. The vertical mixer is the most popular today. It is also called the **planetary mixer** because of the action of its beater, which rotates on an axis in one direction while it moves in a circle around the inside of the bowl in the opposite direction, similar to the rotation of a planet on its axis while orbiting around the sun. The bowl itself does not rotate. Countertop planetary models are usually sized from 5 to 20 qt. (4.7 to 18.9 L) This size is commonly used by smaller operations. They are generally placed on a table or mobile unit so that the top of the mixer bowl is about the same height as the worktable. Floor models in the upright mixers range from a 30- to 140-qt (28.4 to 132.4 L) capacity but in factory-size production units they may be even larger. Medium-capacity units are generally considered to be 30 to 60 qt (28.4 to 56.8 L) and will satisfy the needs of most large food services. The larger units ranging from 80 to 140 qt (75.7 to 132.4 L) are generally used by high-volume institutional food services and bakeries. If one has a larger capacity mixer, but has combination needs, it is possible to get adapter rings that will support a smaller bowl. See Table 19–1 for more information on mixer capacities.

TABLE 19–1 *Capacities of Food Mixers*[a]

Size Mixer Motor	15 qt ⅓ hp	20 qt ⅓ hp	30 qt ¾ hp	60 qt 1 hp	80 qt 1½ hp	80 or 110 qt 2 hp
Kitchen Materials						
Egg whites	1½ pt	1 qt	1½ qt	2 qt	2½ qt	2½ qt
Mashed potatoes	12 lb	15 lb	23 lb	42 lb	55 lb	60 lb
Mayonnaise (qt of oil)	6 qt	10 qt	12 qt	18 qt	24 qt	30 qt
Meringue (pt of water)	1 pt	1½ pt	2 pt	3 pt	6 pt	6 pt
Waffle or hot cake batter	6 qt	8 qt	12 qt	24 qt	32 qt	32 qt
Whipped cream	3 qt	4 qt	6 qt	12 qt	16 qt	16 qt
Bake Shop Materials						
Angel food (8–10 oz cake)	10	15	22	45	60	60
Box or slab cake	15 lb	21 lb	30 lb	52 lb	80 lb	90 lb
Cup cakes	16 doz	22 doz	33 doz	65 doz	90 doz	110 doz
Layer cakes	15 lb	20 lb	30 lb	60 lb	82 lb	82 lb
Pound cake	15 lb	21 lb	30 lb	52 lb	80 lb	90 lb
Short sponge cake	10 lb	15 lb	23 lb	45 lb	70 lb	70 lb
Sponge cake batter	8 lb	12 lb	18 lb	36 lb	54 lb	54 lb
Sugar cookies	26 doz	35 doz	50 doz	100 doz	115 doz	125 doz
Bread or roll dough	16 lb	25 lb	45 lb	70 lb	105 lb	150 lb
Heavy bread dough	—	15 lb	30 lb	60 lb	90 lb	125 lb
Noodle dough	7 lb	8 lb	10 lb	15 lb	35 lb	35 lb
Pie dough	12 lb	17 lb	27 lb	50 lb	62 lb	75 lb
Pizza dough	10 lb	14 lb	21 lb	42 lb	56 lb	56 lb
Raised doughnut dough	—	9 lb	15 lb	30 lb	45 lb	60 lb
Eggs and sugar (for sponge cake)	6 lb	8 lb	12 lb	24 lb	36 lb	36 lb
Fondant icing	9 lb	12 lb	18 lb	36 lb	52 lb	63 lb
Marshmallow icing	1½ lb	2 lb	3 lb	5 lb	7 lb	10 lb
Shortening and sugar creamed	12 lb	16 lb	24 lb	48 lb	60 lb	63 lb

[a]*Volume Feeding Management,* Conover-Mast Publications, 2056 East 42nd Street, New York, NY.

TABLE 19-2   *Beater Attachment Types*

Attachment	Purpose	Uses	Consistency	Speed
Flat beater	Mixing, creaming, mashing	Mixing cakes or frostings, muffins, cookies, and other prepared dessert mixes, pizza dough (nonyeast type), mixing instant mashed potatoes, mashing cooked vegetables	Medium	Medium
Wire whip	Incorporating air	Whipping eggs, egg whites, or frostings	Light	High
Dough arm or hook	Fold, stretch, knead doughs	Knead bread dough, pizza dough (yeast type), bagels	Heavy	Low
Pastry knife	Cutting in shortening	Mixing pie crusts, pastry shells	Heavy	Low

Motors vary in horsepower from 1/6 to 6 hp. More horsepower is required for larger quantities and stiffer doughs. Bagel and pizza dough mixers, for example, have more horsepower than mixers used for general mixing. Mixers usually operate at three or four speed levels (three is the most common), but some have as many as nine speeds. A gear shift lever generally controls the speed selection, although some mixers have a dial connected to a rheostat that can be set at any point between minimum and maximum speed.

Beater attachments are available either as cast aluminum or stainless steel. The most common are the flat beater (also called a paddle), wire whip, dough arm, and the pastry knife. The purpose, uses, consistency of food, and typical speed for each beater attachment are shown in Table 19–2. Examples of each beater attachment are shown in Figure 19.1. Other beater attachments that are less frequently used include wing whips (with wires attached to two to six "wings" extending out from the center of the beater), which are used to whip materials that are too heavy for the wire whip, and sweet dough hooks (a cross between a dough hook and a flat beater), which are used for doughs that are not too high in guten and somewhat less stiff than the doughs that require a standard dough hook.

Bowls may be made of **tinned steel** or stainless steel. Although stainless steel may cost up to three times more than tinned steel, the added cost may be worthwhile because tinned bowls must be periodically retinned, and they have the added disadvantage of darkening the color of some foods (for example, mashed potatoes). In addition, if an operation prepares acidic products, such as tomato-based sauces, stainless steel bowls are a better choice because tinned bowls are less resistant to the acid.

Most mixers are available with timers, either mechanical or electronic. Several models are also available with programmable controls so that the process can be automated, including changes in speed at preset times. Some large mixers even dump the proper amounts of ingredients into the bowl according to the setting of the controls. When the mixing time is up, the mixer automatically stops, the mixer head is slowly lifted, and the bowl is ready for removal after the platform has been unlocked. For safety, motors should shut off instantaneously when the stop button is pressed, mixers should be installed so they are level to prevent tipping or vibration problems, and large mixer units should be fastened to the floor.

Some mixer bowls are insulated and these should be sealed so they are vermin proof. Rims of bowls should be open and easily cleanable. The moving parts and lower portion of the mixer are considered food contact surfaces and should be made of materials and be constructed to meet NSF standards for such areas. It is a good idea for all mixer types to have sealed-in, permanently lubricated motors. Lubricants and foreign substances should not be able to fall into the bowl. The safety guards on mixers need not be removable. Consideration should be given to available servicing and speed of parts replacement.

The mixing arms should be readily removable and cleanable. Wires on whips should be securely attached to the agitator and contacts between wires should be sepa-

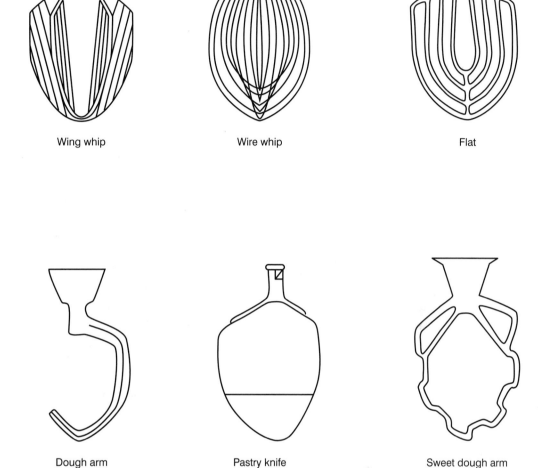

| Wing whip | Wire whip | Flat |

| Dough arm | Pastry knife | Sweet dough arm |

FIGURE 19.1 Beater attachments for mixers.

rable. Attachment points of wires should not be less than two wire diameters. Exposed wound wire fastenings are not acceptable. If rubber or some other plastic material is on the agitator, it should be attached so as to avoid cracks or crevices.

If a grinder or chopper is used as an attachment, it should conform to the standards set for this. For example, knives and plates should be made of suitably hardened high carbon or tool steel. Juicers should be made so they completely drain from the feed screw coupling. Wood plungers for pushing food are not acceptable. They should be made of material that will not break or split off and get into food. The screw cylinder and ring should be made of cast iron or cast iron that is chrome plated or hot tin dipped.

Most surfaces are stainless steel, polished aluminum, or are finished with tough polyurethane or baked enamel. The larger painted units often have a stainless steel backsplash on the front of the column (where food may splash) for ease of cleaning.

Useful options include the following:

- Bowl splash cover
- Wire front bowl guard (which rotates to permit addition of ingredients or removal of agitator)
- Bowl dolly or truck (desirable for moving large-capacity bowls)
- Additional bowls (so that operation can continue while one bowl is being used)
- Pouring chute

- Soup strainer
- Extra high column (permits removal of bowl without removing agitator so bowl changing time is shortened for multiple batches)
- Power-bowl lifter and tilter (important for larger size mixers)
- Lights that reflect into the bowl so one can see the mixing action taking place (lights should be enclosed or shielded)
- Adapters (for converting larger capacity mixers for use with smaller capacity bowls)
- Bowls with hot–cold water jackets
- Bowl scrapers
- Attachments for chopping, grinding, shredding, dicing, and slicing.

Figure 19.2 and 19.3 show two types of mixers.

FIGURE 19.2   A heavy duty 80 qt (planetary) mixer with a bowl guard and power lift to raise and lower the bowl. (*Courtesy of Hobart Corporation, Troy, Ohio.*)

FIGURE 19.3 A spiral mixer used for heavy doughs. A spiral mixer can produce a cooler product in 20 to 30% less time than a planetary mixer. (*Courtesy of Hobart Corporation, Troy, Ohio.*)

CUTTER/MIXERS

The cutter/mixer is a versatile piece of equipment that has a mixing bowl with a motor mounted on the bottom. It is often used just to prepare lettuce for salads, but can be used for variety of purposes. Here are a few of the possible uses:

- Mayonnaise or salad dressing preparation
- Instant potato preparation
- Pizza or bread dough mixing
- Meat loaf mixing
- Bread crumb making
- Ice crushing
- Chopping of cheese
- Chopping of other vegetables

- Cake batter mixing
- Pie dough mixing
- Coleslaw chopping
- Potato salad mixing
- Ham salad mixing.

One of the greatest advantages to the vertical cutter mixer (also called the VCM) is its speed. The shaft turns about 10 times faster than the planetary mixer shaft. Processing times may be ¼ to ⅒ of the time required by a conventional mixer. Some manufacturers make equipment that operates at two speeds (high and low), others only one. The cutting blades are mounted on a removable arm that is attached to the motor shaft projecting from the bottom of the bowl. Two types of blades are available for cutting and kneading purposes. Models range in capacity from 10 to 20 qt (9.5 to 19 L) for countertop models to 25 to 130 qt (24 to 123 L) for floor models. Popular sizes include 20 quart (19 L) and 40 to 60 quart or 37.8 to 56.8 L (for pizza doughs). Many manufacturers make VCMs that can take more than one bowl size with the use of an adapter ring. Bowls may be removable depending on the size of the model. Disadvantages of the cutter/mixer as compared to planetary mixers are that they are noisier, more difficult to operate and clean, and have limited whipping ability.

Cutter/mixers have clamp-down lids and are either made of a transparent material or metal with a slide-back viewing window. Some models are hand operated and others are operated by motor (ranging from 1 to 25 hp). A rotating lever on the top can be used to scrape the sides of the bowl to move the food toward the blades. Models should have an **interlock** with the cover so that the power must be shut off before raising the lid. For emptying, the bowl is simply tilted forward.

Cutter/mixers covers are generally made of polished cast aluminum. Bowls are made of stainless steel or aluminum. The bowl is mounted on a tubular steel frame or cast iron base. Different size and shape blades and attachments are available for different purposes. Narrow blades are used for cutting vegetables, and broader, thicker blades are used for cutting up meats.

Operation is extremely rapid (Figure 19.4). Pizza dough is ready in about one minute, salads take less than 5 seconds, pie dough takes 20 seconds, beef can be chopped in 25 seconds, and cake batters are mixed in 60 seconds. Timers generally permit either continuous operation or up to 5 minutes of operation followed by an automatic shut-off.

Useful options include the following:

- Casters
- Attachments (slicer, dicer, shredder, grater, grinder, cuber, french fry cutter)
- Timer (automatic shut-off is possible with some timers)
- Jogging or pulsing button for momentary on/off action (useful for products that may require a small burst to cut, lettuce for example)
- Two speeds
- Removable bowls
- Strainer basket (allows reuse of water when cutting head lettuce or tender vegetables).

SPIRAL MIXERS

Spiral mixers are used for high-volume dough preparation. Unlike the vertical mixer with a stationary bowl, the bowl rotates in a spiral mixer while the dough arm spins on its axis in a fixed position in the bowl. The largest of the spiral mixers can be up to 245 qt (234 L). Spiral mixers are not as multipurpose as planetary mixers and are generally used only for dough products. The advantage of the spiral mixer for dough products is that they develop the dough at a much faster rate and at a lower temperature than the planetary mixer.

PRODUCTS	MODEL HCM 300	MODEL HCM 450	PROCESSING TIME	PRODUCTS	MODEL HCM 300	MODEL HCM 450	PROCESSING TIME	PRODUCTS	MODEL HCM 300	MODEL HCM 450	PROCESSING TIME
BAKERY ITEMS				**MEAT ITEMS**				Chopped Cheese	10-20 lbs.	15-30 lbs.	30-45 sec.
Bread Dough	12-24 lbs.	18-36 lbs.	2-3 min.	Chopped Sausage	12-25 lbs.	20-40 lbs.	1-2 min.	Chopped Potatoes	10-22 lbs.	16-35 lbs.	15-30 sec.
Cake Batter	15-40 lbs.	25-65 lbs.	2-3 min.	Hamburger	12-25 lbs.	20-40 lbs.	1-2 min.	Cole Slaw	10-20 lbs	20-35 lbs.	30-45 sec.
Cookie Dough	10-20 lbs.	16-32 lbs.	2-3 min.	Liver Paste	12-25 lbs.	20-40 lbs.	2-3 min.	Crushed Ice	10-20 lbs	20-35 lbs.	30 sec.
Fruit Fillings	15-40 lbs.	25-65 lbs.	60-90 sec.	Meat Loaf	12-25 lbs.	20-30 lbs.	1-2 min.	Mashed Potatoes			
Icings/Frostings	21-43 lbs.	25-65 lbs.	60-90 sec.	Mdat Salad	12-25 lbs.	20-40 lbs.	1-2 min.	(Instant Mix)	10-22 lbs.	16-35 lbs.	30-45 sec.
Pie Dough	12-20 lbs.	15-30 lbs.	30-45 sec.					Mayonnaise	10-20 qts.	16-32 qts.	2-3 min.
Pizza Dough	12-24 lbs.	18-36 lbs.	2-3 min.					Potato Salad	20-30 lbs.	25-40 lbs.	1-2 min.
Sweet Dough	12-24 lbs.	18-36 lbs.	2-3 min.	**VEGETABLES/SALADS**		**MISC. ITEMS**		Salad Dressing	10-20 qts.	16-32 qts	2-3 min.
				Bread Crumbs	2-6 lbs.	3-8 lbs.	45-60 sec.	Tossed Salad	4-6 hds.	6-10 hds.	5 sec.
				Cheese Spread	12-25 lbs.	20-40 lbs.	3-4 min.	Vegetable Chunks	5-10 lbs.	10-20 lbs.	15-30 sec.

FIGURE 19.4 A high speed cutter-mixer. The manufacturer's processing times and quantities indicate the high production potential of such a unit. (*Courtesy of Hobart Corporation, Troy, Ohio.*)

FOOD CUTTERS AND CHOPPERS

A food cutter having a rotating bowl with a plow formation on the lid to guide the food under two power-driven knives has been on the market for some time. Its common name is the **buffalo chopper.** It is a useful piece of equipment for general chopping of foods. The fineness of the cut depends on how long the food is allowed to rotate in the bowl. A variety of other grinders, choppers, and specialty cutters are available as well.

For safety it is important that guards on all food cutters and choppers prevent operation when the knives are uncovered. Choose models that can be taken apart for thorough cleaning. Attachments can be obtained for use on a shaft from the motor. These cutters may be procured in bench or pedestal models.

The two-knife cutting assembly and attachment hub should be stainless steel. For the buffalo chopper, the knife and its parts along with the bowl and its cover should be readily removable and when assembled present no areas where food can accumulate. The bowl is generally stainless steel and the bowl cover and housing are aluminum. There should be no square corners, crevices, or exposed threads. (Figure 19.5)

FIGURE 19.5   A rotary chopper (also called a buffalo chopper). Note the rounded corners and edges making for ease in cleaning. They are available with 14 or 18 inch bowl sizes. *(Courtesy of Hobart Corporation, Troy, OH.)*

TABLE 19–3   *Horsepower and Capacity of Buffalo Choppers*

Horsepower	Capacity (lb/min)
⅓	2–3
½	6–7
1	18–20

Cutters should have a safety switch (interlock) that has a guard that makes it impossible to accidentally turn it on. With the buffalo chopper, for example, raising the bowl cover should stop the motor. A red light or other device should also indicate the cutter is working. A motor of about a ⅓ to 1 hp is needed to give heavy-duty, fast action. Bowl rotation should occur about two times a minute. It is wise to specify that the machine should come with an attachment hub so other equipment can be operated with it.

Food choppers or grinders may operate as an attachment on another motor-driven piece of equipment, but for heavy work, independent equipment is preferred. Important selection points are the manner in which the chopper cuts, safety, and sanitary factors. Models are available with grinding capacities as shown in Table 19–3.

The feed screw on choppers and grinders can be made of cast iron or cast steel that is hot tin dipped or chrome plated. Knives and plates are generally stainless steel. The chopper should not allow the accumulation of juices or other substances within the grinding chamber. The holes of plates may be from ⅛ to ¾ in. (3.2 to 19 mm). A feed pan and a plunger should be furnished with the equipment. Chopper cylinders may be horizontal or at a slant to provide gravity flow. Plungers should not be made of wood; a plastic material that does not give any undesirable odor or flavor to the food should be used instead.

Useful options include the following:

- For the buffalo chopper, a three-knife cutting assembly, instead of two knives (increases production by 50%)
- Two-speed motor selection (decreases knife speed, which increases production and lowers processing time)
- Attachments for french fry cutting, dicing, grinding, slicing, grating, and shredding.

FIGURE 19.6   A six-quart food processor that could be used to emulsify, chop, or puree foods. (*Courtesy of Hobart Corporation, Troy, Ohio.*)

FOOD PROCESSORS

Mechanically, these units are similar in many ways to food choppers and cutters. They may be used to emulsify, chop, puree, slice, dice, shred, grate, julienne, and mix. Two sizes of machine are generally available. The smaller size are countertop units and generally use 4- or 6-quart (3.8 to 5.7 L) bowls (Figure 19.6). These units can emulsify and puree, as well as chop and mix. Larger machines are available that slice, dice, shred, french fry, and julienne and can handle up to 90 lb (40.9 kg) per minute. These may be either countertop or floor models depending on size. Floor models are available with casters for mobility. A variety of plates are available that accomplish each of the processing functions. Some units have more than 40 different plates.

Push cylinders should be available and these must meet NSF standards. Interlocks should prohibit operation of the machine until arms, bowls, and covers are properly in place. Food processors generally have aluminum hoppers and housings with stainless steel blades. Plates may be either cast aluminum or stainless steel. Covers are often made of polycarbonate, which allows the contents to be seen without opening the lid. Feeds may be either vertical or at an angle.

SLICERS

Slicers may be completely hand operated, semiautomatic, or completely automatic (Figure 19.7). Hand-operated units are used where the volume is small. In semiautomatic slicers, the knife rotates mechanically by a motor while the carriage is pushed back and forth by hand. Normally they can produce 40 to 60 slices/min. In fully automatic models, electric power drives both the knife and the carriage. Automatic machines may be operated either in the automatic or manual mode. The amount of space (including counter depth) should be measured to make sure that the space allowance is adequate. The carriages on some slicers slide beyond the dimensions of the base.

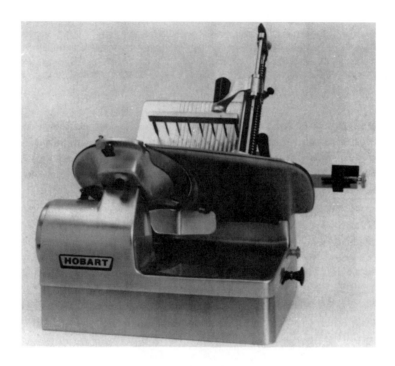

FIGURE 19.7   A modern-type slicer. Note how this unit is constructed for ease in cleaning. (*Courtesy of Hobart Corporation, Troy, Ohio.*)

Hollow grind

FIGURE 19.8   Hollow grind.

Variable-speed machines can be regulated to 1 to 55 slices/min. Some items are better sliced at slower speeds while others may be sliced at faster ones. Slower speeds are used for hot, crumbly foods and the faster ones for firm, solid foods that do not break up easily.

The type of product to be sliced will also affect motor size requirements. Slicers range from ¼ to 5 hp. Slicers intended primarily for slicing cheese should have slightly larger motors. This is not as much of a problem for firmer cheese. In addition, some operators prefer gear-driven motors for tougher slicing needs rather than belt-driven motors.

Knife blade diameters are from 7 to 13 in. (17.5 to 32.5 cm) for most institutional sizes. The diameter of the knife limits the size or diameter of the material sliced to approximately one-half its diameter. If a need for larger diameter blades is anticipated, the larger size should be ordered because slicers cannot be retrofitted later. Larger bladed machines have more versatility but also take up more space. Knives are generally hollow ground (a versatile cutting edge which tapers to a sharp tip on either side of the blade; see Figure 19.8) stainless steel. The steel should take a keen edge and hold it. The knife should be in one piece with a hub for mounting not over 3 in. (7.6 cm) in diameter. The slicer blade should be easily sharpened. Knives should be well guarded and the motor should not work if the guard is not in place. Slicers give variations in slice thickness from a shaved product up to slices that are 1 in. (2.5 cm) thick. The base is generally anodized aluminum.

Most slicers are gravity fed with the carriage on an angle pointing down toward the knife. A weighted plate pushes the food against the rotating blade. A horizontal type slicer is available that is good for slicing juicy items such as rare roast beef. This slicer makes it possible to retain juices that may be as much as 2% of the product. The vertical blade type is less desirable for slicing foods that crumble or fold as they are sliced. For these foods, the angle blade type is preferred.

Some slicers have self-contained portion scales that weigh portions; others have counters that count them. A new model has an electronic portion control system that cuts the exact portion weight desired regardless of variation in size of the material being cut. It turns off automatically when the desired number of portions have been sliced. It can also be operated manually. Portions can be from 0.75 to 9.9 oz. (21.3 to 281 gm). Thickness of the cut can go up to 1¼ in. (3.2 cm). The speed is from 1 to 55 slices/min.

Ease of maintenance and cleaning are factors deserving strong consideration when selecting a slicer. Check ease of disassembly and exposure for cleaning of all parts. Standards prescribed by NSF should be met. The machine should be as safety-proof as possible. A mechanical interlock should require the gauge plate to be closed before the carriage can be removed so that the knife is fully protected during cleaning. Machines should not be operable when guards are not in place. Machines also come with a **no volt release** so that in the event of a power loss, the slicer must be restarted before it continues operation. The machine should be electrically grounded and installed on a firm, level surface. A sharpener should come with the machine.

Useful options include the following:

- Automatic carriages
- Counter (for number of slices that have been cut)
- Rolling stand (so that it may be used in different areas)
- Chute attachments (for irregularly shaped vegetables, such as tomatoes, cucumbers, and onions)
- Specialty slicers that are custom designed to handle only one product, such as tomatoes or onions
- Blade sharpening attachment that is connected to the blade housing
- Stainless steel mesh or Kevlar gloves to improve safety of employees while cleaning the machine
- Juice cup holder
- Slaw tray
- Special locking lift that allows a greater clearance under the machine for cleaning
- Heat lamp
- 15-second automatic shut-off when use stops
- Length of stroke adjustment (allows more efficient slicing of narrow items such as sticks of pepperoni).

VEGETABLE PEELER

Vegetable peelers used to be a fairly common piece of equipment. Today their use has declined. Many potato and vegetable products are purchased preprocessed and/or often served with the skin on. Vegetable peelers are sized from 7- to 60-lb (3.2 to 27.2 kg) capacities. The smallest are table or bench models, while the larger are floor types (Figure 19.9). If desired, they may be mobile so that they can be moved away from the production line when not in use. Automatic timers and adjustable discharge chutes are available. Motors vary from 1/4 hp on the 7-lb (3.2 kg) model to 1 hp for the largest. Right-hand or left-hand operation is possible, but the type desired should be specified. The height of vegetable peelers should be specified so the peeler discharges properly on an inspection table or into a sink (normally 37 in. or 92.5 cm). The production capacity of different sizes operating from 1 to 3 min is given on Table 19–4.

The peeler should be equipped with a safety guard but it need not be removable. The rotating disk should be readily removable. The disk and cylinder area above it should meet food contact surface standards except that the abrasive texture or the cylinder area need not conform to food contact surface requirements for smoothness. The waste strainer should retain most of the waste and not allow it to go into the drainage system. It should be easily removable and cleanable. The machine should be connected to a garbage disposal unit. Back siphonage from the peeler into the water system should not be possible.

FIGURE 19.9   A heavy-duty peeler. This unit would be designed to stand next to a landing table attached to a sink. Loading is from the top. (*Courtesy of Hobart Corporation, Troy, Ohio.*)

TABLE 19-4   *Vegetable Peeler Production Capacities*

Food Item	Bench Model			Floor Model	
	7 lb (¼ hp)	15–20 lb (⅓ hp)	25–20 lb (⅓ hp)	30–33 lb (¾ hp)	50–60 lb (1 hp)
Potatoes	7 lb	15–20 lb	15–20 lb	30–33 lb	50–60 lb
Beets	4–5 lb	10–25 lb	10–15 lb	15–25 lb	25–30 lb
Carrots	4–5 lb	8–12 lb	8–12 lb	15–25 lb	30–45 lb

Note: To obtain kilograms, divide pounds by 2.2.

MEAT UNIT EQUIPMENT

The purchase of preprocessed and prefabricated meat has eliminated the need for meat-cutting units in most food services. Advantages to buying prefabricated meat are cost, convenience, and labor saving. If, however, an operation does have a meat-cutting unit, most will have a power-driven band saw to cut meat and bones. The band saw may also be used for frozen foods. For example, it may be used to divide frozen fish or cut chops from a loin. A typical meat saw will handle meats up to 15 in. (38 cm) high by 13 in. (33 cm) wide. It should be installed in an open area that permits free working around it and removes hazards of bumping or contact with others that are in the area. A landing table or meat block should be nearby.

The blade and wheel cleaner should be readily removable and all areas of the machine should permit easy cleaning. The cabinet, frame, legs, and work surfaces are generally stainless steel. The head unit is generally aluminum. All moving parts except the blade should be enclosed to prevent accidents. In addition, for safety, a pusher plate should be provided to move the food against the saw. Scrap compartments (for collection of waste during cutting) should permit easy cleaning and the tabletop itself should be removable so it can be taken to the sink for cleaning. Many models are floor mounted, but countertop units are also available.

The meat-cutting unit may also have a tenderizer that cuts or pierces meat so it becomes more tender. They may also be used to "knit" together several smaller pieces of meat so that they appear as one solid steak or to "knit" in suet, onions, cheese, or parsley. The machine should be easily cleanable; the cutter and chute should be readily removable so they can be cleaned. Proper safety guards and interlocks should be provided. Normally, slices of meat are fed from the top by gravity to rotating knives inside the machine. The piece of meat comes out the bottom. Cleaning "combs" guide meat between the rollers and automatically prevent accumulation of meat between the knives. Units are available with a stainless steel or chrome-plated finish with stainless steel blades. Some tenderizers also have optional blades to provide scoring of meat. A typical meat tenderizer may be ½ hp.

Patty-making machines are used to make various size and weights of ground meat patties. Some models make up to 1,900 patties an hour. They should make a cleanly formed patty with no sticking or roughness. The machine should be designed for ease of operation and quick cleaning. Disassembly for cleaning should be easy and quick. The machine should not allow the accumulation of food particles in any area. The change over to different mold forms and sizes should be done easily.

EXTRUDERS

Some central kitchens and large kitchens may use extruders to fill pastries or for other purposes. These should be constructed so as to meet the standards of the NSF. They should be easily disassembled and cleaned. All food contact areas should be readily accessible for cleaning. The machine should permit a variation of portion size and also should be able to dispense or extrude materials of different texture and consistency.

ICE CREAM FREEZERS

Freezers for making frozen desserts and drinks operate on the same principle as refrigerators or freezers. The freezing compartment of the machine is surrounded by coils that extract heat from the product to be frozen. A dasher or mixing blade inside the freezing chamber turns and scrapes the frozen material away from the chamber wall. This blade also acts as a whip to incorporate air into the product. Some machines operate at two speeds; one slow speed while freezing and another fast speed to whip the product and incorporate air after the product is nearly frozen. The product is then allowed to flow out of the freezer (at about 17°F or 11°C), a point called **ribbon flow,** so it can be served as soft serve dessert products. Or, this ribbon product can be allowed to flow into containers that are placed in low-temperature chambers (called hardening cabinets) to become a hard-frozen product. Such products should be stored for several days to "ripen" them. Shake machines operate in much the same way as the soft serve machines except that the shakes are served at slightly warmer temperatures.

Examples of soft serve products include ice creams, ice milk, frozen yogurt, frozen custard, sorbet, and sherbet. Machines are available as single-flavor dispensers or twist dispensers, which combine two flavors with a twist effect. Hard-frozen desserts include ice cream, ice milk, frozen yogurt, sorbet, sherbets, and Italian ices. These are often combined with desired flavorings, candy, nuts, or fruit. Manufacturers' stated capacities should be checked carefully. Typical freezers accommodate a batch size of 3 to 10 qt. (2.8

to 9.5 L). Shake freezers are available as single flavor (which either dispense a flavor of the day or dispense a flavor that is later customized by the addition of fruit or syrup flavorings) or multiple flavor (which use a neutral mix and blend the selected syrup flavoring automatically as the shake is dispensed).

It is essential that high sanitary standards prevail in such freezing equipment. All requirements of the NSF should be met and the unit should bear its seal of approval. The equipment should be able to withstand high sanitizing temperatures and all food contact surfaces should be made of noncorrosive materials. Monel should not be permitted. The mix tank should be made of suitable noncorrosive materials (preferably stainless steel) and have a cover that is flanged down at least a ⅛ in. (3.2 mm), fitting snugly over the mix tank opening that is flanged upward ³⁄₁₆ in. (4.8 mm). The cover should slope so any spill or liquid runs off but not into the mix tank. The mix tank should hold the product and deliver it to the freezing chamber at 40°F (4.4°C) or slightly lower. No section of tubing should be over 7.5 ft. (1.2 m) in length and it should be easily removed and cleaned. Manufacturers directions for clean-in-place equipment should be followed carefully.

MISCELLANEOUS BAKESHOP EQUIPMENT

Many operators find specialized equipment, such as **dough dividers** (which portion dough by size and weight), **rounders** (which forms dough into consistent balls for easier handling), and **rollers** or **sheeters** (which flatten dough to a desired thickness and shape), to have sound economic value in labor saving, portion uniformity, and improved quality. A medium-size divider and rounder can shape 1,000 rolls per hour. A motor-driven pie roller rolls pie crust or cookie dough to desired thickness in two operations and in one-third the time required for hand rolling by a skilled worker. The capacity is 200 to 300 per hour. When quantities of sweet breads are produced, a dough roller or sheeter may be used to roll the doughs for final makeup. It may also be used for pizzas, calzones, pita bread, and tortillas, in addition to pastries, danish, and puff pastry. They may be manual or electric, table or floor models. The working length of the roller needs to be considered carefully because they take up a great deal of space. Typical horsepower ranges between ½ to 3 hp. Some can be programmed for 20 different automatic dough handling programs.

Large power sifters are also useful for bakeries and can sift a barrel of flour in 4 to 6 min. Small power sifters have a capacity of 50 lb or 22.7 kg/min. **Proofers/retarders** for yeast dough may also be used. Retarding action in these machines is useful in that they can be switched to retard, recover, and proof so that doughs may be placed in the machine in advance to be ready on a delayed schedule (for example, the next morning). Retarding action is designed to maintain a desired humidity level and refrigerator temperature so that dough is held for an extended period without forming a crust on the surface. Some proofers allow the use of roll-in racks. Others use trays, typical examples hold between 18 (one-door model) and 48 trays (three-door model).

Accurate scales are required in preparing large quantity formulas. In kitchens using 50- or 80-qt (47.3 or 75.7 L) mixers, it is desirable to have a scale that will weigh quickly and accurately from ½ oz to 50 lb (14.2 gm to 22.7 kg). Receiving scales should be able to handle between 50 and 300 lb (22.7 and 136.2 kg). Needed also are **tare adjustment** (which can adjust for container weight so that the product weight only is measured) and a platform size that is large enough for the containers used to measure ingredients.

Beams and counterweight scales requiring adjustment tend to be time consuming. Lightweight spring scales quickly lose accuracy. Electronic digital scales are faster and more accurate, but require a power connection where they will be used (or batteries) and are more expensive, particularly for greater levels of accuracy and greater weight measurements. Other advantages include that they are more compact and take up less counter space. In addition, they are required for **legal-for-trade weighing.** If the scale is used to weigh foods sold to customers by weight (deli meats, cheeses, or salads), the scale must meet legal-for-trade standards. Electronic scales meet these standards, but mechanical scales do not. They are also preferred when precision is required (for example, weighing of steaks).

Purchase considerations should be made on the basis of range of weights to be measured, accuracy requirements, speed and ease of weighing, durability, sanitation, and ability to do easy tare adjustments. Some electronic scales are available with several useful features, including color-coded keyboard with universal symbols, automatic pricing (based on weight or unit, useful for deli operations and salad bars), data storage, and removable stainless steel trays and smooth surface keypads for easier cleaning.

Large bakeshops in some food facilities may require many of the pieces of equipment found desirable by commercial bakers, such as large horizontal mixers, cookie droppers, conveyors, dough chutes, dough hoppers, dividers, molders, panners, pan greasers, automatic depanners, tunnel ovens, and other highly specialized equipment. Consultation with bakery planning specialists is recommended when such an installation is being considered.

CHAPTER SUMMARY

Many pieces of equipment are used in food preparation that have remained relatively unchanged in the last 40 years. Newer additions have included computerized, automated, and/or programmable controls.

Mixers are used extensively in food services. Three kinds are available: planetary or vertical mixers, vertical cutter mixers, and spiral mixers. Grinder or chopper attachments are also available for some models. If food chopping and grinding needs are heavy, food choppers and grinders and processors are also available as free-standing pieces of equipment. Selection should be based on the quality and quantity of production, as well as safety and sanitation factors.

Slicers may be purchased with varying degrees of automation. With semi-automatic units, the knife rotates electrically, but the carriage is moved by hand. With a fully automated model, both carriage and knife are automatically controlled. Different speeds, motor sizes, and knife blade diameters may be purchased.

Vegetable peelers and meat processing equipment are not as commonly used today. If they are used, though, not only is performance important, but safety and sanitation factors as well. Units should be easy to disassemble for cleaning.

Numerous pieces of specialized equipment may be used in a bakeshop. They include dough dividers, rounders, rollers or sheeters, and proofers/retarders. Accurate scales that are easy to use and clean, accurate, and easy to tare are essential. Newer electronic scales have become very common.

REVIEW QUESTIONS

Observe and list the electrical food preparation equipment used in each of the following food operations: fast food, college food service, hospital, school lunchroom, and a fine dining restaurant.

KEY WORDS AND CONCEPTS

buffalo chopper
dough dividers
interlock
legal-for-trade weighing
no volt release
planetary mixer

proofers/retarders
ribbon flow
rollers (sheeters)
rounders
tare adjustment
tinned steel

CHAPTER

20

Cooking Equipment

Specialization of foods in menus and changes in systems of operation have brought about changes in the cooking equipment selected for food operations. Just as there are many types of food preparation, there are specific pieces of equipment best suited to its preparation. Priorities should be carefully examined in relation to its selection. Examination should include such points as quality of food produced, labor requirements, particular adaptation to specific use, speed of heating, control of temperature and humidity, sturdy construction, ease of operation, safety, economy, insulation, ease of cleaning, and suitable capacity for volume required.

OVENS

Probably more change has occurred in ovens in the last 30 to 40 years than in any other kind of kitchen equipment. This should come as no surprise because until this time ovens were pretty much, except for the heat source, the same as those invented by the Chinese in 6000 B.C.

One of the first changes came with the convection oven in which a fan was used to move and distribute heat in a more effective manner. The next step was the introduction of the low-temperature cooking oven, which improved baking performance for meats and some other items. The reel oven made it possible to process more food per square foot of space used. Microwaves, impingers, and infrared ovens made it possible to cook items faster. Induction range tops have provided safer, more efficient cooking for the front of the house. Combination cooking technology in equipment such as combi-ovens has dramatically increased equipment flexibility. Figure 20.1 shows a conventional two-deck oven.

New improvements are also making ovens more efficient and less costly to operate. Better insulation is reducing outer surface skin temperature and heat loss. When the door of a convection oven is opened, the fan stops, which reduces the heat loss. Alternatively, some ovens are said to have a lower heat loss when the oven doors are opened because a wave of forced air is moved across the door opening closing off any heat that might flow out. Better engineering has made it possible to recirculate hot air and combustion gases so as to extract more heat from them. Automatic dampers now close when a gas or oil burning oven stops firing since there is no need to exhaust combustion gases. This closed damper prevents the loss of heat that used to occur in old

FIGURE 20.1   A standard two-deck, six pan per deck, oven. Note the windows in the doors, which permit observation of products without the loss of heat when the door is opened for inspection. *(Courtesy of Hobart Corporation, Troy, Ohio.)*

ovens. The dampers open when the gas or oil starts to burn again. Improved transfer of heat from the heat source has also reduced heat requirements.

Oven Construction

Ovens should be supported on completely welded structural steel frames. Panel bodies should provide support. Outside bodies should be 16- to 18-gauge metal attached to the durable, solid-frame support and should have a durable smooth finish. Inner linings should be 18-gauge rust-proof sheet metal, reinforced to prevent buckling or warping. Linings should be chip-proof. Aluminum steel is being used in some ovens with good success—the high reflectance value of the aluminized steel can help reflect heat and reduce heat loss. Oven interiors should be nontoxic and corrosion resistant. Paint or lacquer finishes are acceptable if they meet other requirements. Oven interiors are considered food contact surfaces.

Racks and rack slide supports should be strongly made. Racks should be able to be pulled out one-half to two-thirds of the way without tilting. Where ovens take heavy loads, rollers may be provided in the ovens to make movement in and out easier. The fronts of ovens should be all one piece. Oven decks more than 36 in. (81.5 cm) wide should have 10-gauge shelving and those under this size should have 14-gauge shelving. Tile or ceramic materials in ovens should be mounted on sturdy steel plates.

Gas- and oil-fired ovens must be vented to allow for the escape of combustion gases. Electric ovens may or may not be vented (cook by light and microwave ovens do not need venting). Most electric ovens have their damper exhaust picked up by a hood or other ventilating device. **Automatic dampering** that closes when the gas or oil burner is not operating can save fuel and reduce heat loss. Heat recirculators also save fuel in any oven. The draft pull-through venting is usually sufficient, especially if the stack runs up to the roof and the stack is higher than any surrounding projection—a nearby building may cause a downdraft if it is higher than the stack. The draft stack should be topped with a draft diverter. Fans can be used to pull out air and heat; this should not be necessary if venting is adequate. Check with local codes to ascertain requirements for rails or other items on the top of ovens. Some codes require tightly sealed sides on gas and oil ovens but the panels must be just laid over the top, so that, should an explosion occur, the force will be directed up. Vapor should be directed up with vented air and not allowed to flow back as condensate. It is wise to have a drain in large ovens so that if moisture does collect it will run off.

The type, quantity, and durability of insulating material are important for economy, evenness of heating, and reduction of heat loss. The thickness of the insulating material is not as important as the effectiveness of it. The *k value*—the amount of heat that goes through 1 sq ft of 1-in.-thick material when there is a temperature difference of 1°F—is important. Some manufacturers can fill a thick wall with cheap insulation that soaks up moisture until the insulation is almost worthless, whereas a reputable one will put in only a thin wall of top-grade material that does the job for the lifetime of the oven. Check the skin temperature of the oven when it is operating at high heat. One should be able to touch the outside surface (skin) without harm. Successful insulating materials have been walls of 5-in. (12.5-cm)-thick and front and rear 3-in. (7.5-cm)-thick compressed thermafiber industrial insulating felt of high density, or a thickness in all these places of 8 in. (20 cm) of Grade X diatomaceous well-packed silica. Large ovens should be packed with insulation during installation and should not be prepacked at the factory. Large ovens should also have their hoods installed over them after installation. Walls surrounding insulation should be tightly sealed so moisture cannot enter. Heat loss around doors should be minimized and break strips should prevent heat from flowing out. Handles of doors should be cool to touch or at least below 125°F (69°C).

Ovens may have recessed lights so products can be viewed more easily. These should have heat-proof lamps sheathed or enclosed by shatter-proof, nonfriable (noncrumbling) material.

Doors should be sturdy and contain windows to give a view of the inside. Doors should easily hold 200 lb (91 kg) of weight and be counterbalanced and not spring shut for easy loading/unloading and cleaning. Hinges should be heavy-duty type. Doors should open level with the bottom of the oven or deck.

Ovens having separate compartments may have a Dutch-door type arrangement so one compartment can be opened without disturbing the other part. Sliding doors can save heat and might be useful on some ovens.

Oven chambers should be vented, dampered, and baffled as required. Heat reflectors may be used to direct heat. Controls should be in front and easily accessible to workers. Some have the knobs or dials recessed so that they will not be damaged by mobile equipment. The thermostat should be capable of settings from 150 to 500°F (71 to 260°C). Check thermostats for variation. Old thermostats should not have a variation of more than ±20°F (11°C) and new solid-state thermostats should not have a variation of more than ±3°F (1.7°C).

Most ovens are heated by gas or electricity; oil may be used in some. Gas-fired ovens of several decks may have only one heat source at the bottom. Studies show that recirculation of heat saves on fuel. A ribbon gas burner with stainless steel inserts is more efficient than the round globe type. These ribbon burners should be set in rows along the bottom and the top of the oven; specific distances between rows is decided by the type of heat desired and the kind of oven. If air combustion chambers are used for each row of burners to premix gas and air, greater efficiency is obtained. Burners that mix the air as it comes into the burner fail to do so completely and thus some gas is lost. Heating elements should be warp-proof. Top and bottom heat in ovens should be independently controlled. Different decks should operate separately also.

The size of the oven should be equated to the facility's needs. This is best determined by taking a series of typical menus and calculating the space needed. Both cooking time and loading or unloading time should be considered. Ovens are sometimes rated based on the number of 18- × 26-in. (45.7- × 76-cm) bun pans they will hold. Thus, what is called an eight-pan oven holds eight bun pans. Manufacturers should be consulted as to their **oven sizing** and production capacities but they usually overstate the latter. It is better to purchase a standard size than to have one of special size made. Some operations may think it better to have two 6-pan ovens than one 12-pan because often the second 6-pan oven may not be needed and then a 12-pan one would only be partially filled. It should be remembered, however, that it takes more heat to heat up two 6-pan ovens than one 12-pan one and this must be considered if the demand is more often closer to the 12-pan need.

Another way of sizing ovens is to indicate their production by pounds of bread per hour. Normally, a gas oven produces a pound of bread for every 500 to 600 Btus it uses, while an electric oven uses 375 to 450 Btus for the same thing. Thus, a 120,000-Btu gas oven would produce 240 lb of bread per hour. It would take about a 35-kW electric oven to do the same thing.

Oil- and gas-fired ovens should be ignited with automatic electronic ignition devices instead of pilot lights. These lighters should be AGA (American Gas Association) approved. Electric ovens should have thermostats accurate to ±3°F (1.7°C) of the desired temperature. Thermostats should give this accurate control at least between the temperatures of 150 and 500°F (65 and 260°C). It should be possible to control the temperature of the top and bottom of the oven separately, and all ovens should be equipped with timers. Ovens may also have computer controls that maintain even temperatures, regulate on/off times, change heat levels during the baking cycle to suit the product, and adjust baking time and temperature according to the oven load. An automatic buzzer sounds when baking is finished. If additional items are added to the oven during the baking cycle, the computer compensates for this addition. A digital display reads out the remaining baking time in minutes and seconds. Some ovens are equipped with **thermocouple** units, which are inserted into foods to give interior temperature readings for doneness. A light or buzzer signals when the proper interior temperature has been reached. Lights may come on to signal the end of baking time.

A good oven should rise to 450°F (232°C) within 20 minutes and should have good recoverability. Proper heat circulation is important. Some high efficiency ovens improve heat circulation with wrap-around heating elements, rather than top and bottom elements. Ovens should be able to cool quickly when a drop in temperature is required. Some ovens may also have uneven baking spots when heavily loaded. Nonshatterable, heat-resistant glass doors that are well insulated are preferred by many operators because they allow better observation of products and reduce door opening, which causes heat loss and higher energy costs.

Oven location should be carefully considered. Ovens require ventilation so they should be located under a ventilation hood. Fire suppression should be available. Refrigerated units should be nearby, but not next to the heat source of an oven because of energy efficiency.

Range Ovens

One of the most commonly used ovens, especially in small operations, is the range oven, which is a unit having a cooking surface above the oven. These should be heavy-duty type with sturdy doors and strong shelving. The range oven is generally used for a wide range of work and so it needs good calibration, insulation, and construction. A nonheat-transferring window in the door is helpful.

All racks or shelving, shelf guides, and decks should be removable or be built in such a manner as to minimize collection of food particles and other foreign matter between guides and the wall. If the need for oven racks is unknown for the future, additional racks should be purchased because the price of these may double later. The burners should be readily accessible and removable so they can be cleaned.

Deck Ovens

Deck ovens are the stationary type where one deck sits on top of the other (see Figure 20.1). Separate decks allow different products to be cooked at different temperatures at the same time. Ovens may be stacked up to three high, but often no more than two stacked ovens are preferable for safety reasons (getting food in and out becomes more difficult). They are sized from 1 bun pan to more than 70 bun pans per oven group. They may be platform mounted (on concrete), on wall-supported brackets, on 6-in. legs for floor models, or 4-in. legs for countertop models.

Base-fired gas ovens containing several decks will have the hottest temperature at the bottom and the coolest at the top. Separately fired decks give the best control and most flexibility for broiling (top heat), baking (top or bottom heat), and roasting needs (both top and bottom heat). Multiple heat conduits for base-fired ovens, however, have made it possible to secure more even heating. Gas-fired ovens should have stainless steel interiors, precision thermostats, and a device that, working as a thermocouple, will turn off the gas automatically when the interior of a roast or other item reaches an established temperature. Gas deck ovens are one of the few pieces of gas equipment that require no electricity.

Conventional deck ovens heated by electricity may be heated by elements buried in the bottom or by elements overhead. The elements may be separately controlled. The best heating elements are made from nickel-chrome alloy for the enclosed tubular type with Incoloy protecting sheathing at the top and bottom of the oven deck.

The depth of a deck is important. Ovens with deep decks and shallow height require a **peel** (which looks like a long handled paddle) to remove items. Given the depth of the oven, considerable space may be required to maneuver the peel.

Ovens should permit easy cleaning. Oven decks made of brick or ceramic material (for hearth-baked pizza) should be nonabsorbent and sufficiently hard so they are not harmed in cleaning. Some oven decks are removable for easy cleaning. Spillage should not be allowed to seep down. Wiring and manifolds should be concealed. The entire unit should allow easy access to the mechanical parts and be easily serviced. Availability of spare parts and servicing affects long-term use of the equipment. Flooring for the deck oven should be considered as well. A double-stacked deck oven can weigh more than 1,600 lb (727 kg) and requires a strong, durable, well-supported floor.

Ovens used for meat roasting are usually 12 to 15 in. (30.5 to 78.1 cm) high, whereas those for bakery products are from 4 to 8 in. (11.6 to 23.2 cm) high. Steam sprays can be used to make hard-crusted breads and some other products. If the steam is over 8 psi a pressure reducer valve should be installed. There should be a condensate reservoir and a thermostatic steam trap. Separate steam generators are available to furnish such steam. Pizza ovens are only about 4 in. high (11.6 cm) and are built to operate at high heat. They should be sturdy ovens built to take the high temperatures used (Figure 20.2).

Cook-and-Hold Ovens

Cook-and-hold ovens were introduced in food services in the 1970s, but the concept of low-temperature cooking of meats has actually been used for thousands of years. Cook-and-hold ovens improve the palatability, tenderness (even for less expensive cuts), and juiciness and reduce shrinkage of roasts of meat and poultry beef. Meat cooked in a conventional oven, for example, may lose up to 30% of its weight, whereas shrinkage in a

FIGURE 20.2 A pizza oven is ruggedly built to take the high heat such ovens must use to properly process the product. Heat loss is reduced because when the door is opened, a flow of hot air comes across the door opening, holding in the oven heat. *(Courtesy of Lang Manufacturing Co., Redmond, Washington.)*

cook-and-hold oven is in the range of 5% to 10%. The difference between the two is largely in the form of moisture loss. The oven will also hold foods at a serving temperature for a long time (up to 24 hours, for example).

Two types are available. One type uses natural convection (no air movement) and maintains a high humidity level (90% to 95% humidity) (Figure 20.3). The other type roasts meats at a slightly lower temperature and uses fans to move air for convection-type cooking and lower humidities (30% to 60% humidity). Cook-and-hold ovens can be either gas or electric. They are also available as mobile cabinets. If they are mobile, corner guards and bumpers are recommended.

Such ovens require good insulation and must hold temperatures within a narrow range. In the past, some health boards did not allow the use of cook-and-hold ovens for certain meat items because the temperatures were thought to be too low to thoroughly cook the interior areas. If cook-and-hold ovens are used properly, however, products should meet health code regulations. FDA food codes should be used to guide time and temperature requirements for cooking and holding of meats. Certain products, for example, such as poultry and ground-meat products require higher final cooking temperatures than beef roasts.

Cook-and-hold ovens have limited ventilation requirements and do not necessarily require placement under a hood. Local code regulations should be checked for **ventilation requirements.**

FIGURE 20.3   A convection oven controlled by the computerized control panel shown on the right. *(Courtesy of Lang Manufacturing Company, Redmond, Washington.)*

Convection Ovens

Developed in the 1950s, a convection oven is a fixed or stationary oven with a fan that circulates heat in the oven. It may be operated with or without the fan. When the fan is turned off, the oven operates as a conventional oven. Two methods of air circulation are possible: **turbulence** (or free flow) or **directed** (or controlled flow) circulation. Special circulating flues and baffling have been introduced in some models to give better heat distribution. The coving of sides and corners is also said to help move heat that might otherwise get trapped in these corners.

Advantages of convection ovens over conventional range style ovens are that convection ovens:

- Cook faster,
- Brown well,
- Make better use of the oven cavity,
- Can cook at lower cooking temperatures,
- Are more energy efficient, and
- Are more compact.

FIGURE 20.4 A convection oven with a two-speed fan shown as a single deck, although it may be stacked as a double deck. *(Courtesy of Southbend, Fuquay-Varina, North Carolina.)*

Disadvantages include increased cooking losses, a thick surface layer on some foods, uneven surface effects and cooking in some ovens, blowing around of fragile batters such as meringues (although fans can be turned off), and higher cost.

Convection ovens have a high productive capacity for the cubic area they occupy. A standard full-size convection oven holds five pans. For rack adjustment, 8 to 11 slides are generally provided. Large roll-in types are available that take a rack of 22 shelves loaded with food. Some ovens are divided into compartments to allow for different baking conditions in each compartment. Because the heat is moving, shelving can be closer together than in other ovens. Some units are also available with nonpressurized steam, microwave energy, or cook and hold ability. Convection ovens can be either gas or electric.

A stainless steel exterior is particularly valuable if the oven location will be near grease-producing equipment because stainless steel is easier to clean. Other surfaces include porcelain enamel. An interlock switch should automatically switch off the fan when the door is opened. If this is not available, the fan should be switched off during loading and unloading of product. Quick utility disconnects and casters make it easier to clean around the oven.

Cooking times and temperatures need to be considered carefully because they impact both quality and yield of the products. Generally speaking, as the temperature is reduced, cooking time and meat yield increase and power consumption decreases. As air movement increases, cooking time decreases. Recipes for conventional ovens must be adjusted either for time or oven temperature or both in convection ovens. Temperatures are often set 25 to 75°F (14 to 42°C) lower and cooking times are often one-quarter to one-half less compared to that of conventional ovens.

Convection ovens may be either half size, full size, or roll-in (Figure 20.4). Half-size ovens may hold up to five half-size racks. Full-size ovens dimensions depend on the manufacturer, but generally may hold up to five full-size racks. Large ovens that can have racks rolled into them are used in the largest food services. This reduces time and labor in loading the oven and unloading it.

General rules of thumb for the number and type of ovens required are based on either the number of meals served per day or on the seating capacity. Individual requirements may vary with the type of operation, the flow of customers, and the menu requirements. Typical rules of thumb suggest a half-size oven if an operation prepares 50 to 100 meals per day, a full-size oven for 100 to 400 meals per day, two full-size units for 400 to 750 meals, three full-size units for 750 to 1000 meals, and a roll-in rack oven for 1,000 or more meals per day. Using seating capacity, one standard oven is recommended for 110 seats and two standard ovens for 225 seats.

Combi-Ovens

Introduced in the 1970s in Europe and in the mid-1980s in the United States, combi-ovens offer tremendous versatility in cooking options. Combi-ovens can be used to cook with steam, hot air, or both. In the hot air mode, they may cook at temperatures as high as 575°F and can even be used for oven frying. The dry convection mode is typically used for products such as pizzas, cakes, and cookies. Variable steam modes may be used for hard- crusted breads, seafood, vegetables, and other delicate foods. Rethermalization is also possible with little drying of the product. The combination mode provides moist heat for baking many pastries and breads and for the roasting of meats. It may also be used for thawing and reheating.

Combi-ovens are available as countertop, stacking models, or roll-in models (Figure 20.5). Capacities range from four 12- × 20-in. (30- × 51-cm) pans (for countertop models) to 40 pans (for roll-in models). The use of roll-in carts is particularly useful for cook-chill op-

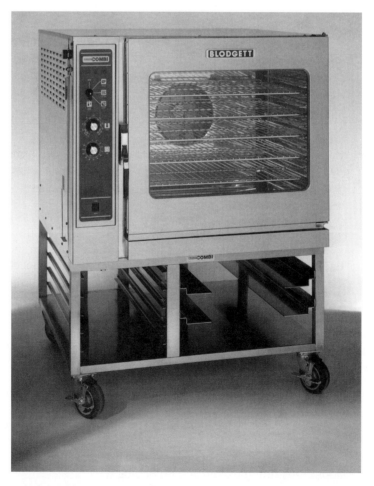

FIGURE 20.5 A single stacking model of combi-oven which can be used in three cooking modes including steam, hot air, or both steam and hot air. *(Courtesy, G.S. Blodgett Corp., Burlington, VT)*

erations. Combi-ovens are available as either gas or electric. All units use pressureless steam that is blown through the cavity. A door interlock is useful to turn off the fan when the door is opened. Steam is produced in a self-contained steam generator and circulated throughout the oven cavity. Because of problems with scale buildup, an **in-line filter** or **water softener** is one way to minimize the need for costly repairs of the steam generator. Another is to use a **flushable generator,** which limits the need for descaling to once a year.

Programmable meat probes decrease the need to continually check for doneness. In addition, combi-ovens may be programmed for 100 different products with up to nine cooking steps to simplify operation. Other useful options include variable selection of amount and temperature of steam used and fan speed (some units may even be used as slow cookers or hot holding units), automatic starts set by timer, self-diagnostics (for trouble- shooting problems), and an indicator light that signals when the steam generator needs cleaning.

Conveyor Ovens

Conveyor ovens have been with us for a long time, but have grown tremendously in popularity during the last 20 years. Although more expensive than deck ovens, they have become particularly popular in bakeries, pizza restaurants, and hot sandwich and bagel operations. All conveyors operate the same way in that foods are loaded onto a moving belt and come out baked at the other end (Figure 20.6). The range of conveyor sizes and different cooking technologies, however, has increased tremendously in the last few years.

Conveyor ovens are available in a wide variety of sizes. Generally size is expressed in terms of width of the conveyor and the length of the heated tunnel. Small countertop

FIGURE 20.6 Two models of high-speed conveyor ovens are shown here. Such ovens with top and bottom heat permit the rapid processing of many products for high-volume units. High-speed conveyor-type pizza ovens of a similar type are also available. *(Courtesy of Middleby Marshall Oven Co., Inc., Morton Grove, Illinois.)*

units have conveyor widths between 14 and 20 in. and tunnel lengths of 18 to 24 in. Large floor units may have conveyor widths up to 32 in. and tunnel lengths between 36 and 70 in. Most conveyor belts are stainless steel wire or mesh.

Different cooking technologies include natural convection, forced convection, infrared, and quartz. Extremely fast cooking ovens are also available that combine both infrared and forced convection cooking. All quartz and infrared conveyor ovens are electric. Natural and forced convection ovens may be either gas or electric. These newer technologies have greatly expanded the number of items that may be prepared in conveyor ovens. The primary advantages given for conveyor ovens are decreased skilled labor requirements (products are conveyed through the machine with no need to monitor them) and consistency (conveyors will turn out the same product with no over- or undercooking).

Forced and natural convection ovens cook between 475 and 550°F (246 and 288°C). Infrared ovens use higher temperatures, between 575 and 650°F (302 and 343°C). Quartz ovens use a very high intensity light and are the newest of the four types. Because of the high-temperature, fast cooking process, the speed of the conveyor is critical. Thickness of the product is also a consideration. Infrared ovens are typically used to cook products that are less than 2 in. thick such as pizza.

Natural convection ovens work by movement of the heated air. Forced convection uses fan-blown hot air to increase the efficiency (similar to a convection oven). In some of the forced convection ovens, the heated air is blown onto the product through small holes as jets or fingers of hot air. Also referred to as **impingers,** the hot air inside impinges or collides with the "boundary layer" of cold air that clings to food to blow it away and speed the cooking process. As an example, a natural convection oven will cook a lobster tail in 13 minutes at 575°F (302°C), a forced air convection oven will cook it in 8 minutes at 375 °F (191°C). Cooking times for infrared and quartz ovens are generally closer to the forced air than the natural convection oven.

Different heat treatments are possible in different parts of conveyor ovens. The longer ovens are more likely to offer this flexibility. In addition, some conveyors allow food to be placed on the conveyor from a side door to heat foods that do not require as long a cooking period (sandwiches heated in a pizza oven, for example). Some machines also have automatic loading and dumping devices.

Smaller conveyor ovens are now being used by food services. (Older conveyor ovens used to be 30 to 35 in. high; newer ovens are 20 in. high.) These conveyor ovens can be purchased in decked design. The most common are single, double, or triple stacked. Some rack ovens move the racks through the oven on a sort of rachet-moving platform. The spiders or carts used should be of tubular, welded construction, built to withstand the high heat without warping or losing strength. The casters should be a durable, high-heat resistant type and the carts should have locks on the casters. Adequate room should be left around the oven to give proper cleaning and also to create some safeguard in case of fire.

Reel Ovens

Reel ovens can move bake shelves around as if on a merry-go-round or ferris wheel (Figure 20.7). They have been used extensively in bakeries for more than 50 years. The latter type is used more since it saves space. Reel ovens can hold 6 to 70 bun pans 18 × 26 in. in size. Some of the smaller ovens are quite compact and save space over deck ovens. The ferris-wheel type should have self-levelers and stabilizers for the shelves. It is better to use the gear-driven model than the chain-driven model. The gear-driven mechanism should be outside the heat area. All reel ovens should be equipped with strong shelving and crossbracing and should be strengthened with support truss rods. They should carry at least 500 lb (227 kg) on each shelf. The shelf surface should be made of expanded sheet metal or solid steel. Reel ovens should have a panel that makes it possible to get into the interior for easy cleaning or repair.

FIGURE 20.7   A large revolving oven used to obtain high production. Note locked entry door on the left which allows a worker to enter and clean when the oven is shut down and cooled. *(Courtesy of Middleby Marshall Oven Co., Inc., Morton Grove, Illinois.)*

Microwave Ovens

Microwave ovens were invented in the 1940s. Their introduction into homes and restaurants increased tremendously during the 1970s and 1980s. Although the microwave oven does not cook all food well, its speed is incredibly useful for some special purposes. Microwaves are usually best used for heating of preprocessed foods, although cooking of many foods is possible in a microwave. Meats, for example, may actually be cooked in a microwave, but different cooking techniques are required compared to conventional ovens. The depth of penetration is from 1.5 to 3 in. (3.7 to 7.5 cm) and foods having greater diameter, such as large roasts, require the use of **standby mode** for heat to be conducted to the full depth. Browning does not occur with microwaves alone. It may be achieved by using infrared lights in the chamber or by post- or prebrowning to achieve a desired appearance and flavor. Other limitations of microwave meat cooking include that the short cooking period does not allow tenderness to develop or blending of flavors. Cooking is sometimes uneven as well. Because of these disadvantages, microwaves are generally not used for the cooking of meat items. On the other hand, combination units that combine convection operation with the microwave have been introduced and these combination units overcome these disadvantages. In addition, metal pans may be used in the combination units unlike standard microwave ovens.

A microwave oven, however, can be highly useful if it is well integrated into certain production systems. A hospital, for example, that utilizes it on a floor to heat hot foods immediately before service may find it very satisfactory. It is often used for quick treatment of foods in fast-food and other operations. In such operations, many foods are prepared ahead of service and held frozen or chilled in portion sizes and then quickly heated for service in a microwave oven. Some use it for quick thawing of frozen foods. Others may use it for heating single-service items, such as slices of pie, rolls, muffins, etc.

Unless the microwave is integrated into a system according to need, it is likely to become an expenditure that gathers dust.

Commercial microwave ovens come in 700- to 2,700-watt models (Figure 20.8). Simple heating of rolls and sandwiches may be done with lower watt models (700 to 800 watts, for example). These are particularly useful at waitstaff stations for quick point-of-service heating. Heating of already cooked, refrigerated food is generally done with models ranging from 900 to 2,200 watts. Fast-food operations may also use these at or near the service line for heating of single portions. Heavy use bulk microwave ovens (2,400 to 2,700 watts) are used to defrost and to cook or reconstitute in bulk. They are not normally used for heating single or small portions. Microwaves manufactured for the home market should never be used in food services. Commercial models are preferred for restaurants because of their power, safety, larger size, and programmability.

Larger microwave ovens may have up to two to four **magnetrons** to improve the reliability and power. Variable power options are essential for versatility. For example, primary cooking is generally done at 90% to 100% power, reheating at 70% to 80% power, defrosting at 30% to 40% power, and warming at 10% to 20% power. Control panels today are typically digital (rather than dials) and computerized so that they can be programmed by touchpad for different foods. Some models also allow tracking of sales of different items (based on the use of a touchpad for a particular food). Doors can be requested to open on the left, right, bottom, or top. Ventilation is generally not required for microwave ovens.

Required cabinet widths for microwaves are approximately 13 to 21 in.; depths may range from 21 to 25 in.; heights range from 14 to 16 in. Higher wattage ovens generally have larger cabinets. Interior size is also important and varies with the manufacturer. Interior compartment size should be evaluated against its intended use (plates versus full-size nonmetallic steam table pans). Large size models are available that will accommodate a large turkey or roast. There is evidence, however, that shrinkage is greater with microwave cooking than with conventional cooking.

For hospitals or other facilities where it would be convenient to heat foods on a served tray, it is possible to obtain a shield that covers the cold food to prevent it from heating while the other foods are quickly heated. The unit is equipped with a thermo-

FIGURE 20.8   A 1,600-watt microwave oven with programmable memory pad selector. *(Courtesy of Hobart Corporation, Troy, Ohio.)*

stat that allows a short bit of heat to build up in the chamber to warm the food as desired and then shut off. In a few moments the heat is on again and then off. This pulsing of the heat cycle gives a more uniformly heated product without some of the excessive heat treatment likely to occur in foods treated in a regular oven.

Government standards have been set for the amount of leakage of energy permitted from microwave ovens. Other safety factors have also been established, such as the door interlock. It is wise also to investigate the availability of servicing and spare parts before purchase. Ease of maintenance, cleanability, safety, and ease of repair should be strong selection factors.

Wood-Burning Ovens

Wood-burning ovens were reintroduced in the 1990s in some specialty restaurants for the cooking of pizza in particular, but also seafood, poultry, vegetables, breads, focaccia, and desserts. Cooking is similar to conventional ovens with the difference that the heat is more intense (up to 750°F or higher) and dryer than a conventional oven. In addition, a smoky wood flavor is added to the products cooked in a wood-burning oven. They are often used as part of the décor or ambiance and are considered one form of display cooking.

Ventilation and exhaust must be specifically designed for the needs of the wood-burning oven. Regular maintenance of the ventilation and exhaust systems must be done more frequently as compared to systems for conventional ovens because of the buildup of creosote and the danger of fires. In 1994, the National Fire Protection Association published the following recommendations for wood-burning (solid fuel) ovens:

- Make-up air requires special attention.
- Solid fuel cooking equipment should be installed on noncombustible flooring materials that extend three feet in all directions from the equipment.
- Solid fuel storage shall not exceed a one-day supply.
- Solid fuel shall not be stored in the same room as the solid fuel cooking equipment.
- Solid fuel shall not be stored in the path of ash removal.
- All solid fuel storage areas shall be provided with sprinkler systems.

Local health and fire departments should be checked for other regulations.

In addition to a higher initial price for wood ovens, wood fuel is also more expensive than other fuels. A reliable supply must be available, and prices will vary greatly. Flooring also must be evaluated. Wood-burning ovens are heavy and require strong floors. Local fire codes should be checked for allowed flooring materials.

Peels are used to move foods in the wood-burning ovens because of the intense heat and the size of oven. A great deal of skill is required to start and maintain fires during the meal period. Skill is also required to move foods around during the cooking process to allow for more even cooking.

Cook by Light Ovens

Introduced in the 1990s, cook by light ovens (developed by the Flashbake Corporation) are one of the newest alternatives for cooking. Cook by light ovens cook at very fast speeds with a combination of infrared and lightwaves produced by quartz halogen lamps that are positioned above and below the product. Examples of its fast cooking include pizza made with a parbaked crust at 45 to 80 seconds (depending on pizza size), pizza made with raw dough at 100 to 150 seconds, nachos and quesadillas at 30 seconds, and cinnamon rolls in 4 minutes.

Cook by light ovens (Figure 20.9) are about the size of a microwave oven and are stackable. In its first installations, ventilation was not required although local health

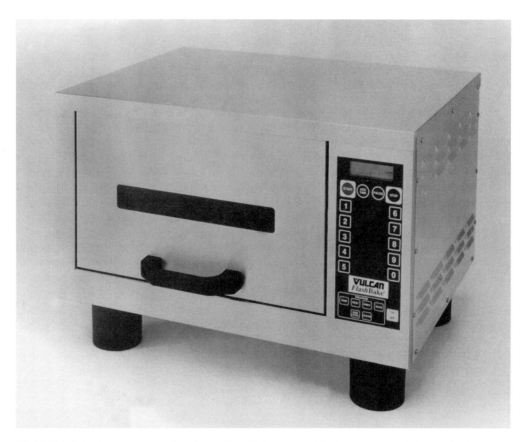

FIGURE 20.9   A countertop electric cook by light oven with observation window which uses seven quartz halogen lamps, four on the top and three on the bottom. *(Courtesy of Vulcan Hart Company, Louisville, KY)*

department regulations should be consulted. Although more expensive to purchase than conventional ovens, cook by light ovens are thought to be more energy efficient because they do not consume power between cooking cycles and because the cooking time is short. They are programmable for the power input and wavelength according to the type of food being cooked.

RANGES AND GRIDDLES

A range consists of a frame used as a mounting for the cooking top and the cooking top itself. Most models include an oven below. The frame should provide sturdy support. At least 16- to 18-gauge metal should be used on all **heavy-duty ranges** with the surface areas of the frame being made of a heavier metal. Heating units should be made of heavy cast iron alloys or other durable material. They may be solid, open, or grills. Surface finish is generally steel, stainless steel, or enamel. Baffling, fins, and venting may be required. Heating should be rapid. A good gas or electrical unit should, in eight minutes from the time it's turned on, bring 1 qt of water at 50°F (10°C) to a rolling boil. Desirable work height of the range will vary, depending on the type of cooking done. For example, ranges intended for use with stockpots must be shorter so that chefs can see into the stockpots.

Gas, electric, and infrared heating units are available. Gas ranges generally cost more than electric, but are less expensive to operate and provide more immediate response to the controls. Infrared models are even more expensive, but maintain the temperature within a few degrees of the dial setting, preheat more rapidly, and maintain a

TABLE 20-1 *Advantages and Disadvantages of Thin and Thick Griddle Plates*

	Thin Plates	Thick Plates
Advantages	Transfer heat quickly	Stronger
	Excellent heat recovery	Less tendency to warp
	Preheat faster	Retain heat longer
	More responsive to temperature adjustments	Distribute heat more evenly
Disadvantages	Tendency to warp	Responds more slowly to temperature adjustments
		Requires more Btus to heat

more constant level of heat with fewer fluctuations. On gas units, thermostat controls (as compared to simple manual controls) are not standard, but are preferable.

Several options in the type of range top are possible. **Open burner tops** or grate tops are the most common option. They are made of cast iron or steel and support the pots above the burner. This type is more energy efficient than closed tops in that there is less metal to heat. Uneven bottoms on pots are not as much of a problem on these burner tops. A sliding tray is generally provided under the open grates to catch food debris and drippings. Gas, electric, and infrared open burner tops are available.

Areas under open top burners should be accessible and easily cleaned. Easy cleaning drip pans that catch spillage, backsplashes that make for easier cleaning, grease guards, and other factors should be checked to see that they are adequate. Cove corners and angles are desirable so grease will not build up there. Grease receptacles should be removable and catch grease without spillage. Troughs and drains should be constructed to adequately carry away all accumulated grease quickly. The grease receptacle should be in full view of the worker, who should be instructed to note when it is full and how to empty it.

A second type of burner top is the **hot top, uniform heat top,** or **closed top.** This type has a plate 12 to 18 in. wide and 0.5 to 1 in. (1.3 to 2.5 cm) thick. Thicker plates will require more powerful burners, but will also even out the heat on the surface. Some units come with separate controls for each 12- in. segment to allow cooking of different products. The advantage with closed tops is that the whole heating surface may be used. Disadvantages include that it is somewhat less energy efficient (there is more metal to heat because of the plate), it takes longer to heat up and cool down, and that heat may be somewhat uneven over the closed top surface in some models.

The third type of surface is a **griddle top.** The griddle top is similar to a closed top, but generally has a stainless steel fence or raised edge around the two sides and the back and a grease trough along the front, side, or rear to scrape excess grease or debris into. Grease troughs in the rear allow more working space in the front of the grill, but are the most difficult to clean. Range tops come in widths from 12 to 36 in. Again, separate controls for each 12-in. segment are desirable.

Griddle or fry top plates may be either "thin" at ⅜ to ½ in. (9.5 to 12.7 mm) or "thick" at 1 to 1.5 in. (25.4 to 38.1 mm) and are generally made of steel. The appropriate choice will depend on the menu and quantity production needs. Operations that griddle many frozen items or those that are constantly cooking at high rates of production (fast-food operations that specialize in hamburgers, for example) require thick griddle plates. The advantages and disadvantages of each type of plate are listed in (Table 20–1).

Chrome surface units are a more recent and expensive option. The griddles have a thin hard coating of chromium on the surface of the steel. They are faster and easier to clean, use less energy, and radiate less heat into the kitchen. They also do not require seasoning with oil because the chromium surface is not as porous as the steel. Their disadvantages include the fact that they require more care and are more likely to be scratched or nicked.

The working top of a griddle should be built in one piece. If that's not possible, then the number of seams should be minimized and closed as tightly as possible. Metal griddle surfaces should have a smooth finish equal to a 125-microinch finish. Spacer or spreader plates should be used to eliminate unsanitary areas. They offer a convenient work surface and are actually required between a fryer and an open top gas range.

Historically, griddles had relatively uneven heat distribution from the center of the griddle to the edges. Newer griddles have improved heat distribution in both gas and electric models by better placement of gas burners, improvements in the electric elements themselves, and the use of more accurate thermostats. Even cooking is still an important purchase consideration, however, and should be evaluated for each model.

Labor-saving tools are available for use at the griddle to reduce time to load and unload items, thus increasing production capacity. For instance, egg droppers are available that will drop a large number at one time. Hotcake dispensers help also. Multiple flippers are available. Production capacities as stated by manufacturers are usually reduced by 40% to allow for time factors that they have not considered. Table 20–2 shows some of the data used by manufacturers that should be decreased 40% when calculating actual production capacities.

The fourth type of surface is called a **ring top** or **graduated hot top.** These are convertible solid tops that allow the top to be used as a solid unit or have one or more circular plates removed to convert it to an open burner cook top for different size pots.

A fifth option is the **French hot plate** (Figure 20.10). It is a solid round plate (diameters range from 6 to 10 in.) that is slightly raised from the cook top surface. French hot plates are used to protect the tubular metal heating elements in electric tops and give more even heat distribution.

In general, closed tops are preferred for continuous heavy cookery production or where many entrees are sauteed to order. Open units are used for speedy, intermittent cookery. Individual types of tops may be combined with units, such as broilers, ovens, fryers, and plate warmers, to meet production needs. Open type units and grills are

TABLE 20-2   *Griddle Capacities for Different Foods*

Menu Items	Griddle Sizes and Units Per Hour		
	24 × 36 in. (60 × 87.5 cm)	32 × 36 in. (80 × 90 cm)	32 × 72 in. (80 × 180 cm)
Hamburger (4 oz or 3½ in. dia. or 114 g and 9 cm dia.)	48	60	90
Tenderloin steak (5 oz or 125 g)	36	45	90
Minute steak (4 oz or 114 g)	18	22	44
Bacon (22 to 32 sli/lb or 454 g)	6 lb (2.72 kg)	7½ lb (3.4 kg)	16 lb (7.3 kg)
Pork sausage portions (1½ oz or 40 g)	45	56	112
Fish cake portions (2 oz or 57 g)	45	56	112
Fried egg portions (2 eggs)	45	56	112
Griddle cakes (4 in or 10 cm dia.)	32	40	80
Fried potatoes (4 oz or 114 g) portions	15–18	20–25	40–50
Ham steaks (5 oz or 142 g)	54	66	132
Liver (3 oz or 85 g) portion	27	35	70
Fried onions (2 oz or 85 g) portion	60	75	150

placed in service lines of cafeterias or behind counter production areas in short-order restaurants. French hot plates are preferred for electric units where many heavy stock-pots are required.

The size and number of ranges should be calculated in terms of menu, volume, and other specialized equipment, available, such as broilers, fryers, and steam equipment. Labor and cooking times are reduced if stocks, soups, and similar items are processed in steam equipment rather than in stockpots on a range top. Range tops are often thought of as modular units and combined in different ways for a variety of needs. One general guideline for determining the number of 36-in. ranges required is based on the number of meals served per day: Under 300 meals may require one 36-in. range, 300 to 500 meals may require two, 500 to 1,000 may require three, and more than 1,000 meals per day may require four. Heavy-duty ranges should usually be selected for normal use. Medium-duty units, which are also called **restaurant ranges,** are used where operational demands are not heavy. Heavy-duty ranges are individual units (32 to 36 in. per section) that are combined to form a bank of machines. Restaurant ranges are built as individual units. Generally the restaurant ranges are smaller (24 to 72 in.).

Mobility in ranges or grills may be desirable. Portable gas counter-type units, for example, are available that may be used for display, buffet, or tableside cooking. Another useful option is the addition of a small broiler or salamander mounted at the top. Other ranges may come with overshelves (useful for storage of plates or tools), warming shelves (generally only available with gas units), or cabinets that are mounted at the back of the range.

Some "smart" electric models are now available that automatically turn down the element when there is no pot on it. Gas ranges are now available with improved systems that actually deliver a mixture of gas and air for better combustion (rather than relying on air available around the burner) so that the burners cook faster, use less gas, and keep the kitchen cooler. Spark ignition is another recent improvement that also helps lower energy costs. Spark ignition eliminates the need to burn fuel continuously to keep the pilot lights lit. Japanese-style teppanyaki models are another recent option. These units heat only a small portion of the griddle and allow the heat to taper off to the edges where it serves as a warm holding area. Grooved griddles are another option that allow the grid lines of a broiler to be simulated. Some of these griddles are made with an attachment that allows cooking on both sides at the same time (clamshell style). Independent thermostats may control the top and bottom. Upper grids are typically set slightly cooler than the main surface grid. The upper grid is generally made of an aluminum alloy and

FIGURE 20.10 A range top showing two French hot plates, a griddle top with backsplash, and an oven below. (*Courtesy of Hobart Corporation, Troy, Ohio.*)

is covered with a nonstick coating. Often these units are smaller in size. They may be used, for example, for finishing of individual grill-type items, such as meats or panini sandwiches. The advantage of the two-sided griddle is that it cooks more quickly because it heats from both sides. Another useful option is ranges that are built with heavy-duty casters. Casters allow for easier cleaning, but are only possible if the ranges are fitted with flexible pipe connections.

Specialty ranges include wok, taco, and stockpot types. Wok, Chinese, or Oriental ranges are useful for rapid individual cookery. Wok ranges have one or more openings or chambers over which woks are placed for cooking at extremely high temperatures. Chambers are available in 10- to 20-diameters. The openings must be sized to be at least 2 in. smaller than the wok pan for a proper fit. Chambers are normally spaced at least 6 in. apart. Wok ranges also contain elements of a sink (faucets are generally specified as one per chamber) that allow the chef to rinse and flush the woks without removing them from the range. Different styles of burners are possible for different styles of cooking. A high back shelf provides an area for woks and utensils. The heat source may be natural, butane, or propane gas. A gas valve at knee level allows the chef to adjust the heat while using both hands to cook. The taco range is similar to the wok range in that the burners are usually set into an open trough, but large pans of cooking oil fit into the trough instead. A stockpot range is another type of range that is more rugged. It is designed for use with one or two heavy stockpots and is set at a lower height (24 in. or 60 cm) so that stockpots are easy to lift on and off.

INDUCTION RANGE TOPS

One of the latest commercial cooking methods to be developed is **induction cooking.** Although the technology was developed 100 years ago, electric induction cooking did not really become available until the 1990s. Below the ceramic cooktop is an **electromagnetic coil.** The coil creates a magnetic field along the ceramic or glass cooktop. When magnetic cookware is placed on top, it creates an electrical resistance to the coil. This resistance excites the molecules in the pan, which start to move so rapidly that the pan gets hot. The actual cook surface never gets hot. Spills on the cooktop are easy to clean up because they also do not heat up. Speed and intensity of heating is controlled by adjusting the magnetic field.

Cookware must be made of magnetic material. Magnetic stainless steel, enameled steel, iron or cast iron pans work, but aluminum, copper, and heat-resistant glass cookware will not unless they have a stainless or ferritic steel base. Flat-bottomed pans work best because pans require direct contact with the induction cooktop to heat.

The advantages include that cooking times are fast (a quart of water goes from room temperature to boiling within 3.5 minutes), it is energy efficient (it only heats the bottom of the pan), it does not have to be preheated, accidental burns from touching the cooktop do not happen (valuable for display cooking), it is easy to clean (the surface is flat and you don't have to wait for it to cool down before wiping clean), kitchens are not heated by ambient heat from the cooktop, and it can be used anywhere (a refrigerator is not heated by the proximity of an induction range).

Many single-burner units are available as portable countertop units. Two- and four-burner tops are also possible. Induction cooktops (Figure 20.11) can also revert to standby mode so that they don't have to stay on full power to resume immediate heating. Ventilation is generally not needed because little heat and grease are given off. For heavy cooking with grease, induction ranges can be used with **ductless ventilation systems.** Local codes should be checked for ventilation regulations.

The latest introductions to induction cooking include heated core pellets for transporting hot plated food to customers in remote locations (hospitals, room service in hotels, etc.) and induction fryers. The fryers use an induction coil embedded in a ferrous

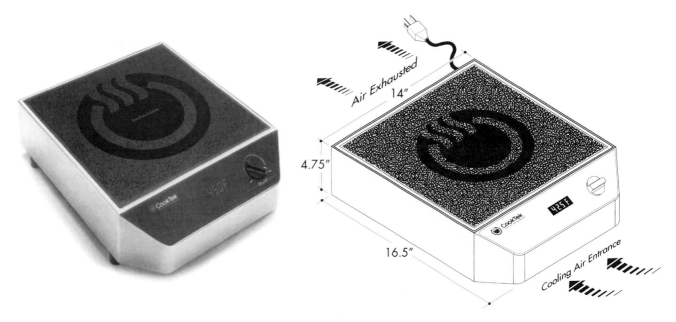

FIGURE 20.11   A single induction cooktop with digital display of cooking temperature and auto shut off to prevent pan from overheating *(Courtesy of CookTek, Chicago, IL).*

tube in the fryer well. When electricity is turned on, it causes electromagnetic agitation, which creates heat and raises the oil temperature for frying.

TILT SKILLETS

Tilt skillets, also called tilting braising pans, provide desirable flexibility in food processing because they may be used as griddles, deep fryers, stew pots, bain maries, and range tops (Figure 20.12). Because of their shallow size, they are a better choice for preparation of items that might be easily crushed in a steam-jacketed kettle. They also simplify cleaning in that they can be used for all steps from browning meat to adding of stock and simmering. Optional perforated pans allow the tilt skillet to operate as a pressureless steamer. It is even possible to bake in the tilt skillet if the product is placed on wire racks about 1 in. (2.5 cm) from the bottom. They operate on electricity, gas, or steam. Some of the higher temperatures are not available if the tilt skillets are steam heated. They should be equipped with a lip and a cover that is **counterbalanced** to prevent it from swinging shut on hands. They should be mounted for easy cleaning around and underneath.

Most tilt skillets vary from 16 to 48 in. (40 to 120 cm) in width, from 24 to 28 in. (60 to 70 cm) front to rear depth, and are 36 in. (90 cm) in work height with a pan depth of 7 or 9 in. (17.5 to 22.5 cm). The tilt mechanism may be operated by a hand wheel or electrically. They should tilt the pan up to 90 degrees from horizontal. Tilt skillets generally come in 10- to 40-gal (38- to 151-L) capacities. Models may be either be countertop or floor models. Many are mounted on an open leg frame with optional casters and quick disconnects for mobility. If casters are used, the tilt skillet must be anchored to the wall so that it won't tip over when tilted. Others are placed above cabinets that offer storage space for pans. Pan bottoms are generally made of aluminum or mild stainless steel. Occasionally they are coated with copper or layered with aluminum for better heat transfer. Other useful options include removable receiving pan support, double or single faucet with swing spout, hot and cold spray hose, timers, and a food strainer for the pouring spout.

FIGURE 20.12   A tilting fry pan or skillet may be used for a variety of cooking. A water connection beside it adds greatly to convenience. *(Courtesy of Market Forge, Everett, Massachusetts.)*

BROILERS, ROTISSERIES, AND SALAMANDERS

Broilers use intense dry heat, provided either by infrared or radiant heating units (Figure 20.13). The most rapid cooking and preheating is by infrared heat. Temperatures will range from 1500 to 1650°F (816 to 899°C). Regular charcoal, wood, gas, or electric units are less efficient but will still produce good results, and they have a long history of use. Conveyor broilers are also possible and are used heavily by fast-food restaurants that serve large volumes of hamburgers. In most cases, broilers cook only one side of the food at a time, but a few models cook food on both sides at the same time. Large volume operations may require a "hotel broiler." Exterior dimensions are usually between 32 and 36 in. (80 and 90 cm) wide, 30.5 and 40 in. (76.3 and 100 cm) deep, and 31 and 61 in. (77.5 and 152.5 cm) high.

Cheese melters and salamanders are small overhead broilers that are usually mounted on an elevated shelf over a range or fry top (Figure 20.14). They are often called backshelf broilers and are generally used to brown au gratin dishes and do other light broiling work. They are not designed for high-volume production. They radiate heat downward and may use gas or electrically heated ceramic or metal elements, or direct gas flame to provide radiant heat. Infrared models produce almost instantaneous heat. They preheat faster, needing only 1 to 1.5 min in contrast to radiant heat units, which may take 15 min or longer. In addition, they are more energy efficient because they need not be kept on while on standby, whereas radiant units must be kept on low. In addition to backshelf mounts, salamanders also come as wall-mounted or countertop units. Wall-mounted, countertop units, floor, and pass-through mounted units are available for cheese melters. Interior size must accommodate the size plates that will be used.

Salamanders and cheese melters are similar except that salamanders are slightly more heavy duty. Cheese melters have a lower Btu rating compared to salamanders. As a result, cheese melters are used to finish off plated foods. In addition to this function,

FIGURE 20.13 A heavy-duty broiler. If the top broiler unit were not there, the unit could have a Dutch oven over the lower broiler, where items that need further cooking could be placed. *(Courtesy of Lang Mfg. Co., Redmond, Washington.)*

salamanders may also be used to broil items that are placed directly on the heavy-duty metal rack. The production rate for a salamander is about one-third that of a larger broiler. They are usually 32 to 36 in. (80 to 90 cm) wide, 16.5 to 22.5 in. (41.3 to 56.3 cm) deep, and 14.5 to 17.5 in. (36.3 to 43.8 cm) high. The dimensions of cheese melters vary tremendously. They range from 24 to 120 in. (60 to 300 cm) deep, 17.5 to 20.3 in. (43.8 to 56.3 cm) deep, and 18.8 to 24 in. (47 to 60 cm) high.

Rotisseries are broiler units that cook food on a rotating spit. Generally, two to seven spits rotate food mechanically in front of one to three burners located in the rear or center of a vertical unit, although rotating hanging baskets, trays, and racks are other options. Batch units or continuous flow cooking is possible. Continuous production units generally require a vertical rotisserie. Rotating skewers are arranged in a ladder formation. Foods nearest the top cook first. As products are removed from the top, the next skewers move up so that raw product can be added at the bottom. Infrared units are also available.

Grease removal is a concern with rotisseries. Some models use a foil lining on the bottom to be changed after each cooking cycle. Some may have removable pans. Others may allow water to be added to the bottom to collect drippings and add humidity to the cooking process. The fat and water are later removed through a drain in the base of the rotisserie.

Glass and other rotisserie surfaces should be easy to clean. Skewers must be easy to remove for cleaning as well. Rotisseries are often placed so patrons can see them operating and be tempted to order the broiled food they are cooking. Internal lighting is available on some models to improve merchandising of the products. These should have

FIGURE 20.14   A salamander does light broiling jobs such as browning and au gratin topping. It is often combined with other cooking units. *(Courtesy of Lang Mfg. Co., Redmond, Washington.)*

heat-proof lamps sheathed or enclosed by shatter-proof, nonfriable (noncrumbling) material. Some units also come with a holding section to keep foods warm after cooking.

Char-broilers use a top grate of cast iron or steel to broil food using one of four types of fuel, charcoal, wood (such as hickory or mesquite), gas, or electricity. Another alternative that is designed to imitate the properties of charcoal or wood is the use of ceramic "briquettes" and pieces of crushed lava rock. They are fired from underneath by gas burners. They are difficult to keep clean and generally must be replaced (along with the cast iron lower grates) several times a year, depending on usage.

Char-broilers provide unique heating in that the meat juices are allowed to drip down onto the heat source during the cooking process to produce a distinctive smoke and flavor. The hot grate produces sear stripes on the food, another characteristic of charbroiled foods. Some models have adjustable grate heights (hotter heat sources such as mesquite wood require a higher grate position) or tilting grate chambers. With tilting grate chambers, the grate tilts slightly so that the majority of the grease runs down the bars into a trough instead of dripping onto the heat source. Enough grease, however, is allowed to drip onto the heat source to produce the characteristic aroma and flavor without producing undue smoke. Another option is a radiant element char-broiler in which metal "tents" cover the gas burners. The dripping fat hits the tents and collects in trays.

Local fire code regulations should be consulted because char-broilers can be a serious fire hazard. Proper ventilation is essential. Some jurisdictions also restrict the type of fuel that may be used. For environmental reasons, some areas do not allow the use of wood fuel sources.

All types of broilers should be easily cleanable. Grease can build up and be burned onto grids, guides, and surfaces. These should be removable and cleanable. Where surfaces are not removable, they should be accessible for cleaning. Areas where vermin might be harbored should be closed tightly. The moving mechanism of the unit should be protected from spillage and the accumulation of food. Drip trays should be removable so they can be cleaned.

Broilers can be wasteful of heat. Therefore, selection should be based on maximum utilization of heat. Some units on the market come to temperature in 3 to 5 min. An infrared broiler achieves broiling temperature in 1.5 min. Others come to broiling temperature in 10 min. Charcoal broilers will generally take longer than this. Flexibility in heating is also desirable. **Zone heating,** for example, will save heating the entire broiler for a few items. Variable temperature controls and separate switches should be provided. Similar savings might be gained through having two smaller broilers instead of one large one, so that only one need be operated when loads are light. Proper concentration and direction of heat is necessary. Reflective linings assist in directing radiant heat. Insulation may reduce heat loss and save energy. Utilization of heat that moves upward can do much to assist in maximizing heat use. For example, a small salamander or cheese melter is often placed above the broiler on which foods are cooked. Some ovens are located above the broiler for baking or for warming foods that are ready for service. Air drafts should not affect flames or cool foods.

Broiler bodies should be made of 16-gauge or better sheet steel rigidly reinforced with sturdy angle supports. Construction should be simple and all welded construction should be specified. Finishes can be those used on ranges. Grids should be rugged, sturdy, and easy to adjust to proper levels from 1.5 to 8 in. (3.8 to 20.3 cm) from the heat source. Grids should pull in and out easily and safety stop locks should be provided. All areas should be easily accessible for cleaning and repair. A sloping grease trough under the grid should catch grease and drippings and conduct them to a grease receptacle. Char-broiler beds should be of heavy construction. The cleanability of the surface of broilers and salamanders should be equal to that of good-quality cast iron.

All heating units and parts should be warp-proof. Some broiler units have lift-out sides for wiping down and cleaning. Wide spaces between grids make it difficult to hold small items and also permit flare-up of flames if grease catches fire. Baffling should prevent heat blast and overly heated sides. The fewer mechanical parts, the less maintenance required usually.

Manufacturers' statements need to be evaluated in terms of specific use. For instance, one claims that a broiler holding nine steaks will broil 90 steaks per hour. If that is true, then the steaks must be very thin or served extremely rare. Another claims that each square foot (0.3 sq m) will produce 20 to 25 lb (9 to 11 kg) of broiled fish, poultry, or steak per hour. Another advertises that on a 600 sq in. (3750 sq cm) grid holding 24 hamburger patties, 420 can be broiled in an hour. This allows slightly less than 3 min of cooking time per patty. Many manufacturers use the surface capacity and cooking time to calculate the quantity that can be prepared, forgetting that there is a load and unload time loss to consider. This is an error frequently made in calculating equipment load capacity.

Good flues are needed to remove smoke, odors, and combustion products. The exhaust blower should be planned to remove a minimum of 500 cfm (14.2 cu m/min) for every sq ft (0.3 sq m) of grid space. Thus a grid 24 × 26 in. or 4.3 sq ft (60 × 65 cm or 0.4 sq m) will require 2150 cfm of exhaust. Exhausts should be covered with filters. Because of flames, exhaust filters should be no less than 48 in. from the food. Filters and ventilation systems represent a considerable fire hazard unless properly maintained and equipped with ducts that have automatic turnoffs or other devices to reduce fire hazards. Local code regulations should be checked. Filters should be removable for frequent washing.

FRYERS

Desirable factors in selection of fryers include tight temperature control, fast recovery time, flavor protection, ease and safety of use, ease in cleaning, sturdiness, and adequate size. Safety is an important factor in selection and also in location of the fryer. The National Fire Protection Association, for example, requires that fryers be located at least 16 in. (41 cm) away from any surface flame cooking equipment. The fryers must be located under an approved hood with a fire suppression system. Local regulations should be checked for other requirements.

Because shortening is such a significant expense in fryer operation and affects product quality so greatly, fryers should be selected that maintain the life of the oil as long as possible. Close temperature control is important as well as convenient and thorough methods of filtering and cleaning.

Good heat recovery is also an important selection criteria. Rapid recovery makes it possible to decrease batch times, increase quantity produced, extend shortening life (because higher standby temperatures are not required), and decrease energy usage (because standby temperatures are lower).

Cold zones are also valuable and are built into most fryers. A **fryer cold zone** is an indented area in the bottom of the fry pot that catches food particles and holds them at lower temperatures to reduce **carbonization** and the subsequent off-flavors and shorter shortening life. Other useful options include melt cycles (which prevent scorching of the shortening and stress on the fryer's heating elements), fry tank covers (which help lengthen the life of the shortening by minimizing contact of the shortening with oxygen and light), food warmer lights (for finished product), and automatic basket lifts.

There are four basic kinds of fryers: deep fat, pressure, conveyor, and air. Deep-fat fryers are the most common and are the traditional type of fryer used in fast-food operations. Countertop models run between 12 and 15 in. (30 and 37 cm) wide and will hold between 30 and 50 lb (13.6 and 22.7 kg) of shortening. They will produce between 25 and 60 lb (11.4 and 27.3 kg) of fries per hour. Floor size models will hold between 35 and 70 lb (15.9 and 31.8 kg) of shortening and will produce between 60 and 100 lbs (27.3 and 45.5 kg) of french fries per hour. Traditionally, fryers were either gas or electric. More energy efficient infrared models were introduced in the early 1980s. Infrared burners are used to heat ceramic plates next to the fry pot, which then transfer heat to the pot and shortening inside. Induction fryers were introduced in the 1990s. The advantages of induction fryers include that they have a colder "cold zone" and cooler flue temperatures because they do not heat the surrounding air. They are also highly energy efficient.

Pressure fryers are typically used by high-volume chicken and fish fast-food operations (Figure 20.15). The pressure in the sealed pot speeds the cooking process and shortens the cooking time. These products may also absorb less fat than deep-fat fryers. A lid seals the fryer tightly after food is added to the hot fat. Fryers should be constructed so that they cannot be opened during the cooking process until after pressure is exhausted. Chicken that normally requires 20 minutes in a deep-fat fryer cooks in pressure fryers in 7 to 9 min. Some manufacturers offer 15-lb (7.3-kg) capacity units with stated production capacities of 90 to 100 lb (41 to 56 kg) per hour. Under actual working conditions with delays and loading and unloading time, capacities may actually be closer to 50 to 60 lb (25 to 27 kg). For flexibility in handling low production periods, some operators find using two smaller pressure fryers preferable to installing one large one. This also permits staggered production. While one is being unloaded another can be loaded, resulting in fresher products and better utilization of labor. One operation found that using a 6-lb and a 15-lb fat capacity pressure fryer met its needs. The capacity of most units is 1 lb of food to every 3 or 4 lb of shortening. In nonpressure fryers this would be 1.5 lb for potatoes and 1.7 for other foods.

FIGURE 20.15 A pressure fryer. The steam developed in the frying under pressure speeds the cooking and also helps to tenderize. *(Courtesy of Henny Penny Corporation, Eaton, Ohio.)*

Conveyor fryers are also used for high-volume operations and are more common in theme parks and concession stands. In conveyor fryers, the product is carried through the fry tank in baskets, and then deposited on to a collection station after cooking. Some fryers produce 100 lb (45 kg) of french fries per hour from a compact countertop unit.

The last type of fryer is the countertop air fryer. These air fryers, or "oil-less hot air fryers" as they are also called, were introduced in the mid-1990s. They were originally introduced for small operations, but larger capacity fryers have since been made available. A typical oil-less fryer batch size is 3 to 5 lb (1.4 to 2.3 kg), takes 4.5 min, and is similar to a 50- lb (22.7-kg) deep-fat fryer. The oil-less "frying" is done in several steps. First, the product is quickly heated until steam is produced. The steam speeds up the heating and prevents the product from drying out. Then the water vapor is vented. Hot air is blown in and browning or crisping occurs. A computer is used to adjust for different loads, sizes of products, and product temperature. One of the primary advantages of such fryers is that they only require a self-contained recirculating hood and do not require the use of grease hoods. Therefore, they can be installed in nontraditional sites. Local regulations should be checked for ventilation requirements.

For determination of fryer requirements, one general rule is that fryers should fry a quantity of product that is one and a half to two times the weight of the fat per hour. Fryer requirements for some fast-food operations are sometimes based on a load of 0.5 lb of french fries per seat per hour. See Table 20–3 for some examples of production capacities of fryers.

Deep-fat fryer baskets should be made of stainless steel or steel covered with 95% or better tin. Welded wire or welded perforated metal can be used. The bottom shelves, if subject to splash or spillage, should have no joints or seams and should have shelf sides turned up 1 in. with corners sealed. Some countertop models do not have built-in drains. This must be considered carefully because they will require manual removal of fat or a reversible pump filtering system.

TABLE 20-3 *Productive Capacities of Deep-Fat Fryers Per Hour*

Item	Fat Capacity of Fryer		
	10 to 15 lb	30 to 40 lb	45 to 60 lb
French-fried potatoes, ⅛ in. thick	21 lb	61 lb	90 lb
Fish fillets, 5 × ½ in.	8–10 fillets	8.8 lb	17 lb
Shrimp	2 lb	5.6 lb	7.75 lb
Chicken, 8-oz portion	4 portions	7 portions	14 portions
1-lb portion	2 portions	3.5 portions	7 portions
Croquettes	2 lb	8.8 lb	14.6 lb
Doughnuts, 2.5-in diameter	16 doz	30 doz	64 doz

Sediment and other material can destroy the efficiency of fat for frying and reduce the quality of the products fried. More attention is being given, therefore, to collection and removal of sediment. Some have deep well indentations that allow the material to settle to the bottom in a "cool zone" of 100 to 200°F (38 to 93°C), which removes it from temperatures that char it. Ease of removing and filtering fat is an important part of fryer selection. A common rule is that the single biggest factor that affects shortening life is how well the shortening is filtered. Frequent filtering may save from 25% to 50% of the fat used and also improve the quality of fried products. If oil volume is large, a filtering machine may be warranted. If the volume is small, simple straining equipment will suffice for removing undesirable materials, but manual filtering is dangerous if not done properly. If an operation can afford a filtering system, it should be purchased. If several fryers are to be used, a portable filter system is an economical alternative. If, however, the operation only has one fryer or has a bank of floor model fryers, the best choice may be to purchase a filter that is matched to the fryers. Such filters fit underneath the fry pots. When used, the shortening is drained into the filter, filtered, and then returned to the fry pots. Filtering may be necessary after every meal or at the end of the day depending on usage. Automatic filtering systems may complete filtering in less than 5 min.

Fryers have also been developed that are semi- to fully automated. Simple automatic controls may include the convenient use of buttons that can be preset and programmed by computer for each product. Fully automatic fryers are intended for high-volume operations. They feature overhead hoppers for holding frozen product that is automatically released in specific amounts. Timers are then used to activate lifts, which remove the finished product from the hot oil and even drain and bag it for serving. Large systems can even be set up for multiple hoppers with different products to be cooked at different times and temperatures. Built-in filter systems complete the process.

A specialty type of fryer is the doughnut fryer. The capacity required should be based on sufficient doughnuts produced to meet peak demands without doughnuts becoming three hours old before sale. Automatic, semiautomatic, or manual machines are on the market. If volume is available and labor can be reduced, the higher cost automatic machine is likely to be worth the price. Ventilation to remove frying odors and cleanability of the machine are important. A hood may be required over the machine to remove unpleasant odors of fat and the volatile fat that saturates surroundings and becomes stale. Most doughnut fryers come equipped with a doughnut dropper. The dropper should be capable of being adjusted to control size. It should make different shapes also, such as French crullers, Bismarcks, Long Johns, etc. Fryers equipped with frying screens should have the screens located between 2 and 3 in. (5 to 7.5 cm) below doughnuts moving over the frying fat. If closer, the doughnuts may stick, crack, or break up. If too deep, the doughnuts may turn over before they should or distort in shape.

STEAM EQUIPMENT

When selecting steam equipment consider (1) the source and character of the steam and (2) the type and capacity of equipment best suited to specific needs. The pressure requirement is important. Some are pressureless, but 5 psi or 15 psi are also used. The steam should be reasonably dry. The condensate may be drained off by having a trap installed close to the reducing valve. Where adequate steam is not available from a central plant, provision may be made for equipment to generate its own steam (**self-contained steam**) or install a boiler near the kitchen (**direct steam**). The latter is preferred if the amount of steam used is great.

Steam generators are categorized according to boiler horsepower (Bhp). Steam requirements vary from one piece of steam equipment to another. One general rule of thumb suggests that 1 Bhp is required for each compartment in the steamer. Many boilers are designed to operate more than one piece of steam cooking equipment, but the capacity of the boiler must be carefully matched to the equipment demands.

Any steam that is used in direct contact with food must be clean or food safe. It must not contain any chemical contaminants. Frequently, a direct steam supply does contain potentially toxic chemicals such as descaling agents, which extend the life of the boiler. In these cases, **non-cooking grade steam** is used to heat potable water in a steam coil heat exchanger unit, thereby creating clean steam without contamination from a central steam supply.

In equipment with self-contained steam, the boilers are either located at the base of the equipment or inside the unit. Scale and lime buildup within these boilers can also significantly shorten the life of the steam generator in regions with hard water. Preconditioning of hard water into the unit is strongly recommended. Manufacturer's recommendations should be consulted for acceptable water hardness and pH levels. Failure to treat water may also invalidate the manufacturer's warranty.

Steamers

When selecting steamers consider size in relation to cooking time and speed to service. Many items, particularly steamed vegetables, should be cooked on a rotation to supply freshly cooked items every 15 or 20 minutes during the serving period. How many persons are to be served per minute? If five portions were served per minute per line of service, 75 orders would be required every 15 min. Both cooking time and handling time to drain, season, pan, and deliver should be counted.

Steamers vary in (1) number of compartments and size, (2) source of steam, (3) type base, and (4) design (Figure 20.16). Widths vary from those in which a 12- × 20-in. (30.5- × 50.8-cm) pan will fit to those taking 18- × 26-in. (45.7- × 66-cm) pans. Compartments may be single or in stacks of two or three (Figure 20.17). Occasionally four stacks may be used, but inconvenient heights for the bottom and top compartments result. Mounting may be on legs, enclosed base, pedestal, or wall mounted. One, two, or three shelves may be in each compartment; they may be stationary or operate to pull out when the door is opened. Those with three shelves are usually designed for 2.5-in.-deep pans or less.

Steamers should be selected with heavy-duty gaskets. When selecting cooking containers, choose those that are suitable for the material to be cooked, will minimize handling, and will permit suitable load size for workers to lift. The use of serving pans can often minimize transfer. Baskets that are tall or flat, requiring only one or two to fit the compartment height, wide or narrow for one or two in the compartment width, and perforated or solid for products with or without liquid, are available. Pans of serving size 2.5 to 4 in. (7.6 to 10 cm) in depth, either solid or perforated, may be obtained.

Steamers should be equipped with timers, safety devices, and pressure gauges (on direct steam models, a pressure gauge should also be installed on the incoming steam

FIGURE 20.16   An array of steam-operated equipment combined with (left) tilting braising pan, two small tilt steam kettles, a large steam kettle with water over, another small tilt steam kettle and two steamers. *(Courtesy of Green Division of the Dover Corporation, Elk Grove Village, Illinois.)*

FIGURE 20.17   A compartment steam cooker with adjustable shelves wide enough for two standard steam table pans placed side by side. *(Courtesy of Market Forge, Everett, Massachusetts.)*

line). They also need an automatic exhaust and a solenoid cutoff. The condensate in compartments should flow to a drain that is trapped near the reducing valve. Condensate is generally eliminated through a floor drain. An air gap is recommended, however, between the steam boiler drain and the floor drain.

Three types of steamers are available. They are pressureless, low pressure, and high pressure. The most commonly used are the pressureless, or atmospheric, steamers. Although not as fast as the high-pressure steamers (the steam temperature is 212°F or 100°C), they have several advantages. One of the primary advantages is that the door may be safely opened at any time. Another advantage is that they are less likely to transfer flavors from one food to another because they are continuously vented and condensate is drained. They are used for a wide variety of food types including fresh vegetables, as well as loose pack frozen and solid frozen block vegetables. See Table 20–4 for examples of cooking times in the different steamers.

Pressureless steamers (Figure 20.18) are sometimes called **convection steamers** because the vast majority use a manifold or fan to force the steam through the cabinet. This improves the efficiency and creates faster heat transfer (similar to that of low-pressure steamers). Pressureless steamers are available as floor or countertop models, gas or electric, and with self-contained or direct steam systems. Typical countertop models will

TABLE 20-4 Examples of Cooking Times in Pressureless, Low-Pressure, and High-Pressure Steamers

Food	Weight per Pan	No. of Pans	Minutes		
			Pressureless	Low Pressure	High Pressure
Green beans	6 lb (2.7 kg)	1–3	10–20	15–20	4–10
		4–6	15–25	20–25	7–15
Carrots	9 lb (4 kg)	1–3	18–21	18–21	6–15
		4–6	21–25	21–25	10–18
Peas	5 lb (2.3 kg)	1–3	5–6	8–10	3–4
		4–6	6–8	10–12	4–6
Potatoes, french fry cut	10 lb (4.5 kg)	1–3	18–21	15–18	7–13
		4–6	21–23	18–20	10–16
Chicken, cut up	8 lb (3.6 kg)	1–3	20–30	18–25	10–15
		4–6	25–35	25–30	15–20
Hamburger, 3 oz.	5 lb (2.3 kg)	1–3	18–22	12–14	8–10
		4–6	20–25	15–18	12–15
Meatloaf	15 lb (6.8 kg)	1–3	40–50	35–40	25–30
		4–6	50–55	40–50	30–35
Turkey, off carcass	10–12 lb	1–3	60–75	50–60	40–45
	(4.5-5.4 kg)	4–6	75–90	45–50	60–75

Source: North American Association of Food Equipment Manufacturers, *An Introduction to the Foodservice Industry*, NAFEM, Chicago, IL, 1997.

FIGURE 20.18 Pressureless steamers ranging in capacity from three to six pans. (*Courtesy of Groen, Jackson, Mississippi.*)

hold three to five 12- × 20- × 2.5-in. (30- × 50- × 6.3-cm) pans. Countertop models require a direct water supply and a drain line. Larger floor models have two compartments and may hold up to 12 to 24 steamer pans and can even be used with 18- × 26-in. (45- × 65-cm) bake pans. Multicavity units are available with multiple boilers that allow greater flexibility in preparing different foods.

Advantages of pressure steamers over pressureless steamers include that they consume less water and energy. Disadvantages include that they are not recommended for cooking frozen block products, they may allow flavor transfer between products cooking at the same time, and they can easily overcook products. Pressure steamers may be either low (5 psi) or high pressure (15 psi).

Low-pressure steamers are often used where all meals must be served at the same time (schools, for example). They deliver steam into the cabinet at 5 psi, which makes the temperature of the steam approximately 227°F (108°C). They are also called compartment steamers and are most often used as floor units with two, three, or four compartments. Each compartment holds up to six 12- × 20- × 2.5-in. (30-× 50-× 6.3-cm) pans. They may be gas or electric, self-contained or direct-steam. The production capacity as stated by manufacturers should be evaluated in relation to needs and cooking times. A broad guide to their selection might be based on data shown in Table 20–5.

High-pressure steamers cook faster because 15-psi pressure (which provides a steam temperature of 250°F or 121°C) is used for cooking, but they actually do not allow the high-volume cooking capacity that compartment steamers do. They can be either countertop or cabinet mounted but all come in the same size. They will only hold up to three 12- × 20- × 2.5-in. (30- × 50- × 6.3-cm) pans. They are best used where rapid cooking of small batches on demand is necessary. They may be electric or gas, direct steam or self-contained.

Combination pressure and pressureless steamers are also available. They are used to first defrost food, then automatically pressurize for cooking. The pressure may be either high or low. Dual-mode steamers are another variation that allow the employee to choose pressureless or pressure cooking via the flick of a switch.

Steam-Jacketed Kettles

Steam-jacketed kettles have been a tradition in both large- and small-volume operations for more than 50 years (Figure 20.19). They can be used to prepare soups, sauces, gravies, stews, and chili. In addition, they may be used to boil pasta, potatoes, eggs, vegetables, and rice. Basically, they can do anything that can be done in a stockpot, but steam-jacketed kettles are faster and have more even heat.

Steam-jacketed kettles contain one kettle inside another with the resulting internal space referred to as the **kettle jacket.** Steam enters the jacket, condenses on the inner wall, transferring its heat to the inner kettle's metal, which is then transferred to the food being cooked. As the steam in the jacket condenses (returns to liquid state), it drains out and is replaced by more steam in direct steam kettles, or regenerated back into steam in self-contained kettles. The steam heats faster and more evenly than cooking done in stockpots because the heat comes up around the sides of the kettle as well as the bottom.

Kettles are shipped from the manufacturer with distilled water (treated with a rust inhibitor) inside. In some cases, anti-freeze is added as well. All self-contained units

TABLE 20-5   *Meals per Hour Cooked in Low-Pressure Steam Cookers*

Number of Meals	Number of Compartments		
200 to 500	1 to 2 compartments	or	1 to 3 compartments
500 to 750	1 to 3 compartments	or	3 to 4 compartments
750 to 1000	1 to 3 compartments or 2 2-compartments	or	4 to 6 compartments
1000 up	1 to 2 compartments/ 500 mls/hr served	or	1 compartment/200 to 300 mls/hr

come with a pressure safety valve that releases steam pressure within the kettle at a preset limit. These pressure safety valves are also used to add more distilled water to the system, if necessary.

The steam entering the jacket determines the maximum operating temperature and cooking speed. Most direct steam kettles operate with 25 lb psi, although large models used in cook-chill operations may use up to 100 lb psi. Most self-contained units use between 15 and 55 lb psi. If cooking includes braising of meats, higher pressure models should be specified. Temperature is controlled by adjusting the thermostat setting or steam valve. Higher steam pressures will create higher temperatures. With 0 psi the temperature of the steam is 212°F (100°C), with 15 psi the temperature is 250°F (121°C), and with 50 psi the temperature is 298°F (148°C). See Table 20–6 for examples of pressure/temperature relations. Direct steam models require a **pressure reducing valve** if the incoming pressure exceeds the kettle jacket rating.

A newer option is the use of oil instead of steam in the kettle, which allows cooking at higher temperatures than in conventional steam-jacketed kettles. Manufacturers claim that less energy is required for cooking and there is no corrosion or scaling. **Thermofluid kettles,** as they are called, are capable of higher temperatures exceeding 350°F (177°C). Thermofluid kettles are available as floor models of 25, 40, and 60 gal (95, 151, and 227 L).

FIGURE 20.19 A steam kettle with a mixer or stirrer. (*Courtesy of Green Division of the Dover Corporation, Elk Grove Village, Illinois.*)

TABLE 20-6   *Pressure/Temperature Relationships in Steam-Jacketed Kettles*

Operating Pressure (lb)	Maximum Temperature
0	212°F (100°C)
2	219°F (104°C)
4	224°F (107°C)
6	230°F (110°C)
8	235°F (113°C)
10	239°F (115°C)
15	250°F (121°C)
20	259°F (126°C)
25	267°F (131°C)
30	274°F (134°C)
35	281°F (138°C)
40	287°F (142°C)
45	292°F (144°C)
50	298°F (148°C)

Source: North American Association of Food Equipment Manufacturers, *An Introduction to the Foodservice Industry,* NAFEM, Chicago, IL, 1997.

Steam-jacketed kettles come in a variety of types, sizes, and styles. They may be gas or electric, countertop or floor or wall mounted (Figure 20.20 and 20.21), direct steam or self-contained. Direct steam countertop models range from 32-oz oyster cookers used for display cooking to 10- to 40-qt (9.5 to 38 L) models. Floor models range from 20 to 150 gal (76 to 568 L). Self-contained models are similar, 10 to 40 qt (9.5 to 38 L) for countertop and 20 to 100 gal (76 to 378 L). One suggested guide for sizing of kettles is shown in Table 20–7.

Some kettles can be tilted (**trunnions**, see Figure 20.22), others are stationary with a **tangent draw-off valve** (positioned horizontally at the very base of the vertical kettle) for draining liquids. Tilting kettles cost slightly more than stationary models, but are easier to empty and also clean. Most gas models are stationary although some manufacturers do offer tilting models. Tangent draw-offs are generally 1.5 to 2 in. (3.8 to 5 cm) in diameter, although 3 in. (7.5 cm) may also be specified if larger chunks of food will be drained, such as stew. They generally have a strainer so that foods do not catch inside during the cooking process.

Most floor models are **two-thirds jacketed** (which take up less floor space) although **full-jacketed kettles** are sometimes used. Full-jacketed models are slightly wider and shallower and are useful for cooking large quantities of more delicate meats, poultry, and vegetables, which are crushed by mass and movement. If the kettles are only going to be filled partway, two-thirds jackets should be specified because they use less energy and do not cause food to burn on the walls near the top. Most kettles are made with 14-gauge, Type 304 stainless steel with a No. 6 or 7 semimirror finish. Covers for floor models should be hinged with an offset of about 45 degrees from the back of the kettle to prevent employees from being burned when they lift the lid. They should also be counterbalanced. Lids for tabletop models are generally totally removable. It is best to have a floor drain under steam-jacketed kettles so that cleaning can be done without having to dispose of the wastewater.

Unless power stirrers are used, 40-gal kettles should be considered the maximum size for the preparation of entrees or other foods requiring stirring. Even this represents a heavy mass of food that can tax the average worker. Kettles ranging from 5 to 20 gal are satisfactory for the rotation cooking of vegetables. Kettles larger than 40 gal may be used for products having a high liquid content, such as for simmering stock.

FIGURE 20.20 Wall-mounted steam equipment presents good appearance and facilitates cleaning. Convenient water supply, adequate drainage, plus good light and ventilation are needed. Note small kettles mounted to empty over sink. *(Courtesy of B. H. Hubbert and Sons, Baltimore, Maryland.)*

FIGURE 20.21 Steel structure that supports wall-mounted equipment shown in Figure 20.28 Cabrini Hospital, Seattle. *(Courtesy of B. H. Hubbert and Sons, Baltimore, Maryland.)*

The cooking capacity of kettles should be based on a maximum load to fill the kettle to about two-thirds to three-quarter full. More than this makes manipulation of food difficult without spillage occurring. Planners use a rough guide that for every 4 lb (1.8 kg) of poultry or 8 lb (3.6 kg) of meat or vegetables, a gallon (or 3.8 L) of kettle is required. Thus, if a kettle capacity is to simmer 80 lb (36.4 kg) of meat, a 10-gal (38-L) kettle would be needed, which, if two-thirds full, would require a 15-gal (57-L) kettle.

TABLE 20-7 *Suggested Kettle Sizes*

Number of Meals Served/Day	Number and Size of Steam-Jacketed Kettles
100–250	One 20 gal (76 L)
251–350	One 30 gal (114 L)
351–500	One 40 gal (151 L)
501–750	Two 30 gal (114 L) or one 60 gal (227 L)
751–1,000	Two 40 gal (151 L)
1,001–1,250	Two 40 gal (151 L) and one 20 gal (76 L) or one 60 gal(227 L) and one 40 gal (151 L)
1,251–1,500	Three 40 gal (151 L) or two 60 gal (227 L)

North American Association of Food Equipment Manufacturers, *An Introduction to the Foodservice Industry,* NAFEM, Chicago, IL, 1997.

FIGURE 20.22 A tilting 40-gal kettle with pan holder. *(Courtesy of Market Forge, Everett, Massachusetts.)*

If kettles are used to make stock or soups, basing size on the volume to be prepared is preferable. It takes 6.25 gal (24 L) to serve one hundred 8-oz portions (one hundred 237-mL or 227-g portions) of soup or stew. If 500 portions are served, 32 gal (121 L) will be required and a 40-gal (151-L) kettle would be the size to specify for this quantity. It may be preferable to install smaller kettles rather than one large one to give more flexibility. If large quantities are prepared frequently, however, it is better to choose an adequate size rather than divide batches.

When selecting kettles, their ability to be emptied safely and easily is important. The type of food to be prepared and whether it can be drawn off or must be poured influence whether a tilt kettle or stationary kettle should be selected. Factors such as control of the degree of tilt on tilt kettles and prevention of splash of hot liquid in draining stationary kettles affect employee safety. Drain boxes also keep fluids from pouring from sufficient distance to splash.

Cleanability of kettles, convenient water supply, and sanitation regulations should be considered. The NSF considers the interior of steamers as food contact areas. For cleaning, a swivel faucet beside the kettles can save many steps by providing water at the work center for cooking and for cleaning. Steam guard handles should be specified. Work heights and widths in terms of normal reach should be considered. Kettles that are so high that workers must stand on ladders to work in them are hazardous. Steam equipment may need a hood over it, and if the equipment is gas fired will need an exhaust to eliminate fumes. If the gas burner is attached by direct flue, a draft diverter should be installed. Kettles that are wall suspended are preferable to floor-mounted units unless they are very large. The equipment plus contents have sufficient weight to require sturdy bridgework for their support. The NSF requires that the area under tilting kettles be easily cleanable and not blocked by the kettle. The kettle should be able to be tilted with a force of not more than 80 lb (36.3 kg).

Useful options include covers (normally standard on stationary floor models, but may be available on some tilting models), kettle-mounted faucet (useful for adding water and for cleaning), Type 316 stainless steel liner (if acid products will be used frequently), mixers (these models are called cooker-mixers or **agitator kettles**) which provide continuous mixing and scraping of the sides of the kettle during cooking, wire basket inserts (which help with product loading and unloading), brush kit (for cleaning the kettle and tangent draw-off), water meter (can be set to measure the number of gallons of water as the kettle is being filled), and cold water cooling (available on direct steam-jacketed kettles either through circulation of cold water or with built-in refrigeration coils).

MISCELLANEOUS SMALL EQUIPMENT

Toasters

Three types of toasters are used: the slot, the conveyor, and bun toasters. The first, with either two or four slots, may be arranged as multiple units (Figures 20.23 and 20.24). They may be fully automatic or hand operated. A variable timer adjusts the length of the toasting period. The units require from 1.3 to 9.8 kW. If the style of cooking is "to order" and not batch cooking, the slot toaster is typically specified.

A gas-heated slot toaster operates by a gravity feed system. Bread is dropped into the toaster and timed by a variable timer. The first slice takes 1 min to toast and succeeding ones 20 seconds. When toasted they fall by gravity from the bottom of the toaster. If an operation requires 150 slices per hour or less, a two-slot toaster is generally adequate. If 151 to 300 slices are needed, a four-slot toaster is required.

Where requirements are heavy and continuous, conveyor models are best used. They may be either gas or electric. The gas model uses 0.003 kW of electricity for driving the motor, and a 4-in. flue. Two ceramic radiants direct heat to the bread as it travels on a small chain-driven platform. Some models operate vertically, others horizontally. Horizontal models generally have greater capacities.

Conveyor toasters produce from 360 to 900 slices of toast per hour. By contrast the production rate for a pop-up slot may only be as high as 60 to 75 per hour. Required voltages may vary from 120 to 440 V or higher. All large units should be equipped with overload cutoffs so toast will not burn when the machine jams. Sanitation and cleaning factors are important. The crumb tray should be easily removable for cleaning and be accessible. A wide variety of settings should be available for very light to quite dark. All

SIDE VIEW

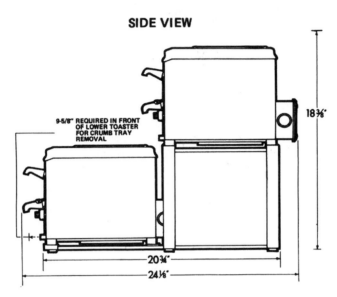

9-5/8" REQUIRED IN FRONT
OF LOWER TOASTER
FOR CRUMB TRAY
REMOVAL

18⅜"

20¾"

24⅛"

FIGURE 20.23   Tandem placement of toasters promotes flexibility in meeting demands, and maintains ability to produce a large quantity of toast within a short time. Units may also be set up in sets of six or more in this manner to give an almost continuous production of fresh product. Such units are sometimes placed in dormitory dining halls and other residence institutions, beside the bread and butter, to permit residents to prepare their own fresh toast. (*Drawings from McGraw-Edison Co., Algonquin, Illinois.*)

electric models should meet the UL requirements and gas models those of the AGA. NSF standards should be met also.

Bun toasters operate the same way that slot toasters do, but have wider slots to accommodate buns, bagels, rolls, waffles, pancakes, or English muffins. Adjustable slots allow the most flexibility. Some have special baskets with retainer bars that prevent bread or buns from curling. The bars should swing out of the way as the bread unloads.

Data on a common gas and electric toasters are shown in Table 20–8.

Toasting may also be done on a griddle, in a broiler, or in a hot oven. A heavy-duty broiler can produce 1,200 slices of bread or half buns toasted per hour.

Waffle Bakers

Waffle bakers may be obtained in single units or in batteries up to six. The shape may be rectangular or round. The baking grids should be made of a nonstick metal that conducts

FIGURE 20.24 When large quantities of toasted breads or other items are needed, a rotating toaster that can take continuous loading is used. *(Courtesy of Wells Manufacturing Co., Verdi, Nevada.)*

TABLE 20-8 *Capacity and Energy Requirements of Common Toasters*

Size in Inches			Capacity per Minute		Energy Requirements	
Width	Depth	Height	Toast	Buns[a]	Electricity (kW)	Gas (Btu input per hour)
18⅜	18⅝	29⅜	6	6–9	2.6	12,000
23⅛	16⅝	29⅜	9–12	12–15	3.6	20,000

[a]Including wiener buns.

heat rapidly and evenly. Lipped grids are best, for they prevent overflow. A flexible or floating-type hinge allows the waffle to expand during baking. Average baking time per iron is 6 min. Bell timers and signal lights that indicate heating and baking time are desirable. Preheat switches and automatic temperature controls on individual waffle irons will permit them to be turned off when not required. Removable drip pans to catch spillage aid cleanup. Each baker requires approximately 750 to 825 watts.

CHAPTER SUMMARY

Significant changes have occurred in cooking equipment during the last 30 to 40 years. Trends in the newer methods of cooking include

- Speed
- Energy efficiency
- Temperature accuracy
- Even heating
- Safety
- Ease of cleaning
- Flexibility
- Mobility
- Automation
- Computerized controls
- Compactness
- Combination cooking technologies.

Cooking equipment should be selected for the quality of food produced, labor requirements, adaptation for specific use, speed, control of temperature and humidity, durability of construction, ease of operation, safety, energy efficiency, ease of cleaning, production capacity, and purchase and installation price.

Many oven options are available today, including traditional range ovens, deck ovens, cook-and-hold ovens, convection ovens, combi-ovens, conveyor ovens, reel ovens, microwave ovens, wood-burning ovens, and the newest—cook by light ovens. Ranges also offer numerous options, including open burner or grate tops, hot tops or uniform heat tops, griddle tops, ring or graduated hot tops, French hot plates, and the newest—induction range tops. In addition, specialty ranges are available including wok, taco, and stockpot ranges.

Tilt skillets offer a flexible alternative for griddling, frying, stewing, and possibly even for steaming and baking. Broilers provide intense dry heat either through infrared or radiant heating units. Smaller cheese melters and salamanders are popular as back-shelf broilers. Rotisseries are used to broil foods while they are rotating on a spit and may help to merchandise food as it cooks. Char-broilers provide unique heating by allowing some of the meat juices to drip onto the heat source to produce a distinctive smoke and flavor.

Fryers differ in their speed, amount of automation, use of pressure, and even the use of oil. The four kinds of fryers include deep-fat fryers, pressure fryers, conveyor fryers, and air (or oil-less hot air) fryers. Doughnut fryers are a specialty kind of deep-fat fryer that may include the use of a conveyor and a variety of useful options including doughnut droppers. Filtering systems are valuable options on frying equipment that greatly extend shortening life.

Steam equipment includes steamers and steam-jacketed kettles (as well as combi-ovens and combination cooking technologies that use steam). Steam may be either self-contained or direct. Steamers may be pressureless (using atmospheric pressure), low pressure (using 5 psi), or high pressure (15 psi). Steam-jacketed kettles may be tilting (trunnions) or stationary and two-thirds jacketed or full jacketed.

The three types of toasters are slot, conveyor, and bun. Conveyor toasters are used for the larger volume operations. Waffle bakers come in single units, but may be combined to total six units.

Many types of equipment exist for each category. Different types are suited to particular volume and quality needs. In addition, numerous options are available to simplify, automate, improve safety, and make cleaning easier. Purchasers should carefully consider all of these values and set priorities for their essential needs.

REVIEW QUESTIONS

1. Observe food operations using a (a) conventional oven, (b) convection oven, and (c) microwave oven and describe how each is used in terms of schedule of use, time periods for specific products prepared, procedures of operation, problems that commonly arise connected with use, and quality of products as affected by baking.
2. Note the type of range surface used in three different food operations and state fuel used, arrangement of top (such as open burner or plates, number and how divided), amount of time range is normally used in food preparation and for what purposes, and suitability of size in relation to amount used.
3. Observe griddles in three different food operations and note size, source of heat, amount and type of heat control, purpose, and amount of use.
4. Observe broiling where gas, electric, and char-broilers are used. State size, amount and type of use, method and ease of control, and care required.
5. Observe gas-fired, electric, and infrared fryers. Note amount and type of use, amount of fat

required, care and handling of fat, ease of operation and cleaning.

6. Observe use of a microwave oven and state how used, kind of quantity of food prepared in a peak hour of service, and quality of food.

7. Observe use of steamers and kettles in three different food operations. Note steam pressure

used, kind of food prepared, length of cooking time, appearance and quality of products, and safety precautions in operating. Describe operating procedure and type of care required in cleaning.

KEY WORDS AND CONCEPTS

agitator kettles

automatic dampering

carbonization

chrome surface units

closed top

convection steamers

counterbalanced

direct steam

ductless ventilation systems

electromagnetic coil

flushable generators

French hot plate

fryer cold zones

graduated hot tops

griddle top

heavy-duty range

hot top

impingers

induction cooking

in-line filters

kettle jacket

magnetrons

noncooking grade steam

open burner tops

oven sizing

peel

pressure reducing valve

restaurant range

ring top

self-contained steam

standby mode

tangent draw-off valve

thermocouple

thermofluid kettles

trunnions

turbulence or directed flow circulation

two-thirds jacketed, full-jacketed kettles

uniform heat top

ventilation requirements

water softeners

zone heating

CHAPTER
21

Serving Equipment

Characteristics in the service of food vary from a simple presentation of food to a consumer standing at a take-out window to the meticulous presentation of meals in fine restaurants. Foods served in each instance are fragile in quality. The consumers' enjoyment of the food is usually tempered by the general appearance and manner in which it is presented. Equipment is needed for the serving of food that will help to (1) preserve food palatability, (2) promote speed of service, (3) ensure sanitation, (4) present a good appearance, (5) provide comfort, safety, and convenience for workers and consumers, (6) give flexibility for adjustment to changes, and (7) provide economical holding and merchandising.

Service needs are variable between restaurants. Some require equipment for its merchandising appeal. Cold dessert or bread display cabinets at the entrance may, for example, increase their sale during the meal or for take-out. Other operations require customer self-service equipment for hot or cold bars or for beverage service. Others may, as part of the merchandising appeal, require equipment for display or exhibition style cooking at the point of service. Finally, some restaurants have expanded the sale of ready-prepared take-out foods for "grab-and-go" meals, also referred to as home meal replacements, and require both hot and cold merchandising cabinets.

HOT FOOD EQUIPMENT

Food warmers are required to keep quantities of prepared food hot for service, to have foods available for immediate service, and to take peak loads off the kitchen. Plates and dish warmers for serving hot food are required.

Soups, gravies, stews, many entree dishes, and some sauces require serving temperatures of about 175°F (79°C). Others, such as sliced meat, roasts, and vegetables, require lower temperatures. All hot foods must be held at a minimum temperature of 140°F (60°C). Moist or dry heat may be required, according to the type of food stored. Length of time foods can be held will determine the most suitable size of container and the space needed in a warming area. Heat used for warming equipment may be electricity, gas, or steam. Insulation of doors and sides should be provided. Dish warming equipment opposite the service counter on the waitstaff side may also be useful. Access doors into such areas should be provided so waitstaff can reach the heated dishes.

Hot food equipment should hold food from 150 to 175°F (65.5 to 80°C), except those used to keep rolls and buns warm. All cabinet-type warmers should have a thermometer installed, which permits the operator to monitor the air temperature within the cabinet. They should also meet other requirements of the NSF and FDA.

Food warming equipment used in cafeterias is usually combined with service counters. Merchandising is an important component in service areas. Rectangular or square hot table containers will give more food holding capacity than round containers and will present a more attractive food display. Flexibility in serving counters is also needed. All possible menu variations should be considered when selecting a hot table. Proper placement of foods and dishes should be considered to enable workers to work to the best advantage with their right and left hands. Placement of dish leveling equipment in the counter is often useful. Time may be saved by having dishes in dispensers at right angles to the serving counter.

Steam tables can be selected from many offerings in standard stock and need not be custom built. Steam tables are 24 to 32 in. (60 to 76 cm) wide and frequently come equipped with an 8-in. (20-cm)-wide, 2-in. (5-cm)-thick laminated maple cutting board or stainless steel shelf used as a plate rest. Openings in the steam table should be supported by channeling of angle support. The steam table frame and legs should provide adequate support as well.

Steam tables may be heated by hot water or by dry heat provided by gas or electricity. Both have proven satisfactory. The dry tables are often preferred because there is no steam to build up heat and no condensation on the steam table equipment or breath guards.

Hot food tables used for customer self-service may be either dry or steam type. **Breath guards** (or sneeze guards as they are sometimes called) should be used with all self-service hot and cold food bars. They are used as a canopy over the serving bar and are typically 10-in. (25.4 cm) in width. Some breath guards are attached to the bar units (either permanently or with clamp-on attachments), some are freestanding, others are suspended from the ceiling. Many of these incorporate lighting to improve merchandising. **Tempered glass** is the most expensive material used for the breath guards, but less expensive plastic is available as well. **Plastic** has the added advantage of being lighter in weight, but more care must be taken in cleaning so as not to scratch it.

A **bain marie** is an open hot water bath having a perforated false bottom on which containers of food may be set. It is usually near or a part of the cooks' section. More recently, rotation cooking yielding a continuous supply of freshly cooked food has reduced the use of bain maries. Where they are employed, the use will be heavy, and they should be constructed of 14-gauge stainless steel tops with supporting channeling and frame work sufficient to support weights given during use. Water-bath types are most desirable. Width is usually between 24 and 30 in. (61 and 76 cm). The depth of water chamber is usually 10 in. (25 cm). The length is sized according to needs as indicated by the production chart.

Heated pass-through compartments are convenient for use in cafeterias and other operations where service is from a counter. Pass-throughs should be well insulated. Some may be equipped with blower fans to spread the heat throughout. Humidity controls are also useful for extended holding in humidified hot holding cabinets (Figure 21.1). Pass-throughs may be sized to hold mobile carts of food or individual pans of food (Figure 21.2). Good door insulation and seals should be provided. If doors are hinged and open from the bottom, construction of the door should be rugged to hold weights and wear given when it is open. Other hot food holding cabinets are designed with glass doors or windows for merchandising purposes and maintain food with acceptable quality between one and four hours depending on the food and the holding conditions.

The growth of central commissaries and satellite units has led to the need to be able to transport food in mobile equipment that will help maintain quality and reduce sanitation hazards. Generally speaking, two different types of systems for maintaining temperature have evolved. The first is **passive temperature maintenance** and relies on

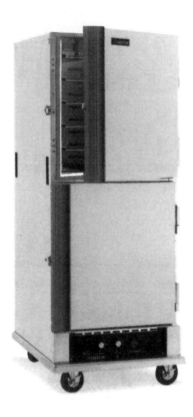

FIGURE 21.1 An insulated, humidified hot holding cabinet that will hold food at approximately 200°F (93°C). *(Courtesy of CresCor, Mentor, OH).*

FIGURE 21.2 A roll-through unit that permits loading from one side and removal from the service side. *(Courtesy of Hobart Corporation, Troy, Ohio.)*

insulation to maintain the temperature of food when it is placed into the cabinet. The second is active temperature maintenance and provides heating or cooling during the transporting process. The number of different models within each category is huge. Food carts, insulated tote boxes, thermal retention trays, and units that use heated disks underneath plated food are just a few of the examples. Important selection points for this equipment in addition to temperature retention are ease of cleaning and sanitizing plus durability that will withstand the hurried, oft repeated, and sometimes rough handling it is likely to receive in the transporting of food.

Food and beverage holding boxes that use passive methods of maintaining the temperature of food are generally made of stainless steel or polyethylene. Insulation is generally polyurethane foam or fiberglass. Interiors should have coved corners and no rough edges, seams, or places where soil can collect and be difficult to remove. Covers are usually double walled and insulated similar to the walls in the rest of the unit. Faucets on beverage containers are typically made of black nylon, stainless steel, or chromed brass. Units should have faucets recessed to prevent them from being broken during transport. In addition, some units include a guard over the faucet.

If units are not mobile, they should be easily portable or combined with suitable mobile equipment for ease of movement without excessive lifting and/or carrying. The equipment should be tested for its ability to maintain the desired temperature for the required period of time. Typical insulated units (with no added heat through electricity or canned heat) lose about 3 to 4°F (1.7 to 2.2°C) per hour. Although this loss appears minimal, FDA standards require that potentially hazardous foods (such as meats, poultry, and fish) be maintained below 40°F (4.4°C) or above 140°F (60°C). If foods will be held for long time periods, this heat loss may be a significant concern. Table 21–1 lists the temperature maintenance standards established by a manufacturer of this type of equipment.

Useful options include color options in plastic units (darker colors may be selected for high-volume areas because they are less likely to show stains), condiment holders, plastic dollies for nonmobile units, stacking ability, double units or insulated dividers (which offer both hot and colding capability), raised spigots (which allow the use of larger size cups under the faucet), and faucet guards (to prevent breakage during transport).

The use of mobile food cabinets that use active methods to maintain the temperature of food has grown tremendously. Holding equipment can be set for thermostatic control and humidities can be regulated. They are generally operated on electricity with blower fans to better distribute the heat, but bottled gas or canned heat can be used if electricity is not available or too expensive. Many units contain a water pan to provide some humidity and prevent drying out of products.

Mobile cabinets are generally made of aluminum or stainless steel (Figure 21.3). Heights range from 30 to 73 in. (76 to 185 cm) and widths from 22 to 81.5 in. (56 to 207 cm). The number of pans that each cabinet holds will vary from small units which accommodate four 12- × 20-in. (30- × 51-cm) pans, to large units, which hold thirty-eight 18- × 26-in. (46- × 66-cm) pans. If casters are used, the ball bearing type

TABLE 21–1 *Recommended Food Temperatures at Loading and After Holding*

At Loading	1 hr	2 hr	3 hr	4 hr	5 hr
Hot 170°F	163°F	162.2°F	161°F	160.5°F	160°F
(76°C)	(72°C)	(71.6°C)	(71°C)	(70.7°C)	(70.4°C)
Cold 33°F	33.5°F	34°F	35.2°F	36°F	37°F
(.6°C)	(.8°C)	(1.1°C)	(1.7°C)	(2.2°C)	(2.8°C)
Frozen— 10°F	−9.6°F	−8.2°F	−7.1°F	−6.0°F	−5.4°F
(−23.1°C)	(−22.9°C)	(−22.1°C)	(−21.5°C)	(−20.0°C)	(−18.7°C)

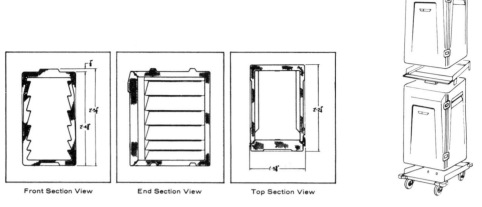

Front Section View   End Section View   Top Section View

FIGURE 21.3   A food carrier manufactured to receive a six 12- × 20- × 2.5-in. (30- × 50- × 6.25-cm) pans or five 4-in. (10-cm)-deep or three 6-in. (15-cm)-deep pans, and the stacking of the units loaded with portioned food ready for transport.

are considered the most durable. Two fixed and two swivel casters are thought to provide the greatest control in movement.

Useful options on mobile cabinets include Dutch doors (which allow only a portion of the cabinet to be opened in order to retain more heat), see-through doors (which allow merchandising in service areas and minimize door opening on proofing cabinets where products require more observation), rack or pan slides, corner or wrap-around bumpers (which protect doors, walls, and other areas during movement), security locks, top warmers (which allow service of food from the top of the cabinet), foot pedal-operated doors, drains, locking casters, and larger size casters (casters typically range from 3 to 8 in. or 8 to 20 cm, with the larger size casters providing easier movement for heavier cabinets or difficult flooring materials such as carpeting).

Interior dimensions of all food units should be checked to make sure that they will be suited to pans, plates, or trays that will be placed inside. Mobile cabinets and holding equipment should be able to tolerate cleaning with standard detergents and a water temperature of 180°F (81°C). If temperatures greater than 185°F (85°C) will be used, polyurethane containers should not be purchased because the plastic tends to soften under high heat conditions. Abrasive cleaners should not be used on polyurethane containers either.

Many small specialized types of food warmers are being used. Roll warmers are popular for holding hot breads and many other foods. Those of 12- to 32-doz capacity require 0.8 to 1.2 kW. They may be used in food operations for hot pies, premade hot sandwiches, and other hot foods in addition to breads. Drawer-type warmers are convenient when located near the grill or hot table in the serving area. They are available either as single-, double-, or triple-drawer models. Some units allow separate temperature and humidity controls for each drawer. Soup warmers can be round, square, or rectangular units that accommodate inserts for holding soups. Countertop models range in size from 4 to 11 qt. (3.8 to 10.4 L). Most models use electrical elements immersed in water, which in turn heats the soup. Models using water are generally preferred because of the evenness of heating which is important for cream soups and thicker sauces.

Infrared tube or bulb units can be used to keep food warm (Figure 21.4). They are particularly useful when holding plated meals at serving temperatures until waitstaff pick them up for service. Another common use is to maintain hot crisp french fries in fast-food restaurants. These warming units use quartz or metal filaments, which give off infrared heat waves. About 90% of the electricity is turned into heat. Infrared warmers

FIGURE 21.4 Infrared heat lamps such as these are simple units that will keep food warm while it is waiting for pick up or other service needs. (*Courtesy of Franklin Products Corporation, Northbrook, Illinois.*)

generally place the bulbs between 10 and 18 in. (25 to 46 cm) above the food. Flexibility is gained if the height above the food is adjustable. Some bulb units are mounted on swivel bases that slant the heat waves so that they cover a larger area than if placed facing directly down. Properly placed, infrared warmers can maintain crisp french fries for about 15 min. Other foods may be held for up to 25 min. Tube heaters are usually less attractive than bulb arrangements but they can be hooked together to give considerable heating diversity. Stainless steel shelving is the best choice for use with infrared heaters. Wood, some plastics, and other fusible materials may be harmed by the heat. All heating devices should be checked for ease of cleaning, maintenance, and expected life. Some units are guaranteed for a longer operating life than others.

Another type of specialty warmer may be a pizza-by-the-slice service cabinet. The unit typically has four walls of glass with shelves that revolve to display the pizza. When the door is opened, the rotation stops. Some cabinets offer humidity control so that humidity can be kept low in order to keep the pizza crust crisp. Cabinets intended for short-term holding use infrared bulbs or heat strips in the top of the cabinet. Those intended for longer term holding may provide heat from below as well as above.

Heated dishes for serving are a problem if repeated handling of dishes is necessary. Care should be taken in their placement, heating, and use in order to minimize handling. If dishes are loaded into mobile equipment at the dish machine and moved into heated chambers at service areas, much handling is eliminated. Sturdy construction is needed in mobile dish carts to bear the heavy weight of dishes. Dish warming equipment should be well insulated and have placement planned for ease of use and labor savings.

COLD FOOD EQUIPMENT

The need for safe holding of cold food near or in service areas has grown in the last 30 years with the introduction of the salad bar. The popularity of salad bars has varied over the years, but where used they are more versatile than when originally introduced. Many more types of food are offered, often in combination with hot food. Cold food bars typically come in 4- or 6-ft widths (122 to 183 cm) with a height of 52½ in. (133 cm) and a depth of 33¼ in. (84 cm). Youth or children models are also available that offer a depth of 20⅛ in. (51 cm), a tray slide height of 28 in. (71 cm), and a total height of 45¾ in. (116 cm). Countertop or floor models are available. Countertop models are easier to move from one area to another or store between service periods. Floor models are available with 4- or 5-in. (10.2- or 12.7-cm) casters, but these are not as mobile and are most useful for moving the unit for cleaning. Figure 21.5 shows a dessert trolly that has internal cooling.

Cold food bars may be made from a variety of materials, including plastic, metal, or wood. Pans should be 16-gauge metal or equivalent strength in plastic. Pans should be pitched ⅛ in. to the foot for drainage. Metal counter tops should be turned down 1¼ in. into the pan and welded. Composition breaker strips should be installed under the countertop turndowns on all sides. In mechanical units, dehydrated seamless copper cooling evaporator coils should be installed and encased in hydrolene.

Breath or sneeze guards are required for all customer self-service cold food bars. Requirements for construction are the same as for the breath guards for hot food bars. One additional concern is with the type of lighting. Fluorescent lighting is generally preferred for cold bar units because it gives off little heat. In addition to the heat given off by lighting however, the color impact on the food should be considered. Some kinds of fluorescent lighting, for example, tend to give foods a more gray, less appealing color.

Four general types of cold food bars are available. They include ice-cooled, mechanically refrigerated units, or those that use a combination of both methods, and convected cold air **(air curtain)** models. Ice-cooled units are popular because they are considerably less expensive to purchase than refrigerated units, but ice-cooled units require more labor for filling and emptying and, of course, ice. According to the FDA Food Code, all four types of cold food bars should hold cold foods at 35°F (1.7°C) so they will be served at not over 40°F (4.4°C).

In ice-cooled food bars, the food is kept cold by filling the food bar with ice. Because of this, the sides and bottom of the wells are insulated, typically with expanded **polystyrene** or closed-cell **polyurethane.** Double-wall construction in the molded units may also be used to provide additional insulation. Ice-cooled units will require a drain with a stopper or petcock. Drain hoses must be at least a minimum of 0.5 in. (1.3 cm) according to NSF standards. They may be drained periodically by employees or the drain hose may lead to a tub inside the salad bar or to a permanent connection. If a permanent connection is used however, an air gap must be set up so that there is no direct connection to a sewage drain. Cold food bar well sizes vary, but generally fit standard pan sizes, such as 12 × 20 × 4 in. (30.5 × 50.8 × 10.2 cm). Typical models are for three, four, or five pans. Custom refrigerated units range from two to six pan sizes. Adapter bars are used to accommodate fractional size food pans. In addition, some units have false bottoms of 16-gauge metal in the well (perforated insert) that allow water to drain from the ice, slowing the melting process.

Other useful accessories include a **template,** which covers the iced bottom section and allows bowls or pans to be attractively fitted into cut-out openings and slows the

FIGURE 21.5 A dessert trolly that is refrigerated by eutectic frozen blocks. The construction is such that a fresh appearance is retained on the product longer. *(Courtesy of Lentia Manufacturing Ltd., Port Coquitlam, B.C., Canada.)*

melting of ice; refrigerated cabinets for storage under the bar; plate or tray rests for customers as they move through the line; countertop boards for slicing of breads or meats; or well organizers for individual juice glasses, dessert or salad plates, etc.

Refrigerated units may have refrigeration lines built into the sides and/or bottom of the well. Others may be connected to refrigeration units some distance away with well-insulated lines running to them. Refrigerated units are similar in size, construction materials, and accessories to the ice-cooled units. Because of the machinery required for the refrigeration lines, refrigerated countertop units are not possible.

Some units are convertible for either hot or cold service with the flip of a switch. These units may require a short time period for temperature adjustment. The unit converts to a hot food bar with electric heating elements or with a hot water booster and water pumps. Combination units may even allow both hot and cold service at the same time by the use of snap-in heated sections.

Another more recent alternative is the air curtain model in which cold air is circulated or convected around the food well from ducts at the surface of the unit. A fan is installed on one side of the cabinet to force the air over the surface of the food to the other side of the cabinet where holes act as air inlets to return and recycle the air. The advantage of the air curtain units is that food temperatures are kept more constant.

Useful accessories for a food bar include the following:

- **Ice guards** (ice guards are used as holders for the crocks so that crocks may be easily replaced without losing their position within the ice)
- **Crock inserts** (which fit into crocks and lift the product up so that less is displayed when turnover of the product is slow)
- Tight-fitting lids (which allow crocks to be more easily stored or protected between services)
- Specialty tongs (pasta tongs, spring tongs, salad tongs, meat tongs, etc.).

Pans, bowls, and crocks used in hot and cold food bars may be made of a variety of materials ranging from stainless steel to various types of plastic resins. Types of plastic resins have greatly expanded. Some high-temperature plastics, such as **polysulfone,** are now available that tolerate temperatures from −40°F (−22°C) to 300°F (149°C). Stainless steel units are more durable and commonly used, but if placed directly on ice may get too cold for delicate raw vegetables. High-temperature plastics are less likely to develop bent corners (which produce inefficient seals on steam tables), are lighter in weight, and quieter when pans are being washed or stacked. On the other hand, extra care is required in cleaning of plastic so it is not scratched.

In service areas, cold merchandise cabinets may also be used to keep foods fresh and ready to sell. They are popular in delis and take-out food areas, including those that provide home meal replacement food. Tempered glass fronts and sides provide a convenient view of the displays. Other materials are generally stainless steel and aluminum. Both refrigerated and freezer models are available. Countertop models average 18 to 22 in. (46 to 56 cm) high, 16 to 20 in. (41 to 51 cm) deep, and 3 to 5 ft (91 to 152 cm) long. Floor models range from 3 to 12 ft (91 to 366 cm) long. Doors are generally swing type or sliding doors. Open cases with no doors (air curtain models) are sometimes used in customer self-service areas. Some models offer a revolving shelf option. Cabinets should be insulated with polystyrene or polyurethane foam. Freezer units may have heated glass and door frames to minimize condensation and keep doors from freezing shut. Locks and self-adjusting magnetic seals are also available.

COFFEE EQUIPMENT

Coffee brewing has changed considerably since the 1980s with the resurgence of interest in specialty coffees. The introduction of flavored coffees, **espresso,** and **cappuccino** has required the addition of specialty pieces of coffee brewing equipment. Smaller volume equipment has also become more common. Espresso, in particular, is generally produced on a brew-to-order service. Passive holding of coffee using airpots has also become popular so that a wider variety of flavored coffees may be prepared in advance with less deterioration in quality than if held in heated units.

Quality coffee has always been associated with equipment that keeps it fresh. Because quality deteriorates the longer the coffee is heated and exposed to air, proper sizing of equipment for coffee needs is one of the most important factors in maintaining coffee at its peak of quality. Both brewers and urns are commonly used to produce coffee. **Coffee brewers** produce smaller volumes. They typically brew up to 12 cups per batch. **Coffee urns** are used in larger volume operations. They typically brew 75 to 500 cups per batch, but even higher production equipment is available that brews 9,000 cups per hour. A common guide suggests that operations that use up to 40 lb

(18.2 kg) of coffee and produce 80 to 120 gal (302 to 454 L) of brewed coffee can use brewer(s), whereas a volume between 40 and 60 lb (18.2 and 27.2 kg) with a production of 80 to 120 gal (303 to 454 L) will require a single urn; beyond this amount, a double urn will be required. Because urns will not brew smaller quantities of coffee, operations with combination needs should consider both a brewer and an urn.

Both manual and automatic brewers are available. **Manual** brewers, which are also called pour-over units, are used where a direct hookup to a water line is not possible. For these machines, the employee must pour fresh water into the tank to force hot water (previously poured in and heated) through the spray head and onto the coffee bed. **Automatic** brewers require a water hookup and do not require manual filling. A tank-style brewer holds water at the correct temperature in a heating tank until a brew button is pushed. When the button is pushed, new water flows into the bottom of the tank forcing the hot water out the top and onto the coffee bed. A second type uses a **flash heater** to heat water as it flows from the water line onto the coffee bed. Most controls are preset at the factory with brewers so that little adjustment for quantity or temperature of water can be done. Many brewers also have one or more warming plates to hold the coffee pots at serving temperature. Extra warming plates can be ordered for holding prepared pots. Instead of warming plates, some models also allow direct filling of insulated airpots, which maintain the temperature without the addition of heat.

Urns produce larger quantities of coffee. In addition, they hold coffee in a fresh state longer than brewers. Careful temperature control and an air pump that aerates coffee allows them to hold coffee in a fresh state from 1 to 1.5 hours. Finally, urns have the advantage of adjustable controls. In some models, adjustment can be made to the amount of water that goes through the coffee bed, timing, temperature of water, and depth of the coffee bed.

Adjustments are useful for quality control, cost considerations, and regional preferences. For example, recommended ratios of coffee to water range from 1 lb (0.45 kg) of coffee to 1.75 gal (6.6 L) to 1 lb (0.45 kg) to 3 gal (11.4 L) of water. Temperature of brewing water should be maintained between 195 and 205°F (91 and 96°C) and holding temperature around 185°F (85°C). Coffee beds are usually 6 in. (15.2 cm) or less in diameter and should be between 1.25 and 1.75 in. (3.2 and 4.4 cm) deep. Brewing time is critical as well. Sweeter flavors are the first to be extracted from the coffee with bitter flavors emerging next. Optimum brewing time must balance the two to produce the best quality.

Two types of urn models are available. **Pump** models hold water at the correct temperature until it is used. **Exchanger** models pump fresh water into the unit and quickly heat it to the proper temperature at the time of use. Pump models have the advantage of being less vulnerable to damage from lime buildup caused by evaporation. Exchanger models, on the other hand, have the advantage of brewing with fresh water, which is important for high-quality coffee. Urns usually have a heated water jacket surrounding the coffee holding tank. Heat may be supplied by electricity, gas, or central steam system.

The quality of coffee produced also depends on the ability to fully clean the equipment and remove residual oils or off flavors. The inner shell or the container in which the coffee is made must be of highly durable material that is non-toxic and will not react with the coffee brew to give off-flavors. Inner shells may be made of stainless steel (20-gauge steel, for 2- to 5-gal capacity urns and 18 gauge over that size), heat resisting glass, china, or earthenware. Stainless steel is the most frequently used because it can be drawn. Drawing gives no seam construction, although new welding techniques now provide almost indestructible welds. Furthermore, stainless steel is a highly durable, noncorrosive material that will not react with a coffee brew to create an undesirable flavor. Glass, earthenware, and vitrified stone are excellent for coffee containers. However, they are somewhat fragile and spare containers should be carried when they are used. They can only be made up to certain sizes. Earthenware crazes and off-flavors can result from captured oxidized essences in the **crazing.** Complete drainage of inner shells should be specified.

Equipment interiors should be readily cleanable. Valves should be of the sanitary type and easily disassembled for cleaning. There should be no sharp corners or crevices in them. Draw-off tubes should be either tangential or vertical and of one piece. Tubes should be the same size as the outlet. Strainers should be removable and be made of perforated metals. Drip-collecting drains should be easily removable. Faucets should permit thorough cleaning.

All urns should be specified with gauges to indicate capacity. Faucets and fittings should be of top quality and nonslip, nonleak type (Figure 21.6). Plastic or insulated parts should be provided where necessary to prevent hands from touching hot areas.

Leachers or containers to hold coffee grounds during coffee making are available as rings to hold coffee bags, stainless steel filters using filter paper bottoms, or stainless steel units that have a series of perforated stainless steel sheets placed one over another to give an effective low-process leach action.

Urn stands are usually enclosed and supplies of cups and saucers are kept in the heated enclosure on mobile equipment. A 4-in. (10.2-cm)-wide, 2-in. (5.1-cm)-deep drain is usually provided across the top under the urn faucets. This area should be pitched to a drain. A nonsplash louvered drain plate (removable) should be specified to keep the level of this drain area flush with the tabletop. Usually a marine edge is specified for the top. Service openings should be raised integrally to provide a seamless escutcheon, through which the service lines can be brought and leakage avoided. Specify 14-gauge tops for heavy-duty units. Bracing and frame support are required.

Specifications for coffee urns should state the type of heat to be used, thermostatic control, and service cut-outs required. Steam heat usually requires coils in the boiler of the urn. Electrical heaters should be of the threaded immersion type, and specifications should require safety cutoffs if the boiler becomes empty. Draw-offs should not leave immersion heaters exposed. If gas is used, standard speed burners should be specified. If urns are to be self-service, specifications should state that the urn be equipped with a goose-neck overflow to prevent hot water and steam spillage on patrons while at the urn. If urns are to be used for double service, the specifications should also state that both sides are to have draw-off faucets.

Espresso coffee machines produce coffee by forcing hot water under high pressure through a bed of very finely ground coffee (Figure 21.7). The process is done in smaller volume. Typically coffee beans are ground at the time the coffee is brewed, then portioned, and placed in a filter. Then water is heated to 200°F (93°C) and forced over the coffee at a pressure of 135 to 150 psi. In 15 to 20 seconds, a 2- to 3-oz (59- to 89-mL) cup of espresso is ready. Filter baskets may hold one, two, or three servings of espresso. Larger quantities of espresso are produced by increasing the number of **espresso brewing heads** or groups. Espresso machines are generally available with up to four groups. Capacities of equipment will vary with each manufacturer with some as low as 60 cups per hour. Other models may produce up to 750 cups per hour. Brewing pressure may be supplied with a manual lever, a hydraulic piston, or a small pump. Some models include separate steam generators, which increase the production capacity. Espresso machines are available that produce up to 22 different espresso-type beverages (including single shot, double latte, single decaffeinated cappuccino, etc.) with the push of a button.

Grinding and measurement of the coffee is more critical for espresso than for regular coffee. Espresso is ground very finely, down to 4.5 million particles per gram. The coffee is ground so finely that humidity will affect the rate at which water flows through the grounds and the resulting coffee quality. Because of this, grinders should be adjustable, coarser grinds being preferred for higher humidity days. In addition espresso ground coffee differs from regular coffee in that it is roasted to a greater degree.

The two **grinder compartments** are the hopper for beans and a doser for ground coffee. The doser is so named because it dispenses an accurately measured amount of coffee when a filter basket is inserted. Automatic and semiautomatic models are available. Automatic grinders automatically refill the doser when it gets low, whereas semiautomatic models require an employee to press a button or switch when the doser is empty.

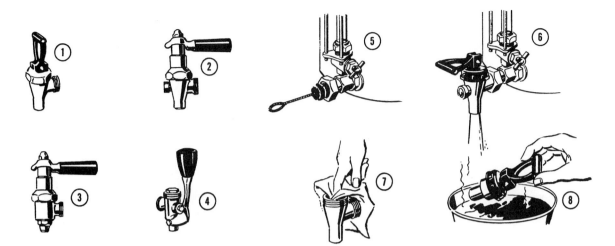

The coffee urn faucet is one of the few moving parts of the urn and beyond question the hardest working part—it may operate up to 288 times to only one time for another part. As such, it is truly the heart of the urn and should be prime consideration when buying new equipment or modernizing old. Faucets vary in style and material. Brass, stainless steel and nylon are the most common materials. Popular styles are:

Self-closing (with either flexible seals or "O" ring seals) (Fig. 1)

Key-cock (with either ground metal plugs or metal plugs or metal to rubber seals) (Fig. 2 & 3)

Push-pull (with metal to rubber seals) (Fig. 4)

Here is your check list guide to purchasing or specifying the proper faucet for your application. When in doubt as to which faucet to buy, be sure to consult with your urn or faucet supplier.

1. Style or type of faucet best suited to YOUR purpose.
2. Service life of faucet.
3. Construction of faucet with regard to sanitation.
4. Ease with which faucet may be maintained in proper operating condition.
5. Availability of replacement parts.
6. Initial cost and cost of maintenance.
7. Reputation and guarantee of manufacturer.
8. Design and appearance.

Once you have obtained the proper faucets, the quality of your coffee is governed in large part by your standards of cleanliness. Good coffee cannot be made in unclean equipment—when you brew a "bad" batch of coffee, do not be too hasty in condemning the roast or the urn manufacturer. Check the condition of the urn, and in particular, look to see whether your faucets have been cleaned properly. Set forth below are the salient points in caring for and cleaning the faucets and fittings on your urn equipment.

1. Rinse with clear water after each batch of coffee. (Fig. 6)
2. EACH DAY remove faucet from shank. Clean through shank into urn, brushing out all coffee deposits. Scrub inside of faucet with hot water and urn cleaner. Rinse in clear hot water. Assemble faucet to shank and partially fill urn with clear water. (Fig. 5 & 7)
3. EACH WEEK remove faucet from shank and disassemble as recommended by manufacturer. Scrub all parts in hot water with urn cleaner. Scrub shank clean with urn brush. Assemble faucet to shank and rise by passing hot water through entire unit. Place a few gallons of clear water in urn. (Fig. 8)
4. When in doubt as to how to clean your faucet, write direct to the faucet manufacturers, or to the urn manufacturer, for explicit instructions.

Addresses of major coffee urn faucet manufacturers:

Economy Faucet Company, 11 New York Avenue, Newark, New Jersey.

Tomlinson No-Drip Faucet Co., 1601 St. Clair Avenue, Cleveland 14, Ohio.

Wyott Manufacturing Company, P.O. Box 898, Cheyenne, Wyoming

Bunn-o-matic Corp., 1400 Stevenson Drive, Springfield, IL 62703

Brewmatic Company, 20333 South Normandie Ave., Torrance, CA 90509-2959

Wilbur Curtis Co., 1781 N. Indiana Street, Los Angeles, CA 90063-0901

FIGURE 21.6 Faucets play a major role in coffee quality *(Courtesy of Food Service Magazine, Madison, Wisconsin.)*

FIGURE 21.7   An automatic espresso/cappacino machine with two heads made of highly polished steel and copper. (*Courtesy of Kaldi Gourmet Coffee Roasters, Wilmington, NC*).

Manual, semiautomatic, automatic, and **superautomatic** espresso machines are available. Manual machines only make one cup of espresso at a time and require the employee to pull a lever that operates springs, which force the water through the group. Semiautomatic machines brew up to two cups at a time and use an electrically operated pump to force water through the group. The employee must switch the pump off after brewing. Automatic espresso machines are like the semiautomatic machines in that they also produce two cups at a time. Unlike the semiautomatic machines, however, the pump is automatically switched off at the proper time after brewing. Some automatic machines also have sensors that determine the size of cup that has been placed beneath the head to ensure portion control. In addition to pump control, superautomatic machines automatically grind, pack, and dispose of used coffee grounds and sterilize themselves before the next brew. They also may automatically top the coffee with steamed milk for cappuccino.

Production of cappuccino is somewhat more complex than straight espresso. Cappuccino is composed of equal parts espresso, steamed milk, and frothed milk. As a result, cappuccino or latte generally takes two to three times as long to brew. Steaming and frothing of milk is done by combining high-pressure steam and cold milk. Steam is provided through one or two 5- to 8-in. (12.7- to 20.3-cm)-long stainless steel wands. Units are available that use either freeze-dried or fresh fluid milk.

Improvements in coffee technology have also offered other alternatives to traditional coffee brewing. Instant machines are available that use a concentrated **liquid** or **freeze-dried powder base.** Although not authentic brewing, some operations prefer these machines for their simple operation, lower cost, ease of cleanup, and fast brewing. Iced coffee machines are another alternative. The typical machine is a refrigerated unit, which combines coffee concentrate, milk, and ice. Brewing models are also available.

Useful options on coffee machines include built-in water softeners (for lime problems) or filtration systems (to reduce chlorine content because of its effect on coffee flavor); premeasured regular or espresso ground coffee in vacuum-sealed pouches; microprocessors for more accurate measurement; color-coded faucets for regular and decaffeinated coffee; airpots (airpots can maintain coffee temperature and quality for up to 10 hours as compared to coffee brewing equipment in which the coffee starts to turn bitter within 18 to 25 min) or thermal servers (which include an outer gauge to indicate how much coffee remains); insulated urns (which allow better maintenance of coffee temperatures); smart machines that keep track of the number of cups served or interface with cash registers; and surge suppressors and fused circuits.

SOFT DRINK EQUIPMENT

Carbonated beverage dispensers are extremely varied. Countless combinations of mix systems, propulsion systems, and valve delivery systems are possible. Carbonated beverage dispensers can be divided into the two types of postmix and premix.

Postmix soft drink systems move a syrup concentrate through a chilled line to the dispensing head. A separate line is used to carry filtered and carbonated tap water to the head where it is mixed with the syrup. Most systems use carbon dioxide and a small amount of high-pressure air to propel liquids through the system. Syrup is generally provided from 3- or 5-gal (11.4- or 18.9-L) tanks. Tanks may be connected in series to reduce the number of times that tanks must be changed. **"Bag-in-the-box" soft drink dispensing systems,** which use plastic bags and a spigot inside a corrugated board frame, come in 5-gal (18.9-L) capacities. They require less space and are easier to handle than traditional metal canisters, but require disposal when they are empty in comparison to the canisters, which are refilled. Advantages of postmix systems include that they require less space than premix systems and that the concentrate is less expensive. The disadvantage is that the equipment is more complicated.

Premix soft drink systems are different from postmix in that the beverage is already mixed and requires only one line to the dispensing head. Carbon dioxide is still generally used to propel the mixture through the line. The advantage to premix is that the equipment is less expensive and simpler; its disadvantage is that the product requires more storage space.

A variety of models are available for both systems. Dispensing heads range from a single-valve model to 12-valve models. Ice dispensing chutes are also included in many units. Useful options include automatic portion control, including variations for different size beverage containers and faucet guns attached to a flexible hose for bar or other high-volume areas (selection of beverage is made on the faucet gun through a choice of buttons).

Beverage cooling systems should also be selected carefully based on volume requirements. Cooling systems may be either mechanical refrigeration or **cold-plate systems.** Cold-plate systems are less-expensive than mechanical refrigeration, but are not as well suited for high-volume operations. In cold-plate systems, a metal plate is chilled by ice. The plate in turns chills the syrup and water lines. Temperature control is important because carbonation fails at a product temperature above 40°F (4.4°C) so that the soft drink tastes flat. Larger plates generally chill the product more effectively. Volume also affects the choice of carbonator. Typical medium volume operations use a ¼-hp unit. If volumes of more than 100 gal (378 L) per hour are required, additional power is necessary.

In addition, soft drink systems should be made of nontoxic and corrosion-resistant materials. They should be easily cleanable and tubes leading from them to the dispensing equipment should be readily removable and cleanable. They should require little maintenance and be easily serviced. For health reasons, carbon dioxide or carbonated water should not touch any metal containing copper or even small parts of copper. Finally, soft drink equipment should allow for sanitary dispensing without contamination. For example, where reuse of glasses is allowed by customers, consideration should be given to the activation lever or button in machine. Pushing a button on a panel above the dispensing nozzles is generally preferred as compared to a lever that is activated when the glass is pushed up against it. In addition, longer levers are preferable over shorter levers in that the top of the reused glass is less likely to touch the dispensing nozzles.

TABLES AND CHAIRS

Dining areas can be enhanced in appearance and comfort by the attractiveness of the tables and chairs selected. Flexibility is desirable as to the total number that can be seated and the seating arrangement. Storage may be an important consideration if removal from the room is likely to occur for periodic cleaning of the floor or for use of the room for other purposes. You should consider whether chairs will need to be moved or stacked regularly for floor cleaning. Proper initial provision may help to reduce scarring that will spoil appearance.

Tables vary in height, size, and shape. The height may be as low as 17 in. (42.5 cm) for a coffee or cocktail table or as high as 30 in. (75 cm). Tables from 26 to 30 in. (65 to 75 cm) are considered standard depending on patron size and need. Table surface size is gauged in terms of individual place settings, which vary from 20 to 30 in. (51 to 75 cm). The smaller allowance is made for children and for crowded banquet space. A normal place-setting allowance is 24 in. (61 cm) of linear space. Tables over 42 in. (107 cm) long should have at least six legs, unless they are sturdy, banquet, folding tables. The bearing weight of food, dishes, and individuals leaning on the tables should be considered in specifying the number of legs and top strength. The table legs should be equipped with levelers and also have nonfriction-type **glides** or plastic **boots** on the bottom of the legs to prevent marring floors.

A strong, mar-resistant surface is desirable for tabletops. Plastic-impregnated wood is attractive and acceptably durable. Plastic makes a good cover and gives softness. It reduces the need for tablecloths or doilies for informal service. If the top is plastic over plywood, specify that the plastic be not less than $\frac{1}{16}$ in. (1.6 cm) of high-pressure thermosetting, chip- and stain-resistant laminated plastic. The plywood should be 1 in. (2.5 cm) thick, 5 to 9 ply. Plywood can be covered also with a hardwood such as Luan mahogany or other similar beautifully grained wood and finished with a durable, nonstain finish. Countertops should be fairly resistant to scratching, alcohol, or water damage, as well as resistant to burns from cigarettes or cigars. Folding tables need to be specified to have suitable tops with a strong, welded-steel base.

The best weight for a chair is from 10 to 12 lb (0.5 to 5.5 kg), unless heavier or lighter ones are needed for special purposes. Armchairs usually weigh between 15 and 22 lb (6.8 and 10 kg). Folding chairs should fold easily and stack well.

Chairs may be made of wood, plywood, plastic-impregnated wood, plastic, or metal. Strength of material and workmanship are important to durability. A number of hardwoods are suitable for chairs, the best being birch, hard maple, walnut, and oak. Walnut may have reduced life because it can dry out and split. Birch can be strengthened by impregnating it with plastic. This gives a highly serviceable chair. Bentwood chairs are best made of hard elm. The more wood that is exposed on chairs, the higher the cost. Molded plywood, 7 ply, $\frac{5}{8}$ in. (16 mm), gives a strong chair. The crossing of the grains of wood in plywood increases strength. Molded rigid urethane is the strongest plastic used for chairs. A high-impact polystyrene can be used also for legs and backs. Fiberglass has good durability. Plastics can be combined with wood or metal effectively.

Metal chairs can be made from cast aluminum; tube aluminum, either square or round; chrome; baked enamel; or steel or wrought iron. Aluminum can be anodized to take different colors, but scratches will show through the color to the silver color of aluminum. Tubular chairs should have stainless steel or other glides to reduce marring of floors. Metal pins are satisfactory on wooden chairs. Some glides may be cushioned with a rubber gasket between the glide and chair foot. Metal legs should be provided with proper glides also. Leg bottoms should be broad enough to give secure footing and not pierce or dent the flooring. **Ball feet** may be put onto some chairs. These are good for use over a rug, especially long-fiber shag rugs. Luxury chairs may be of the swivel type.

Durability and appearance are influenced by the workmanship on chairs. Metal chairs should be welded with strong, smooth welds. Seats may be fastened to metal frames with screws or bolts. Wooden chairs may be glued, with screws used at points of stress. All chairs should be examined to determine strength at points of stress, such as where the back joins the seat and where the legs join the seat. Legs should be reinforced by spreaders below the seat. Strong bracing will be required to withstand stress created when occupants tip their chairs back. One test is to turn a chair over, note its junctures, and test its strength by placing one leg on the floor at a time and pressing down as hard as possible. Note any give or yielding. Note how the legs are jointed to the seat. They should fit tightly, be well reinforced, and be securely fastened. In armchairs, note how arms are fastened to the chair and whether they are strong enough to take stress. Both concave and straight backs give satisfactory use if properly made and fastened to the chair. Concave backs tend to be more comfortable than straight backs.

Durability and appearance are influenced by the chair's finish. Poorly finished wood tends to splinter and wear quickly and show mars more readily. It is also likely to snag clothing. Spray finish on wood is less expensive than rubbed or glazed finish but not as beautiful. If chairs are of the stacking type, check to see that they will not experience excessive wear at corners or points of contact. Note the amount of play possible when several chairs are stacked together. They should fit securely so that they will not topple or rub when moved or handled. It is advisable to select dollies or other mobile equipment on which they fit and are suitable for moving chairs and tables.

Chairs should be easily cleaned and dusted. Coverings should be durable, burnproof, and soft and should hold their shape when stretched. Padding should have good resilience. It is usually specified as from 1.5 to 2 in. (3.75 to 5 cm) thick, with some as thick as 4 in. (10 cm). Cotton is durable and has good resilience. It may be combined with foam rubber under it. Leather as a covering is attractive in appearance and gives good wear, but is costly. Fabrics are durable and less expensive, but care needs to be taken in their selection for suitable pattern and color that will harmonize and not show stain. The fabric should be treated to be stain resistant, and should be easily cleanable. Many plastics have a soft, beautiful sheen and are easily cleaned. Some will stretch. Vinyl that has been perforated fits well to padding and permits good transfer of air on impact. If seats have springs under them, barbed nails should be used for fastening so that they will not fall out.

Tables and chairs should be selected together. Sizing should be based on need. Small children need lower tables and lower chairs. Large individuals do not like either undersized or oversized units. Flexibility should be sought. An 18-in. (45-cm)-high chair should be selected for a 30-in. (75-cm)-high table and a 17-in. (43-cm) chair for a 29-in. (73-cm) table. Standard chairs are from 16 to 18 in. (40 to 45 cm) high at the seat. Legs at the base should be a minimum of 14 in. (35 cm) apart. The seat should be 14 in. (35 cm) deep and 16 in. (40 cm) wide. The height of the back from the seat should be 16 to 17 in. (40 to 43 cm). The overall height of the chair is generally from 29 to 34 in. (73 to 75 cm). Sizes will vary in arm chairs.

Tables and chairs selected for meeting and board rooms may vary from those used in dining rooms. They need to be appropriate to the area. A luxurious board room of a corporation, where meals may be served occasionally, should have a substantial table and comfortable chairs. Those used in a fast turnover restaurant are likely to be lighter and less sumptuous. Some examples of suggested tables sizes are shown in Table 21–2.

The size chosen for tabletops needs to be determined in relation to the type of meals served, the manner of service, and the type, size, and number of pieces of tableware that will be on the table during the meal. In cafeterias the tabletop dimensions will be influenced by the size and shape of the trays used and the number of individuals to be seated at a table. Tables 42 to 48 in. (106 to 122 cm) long and 30 in. (75 cm) wide give good flexibility for institutional use.

Round tables may be desirable for banquet use. These usually seat 8 but they are available for 6 and 12 also. The cabaret tables usually stand on a center base, which eliminates legs. To prevent tipping, a 30- to 36-in. (75- to 90-cm) top is generally placed on a pedestal over a 19.5- to 22-in. (48.5- to 55-cm)-diameter base. They should weigh from 50 to 60 lb (23 to 27 kg) for best stability. They should have both levelers and glides. Folding tables may be 30 in. (75 cm) square or 30 in. (75 cm) wide and from 36 to 96 in. (90 to 240 cm) long for banquet service. They should be equipped with lock legs. Some tables used for banquets are as narrow as 18 in. (45 cm). This width permits them to be used as writing tables during meetings and then put together to form a 36-in. (90-cm) width. When covered with silence cloths and tablecloths they can be used for both purposes very well. In rare instances these tables may be as narrow as 15 in. (38 cm).

TABLE 21-2 *Suggested Table Sizes*

Number of People	Cafeteria	Fine Dining
2	24 × 30 in. (61 × 76 cm)	$^{24}\!/_{30}$ × $^{30}\!/_{76}$ in. ($^{61}\!/_{61}$ × $^{61}\!/_{61}$ cm)
4	30 × 30 in. (76 × 76 cm)	$^{36}\!/_{42}$ × $^{36}\!/_{42}$ in. ($^{91}\!/_{107}$ × $^{91}\!/_{107}$ cm)
6	30 × 72 in. (76 × 183 cm)	48-in.-diameter round (122 cm)
8	30 × 96 in. (76 × 244 cm)	60- or 72-in.-diameter round (152 or 183 cm)
10	30 × 120 in. (76 × 305 cm)	96-in.-diameter round (244 cm)

Source: North American Association of Food Equipment Manufacturers, An Introduction to the Foodservice Industry, *NAFEM, Chicago, IL, 1997.*

In selecting equipment for dining areas, the use of platforms should be considered. These can be purchased in different sizes and heights. Some may stack so tiered arrangements can be made. They should be strong and durable and able to take the bearing weights. If equipped with legs, check to be sure that they are strong and will support the stress given them.

COUNTERS

Counters may be required as work areas or for food display. They may provide a base for certain pieces of equipment or may be combined with steam tables, cold pans, a fountain, urn stands, or other serving equipment.

Cafeteria counters are usually 34 to 36 in. (13.6 to 14.4 cm) high and 24 to 30 in. (9.6 to 12 cm) wide, with about a 12-in. (.5 cm)-wide tray slide. If a work ledge or cutting board is on the working side, the overall width will be approximately 44 in. (17.6 cm). For strength, most counters should be mounted on frames of 1½ × 1½ × $^{3}\!/_{16}$-in. (.6 × .6 × .08 cm) galvaneal angle finished with two coats of silvertone lacquer or aluminum paint. For heavy wear, 14-gauge stainless steel tops are specified and lighter gauge or other materials where wear will be lighter. Metal tops should have edges turned down 1.5 to 2 in. (.6 to .8 cm), bull-nosed and designed for good sanitation. If field joints are necessary, hairline joining with a metal cover should be specified. No bead or rivet heads should show. Panels enclosing the counter may be of 18- to 20-gauge stainless steel, 1.25-in. (.5 cm) formica, or vitreous enamel. The counter may be mounted on 6- to 8-in. (2.4 to 3.2 cm) legs, either stainless steel, white metal, or vitreous enamel, on a 14-gauge stainless steel front platform or a solid masonry base. **Cantilever mounting** is recommended, or the counter may be suspended between columns. Openings should be planned as required, such as ice cream cabinet, cold pans, and so forth, and utilities or services should be provided as needed. A three-bar (with 1-in. or .4 cm OD bars) 12- to 16-gauge tray slide, should be mounted on white metal brackets that are spaced on centers not to exceed 42 in. (16.8 cm) if trays are to be moved in front of the counter.

Open food displays must be shielded by vertical or slanted sneeze guards; these may be hinged for ease in cleaning. The guards should be supported on brackets on 42-in. (16.8 cm) centers and should be vented to prevent steaming. There is usually a landing shelf over the guard. Shelving, if provided under the counter, should be 18-gauge stainless steel or 16-gauge galvaneal and removable; however, consideration should be given to use of mobile, undercounter storage instead of fixed shelving.

Stools may or may not be required at counters where patrons eat. Seats that are cantilevered make for ease in cleaning. Counters are frequently built of wood with a masonry base and a countertop of vinyl, linoleum, or hard plastic. A very satisfactory top is made of high-pressure sealed laminate. Stools for the counters 42 in. (107 cm) high may be raised on a pedestal from the floor level and a foot rest provided or they may be set on a masonry base, 8 in. (20 cm) high. The first is considered best from the standpoint of safety.

If the cashier station is a part of the counter, a space at least 30 in. (12 cm) wide should be provided. An electrical outlet will be needed for an electric cash register. A drawer approximately 20×20 in. (8×8 cm) should be provided. A foot rest may be installed if desired.

A variety of cash registers are available to fit specific needs. They speed calculation and minimize error by indicating correct change. Most permit itemizing so that number and kind of items can be tallied. The machine selected should be simple to operate, especially if a number of different personnel are to use it. It should provide a tape for records in counting cash and for bookkeeping. Separate drawers may also be required for the different persons using the machine.

Cash registers are available that can be preset for specific items at different prices and a different number of units sold. Thus a fast-food operation may sell a plain hamburger and a deluxe hamburger. Each can be priced into the machine. The price for one to five of each on an order may be totaled so that if a certain number are sold, only one ring up is needed. For the hamburger selling at $1.90, the machine may be set so if three are sold, only a 3 multiplier button need to pushed down along with the plain hamburger key to print the cost of sale as $5.70.

It may be desirable to specify a **reset counter.** This moves ahead each time a total is cleared. Such a device makes it difficult for employees to manipulate cash and furnishes management a record of operation for times during which they have been unable to supervise employees. Customer counters are available and, as with the cash reset counter, move ahead each time a customer count is taken, making a traffic tally. An instant loading of tape saves time during busy periods over one that must be rethreaded while customers wait.

Newer "point of sale" (POS) equipment is now used extensively in some operations, such as fast food restaurants (see Figure 21.8). The development of touch based screens and computer POS software has greatly expanded the capabilities of these newer POS systems as compared to traditional cash register systems. Some of the options for the new POS systems include:

- data processing for numerous areas including sales, inventory, labor scheduling, hotel systems interface, advance reservations, etc.
- comprehensive data reporting
- data transfer to kitchen to place orders (to eliminate trips to and from the kitchen)
- credit card processing
- printer routing (to the place where an order may be filled for a customer)
- audit trail capabilities
- ability to work as stand alone units or as multiple points of sale
- graphics (which decrease employee training time)
- numeric code entry to track which employee conducted the transaction
- user customizable screens (for daily, weekly, or monthly menu changes)
- coupon printing (to encourage the sale of complementary items).

Check tallies can provide useful information for management pertaining to popularity of menu items, volume served from day to day, and income. Consideration should be given to speeding the tallying of checks. The availability of a calculator may help employees to more quickly tally checks without error. A quick food tallying register that prints out the item, prices , and totals it with an identifying number and date is available. Time stamping is also usually included. The slip or a duplicate may be given to the guest. The tallying register dollar total should coincide with the cash register total. The machine may be connected also to an ordering system so orders are immediately transferred to the kitchen or production area. A variation of this system is one that allows customers to enter their own orders. The machine notifies production of the order, prints out the check, totals it, and may give other information if desired. A memory storage unit

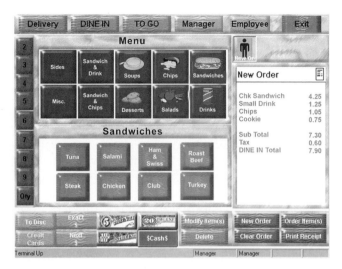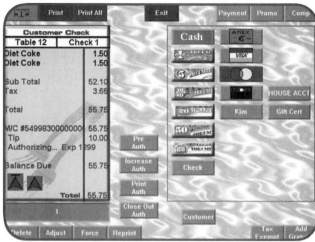

FIGURE 21.8   A point of sale system (POS) that is compatible with computer software. Such programs can use touch screens with icons or text to speed data entry. Numerous reports are possible from such systems, including restaurant sales, check in/out times, payment reports, server sales, labor reports, and item availability. *(Courtesy of Ibertech, Bedford, TX)*

can be added so management may have retrievable information on items sold, numbers served, peak periods, and other information.

CHAPTER SUMMARY

Point-of-service needs vary tremendously between restaurants from holding cabinets to self-service hot and cold food bars, to exhibition cooking, to transport equipment to display cabinets. Food must be kept safely during service. Temperatures for potentially hazardous foods must be kept below 40°F (4°C) or above 140°F (60°C). Protection from contamination should also be provided. In self-service areas, for example, breath guards are required above both hot and cold food bars.

Many specialty pieces of equipment are available for both hot and cold holding. Moist or dry heat is available for hot food tables and holding cabinets. A variety of sizes are also available including both countertop and floor models. Insulation is an important selection factor for both hot and cold holding equipment. In passive temperature maintenance equipment, adequate insulation is essential because no heat or cold is added during the holding period. Mobile equipment has become more popular. The maneuverability of casters and bumper guards is an important feature. Interior dimensions should be carefully considered on pieces of holding equipment. In addition to total capacity, dimensions should be compared to pans, plates, or trays that will be placed inside. Ease of cleaning is another critical selection factor.

Four types of cold food bars are possible: ice-cooled, mechanically refrigerated units, combination units, and convected cold air (air curtain) models. A variety of useful options on these include templates, plate or tray rests, adapter bars for fractional size pans, well organizers, ice guards, crock inserts, tight-fitting lids, specialty tongs, and countertop boards for slicing of breads or meats.

Coffee brewing equipment has changed dramatically in the last 10 years with the renewed interest in flavored coffees, espresso, and cappuccino. A variety of manual to superautomatic models are available requiring different skill levels to operate. Quality of the coffee produced depends on a number of factors related to brewing and holding including length of brewing or holding time, grinding of beans, ratio of coffee to water, temperature of the water, depth of the coffee bed, and satisfactory cleaning of equipment. Espresso machines produce smaller quantities of specialty coffee using high pressure to force the hot water through a finely ground coffee. Cappuccino incorporates frothed and steamed milk into the espresso. Alternatives to traditional brewing of coffee include the use of concentrated liquids or freeze-dried powder bases.

Carbonated beverage dispensers may be either premix or postmix systems. Postmix systems require less space, but require more complicated equipment. Equipment for premix systems is less expensive, but more storage space is required for the product. Cooling systems and carbonators should be selected based on volume.

A variety of chairs and tables are available. Materials include wood, plastic, metal, or a combination of these. Size, durability, ease of movement, and safety are important considerations in addition to appearance. Tables and chairs should be chosen to complement each other. Sizes and materials selected will vary with the style of foodservice. Other service area needs may include counters and cash registers.

REVIEW QUESTIONS

1. Note type of seating and material used in three different dining areas. Evaluate seating from standpoint of (a) comfort, (b) amount of care required, (c) ease of handling by customers and employees, (d) ease of cleaning, (e) appearance, and (f) durability.
2. Note the table height and dimensions in three different dining areas. What is the material of the tables and how is it finished? Do the tables have glides? What housekeeping care is required for the tables? Are the tables attractive?
3. Observe two cafeteria counters and state (a) height, (b) width, (c) arrangement of top, (d) storage areas for food, serving tools, and dishes, (e) work space, (f) sanitary protection, (g) appearance, (h) convenience features, and (i) care required.
4. Locate five examples of equipment used for retaining desired temperature in food and state how they are used in a (a) commercial restaurant, (b) hospital, (c) school food service, and (d) for transporting food. Evaluate each in terms of (a) effectiveness, (b) convenience, (c) sanitation aspects, and (d) appearance.
5. Note the beverage equipment used in three different dining areas, and state (a) brewing method, (b) amount brewed at one time, (c) greatest length of holding period, (d) total time required (worker time spent each brewing period times the number of times brewing is done), (e) adequacy of volume and serving speed, (f) location convenience of brewing equipment (for brewing and for service), and (g) coffee quality.

KEY WORDS AND CONCEPTS

active temperature holding equipment
air curtains
air gap
"bag-in-the-box" soft drink dispensing system
bain marie
breath guards
cantilever mounting
cappuccino
coffee brewers
coffee urns
cold-plate beverage cooling system
crazing
crock inserts
espresso
espresso brewing heads
exchanger coffee urn
flash heaters

grinder compartments
ice guards
leachers
liquid and freeze-dried coffee base
manual, semiautomatic, automatic, and superautomatic machines
passive temperature maintenance
plastics, such as polysulfone, polyurethane, polystyrene
postmix soft drink systems
premix soft drink systems
pump coffee urn
reset counter
table ball feet
table leg boots or glides
tempered glass
template

CHAPTER
22

Refrigeration and Low-Temperature Storage Equipment

Suitable cold storage is an essential for preserving materials and ensuring good sanitation. The use of refrigeration and low-temperature storage has greatly increased in the last 40 years or so. The amount needed will vary with the type of food offered in different facilities, and an allowance should be made as a margin of safety and for flexibility. Current use of frozen foods has increased the need for more low-temperature storage than formerly required. The manner in which it is used influences its location in the layout and the type of unit. See Table 22–1 for an example of refrigerator and freezer types.

TABLE 22–1 *Average Number of Refrigerators or Freezers per Food Service*

Type of Unit	All	Hospital	College	School
Refrigerator				
Upright	6	4	6	11
Under-counter	3	2	3	6
Walk-ins	3	3	4	5
Pass-throughs	5	2	4	14
Freezer				
Uprights	4	2	4	7
Under-counter	5	1	2	7
Walk-ins	2	3	2	3
Pass-throughs	7	1	2	4

Source: Adapted from Freezers & refrigerators. (1994). Foodservice Director, 7(6), 154.

REFRIGERATION SYSTEMS

The equipment required to lower temperatures is a motor, a **compressor,** a condenser, an evaporator, controls, valves and other subsidiary equipment, and an insulated enclosed area. Temperatures are lowered by taking advantage of the thermodynamic property of liquids that requires heat to expand or contract. The heat absorbed in the refrigerated area is given off at the condenser in the compression-type units. These condensers for cooling require either air or water. Large machines usually have **water-cooled condensers,** while self-contained units have **air-cooled condensers.** Machine rooms where motors and condensers are located should have water piped to them, have drains, and be well ventilated. If air-cooled equipment is placed there, a drain is needed to carry away condensate. Machines are also available that offer condensate **evaporators** that utilize the heat of the hot return refrigerant line or electric evaporators. These make the location of the refrigerator more flexible by eliminating plumbing requirements. Diagrams showing the basic components of both a refrigeration and absorption cooling system are shown in Figures 22.1 and 15.4, respectively.

Special refrigerated and low-temperature areas may be required to avoid flavor absorption by different foods and to give required variable temperatures and humidity. Table 22–2 indicates recommended temperatures and relative humidity levels. Up to five general types of temperature ranges may be used: standard refrigerator temperatures (less than 40°F or 4.4°C), freezer temperatures (less than 0°F or −17.8°C), ice cream freezers (6 to 12°F or −14.4 to −11.1°C), and two units that use forced air to more rapidly cool products, blast chillers and blast freezers (−20 to −40°F or −28.9 to −40°C). Some planners of food services are recommending −10°F (−23°C) for longer storage of frozen items. For the greatest energy efficiency, freezers and blast freezers should be located inside other refrigerated storage, separated by an inner door.

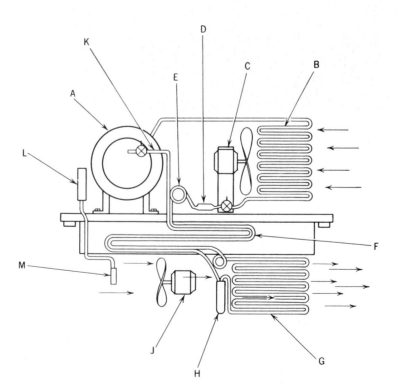

FIGURE 22.1   General schematic of refrigeration assembly: (A) condenser, (B) cooling coils, (C) fan, (D) expansion coils, and (E) refrigeration fan.

TABLE 22–2   Recommended Conditions for Refrigerated and Low-Temperature Areas

Foods	Temporary Storage (°F)	Holding Storage (°F)	Recommended Relative Humidity (%)
Vegetables and fruits	36–42	32–36	95
Meats	34–38	32–36	85
Fish	30–40	30–40	85
Eggs	36–40	31–40	95
Butter and cheese	38–40	35–40	85
Bottled beverages	35–40	35–40	—
Frozen foods	10–30	0––10	—
Ice cream	6–12 (for dishing)	0––10	—

Large refrigerator and low-temperature units are usually operated with the motor, compressor, and condenser located in a remote area. If more than 20 to 30 ft (6.1 to 9.1 m) away, the pipes carrying refrigerant should be insulated. In addition, the areas themselves will require electrical current for light and blower fans and drainage must be provided for moisture runoff. Drainage lines for condensate should not be connected directly to sewers but should include an air gap to prevent contaminants from returning up from the sewer lines into the refrigerated area.

Full air-duct controlled air flow usually gives the best temperature control, especially if a dual fan and coil system is installed. Freezers should hold a steady -10 to $-12°F$ (-23 to $-24°C$). In humid climates, it is desirable to have **anti-sweat heaters** around door openings, to prevent them from freezing shut and being difficult to open. A vent system should be installed in walk-ins where odor or humidity may be a problem. The amount or size of the coil installed should be calculated to give 80% relative humidity. A thermometer installed in the equipment should be accurate to within 3°F (1.7°C) and easily readable. An indicator light mounted in the door or the face of the cooler should indicate when power is on or off. Some units include a sound system to notify when the inside temperature goes too high. A safety latch for inside openings should be installed in walk-ins to prevent individuals from being locked in. Refrigeration coils and condensing units should carry a five-year minimum guarantee.

Air-cooled units are used for smaller requirements, whereas the larger condensers are usually water cooled. In quite large installations the heat from condensers may be used for other purposes such as heating water. Top-mounted installations for reach-ins provide better utilization of space than either bottom- or side-mounted units. Adjustable shelving is desirable, and half an inch of spacing is most versatile. Roll-ins are desirable because they reduce handling of material. Their location should be considered in relation to preparation and service sections. Even if roll-ins fill most refrigeration needs, there is likely to be some need for standard adjustable shelving.

Requirements for coolant and insulation material used in refrigerated and freezer units have changed since many units were installed. CFC compounds that deplete ozone have been banned. As of the end of 1995, the manufacture of **CFC refrigerants,** such as R-12 and R-502, ceased. In addition, the use of CFC-11 as one of the major blowing agents in rigid foam insulation used in refrigerators and freezers was banned. Options for equipment that previously used CFC refrigerants have included these: continuing to use the existing refrigerants at dramatically increased cost as the supply dwindles (until the equipment itself must be replaced); retrofitting the existing equipment to **HCFC refrigerants** (also scheduled for phase-out in new manufacture in 2010 and for service applications in 2020) or **HFC refrigerants** (this generally requires a new compressor and seals); or buying new equipment that meets current guidelines. Costs vary tremendously for each of these alternatives.

Door **gaskets** should be grease-proof vinyl and easy to clean and change. If space for door openings is too limited, sliding doors may be used. Doors should be self-closing. Recessed handles are useful if aisle spaces are narrow. Glass or Plexiglas doors or windows in doors reduce door opening in search of items. Locks may be useful where security is necessary. The finish should be durable, easy to clean, and retain good appearance in spite of repeated cleaning. Stainless steel, although costly, is durable and retains a bright appearance. Some of the high-temperature baked acrylics give good service. Units chosen should be fully NSF approved.

Useful options include built-in alarm systems (if temperatures rise too high); indicator lights for power, defrost, and malfunctioning; **strip curtains** (to minimize air loss when the door is opened); re-hingeable doors; adjustable shelves; **pressure relief vents** on freezers (which minimize the vacuum effect created when warm air enters the freezer and is then cooled); foot pedal openers for opening doors when one's hands are full; **diagnostics capability;** programmable defrost cycles; and door snubbers (which pull the door closed when it gets close to the point of closing).

TYPES OF REFRIGERATION EQUIPMENT

Types of refrigerating or low-temperature units include (1) reach-ins, (2) walk-ins, (3) blast units, (4) specialized units, and (5) ice-making equipment.

Reach-Ins

Reach-ins may fulfill all the storage needs in a small operation. In large operations they are used for storage needs within a work center and walk-ins are used for central storage. In some operations, reach-ins may even be built into the side of the walk-in (Figure 22.2). Reach-ins may be refrigerated or freezer units. Some units are convertible between the two with the flip of a switch. Upright reach-ins range from 78 to 84 in. (198 to 213 cm) in height and are 32 in. (81 cm) deep. Each compartment is about 28 in. (71 cm) wide. Single-compartment units generally hold 21.5 cu ft (0.6 cu m), double compartments hold 46.5 cu ft (1.3 cu m), and triple compartments 70.0 cu ft (2.0 cu m). Proper sizing of reach-ins to meet specific needs is important. A general guide for amount of reach-in space is shown in Table 22–3.

Slide doors or windows may be required. Right or left door openings should be indicated. Lights should be specified. Lights must be shielded or covered with a shatter-resistant coating.

Insulation for refrigerators and low-temperature units should be 3 in. (7.6 cm) and 3 to 6 in. (7.7 to 15.2 cm), respectively, and of the moisture-resistant, nonsettling type. Outside and inside seams should be welded. Coving on interiors and exteriors should be ⅝ in. (1.6 cm). Walls are generally stainless steel, aluminum, plastic coating over galvanized steel, or one-piece ABS plastic. Stainless steel is considered the most durable. Sturdy construction of doors, hardware, and fixtures is a requirement. Doors may be full or half length and should have strong catches. Shelving should be adjustable. Door gaskets should provide reasonable wear and be replaceable. Hinge locking devices (which hold the door open past 90 degrees for easier loading and unloading) and an **adjustable strike** (the plate that the door hits upon closing) should be specified. **Magnetic strips** on the door frame provide a tighter seal. Stainless steel or heavy chrome-plated brass or bronze should be the metal used for hardware. Rust-proof drains with bell-type drain traps or air gaps should be provided.

Reach-in freezers may be of the upright or chest type. **Upright freezers** are the most commonly used. They cost slightly more and will lose more refrigerated air than **chest**

FIGURE 22.2   A reach-in compartment that is a part of a walk-in refrigerator. (*Courtesy of George Bunby & Associates, Seattle, Washington.*)

TABLE 22-3   *General Guide for Reach-in Space*

Size of Operation (No. of Seats)	Refrigeration		Freezer	
	Units	Compartments/Unit	Units	Compartments/Unit
Under 50	2	2	1	2
50–100	3	2	1	3
100–250	3	3	2	2
250–500	4	3	2	3
500–750	5	3	2	3

Source: North American Association of Food Equipment Manufacturers, An Introduction to the Foodservice Industry, *NAFEM, Chicago, IL, 1997.*

freezers, but they have the advantage of being easier to defrost, take less floor space, and are easier to use for storage and removal of items. The upright must have space provided for open doors. The chest type may provide additional counter space if mobile and located under a counter where it can be pulled out, or drawers may be provided.

Pass-throughs open from both sides. If they cannot be located adjacent to both production and service areas, they should be designed to hold mobile carts that can be loaded in the production area and rolled to the pass-through. Tight seals between doors and the floor should be made if mobile units are rolled in.

Certain preparation areas may have specialized needs. Bakeshop refrigerators, for example, should be designed to take slide-in equipment in addition to stored supplies. Some areas may require refrigerators sized for mobile equipment. Service areas may require counter or backbar refrigeration. Drawer-type units are useful near broilers and other preparation areas and in service counters. Waitstaff units frequently are provided

TABLE 22–4   A General Guide for Walk-in Space Needs

Type of Operation	No. of Walk-Ins	Area
Fast-food restaurant	1	90–120 sq ft (8.4–11.2 sq m)
Small restaurant	1	120–150 sq ft (11.2–14.0 sq m)
Medium restaurant	2	180–240 sq ft (16.7–22.3 sq m)
Large restaurant	3	240–400 sq ft (22.3–37.2 sq m)
Large institution	3	400–600 sq ft (37.2–55.8 sq m)
Large hotel, restaurant with complex menu and catering	4	600–900 sq ft (55.8–83.7 sq m)

Source: North American Association of Food Equipment Manufacturers, An Introduction to the Foodservice Industry, *NAFEM, Chicago, IL, 1997.*

with small units for creamers, butter or margarine, desserts, salads, and other items. Low-temperature storage may also be needed for ice cream. Beverage dispensers are also often placed where service is required. Where quantities of frozen cooked foods, meats, vegetables, fruits, and other foods are used, freezer reach-ins may be located within the work center. Usually temperatures just below freezing are desirable.

Walk-Ins

Walk-ins are usually designed to carry large quantities of food and are usually used for storage in central areas. Location of walk-ins should be such as to make delivery of foods from receiving to production and to service units as short and easy as possible. They should be located where they can be easily supervised. They may be an integral part of the building and as such are often constructed of concrete or they may be knockdown or prefabricated rooms put up in sections. Temperature and humidity conditions should be carefully planned. The usual number of walk-ins used by a large food service is three— one for fruits and vegetables; one for meats, poultry, and fish; and one for dairy products, although more may be added if specialized requirements make this desirable. Frequently a salad walk-in and occasionally refrigerated garbage rooms are provided. Bakers' walk-ins are sometimes located close to the bakeshop. Small operations find one walk-in sufficient but optimum storage conditions do not prevail for all types of foods. A general guide for amount of walk-in space by type of operation is shown in Table 22–4. Another common guideline is to allow 1 to 1.5 cu ft per person served per day. Walk-ins are used in large operations. Many operations install a walk-in if they serve 300 to 400 meals per day or more. Smaller operations may use reach-in units instead. Walk-in freezer space is generally calculated at one-half the required refrigeration space. If quantity of food to be stored is known, storage needs may also be estimated from these. Generally, an average of 28 lb (12.7 kg) of food may be stored per cubic foot (0.03 cu m) of storage space.

Refrigerated walk-ins should have 2- to 3-in. (5.1- to 7.6-cm)-thick good insulation and walk-in freezers at least 4 in. (10.2 cm). Vapor-proof, easily cleanable, durable walls, ceilings, and floors should be installed. Typical walls are aluminum or galvanized steel with urethane insulation. Insulated floors are particularly critical for walk-in freezers to increase operating efficiency and prevent condensation and freezing of water on the floor. The floor should be on a level plane with the outside floor and insulation should be installed below floor level. If the outside floor is not at the same level, a ramp may be installed in order to roll carts into the walk-ins. Sturdy well-insulated doors with heavy-duty, corrosion-resistant, lock-type hardware should be used. Magnetic seals and self-closing hinges are typical. Inside emergency opening devices should be provided. Meat rails, shelving, and other equipment used to hang food or shelving on which foods are

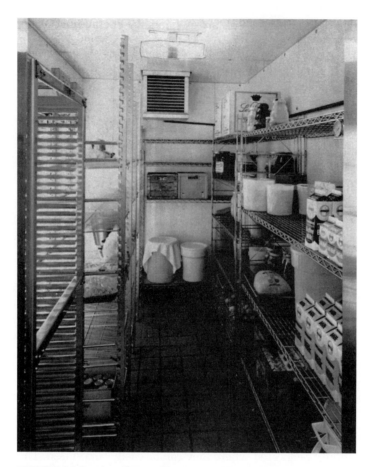

FIGURE 22.3   A walk-in refrigerator with adjustable wire shelving and a quarry tile floor. *(Courtesy of George Bunby & Associates, Seattle, Washington.)*

placed should be adjustable, durable, sturdy, and made of noncorrosive-type materials. Slatted or open welded wire shelving is preferred for better circulation of air (Figure 22.3). An outside temperature indicator should be provided and be accurate to within ±3°F (±1.7°C). Some operations locate the walk-in freezer inside the walk-in refrigerator to improve energy efficiency.

Walk-ins may be either prefabricated or built in. Built-in refrigerators and freezers are generally more expensive. They are usually constructed with glazed tile or fiberglass walls, a tile floor, and an aluminum or stainless steel ceiling. A number of prefabricated walk-ins can also be purchased, some of which are as large as refrigerated buildings. They should be specified for standard heights. A typical unit is 8 × 12 ft (2.4 × 3.7 m), but units are available as low as 6.5 ft (2 m) and as high as 11 ft (3.4 m). The systems may require from ⅓- to 10-hp motors. Rigid urethane insulation at least 4 in. (10 cm) thick with a 0.029 U factor[1] and a UL 25 low flame spread, nonburning rating should be specified. Walls should be rigid and of light reflective material tightly joined to allow no moisture penetration. Standard finishes for interiors and exteriors are 24-gauge bright galvanized steel or white painted steel, 0.040 embossed patterned aluminum, 22-gauge Type 304, No. 2B finish stainless steel, or anodized aluminum. In many instances these same requirements can be applied to other refrigeration put into the facility.

---

[1]This would be a 0.116 (4 in. × 0.029 = 0.116) k factor, which compares with a urethane slab (0.139 k), Styrofoam slab (0.25 k), or corkboard (0.270 k), which would give U values, respectively, of 0.056, 0.100, and 0.108. U coefficients quantify the amount of heat that will flow through one square foot of refrigerator wall per hour for each degree Fahrenheit difference in temperature between the inside and the outside of the refrigerator. Lower U coefficients are preferred over higher U coefficients.

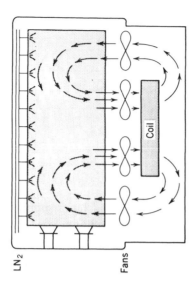

FIGURE 22.4 Rapid freezing may be accomplished by circulating air temperature as low as −20°F and also by injecting liquid nitrogen into the compartment at a temperature of −320°F.

Walk-ins of the knock-down or fabricated type are used when walk-in space is required and cannot be furnished by integral construction. Standards should be equivalent to that required for integral walk-ins. They should be designed to handle mobile equipment. Modular planning based on equipment use and portion sizes will greatly assist in achieving better utilization of expensive space.

Blast Chillers and Freezers

Blast chillers rapidly cool foods using a convected air system. They are a standard piece of equipment in cook-chill systems where they are used for almost any kind of food product. They are an essential part of the cook-chill system for foods that cannot be handled by a tumble chiller (fried chicken, pork chops, etc.). Blast chillers cool foods more rapidly than standard refrigerators. They can, for example, chill food from 165°F (73.9°C) down to 38°F (3.3°C) within 90 minutes. **Blast freezers** are also available to more rapidly freeze foods (in order to produce large volumes of higher quality, safer foods) and operate at −20 to −40°F (28.9 to 40°C) (Figure 22.4). Blast chillers and freezers are constructed of similar materials to standard refrigerators and freezers and use either air- or water-cooled compressor systems with a higher horsepower rating than "nonblast" systems.

Specialized Equipment

Specialized equipment in frozen dessert (ice cream, frozen yogurt, shakes, etc.) restaurants may be very similar to reach-ins. A frozen dessert restaurant, however, must provide for different refrigeration and freezing needs and, for that reason, two or more units may be required. Refrigerated space at about 40°F (4.4°C) for whipped cream and other food must be provided. Syrup racks must also be kept refrigerated. **Ice cream freezers** must cool to 6 to 10°F (−14.4 to −12.2°C) for dishing rather than the standard freezer temperatures of 0°F (−18°C) used for ice cream storage. Equipment should meet NSF standards.

For cafeteria and other customer self-service areas, cold pans may be required for displays of salads, juices, sliced fruits, desserts, or other chilled foods. Display refrigerators or cases are frequently used for foods to be held at temperatures of 40°F (4.4°C) or below. Wall-type refrigerators are now on the market. Glass walls and doors should be made of double or triple glass to provide insulation and prevent clouding. Cold display cabinets are also common for certain take-out markets, including those that provide home meal replacements.

In customer self-service areas, refrigerated fruit juice dispensers that hold 2.5 to 5 gal (9.46 and 18.92 L) are available. They are usually equipped with small self-contained refrigerating units. Carbonated beverage dispensers come in various sizes and vary in the number of drinks of different kinds they will deliver. Most dispensers will dispense from one to six kinds, and a few may dispense more. Some require two-handed operation where the operator holds the glass in one hand and pulls the lever down to fill it. Some operate by pushing the glass against the flow release, thus permitting one-hand operation. Where disposable cups are used, it is important for the push release to operate easily enough to not crush the cup.

The size of the machine purchased should be equated to demand. For large-volume operations, machines are available that initially produce 600 drinks per hour and then have a recovery of 300 drinks per hour. Most models dispense two to six drinks per minute. Countertop units are available, and where space is limited models may be obtained to fit under the counter. Mobile units are available also. Counter models have the advantage of promoting impulse sales. Locating a dispenser over a sink eliminates the need for a drip tray and a container to hold the dripped liquid.

Stainless steel construction or high-temperature baked acrylic finishes present a good appearance and are easy to clean. Drip trays should be easily removable for cleaning. Cleaning nozzles can be purchased as additional equipment. A carbonation tester should be purchased if the machine does not have one.

Bulk milk dispensers may be used. These units are self-contained refrigerated units that hold from 2.5 to 5 gal (9.5 to 18.9 L). They should possess many of the features mentioned for carbonated beverage dispensers. Milk dispensers should be easily cleanable, either in place or disassembled, and removable parts should be easy to access. The machine should be of the type that dispenses milk from the original container and not be one into which milk is poured from the original container. It should hold milk at 40°F (4.4°C) ± 3°F (1.7°C) or less when in an area of 110°F (43.3°C) or less. Milk at the delivery point should not be more than 40°F (4.4°C). Dispensing tubes should be capable of being connected to dispensing equipment in the machine without contamination; the tube should be single use. They should close completely under 15-lb (6.8-kg) shutoff weight without leakage. The NSF standards in its Standard No. 20 should be followed.

Cream dispensers are usually insulated units holding from a quart to three quarts of cream. Many are operated by a hand pump that delivers a set amount of cream. They are usually placed at coffee dispensing units so delivery can be made at the same time that coffee is drawn.

The use of large amounts of drinking water at about 40°F by customers places heavy demands on refrigeration equipment; careful sizing is required to meet demands. Tank or storage coolers, instantaneous coolers, or a combination of the two are used. These can usually be provided from standard stock equipment for either a bubbler drinking-type fountain or glass filler type. Water stations may be placed at islands for self-dispensing in cafeterias or at strategic spots for waitstaff. The estimated quantity of chilled water required per person served is 10 to 12 oz (296 to 355 mL). Peak demands should be ascertained and equipment sized to meet this need. Ice is frequently required in addition to chilled water so that storage and dispensing must be provided close to the water source.

The use of vending machines has increased in the past few years and it is expected this trend will continue. While such units save labor, they also present other problems since employees are no longer there who would normally supervise this service. As a result, sanitation problems have sometimes increased.

The construction of vending machines should follow the general principles of good construction and design and materials cited previously for other foodservice equipment. All food contact areas should be readily accessible and easily cleanable either in place or when disassembled. Removable parts should be readily removable.

Where tubes, valves, or other attachments cannot be removed, it should be possible to flush the equipment with a sanitizing solution to obtain adequate clean-in-place cleaning. Foods should be able to be added or removed in a sanitary manner. All openings for food removal should be designed to minimize contamination from dust, seepage, or other substances and to minimize the handling or touching of food contact surfaces. Disassembly and reassembly ease for cleaning should be checked. All spigots, spouts, and faucets should be the nondrip type. They should meet standards of the U.S. Public Health Department and NSF.

If beverages or foods are delivered to the patron in bulk, there should be a self-closing door or panel that protects against the entrance of vermin, dust, or other contaminants. The closure device should fit so snugly that no cracks or openings larger than $\frac{1}{16}$ in. (1.6 mm) exist. Outlets of delivery tubes should be protected from normal manual contact. A door or closure device may not be needed when only a dispensing tube and waste drainage vent are used. Dispensing trays or compartments for packaged goods such as candy, cookies, and cupcakes should be rodent proof.

Construction should be such as to safeguard against the spillage of hot liquids and other foods, which could cause severe burns. Rough or sharp edges should not be permitted nor projections or other factors that can cause surprise accidents. Piping should not react with carbonated water. Water and plumbing design and materials should conform to NSF codes. Hot water heaters in vending units should not go over 210°F (99°C) and should be equipped with proper relief valves and overflow pipes. A gooseneck unit should carry overflow water into a drain so patrons cannot get burned. Glass that might shatter should not be permitted. All vending machines should be sturdy and not be able to be tipped over.

Refrigerated units should maintain an even temperature of 40°F (4.4°C) or lower and should not be in areas where ambient temperatures are above 100°F (37.8°C). Hot foods must not be held lower than 140°F (60°C), and the machine should not be in an area lower than 50°F (10°C). If the hot food is a dairy product, the temperature on dispensing should not be lower than 160°F (71°C). Cutoff controls should prevent the machine from dispensing food when temperatures do not conform to these temperature requirements. Temperatures must hold to ±3°F (1.7°C); some recording device should make the temperature visible to supervising personnel. The vending part of the machine should be completely sealed off from their heating or refrigeration units. Where machines both refrigerate and heat, the requirements for temperature at service are the same, and the reduction to a refrigerated temperature or the raising to a hot serving temperature should also conform to these requirements. A complete sanitation manual should come with the machine so all phases of operation will be known to operating personnel.

All dispensing or vending equipment dispensing liquid food should have collection and drainage units for drip, spillage, overflow, or other waste. Drip pans may be used with some units. Machines connected to water should have an automatic shut-off mechanism should the machine fail to dispense water. Waste containers should be placed in machines only for the collection of coffee grounds, coffee containers, tapes, and other solid materials; otherwise, all trash and food should be deposited in containers outside the machine. All storage units should be leak proof and be readily removable, easily cleanable, and corrosion resistant—often these are plastic. When dispensing units have internal collection, they should have an automatic turnoff of the dispensing mechanism when a waste container becomes filled. The cutoff point should come before the container is completely filled so as to avoid spillage.

ICE MAKERS

Most food services have ice making equipment. In large hotels, restaurants, or cafeterias, huge equipment is required; the equipment may be located outside the dining room area and delivery of ice is made as required to storage and dispensing units. In others, ice making equipment is located closer to the point of use. Under-counter units are even available for small capacity needs. If condensers are located remotely, ice making units are quieter for use in service areas. Purity is essential. Sanitary and well-insulated facilities should be provided for ice storage and dispensing.

Ice makers to make ice in block or bulk form that can be broken up in sizes by chippers or crushers are available. Capacities run from 40 to 4,000 lb (18 to 1,816 kg) per day. Cube makers may be purchased and some may be adjustable to freeze cubes as small as ¼ in. or as large as 1 in. (0.6 to 2.5 cm). Bin storage capacities range from 400 to 800 lb (181 to 363 kg). Crushed or flaked ice machines may be obtained also. Self-contained units freezing 20 to 600 lb (9 to 272 kg) of ice per day may be obtained. Electricity, cold water, and drainage must be provided. Insulated mobile carts having thermostatic controls to turn off automatically when the cart is full are also on the market.

Ice shape and size affect how fast it melts. Cube ice lasts longer in drinks, which makes this form desirable for take-out drinks or drinks to be held before consumption. Flake ice cools the drink faster, but unfortunately melts faster. Several **ice shapes** are possible, including these:

- Cylindrical or hollow center cubes (common for all-around use)
- Lenticular (lens shaped, used in clubs and bars)
- Mini cubes (sometimes used instead of crushed or flaked)
- Full-size square cubes (often used in clubs and bars)
- Flaked (used in salad bars and blended drinks).

Small cubes or flakes pack well in a glass and take up more space so that the glass appears full with less beverage. Standard fill of ice per glass is often calculated as 40% to 50% of the capacity. For example, a 10-oz (296-mL) cup would contain 3.8 to 5 oz (108 to 142 g) of ice; a 12-oz (355-mL) cup would hold 4.5 to 6 oz (128 to 170 g) of ice. The 40% ice rule can also be used to determine capacity needs. For example, 40% of cup capacity multiplied by the number of drinks served per day of each size cup should offer an estimate to use when determining capacity needs. Average use guidelines are also sometimes used to calculate capacity requirements. For example, the average restaurant customer uses between 1.5 and 3 lb (0.7 and 1.4 kg), a salad bar uses 15 lb (6.8 kg) of ice per square foot (929 sq cm) when packed 4 to 6 in. (10.2 to 15.2 cm) deep, hotel customers require 5 lb (2.2 kg) per room, and cocktail lounges use 3 lb (1.4 kg) per customer. A final guide suggests taking the weekly volume divided by seven days multiplied by 1.2 (to allow a 20% safety margin for increased use) to determine average daily use of ice. Actual consumption will vary with the menu, nonfood use of ice (such as in salad bars, storage of fresh fish, etc.), and even with the weather so that these guidelines are only used as estimates.

Machine production capacity also varies. Flake machines usually produce more ice per day than cube machines. Machines should carry a guarantee of performance including the amount they make in an hour or day. Machine capacities, however, are often overstated by the manufacturer in that they may be based on a 70°F (21°C) room temperature and water flowing into the machine at 50°F (10°C) or 60°F (15.6°C). Because production drops with higher room and water temperatures (during the summer for example), such capacities may easily be overstated by 10% to 15% for actual use. More realistic guidelines use a 90°F (32°C) air temperature and 70°F (21°C) water temperature.

Some operations with uneven needs may purchase lower capacity machines with larger storage bins so that ice is produced and stored during off periods. This is generally a less expensive option than purchasing a larger production capacity to handle the peak demand requirements.

Large machines are usually water cooled, but some are air cooled. Combination air- and water-cooled units are also available. Adequate drainage is required on water-cooled units. The cost of water for the water-cooled units should also be considered. CFC refrigerants in ice machines are under the same regulations as refrigerators and freezers, described previously. Installation at point of use is desirable. One machine on the market manufactures ice and delivers it via pipes to other areas. Bins should be well insulated and be able to hold ice in a refrigerated area for almost a week. Polyethylene is an acceptable plastic material for bins, trays, and other contact surfaces. Stainless steel, aluminum, and galvanized steel are also available. The construction and materials of ice machine equipment should follow standards established by NSF in Standard No. 12.

Vermin, dust, dirt, splash, or drainage should be excluded from the ice machine by proper construction. It should be easily cleaned and maintained and serviced. Where direct cleaning cannot occur, it should be possible to cleanse by circulating cleaning solutions through the equipment.

Useful options include self-cleaning systems, water filtration systems, machines that make two different forms of ice (cubes and crushed, for example), ice dispensing machines that automatically dispense ice into portable containers for hotel customers at the push of a button (rather than the bin method, which may become contaminated more easily by customers during self-service), ice scoop holders, stacking models (which can be stacked two high to double the output), **ice caddies** (insulated containers with casters that can hold or transport up to 175 lb or 79.4 kg of ice at a time), indicator lights (to signal proper functioning, malfunctioning, or cycling phase), bin sensing (which tells the ice maker to stop making ice when it is full), and **inlet chillers** (which prechill the water before it enters the ice machine for faster ice production).

CHAPTER SUMMARY

Refrigerated and freezer storage is required for maintaining the quality and safety of foods in storage. The amount of storage required differs between operations, but has increased during the last 40 years. Refrigeration equipment requires a motor, compressor, a condenser, an evaporator, controls, valves, and an insulated enclosed area. Condensers may be air or water cooled. Air-cooled units are generally used for smaller units. Condensers may also be installed at the unit or remotely. Remote locations generally offer more quiet operation. The manufacture of CFC refrigerants was banned at the end of 1995 and affects maintenance of existing equipment. New equipment is being manufactured with non-CFC-containing refrigerants.

Cold holding equipment may include reach-ins (either uprights or chest types), walk-ins, or a variety of specialized units that include pass-throughs, drawers, display cabinets, roll-ins, ice cream freezers, wall-type refrigerators, cold beverage dispensers (juice, carbonated beverages, and milk), cream dispensers, and vending machines. Walk-in units are used by operations that produce large quantities of food. More moderate size operations may use reach-ins. In large operations, reach-ins are used in the individual work centers in addition to the walk-in units, which are located more centrally. All cold holding equipment should be designed to be durable, work efficiently at keeping the appropriate temperature and humidity, and be well insulated, easy to clean, and sized to meet demand.

Ice machines can also be either air or water cooled. Capacity requirements can be calculated in a number of ways. Manufacturers' stated capacities should be evaluated carefully for actual use conditions. Production capacity of ice machines is generally less during the summer because of higher ambient temperatures. Some operations with uneven demands choose to purchase somewhat smaller capacity machines and larger bins to even out the production schedule. Choice of the most appropriate ice shape and size will vary with each operation. Cylindrical or hollow center cubes are common for all-around use. Smaller size cubes or crushed ice occupy more space in a glass compared to the beverage than do larger ice cubes.

REVIEW QUESTIONS

1. Observe the refrigeration equipment in two large food operations and list items of equipment with specifications for size, capacity, type, temperature maintained, and how used. Where is each located?

2. Write the specifications for the refrigeration equipment for a specified food operation.

KEY WORDS AND CONCEPTS

adjustable strikes

air-cooled condensers

anti-sweat heaters

blast chillers

blast freezers

chest freezers

CFC refrigerants

compressor

diagnostics capability

evaporators

gaskets

HCFC refrigerants

HFC refrigerants

ice caddies

ice cream freezers

ice shape

inlet chillers

magnetic strips

pass-throughs

pressure relief vents

reach-ins

strip curtains

U coefficients

upright freezers

walk-ins

water-cooled condensers

CHAPTER

23

Cleaning or Housekeeping Equipment

DISHWASHERS

Satisfactory dishwashing occurs when cleaning and sanitizing render "eating and drinking utensils free of soil, wash water, and detergent, leaving them clean, sanitized, and reasonably dry."[1] The steps needed to do this are usually to (1) prescrape (before dishes and utensils are put into the machine), (2) prewash (rough soil is removed in the dish machine), (3) wash with detergent (remaining soil is removed), (4) rinse (to remove wash water), (5) sanitize (using a spray of fresh hot water or water containing an approved chemical solution), and (6) air dry. Sometimes blowers or dryers are used to help dry the ware (Figure 23.1). The prewash is sometimes omitted in the machine and is done manually using a sink with a perforated soil collection basket or using a mechanical pump to remove the rough soil from the dishes.

Machine types are categorized by the type of sanitizing done (hot water or chemicals), the number of tanks, and the way the ware goes through the machine. With chemical sanitizing machines, a chlorine-containing sanitizing agent is used as part of the final rinse. Temperature of the final rinse is set between 120 and 140°F (49 and 60°C) to allow for efficient action without vaporization of the chemical. The lower water temperature dish machines require less energy compared to hot water sanitizing dish machines and do not require the purchase of a booster heater. They do, however have higher chemical costs. Low-temperature dish machines are also associated with dishes not drying adequately, particularly in humid kitchens, and they may not remove heavy grease as well as hot water machines. In hot water machines, the final rinse temperature must be between 180 and 195°F (82 and 91°C), which requires a booster heater. Temperatures above this are not used because the water starts to turn to steam and does not contact the dishes for proper sanitizing action.

---

[1]NSF Standard No. 3.

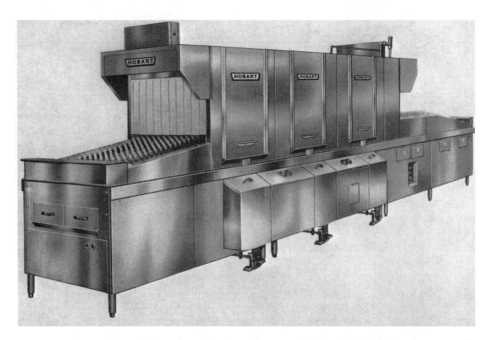

FIGURE 23.1   A large dishwashing machine that would be installed in very large installations to handle a mass of dishes. A blower could be placed on the unloading rack end to help dry dishes as they emerged from the machine. (*Courtesy of Hobart Corporation, Troy, Ohio.*)

Dishes move through dish machines either by means of a stationary rack in the machine or on a conveyor (moving belt machines). Some conveyors require the use of racks. Other conveyors have pegs (these machines are often called **flight machines**) between which dishes are placed. Racks can still be used with these machines for flatware and other smaller items.

Machine types are differentiated by the way the ware goes through the machine as well. Basically, there are **stationary rack-type machines** and moving belt ones. The conveyor type takes racks into which dishes are placed or takes dishes directly on the moving conveyor belt (Figure 23.2). For larger operations, an additional feature on some machines is an automatic unloading mechanism for such items as trays. Automatic loading systems are also available that automatically feed stacked dishes into the machine. In stationary rack machines, the dishes must be manually placed in the racks and then put into the machine manually. Stationary rack machines are often called "counter type" because they are often put into counters for limited dishwashing needs. For most of these small machines, the racks are filled with ware and then placed inside the machine, the door is closed, and the wash cycle is started either manually or automatically. For smaller operations, under-counter dish machines are also available. These have doors that open to accommodate a rack of dishes similar to the design of home models of dish machines. Capacities range from 18 to 40 racks per hour or 450 to 1,000 dishes per hour.

Some moving belt machines use a circular or carousel style belt and will continue to run dishes through unless they are removed. **Carousel machines** are more space efficient compared to traditional flight machines, but have a serious defect in that workers frequently handle soiled and clean dishes without hand washing in between since the two areas are together (Figure 23.3).

As a conveyor belt moves through the machine it automatically activates prewash, wash, rinse, and final rinse cycles. Conveyor speeds vary from 5 to 15 ft (1.5 to 4.5 m) per minute. Eight feet (2.14 m) per minute equals approximately 40 spaces on the conveyor belt or 40 cafeteria trays used by patrons to carry food; this would yield about 2,400 trays per hour provided every space was filled. The time of wash and rinse are regulated by the conveyor speed and this speed, in turn, regulates the quantity of water directed at the dishes to get the proper cleansing and sanitizing action. When specifying these ma-

FIGURE 23.2 A heavy-duty three-tank dish machine with a conveyor-type belt that can carry dishes and other items on the belt or the conveyor can be specified for holding loaded racks. Note the prominent display of temperature gauges on the top of the machine. *(Courtesy of Hobart Corporation, Troy, Ohio.)*

chines a statement should be made about desired belt width if the need will arise to put wide baking sheets or similarly wide equipment through the machine. Belt widths up to 60 in. (152 cm) are available.

A dish machine cleans by water pressure between 15 and 25 psi. Moving or nonmoving spray manifolds above and nonmoving usually below drive water against the units and remove soil. In the wash area, detergents promote removal of soil, but about 70% of the cleaning is due to force of the water.

Research has shown that a low bacterial count on washed dishes is promoted by adequate prerinsing that reduces soil from being carried into the wash solution. Preflush or prerinse machines are often used with dish machines to remove a large part of the food and grease from items. Good waste retention is needed in this area and usually perforated racks are located below that can be easily removed to get rid of soil caught on them. The machines are usually connected to the water system with a mixing valve that yields the proper water temperature. The valve should be capable of adjustment. Manual prewash can be done by scraping under a trigger-valve spray or on a rack of dishes placed over a sink located near the machine opening. As noted, a perforated basket should be in the sink to catch waste, or a disposal unit should be placed underneath the sink to take care of this rough soil (see Figure 23.4). Many dishwashing units require a presoak sink for soaking ware that is heavily soiled.

A single-tank machine has a cycle of washing and rinsing that starts when the machine is turned on. Single-tank machines may be obtained with a prewash cycle. A two-tank machine usually has wash, rinse, and final rinse stages. Water from the final rinse flows into the rinse and the overflow from the rinse flows into the wash section, thus keeping up a constant flow of clean water on down through the machine. A standard overflow in the wash section permits grease, soil, and scum to flow out the drain. The dilution of the wash water requires that a detergent be added as this dilution occurs. A three-tank machine has prewash, wash, rinse, and final rinse stages and operates much the same as a two-tank machine.

Open-end machines require splash curtains at each end and sometimes curtains are needed between compartments to prevent wash or other water getting into the wrong compartment. Curtains should not be held open by objects in the racks or belts;

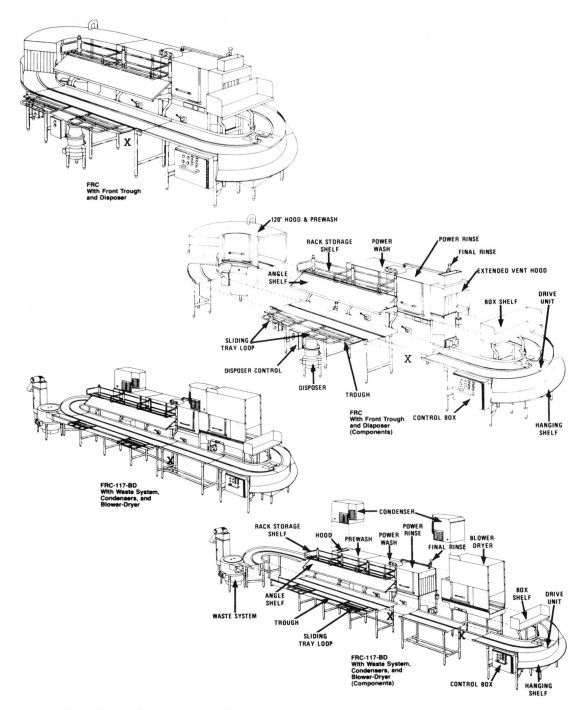

FIGURE 23.3 Various line drawings of dishwasher arrangements using the circular type arrangement. Note the use of a blower-dryer arrangement in the drawing on the lower right. A handsink is recommended for placement at point "X" so workers will not handle clean dishes with hands still unwashed after handling soiled ones. *(Courtesy of Hobart Corporation, Troy, Ohio.)*

this is likely to occur when a section is very short and tall items such as cafeteria trays are washed.

Water temperatures in each compartment are critical for performing proper cleaning and sanitizing. Machines are usually connected to the water system with a mixing valve that yields the proper water temperature. A variation from the critical temperature up to ±3°F (1.7°C) can be allowed. **Booster heaters** using gas, electricity, or steam may be required to give the proper temperatures. Infrared gas heating is available as

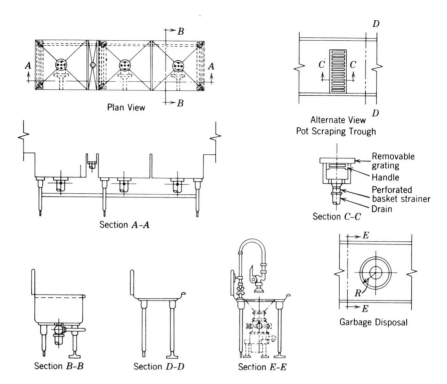

Plan View

Section A–A

Section B–B   Section D-D   Section E-E

Alternate View
Pot Scraping Trough

Removable
grating
Handle
Perforated
basket strainer
Drain
Section C-C

Garbage Disposal

FIGURE 23.4 Sinks for manual pre-rinsing and washing dishes or pots and pans. Maximum water temperature for manual washing in first sink is 120°F (49°C), second sink temperature is to 140°F (49 to 60°C) and for rinsing in third sink a minimum of 170°F (82°C) for 30 sec. Immersion basins are used for second and third sinks. A thermometer should be available to record temperatures. An alternative to having a third sink is to have a final rinse cabinet with nozzle spray delivering 10 gpm at 180°F (82°C) at the manifold for 5 sec of 5 gpm per sec. (*Courtesy of U.S. Department of Defense, Military Handbook 740.*)

well. The size of the booster depends on the temperature of water to be delivered at the machine.

Ultrasonic dishwashing machines have also been developed that use water at lower temperatures and with less detergent. The ultrasonic machine generates sound waves that produce microbubbles that implode on the dish surface at a rate of 40,000 times per second to produce a mechanical scrubbing action that improves the cleaning action of the water and detergent.

If a machine has a prewash cycle, the prewash temperature should be 100 to 120°F (38 to 49°C). This softens fats but is not hot enough to cook food onto the utensils. The wash water should be 140 to 160°F (60 to 71°C), rinse temperatures 160 to 180°F (71 to 82°C), and final rinse 180 to 195°F (82 to 91°C) for 10 seconds. Temperatures higher than 195°F (91°C) tend to vaporize the water and the vaporization can interfere with the force of the water. At each critical area, a thermometer or other temperature-measuring device should be located so workers can see whether temperatures are correct. Some machines have warning lights or tone signals that work when the temperature is not right.

Considerable energy is lost by machines that are left on when no dishes are being washed. A **final rinse trip device** that allows rinse water to flow only when dishes are in the machine helps save hot water. An **idle pump shut-off** device reduces energy use of pumps and the loss of heat from water—it shuts the pumps down when no dishes are going through the machine. When dishes go through, the pumps start up again.

The dispensing mechanisms for detergent, sanitizing agent, and chemical drying agent or other rinse additives may be done differently for each machine. Detergent dispensing is either semiautomatic or automatic. **Semiautomatic chemical dispensing**

systems require the operator to fill a small reservoir in the machine with detergent, which is then dispensed as prompted by electronic probes in the dish machine. **Automatic chemical dispensing systems** operate on the same principle, but do not require the operator to fill the reservoir because detergent is dispensed directly from the shipping container. Rinse agents may be injected into the dish machine by the action of the rinse water, fed by a small electric motor, or dispensed as part of the dish machine's detergent dispensing system. A buzzer or other device should indicate when proper solutions are not being maintained. The dispensing device should not be affected in any way by the corrosive properties of the substances used. It also should not allow free flow or siphonage into the dish machine. Dispensing devices should dispense uniformly with an output ±10% of the desired standard. They should be mounted to allow easy cleaning of surrounding areas and not harbor vermin. They should be set to operate at proper water pressures and be useful for a period of operational life as established in NSF Standard No. 29. Other standards in the NSF manual should be required as well. A data plate should be attached to the dish machine that states the specific requirements for satisfactory operation. Dispensers should be in full view of operating personnel. Machines should be made of corrosion-resistant material. Operating manuals should also be provided by manufacturers.

Most machines use from 8 to 10 lb (3.5 to 4.5 g) of detergent per 1,000 meals. This gives a concentration of about 0.20% to 0.25% by weight in the wash solution. Permissible range is considered to be from 0.15% to 0.40%. Too much detergent can actually reduce cleaning action. Sudsing retards cleaning by reducing water pressure.

To aid in drying, some machines use a chemical rinsing agent; this gives better water runoff and reduces spotting. From 75 to 200 ppm are needed to do the job. Rinse water containing this chemical should flow at the rate of 4 to 15 gal (15.1 to 56.8 L) per minute and 15 to 25 psi. The chemical dispensing system should be capable of adjustment from 6 to 8 oz (170 to 227 g) of rinse aid fluid for about every 1,000 meals. The specification for the machine should give the exact requirements. Some machines use blowers at the end of the machine to dry ware.

The allowed bacterial counts on utensils after dishwashing are from $30/cm^2$ (American Hospital Association) to $100/cm^2$ (Mallman and USPHS). A well-equipped and properly maintained dishwashing unit usually gives lower counts than these. Silverware usually gives higher counts than other tableware.

Appropriate racks should be used for each type of dishware. Glass stemware or tall glasses require racks with tall partitions. Cups are placed in special racks that protect their handles. Cutlery uses plastic holders as it passes through the dish machine a second time. Standard dish racks are 20 × 20 in. (51 × 51 cm). Most racks are made of plastic because it is lightweight, rust proof, chemical resistant, quiet, and minimizes breakage.

Many factors influence the size requirements of dish machines for operations. The quantity of dishes is the most significant factor, but the speed at which dishes are returned for service may also influence sizing. Some operations may demand excess sizing to obtain rapid return of dishes. Others may have an inventory sufficient to satisfy the complete requirements for a meal and dishes can accumulate and be washed during lull periods. This gives a more even use of full-shift dishwashing labor. Glass machines, silver-washing machines, and other units reduce requirements. Adding pots and pans to the dishwashing load increases the total load. Using paper goods reduces the load. Dish machines are usually operated at only 70% of maximum capacity. A careful analysis of specific conditions in each installation is necessary to establish dishwashing requirements.

Freshwater and Steckler[2] suggest the following standards to size machines:

[2]John Freshwater and David M. Steckler, *Evaluation of Dishwashing Systems in Food Service Establishments,* Marketing Research Report No. 1003, USDA, Washington, DC, October 1973.

- When the number of pieces is 1,400 per hour, install a single-tank machine.
- For 3,000 to 5,200 pieces per hour, install either a 180 rack per hour carousel or a two-tank rack machine.
- For 7,000 to 9,000 pieces per hour, install a large carousel or a three-tank conveyor- or flight-type machine.

Capacities beyond this are generally always handled with a flight type of machine. Modern flight machines can wash up to 13,000 to 24,000 dishes per hour.

To determine the number of dishes for washing, an estimate based on the type of operation can be used. The average limited menu operation will have 5 to 8 dishes per customer for breakfast and 7 to 10 dishes per customer for lunch and dinner. Restaurants with more extensive menus may have 12 to 14 dishes per customer. Cafeteria operations will have 20% less than this. Fine dining operations use more, up to perhaps 12 to 20. Normally, three partial meals can be counted as one meal. In addition to these dishes, flatware and other items that are not used for individual service must be added to the dishwashing load. These per-customer estimates are then multiplied by the number of anticipated customers in a given time period. Finally, this figure may be divided by the capacity of the dish machine during the same time period. On the average, about 20 to 25 pieces can be loaded into a basket. In a 19¾- × 19¾-in. (50- × 50-cm) basket, the following pieces can be loaded: 14 dinner plates, 28 pie plates or saucers, 20 cups, 10 soup bowls, 36 glasses, or 50 pieces of flatware.

Machines made of galvaneal last 7 to 10 years or longer. Stainless steel has double this life expectancy. Frames should be made of durable, rigid angle construction, and bodies and tanks should be no lighter than 16-gauge metal on smaller machines and no lighter than 14 gauge on larger ones. Bodies of galvaneal should be no lighter than 12 gauge on any type of machine. All interiors (spray arms and so forth) should be constructed of metal or stainless steel. All welded construction should be specified. Motors should be the splash-proof type and installed so as to be away from steam and moisture. The motors should be the sealed-in type and protected from overloads. Conveyor-type machines should be equipped with an **adjustable friction clutch** that stops operation in case of a jam. Plumbing should conform to local codes and necessary vacuum breakers should be provided. Machines that meet the standards of the Plumbing Engineers Testing Laboratories usually meet local requirements. Tanks should be provided with adequate size drains protected against plugging by perforated overflow caps or similar devices. Well-pitched drainage from the tank bottoms should be provided. All other areas should have no standing water after drains have been opened. Tanks should be suitably baffled to prevent undesirable overrun occurring from one tank to the other. Separation of tanks by air space should be provided so that there will be no heat transfer from one tank to the other. The number of standard items furnished and the number of extras should be ascertained. If the extra equipment required is written into the specifications, the cost is usually less than when it is purchased separately. All wash and rinse operations should have accurate temperature indicators and automatic thermostats for controlling temperatures. Automatic cycle machines should have signal lights indicating on and off operation. **Scrap trays** should be provided and basket-type machines should come with three or more standard sized baskets. The necessary booster heaters with thermostats, line strainers, relief valves, steam traps, solenoid steam valves, hot water pressure regulators, and pressure gauges should be specified. Exhaust ducts should be provided and hoods may be added to carry away steam and heat. Pumps should be guaranteed against leakage. Sanitary-type feet should be provided.

Dish machines are made for corner, wall, or center installation and specifications should state the location so that doors and panels can be properly located. Machines installed against a wall should have easy access to all machinery and other equipment from the open side. Conveyors should be made of stainless steel. **Peg-type conveyor belts** may have nylon links and pegs. Polypropylene plastic conveyors have proven satisfactory against wear. All plastics should conform to the NSF Standard No. 14 for plastics. Doors should be counterbalanced, easily opened, and nonleaking. The machine should be easily cleaned inside and out. Spray arms should be easily detached and cleaned. Hose attachments should be provided. If gas heaters are used, flues should be provided. Service, spare parts, and easy maintenance should be checked. The type of heater used for boosters and tanks, electrical current, water pressure, and other factors for proper regulation of the machine should be stated. Shipment should be specified in sections if the machine is so large that it cannot be brought into the building for installation as one unit.

All interior materials should be smooth, noncorrosive to detergents and other substances, nontoxic, and easily cleaned; parts that must be removed for cleaning should remove easily. Different sections of the country will require different materials inside because of the kind of water used, and the machine purchased should suit the water conditions of the local area.

Every machine should be delivered with a **data plate** that gives the following information:

1. Name of manufacturer or trade name
2. Model number of feeder
3. Type of signal
4. Duration of signal (if applicable)
5. **Feed rate** (mL/second) (When the feeder is listed with a variable feed rate and/or feed time, the manufacturer will be required to provide supply delivery data.)
6. Line pressure (if applicable)
7. Type and concentration of chemical solution(s) to be delivered.[3]

Machines should be delivered with at least three operating manuals.

Specifications should include (1) manufacturer and model number—the model number refers chiefly to design, size, and capacity; (2) body material—galvanized or stainless steel; (3) direction of travel—in and out as in a counter model, at right angles for corner installation, and right to left or left to right; (4) electric current—voltage, current cycles and phase; (5) method of heating—manual or thermostatic control of gas, electricity, or steam; (6) booster heater for rinse water—internal or external and whether it uses gas, electricity, infrared, or steam; (7) racks in excess of standard equipment listing type—such as plate, cup, or glass, cutlery racks, and the required number of each; (8) approval—NSF and UL; (9) special accessories, such as ventilating cowls, locked selector switch, and time control; and (10) date and place of delivery.

Useful options vary tremendously with the style of machine, but can include automated de-liming; built-in booster heaters; blow dryers; a **door interlock safety feature** (which prevents operators from opening the dish machine while parts are moving); **exhaust condenser coils** (which help to eliminate steam vapors); automated dispenser controls (which can be programmed for different cleaning needs); diagnostics (which notify operators that wash tanks are dirty, tanks have been idling too long, etc.) including printouts of operating status; extended conveyors; and water filters. Water consumption will vary with each machine and should be considered when making a purchase decision.

POT AND PAN WASHERS

Many operations still wash pots and pans manually, but the use of automatic washers is increasing. Pot washers function in much the same way as dish machines with a couple of exceptions. The motors for pot washers are generally larger to create a high enough

---

[3]NSF Standard No. 29.

FIGURE 23.5   A heavy-duty pot and pan washer. A soiled table area and clean table area would be attached to this unit. *(Courtesy of Metal Wash Machinery Corporation.)*

velocity of water to remove crusted foods. Motors for pot washers range from 5 to 10 hp, whereas dish machines usually only require 2 to 3 hp. Second, the internal size of pot washers is larger to accommodate the large pots and pans as compared to standard dish machines.

The machines should have good construction that is even heavier in some ways than dishwashers (Figure 23.5). Machines should be provided with proper controls and auxiliary equipment. Continuous conveyor- or rack-type machines are available. Some machines have moving spray arms, while others have fixed ones. The largest machines operate on load, wash, rewash, pumped rinse, and final rinse cycles. Wash temperatures are 150 to 160°F (66 to 71°C), pumped rinse 160°F (71°C), and final rinse 180 to 195°F (82 to 91°C).

Soaking, scraping, and prewash units are often required with the machine. Adequate table space to hold soiled pots and pans is necessary. Space also needs to be provided for scraping and preliminary work before washing and an adequate drying table must be present. The scrap unit should have a perforated collection basket in a sink with perhaps an overhead spray. If no basket is provided, the sink usually will have a disposal under it. If a recirculating prewash unit is a part of the machine, it should recirculate at least 2 gal (7.6 L) of water per minute from the wash tank, or power rinse tank overflow, or the final rinse depending on where this reused water is taken. Noncirculating or fresh water types should deliver 6 gal (22.7 L) per minute. The water pressure should be at least 15 psi.

The pot and pan washer should maintain the proper temperature within ±3°F (1.5°C). Temperatures should be maintained automatically and booster heaters may be required to do this. Some of the better washers are being insulated to reduce heat loss.

Conveyors or racks should minimize obstruction of spray water so as to provide the most effective washing. The volume of water delivered for washing differs for the various types of machines. The majority operate at 20 psi. The volume of water delivered will vary with the machine and whether it is used in the wash, pumped rinse, or final rinse stage. Some large machines use considerable amounts of water.

Machines will need venting to carry away heat and moisture. The large washers need from 300 to 450 cfm of air exhausted, calculated at either 0.5 or 1 in. of static pressure. Strainer baskets to catch food soil should be provided.

GLASS WASHERS

Separating glass washing from dishwashing is recommended for many operations. It may be satisfactorily combined with dishwashing if the water is fairly soft, the dishes are prewashed well, the dish load is not too heavy, and a good detergent is used. Typical glass washers are single-tank machines using chemical sanitizers so that glasses are cool for use with cold drinks. Conveyor models are available, as are units that rotate the wash deck within the machine. Advantages to the use of glass washers are lower labor costs, less breakage and chipping, and a faster supply of glasses. Manual washing is still done in some operations, especially in counter units, fountains, and bars. Local public health codes require the same washing and sanitizing conditions for manual dishwashing of glasses as are required for dishes. Small manually operated brush units that can be placed in a sink for washing the glasses are available. Local health code regulations should be checked regarding their use, however. A new mechanically driven brush machine using cold water is also available.

SILVER WASHERS

Because flatware directly touches a customer's mouth, it is run through a standard dish machine twice. The first time, the flatware goes through the dish machine spread flat on a rack. The second time it passes through the dish machine standing in perforated plastic holders with the eating portions up (the bowl of the spoon, the cutting edge of the knife, and the tines of the fork). After the second time through the dish machine, the silverware is tipped upside down into new clean plastic holders so that only the handle portions are touched when silverware is removed. The flatware is therefore washed, rinsed, and sanitized twice. Many operations use a wetting agent in the rinse to retain the flatware's polish and prevent spotting.

One mechanical silver washer on the market is a tumble type that completes an automatic cycle of wash, rinse, and dry (200°F or 93°C air) in 3.5 minutes. From 150 to 300 pieces of flatware are washed in a cycle. Water usage is 3 gal (11.4 L) per cycle. A 30-ampere, 115-V, 60-cycle current is required.

Silver burnishers of the barrel type using shot are frequently required in operations having a large quantity of silver. Models are made that burnish 75 to 500 pieces of silver flatware at a time.

CAN WASHERS

The time used to wash, scrub, and hose a large number of garbage cans manually can be significant. Can washers can be substantial labor savers. A can washer that operates with hot water at 20 to 35 psi and low steam pressure is available. It will wash cans up to 21.75

in. (55.2 cm) in diameter. The dimensions are 21¾ in. (55.2 cm) for the bowl and overall height of 25.5 in. (64.8 cm). It should be installed in an area where there is a watertight floor with good drainage and where it will not be in the line of traffic.

DISPOSALS AND PULPERS

The use of different types of disposals or disposers has increased in the last 20 years. Disposals generally use a revolving turntable that grinds or minces refuse and flushes it into the sewage system. A 0.75-hp revolving turntable disposal can dispose of 300 to 600 lb (136 to 272 kg) of waste per hour. A 2-hp motor can double this capacity. Disposals generally have a high water requirement that may not be desirable in areas where water is not plentiful. Careful consideration needs to be given to many factors before final selection is made.

The use of disposal units eliminates the labor required in handling garbage. Most disposals operate by using running water to carry food into spinning gears that shred it into small pieces. As the size grows smaller, it is forced down into smaller and smaller orifices until it is about ⅛ in. (0.3 cm) in size, and then is flushed into the sewer. Some large disposals have screw-type shafts that force the waste into grinders. Disposals should not be connected to grease traps, and drains should have a pitch of at least ¼ in. (0.6 cm) per foot (30.5 cm). Two- to 3-in. (5.1- to 7.6-cm) drains are required (Figure 23.6). The power required to operate the disposal may vary from 0.5 to 5 hp. Water consumption is significant. For the smaller units, water consumption ranges from 2 to 3 gal (7.6 to 11.4 L) per minute; the larger sizes require 8 to 10 gal (30.3 to 37.8 L) per minute.

Small disposals are frequently installed at origin points of garbage, such as soiled dish tables, pot and pan sinks, vegetable or salad preparation units, and butcher shops. Small disposals will have difficulty grinding bones, milk cartons, asparagus, celery, and artichoke leaves, but the larger models have little difficulty with most food and paper wastes. Although ½-hp models may be adequate to handle light wastes, a 5-hp unit is generally recommended where the quantity of waste is sizable.

Disposals installed in soiled dish tables and other areas should be provided with a stainless steel cone with a rubber garbage block, overhead spray, and a built-in silver guard. A compact model is desirable. Quietness of operation is also an important selection factor. Controls should be easy to operate and should be installed in a place convenient to the operator. Central installations might be on tables where waste is dumped and then fed into the disposal.

Selection of disposals is based on the type of waste to be handled, capacities of available machines, repair and spare parts service, protection against accidental entry of flatware, balance, freedom from vibration, antisplash guards, noise control, accessories, and maintenance cost. In addition, before selecting a disposal, local codes should be checked. Some local codes do not allow a disposal to be connected to the public sewer system because of the large quantity of refuse generated and the capacity limitations of the public sewer system.

In pulpers, water and waste (both food and paper) are mixed together and ground into a slurry. The slurry is sent to an extractor where water is removed and returned to the pulper to be reused in the next pulping with added fresh water. The semidry solid waste is sent to a garbage container for disposal. Because the pulping system does not flush wastes into the public sewer system, it is preferable where regulations restrict the use of disposals and water resources are limited. An added benefit of the pulpers is that the weight and volume of the waste is reduced through the removal of water to produce significantly less waste. Pulpers do, however, generally cost more than conventional disposal systems. Capacities of pulpers range from 600 to 1,000 lb (272 to 454 kg) of waste per hour.

FIGURE 23.6   A heavy-duty disposal. Such units should not be connected before sewage goes through the grease trap but should be connected after. If connected before, the grease trap clogs with the fine sediment and plumbing problems occur. *(Courtesy of Hobart Corporation, Troy, Ohio.)*

TRASH COMPACTORS AND CAN CRUSHERS

Trash compactors and can crushers are mechanical devices that compress waste so that the volume is greatly reduced (Figure 23.7). If inside trash compactors and can crushers are used, one advantage is that it is easier to carry the compacted waste to the outside waste containers. Trash compactors are also available as part of the outside waste holding container. The primary advantage to the use of compactors is that they decrease waste hauling fees if fee rates are based on the volume and frequency of waste removal.

CHAPTER SUMMARY

Satisfactory dishwashing can be done either by hand or in a variety of dish machines. The same basic steps are used for all of these. The steps are to prescrape, prewash, wash, rinse, sanitize, and air dry. Machines can be categorized by:

- Type of sanitizing (hot water or chemicals)
- Number of tanks (single, double, or triple)
- Movement of ware through the machine (stationary or conveyor)
- If used, type of conveyor (belt or peg, straight line or carousel)
- Method of heating water (gas, electricity, steam, or infrared).

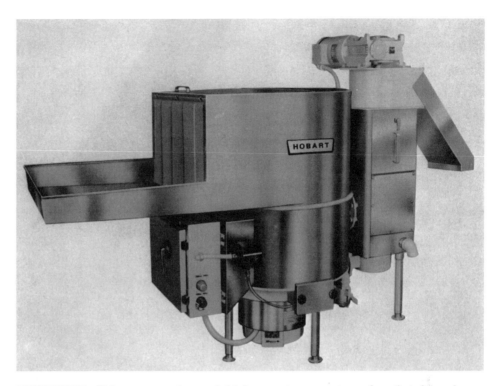

FIGURE 23.7 If the amount of waste is high, a waste compactor such as that shown here may be preferred to a disposal. Both wet and dry waste can be processed in such a unit. The compactor extracts moisture from the wet material leaving it in a semi-dry solid state. (*Courtesy of Hobart Corporation, Troy, Ohio.*)

For effective cleaning and sanitizing, all steps of the dishwashing process must be done properly. Water temperature and concentration of chemicals are critical. Prewash temperatures should be 100 to 120°F (38 to 49°C), wash water should be 140 to 160°F (60 to 71°C), rinse temperatures 160 to 180°F (71 to 82°C), and final rinse 180 to 195°F (82 to 91°C) for 10 seconds for hot water sanitizing machines. For chemical sanitizing machines, the final rinse temperature is between 120 and 140°F (49 and 60°C) to allow for efficient action without vaporization of the chemical. Thermometers should be located in each tank so workers can see whether temperatures are correct. Warning lights or audible signals for temperature and chemical concentration problems are also useful. A data plate on the machine should list all temperature and chemical requirements.

Sizing of dish machines may be done in several ways. Factors that influence sizing include the quantity of dishes available, speed at which dishes must be returned to service, amount of pots and pans to be washed, style of food service, capacity of the dish machine, and number of anticipated customers.

Dish machines should last for a minimum of 7 to 10 years. Stainless steel machines may last twice as long as other machines. Dish machines should be durable, easily cleaned, and made of smooth, noncorrosive, nontoxic materials. Specifications should include the manufacturer and model number, body material, direction of operation, electric requirements, method of heating, booster heater requirement, racks, special accessories, and date and place of delivery.

Specialty washers, such as pot and pan, glass, silver, and can washers are more common in large operations. The operation of pot and pan washers is similar to standard dish machines except that they have larger motors, larger interiors, and may include some heavier construction. Advantages to the use of glass washers are lower labor costs, less glass breakage, and a faster return to service of the glasses. Can washers reduce labor costs significantly.

Disposals and pulpers may be used to handle food and paper waste. Disposals are less expensive, but use large quantities of water and may be restricted by local regulations because of the volume of waste material that is sent to public sewer systems. Pulpers are more expensive, but often preferred because they use less water and produce a semidry waste material that is disposed in a waste container and not the public sewer system. Advantages to the use of trash and can compactors include that they decrease waste hauling fees if fee rates are based on volume and frequency of waste removal.

REVIEW QUESTIONS

1. Obtain a copy of an operation and/or maintenance video for each of the pieces of equipment discussed in this chapter. (Many of these are available to instructors at no charge from the manufacturers.)
2. Observe and list dishwashing equipment used in three different food operations, such as college food units, a commercial restaurant, a hospital, or a school lunchroom.
3. Describe the equipment used in dish handling for each of the three different food operations and observe each of the following
   a. Removal from dining area.
   b. Scraping, stacking, and prerinsing.
   c. Type and size of dishwasher used.
   d. Method of detergent dispensing.
   e. Rinsing agent used and how applied.
   f. Water temperatures maintained, as taken from thermometer reading on the machine.
   g. Possibility of contamination due to handling methods; explain where and how it may be corrected.
   h. Time allowed for air drying.
   i. Drying problems due to type of tableware, and how corrected.
   j. Methods used for transportation and storage.
4. Describe and evaluate the pot washing procedure followed in each of the three different foodservice operations.
5. Are disposals used in the three foodservice operations? If so, where are they located, what sizes are used, and for what purpose? Are compactors used? What horsepower is used for each disposal?

KEY WORDS AND CONCEPTS

adjustable friction clutch

booster heaters

carousel machines

data plate

door interlock safety feature

exhaust condenser coils

feed rate

final rinse trip device

flight machines

idle pump shut-off

peg-type conveyor belts

scrap trays

semiautomatic and automatic chemical dispensing systems

stationary rack-type machines

CHAPTER
24

Auxiliary Equipment

The auxiliary equipment in food facilities supports the essential foodservice activities in conjunction with other items in work sections. Size, design, and structure that meet specific needs are important for satisfactory use.

HOODS

Hoods are used for the removal of heat, grease, moisture, and steam. The removal of odors and pollution products from air exhausted from kitchens has received increased emphasis in recent years. Pollution control devices are available that can be placed into ventilators and hoods. These operate both with hot water spray from nozzles and **electrostatic precipitator cell units.** In some cases, activated charcoal units can be added. In addition, some of the units contain fire control devices that have automatic closing dampers and a fine spray of water to put out fires. Figure 24.1 shows a drawing of a ventilator with the pollution and fire control units installed. Pollution control units are available also that can be installed in the duct system on the roof (Figure 24.2). Water requirements tend to be high and this may present a problem in some areas. For instance, a device exhausting 180,000 cfh will require 34.5 gpm at 60 psi for both pollution and fire control, if both are operating.

The size and placement of the hood in relation to heat and pollutants to be removed are important (Figure 24.3). The closer the suction is to the object to be removed the more effective it is likely to be. For this reason, low hoods over griddles and fryers are favored. Canopies should usually have about a 2-in. (5-cm) overhang for each foot above the equipment. The usual clearance of high canopies is 5 ft (1.5 m) above equipment and a minimum of 6 ft 3 in. (1.60 m) where workers pass under it. To work properly, canopies should be at least 2 ft (61 cm) from the bottom edge to the top and one outlet should be provided for every 6 to 18 linear feet (1.83 to 2.44 m) of canopy. Low canopies of the backshelf type sit about 18 to 22 in. (45 to 55 cm) above the equipment and give the strongest pull of air where it is most needed. They may vary from 200 cfm to a high of 350 cfm per linear foot of appliance. The National Fire Protection Association recommends that all hoods be equipped with **grease filters** or be provided with a fire extinguishing system that meets their Standard No. 96 requirements. Filters should not be installed less than 3.5 ft (1.05 m) above an open flame and not less than 4.5 ft (1.35 m) above charcoal flames.

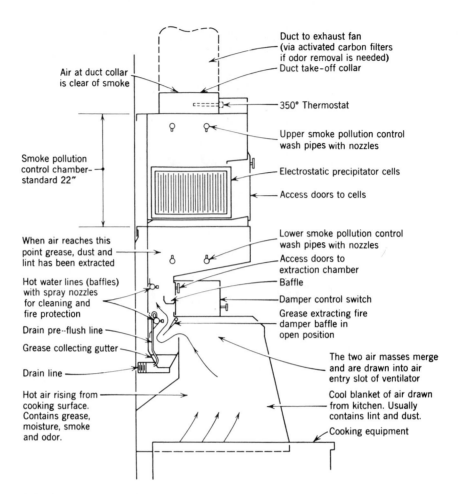

FIGURE 24.1 A ventilator equipped with a fire and pollution control unit. Air drawn into the fire damper baffle is made to move in a circuitous route, which throws grease and lint into the baffle, collecting it there. The 350°F (75°C) sensing thermostat at the top triggers the damper-closing unit and the fine water spray in case of fire. As the air moves up it passes through the electrostatic precipitator cells and washing sprays, which removes smoke and other pollution products. *(Courtesy of Gaylord Industries, Inc., Tualatin, Oregon.)*

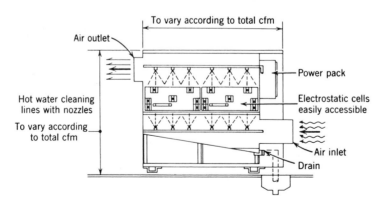

FIGURE 24.2 A roof-mounted pollution control unit. Note that the air enters from below on the duct system and passes through a water and electrostatic precipitator cell cleaning unit and then out where it is exhausted into the atmosphere. This unit, unlike the one shown in Figure 24.1, does not contain the fire control device. *(Courtesy of Gaylord Industries, Inc., Tualatin, Oregon.)*

FIGURE 24.3 Hoods designed for steam equipment. *(Courtesy of Cleveland Range Co., Cleveland, Ohio.)*

Canopies or hoods should be integrally constructed with easily accessible surfaces and be free of crevices, trim, or other projections. The surface of the unit should be smooth and easily cleanable; drip catchers or gutters should be constructed so as to be easily cleanable and over 1.25×1.25 in. (3.2×3.2 cm) in size so access is easily possible. Filters or baffle vans, turning vanes, and sliding dampers should be installed to prevent drippage into food and should be removable for cleaning. The standards of NSF Standard No. 2 should be followed. Drainage holes or other devices should be provided to drain away condensate. An automatic device should close dampers and vents when temperatures go over 360 to 400°F (182 to 204°C). Hoods should be rigidly supported to equipment, wall, or ceiling. Marine type or sealed-in vapor-proof lights should be installed as required for proper illumination.[1]

The air flow over the front of the equipment should be checked and reduced if the ventilator air flow is excessive. Too much air flow over equipment wastes heat. Too much air flow over food can cool it and even dry it out.

POT RACKS

Pot racks may be the overhead bar type or shelf type. Overhead racks can have one, two, or three bars formed in a straight line, oval, half-oval, or revolving round forms. Where three bars are used, two form an oval and a third is centered for support at a distance approximately 12 in. (30.5 cm) below the level of the others. Stainless steel 2×0.25 in. (5.1×0.6 cm) thick, seamlessly welded, ground, and polished is recommended. Drop-forged pot hooks of stainless steel are riveted on 6-in. (15.2-cm) centers on each side of

---

[1]For further discussion, see E. A. Jahn, *Commercial Kitchen Ventilation*, American Gas Association, 420 Lexington Ave., New York.

all three bars. The stainless steel ceiling hangers are flanged over and bolted to the pot rack. Where ceiling hangers are more than 48 in. (122 cm) long, they are cross-braced. Less durable and expensive models may be made of iron painted with two coats of aluminum paint or steel that has been lacquered black.

Mounting may also be by means of a pipe support that passes through the table with the rack firmly attached to the table structure. Revolving racks are sometimes used where space and reach are limited. Heavy, bulky items should be stored on shelves that minimize lifting and do not overload hanging pot racks. Spacing should be planned for large equipment, such as mixer bowls. Some items may be hung from hooks.

Adjustable, portable shelving of perforated sheet metal, metal bands, or pipe is suitable for pot and pan storage units. Solid metal shelving does not permit good circulation of air. These racks should be mobile in most instances. To support the weights required, the structure should be sturdy. Smooth, easily cleanable surfaces are desirable. The height and balance should be such as to permit an easy reach to pots and should not be top heavy.

SHELVING

Shelving may come in many forms and be for a variety of storage materials. Most shelving should be adjustable and removable. Surfaces should be smooth. The framework may be angle or pipe and sectional or completely detachable for removal from the storage area for complete scrubbing and cleaning. Materials commonly used are aluminum alloys and galvanized and stainless steels. Shelving may be mobile.

CABINETS

Enclosed units may be constructed as separate units or incorporated as a part of other equipment, such as serving counters or worktables. Doors may need to open out to expose the full width of a shelf area or they may slide in opposite directions. Shelves should be removable for easy and thorough cleaning. If food is to be stored and good ventilation is required, louvers or openings should be placed for proper air circulation. Material may be aluminum alloys or galvanized or stainless steel. The required gauge will depend on the size of the cabinet, condition of wear, and material used.

Proof boxes are a special type of cabinet used in the bakeshop. Gas, steam, or electricity is required to maintain a temperature of 90 to 100°F (32.2 to 37.4°C) and to operate an evaporator to maintain a relative humidity of 80% to 85%. Because of the high humidity, nonrusting metals should be used. Mobility is desirable to enable the baker to fill the proof box at the bench, move it away while proofing, and then move it to the oven for baking. Size should accommodate available pans. The interiors of proof boxes are considered food contact surfaces.

SINKS

Sinks as individual pieces of equipment are available as standard stock equipment with or without drainboards (Figure 24.4). They are frequently incorporated into worktables for work centers. Pot and pan and vegetable sinks may be sized larger than normal, while counter and utility sinks may be smaller. In a pot sink, three compartments are required. Compartments 24 × 28 × 14 in. (61 × 71 × 36 cm) deep are large enough for stan-

FIGURE 24.4   A well-constructed general-purpose sink. *(Courtesy of S. Blickman, Inc., Weehawken, New Jersey.)*

dard baking sheets, roasting pans, and similar large equipment. The depth of the sink should be studied; 16 in. (40.6 cm) may be too deep for some purposes and 12 or 14 in. (30.5 or 35.6 cm) would be better. The distance from the bottom of the sink to the floor, plus the overall height, will dictate whether or not the sink is at a convenient work level. Where tall workers are employed sinks of 38 in. (96.5 cm) are used and the sink bottoms are 22 in. (55.9 cm) off the floor. Sink bottoms should be 27 in. (68.6 cm) from the floor for women and 29 in. (73.7 cm) for men. Soak sinks may be 6 in. (15.2 cm) deeper but workers should not put hand tools in them.

Good construction is required for sinks. A 3-in. (7.6-cm) raised edge is frequently used above the drainboard where spillage may occur. Compartment walls should be of one-piece double construction. **Backsplashes** should be integral with tops of sufficient height and sealed tightly to the wall or 4 in. (10.2 cm) away from the wall for easy cleaning.

Strong bracing should be given drainboards. The minimum pitch should be ⅛ in. (0.3 cm) per foot. Corrugated drainboards are used where inverted glasses are allowed to drain. Corrugations should be not less than 3⁄32 in. (0.2 cm) deep and sufficiently wide for ease of cleaning. Drainboards for clean and soiled items should be separate; if they are parallel the clean utensil section should be at least ½ in. (1.3 cm) above the dirty utensil section. Sliding drainboards should be constructed to prevent seepage or overflow and should be easily cleanable.

Specifications for sinks should state type of outlet, drain, overflow, and drillings to be made for hot and cold water. The drilling is usually done on 8-in. (20.3-cm) centers for each compartment unless swinging faucets are used. Faucets are usually not furnished and should be specified if desired. Drains are usually 2 in. (5.1 cm). Air gaps must be provided. Drains should have removable strainers with or without remote control. Drains should have cleanouts before drainage pipes enter inaccessible areas. Fittings should be of corrosion-resistant materials. Sinks for manual washing of dishes should have three units—one for washing, one for sanitizing, and one for rinsing. The National Sanitation Foundation's recommendations for sink construction should be closely followed. Utility sinks or curbed floor drains should be available for dumping of mopwater. Floor sinks should be recessed 6 to 8 in. (15.2 to 20.3 cm) and easily cleanable.

TABLES

Working surfaces should be carefully planned in relation to work center needs, height, available space, surface material, and storage facilities. Although certain large, sturdily built tables in fixed locations may be required, smaller mobile units add greatly to flexibility and convenience.

Finish of **table edges** is important. Some of the edges recommended for tables, sinks and curbs are as follows:

1. *Fully rounded with bullnosed corner.* Edges are rolled 1.5 in. (3.8 cm) in diameter so all radii are equal horizontally and vertically and corners are fully rounded and integral with top and side rolls.
2. *Raised rolled edge.* Similar to above, except edges are raised 0.375 in. (0.9 cm) before forming edge rolls. This is useful as a curb against spillage.
3. *Inverted V edge.* The edges are integrally raised 0.5 in. (1.3 cm) and then bent down 2 in. (5.1 cm) to form a straight sided edge and then straight back 0.5 in. (1.3 cm). The corners are mitred, welded, ground, and polished to be in harmony with the top. This edge furnishes a curb against spillage, such as might occur on an urn stand.
4. *Recessed curb.* The edge may be formed like the inverted V edge except that it is not raised and the 2-in. (5.1-cm) apron is recessed through the center 0.5 in. (1.3 cm).
5. *Curbs and vertical corners.* The edges of dish table curbs and sinks may be rounded in a manner similar to that described for fully rounded edges, and the vertical edges or corners may be coved on a 1-in. (2.5-cm) radii or formed into a square corner. The coved edges are preferred for ease of cleaning.

Large tables that receive heavy usage should be constructed of 12- to 14-gauge stainless steel, with channeling and bracing used as required for sturdiness. The stainless steel top may be satisfactorily used for all types of cooking and pastry work. Some people prefer wood surfaces, however, for the tables in the baking section and the pantry. If allowed by local sanitation regulations, wood tops should be made of 3-in. (7.6-cm) sectional hard maple, glued and bolted, with concealed metal tie rods. Flush dowels should conceal the head and burr of the tie rods. Local sanitation regulations should be checked for guidance, because many health departments restrict the use of wood and do not allow it for wood table surfaces or cutting boards. If it is allowed, it must also be maintained in good shape with no open seams or cracks, gouges, or chips.

Figures 24.5 and 24.6 show different types of table setups.

Table widths vary from 15 in. (38.1 cm) for a mobile unit to 30, 36, and 42 in. (76.2, 91.4, and 107 cm) for large tables. The length varies widely. They should be amply supported with legs to provide sturdiness and prevent sagging. If over 7 ft (2.1 m) long, six legs are recommended or strong channeling must be provided. Heights of tables should be adjusted to job requirements. Small tables that may be pulled over the lap are convenient for vegetable or pantry workers who may sit down while working. Even heights of 40 in. (102 cm) are desirable for certain tasks. Tables may be constructed to stand on a platform 14 to 18 in. (35.6 to 45.7 cm) high. The durable floor material may form the bottom shelf. Plans should be made for toe space and for coving at the floor.

Ingredient tables for bakers and cooks should have spice drawers located in a high shelf position, with equipment drawers and either tilting or rolling bins under the top. A hanging pot rack should be suspended above it. Space for the scales may be allowed at the end of the table next to the mixer or a separate, small, portable table planned to fit between the ingredient table and the mixer. For large facilities, which are likely to measure sizable quantities into the mixer, mobile bins are preferred. Where small amounts are used, such as flour for thickening by a cook, tilt bins that permit one-handed operation for opening are better. Where rolling bins are used, the spacing for small drawers should harmonize with the width of the bins. A stretcher should be spaced under the

FIGURE 24.5   A salad work center with shelves for equipment. *(Courtesy of Southern Equipment Co., St. Louis, Missouri.)*

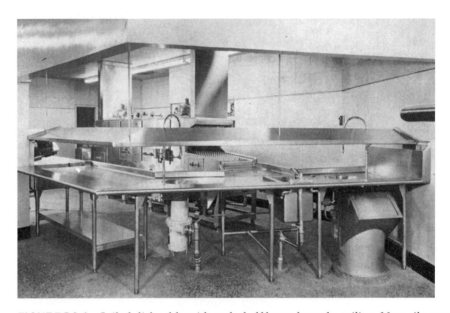

FIGURE 24.6   Soiled dish table with rack shelf hung from the ceiling. Note silver soak sink. *(Courtesy of G. S. Blakeslee and Co., Chicago, Illinois.)*

table where rolling bins are used, so that it will serve as a stop to position the front of the bin flush with the face of the table.

Tables should permit complete cleaning and be built with smooth, cleanable surfaces free from crevices where soil may lodge. Wall mounting facilitates cleaning. Drawers should be vermin and dust proof. Work tables need to be equipped with drawers, shelves, or open space that will best fit the needs in the work center.

Wood cutting boards or tabletops should meet NSF standards as outlined in Standard No. 2. If allowed by local health department regulations, they must, for example, be made of suitable hard wood with strips not over 1.75 in. (4.4 cm) wide, strongly bonded to a ± 0.002-in. (0.05-mm) variation, and bonded with substances that meet the requirements of U.S. Commercial Standard CS 233-60. Bonded joints should equal or exceed a sheer strength of 1,800 psi. The surface should be smoothly machined or sanded, straight grained and free of knots, decay, warp, larva channels, open checks, or splits. The units should be easily scrubbed and sanitized.

Dish tables receive rugged use in most operations. They should be strongly built of 12- to 14-gauge stainless steel and braced laterally with 3-in. (7.6-cm) wide channeling. Legs should be 1.625-in. (4.1-cm)-OD, 10-gauge metal. Shelf bracing underneath should be kept at a minimum to give ease of cleaning under and allow use of mobile equipment. Catch-all space should be avoided. Edges are usually turned up 3 in. (7.6 cm) and rolled on a 1.5-in. (3.8-cm) diameter with bullnose corners but may be left open and flashed into dish machines of the basket type. Backsplashes of 10 in. (25.4 cm) are sometimes used when the tables are placed against the wall. If necessary, tray rests for unloading soiled dishes should be provided for dish delivery. Good bracing should be provided for the rests. Overhead shelves should be provided for glasses and small dishes. A slightly turned edge on the opposite side will prevent items being pushed off in loading. Overhead shelves should be 14-gauge and edges should be rolled. If glasses and other small dishes can be directly loaded into baskets standing on shelves or tale space, labor time is saved.

It is desirable for conveyor tops to be integral with the rest of the table but space must be left open for passage of the belt. A hole for garbage and waste or garbage disposal is usually provided near the dish machine where stacking or loading will occur. Scrap blocks should be made of grease-resistant NSF-approved material and should be removable. The hole should be constructed to prevent refuse from falling outside the garbage receptacle and the edge should be integrally raised 0.5 in. (1.3 cm) to prevent leakage.

Drainage should be provided near the machine and the table should be sloped to the drainage. Sometimes a depression 4 in. (10.2 cm) deep and 6 in. (15.2 cm) wide is placed across the entrance of the table into the machine. A removable perforated basket is placed over this level with the table top. Drainage may go into disposals. Other drainage areas may have to be provided on large tables. Preflush sinks may be required and these should be at least 8 in. (20.3 cm) deep and sized properly for the baskets used. A strainer basket (Figure 24.7) and overhead spray assembly may need to be provided. Soaking sinks may also have to be provided; the size required will depend on the estimated number of dishes encrusted with egg or other materials that will have to be soaked. Soaking sinks are also used for bleaching coffee cups and so forth. It may be desirable to have table flush covers for the sinks. Removable strainers should be installed in drains and sinks.

The clean dish table on rack-type machines should be adequate to hold the dishes until they are dry. It is usually calculated that 60% of the table space of this type should be for clean dishes and 40% for soiled. Mobile tables should be provided, along with other mobile storage equipment at the clean dish ends of basketless machines. The sizing of the table and shelves to be used for working space and dish storage will depend on the way the work is to be done in the unit and the amount of dishes that will arrive in specified periods. If dishes are to be stacked only during peak periods and then washed during lulls, more soiled dish space will be required. Sound-deadening under all tabletops should be provided where noise may be a problem.

CHAPTER SUMMARY

Auxiliary equipment plays an important support role in the production of food in work centers. Hoods are required for removal of heat, grease, moisture, and steam above cooking areas. Pot racks, shelving, and cabinets facilitate storage of needed equipment and food in convenient areas. Sinks and tables must be durable, corrosion resistant, strong, sanitary, and easily cleanable. Stainless steel construction is often preferred, but other materials may be acceptable as well. No openings or crevices should allow for soil or pests to gather. Edges should be finished appropriately. National Sanitation Foundation standards should be used for all auxiliary equipment.

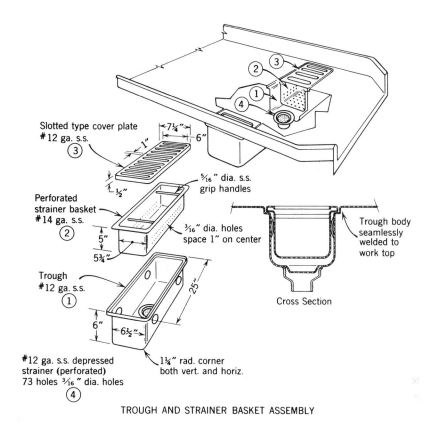

Slotted type cover plate
#12 ga. s.s.
③

Perforated
strainer basket
#14 ga. s.s.
②

⁵⁄₁₆" dia. s.s.
grip handles

³⁄₁₆" dia. holes
space 1" on center

Trough body
seamlessly
welded to
work top

Cross Section

Trough
#12 ga. s.s.
①

#12 ga. s.s. depressed
strainer (perforated)
73 holes ³⁄₁₆" dia. holes
④

1¼" rad. corner
both vert. and horiz.

TROUGH AND STRAINER BASKET ASSEMBLY

FIGURE 24.7   Detail of trough and strainer basket assembly for draining soiled dish table. *(Courtesy of S. Blickman, Inc., Weehawken, New Jersey.)*

KEY WORDS AND CONCEPTS

electrostatic precipitator cell units

grease filters

splashbacks

table edges

REVIEW QUESTIONS

1. Observe hoods in five food operations, and describe the following:
   a. Location, giving height above source of heat or pollution.
   b. Size in relation to area to be ventilated.
   c. Type of filter and how cleaned.
   d. Effectiveness in removing heat and pollutants.
   e. Comfort for workers in terms of location and draft.

2. Observe the pot and utensil storage in the five food operations and describe the following:
   a. Location in relation to work sections.
   b. Convenience in finding items required for work.
   c. Adequacy in terms of number of items handled and sanitation protection.

3. Write specifications for a custom-built pot sink, cook's table, and storeroom shelving.

CHAPTER

25

Transportation and Mobile Equipment

Transportation devices to carry loads, save steps, lessen fatigue, and reduce labor can do much to reduce labor costs and speed accomplishment. The convenient transport of materials and equipment by workers and the flexible movement of equipment for forming good work centers can greatly improve productivity. Rehandling of stored equipment and supplies can be reduced through the use of mobile units. Careful evaluation of means for increasing mobility is important. In the planning, care should be taken to see that storage space for **mobile equipment** is available and aisles and work areas are sufficiently large to allow for their entry and use in the work center.

CONVEYORS AND ELEVATORS

Vertical conveyors, elevators, or dumbwaiters for movement of materials are frequently required and unless planned to suit the need can be the cause of much delay and confusion in the movement of supplies and meals. Subveyors may make it possible to utilize space that otherwise would not be available. The location of dishwashing sections or food production areas, such as bakeshops, on another floor than the serving area becomes feasible when good vertical transportation is available. The location of banquet rooms or other special dining spaces above or below production areas also becomes possible when good vertical transportation is available. Systems may be devised with push-button control for sending foods or supplies to the location where desired. Elevators, dumbwaiters, or tray belts should be installed according to need and as part of an operational plan. Motorized conveyors may operate as belts or tracks horizontally under counters, at working level, or overhead, and as vertical carriers (Figures 25.1 and 25.2).

A reliable firm or specialist should be consulted before designing a conveyor or elevator system. Specific information will be required, such as number of people or items to be transported, the time limitations, speed, size of tray, tote boxes, number of floors to be served and floor heights (floor to floor), length of take-off or feeder belts (if any are required), type of service wanted (up, down, reversible), electric current available, and a sketch or plan of operation. A durable, easily maintained, easily cleaned, smooth func-

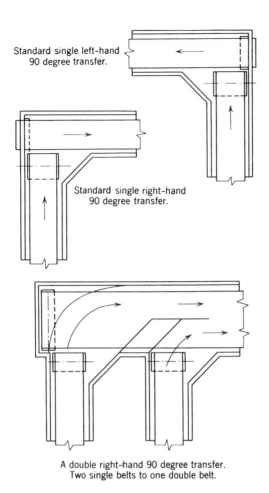

Standard single left-hand 90 degree transfer.

Standard single right-hand 90 degree transfer.

A double right-hand 90 degree transfer.
Two single belts to one double belt.

FIGURE 25.1 Horizontal 90-degree transfer on conveyors. *(Courtesy of Samuel Olson Manufacturing Co., Chicago, Illinois.)*

FIGURE 25.2 An example of vertical and horizontal movement in movement of hospital trays.

tioning system is desired. All areas should be easily accessible for cleaning and maintenance. Entry and exit areas should be of stainless steel. A rigid frame support should be provided for subveyor and conveyor housings and belt chassis.

The most popular uses for which conveyors have been employed include the assembling of meals, such as hospital trays and school lunches, the removal of soiled dishes from dining areas, the delivery of supplies and equipment to serving stations, and the distribution of hospital trays to patient floors. The movement of soiled dishes by these means not only saves steps but also speeds work, lessens noise and unsightliness in dining areas, and may reduce breakage. The speed of the conveyor can be controlled to permit proper handling. A speed of 15 feet per minute (fpm) will space trays and dishes from a cafeteria or hospital service so that workers can work at a normal rate when scrapping, sorting, and stacking. Subveyor and conveyor systems are usually planned to deliver approximately 60 to 75 dishes per minute or approximately ten 14×18-in. (35.6×45.7-cm) trays onto a soiled dish table per minute. Pile-up and excess speed will increase breakage. Important values of conveyors in connection with soiled dish handling are the keeping of waitstaff and other outside personnel out of this work section, the reduction of noise, and the utilization of space to the best advantage (Figure 25.3).

Belt Conveyors

Care should be taken when selecting and installing belt material. Attention should be paid to its general design, which should provide good sanitation. The belt should be made of sturdy material that is relatively nonabsorbent to grease and liquids, nontoxic, and with sealed sides that permit no raw edges. It should be installed to allow for complete cleaning above and below. The belt support, pan rollers, driving mechanism, and pulleys should likewise be easily cleanable. Where drip may occur, proper pans or

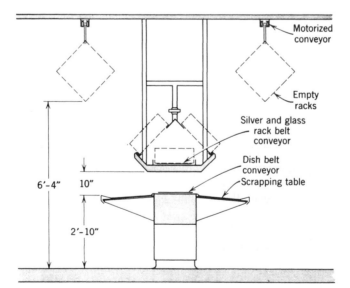

FIGURE 25.3 Conveyors save time and labor in a large dishwashing operation at the Houston Club in Texas. This cross-section view gives a good picture of how three separate conveyors are incorporated into the soiled dish table at the Houston Club. The belt running through the center of the table at table height brings incoming trays of soiled dishes. Glasses and cups are sorted and placed in racks held at an angle on second level, a conveyor through the center of this section carries filled racks to the machine. The overhead unit carries a supply of empty racks. In addition, an overhead gravity unit is connected to the end of the dish machine to move large silver pieces. (*Courtesy of Institutions Magazine, Chicago, Illinois.*)

devices should be installed to catch it. Strainer baskets in drains should be removable. Belt lacing or juncture fastenings are considered food contact surfaces. Motors should be protected against splash or spillage and located in the best possible place for protection against soil. **Limit switches** to stop a vertical conveyor should be installed to prevent pile-up when trays are not removed from a belt that is being supplied by a vertical conveyor. Spillage sometimes occurs inside vertical shafts and provision should be made for regular cleaning of the shafts. Care should be taken with ventilation to prevent the possibility of chilling drafts occurring where food is to be transported.

Specifications for belt conveyors should indicate (1) width of belt, (2) length of belt, (3) belt material, (4) directional movement and whether it is one way or reversible, (5) location of head, and (6) placement and completeness of access to machinery. Vertical conveyors may be ascending, descending, and reversible. The widths may vary to accommodate standard-sized cafeteria and hospital trays, bus boxes, and oval trays. Movement may be controlled by means of a floor selector that stops the conveyor at the desired location or it may be continuous. Specifications should indicate all points where choices for location need to be selected.

Track Conveyors

The overhead, track-type conveyor may be motorized or manually operated. The track may be straight or curved.

Roller Conveyors

Roller conveyors may move by gravity or be activated through friction from a motor-driven belt. The amount of friction may be controlled so that action can be held up when desired by light pressure of the hand or load pile-up. **Gravity conveyors** may be the roller or skate-wheel type. The rollers may be made of hardwood, plastic, or light metal. They may also be rubber covered. The diameters of the rollers range from 0.75 to 6 in. (1.9 to 15.2 cm) and lengths vary according to need. They may have precision ball bearings or bronze bearings inside or use external bearings. Gravity rollers are considered to be the most economical of all conveyors for handling of supplies and therefore are widely used. They may be straight, curved, or spiral and at varying degrees of pitch.

GRAVITY SLIDES OR CHUTES

Gravity slides or chutes require pitch for ease of movement. The pitch should be at least 2.5 to 3 in. (6.3 to 7.6 cm) per foot (30.5 cm). Spiral chutes may be fully enclosed or open, and used between floors for handling bags, boxes, and other wrapped materials. Open containers, those that are too light or fragile, and those that are wired wrapped may not slide well or safely. Gravity rollers are better for these items and have more general use than the slides, but they are more expensive to construct.

ELEVATORS AND DUMBWAITERS

The movement of food carts or trucks and other sizable objects from one floor to another frequently requires the use of an elevator or **dumbwaiter.** Models of widely differing sizes, speeds, and degrees of refinement are available. Elevator doors of a double-leaf flush type, equipped with an automatic opening and closing device, are desirable for food operations. Dumbwaiters are often used in hospitals for sending food to service kitchens from the main kitchen and for movement of small tray carts to patient floors. It is important to consider load capacity, space requirements, draft protection, sanitary features, and desired operating speed when choosing this equipment. If banquet areas are used for exhibits or trade shows, a heavy-duty elevator, sized to meet the space and local demands, must be installed. These elevators are usually slow moving and if they are used for food transport, the food should be placed in mobile insulated units. Chilling drafts or air currents through shafts of vertical transport equipment should be avoided. Food should not be transported in guest elevators. If mobile equipment is transported in elevators or dumbwaiters, self-leveling equipment should be installed. High-speed dumbwaiters may be used for transfer of bulk foods or trays on small carts. Proper sizing with tray slides or shelf space for pans is desirable.

Planners may have to indicate to elevator or conveyor consultants the basic needs of the facility for transport and therefore should know what some of the requirements are in such planning. Adequate service must be obtained at a minimum cost. Costs of transport can be high and maximum efficiency is needed. The cost of installing an elevator system in a 30-story building may be 10% of the total construction cost.

The number of individuals or units to be moved in an hour is usually taken as the basis for calculating elevator needs. Normally in hotels 12% to 15% of the hotel capacity is considered moved to the destination in five minutes of elevator operation. In a normal hotel, the number of rooms times 1.3 is often used to calculate the number of people to be moved. In a hotel catering to conventions 1.7 is usually used. If carts plus individuals are moved as in foodservices, the number of units and space required for both must be calculated. For restaurants and other facilities transporting people only, the capacity of the dining areas and the turnover rate plus flow of traffic can be used to establish numbers to be carried. In office buildings, estimates are frequently based on the footage of space. Normally one individual is considered as the occupant of every 90 to 110 sq ft of space (8.4 to 10.2 sq m), but if the occupants are largely secretaries and clerks, 50 sq ft (4.6 sq m) is used. Thus, a floor having a large number of clerks and secretaries with 7,500 sq ft (696 sq m) would require movement of 150 people.

An **elevator wait time** of 40 to 70 sec is considered normal. Elevator travel time for people in a building should not be more than 1 to 1.25 min. If over this, the longer the time, the greater the annoyance. Speeds of cars must be varied according to the distance traveled. The type of clientele may also dictate elevator speed—or the type of food, if food is the main product transported. Some facilities cater to people who are in a hurry and have only a limited amount of time for a lunch period, others may specialize in a more leisurely type of service.

Floor heights are usually calculated as being from 9 to 12 ft (2.7 to 3.7 m). A car going 10 floors would travel 90 to 108 ft (27 to 33 m). Normally cars will travel from 400 to 600 fpm but systems are installed in which cars travel from 250 to 1,400 fpm.

The number of individuals to be transported must be indicated. If a 200-room convention hotel is being planned and 15% of the occupants are to be moved in 5 min (300 sec) with a 50-sec wait, the number to be moved would be $1.7 \times 200 \times 0.15$ or 51, which probably would be rounded off to 50 moved every 5 min. If the hotel is 10 stories high with 12 ft (3.7 m) for each floor, the distance of travel is 120 ft (36.6 m). An expert is likely to recommend on this basis cars of 2,500- or 3,000-lb (1,135- or 1,362-kg) weight capacity that carry, respectively, 17 or 20 people. It is usual to calculate car capacity as only 80% of maximum and thus each car would be considered to hold 14 or 16, respectively. The engineer now checks standard tables and finds that a 2,500-lb (1,135-kg) car will take 120 sec for a round-trip at a speed of 400 fpm and 110 sec at 600 fpm, while a 3,000-lb (1,362-kg) car will require, respectively, 135 and 124 sec. Thus the 2,500-lb (1,135-kg) car in 5 minutes can make 2.5 trips at 400 fpm and 2.75 trips at 600 fpm; the 3,000-lb (1,362-kg) car will make, respectively, 2.25 and 2.4 trips. A summary is given in Table 25–1.

However, a 50-sec wait has been specified and since the fastest round-trip is 2.75 trips every 300 sec or over 100 sec per trip, the engineer may recommend a compromise of a slightly longer wait using two 2,500-lb (1,135-kg) cars, which would move

TABLE 25–1 *Number of People Transported in Five Minutes*

	400 fpm	600 fpm
2,500-lb car	35[a]	38
300-lb car	36	38

[a] 2.5 trips in a 2,500-lb car holding 14 people equals 35 people transported in 5 minutes.

70 people in the time allowed. The engineer could present information using larger cars at higher speeds using only one car. Based on cost, this might be shown to be the most favorable system except that with only one system and a breakdown the whole hotel would be immobilized except for the stairways. This might cause the planners to choose the two 2,500-lb (1,135-kg) cars.

Similar calculations would be followed if the transport required was for food or other items on service elevators. Engineers use rather complex formulas for making calculations, but basically the calculations made will be based on the type of information given here.

Space needs for elevators at entrances must be well planned. The location of the elevators in relationship to rooms or spaces they are to serve must also be considered. Elevators may be banked in a row or opposite each other. The minimum distance between elevators across from each other should be 6 ft (1.83 m) but for a normal lobby, hall, or other waiting area the minimum set is 10 ft (3 m). Good visibility should be provided around doors so people moving in or out of the elevators have a view of the area. Some elevator systems are computer controlled so that they may be changed in circuit to meet service demands.

Escalators are used when distance of travel is not great, such as several floors. Department stores use them so that patrons can see merchandise on the floors and also to provide good transportation between floors. They have the advantage of providing instant and independent travel, unless a line forms at the boarding area.

Dumbwaiter requirements will be based on the quantity and type of items to be transported, and time requirements. Normally, speeds from 50 to 300 fpm are used. If the quantity is large and the distance for transport is not great, a geared elevator or an elevator operated by hydraulic lift may be used. Freight elevators must be considered also on the basis of the weight per square foot they must carry.

MOBILE EQUIPMENT

Casters for Mobile Equipment

Much of the durability and satisfaction in use of mobile equipment depends on the quality of caster on which it moves. They should be (1) easy rolling; (2) durable; (3) moisture, chemical and grease resistant; (4) quiet; and (5) adequately sturdy to support the required weight, yet not damage flooring. Steel wheels can be hard on flooring. When specifying, state (1) wheel diameter, which should be as large as practical; (2) type of tread, such as rubber or hard tread; (3) ball bearing; (4) finish, such as cadmium plated or other; (5) type of adapter, such as stem, plate, or other fitting; and (6) swivel or rigid. If needed, **wheel locks** may also be specified.

The larger the wheel diameter the easier the movement of a load. Casters, 5 in. (12.7 cm) in diameter, are popular for carts and other mobile equipment. The rubber tires may be solid, **pneumatic,** or semipneumatic and the hard treads may be of steel, aluminum, or plastic. The finish may be enameled or cadmium plated, which is preferable for rust proofing. Four **swivel casters** are selected when it is desirable to maneuver a piece of equipment into a space using sideways as well as forward and back motion. Two rigid casters at one end assist in guiding equipment when movement is in a direct line. **Wheel locks** on two wheels help to fix the position of **portable equipment.** It is important to note appropriate sturdiness in fork and axle. If these are too light for trucks transporting heavy loads, they are likely to become bent or give way. The requirements of NSF Standard No. C-2 (p. 11) for casters should be met.

Bumpers

Bumpers on equipment, walls, and doors will be essential in preventing scarring if a great deal of mobile equipment is used, particularly if equipment is heavy and difficult to maneuver (Figure 25.4). Equipment bumpers are made of rubber molded to the desired forms. They may be corner bumpers to cover the vertical edges or placed at baseboard height to hold equipment from hitting the wall or other objects. Doughnut-shaped bumpers may be placed on the shaft above the casters and on cart or truck handles. They may be made of a 1-in. (2.5-cm)-OD encircling rubber doughnut set in a 1.25- × 0.5- × 0.125-in. (3.2- × 1.3- × .3-cm) seamless channel from the same metal as the uprights. The channels should be connected to the chassis by 2- × ³⁄₁₆-in. (5.1- × 0.5-cm) screws. They will add approximately 5 in. (12.7 cm) in length and 4 in. (10.2 cm) in width to the overall dimensions where used on the caster shaft.

Continuous rubber bumpers around the bottom of equipment serve as effective protection. These bumpers may be procured in widths varying from 0.625 to 1.25 in. (1.6 to 3.2 cm) and in depth from 0.5 to 1.125 in. (1.3 to 2.9 cm). They are molded on a steel strap or bar and may or may not be set in a channel. The size and weight chosen must be adequate for bumpering the size and weight of the mobile equipment.

Doors to garbage rooms, receiving, and storage need protection from the movement of heavy mobile loads. Steel, either galvanized or stainless, in 1-in. (2.5-cm) pipe or sheet form may be used. Stainless steel of 16 or 18 gauge fitted tightly over a 1- × 3-in. (2.5- × 7.6-cm) board serves as effective wall protection. It should be positioned at a height to give maximum protection.

Construction Standards

Flexibility of many pieces of equipment can be increased by placing them on casters (Figures 25.5 and 25.6). Large equipment may be mounted directly on casters and smaller pieces on a mobile base or table (Figure 25.7). Attention should be paid to securing proper working height. Food cutters, slicers, and small mixers are usually satisfactory on tables that are 18 to 24 in. high (45.7 to 61.0 cm). One under-shelf in such tables, 8 to 10 in. (20.3 to 25.4 cm) above the floor, will be convenient for use and add rigidity and strength to the frame. A drawer 4 to 5 in. (10.2 to 12.7 cm) deep may be hung under the top for storage of small equipment.

Carts may be factory or custom built in a wide variety of sizes and designs. They may be made of aluminum, galvanized iron, or stainless steel in various gauges. The supports or frames may be continuous tubing, tubing used for uprights only, and **angle frame.** Materials are sometimes combined. For example, a **tube frame** of aluminum tubing and stainless steel shelves may be satisfactory for a lightweight cart. Heavy use requires sturdy, durable materials and gauge. Sixteen-gauge metal should be used for galvanized steel and 18 gauge for stainless steel, and 1-in. (2.5-cm)-OD × 16-gauge wall tubing. Utility carts may have two or three shelves and may be approximately 36 in. (91.4 cm) high. To lessen delivery costs these models are designed for compact shipment and local assembly. The length and width should be sized in terms of use. If it is to be used

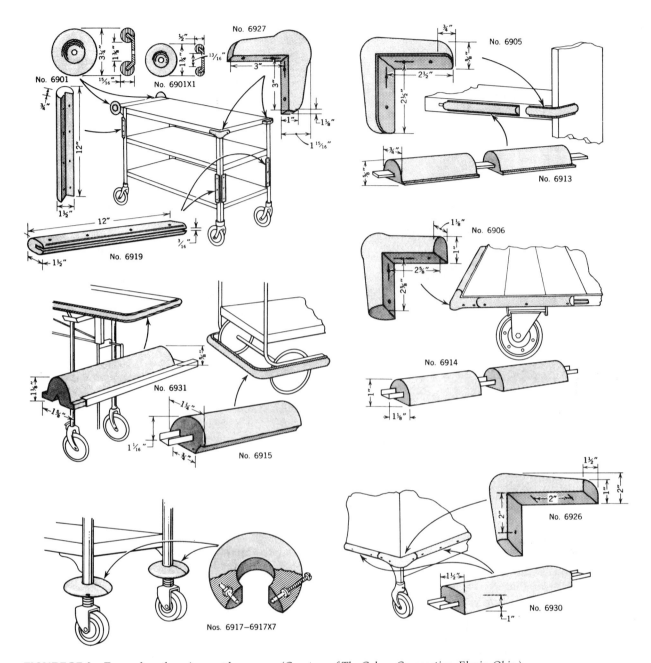

FIGURE 25.4 Examples of equipment bumpers. *(Courtesy of The Colson Corporation, Elyria, Ohio.)*

for bussing dishes, care should be taken to select bus boxes, so that one or two boxes will fit well on a shelf. Tray carts may have four to eight shelves each to hold one tray, and from four to six shelves each to hold from three to five trays. Ease of maneuvering should be considered when selecting them.

The sturdiness of construction should be in proportion to the load that a cart will be required to carry. A cart 5 to 6 ft × 30 in. (1.5 to 1.8 m × 76.2 cm) wide carrying a moderate load should have an angle frame of 1½ × 1½ × ⅛ in. (3.8 × 3.8 × .3 cm). Shelving should be not less than 16 gauge and should be turned down 1 to 1½ in. (2.5 to 3.8 cm) on the edges with edges sealed. Angle support may be necessary under the shelving for support if very heavy loads are to be handled. A cart such as this with five shelves will be about 5½ ft (1.7 m) high with shelves on 8 in. (20.3 cm) centers and is suitable for dish transport but may have to have 12-gauge shelves.

FIGURE 25.5   Mobile equipment facilitates one-motion storage.

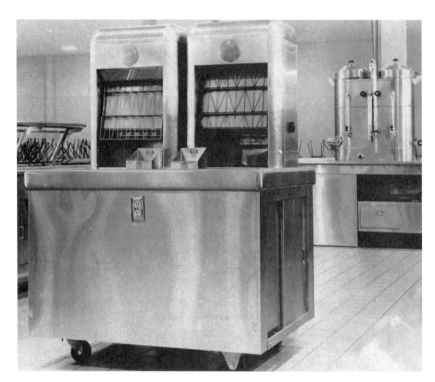

FIGURE 25.6   Mobility of toasters makes it possible to obtain variation in service needs behind a service counter.

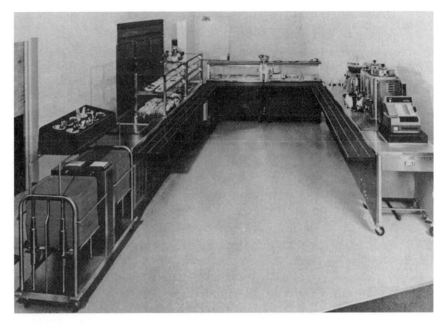

FIGURE 26.7 Attractive mobile counters used for service in a multipurpose room.

FIGURE 25.8 Dollies provide convenient transportation for many items, such as milk cases or cup and glass racks.

DOLLIES AND PLATFORM TRUCKS

The **dolly** consists of a metal frame with casters, of a size to fit garbage cans, one or more milk cases, or cup and glass racks (Figure 25.8). It may or may not have a handle. They are usually constructed of steel.

The **platform truck** is almost synonymous with the dolly and the names may, in certain instances, be used interchangeably. Generally the platform truck is considered to be one of greater size, sturdier build, and equipped with handles. The platform may be of aluminum, wood, or steel and the fittings of aluminum, steel, or stainless steel. Size and sturdiness of build should be governed in terms of intended use, and the size and weight governed in terms of whether a man or woman will be using the equipment. The platform truck generally used by the receiving and storage clerk is 4 to 5 ft long (1.2 to 1.5 m) and 2 ft 3 in. (0.7 m) wide. The casters may be equal in size and located at the four corners. All may be swivel casters, or the two front ones swivel and the back ones **stationary casters**. For easy maneuverability, the casters may be in a diamond formation with two larger stationary ones on the two sides of the truck and smaller swivel casters in the center of the ends.

LIFT TRUCKS

A hydraulic lift may be used as a part of a hand cart that can be used conveniently by smaller workers, or as a lifting device for the movement of pallets on which heavy loads of food supplies are stored. Lift trucks are available in varying sizes and selection should be made in terms of specific use.

MOBILE RACKS AND CABINETS

A framework or rack designed to fit modular containers of a specified size that are supported on ledges in the framework may be mounted on casters. The framework is usually of angle construction of aluminum, galvanized steel, or stainless steel, with ledges formed by angles or corrugations of like metal. The racks may be open or closed, heated or unheated. For flexible use it is important that they be planned for modular pans, such as the standard steam table pans, baking sheets, and trays. Excess height that is impossible to see over and racks that tip easily should be avoided. They may be chosen for cabinet or under-counter use. These racks are very useful for storage, for holding materials during preparation to reduce space required in work centers, and for predishing of portions for service. NSF Standard No. 2 should be followed.

TRUCKS

The terms *cart* and *truck* are often used interchangeably and are frequently applied to mobile racks also. The term *truck*, as it is used here, refers to heavier, more complicated structures, designed for specific purposes, such as mop trucks, food trucks for hot or cold foodservice, and dispensing units. A wide variety of trucks that are equipped for hot and cold food and beverage service are offered for hospital and industrial foodservice.

Hot or cold food trucks should be well insulated and where electrically heated should have a signal light to indicate when electricity is on or off. Food trucks should have 14- to 16-gauge tops and 18-gauge bodies with an angle frame inside where necessary for rigid support. Shelves may be included underneath the top. Mobile canteens should be built of 3-in. (7.6-cm) ship channel chassis reinforced with 18-gauge angle iron for the superstructure. The design should be based on the food items to be offered, such as hot and cold beverages, hot rolls, doughnuts, sandwiches, candy, and cigarettes. The units may be open or enclosed.

FIGURE 25.9 A mobile sorbet trolley, which has each pot of ice cream or sherbet held frozen by an individual eutectic block. Frozen desserts can be held up to six hours. *(Courtesy of Lentia Manufacturing Ltd., Port Coquitiam, B.C., Canada.)*

Self-leveling units may be stationary or portable, and unheated, heated, or refrigerated. They are used for cup, glass, tray, bowl, bread, and plate dispensing. One-motion storage of items from the dishwashing is possible when such units are mobile. Space requirements will depend on the measurements of the item dispensed, whether the truck is open or enclosed, and whether heated, refrigerated, or neither. Space should be allowed in work centers and in relation to other equipment according to desired use.

Facilities in which mobile equipment is used should be planned for its use. Automatically opening doors, sufficiently wide aisles, adequate space in work areas, flush floor walk-ins, and protected corners are essential. Storage areas for the mobile equipment must be planned but if mobile equipment takes the place of fixed shelving, then space may be found along walls.

PORTABLE CARRIERS

The term **portable** has frequently been applied to any piece of equipment that may be moved. It is used here to signify those items that may be carried, and the term *mobile* is applied to those that are moved on wheels or casters.

Many times amounts to be transported are small enough to be moved quickly and easily by hand or on a mobile base. Cases, cabinets, and some insulated containers have been designed for such use (Figures 25.9 and 25.10). They may be shaped in such

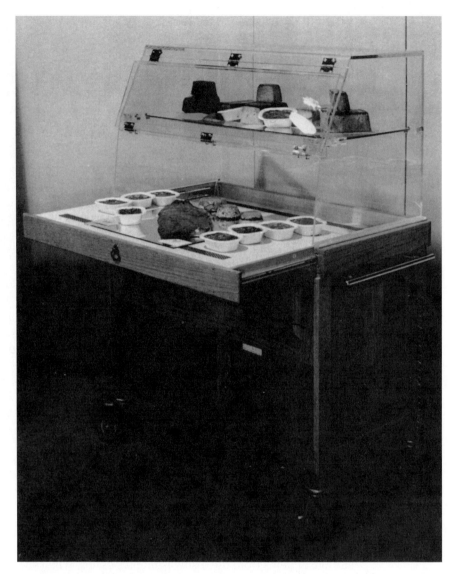

FIGURE 25.10   A mobile condiment cart. *(Courtesy of Lentia Manufacturing Ltd., Port Coquitlam, B.C., Canada.)*

a manner as to permit stacking on dollies or special carts. The cabinets may be equipped for electric or canned heat and designed for the standard hot table pans or baking sheets. Pie cases may have shelves or slides to fit 8 or 10 pie pans of standard size. These have a handle in the top and the cabinets a handle at each end for carrying. Insulated cabinets are used in hotels for room service meals, and may be transported by cart or under a drop-leaf table. It is important that items carried be as light in weight as practical. Aluminum or a light gauge of stainless steel is often used for that reason.

Vacuum-insulated containers made of 18-8 stainless steel are available in groups of two to four food pan assemblies varying in size from 1.5 to 5 gal (5.7 to 18.9 L) or single pan units having an 11-gal (41.6-L) capacity. Thermos jugs equipped with a faucet for beverages vary in size from 2 to 10 gal (7.6 L to 37.8 L) capacity. Accessories are available to use in connection with them, for moving via a hand cart, heating by means of a rod, and for filling, pumping, and cup dispensing.

CHAPTER SUMMARY

Transportation equipment, such as conveyors, elevators, carts, trucks, mobile cabinets, and dollies, moves materials and equipment more efficiently, which reduces labor and speeds accomplishment. Conveyors may move vertically or horizontally. They may use a track, rollers, belts, or gravity slides. Elevators are useful for vertical movement of materials, equipment, and people. They must be sized appropriately. Calculation of needs is based on volume (of people, carts, etc.) to be moved, optimum waiting times, speed of cars, size of cars, floor heights and number of floors for which transport is required. Location of the elevator must also be well planned.

The best mobile equipment is easy rolling; durable; moisture, chemical, and grease resistant; quiet; and adequately sturdy. Wheels or casters are a critical factor in their maneuverability and should be selected with care. Bumpers may help prevent damage to equipment and walls. Frames should be sturdy and support the weight of materials to be moved without tipping.

REVIEW QUESTIONS

1. Visit three cafeteria-style foodservices and study their tray return procedures. Do they use a conveyor belt? What is the approximate width and length? What is the belt material? Does it move vertically or horizontally? How fast does it move? How many trays does it take at one time? Finally, evaluate the tray return equipment for ease of cleaning and sanitation.
2. Evaluate five carts, hand trucks, or mobile pieces of equipment. What size casters do they have? What are the casters made of? Do the wheels swivel or are they fixed? Are there wheel locks? Are there any bumpers? If so, what size are they, what are they made of, and how far out do they project from the equipment? Are there any problems with movement associated with the wheels? See if you can determine what might be causing these.
3. Using standard calculations, how many individuals would need to use elevators in a 5-minute time period in a 300-guest hotel property? How many people in a hotel catering to conventions? Would patrons have to wait longer than 1 minute for an elevator traveling from the 12th floor to the first floor if floors are 12 ft (3.7 m) tall and the elevator is traveling 500 fpm?

KEY WORDS AND CONCEPTS

angle frame
dolly
dumbwaiters
gravity conveyors
limit switches
normal elevator wait time
mobile equipment

platform truck
pneumatic tires
portable equipment
stationary casters
swivel casters
tube frames
wheel locks

CHAPTER

26

Utensils and Tableware

Small equipment and tableware may claim 20% to 30% of the budget for food facility equipment. Although the amount spent for individual items may appear negligible, the large quantity makes an impressive total. The items are numerous and differ widely in character and use. Careful selection is significant to work efficiency, initial cost, and operation expense.

SELECTION

The important selection points for this equipment are as follows:

1. *Satisfaction for specific use.* Is it convenient, safe, and sanitary to use? Will it enhance quality or quantity in production or service? Will it save labor or make work easier? Is it essential?
2. *Appearance.* Is it attractive in itself and harmonious with the other equipment?
3. *Durability.* Is it satisfactorily durable in relation to functional needs for specific use and volume of work? Will operating expenses be appropriate in terms of repair, renewal, and replacement?
4. *Cost.* Selection should be evaluated in terms of initial investment and of probable operation (i.e., replacement, maintenance) costs. Can its purchase be justified economically?

Small equipment and tableware are usually made according to factory specifications. Manufacturers furnish brochures giving descriptions and pictures of the majority of items. Actual selection can often be made from displays in dealers' showrooms. Valuable records of use may be gained from those who are using specific equipment. Even with items that are small and "expendable," the initial selection will be important in establishing a pattern to be followed for many years. A change of make, material, or design may result in a heterogeneity that is unattractive and inconvenient. Changing an entire set of tableware or serving equipment, for example, may add greatly to expense.

MATERIALS

The material of which utensils and tableware are made will strongly influence durability, utility, beauty, and cost. Normally this ware is subjected to fairly vigorous hammering through repeated use and rapid handling. On the other hand, massive utensils that may be quite durable are heavy to handle and may cause serious fatigue. Each of the materials in popular use has specific advantages and disadvantages in relation to its intended use.

Aluminum

Aluminum utensils are relatively inexpensive, light in weight, and conduct heat rapidly. The metal is soft and can be damaged through rough treatment or by cleaning with coarse abrasives and alkalis. With suitable care, however, aluminum will withstand many years of active use. Lightweight ware dents easily and may be bent out of shape through heavy use. Aluminum has a bright appearance that may last through the use of mild cleaning methods. It has high thermal conductivity and distributes heat evenly. It is sometimes used as a core or as a covering over other metals that conduct heat less well.

Many utensils are made from sheets of fairly pure aluminum and from spun, **drawn,** and punched, pressed aluminum. Certain heavy pots and pans are cast. Alloys are used with aluminum to develop greater hardness and corrosion resistance. Anodized or surface-hardened material is used extensively. The cast utensils should be made from aluminum that conforms to the TS-4021 Standards of the National Bureau of Standards. This type will resist staining and corrosion under normal use.

Copper

The satisfactory heat conduction of copper has caused it to be used as a core or as a covering over metals that are less efficient in heat conduction. It stains and discolors readily, requiring extra effort in maintenance. The green rust on copper, known as **verdigris,** is poisonous. Copper is a soft metal that can be scratched or dented. It has a beautiful warm color when polished. When used where it will not be subjected to friction, it may be lacquered to preserve its bright appearance. It should not be used in contact with acidic foods or beverages (such as a pH below 6 according to the 1999 FDA Food Code).

Cast-Iron

Cast-iron utensils are made from molten gray iron poured into a mold. It is a close-grained metal that may be machined to produce a smooth finish. The exteriors are black. The cost is comparatively low. Utensils of this material may break or crack if dropped on a hard surface. In addition, the FDA Food Code only allows **cast iron** to be used as a food contact surface if it will be heated (skillets, pans, grill tops, etc.). A suitably heavy weight is an important factor for even heat distribution and for sufficient sturdiness to withstand commercial use. The cast iron will rust unless protected by a thin film of salt-free oil, especially where it is allowed to stand without use for a considerable period of time.

Sheet Steel

Many pieces of kitchen utensils are made of **sheet steel,** such as roasting pans, bread pans, pie tins, baking sheets, muffin pans, and light skillets. They are relatively inexpensive. The steel rusts readily and certain protective covering is required. Lacquer finish is frequently used as a protection when it is manufactured. This is usually burned off before the item is used. The steel that is not otherwise covered should be given a thin film of oil to prevent rusting if the item is to stand for a long period without being used.

Utensil Steel

Steel can be hardened by heating it to temperatures greater than 1500°F (815°C) and then suddenly cooling it by plunging it into water. It can also be given hardness by adding carbon; the carbon gives the iron more density. Many kitchen utensils and tools require the hardened steel, referred to as **utensil steel.**

A **high-carbon steel** is used for knives and other cutting tools. It takes a good edge and wears well but it will stain and also rust. Cutting tools are usually assigned a hardness anywhere from around C-56 to C-58.[1] Steel with a hardness of C-52 gives a cutting edge that is soft and will not hold up well but it does take a new edge easily. From about 0.9% to 1.1% carbon is required to give this degree of hardness. Tools that must be hard and yet flexible such as bowl knives, spatulas, and turners will have steel with the lower amount of carbon, whereas knives that must retain a good cutting edge will have the higher amount. Lower, cheaper carbon steels are what are referred to as **cold rolled** and are not hardened and tempered. They make poor kitchen utensils and should not be used. A high-carbon steel containing some vanadium and some chromium resists staining and rusting better than good quality high-carbon steel and still holds a hard, durable cutting edge. Stainless steel may be used for tools and utensils. It is too hard to be easily sharpened but it resists stain and rusting and holds a hard, durable cutting edge. If some carbon is added to stainless steel, the metal is softened so it can be sharpened more easily yet will still resist staining and rusting; it loses flexibility but the cutting edge is very durable. It is probably the best metal to use for many kinds of tools in the kitchen. It must be properly hardened and tempered to attain these desirable qualities.

Tin

Tin coating is used on many pieces of steel utensils. This supplies a bright finish and one that is resistant to rust. Tin is soft and a thin coating will wear off in a fairly short period of use. It is more desirable to discard light inexpensive pieces, such as pie tins, rather than to have them re-tinned. Large bowls, such as those used for mixing machines, colanders, and similar utensils may be re-tinned. Small utensils, such as pie tins and muffin pans, are usually made of tinned sheet steel. Hot dipped tinware should be specified for commercial use.

Porcelain Enamel

Porcelain-enamel utensils are made from sheet steel covered with one or more layers of porcelain enamel. They have very limited use and acceptance in commercial establishments because of their tendency to chip, heat craze, or crack. This ware is inexpensive, highly resistant to food acids, and easy to clean. Commercial standards for porcelain-enamel equipment are published in National Bureau of Standards publication TS-4482.

Stainless Steel

Bright, durable, easy-to-clean, rust-free **stainless steel** holds a popular place as a material for both kitchen utensils and tableware. It has many good features and some less fa-

---

[1]"C" stands for carbon. The amount of carbon in steel accounts for its hardness. The "C" standards have been established to indicate amounts of carbon in steel and therefore its hardness or softness.

vorable ones. Its major drawbacks are seen in terms of weight, cost, and slow, spotty heat conduction. It reflects radiant heat away and so is seldom used for baking utensils. "Hot spots" develop in stainless steel cooking utensils. It distributes heat poorly and those surfaces in contact with the heating surface carry heat directly into the food. Better heat distribution is secured by laminating layers of stainless steel with a core of a metal such as copper or sheet steel that conducts heat well. Copper or aluminum may also be used to cover the bottom of cooking pots. This laminated metal is known as **cladded metal.** Sometimes stainless steel utensils are covered on the outside with a layer of copper by means of electroplating.

Its durable, attractive appearance is an important asset of stainless steel. It can withstand rugged use and vigorous cleaning methods. The gauge of metal should be suitable in relation to size of the item and the intended use. Many of the pans, for example, should not be less than 16 gauge. Most of these utensils are drawn.

Stainless steel flatware for table use is usually made of a high-grade **alloy** of chromium, steel, and nickel. Nickel gives it a whitish, silvery luster. Cheaper grades, which lack nickel, have a blue metallic color. The lower quality of flatware is made by **punch pressing** the shapes from sheets of stainless steel. The thickness is the same throughout. It can be detected readily by the somewhat rough appearing edges and the pebbly appearance where the press cut through the metal around handle edges and between fork tines. This ware is usually poorly balanced. Stainless steal flatware may be given a chromium high-luster finish, which adds to the beauty and durability of the product.

The more expensive stainless steel flatware is **fashioned** or graded. Handles, spoon bowls, and fork tines are tapered and the finish is smooth and even. This flatware is usually reinforced at stress points. Graded ware usually has simple smooth flowing lines and is quite attractive. Patterns used with stainless steel are usually simple, and pressed ware may have slightly embossed designs. The finishes are bright, semidull, and satin.

The strength of stainless steel is greater than that of similar weight silverplate. Strength can be tested by bending the spoon bowl where it joins the handle or by placing one of the outside tines on a hard surface and pushing. Good ware can be bent only with great difficulty. Flatware knives should be made of a single piece of stainless steel. Stainless steel blades with silverplated handles are sometimes found in knives. The blade should be set into the handle with solder, not cement, for the knife to give adequate wear.

Silverplate

The character of the base metal is important to the durability of silverplated ware. The most rugged treatment given this ware is during collection in the dining room and during washing. The silverplating is soft and contributes little to sturdiness. Nickel silver is the standard metal for the base and the alloy should contain as much as 18% nickel for satisfactory rigidity and toughness. Silverplated pieces on bases having 12% nickel bend and dent easily. The silver peels from the steel as soon as the steel has attracted moisture under the plating.

The nickel silver blanks pressed from sheet metal are rolled and formed to have proper shape, size, and balance. They are trimmed and polished to have smooth edges and polished surfaces free from roughness or pebbles that would be unpleasant in use and be points where extra wear might occur. Plating methods used by the leading silver manufacturers differ, but approximate specifications for quality are as follows:

Standard plate (or A1): Five ounces (142 gm) of silver are used for plating one gross of teaspoons and in like proportions for other items.

Half standard plate: Approximately one-half of the standard plate silver content, or 2.5 oz (71 gm) of silver, is used for plating one gross of teaspoons.

Triple plate: Six ounces (170 gm) of silver are used for plating one gross of teaspoons.

Extra heavy hotel plate: Eight or more ounces (227 or more grams) of silver are used for plating one gross of teaspoons. This ware goes through more preparation and finishing processes to toughen it and give it a hard finish than that used in lower grades.

Banquet plate: This uses one-half the quantity of silver used for extra heavy hotel plate. It is produced in a few items only. The weight of the blank and finish are identical.

Hotel plate: This type of plate may be reinforced at points where the greatest wear is likely to occur, such as at the bottom of the spoon or fork bowl. The reinforcing may be by means of an inlay of silver or by spot plating before applying the general plating.

Pieces of table flatware are "intimate" pieces that directly influence dining pleasure. The items are handled and carried to the lips. Attractiveness, a smooth clean surface, and comfortable balance are important. A gritty or greasy feel and tip heaviness create a poor impression and spoil enjoyment of the food. The design may be plain, semi-ornate, or ornate and the finish may be a bright, butler, or satin finish to meet varied tastes and fit into a specific decorative plan.

China

The term *china* has sometimes been used to include all of the clay or ceramic materials found in food facilities. There are four distinct types of clayware: (1) **Earthenware** is an unvitrified, soft porous product that may or may not have a glaze. (2) **Pottery** has a glaze and the clay from which the body is made is of slightly better quality than earthenware. These two types of clayware are not suitable for use in food establishments except for decorative purposes. (3) **Stoneware** is vitrified and has a glazed surface. The clay is coarser than that used for porcelain. Its use is most suitable for heavy serving dishes, beverage containers, and kitchen crockery. (4) **Vitrified china** and porcelain are synonymous. The body of the ware is made of a fine quality of clay, which is fired to vitrification in the bisque. It has a **glaze** applied that upon refiring forms a transparent glassy surface. The number of times china is fired will be influenced by the colors used for decoration. The number of colors, the intricacy of the pattern, and the amount of handling required have a strong influence on price. The quality of the body and the glaze and the strictness of the grading also affect price.

The life of china depends on several factors. The body of the ware must be strong enough to withstand the repeated hammering of normal use and the glaze must be tough in resisting friction from the weight of other dishes stacked on it or sliding over it. The edge of coffee cups that are repeatedly stacked often become etched so that they are unpleasant to use even when they are not chipped or broken. Unless a sturdy glaze is used, the centers of plates will wear from repeated cutting of food and from stacking, and will be dull and unsightly. It is important that dishes stack evenly to reduce the danger of stacks tipping or sliding, resulting in breakage.

The weight of the china and the shape of the edge will influence the strength of dishes. Lightweight china used in homes is practical only where it can be given gentle care. The appeal of its beauty and delicacy is sufficient to promote its use in exclusive establishments. Semi-heavy china with a slight rolled edge and the institution weight have correspondingly greater sturdiness. Certain of the scalloped edges appear to have more strength than the plain circle.

The grading of china is of concern to the extent that it influences appearance, sanitation, roughness that may cause scarring of surfaces on which it is placed, and irregularities that cause poor stacking. Common defects include (1) crookedness caused by warping or uneven shrinkage; (2) **crazing,** which refers to cracks in the glaze; (3) denting, which refers to cracks in the body under the glaze; (4) pinholes or tiny depressions in the glaze; (5) spots and stains caused by a particle of iron in the clay or other discoloration of the slip; (6) white patches caused by accidental splashes of slip or poor mixing of the glaze; (7) unevenness in color; and (8) scars caused by marks of the stilts on which dishes rest during firing of the glaze.

The National Bureau of Standards has established tests for satisfactory strength on the basis of various temperature, shock, and impact tests. China should also meet the requirements of the federal specification "China, Vitrified, M-C-301d," which requires that a piece of china that is 2.5 in. square (16.25 cm^2) after boiling 5 hours and soaking in water 20 hours more should, on small ware, not absorb more than 0.2% water, and on large ware, not more than 0.5% water. Low lead and cadmium content should also be specified to meet the requirements of the U.S. Potters' Association for these substances. The NSF standards on shape, contour, cleanability, durability, and condition of surfaces as set forth in Standard No. 36 should be met.

Table 26–1 indicates the quantities of china normally required by various types of food services.

Buyers should specify carefully and examine the wares purchased. The grades based on strict selection include (1) selects, which appear perfect to a careful grader; (2) firsts, which are almost perfect; (3) seconds, which have minor defects that are conspicuous; (4) thirds, which possess obvious blemishes of a type that do not weaken or eliminate the ware for possible use; and (5) culls or lumps, which are badly warped, chipped, or scarred. **Run of the kiln** may include the two top grades and the best of the seconds.

Manufacturers of vitrified china identify their products with **backstamps.** Terms used to designate pieces commonly used commercially differ in certain instances from those used for home ware. Specification for items should indicate item name, size, weight, pattern, shape, and such other qualities that may identify choice such as body color or rim style.

Dealers often select patterns they have found to be or believe will be popular and carry them in **open stock.** Large-quantity shipments of this ware usually yield a price advantage over patterns used exclusively by one establishment in a local area. The length of time that the ware will be carried in open stock will largely depend on continued popularity. Designation of size should be given by exact measurement in terms of overall diameter or weight of contents. Using the old method of measuring the bowl of a plate—inside the rim—may lead to error. Slight measurement changes on reordering of dishes may interfere with the use of leveling equipment or result in unsatisfactory stacking (Figure 26.1).

Glass

In the past the use of glass was largely limited to bowls and beverage service. Today complete sets of dinnerware are available in glass. The cost, use, and durability of glass compare well with that of china. The designation of size and shape is made in a similar manner to china for both table and oven ware. The formula for certain items designed for cooking combines glass and plastic in such a manner as to develop outstanding toughness and resistance to rapid, extreme temperature changes. The glass used for glass cooking utensils contains metal and other compounds that give them resistance against heat and shock and makes them better heat conductors. Glass utensils are easy to clean, are extremely resistant to corrosion, but are fragile.

The glass commonly used for water or beverage glasses and salad or dessert plates may be classified by composition as **lead** or **lime glass** and **rock crystal,** and by shaping as blown or pressed glass. Rock crystal, a potassium and lead silicate, is beautifully clear and shining. It is of top quality and price and is used only in a few food establishments. Lead glass, which is widely used, is less brittle than lime glass and may be shaped into the desired form by blowing molten glass into a mold. Molten lime glass is deposited in a mold, pressed, polished, and tempered.

TABLE 26-1   Quantity of China Required by Various Foodservices

Item Description	Dining Room Service (Rest., Hotels Clubs)	Counter Service/ Fast Food Table Service (Coffee Shops, Diners, Restaurants)	Tray Service (Cafeterias, Colleges, Schools, Hospitals Nursing Care Homes, Contract Feeding)	Catering Service (on/off premises)
Trade Name/Usage	Dozens per 100 seats	Dozens per 100 seats	Dozens per 100 seats/beds	Dozens per 100 seats
Plate #3/"C" Hor d'oeuvres, bread and butter, salad,	27			
Plate #4/"D" Dessert		21		18
Plate #5/"F" Hors d'oeuvres, salad, dessert	24	36	36	24
Plate #6/"H" Breakfast, brunch lunch, sandwich,			21	
Plate #7/"I" Small dinner	18	15		
Plate #8/"J" Dinner, roast beef, steak, lobster, fowl, pasta,	18	Depending on need, 15 doz. in lieu of #7 plate (option)		15
Plate #10/"K" Service plate				
Great Plate Lg/M/Sm Roast beef, pasta,				
Dish #7/"G" Burger 'n' fries,		12		
Dish #8/"T" Steak, lobster, fowl, fish	9			

Item	Description				
Cup, tea	Use together for coffee, tea, hot chocolate service	24	36	21	18
Saucer, tea		24	36	21	18
Newport cup	Use with or without saucer for coffee, tea, hot chocolate service				
Viennese cup		24 (option)	36 (option)	21 (option)	18 (option)
Java mug					
Bouillon, unhld.	Soup	12	9		12
Saucer, tea	Underliner for bouillon	12			12
Plate #7, rim deep	Spaghetti, clams, soup, chili, cereal	6			12 (option)
Plate #8/"J"	Underliner for #7 rim deep	6			12 (option)
Fruit #3½/"A"/"B"	Side vegetable, fruit, ice cream	24	36	36	24
Bowl, coupe deep	Soup, deep dish dessert, salad, shortcake, cereal, etc.	9	12	24	15
Bowl, grapefruit, small					
Bowl, grapefruit, large					
Bowl, salad					
Nappy					
Plate #5/"F" or 4/"D"	Underliner for bowl	9			15 (option)
Cup, A.D.	Use together for after dinner coffee, etc.	6			
Saucer, A.D.		6			
Bouillon, unhld.	Sugar	6	6		6

The recommended quantities will provide adequate opening inventory. Provided you *rotate* items in service correctly and *maintain* adequate inventory levels, your replacement costs will be minimal. Properly used, Syracuse China will cost as much less than 1% per meal.
Source: Courtesy Syracuse© China Corporaton, Syracuse, New York.

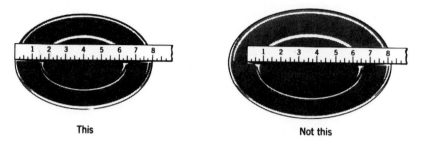

This   Not this

FIGURE 26.1   To get the size of dishes, measure the overall diameter.

Judgment of quality in glassware can be based on five points: (1) Good glassware has a lustrous appearance and clarity that give it a clean sparkling look free from cloudiness or discoloration. (2) The edges should be smooth and regular. (3) The shape should be well balanced and symmetrical. (4) Defects such as waviness, specks, and bubbles should be at a minimum. (5) Where pattern is used, it should show skillful craftsmanship.

Breakage and surface wear of glassware and cups are minimized by washing, handling, and storage in racks. Metal racks with plastisol covering of areas that come in contact with the dish are desirable.

Table 26–2 lists items in quantities commonly needed and the number of racks required for handling them.

Plastics

The development of plastics has brought many valuable qualities to ware used for small equipment and table service in institutions. Its use has yielded sanitary and heat-proof handles for tools and utensils, plus lightweight, attractive durable trays, buckets, bowls, garbage cans, and numerous other kitchen items. Its low heat conductivity makes it an effective insulator. This quality, on the other hand, means that it does not absorb enough heat to dry quickly when coming from the dishwasher. It tends to muffle sound and is therefore quiet to use. It does not break easily. It is frequently combined with other materials, such as wood, metal, or textiles, to improve its strength. A tray having an excellent service record is composed of synthetic resin and tough wood fiber.

Melamine alpha-cellulose-filled tableware is made from plastic, paper pulp, and color pigments. It should be of the heavy-duty type and should comply with Commercial Standards CS173-50 as published by the U.S. Department of Commerce. Melamine ware is made by subjecting the raw plastic mixture to high pressure and temperatures. Decorations can be implanted in the ware and such decorations should be an integral part of the ware and as durable as the undecorated portion. Plastic ware should be resistant to cracking at dry heat when placed in 170°F (76.6°C) for eight hours and against corrosion from boiling sulfuric solutions.

Plastic trays and tableware from the various manufacturers vary in toughness of surface and imperviousness to absorption, buckling, and cracking. Examination of specific makes that have been in use for some time is recommended before making a selection. If this dinnerware is contemplated, note how well the ware withstands cutting of food on the dish and friction characteristic of normal use. Minimum standards have been worked out by leading manufacturers and the National Bureau of Standards for thickness, finish, and resistance to acid, boiling water, and dry heat.

The use of color in plastics offers opportunity for color coding that reduces search by workers for specific equipment. Handles of different color that identify size of scoops or dishes, for example, is a convenience. Plastic cutting boards that are color coded for each product use may also help prevent cross-contamination (red for meats, green for vegetables, etc.). Color coding is a feature that could be exploited more fully and with greater standardization by equipment manufacturers.

TABLE 26–2   Glasses, Cups and Racks Required for Washing and Storage[a,b]

	Coffee Shop		Dining Room			Banquet Room			Cafeteria			Fountain	
Number of Seats	100	200	100	200	300	100	200	300	100	200	300	25/50	75/100
5-oz juice	144	252	144	252	350	144	256	360	108	216	329	72	144
36/rack	4	7	4	7	10	4	7	10	3	6	9	2	4
10-oz water	300	500	300	500	700	200	300	450	300	600	900	100	200
25/rack	12	20	12	20	28	8	12	18	12	24	36	4	8
12-oz iced tea	200	300	200	300	400	150	250	400	200	400	600	100	200
25/rack	8	12	8	12	16	6	10	16	8	16	24	4	8
7-oz beverage												108	216
36/rack												3	6
12-oz malted												75	150
25/rack												3	6
10-oz goblet			300	500	700	200	300	450					
25/rack			12	20	28	8	12	18					
5½-oz sherbet			150	250	360	150	250	350	100	200	300	75	150
25/rack			6	10	14	6	10	14	4	8	12	3	6
4½-oz fruit cocktail			150	250	350	150	250	350	100	200	300	75	150
25/rack			6	0	14	10	0	1	4	8	12	3	6
4½-oz parfait			144	252	360	144	252	360	108	216	324	72	144
36/rack			4	7	10	4	7	10	3	6	9	2	4
5½-oz champagne						150	250	350					
25/rack						6	10	14					
Cups	300	500	300	500	700	160	280	400	300	600	900	100	200
20/rack	15	25	15	25	35	8	14	20	15	30	45	5	10

[a]Courtesy of Seco Company, St. Louis, Mo.
[b]Rack size is approximately 19¾ by 19¾ in.

SELECTION OF TABLEWARE

The quantity of flatware and dishes required will depend on the following parameters:

1. The number of customers served
2. Type of service
3. Menu items
4. Length of serving period
5. Duration of peak serving period
6. Speed of service or turnover
7. Speed of wash and sanitizing and return to service
8. Allowance for loss and breakage.

Some operations carry 1.5 times their seating capacity in flatware and dishes. Other operations find they must carry four or five times the seating capacity to have adequate supplies. This is especially true in operations with a fast table turn. One industrial cafeteria chain found that carrying an inventory to satisfy the full needs for a meal period reduced breakage and replacement costs by more than 25%. The inventory carried will depend on the item. The ordinary operation would not carry two times its seating capacity in oyster forks, iced tea spoons, creamers, or relish trays. Yet a facility might find it advisable, if it catered to heavy coffee breaks, to carry four times the seating capacity for those pieces of tableware used most commonly. (Table 26–3).

Many types of dishware are used in food services. Appearance is important. Design and color must be satisfying to the customers and blend with the design and

TABLE 26–3   *Suggested Inventory of Flatware and Dishes, in Dozens*

Dining Room Capacity	50	100	200
Plates, dinner	8	12	24
Plates, salad, dessert, and liner	12	24	45
Plates, bread and butter	8	12	24
Bouillon cups	5	10	18
Grapefruit or oatmeal nappies	5	8	12
Cups	9	20	35
Saucers	8	16	32
Fruits	7	12	24
Utility knives	6	12	20
Utility forks	8	16	30
Teaspoons	10	20	40
Dessert spoons	3	5	10
Bouillon spoons	3	8	12

decor of the facility and other table appointments. Durability and sanitation should receive consideration, along with weight and size. Heavy dishes make heavy loads for workers. Size is important in properly presenting food portions and in giving food an attractive appearance. Weight and size must be remembered in relation to dispensing equipment. Price may be a governing factor in purchasing.

SELECTION OF UTENSILS

Good pots and pans should be designed to suit their intended use. They should be heavy enough gauge to be durable, yet light enough to be handled easily. Cooking utensils should be made of materials that conduct heat rapidly and give good heat distribution. Bottoms should be flat rather than round if used for cooking so that they conduct heat well from the heating surface. They should resist bending or denting. Covers should fit; spouts should have nondrip edges and pour well; and rims should be smoothly turned and finished. There should be no rough or sharp edges. Handles should be firmly attached, be heat resistant, be fitted to the hand, and in such a position as to give good leverage in lifting. Extra strength should be given handles by riveting where necessary. They should be easy to clean, with no cracks or crevices. The material from which they are made should be of noncorrosive material.

Quantities and sizes required should be selected after analysis of requirements. Capacities of pots and pans are most usually stated in liquid quarts filled to the brim with a 5% plus or minus tolerance measured to the point of first overflow. Capacity of much coffee equipment is usually stated in terms of 5-oz (148 ml) cups.

Dish tote boxes should be water tight and made either of heavy plastic or 20-gauge metal bent over ⁵⁄₁₆-in. (0.8 cm) in diameter brass wire at the top (Figure 26.2). All boxes should possess good grip handles or rims. They should be chip and warp proof and sufficiently sturdy to support probable loads. Reinforcing with a center metal band of 1.5-in. (1.3-cm) , 12-gauge metal gives added strength.

Knives are of such importance to a production worker that many cooks and chefs own their own. Even the lowly paring knife offers variety for selection, and one should be chosen that has (1) a good blade that will receive and hold a sharp edge, (2) a shape of blade that will be effective for intended use, and (3) a handle that is comfortable to hold and sanitary. Vegetable workers grip knife handles tightly for long periods of time.

FIGURE 26.2 Plastic tote boxes should be light in weight, sturdy, and chosen to fit the transportation equipment.

The handle needs to be large enough so that hands will not become cramped. For the salad worker, the blade must be sharp and also stainless. A salad knife needs a sharp, slender, stainless blade long enough to cut through a head of lettuce or cabbage. A blade 7.5 to 8 in. (19 to 20 cm) is satisfactory, and the cutting edge should be straight, curving slightly toward the tip for slicing or making julienne strips.

The French knife has many uses. It is especially good for dicing and chopping. It should be selected with (1) a good quality carbon steel blade that will receive and hold a sharp edge, (2) a weight and balance in the knife that promote easy handling, (3) the proper length of blade for intended use, and (4) a well-made, sanitary handle. The volume and kind of materials to be cut will influence the weight and length of blade desirable. Sanitary, easy-to-clean construction is important for all knives.

Knives should be made of either high-carbon stainless steel or stainless steel containing some vanadium and chromium. Good balance of the knife and contour of the handle or grip are requirements. The handle should have an angle of 19 degrees to best fit the working position required (Figure 26.3). The lower part of the handle toward the cutting edge should have a safety shoulder guard to prevent the hand from slipping onto the blade should the knife suddenly come on some unexpected resistance. The handle should be made of a smoothly finished piece of hardwood in which the tang (the part of the knife in the handle) is fastened securely to the handle by at least three rivets. A plastic, molded handle of hard polypropylene given a textured finish for aiding the grip is also satisfactory. It is both low and high temperature resistant. The various **knife grinds** are (1) hollow, (2) flat, (3) taper or V, (4) rolled edge, (5) cannell, and (6) concave. Some special knives may have scalloped edges or serrated edges. The taper or V grind gives good sharpness along with durability and can stand up to the rugged treatment experienced during chopping or cutting, which causes side strain. Hollow and concave grinds are not as durable although for special uses, they may be specified. The three grinds specified for most professional knives are the V, the rolled edge and the cannelled edge. Some knives specified as having *tip-breakthrough* have tips that give a penetrating action to the knife tip.

The choice of modular pans appropriate for a variety of uses and that will fit special equipment in which they are to be used is recommended. It is very convenient to have the 12- × 20-in. (30.5- × 50.8-cm) serving pan fit not only the serving table but also

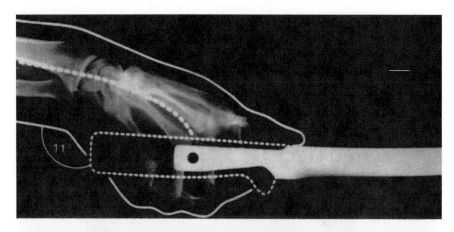

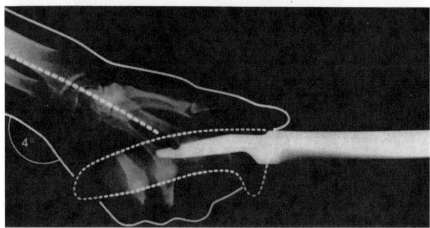

FIGURE 26.3   The top photo shows how the hand must be bent to an 11° angle causing extra stress and tension in the wrist and forearm and a reduction in wrist motion. The bottom photo shows how having the handle at a 19° angle requires only a 4° wrist turn allowing more energy to be used and reducing tension and stress. (*Courtesy of Chicago Cutlery Consumer Products, Inc., Minneapolis, Minnesota.*)

a mobile rack, steam table and oven compartment, and the storage area. The choice of major equipment should be tied in with this plan in order for it to be fully effective.

CHECKLIST OF SMALL EQUIPMENT

Items of small equipment for consideration when preparing lists for initial estimates include the following.

For the Delivery and Storage Area

Box opener

Box cutter

Crowbar

Hammer

Pliers

Scales

Scoops, grocer type, aluminum

Screw driver

Spindle or clip board
Step ladder
Storage containers, such as cans or bins.

Vegetable Preparation Area
Boards for cutting, 15 × 20 × 1¾ in. (38 × 51 × 4 cm), maple or plastic
Bowls, mixing
Colander
Cutter and grater (may be machine attachments)
Hand parer with swivel-action blade
Knife, French, 10- or 12-in. (25- or 30-cm) blade
Knives, paring
Knives, utility, 6-in. (15-cm) blade
Mobile storage units with removable pans or lugs
Potato ball cutter
Potato eyer knife
Pots, stock, aluminum, 15 qt (14 L), shallow
Vegetable brushes.

Meat Preparation
Brush, steel, block
Cleaver, 7- or 8-in. (18- or 20-cm) blade
Knife, French, 10- or 12-in. (25- or 30-cm) blade
Knife, slicing
Knife, steak or butcher
Knives, boning, light
Pans, stainless steel (s/s), 12 × 20 × 1 or 2 or 2½ in. (30 × 51 × 2.5 or 5 or 6 cm)
Saw, butchers, 24 in. (61 cm)
Sharpener, knife, electric
Steel, butchers, 12 to 14 in. (30 to 36 cm)
Trays or baking sheets for portion-ready meat.

Cooking Section
Board, cutting, 12 × 20 × 1¾ in. (30 × 51 × 4 cm)
Boiler, double aluminum
Bowls, mixing, s/s, 1½ , 3, 5, 8, and 13 qt (1.4, 2.7, 4.6, 7.3, and 11.9 L)
Canister set
Casseroles, individual 5, 6, or 8 oz (148, 177, or 236 ml)
Colander, large aluminum or s/s
Counter pans, s/s to fit No. 200
Cutter, biscuit, 2 or 2 1/2 in. (5 or 6 cm)
Dredges, aluminum
Fork, cooks, 12 and 20 in. (30 and 51 cm)
Knife, carving
Knife, French, 10- and 12-in. (25- and 30-cm) blade
Knife, slicing
Knife, utility, 6-in. (15-cm) blade

Knives, paring

Ladles, s/s, 2, 4, and 8 oz (59, 118, and 236 ml)

Measures, aluminum with pouring lip, cup, pint, quart, and gallon

Paddles for stirring in stock kettles (24, 36, 48 in. or 61, 91, 122 cm)

Pans, bake, aluminum, 12 × 20 × 4 in. (30 × 51 × 10 cm)

Pans, dish, aluminum, 14 or 20 qt (13 or 19 L)

Pans, frying, cast iron or aluminum approx. (8,10, and 12 × 2 in. or 20, 25, and 30 × 5 cm)

Pans, roasting, 16 × 20 × 5 in. (41 × 51 × 13 cm) with lugs

Pans, sauce, aluminum or s/s, in 1, 2, 6, and 8 qt (0.9, 1.9, 5.7, and 7.6 L)

Pot, stock, aluminum or re-tinned steel or s/s

Scales, utility

Scoops, s/s, Nos. 12, 16, 20

Skimmer, s/s, 5 in. (13 cm)

Spatulas, 6-, 8-, 10-in. (15-, 20-, 25-cm) blades

Spatula, offset

Spoons, measuring, s/s or aluminum

Spoons, serving, s/s, perforated or slotted

Spoons, serving, s/s, solid

Stool

Steamer baskets, tall, narrow, or wide; solid or perforated

Strainers, Chinese, s/s

Thermometer, meat

Trucks, kitchen, 3 deck

Turner, utility, s/s

Whip, wire, 8, 12, 16, 24, 36 in. (20, 30, 41, 61, 91 cm), sanitary handle.

Bakery Section

Beaters, egg rotary

Bowl, mixing, s/s, 12 and 25 qt (11 and 24 L), and mobile stand

Brushes, pastry

Corer, apple

Cups, custard, 4 or 5 oz (118 or 148 ml)

Cutters, biscuit, 2 or 2 1/2 in. (5 or 6 cm)

Cutters, cookie assorted

Divider, dough (chopping knife)

Knife, French, 10- or 12-in. (25- or 30-cm) blade

Knife, paring

Knife, utility, 6-in. (15-cm) blade

Measures, aluminum, pouring lip, cup, pint, quart, and gallon

Muffin pans, aluminum or retinned steel, 2 1/4 in. (6 cm) in diameter

Pans, aluminum or re-tinned steel, 18 × 26 × 1 in., 12 × 20 × 2 1/2 in., 12 × 20 × 1 in., 8 × 8 × 2 in., 10 × 4 × 4 in. (46 × 66 × 2.5 cm, 30 × 51 × 6 cm, 30 × 51 × 2.5 cm, 20 × 20 × 5 cm, 25 × 10 × 10 cm)

Pans, pie, aluminum or retinned steel, 9-in. in diameter × 1¼ in. (23 × 3 cm)

Pans, tube, aluminum, 3½ in. (9 cm)

Pastry bags

Pastry tips, set

Peel, if needed

Rolling pin, revolving handles 15 × 3½ in. (38 × 9 cm) in diameter

Scales

Scoops, grocer, aluminum, 1 lb (454 g)

Scoops, ice cream, s/s with plastic handle, Nos. 20, 30, and 40

Scraper, dough

Scraper, rubber, large

Sieve, flour, aluminum, 14 in. (36 cm) in diameter

Spatulas, s/s, 6 and 10 in. (15 and 25 cm)

Spice cans

Spoons, measuring, s/s or aluminum

Spoons, mixing, wooden

Spoons, serving, solid, s/s

Stools, kitchen

Whips, wire with sanitary handle, 8, 12, 16, 24 in. (20, 30, 41, 61 cm).

Salad and Sandwich Preparation

Board, cutting, 15 × 20 × 1¾ in. (38 × 51 × 4 cm)

Bowl, hardwood, 15 or 17 in. (38 or 43 cm)

Can opener, heavy-duty table model

Colander, large, s/s or aluminum

Cutter, melon ball

Egg slicer

Knife, chopping, two curved blades

Knife, French, 12-in. (30-cm) blade

Knife, paring

Knife, salad or utility type, 6- or 7-in. (15- or 18-cm) blade

Ladle, 8 oz (236 ml)

Measures, aluminum with pouring lip, cup, pint, quart, and gallon

Molds, individual, aluminum

Pans, dish, s/s, 14 qt (13 L)

Pans, steam table or pudding

Pans, round bottom mixing, s/s, 15 in. (38 cm) in diameter

Scoops, Nos. 12, 16, 20, and 30

Spoons, measuring, s/s or aluminum

Spoons, serving, perforated, s/s

Spoons, serving, solid, s/s

Spatula, sandwich spreader

Spatulas, wide blade, s/s, 6 and 10 in. (15 and 25 cm)

Tongs, s/s, 6 and 8 in. (15 and 20 cm)

Trays.

Serving Section

Ash trays, glass

Board, cutting, 13 × 16 × 1½ in. (33 × 41 × 4 cm)

Board, menu

Bottle opener

Bus boxes

Bus carts
Can opener, table or wall type
Clock, electric
Coffee decanters
Container, butter
Container, eggs
Cooker, egg, electric
Counter pans, s/s
Cream dispenser
Dish racks for storage and dollies
Dish storage carts
Dishes
Drip-cut servers, 16 oz, 32 oz (.5, .9 L)
Fork, serving, s/s, 2-tine, 12 in. (30 cm)
Glassware
Knife, salad or utility
Ladles, s/s 2, 6, or 8 oz (59, 177, or 236 mL)
Paper napkin dispenser
Pie server, offset, s/s
Pitchers, 3 3/4 or 4 qt, s/s (3.4 or 3.7 L)
Salt and pepper shakers
Scoops or dishers, Nos. 12, 16, 20, 30
Silver dispenser
Spoons, bouillon
Spoons, dessert
Spoons, serving, perforated, s/s 13 in. (33 cm)
Spoons, serving, solid, s/s, 13 in. (33 cm)
Sugar dispensers
Teaspoons
Tongs, Pom, 6 and 9 in. (15 and 23 cm)
Trays, plastic 14 × 18 in. (36 × 46 cm)
Turner, utility, s/s
Utility forks
Utility knives

Housekeeping Section

Aprons, Indian head, twill or duck bib and butchers
Broom
Brush, floor
Brushes, assorted clean-up
Cans, garbage and trash with dollies
Containers for detergents, s/s
Counter towels
Dish racks
Hot pads
Kitchen towels
Mop truck or pails on dolly
Mops, dry

Mops, wet

Pan, dust

Scraper, plate, rubber

Wastebasket

Tablecloths

Table pads

Uniforms

Office Section

Bookcase

Calculator

Cash box

Chair, posture type

Computer and printer

Desk

Files, recipe, inventory, letter

Filing cabinets

Lamps

Telephone

Typewriter and stand

Wastebaskets

CHAPTER SUMMARY

The price of small equipment and tableware may appear to be small, but the quantity that is purchased represents a significant portion of the budget for a foodservice operation. Selection should be based on satisfaction for specific use, appearance, durability, cost, and, of course, sanitation. The material from which the equipment is made strongly influences all of these factors. Equipment that is used for cooking should be nontoxic, light in weight, durable, noncorrosive, resistant to cleaning chemicals, and conduct heat rapidly. Stainless steel is favored for many applications, but other materials such as aluminum, cast iron, sheet steel, and utensil steel may give satisfactory performance for specific uses.

Flatware ranges in durability, price, and attractiveness. Less expensive flatware is punch pressed. Somewhat more expensive flatware is fashioned or graded. Silverplating is more attractive as well as more expensive and may be done to different levels such as standard plate, half standard plate, hotel plate, or banquet plate.

Four general types of china are available: earthenware, pottery, stoneware, and vitrified china. Only stoneware and vitrified china are suitable for foodservice use. Important factors to consider in china selection are glaze, weight, grading, strength, shape, contour, cleanability, and durability. Open stock china is generally less expensive to purchase.

The use of glass has expanded beyond bowls and glasses into table and oven ware. Glass is easy to clean and resistant to corrosion, but is fragile. It is classified by composition as lead or lime glass, or rock crystal.

The use of plastics has also expanded in recent years with the development of heat-resistant plastics. A wide variety of applications include handles on utensils, plastic utensils, buckets, bowls, trays, and tableware. Color coding for use is also possible.

The amount of tableware needed by a food service depends on eight factors: the number of customers served, type of service, menu items, length of serving period, duration of peak serving period, turnover, speed of washing and sanitizing, and allowance for loss and breakage. The design and appearance of dishware are extremely important in its selection, as well as its durability, sanitation, and weight.

Good knives are essential for cooks and chefs. Because of their importance, knives should be selected with a good blade that will receive and hold a sharp edge, a shape that matches its intended use, and a handle that is comfortable and sanitary. Safety of use should be considered in construction of the handle. Special knife edges and grinds are available for different cutting and slicing purposes.

REVIEW QUESTIONS

1. Prepare a list of utensils for a specified food operation with sufficient specifications for purchase.
2. Obtain prices for the equipment.
3. List tableware required for the food operation in quantities required for an initial purchase in relation to the anticipated number to be served.
4. Indicate the type and amount of storage space required for the quantity of tableware listed.
5. Visit tableware showrooms and compare prices of different patterns. On what are the price differences based?

KEY WORDS AND CONCEPTS

alloy
backstamps
banquet plate
cast iron
cladded metal
cold rolled
crazing
drawn
earthenware
extra heavy hotel plate
fashioned
glaze
half standard plate
high-carbon steel
hotel plate
knife grinds

lead glass
lime glass
open stock
pottery
punch pressing
rock crystal
run of the kiln
sheet steel
stainless steel
standard plate
Stoneware
triple plate
utensil steel
verdigris
vitrified china

APPENDIX

Abbreviations

AC   alternating current
AGA   American Gas Association
AH   absolute humidity
AHA   American Hospital Association
ASHRAE   American Society of Heating, Refrigerating, and Air Conditioning Engineers
AWG   American Wire Gauge
amp   ampere or I
Bhp   boiler horsepower
Btu   British thermal unit
Btuh   British thermal units per hour
c   cycle
cfh   cubic feet per hour
cfm   cubic feet per minute
cm   centimeter
cp   candlepower
CU   coefficient of utilization
cu ft   cubic foot or feet
°C   degree Celsius
D^2 square of distance
dB   decibel
DC   direct current
dia   diameter
ft-c   foot-candles
fpm   feet per minute
fL   foot Lambert
FM   frequency modulation
ft   foot or feet
°F   degree Fahrenheit
g   gram
gal   gallon
gpm   gallons per minute

hp   horsepower
HTM   heat transfer value
Hz   Hertz (sound vibration)
I   ampere
ID   inside dimension
IES   Illuminating Engineering Society
in.   inch
IPS   inside pipe size
K   degree kelvin
kg   kilogram
kL   kiloliter
kW   kilowatt
kWh   kilowatt hour
L   liter
lb   pound
lm   lumen
m   meter
m^2 square meter
m^3 cubic meter
MCM   thousand circular mills (wire)
MF   maintenance factor
mL   milliliter
min   minute
mm   millimeter
MRH   mixing ratio humidity
nm   nanometer (light waves)
NSF   National Sanitation Foundation
oz   ounce
ppm   parts per million
psi   pressure per square inch
qt   quart
R   resistance (electricity)

RH   relative humidity
sec   second
SH   specific humidity
sq cm   square centimeter
sq ft   square foot or feet
TV   television
UL   Underwriters Laboratory

USPHS   U.S. Public Health Service
V   volt
vol   volume
W   watt
Wh   watt hour
wt   weight
yd   yard

B

Feasibility Study

FEASIBILITY STUDY

1. Country and State
   a. Economics
   b. Trends
   c. Travel
   d. National promotional agencies
2. Community
   a. Economics
   b. Population trends
   c. Transient traffic statistics
   d. Transportation facilities
   e. Local attractions
   f. Civic promotional agencies
   g. Zoning and building regulations
   h. Real estate tax rates and assessment bases
   i. Alcoholic beverage and other monopolies
   j. Social usage
   k. Availability of materials and supplies (operating)
   l. Labor
      (1) Supply
         (a) Supervisory
         (b) Technical
         (c) Common
      (2) Wage trends
      (3) Labor legislation in effect and pending
   m. Earthquake history of area and other disaster hazards
3. Local Hotel, Club and Restaurant Factors
   a. Existing facilities
      (1) Names and locations
      (2) Capacities
      (3) Present demand for their services and facilities
      (4) Prevailing room rates and food rates
      (5) Associations

        (6) Trade schools

        (7) Development of regional resort areas

   b. Future competition

        (1) Contemplated plans for hotels, clubs, restaurants

        (2) Contemplated plans for enlargement of present facilities

        (3) Current competitive economics

Local Equity Group

1. Identity
2. Responsibility
3. Associations and Connections
4. Experience
5. Availability of Bank Guarantee or Government Guarantee

Physical Aspects

1. Site
   a. Advantages
        (1) Size and shape of lot
        (2) Location in relation to business, amusement and social life of city
        (3) Accessibility: public carrier availability
        (4) Traffic and circulation habits of local inhabitants in that area
        (5) Character of neighborhood
        (6) Physical contours of site
        (7) Ground characteristics which have direct bearing on cost of building foundation and on building maintenance (necessity for pump, etc.)
        (8) Shop rental possibilities
        (9) Direction of expansion of city
        (10) Parking facilities
        (11) Zoning
        (12) Building restrictions
        (13) Information on disturbing noises from nearby installations such as railroads, airports, factories, churchbells, street traffic, etc.
        (14) Include map of city showing location of proposed hotel, RR station, airport location, American embassy, churches, airport, beaches, bus stations, other hotels, business center, etc. (map published by City Planning Commission or similar group)
        (15) Photographs of competitive units
        (16) Aerial photograph of site and/or adjacent areas
   b. Disadvantages
        (1) Related to items (1) to (12) of site advantages.
        (2) Other
   c. Alternates
        (1) Location
        (2) Advantages—see site advantages
        (3) Disadvantages—see site advantages
        (4) Other
2. Building
   a. Type
        (1) Transient, semiresidential, resort
        (2) Materials
           (a) Kind
           (b) Availability
           (c) Building to be earthquake proof and fireproof

       (3) Style: colonial, contemporary, etc.

       (4) Heat, ventilation & air conditioning

          (a) Climate, seasons—extremes and average temperatures and humidities

          (b) Local demands and habits

          (c) Extent of air-conditioning and ventilation of rooms, public spaces, work spaces, including barber and beauty shops, etc.

          (d) Extent of heat insulation

  b. Size

       (1) Number of rooms by types and size

       (2) Height of building

       (3) Number of stores and concessions

       (4) Number, type and size of public rooms

          (a) Restaurants

          (b) Ballroom and private dining rooms

          (c) Bars and cocktail lounges

          (d) Lobby and similar space

       (5) Ratio of public room to guest room space

       (6) Other facilities

          (a) Grounds—tennis courts, golf course, etc.

          (b) Garage

          (c) Swimming pool

          (d) Turkish baths

          (e) Health features in connection with climate, mineral springs, etc.

          (f) Barber shop

          (g) Beauty parlor

  c. Hotel services and facilities requirements

       (1) Laundry

          (a) Guest laundry

          (b) House laundry

       (2) Valet

       (3) Dry cleaning

       (4) Electrician's shop

       (5) Carpenter's shop

       (6) Upholstery shop

       (7) Paint shop

       (8) Radio

       (9) Circulating iced water

      (10) Bakery

      (11) Plumber's shop

      (12) Mechanic's shop

      (13) Silverware cleaning and polishing

      (14) Locksmith

  d. Utilities and sanitation

       (1) Power

          (a) Availability

          (b) Rates

          (c) Type current-power-light

       (2) Water

          (a) Availability

          (b) Rates

          (c) Potability and suitability for laundry boilers (treatment necessary?)

          (d) Permit and taxes on artesian wells

          (e) Pressure and temperature extremes

       (3) Heat
         (a) Type: steam, hot water, radiant, air, etc.
         (b) Fuel—its availability and cost
         (c) Process steam for kitchens, laundry, etc.
         (d) Fuel for kitchens & bakery
       (4) Telephones
         (a) Availability
         (b) Rates
         (c) Bilingual operators on city exchange? hotel exchange?
         (d) Other communication or signal systems, such as pneumatic tubes, telautographs, hall signals for maids, etc.
       (5) Sanitation
         (a) Code
         (b) Prevailing standards and requirements
         (c) Existing and planned waste disposal methods
       (6) Refrigeration
         (a) Types for food
         (b) Types for garbage
         (c) Ice cream manufacturer storage
       (7) Fire alarms, fighting equipment & escapes
     e. Estimated construction time (schedule)
       (1) Demolition
       (2) Foundation
       (3) Building
       (4) Equipment
3. Furniture & Furnishings (by classes)
4. Acoustical Treatment of Public Rooms and Guest Rooms

Financial Aspects

1. Estimate of Capital Required
   a. Land
   b. Building
   c. Furniture and furnishings
   d. Working capital and other (incl. organization, financing and pre-opening expenses)
2. Operational Estimates
   a. Estimate of capacity utilization
   b. Estimate of percentage of permanent guests
   c. Proposed average room rate by seasons, including proposed allowances and discounts, if any
   d. Food and beverages
      (1) Costs
      (2) Proposed sales prices
      (3) Estimated volume of sales
   e. Estimated net income from sources other than rooms and food and beverages
      (1) Cigarstand
      (2) Newsstand
      (3) Candy and soda shop
      (4) Telephone
      (5) Valet
      (6) Check rooms and washrooms
      (7) Porters
      (8) Barber shop

        (9) Beauty parlor
      (10) Baths
      (11) Florist
      (12) Guests' laundry
      (13) Store rentals
      (14) Other (detail)
   f. Salary and wage rates
   g. Pre-opening and other organizational expenses
   h. Real estate taxes
   i. Income taxes
   j. Management fees

3. Proposal for Financing
   a. Estimated amount of equity capital required
   b. Estimated amount of export-import bank loan required
   c. Estimated time schedule for capital outlay
   d. Estimated money to be spent in the United States
   e. Estimated money to be spent in other countries

Market Analysis

1. Determination of visitors by categories
   a. Tourists
   b. Vacationers
   c. Business travelers
2. Sources for gaining such information

Miscellaneous

1. Import Duties
2. Excise Taxes
3. Labor Laws
4. Trade Agreements and Treaties
5. Government Regulations and Exemptions Affecting Hotel Importations, etc.

Conclusions

1. Opinions and Recommendations

APPENDIX

Safety Checklist

SAFETY CHECK LIST	*The Following Checklist Covers Both Physical Properties and Work Practices*		
Area	**Yes**	**No**	**Comments**

I. Receiving Area:

   A. Are floors in safe condition? (Are they free from broken tile and defective floor boards? Are they covered with nonskid material?)

   B. Are employees instructed in correct handling methods for various containers, etc., that are received?

   C. Are garbage cans washed daily in hot water?

   D. Are garbage cans always covered?

   E. Are trash cans leakproof and adequate in number and size?

   F. If garbage disposal area is adjacent to or part of the general receiving area, is there a program that keeps floors and/or dock areas clear of refuse?

   G. Is there a proper rack for holding garbage containers? Are garbage containers on dollies or other wheel units to eliminate lifting by employees?

   H. Are adequate tools available for opening crates, barrels, cartons, etc. (hammer, wire cutter, corrugated board box openers and pliers)?

   I. Is crate, carton, and barrel opening done away from open containers of food?

SAFETY CHECK LIST   *Continued*

Area	Yes	No	Comments

II. Storage Area:
- A. Are shelves adequate to bear weight of items stored?
- B. Are employees instructed to store heavy items on lower shelves and lighter materials above?
- C. Is a safe ladder provided for reaching high storage?
- D. Are cartons or other flammable materials stored at least two feet from operating light bulbs?
- E. Are light bulbs provided with a screen guard?
- F. Is a fire extinguisher located at the door?

III. Pots and Pans Room or Area:
- A. Are duckboards or floor boards in safe condition (free from broken slats and worn areas that could cause tripping)?
- B. Are employees properly instructed in use of correct amounts of detergent and/or other cleaning agents?
- C. Are adequate rubber gloves provided?
- D. Is there an adequate drainboard or other drying area so that employees do not have to pile pots and pans on the floor before and after washing them?
- E. Do drain plugs permit draining without the employee placing hands in hot water?

IV. Walk-in Coolers and Freezers— (Refrigerators):
- A. Are floors in the units in good condition and covered with slip proof material? Are they mopped at least once a week?
- B. If floor boards are used, are they in safe conditions (free from broken slats and worn areas that could cause tripping)?
- C. Are portable storage racks and stationary racks in safe condition (free from broken or bent shelves and set on solid legs)?
- D. Are blower fans properly guarded?
- E. Is there a bypass device on the door to permit exit if an employee is locked in?
- F. Or, is there an alarm bell?
- G. Is adequate aisle space provided?
- H. Are employees properly instructed on placement of hands for movement of portable racks to avoid hand injuries?
- I. Are heavy items stored on lower shelves and lighter items on higher shelves?

SAFETY CHECK LIST *Continued*

Area	Yes	No	Comments

    J. Are shelves adequately spaced to prevent pinched hands?

    K. Is the refrigerant in the refrigerator non-toxic? (Check with your refrigerator service person.)

V. Food Preparation Area:

    A. Is electrical equipment properly grounded?

    B. Is electrical equipment inspected regularly by an electrician?

    C. Are electrical switches located so that they can be reached readily in the event of an emergency?

    D. Are the switches located so that employees do not have to lean on or against metal equipment when reaching for them?

    E. Are floors regularly and adequately maintained (mopped at least three times weekly and waxed with nonskid wax when necessary; are defective floor boards and tile replaced when necessary)?

    F. Are employees instructed to immediately pick or clean up all dropped items and spillage?

    G. Are employees properly instructed in the operation of machines?

    H. Are employees forbidden to use equipment unless specifically trained in its use?

    I. Are machines properly guarded? (Check with the manufacturer if there is a question.)

    J. Are guards always used by all employees?

    K. Is a pusher or tamper provided for use with the grinder?

    L. Are mixers in safe operating condition?

    M. Are the mixer beaters properly maintained to avoid injury from broken metal parts and foreign particles in food?

VI. Serving Area:

    A. Are steam tables cleaned daily and regularly maintained (gas or electric units checked regularly by a competent service person)?

    B. Is safety valve equipment operative?

SAFETY CHECK LIST *Continued*

Area	Yes	No	Comments

C. Are serving counters and tables free of broken parts and wooden or metal slivers and burrs?

D. Do you have regular inspection of:
Glassware?
China?
Silverware?
Plastic equipment?

E. If anything breaks near the food service area, do you remove all food from service adjacent to breakage?

F. Are tray rails adequate and set to prevent trays from slipping or falling off at the end of corners?

G. Are floors and/or ramps in good condition (covered with nonskid material, free from broken tile and defective floor boards)?

H. Are these areas mopped at least three times weekly and waxed with nonskid wax when necessary?

I. Is the traffic flow set so that patrons or workers do not collide while carrying trays or obtaining foods?

VII. Dining Area:

A. Are floors free from broken tile and defective floor boards? Are they covered with nonskid wax?

B. Are pictures securely fastened to walls?

C. Are drapes, blinds, or curtains securely fastened?

D. Are chairs free from splinters, metal burrs, broken or loose parts?

E. Are floors "policed" for cleaning up spillage and other materials?

F. Is special attention given to the floor adjacent to water, ice cream, or milk stations?

G. Are vending machines properly grounded?

H. If patrons clear their own trays prior to return to dishwashing area, are the floors kept clean of garbage, dropped silver, and/or broken glass and china?

I. If trays with used dishes are placed on conveyor units, are the edges guarded to keep from catching fingers or clothing?

SAFETY CHECK LIST   *Continued*

Area	Yes	No	Comments

    J. If dishes are removed on portable racks or bus trucks, are these units in safe operating condition (all wheels or casters working, all shelves firm)?

VIII. Soiled Dish Processing Area:
    A. Are floors reasonably free of excessive water and spillage?
    B. Are floor boards properly maintained and in safe condition (free from broken slats and worn areas that cause tripping)?
    C. Are all electrical units properly grounded?
    D. Are switches located to permit rapid shutdown in the event of emergency?
    E. Can employees easily reach switches without touching or leaning against such metal units as tables and counters?
    F. Are switches readily accessible?
    G. Are employees carefully instructed in the use of detergents to prevent agitation of dermatitis, etc.?
    H. Do you have a program for disposition of broken glass and china?
    I. If a dishwashing machine is used, is the take-off board set to prevent fingers or hands from being caught?
    J. Where controls are in passageway, are they recessed or guarded to prevent breakage or accidental starting?
    K. Are racks in safe condition (if wooden, free from broken slats and smoothly finished to eliminate splintering; if metal, free of sharp corners that could cause cuts)? Are these racks kept off the floor to prevent tripping?

IX. Don't Overlook:
    A. Lighting, is it adequate in the
    Receiving area?
    Storage area?
    Pots and pans area?
    Walk-in coolers and freezers?
    Food preparation area?
    Cooking area?
    Serving area?
    Dining area?
    Soiled dish processing area?

SAFETY CHECK LIST   *Continued*

Area	Yes	No	Comments

B. Doors—do they open into passageways where they could cause an accident? (List any such locations).
Are fire exits clearly marked and the passage kept clear of equipment and materials? (List any violations).

C. Stairways and ramps:
Are they adequately lighted?
Are the angles of ramps set to provide maximum safety?
If stairs are metal, wood, composition, or marble, have abrasive materials been used to provide protection against slips and falls?
Are pieces broken out of the nosing, or front edge, of the steps?
Are clean and securely fastened handrails available?
If the stairs are wide, has a center rail been provided?

D. Ventilation, is it adequate in the
Receiving area?
Storage area?
Pots and pans area?
Walk-in coolers and freezers?
Food preparation area?
Cooking area?
Serving area?
Dining area?
Soiled dish processing area?

E. Shoes:
Do employees wear good shoes to protect their feet against injury from articles that are dropped or pushed against their feet?

F. Clothing:
Is their clothing free of parts that could get caught in mixers, cutters or grinders?

G. Is the extinguisher guarded so that it will not be knocked from the wall?

H. If the door is provided with a lock, is there an emergency bell or a bypass device that will permit exit from the room should the door be accidentally locked while an employee is in the room?

APPENDIX

Instructions to Bidders

Proposals, to be entitled to consideration, must be made in accordance with the following general instructions:

1. Examination of Site and Documents

Before submitting a proposal, the bidder shall:
(a) carefully examine the drawings and specifications,
(b) read thoroughly the existing conditions and limitations,
(c) include in the bid sums sufficient to cover all items required by contract and shall rely entirely upon his or her own examinations in making the proposal.

2. Interpretations

Should a bidder find discrepancies in, or omissions from, the drawings or specifications, or be in doubt as to their meaning, he or she should at once notify _____ hereinafter referred to as _____, who will send written instructions or addenda to all bidders. _____ will not be responsible for oral interpretations. Questions received less than 48 hour before bids close cannot be answered. All addenda issued during the time of bidding will be incorporated into contract. Address all communications to _____.

3. Form of Bid

The proposal shall not contain any recapitulation of the work to be done. Numbers shall be stated both in writing and in figures.
The completed proposal shall be without interlineation, alteration or erasure. Bidder shall present bid by item. Bidder may also give a total bid for all items or for any group if the total price is less than the sum of item bids. If a bid for a group or all items is given it should be clearly indicated what items are included in such a bid. No bidder may bid on a part of an item. _____ reserves the right to accept or reject any item, group or total bid.

4. Alternates

Alternate bids, other than those called for in the specifications and listed in the bid form will not be considered.

5. Signature

Each bid must be signed in longhand by the bidder. Bids by partnerships must be signed with the partnership name by one of the partners, followed by the signature and designation of the partner signing; bids by corporation, followed by the name of the state of incorporation and by the signature of the president, secretary or other person authorized to bind it in the matter. The name of each person signing shall be typed or printed below the signature.

6. Bid Guarantee

As a guarantee that if awarded the contract the bidder will execute same and furnish bond required by the specifications, each bid shall be accompanied by:
(a) a certified check, or
(b) a bank cashier's check
made in the name of _____

7. Modifications

No oral, telephone, facsimile, or e-mail bids or modifications will be considered.

8. Disposition of Bid Guarantees

The successful bidder's check will be retained until the bidder has entered into contract and furnished the required bond. The owner reserves the right to hold the bid guarantees of the two next lowest or preferred bidders until the successful bidder has done so, or for a period of thirty (30) days, whichever is the shorter time. Checks of all other bidders will be returned as soon as practicable after bids are opened. Should a bidder fail to enter into contract and furnish bond within ten days after the proposal has been accepted, the bid guarantee shall be forfeited to the owner as liquidated damages, not as a penalty.

9. Evidence of Qualification

Upon request of the owner, a bidder whose proposal is under consideration for the award of the contract shall submit promptly satisfactory evidence of financial resources, experience, and the organization and equipment available for the performance of the contract.

10. Withdrawal of Bids

Any bidder may withdraw the bid, either personally or by written request, at any time prior to the time set for the bid opening. No bid may be withdrawn or modified after the time set for the opening thereof, unless and until the award of the contract is delayed for a period exceeding thirty (30) days.

11. Division of Responsibility

Attention of bidders is called to parts 1–09 and 1–10 of the specifications for kitchen fixtures and equipment, Section I, General.

12. General Provisions

Provisions of the General Condition for the Construction of Buildings, 6th ed. AIA Form A2 revised 9–1–51 (hereinafter called *General Conditions*) shall apply to this contract, except that articles 28 and 31 shall be omitted. The word architect in these general conditions shall be interpreted to mean the _____.

SPECIAL PROVISIONS

1. General Statement

The following paragraphs refer especially to this particular project. They are a part of the standard *General Instructions* immediately preceding, and shall supersede same whenever they are in conflict.

2. Number of Specified Items Required

Whenever, in these specifications an article, device or piece of equipment is referred to in the regular number, such reference shall apply to any such article as are shown on drawings or required to complete the installation.

3. Abbreviations

The work "approved," as used herein, means "approved by _____" and "for approval" means "approval of the _____ at _____."
"ASTM Specifications" means Standard Specifications for the American Society for Testing Materials, 100 Barr Harbor Drive, West Conshohocken, Pennsylvania, 19428-2959.
"Selected" means "selected by."
Where the words "or equal" are used, _____ is the sole judge of the quality and suitability of the proposed substitutions.

4. Approval of Substitutions

Requests for approval of a different material or articles other than that specified shall be accompanied by samples, record of performance, certified copies of tests by impartial and recognized laboratories, and such additional information as _____ may reasonably request. Such samples and data shall be furnished sufficiently in advance to allow time for investigation before a decision must be made. When _____ approves a substitution, it is with the understanding that the contractor guarantees the substituted article to be equal to or better than the one specified.

If the supplier or bidder submits a proposal on items that are not in exact accordance with the specification—such alternate bid must include the manufacturer's name and model number of the particular item submitted. In addition to this, all such bids are to be fully explained, supported by, and accompanied with complete detailed information drawings and descriptive literature that may be applicable, and provided further that such explanatory information, drawings, and literature shall set forth and fully describe in every respect and detail, any proposed deviations or departures from the applicable manufacturer's specifications or numbers noted herein. All equipment furnished as equal to the items specified must be equal in quality, finish, operating features, etc., to the items specified and approved by owner.

5. Sub-Contracts

Divisions in these specifications conform roughly to customary trade practice. They are used for convenience only. _____ is not bound to define the limits of any sub-contract.

6. Checking of Drawings

Contractors shall carefully study and compare all drawings, specifications, etc., furnished to them by _____ and shall check dimensions, materials and methods of construction, bringing into play the skill and experience for which they are compensated under this contract. They shall report to _____ for rectification of any errors, inconsistencies or omissions they may thus discover, and shall do no work in connection therewith until directed by _____ as to how to proceed. Contractors may inspect building at _____.

7. Prior Use or Occupancy

The owner reserves the right to use or occupy the building or any portion thereof, or to use equipment installed under the contract, prior to final acceptance. Such use or occupancy shall not constitute acceptance of the work or any part thereof.

8. Fire Insurance

The owner assumes no risk for loss by fire to any portion of the building or equipment thereof, whether completed, in process of construction or installation, or stored on the premises, during the life of any contract for any portion of the construction. The making of partial payments to the contractors shall not be construed as creating an insurable interest by or for the owner, or as relieving the various contractors of their sureties of responsibility for loss by fire or other casualty occurring prior to final acceptance of the building. This paragraph supersedes Article 29 or the *General Conditions.*

9. Payment for Drawings and Specifications

For construction purposes, two sets of drawings and specifications covering the contractor's own work and one set each of the subcontractor's work will be furnished to the owner without charge. Additional copies will be furnished by

_____ upon payment to the contractor for the cost of reproduction. This paragraph supersedes Article 4 of the *General Conditions, AIA 2, revised* 9-1-51.

10. Delivery must be made 60 days after day of letting contract.

11. Limit of Operations

Construction operations and parking of cars shall be confined to areas designated by owner. Routing of trucks shall be as directed. This paragraph amplifies Article 42 of the *General Conditions, AIA Form 2*, revised 9-1-51.

12. Bond

Secure and pay for surety bond issued by State-Licensed Bonding Company, in form bound herewith, in the following penal sums:

Performance clause	100% of Contract Sum
Payment clause	100% of Contract Sum
Maintenance clause	100% of Contract Sum

13. Test Samples

Furnish samples of materials for testing if and when requested.

14. Itemized Schedule of Costs

Successful bidder shall prepare a complete detailed breakdown of costs. Sum of all items shall be equal to contract price. This shall be furnished to _____ within 15 days of notification of award. Minor additions or deductions will be based upon this breakdown. Example of such a breakdown required would be on standard equipment and fabrication required for fabrication and installation of service counter.

15. Shop Drawings

Supplementing Article 5 of the *General Conditions, AIA Form 2*, revised 9-1-51, the words "such other copies as may be needed" at the end of the second sentence shall mean "three other copies" making a total of five corrected copies required, two of which will be returned to the contractor.

16. Equipment Lists

Successful bidder shall prepare complete lists of all equipment to be installed, giving maker's name and catalogue numbers and obtain the approval of _____ before ordering. See also paragraphs 3 and 4 of Special Provisions regarding substitutions, (4) *Approval of Substitutions*.

17. Time for Completion

The work under this contract shall be commenced on a date to be specified in a written order to the contractor to proceed, and shall be delivered within 75 consecutive calendar days from and after said date stated in the contractor's bid for the work, or as hereinafter to be agreed upon: the agreement to govern in case of discrepancy.

18. Liquidated Damages

For each calendar day after the date above fixed for completion that the work remains uncompleted, the contractor shall pay the owner the sum of $50.00 as fixed, agreed, liquidated damages, and this sum is not to be construed as in any sense a penalty. Should an extension of time be granted to the contractor, the contractor shall indemnify and save the owner harmless from any other contractor caused by such extension.

19. Use of Premises

The owner will provide adequate space for uncrating and assembling equipment within the building. This contractor shall confine materials to spaces allotted and shall not unreasonably encumber the building premises.

20. Progress Schedule

Prepare, on form satisfactory to _____, a construction progress schedule. Show proposed dates of submission of shop drawings, resubmission of shop drawings, fabrication period, shipping period, installation period. This shall be furnished to _____ within 15 days of award of contract.

21. Work Not Included in This Contract

The following work will be performed under separate contracts operating concurrently with the work of this contract, and is not included in this contract:
(a) Plumbing, heating and ventilating
(b) Electrical work
(c) General construction work
(d) Furnishing
(e) Casework

22. Damage

If the owner should suffer damage in any manner because of any wrongful act or neglect of the contractor or of anyone employed by the contractor, the owner shall be reimbursed for such damage.

Claims under this clause shall be made in writing within a reasonable time at the first observance of such damage, except as expressly stipulated otherwise in the case of faulty work or materials, and shall be adjusted by agreement or arbitration.

23. Signs

No signs shall be placed on the property.

24. Available Materials

_____ has attempted to avoid use of unavailable materials; it will therefore consider that the contract sum is based on furnishing all materials exactly as specified. Should it develop that any material specified is unobtainable and a substitution necessary, an equitable adjustment of the contract sum will be made.

25. Overhead and Profit on Changes

The value of extra work authorized pursuant to Article 15 of *General Conditions* shall be the actual cost of the additional direct labor, materials and subcontract work involved, plus an allowance for overhead and profit as follows:

1. When the total cost of an authorized extra, including overhead and profit, is less than $500.00 the allowance for overhead and profit shall not exceed 25% of the actual cost.
2. When the total cost of an authorized extra, including overhead and profit, exceeds $500.00, the allowance for overhead and profit shall not exceed 20% of the actual cost.
3. When an authorized extra excludes the furnishing and delivery only of an equipment item costing the contractor more than $300.00, the additional allowance to the contractor for purchasing and handling such an item shall not exceed 10% of the purchase price.

26. Guaranty

All equipment covered by this specification and accompanying drawings shall be guaranteed, for purposes intended, in writing, for one year from date of final acceptance. Any defect in material or workmanship shall be promptly rectified by this contractor without cost to the owner during this period.

27. Instructions for Use of Equipment

This contractor shall furnish complete printed instructions for the proper use of all equipment furnished under this contract and in addition the contractor shall furnish a duly qualified instructor for a period of one week, to instruct persons designated by the owner, in the proper operation of all equipment furnished.

28. Architectural Supervision

Architectural supervision of this kitchen contract for equipment shall be performed by _____.

Specifications for Kitchen Fixtures and Equipment

SECTION 1—GENERAL

1-01 Scope of Work

The contractor shall furnish all fixtures and equipment as listed in the acceptance of bid according to specifications and as shown on the drawings. Shipment shall be to _____ (address). Delivery must be made within 60 days of letting of the contract.

1-02 Work by Others

A. The mechanical contractor of the _____ will provide all waste, vent, gas, steam and condensate return services. Piping by mechanical contractor will be complete to floor level or above so that connection can be conveniently made by equipment contractor. All plumbing lines and fittings shall be stainless steel, chrome or nickel covered from floor connection to equipment. No lead or iron pipe fittings shall be visible unless authorized by _____.

B. The electrical contractor will furnish necessary writing, conduit connections to floor level or slightly above so that convenient connection can be made to all kitchen equipment or fixtures.

1-03 Samples Required

Where applicable the successful bidder shall deliver and set up at the place designated by _____ samples of the following:

A sectional portion of a stainless steel sink and drain board with back splash showing all pertinent construction features such as:

Welding

Forming

Finishes—exposed and unexposed

The sample is to be typical of the type of work the bidder intends to use for all stainless steel construction.

The successful bidder shall furnish samples as requested by _____.

Samples will be retained until acceptance of work.

1-04 Inspection

Equipment will be inspected by the _____.

Any equipment or fixtures not in accordance with specifications and drawings shall be promptly replaced at no cost to the owner.

1-05 Materials

A. Stainless Steel:
  1. All sheets to be commercial 18-8 stainless steel, U.S. Standard gauges as noted herein or called for on drawings.
  2. Unexposed reinforcing is to be 12 gauge galvanized iron or heavier with 1 coat zinc chromate painted over with 2 coats silver-tone or aluminum lacquer. Reinforcing and lateral bracing on tops and drains easily visible shall be 12 gauge 18-8 stainless steel and approximately 3" wide. This is to be integrally welded to tops and drains with evidence of weld removed.
  3. Finishes: #2B on shelving or where concealed. Elsewhere, #4.
  4. Sheets to be stretcher leveled, non-magnetic, free of buckles, warps, scratches and other surface imperfections.
B. Galvanized Steel: To be copper bearing steel, "Armco," "Toncan," or equal, U.S. Standard gauges as called for, sheets free from buckles, warps, scratches and other imperfections. All galvanized steel parts to be finished with two (2) coats of silver-tone lacquer.
C. Plywood: Douglas Fir, Waterproof Grade.
D. Hardwood Top: Kiln dried northern hard maple. Selected edge grain.
E. Formica: To be bonded to ¾" waterproof plywood with proper waterproof adhesive and under even and proper pressure in a press. Panels as manufactured by the Colotyle Corp., or equal.

1-06 Workmanship

A. All jointing and connections to adjacent surfaces shall be done in such a manner as to render all parts easily cleaned, dust and vermin tight, and to present a neat finished appearance. Back splashes and other surfaces adjoining walls shall be *tightly* fastened to wall. Fastening shall be by stainless steel screws, flathead counter sunk to be flush with surface. Screws to be 6" on center (from center of screw to center of next screw) around edges of equipment. General contractor shall furnish at proper location within wall strong wooden backing for the attachment of these screws. Gaps ⅛" or smaller at bases and walls are to be sealed with caulking, A. C. Horn Co.'s "Vulcatex" or approved equal. Fixtures shall be solidly braced and reinforced where necessary.
B. Welds to be heli-arc type and shall be homogenous with parts welded, free from imperfections of any kind. Welding rods used are to be of same material as parts welded, and filler pieces of filling with solder will not be acceptable. Excess metal shall be ground off and joints finished smooth to match adjoining surfaces. Field joists will not be accepted except as noted.

All equipment is to be all-welded seamless construction with all joints, crevices, etc., eliminated and all traces of welding removed.

C. Brake folds shall be free of textured appearance or other imperfections.

D. Sheared edges shall be free of burrs, slivers, etc., and shall be smooth to touch.

1-07 Standard Materials and Construction: Shall be as listed below unless otherwise noted.

A. Stainless Steel Drains, Table, and Counter Tops: Shall be of the gauge specified except where noted, with edges 180° to ¾″ outside radius, and corners bull nosed to same radius, mitred, welded and ground smooth. Backs shall be made integral and of same gauge metal as tops, with intersections rolled to ¾″ radius. Where insets are to be made into countertops, and are not to be welded, the seal shall be made with latex gaskets. All tops, drains, or table tops where specified shall be reinforced or braced with 12-gauge black iron with zinc chromate painted with aluminum 8″ × 2″ channel welded to underside. Channels shall run full length of center right angle to braces running from front to back. 1″ OD stainless steel tubing shall be welded to channels on approximately 4′ centers. Such reinforcing or bracing is to be provided wherever in specifications substantial support is specified for extra heavy loads such equipment shall bear.

B. Stainless Steel Sinks: Sinks shall be gauge specified with edges rolled 180° to ¾″ radius. Backs and drainboards are to be made integral and of the same metal, with all intersections rolled to ¾″ radius. Drains are to be Blickman LHO-50-C or approved equal. Supply fixtures to be American Standard San. B900 swing spout faucet or approved equal, except where noted otherwise. Each sink compartment to be provided with overflow consisting of 1¼″ whitened brass piping leading from overflow aperture at rear of compartment in bronze fittings. Aperture shall be covered with stainless steel strainer.

C. Legs: To be 1¼″ OD stainless steel tubing, No. 12-gauge. At top they are to be threaded into white metal flanges and braced where shown with 16-gauge stainless steel gussets which are welded to fixture. At bottom, legs are to be fitted to adjustable white sanitary feet. Legs are not to be threaded. Legs are to be seamless.

D. Bodies: Bodies shall be made of 20-gauge stainless steel #4 finish unless otherwise stated. Bodies shall be formed in angles at top not less than 1½″ wide. Bottom shall be formed into channel not less than 4″ wide and wider to suit base overhand and 1¼″ turned up web. All bodies unless otherwise stated shall be supported on base provided by others. All pilasters, center and ends, shall be turned 1½″ with ¾″ web; shelves and bottom shall butt turned in edge to form uniform construction. Bodies shall have channel supports of 14-gauge black iron approximately 3″ wide as required, primed and painted with zinc chromate painted with 2 coats of aluminum. Where bodies are specified to be made with formica, bracing shall be adequate to bear weights to which equipment will be subjected. No rough edges must show. Workmanship must be top grade.

E. Pipe Braces: Where shown use 1″ OD seamless stainless steel tubing, 14-gauge.

F. Pipe Shelves: Shall be 1″ OD seamless stainless steel tubing, 14-gauge spaced not over 4″ outside center. Entire pipe understructure shall be seamlessly welded, ground smooth, and polished.

G. Intermediate Shelves: 18-gauge stainless steel or galvanized steel or formica as noted. Where marked adjustable, use stainless steel adjustable clip brackets and slotted holes ½″ outside center through divider panels. All shelves shall be turned in from edge of body.

H. Sliding Doors: 18-gauge stainless steel front face, 20-gauge galvanized steel back face, filled with approved sound deadening material or, where specified, with insulating material or formica as stated. Doors are to be removable for cleaning. Hardware is to be as follows:

1. Track: Overhead type formed in body; provide stop to keep doors closed.
2. Door sheaves: Ball bearing 1¼ diameter, case hardened steel. Sheaves to be dipped in hard oil and track to be filled with same.
3. Bottom guides: Brass roller pins at center of door (neoprene or nylon acceptable), fitting into groove at bottom of door, except where detailed differently. Groove to be open to permit dirt to drop through.
4. Rubber bumpers: as specified.
5. Handles: Die-pressed stainless steel recesses in door face, Blickman type or equal.

I. Hinged Doors: Door construction to be same as sliding doors above. Hardware is to be as follows:

1. Hinges—stainless steel continuous piano hinges ¾″ leaf.
2. Catches—heavy duty "Snuggler."
3. Locks—Corbin #0666. Polished chrome finish.
4. Pulls—white metal of approved design.

J. Exposed Panels: Including access panels—16-gauge stainless steel or formica.

K. Backs and Dividers: 18-gauge stainless steel or galvanized steel or formica or plywood as noted.

L. Electric Outlets and Switches: Indicated to be of adequate capacity with plates and housings of satin finish stainless steel or heavy chrome plate.

M. Plumbing and Electrical Conduit: All plumbing pipe and fittings, refrigeration tubing, electrical conduit, etc. furnished by kitchen equipment contractor shall be stainless steel, chrome or nickel covered except where brass or other type fittings are specified.

1-08 Utilities

Electric—110-208 volt 60 cycle; 3 phase motors ½ hp or over to be 208 volt 3 phase. Smaller than ½ hp to be 110 volt, single phase.

1-09 Kitchen Equipment Contractor

To co-operate to the fullest extent with other crafts involved. It will be the contractor's responsibility to cut all holes necessary for piping, conduit, traps, etc., location of valves, controls and switches for convenient operation and to provide proper space for piping, etc., in fixtures so that piping will not interfere with the function of the fixtures.

1-10 Field Joints

Only where specified.

   In specifications the following codes may be mentioned. A short summary of these may help to explain their use in these specifications.

1. National Electrical Code. Used to indicate requirements for wiring and other electrical details. In some cases, local codes may supersede this national code. If so, spell out the details.
2. NSF. The National Sanitation Foundation standards that apply to all equipment.
3. BISSC. This is a code similar to that of the NSF codes but applies only to bakery equipment. ANSI sets safety standards for bakery equipment.
4. USDA. The United States Department of Agriculture requires that cooked meat products shipped across interstate lines must have been prepared in an oven approved by it.
5. Airlines feeding. The Department of HHS, Public Health Service, has a special code that applies to foodservice for transportation units. One of the requirements is that ovens should be securely grouted to floors.
6. UL. The Underwriters Laboratories approval is required on all electrical equipment.
7. AGA. This is the American Gas Association code of standards that all gas equipment must meet.

   Specifications should not require that anything be OSHA approved. OSHA does not give pre-installation approval or approval on any equipment. It only is a factor *after* an operation has been built and equipped. Manufacturers also should not be required to meet OSHA standards except for safeguards on equipment. The specific safety factor required in the equipment should rather be detailed in the specification for the equipment.

APPENDIX F

Estimated Space Requirements for Paper Supplies

Estimated Space Requirements for Paper Supplies

Item	No. to Case	Case Dimensions in Inches (Length-Width-Height)	Cubic Feet (Per Case)
Hot food containers			
8 oz squat	1000	$20\frac{3}{16} \times 16\frac{1}{4} \times 29\frac{9}{16}$	5.4
10 oz squat	500	$21\frac{15}{16} \times 9\frac{1}{16} \times 39\frac{5}{16}$	3.4
12 oz squat	500	$22\frac{1}{4} \times 9\frac{3}{16} \times 29\frac{3}{4}$	3.5
Freezing containers			
16 oz squat	500	$24\frac{1}{8} \times 9\frac{15}{16} \times 30$	4.2
16 oz squat lids	2000	$22\frac{1}{4} \times 11\frac{5}{8} \times 9\frac{1}{4}$	1.4
32 oz squat	500	$25\frac{1}{2} \times 20\frac{1}{2} \times 18\frac{15}{16}$	5.7
32 oz squat lids	2000	$23\frac{13}{16} \times 13\frac{1}{8} \times 9\frac{7}{8}$	1.8
Cold cups			
6 oz—2 piece	2500	$11\frac{1}{4} \times 14\frac{1}{4} \times 23\frac{1}{2}$	2.8
6 oz—Cone	5000	$17\frac{1}{4} \times 13\frac{7}{8} \times 20\frac{7}{8}$	2.9
5 oz—2 piece	2500	$13\frac{13}{16} \times 13\frac{13}{16} \times 15$	1.7
5 oz—Button bottom	2500	$13\frac{13}{16} \times 13\frac{13}{16} \times 15$	1.7
5 oz—Cone	5000	$16\frac{5}{16} \times 13\frac{1}{8} \times 20\frac{5}{8}$	2.6
5 oz—Pleated	2500	$13\frac{13}{16} \times 13\frac{13}{16} \times 15\frac{5}{8}$	1.7
10 oz—2 piece	2500	$16\frac{7}{16} \times 16\frac{7}{16} \times 24\frac{1}{4}$	3.8
9 oz—2 piece	2500	$15\frac{13}{16} \times 15\frac{13}{16} \times 23\frac{15}{16}$	3.5
10 oz—Round bottom	3000	$15\frac{7}{8} \times 12 \times 21\frac{3}{8}$	2.4
10 oz—Cone	3000	$15\frac{7}{8} \times 12 \times 21\frac{3}{8}$	2.4
Dessert dishes			
4 oz—Pleated	3000	$20\frac{1}{16} \times 16\frac{1}{8} \times 15\frac{7}{8}$	3.0
6 oz—Pleated	5000	$20\frac{1}{16} \times 20\frac{1}{16} \times 19\frac{5}{8}$	4.6
5 oz—2 piece	2500	$20\frac{1}{16} \times 16\frac{1}{16} \times 13\frac{1}{8}$	2.45
7 oz—2 piece	2500	$21\frac{1}{16} \times 16\frac{13}{16} \times 13\frac{7}{8}$	2.84

Portion cups

No.

050 (½ oz)	5000	13⅝ × 7⁹⁄₁₆ × 11¾	0.7
050S (½ oz) Squat	5000	13⅝ × 9¾ × 15¼	1.2
075S (¾ oz) Squat	5000	13¾ × 8½ × 13¼	0.9
075 (¾ oz)	5000	13⅝ × 11 × 17¼	1.5
100 (1 oz)	5000	14 × 9⁷⁄₁₆ × 14¾	1.1
125 (1¼ oz)	5000	13⅞ × 10¼ × 16	1.3
200 (2 oz)	5000	14 × 11⁵⁄₁₆ × 17¾	1.6
250 (2½ oz)	5000	14⅛ × 11¼ × 19¼	1.8
325 (3¼ oz)	5000	14¼ × 13½ × 21	2.3
400 (4 oz)	5000	14¾ × 14¼ × 23	2.8
550 (5½ oz)	5000	16¹⁵⁄₁₆ × 14⅜ × 26¾	3.8

Plates

9 inch	1000	20⅞ × 18⅜ × 9⅞	2.2
8 inch	1000	22⅜ × 16⅜ × 8⅞	1.9
7 inch	1000	22⅜ × 14⅝ × 8	1.5
6 inch	1000	19 × 12 × 6	1.0

Bibliography

"A Pan for All Seasons," *Foodservice Equipment and Supplies Specialist,* Vol. 47, No. 10, September 1994, pp. 71–72.

Almanza, Barbara A., and Ghiselli, Richard, "Environmentalism and the Hospitality Industry," in Richard Teare, Bonnie Farber Canziani, and Graham Brown (eds.), *Global Directions,* Cassell, London, 1997.

American Gas Association, *Commercial Kitchens* (6th ed.), American Gas Association, Arlington, VA, 1979.

"Americans with Disabilities Act—Answers for Foodservice Operators," National Restaurant Association, Washington, DC, 1992.

"Any Way You Slice It," *Foodservice Equipment & Supplies Specialist,* Vol. 99, No. 10, 1996, pp. 110–111.

ASHRAE, *1997 ASHRAE Handbook—Fundamentals,* American Society of Heating, Refrigerating, and Air Conditioning Engineers, Atlanta, GA, 1997.

Association of Plastics Manufacturers in Europe, "What Are Plastics?" *http://apme.org/plastics.html,* 1998.

Avery, Arthur, "Gas Ranges," *Cooking for Profit,* No. 508, Sept. 1993, pp. 16–17.

Avery, Arthur, "Convection Ovens," *Cooking for Profit,* No. 501, February 1993, pp. 16–17.

Avery, Arthur C., *Foodservice Equipment,* John Wiley and Sons, New York, 1980.

Avery, Arthur C., "Mix It Up," *Pizza Today,* Vol. 11, No. 10, October 1993, pp. 58–59.

Avery, Arthur C., "Simplified Foodservice Layout," *Cornell Hotel and Restaurant Quarterly,* Vol. 9, No. 1, May, 1968, pp. 114–116.

Avery Arthur C., "Traffic Flow—Good Layout Cuts Costs, *Cornell Hotel and Restaurant Quarterly,* Vol. 2, No. 1, 1961, pp. 51–60.

Bendall, Dan, "Holding and Serving Equipment," *Restaurant Hospitality,* Vol. 81, No. 1, 1997, pp. 65–66, 68.

Bendall, Daniel, "The Ice Machine Cometh," *Restaurant Hospitality,* Vol. 75, No. 3, 1991, pp. 120–121.

Bertagnoli, Lisa, "Fry, Fry Again," *Foodservice Equipment and Supplies Specialist,* Vol. 49, No. 4, 1996, pp. 59–60.

Bertagnoli, Lisa, "Weighing Your Scale Options," *Foodservice Equipment & Supplies Specialist,* Vol. 49, No. 1, 1996, pp. 69–70.

Biagini, David, "Styled for Service: In-Room Bars & Ice Machines," *Hotel and Resort Industry,* Vol. 17, No. 10, 1994, pp. 32–36.

Blickman, Bruce, "Good Kitchen Design Aids Efficient Service," *Club Operations,* Vol. 3, 1964.

Blumenthal, Dale, "Is that Newfangled Cookware Safe?" Fact Sheet HE 8469, University of Florida, Florida Cooperative Extension Service, Gainesville, FL, 1994.

Borsenik, Frank D., and Stutts, Alan, *The Management of Maintenance and Engineering Systems in the Hospitality Industry* (4th ed.), John Wiley and Sons, New York, 1997.

"Cabinets in Motion," *Foodservice Equipment & Supplies Specialist,* Vol. 47, No. 10, 1994, pp. 47, 109–110.

"Cooking Equipment: Steam Jacketed Kettles," *Foodservice Equipment and Supplies Specialist,* Vol. 43, No. 8, 1990, pp. 50–51.

Cooper, C., "Kitchens by Design," *Hotelier,* Vol. 6, No. 6, 1994, pp. 23–24.

Correll, John, "Ovens for the New Age," *Pizza Today,* Vol. 12, No. 5, 1994, pp. 48–49.

Cummings, Gil, "A Case for Salad Bars," *Restaurant Business,* Vol. 84, No. 9, June 10, 1985, pp. 206, 208.

Dale, J. C., and Kluga, Theodore A., "Pull the Plug on High Utility Costs," *Hotel and Resort Industry,* Vol. 13, No. 5, 1990, pp. 48–51.

Dana, Arthur W., *Kitchen Planning for Quantity Food Service,* Harper & Brothers, New York, 1949 (out of print).

Donovan, A. C., "Developing, Testing, and Evaluating a Dishwashing Facility," *Hospitals,* Vol. 42, No. 12, June 1968.

Dreyfuss, Henry, *Designing for People,* Simon and Schuster, New York, 1970.

Durocher, Joseph, "A Wide Range," *Restaurant Business,* Vol. 95, No. 15, 1992, pp. 238, 242.

Durocher, Joseph, "Real Cut-ups," *Restaurant Business,* Vol. 91, No. 2, 1992, pp. 140–142.

Durocher, Joseph, "Squeaky-Clean," *Restaurant Business,* Vol. 93, No. 16, 1994, pp. 174, 178.

Durocher, Joseph, "Steam Esteem," *Restaurant Business,* Vol. 93, No. 12, 1994, pp. 158, 160.

Flambert, Richard, "Programming the Design of School Lunch Facilities," Duke Manufacturing Company, St. Louis, MO.

"Fond of Fried Foods," *Foodservice Equipment and Supplies Specialist,* Vol. 49, No. 10, 1996, pp. 43–44.

Food and Drug Administration, *1997 Food Code,* U.S. Department of Health and Human Services, Washington, DC, 1997.

Food and Drug Administration, *1999 Food Code,* U.S. Department of Health and Human Services, Washington, DC, 1999.

Frable, Foster, "Clearing Up Confusion on CFC Refrigerants," *Nation's Restaurant News,* Vol. 28, No. 35, 1994, pp. 40, 117.

Frable, Foster, "Fire Up Woodburning Equipment," *Nation's Restaurant News,* Vol. 28, No. 30, 1994, p. 35.

Frable, Foster, "You're Getting Warmer: Rethinking Dishwashing," *Nation's Restaurant News,* Vol. 29, No. 21, May 22, 1995, p. 54, 61.

"From the Warming Front," *Foodservice Equipment & Supplies Specialist,* Vol. 49, No. 10, September 1996, pp. 76–77.

Giampietro, Frank N., "Designing Foodservice Areas for Maximum Production," *Journal of Foodservice Systems,* Vol. 1, No. 2, 1980, pp. 84–88.

Ghiselli, R., Almanza, B., and Ozaki, S., "Foodservice Design: Trends, Space Allocations, and Factors that Influence Kitchen Size," *Journal of Foodservice Systems,* Vol. 10, No. 2, 1998, pp. 89–105.

Hicks, Jennifer, "Exploring the Chinese Range," *Foodservice Equipment and Supplies Specialist,* Vol. 46, No. 3, 1993, pp. 51–52.

Hicks, Jennifer, "More Choices Shopping Steam Pans," *Foodservice Equipment and Supplies Specialist,* Vol. 49, No. 7, June 1996, p. 65.

Hicks, J., and Ward, B., "Designing for ADA," *Foodservice Equipment and Supplies Specialist,* Vol. 47, No. 12, 1994, pp. 38–44.

Hirshfield, Jeff, "Coolant Solution," *Foodservice Director,* Vol. 15, No. 9, 1992, p. 144.

"In Step with Warming Trends," *Foodservice Equipment and Supplies Specialist,* Vol. 47, No. 10, September 1994, pp. 87–88.

"It's All the Range," *Foodservice Equipment and Supplies Specialist,* Vol. 49, No. 10, 1996, pp. 62–63.

Johnson, Brad A., "Taking the Bar Exam," *Foodservice Equipment and Supplies Specialist,* Vol. 48, No. 7, June 1995, p. 64.

Kazarian, Edward, *Foodservice Facilities Planning* (3rd ed.), Avi Publishing, Westport, CT, 1989.

Kazarian, Edward, *Work Analysis and Design for Hotels, Restaurants, and Institutions*, Avi Publishing, Westport, CT, 1969.

Kearney, Deborah S., *The ADA in Practice* (rev. ed.), R. S. Means Company, Kingston, MA, 1995.

Kotschevar, L. H., "How to Apply Work Simplification to Foodservice," in J. Wilkinson (ed.), *Increasing Productivity in Foodservice*, pp. 147–180, *Institutions/Volume Feeding Magazine,* Chicago, IL, 1973.

Lampi, Rauno, "Energy Saving Equipment," *Journal of Foodservice Systems,* Vol. 1, No. 1, 1980, pp. 25–29.

"Let There Be Salad Bars," *Foodservice Equipment and Supplies Specialist,* Vol. 49, No. 10, September 1996, pp. 81–82.

Liberson, J., "Cooking Up New Kitchens," *Lodging,* Vol. 21, No. 2, 1995, pp. 69–72.

Means, R. S., *Means Square Foot Costs—17th Annual Edition*, R. S. Means Company, Kingston, MA, 1996.

Merritt, Frederick S., and Ambrose, James, *Building Engineering and Systems Design* (2nd ed.), Van Nostrand Reinhold, New York, 1990.

Metz, C. L., "Kitchens for the Nineties," *Lodging Hospitality,* Vol. 47, No. 8, 1989, p. 98–100.

Mundel, Marvin E., *Motion and Time Study* (3rd ed.), Prentice Hall, Columbus, OH, 1960.

National Sanitation Foundation Testing Laboratories, "Descriptive Details for the Guidance of Technical and Supervisory Personnel."

Nickel, C. R., "Should You Hire a Foodservice Consultant?" *Cooking for Profit,* No. 468, p. 9, 1990.

North American Association of Food Equipment Manufacturers, *An Introduction to the Foodservice Industry,* NAFEM, Chicago, IL, 1997.

Patterson, Patt, "A Frozen Asset: Choosing the Right Ice Machine," *Nation's Restaurant News,* Vol. 27, No. 15, 1993, pp. 49–50.

Patterson, Patt, "It Could Be a Loooong Way from the Kitchen," *Nation's Restaurant News,* Vol. 27, 1993, p. 31.

Patterson, Patt, "Technology Catches Up with Commercial Ranges," *Nation's Restaurant News,* Vol. 27, No. 21, 1993, p. 30.

Pavesic, D. V., "Foodservice Production and Work Analysis Design," FSS 3423, Division of Continuing Education, University of Florida, Gainesville, FL, 1982.

"Proper Use and Maintenance Ensure Hot-Holding Equipment Efficiency," *Independent Restaurants,* Vol. 48, No. 5, May 1986, p. 80.

Ramsey, Charles George, and Sleeper, Harold R., *Architectural Graphic Standards* (6th ed.), John Wiley and Sons, New York, 1956.

Rogers, Monica, "Keep Deep-Fryers Up and Frying," *Restaurants and Institutions,* Vol. 106, No. 21, 1996, pp. 72, 76, 82.

Rogers, Monica, "Kitchen Technology Moves Forward," *Foodservice Equipment and Supplies International,* Vol. 4, No. 2, May 1996, pp. 25, 28–31.

Rowe, M., "Kitchens Go Compact," *Lodging Hospitality,* Vol. 47, No. 8, 1991, pp. 89–90.

Scoviak-Lerner, M. "How Renovated Kitchens Can Increase Productivity," *Hotels,* Vol. 24, No. 6, 1990, pp. 66–70.

Segeler, C. George, and Setchell, J. Stanford, *Commercial Kitchens* (rev. ed.), American Gas Association, New York, 1978.

"Serving Equipment: Warming and Holding Equipment," *Foodservice Equipment & Supplies Specialist,* Vol. 39, 1986, pp. 97–98.

Slomon, Evelyne, "Roaring Success," *Pizza Today,* Vol. 12, No. 9, 1994, pp. 30–32.

"Slow Cooking Stays Current," *Foodservice Equipment and Supplies Specialist,* Vol. 47, No. 10, September 1994, pp. 47–48.

Specialty Steel Industry of North America, "Stainless Steel," *http://www.ssina.com/stainless.html*, 1998.

Stein, Benjamin, and Reynolds, John S., *Mechanical and Electrical Equipment for Buildings* (8th ed.), John Wiley & Sons, New York, 1992.

"Storage & Handling Equipment: Walk-In Refrigeration," *Foodservice Equipment and Supplies Specialist,* Vol. 43, No. 7, 1990, pp. 97–98.

"The Grill of It," *Foodservice Equipment and Supplies Specialist,* Vol. 49, No. 10, 1996, pp. 45–46.

"The Reliable Convection Oven," *Foodservice Equipment and Supplies Specialist,* Vol. 47, No. 10, September 1994, pp. 67–68.

"The Versatile Mixer in Action," *Foodservice Equipment and Supplies Specialist,* Vol. 47, No. 10, September 1994, pp. 123–124.

Ullman, Lisa, "Transporting At Safe Temperatures," *Foodservice Equipment and Supplies Specialist,* Vol. 47, No. 7, June 1994, pp. 55–56.

Ullman, Lisa, "Worth the Weight," *Foodservice Equipment and Supplies Specialist,* Vol. 45, No. 1, 1992, pp. 61–62.

Ursin, C., "Making the Most of Cramped Kitchens," *Restaurants USA,* Vol. 13, No. 6, 1993, pp. 18–21.

Vin Vin, Quetya, "Keeping Your Cool," *Restaurants and Institutions,* Vol. 107, No. 21, 1997, pp. 88, 92.

Walter, Thomas R., Putz-Anderson, Vern, Garg, Arun, and Fine, Lawrence J., "Revised NIOSH Equation for the Design and Evaluation of Manual Lifting Tasks," *Ergonomics,* Vol. 36, No. 7, 1993, pp. 749–776.

Ward, Brian, "Life Without CFCs," *Foodservice Equipment and Supplies Specialist,* Vol. 48, No. 3, 1995, pp. 65–66.

Watson, T., "Renovation, Same Space, New Place," *Restaurant Business,* Vol. 65, No. 6, 1996, pp. 48–54.

West, Bessie B., Wood, Le Velle, Harger, Virginia F., and Shugart, Grace S., *Food Service in Institutions* (5th ed.), John Wiley and Sons, New York, 1977.

Yuhas, B., "The Kitchen: More Is Less," *Restaurants and Institutions,"* Vol. 103, No. 30, 1993, p. 104.

Answers

ANSWERS TO SELECTED REVIEW QUESTIONS

Chapter 12

8. First question: $1.5 \times 120 = 180$ W. Second question: $12,500/208 = 60$ amps pulled $\times 1.25 = 75$-amp breaker in the panel to provide 25% over actual demand.

Chapter 13

6. Fourteen fixtures are needed; 51 sq ft or a space 7.1×7.1 ft $(2.1 \times 2$ m$)$.

Chapter 14

4. $35 \times 2.3 = 80.5 \dfrac{250 - 80.5}{2.3} = 86.5 + 20 = 106.5$ lb

Chapter 15

2. 12,489 Btu for the beans and 2,143 Btu for the noodles.
3. (a) 50 Btu, (b) 24.65 Btu, (c) 22.20 Btu.

Index